Critical Environmental Politics

CW00548319

The aim of this book is to review central concepts in the study of environmental politics and to open up new questions, problems and research agendas in the field.

The book does so by drawing on a wide range of approaches from critical theory to poststructuralism, and spanning disciplines, including international relations, geography, sociology, history, philosophy, anthropology and political science. The 28 chapters cover a range of global and local studies, illustrations and cases. These range from the Cochabamba conference in Bolivia to climate camps in the UK; UN summits in Rio de Janeiro and Johannesburg to climate migrants from Pacific islands; forests in Indonesia to Dutch energy governance reform; indigenous communities in Namibia to oil extraction in the Niger Delta; and survivalist militias in the United States to Maasai tribesmen in Kenya.

Rather than following a regional or issue-based (e.g., water, forests, pollution, etc.) structure, the book is organized in terms of key concepts in the field, including those that have been central to the social sciences for a long time (such as citizenship, commodification, consumption, feminism, justice, movements, science, security, the state, summits and technology), those that have been at the heart of environmental politics for many years (including biodiversity, climate change, conservation, eco-centrism, limits, localism, resources, sacrifice and sustainability), and many that have been introduced to these literatures and debates more recently (biopolitics, governance, governmentality, hybridity, posthumanism, risk and vulnerability).

Features and benefits of the book include the following:

- explains the most important concepts and theories in environmental politics;
- reviews the core ideas behind crucial debates in environmental politics;
- highlights the key thinkers – both classic and contemporary – for studying environmental politics;
- provides original perspectives on the critical potential of the concepts for future research agendas as well as for the practice of environmental politics.

Each chapter is written by leading international authors in their field.

This exciting new book will be essential reading for all students of environmental politics and provocatively presents the field in a different light for more established researchers.

Carl Death is Senior Lecturer in International Political Economy at the University of Manchester, UK.

Interventions
Edited by Jenny Edkins
Aberystwyth University,
and Nick Vaughan-Williams, *University of Warwick*

'*As Michel Foucault has famously stated, "knowledge is not made for understanding; it is made for cutting". In this spirit, the Edkins–Vaughan-Williams Interventions series solicits cutting-edge, critical works that challenge mainstream understandings in international relations. It is the best place to contribute post-disciplinary works that think rather than merely recognize and affirm the world recycled in IR's traditional geopolitical imaginary.*'
Michael J. Shapiro, University of Hawai'i at Mānoa, USA

The series aims to advance understanding of the key areas in which scholars working within broad critical post-structural and post-colonial traditions have chosen to make their interventions, and to present innovative analyses of important topics.

Titles in the series engage with critical thinkers in philosophy, sociology, politics and other disciplines and provide situated historical, empirical and textual studies in international politics.

Critical Theorists and International Relations
Edited by Jenny Edkins and Nick Vaughan-Williams

Ethics as Foreign Policy
Britain, the EU and the other
Dan Bulley

Universality, Ethics and International Relations
A grammatical reading
Véronique Pin-Fat

The Time of the City
Politics, philosophy, and genre
Michael J. Shapiro

Governing Sustainable Development
Partnership, protest and power at the world summit
Carl Death

Insuring Security
Biopolitics, security and risk
Luis Lobo-Guerrero

Foucault and International Relations
New critical engagements
Edited by Nicholas J. Kiersey and Doug Stokes

International Relations and Non-Western Thought
Imperialism, colonialism and investigations of global modernity
Edited by Robbie Shilliam

Autobiographical International Relations
I, IR
Edited by Naeem Inayatullah

War and Rape
Law, memory and justice
Nicola Henry

Critical Environmental Politics

Edited by Carl Death

Routledge
Taylor & Francis Group

LONDON AND NEW YORK

First published 2014
by Routledge
2 Park Square, Milton Park, Abingdon, Oxon OX14 4RN

and by Routledge
711 Third Avenue, New York, NY 10017

Routledge is an imprint of the Taylor & Francis Group,
an informa business

© 2014 Carl Death, selection and editorial matter; contributors, their
contributions.

The right of Carl Death to be identified as editor of this work has been
asserted by him in accordance with the Copyright, Designs and Patents
Act 1988.

All rights reserved. No part of this book may be reprinted or reproduced or
utilised in any form or by any electronic, mechanical, or other means, now
known or hereafter invented, including photocopying and recording, or in
any information storage or retrieval system, without permission in writing
from the publishers.

Trademark notice: Product or corporate names may be trademarks or
registered trademarks, and are used only for identification and explanation
without intent to infringe.

British Library Cataloguing-in-Publication Data
A catalogue record for this book is available from the British Library

Library of Congress Cataloging-in-Publication Data
Critical environmental politics / edited by Carl Death.
    pages cm. — (Interventions)
  Includes bibliographical references and index.
 1. Political ecology. 2. Environmentalism—Political aspects.
3. Sustainable development—Political aspects. 4. Critical theory.
I. Death, Carl.
  JA75.8.C76 2013
  333.7—dc23
  2013016829

ISBN: 978-0-415-63103-7 (hbk)
ISBN: 978-0-415-63122-8 (pbk)
ISBN: 978-1-315-88307-6 (ebk)

Typeset in Times New Roman
by Apex CoVantage, LLC

Contents

Contributors

Susan Baker is Professor in Environmental Policy at the Cardiff School of Social Science and Lead Academic, Sustainable Places Research Institute, Cardiff University. Her research focuses on the interrelationship between social and ecological processes, with emphasis on climate change and biodiversity loss. She has published extensively in this field.

Patrick Bond directs the Centre for Civil Society and is Senior Professor at the University of KwaZulu-Natal, Durban, South Africa. He authored *Politics of Climate Justice* (UKZN Press, 2012).

Andrew Brooks is Lecturer in Development Geography at King's College London. His work investigates connections between spaces of production and places of consumption, and includes publications in *Development and Change*, *Geoforum*, *Geographical Journal* and the *Journal of Southern African Studies*.

Raymond Bryant is Professor in Geography at King's College London. His work includes *Nongovernmental Organisations in Environmental Struggles* (Yale University Press, 2005) and *Handbook of Political Ecology* (co-edited with Soyeun Kim, Edward Elgar, 2014).

Bram Büscher is Associate Professor of Environment and Sustainable Development at the Institute of Social Studies, Erasmus University, and is a visiting Associate Professor at the Department of Geography, Environmental Management and Energy Studies of the University of Johannesburg. He is the author of *Transforming the Frontier: Peace Parks and the Politics of Neoliberal Conservation in Southern Africa* (Duke University Press, 2013).

Mark Charlesworth is an Honorary Research Fellow in the School of Social Sciences at Keele University.

Erika Cudworth is Reader in Political Sociology and Critical Animal Studies at the University of East London. Her publications include *Developing Ecofeminist Theory* (Palgrave, 2005), *Social Lives with Other Animals* (Palgrave, 2011) and *Posthuman International Relations* (with Steve Hobden, Zed, 2011).

Simon Dalby is CIGI Chair in the Political Economy of Climate Change at the Balsillie School of International Affairs, Waterloo, Canada, and author of, among other works, *Security and Environmental Change* (Polity, 2009).

Carl Death is Senior Lecturer in International Political Economy at The University of Manchester. His work includes *Governing Sustainable Development: Partnerships, Protests and Power at the World Summit* (Routledge, 2010).

Tim Forsyth is Professor in Environment and Development at the London School of Economics and Political Science. His work includes *Critical Political Ecology: The Politics of Environmental Science* (Routledge, 2003).

Kevin Grove is Lecturer in the Institute of Geography and Earth Sciences at Aberystwyth University. He has recently published articles in *Security Dialogue* and the *Annals of the Association of American Geographers,* among other interdisciplinary journals.

Emma Hinton is a Research Fellow in the Third Sector Research Centre at the University of Southampton. Her research focuses on understanding the nature and impacts of pro-sustainability behaviour change initiatives.

Stephen Hobden is Senior Lecturer at the University of East London where he teaches courses on International Relations Theory and on China in world politics. His most recent publication (together with Erika Cudworth) is *Posthuman International Relations* (Zed, 2011).

James Igoe is Associate Professor of Anthropology, and a Mellon Fellow at the Institute of Humanities and Global Culture at the University of Virginia. He has conducted extensive research on capitalism and conservation and is part of a Leverhulme funded network for the study of value at the University of Manchester. His forthcoming book, *Spectacle of Nature, Spirit of Capitalism,* examines the role of commodified images in Western imaginaries of nature.

Thom Kuehls is Professor of Political Science at Weber State University in Ogden, Utah. His work includes *Beyond Sovereign Territory: The Space of Ecopolitics* (University of Minnesota Press, 1996).

Gabriela Kütting is Associate Professor in Political Science and Global Affairs at Rutgers University, Newark. Her work includes *The Global Political Economy of the Environment and Tourism* (Palgrave, 2010) and *Environmental Governance, Power and Knowledge in a Local-Global World* (with Ronnie Lipschutz, Routledge, 2009).

Karen Litfin is Associate Professor of Political Science at the University of Washington in Seattle. She has written on stratospheric ozone politics, climate politics, the greening of sovereignty and Gaian governance. Her most recent book is *Ecovillages: Lessons for Sustainable Community* (Polity, forthcoming 2013).

Eva Lövbrand is Associate Professor at the Centre for Climate Science and Policy Research at Linköping University. Her work has been widely published in journals such as *Global Environmental Change, Science, Technology and Human Values, Critical Policy Studies* and *Global Environmental Politics.*

Timothy W. Luke is University Distinguished Professor of Political Science at VirginiaTech and is the author of numerous books and articles. The most recent include *A Journal of No Illusions: Telos, Paul Piccone, and the Americanization of Critical Theory* (Telos Press, 2011) and *There is a Gunman on Campus: Tragedy and Terror at Virginia Tech* (Rowman & Littlefield, 2008), both with Ben Agger.

Katie McShane is Associate Professor of Philosophy at Colorado State University. She has published papers in *Environmental Ethics, Environmental Values, Ethics & the Environment* and *Philosophical Studies.*

Chris Methmann is a research fellow at the Institute for Political Science, University of Hamburg. He works on global climate politics, climate security and climate-induced migration. Most recently, he co-edited *(De-)Constructing the Greenhouse. Interpretive Approaches to Global Climate Governance* (Routledge, 2013).

Angela Oels is temporary Associate Professor in Political Science (International Relations) at the Fernuniversität Hagen, Germany. Her work draws on a Foucaultian governmentality framework and focuses on climate change as a security issue. She has published in *Geoforum* and the *Journal of Environmental Policy & Planning.*

Chukwumerije Okereke is Reader (Associate Professor) in Environment and Development at the School of Human and Environmental Sciences, University of Reading, UK. He is also a Fellow of the Environmental Change Institute at the University of Oxford.

Cristiana Olcese is Fellow in Sociology at the London School of Economics. Her research interests lie at the intersection between culture and social movements. She has published in *Mobilization* and the *BJS*, and contributed to a series of edited volumes.

Matthew Paterson is Professor of Political Science at the University of Ottawa. His latest book (with Peter Newell) is *Climate Capitalism: Global Warming and the Transformation of the Global Economy* (Cambridge University Press, 2010).

Luigi Pellizzoni is Associate Professor in Environmental Sociology at the University of Trieste. His recent work includes editing *Neoliberalism and Technoscience: Critical Assessments* (Ashgate, 2012).

Nancy Peluso is Henry J. Vaux Distinguished Professor of Forest Policy at the University of California, Berkeley. She is author or co-author of more than 60 peer reviewed articles and a number of books, including, with Michael Watts, *Violent Environments* (Cornell University Press, 2001).

Stephan Price completed his PhD on the British environmental movement and climate change in 2013, and continues to carry out research and teaching on climate politics and the sociology of science.

Alan P. Rudy is Assistant Professor of Sociology at Central Michigan University. His collaborative work includes *Universities in the Age of Corporate Science* (Temple University Press, 2007) and *Natures, Environments and Social Theory*, with Damian White and Brian Gareau (Palgrave/MacMillan, forthcoming).

Clare Saunders is Senior Lecturer in Politics at the Environment and Sustainability Institute, University of Exeter. Her recent books are *Environmental Networks and Social Movement Theory* (Bloomsbury, 2013) and *Politics and the Environment* (with James Connelly, Graham Smith and David Benson, Routledge, 2012).

Johannes Stripple is Associate Professor at the Department of Political Science, Lund University, Sweden. His recent research has covered European and international climate policy; carbon markets; renewable energy; sinks; and scenarios and governmentalities around climate change, carbon and the Earth System.

Paul Wapner is Professor of Global Environmental Politics in the School of International Service at American University. His latest book is *Living through the End of Nature: The Future of American Environmentalism* (MIT Press, 2010).

Michael Watts is Class of 63 Professor of Geography and Development Studies at UC Berkeley where he has taught for 35 years. A new edition of his book *Silent Violence* has just been published (University of California Press, 2013).

Damian White is Associate Professor and Head of the Department of History, Philosophy and Social Science at the Rhode Island School of Design. He is the author of *Bookchin: A Critical Appraisal* (Pluto, 2008) and *The Environment, Nature and Social Theory* (Palgrave Macmillan, 2014) with Alan P. Rudy and Brian Gareau.

Mark Whitehead is Professor of Human Geography at Aberystwyth University. His work includes *Spaces of Sustainability: Geographical Perspectives on the Sustainable Society* (Routledge, 2006).

Acknowledgements

This volume owed its inception to the encouragement of Jenny Edkins, for which I am very grateful. The assistance throughout of Nicola Parkin and Peter Harris at Routledge has been invaluable. It has been a privilege to work with this group of contributing authors, who gave generously of their time not only in producing such fine chapters but also in a process of mutual peer-review, which helped give the volume its cohesion, and their patience and enthusiasm throughout was greatly appreciated. Additional peer-reviewing was selflessly provided by Megan Daigle, Daniel McCarthy, Erzsebet Strausz and Aoileann Ní Mhurchú. An edited volume such as this proceeds in fits and starts, and I have been very aware of the influence of a number of particularly critical and political environments in which this book took shape. These include the ever-inspirational Dyfi valley in Mid-Wales and the Department of International Politics in Aberystwyth, to which I will always owe an unpayable debt. The book was also shaped by the happiness of a one-bedroom apartment in an old cotton mill in Manchester, and by the hot sunny hills surrounding Stellenbosch. Near completion, it was a first-time visit to the incomparable Yosemite Valley that re-impressed the importance of critical environmental politics upon me. Fittingly, upon gazing into this valley during his first summer in the Sierra, John Muir (2003 [1911]: 135–6) wrote, 'How vast it seems, how short human life when we happen to think of it, and how little we may learn, however hard we try!' This book is offered in that spirit.

1 Critical, environmental, political

An introduction

Carl Death

Introduction

Making the familiar appear strange and bringing the unfamiliar into clearer focus are both core functions of critical scholarship. Often, both these tasks are a matter of perspective. As the image on the front cover of the paperback edition of this book demonstrates, an unusual perspective can put commonplace sights and activities into question. Similarly, by shifting one's position, or looking through a differently shaped lens, frequently unacknowledged or unrecognised aspects of the world around us can crystallise into view. This book is intended to present new approaches to deeply familiar concepts and issues, as well as to illuminate the potential of newer concepts and theories for the study of environmental politics.

Both tasks are urgently needed. Contemporary global politics is characterised by a telling contradiction and a worrying paradox. We are – as a number of the contributors to this book point out – living through an unprecedented era of environmental change. It seems that the impact of human activities on our planetary environment is now so great, and we are directly affecting the atmosphere, ecosystems, species viability, chemical cycles and biological processes to such a degree, that our age has been termed the *Anthropocene* (Cudworth and Hobden 2011: 114; Dalby 2009; Lövbrand, Stripple, Johannes, and Wiman 2009). Environmentalists have long warned us of the importance of natural stewardship for future generations, but for the majority of the planet's inhabitants the natural environment remains an ever-present concern: food shortages, floods, droughts, storms and hurricanes, diseases, pollution, industrial accidents, and the threat of chemical, biological, nuclear and conventional weapons make much of our world highly dangerous at the moment, never mind in the future. If the warnings of cautious climate scientists are to be believed, and the trajectory of prevailing models of economic development continue, then even the wealthiest of the planet's population (including the majority of those reading this book) will soon realise the degree to which our environment remains precarious and dangerous. As Michel Foucault famously observed, 'modern man is an animal whose politics places his existence as a living being in question' (1979: 143).

Yet this raises a paradox: *we all know this.* In most places, long-term trends indicate that the number of people who know and care about environmental issues is rising (Blühdorn and Welsh 2007). Even those who do not claim to care about environmental issues when asked by survey-makers usually *do* care when food prices rise or energy supplies falter, when there is dumping in local rivers or there is an acrid taste in the air. The environmental movement has devoted itself to making these changes visible to people and, in some cases, explaining why they are happening and what should be done about it. Membership of many environmental groups is higher than ever before. Politicians in all countries profess concern about climate change, natural resources, sustainability, 'green technologies', energy and tourism (Carter 2013). Our leaders and political representatives devote substantial amounts of time and energy to negotiating texts, making speeches, passing laws and creating state agencies with environmental intent.

And yet . . . Progress against even the modest targets we have set – stabilizing greenhouse gas emissions at a level that will prevent dangerous anthropogenic interference with the climate system, reversing the loss of biodiversity on the planet, halving the proportion of the global population without access to clean water and sanitation, slowing rates of deforestation and over-fishing – is rarely encouraging. The massive growth in environmental awareness and governance since the Stockholm UN Conference on the Human Environment in 1972 has been paralleled by increasing environmental degradation and precious few successes to sustain our faith. Because of this, many talk of 'an era of post-ecologism' and 'a politics of unsustainability' (Blühdorn and Welsh 2007; Blühdorn 2013), the 'End of Nature' (McKibben 1989), the 'end of environmentalism' (Wissenburg and Levy 2004), or the 'death of environmentalism' (Shellenberger and Nordhaus 2004).

It is for this reason that a critical project of making the familiar strange and the unfamiliar clearer is so necessary. Our current forms of social living and organisation are not working for the majority of the human population; furthermore, our impact on many non-human populations is hardly conducive to their health and viability. Whilst we must be careful not to overstate the power and potential of intellectual and conceptual activity, at the very least it is important to try to think more clearly and more imaginatively – more critically – about the causes, rationalities, relationships, practices, subjectivities and politics of the environmental crisis. Why should we care? Because, as environmental justice activists insisted in the 1980s and 1990s, the environment is where we all live (Schlosberg 1999, 2013), and, as Milja Kurki has pointed out, '[d]espite its sceptical outlook, critical and philosophical theory is still valuable in reminding us that, while it does not seem so, we do not live in a world without any alternatives' (2011: 146).

This volume is an examination of the concepts and literatures that we might find useful in this task of thinking more clearly, imaginatively and critically about environmental politics. The contributing authors come from a variety of different disciplines and perspectives, and as such, the book does not seek to set out a coherent 'eco-project' or unified 'eco-politics', but instead, each chapter takes a key concept and discusses how it has been, and might be, used by those studying, researching and practicing environmental politics. The book does not have a linear structure (indeed, the chapters are ordered alphabetically, rather than thematically), and there is no conclusion. As such, it might be best to think of its organisation as more akin to a rhizome than a tree. Deleuze and Guattari (1987) contrast rhizome structures – networks that sprout up like fungi or tubers – to the arboreal structure of a sturdy oak with roots, a single trunk and a canopy of spreading branches (see also Schlosberg 1999: 96–7).

Accordingly, the concepts discussed here should be seen as a tool-kit from which one is invited to pick and choose according to the problem, issue, or interest at hand. Not all these tools are easily combined and used together, and some may prove counter-productive. Other problems may require 'loosening' with some tools, 'deconstructing' with others, before 'rebuilding' with yet more. Moreover, it is inevitable that this is just one box with a limited selection of tools: there are many more not included here, and all of those that are present could have been designed and deployed differently.

However, this paean to plurality does not mean the selection here is ad hoc or random. The following sections of this introductory chapter therefore explain the rationale behind the volume in terms of a brief discussion of the three key terms in the title: critical, environmental and politics. The final section explains a little more about the range and selection of the chapters.

Critical

In some senses, of course, all good research should be critical: reflexive, questioning, testing answers carefully and thoroughly, rigorous, and dealing with important issues. Few would argue they engage in *uncritical* environmental politics. But this volume seeks to be critical in a more specific sense, and this can be explained through three dimensions of the term: the theoretical *traditions* drawn upon, the *type* of questions asked, and the *ethos* of critique pursued.

In the first place, and perhaps most straightforwardly, this volume is situated in a broader tradition of critical theorising in the social sciences. Whilst, as with all theoretical approaches, there are always gatekeepers seeking to police boundaries and establish particularly narrow avenues as belonging to 'Critical Theory' proper, in this volume a broader interpretation of critical theory is adopted. Three intellectual traditions are particularly prominent in this collection, but even they do not exhaust or constrain the influences drawn upon. These three traditions are the Marxist/Gramscian, the Frankfurt School, and poststructuralism, each of which is associated with particular authors and concepts. There are differences between these approaches, but they can all be broadly identified with a common attitude of critique, seen by Immanuel Kant as characteristic of modernity itself (Kant 1949 [1784]; see also Brown 1994; Foucault 2010: 7–21; Hutchings 2001: 79).

In 1843 Karl Marx set out the project of critical theory as the '*ruthless criticism of the existing order,* ruthless in that it will shrink neither from its own discoveries, nor from conflict with the powers that be' (Marx 1843). The Marxist tradition has tended to dominate critical approaches in the social sciences, and the influence of Marx's thought is evident in a number of chapters in this volume (including, but not limited to, those by Büscher, Bond, Brooks and Bryant, Cudworth, Igoe, Luke, Methmann and Oels, Paterson, and Watts and Peluso). Thinkers influenced by Marx and Antonio Gramsci tend to interpret critical thought and praxis as closely linked, and as necessarily aligned with counter-hegemonic social forces in a project of political change and economic transformation (Bryant 1998; Harvey 1996; Peet and Watts 1996a; Peet, Robbins and Watts 2011). Drawing on Gramsci, Robert W. Cox made a famous and widely quoted distinction in 1981 between 'problem-solving' and 'critical' theory: if the former 'takes the world as it finds it', then the latter 'stands apart from the prevailing order of the world and asks how that order came about' (1981: 129). Thus 'critical theory can be a guide to strategic action for bringing about an alternative order, whereas problem-solving theory is a guide to tactical actions which, intended or unintended, sustain the existing order' (Cox 1981: 130).

This distinction echoes that drawn by Max Horkheimer in his classic 1937 essay between 'Traditional and Critical Theory' (1982 [1937]). Horkheimer was also working very much in the Marxist tradition, but he is now associated with a group of critical theorists who have gone beyond Marx in a number of important ways and are collectively known as the Frankfurt School. Deeply concerned with the 'dark side' of modernity – including the tendencies towards totalitarian conceptions of 'progress' and instrumentalist visions of science in some branches of the Marxist and communist tradition – theorists associated with the Frankfurt

School, such as Horkheimer, Theodor Adorno, Herbert Marcuse, Jürgen Habermas and Ulrich Beck, have drawn attention to the perils of technology and the environmental risks of industrial society. Critique, for these 'Critical Theorists', is an immanent and reflexive process in which the contradictions of modernity can be illuminated and potentially ameliorated through (especially in Habermas's work) processes of dialogue, learning and democracy (Habermas 1984; see also Beck 1992, 1995; Foucault 1997: 298; Linklater 2001, 2007: 45–6; Schlosberg 1999: 76–90; Wyn Jones 1999). Andrew Linklater, for example, calls for a critical theory that 'identifies the prospects for realising higher levels of human freedom across world society as a whole' (1990: 7). The influence of the Frankfurt School in some form or another can be discerned in a number of chapters in this volume (including, but not limited to, those by Baker; Hinton; Kütting; Litfin; Price, Saunders and Olcese; and Whitehead).

Poststructuralist theorists are sometimes positioned (by themselves and others) as antithetical to both Marxist and Frankfurt School traditions of critical theory, and it is true that there are very different understandings of key concepts such as subjectivity, truth, and freedom/emancipation in these traditions. However, there are also many commonalities, particularly when it comes to the practice of critique in intellectual thought (Ashley and Walker 1990; Brown 1994; Linklater 2001). Of the three approaches or traditions discussed here, the poststructuralist branch is also the hardest to portray as a distinct tradition. It is not a homogenous approach, and it is used here more as an umbrella grouping for a range of theorists, including Michel Foucault, Gilles Deleuze and Felix Guattari, Bruno Latour, Donna Haraway, and several others. Thinkers in this tradition tend to be more sceptical towards the Enlightenment project than either Marxists or Frankfurt School theorists, and they are less willing to proclaim new political projects or progressive alternatives as emancipatory (see Blühdorn 2007: 259–60; Hindess 1996: 149; Mouffe 2005: 34). For example, Foucault made it clear that

> I have always been somewhat suspicious of the notion of liberation, because if it is not treated with precautions and with certain limits, one runs the risk of falling back on the idea that there exists a human nature or social base that, as a consequence of certain historical, economic, and social processes, has been concealed, alienated, or imprisoned in and by mechanisms of repression. (1997: 282)

However, there is a shared critical concern with the role of thought and theory (whether this is termed *discourse, ideology, rationalities, worldviews,* etc.) in supporting an inequitable and harmful status quo and a shared commitment to making familiar things strange and unfamiliar things more easily visible (Comaroff and Comaroff 2012: 19; Edkins 1999; Hindess 1996: 145–6). Chapters in this volume particularly influenced by poststructuralist thinkers include, but are not limited to, those by Dalby, Death, Forsyth, Grove, Hobden, Kuehls, Lövbrand and Stripple, Luke, Pellizzoni, Methmann and Oels, and Rudy and White.

An inspiration from, or intellectual debt to, one or more of these traditions is thus one way to distinguish the contributions to this volume as *critical* in distinction to other approaches to the study of environmental politics. But a card-carrying affiliation to a particular tradition is not a particularly *critical* attitude, and none of the volume contributors present themselves in this way. Rather, a second and perhaps better way of establishing their critical character is to observe that all the chapters in this volume, to a greater or lesser extent, are aware of and sensitive to four particular *types* of question. These four questions concern the role and reflexivity of the scholar, the presence of conflict or contradictions within society, a 'big-picture' perspective, and the importance of normative, moral and ethical issues.

First, the contributions to this volume are not characterised by positivist approaches to science, in which the objective observer tests theories against empirical data (Ashley and Walker 1990; Beck 1992; Brigg and Bleiker 2010; Brown 1994; Escobar 1995: 130; Lapid 1989; Linklater 2001: 25, 2007: 45–6; Wyn Jones 1999: 18–21). Rather, the influence of post-positivist methodologies, meta-theoretical reflection, and philosophical enquiry is more evident here. As Cox suggests, critical theory is 'more reflective upon the process of theorising itself' (1981: 128). An important tenet of critical research methods is that the author is present within both the social world under study and the text produced through that study. Moreover, many critical theorists, including Gramsci and Marcuse, paid close attention to the role played in social change by intellectuals and academics themselves (Kurki 2011: 139; Wyn Jones 1999: 9).

Second, the critical approaches collected here tend to share a perspective on society that is attuned to the presence of conflict and contradictions. Famously, of course, for Marx and Engels '[t]he history of all hitherto existing society is the history of class struggles' (Marx and Engels 1848; see also Mouffe 2005; Rose 1999: 227). As Linklater explains, 'critical theory endeavours to identify counter-hegemonic or countervailing tendencies that are invariably present within all social and political relations' (2007: 48–9). Whether these are interpreted in terms of class conflict, or environmental degradation, or violence and hegemony, or fractured subjectivity, such perspectives on the world draw attention to the fundamental role of power relations. Whilst there will be many different accounts of the possibility or desirability of emancipatory politics, all critical perspectives tend to share a concern with the inequalities, injustices and violences of the here and now.

Third critical theory as defined here is concerned with 'big picture' analysis: the attempt, however incomplete and partial and doomed to failure, to address significant trends, discursive tropes and silences, systemic characteristics, and features of the social world in some kind of holistic way. As Cox defined it, critical theory seeks to examine the 'social and political complex as a whole' (1981: 129). It is necessary to be quite careful and specific here, because this should not be read as meaning that critical analysis must necessarily focus on structural power relations, underlying explanations, great power politics, or the 'big events' of politics and social life. It is perfectly possible to present a critical analysis of the small-scale, the grassroots, the everyday, the private and the apparently insignificant, whilst retaining a 'big picture' perspective in the way I mean it (Magnusson 2003). The alternative to such a 'big picture' or holistic approach, however, is an atomistic approach in which arbitrary conceptual divisions – between the national and international, nature and society, economy and politics, public and private, self and other, etc. – are taken as self-evident, such that it is possible to conduct relatively self-contained, laboratory-style analysis in which variables are controlled and the dimensions of a problem are easily restricted (Lapid 1989; Norgaard 1994; Wyn Jones 1999: 28). In contrast, the contributions to this volume share a concern with the broader social world – or even with the broader social/natural world – that is a characteristic of critical theory in contrast to problem-solving theory. As Richard Norgaard points out, '[o]ur ability to comprehend as a whole is all that matters in the end' (1994: 9).

Fourth critical approaches recognise that it is impossible to completely separate morality and ethics – normative judgements – from arguments and analysis (Cox 1981; Hutchings 2001: 81; Lapid 1989; Norgaard 1994). Whilst the chapters vary in terms of the degree to which they set out explicit normative positions and commitments, and from where they derive these positions, a critical environmental politics must be motivated by a personal and political assertion that these issues are important and that they involve value judgements and ethical commitments. For this reason all authors were asked to be explicit about what they saw as the critical potential of their concept. This was interpreted in different ways by different authors, but they all come to some position on where the most important directions of future action or analysis should lie.

Indeed, this is the final, and broadest, way in which this volume has a shared sense of being critical. There is a critical *ethos* that motivates it: these issues are important, too important not to be studied, however we define and approach them. More than that, a critical ethos is one committed to unsettling conventional ways of seeing and doing things; casting things in a new light; making quick judgements and small violences more problematic; increasing the political and conceptual resources available to those who have been marginalised, silenced, or damaged; and disrupting the status quo (Amoore 2008; Brassett 2009; Escobar 1995; Hutchings 2001: 87; Inayatullah and Blaney 2004: 4–5; Rose 1999). For Foucault, '[c]riticism consists in uncovering that thought and trying to change it: showing that things are not as obvious as people believe, making it so that what is taken for granted is no longer taken for granted. To do criticism is to make harder those acts which are now too easy' (2000: 456). Making the familiar appear strange and bringing the unfamiliar into clearer focus.

The topic of environmental politics lends itself to such a critical ethos. It has tended to be on the margins of the social sciences, and it is still a somewhat marginal realm of political practice (witness the junior status of most Environment Ministers and the low profile of 'environmental' conferences and stories in the mainstream media, most of the time). Most observers end up conceding that quite fundamental changes to the status quo are necessary to deal with the environmental damage our species has caused, although certainly far from everyone is convinced here. By virtue of this, it is possible to suggest that even an author not drawing on the three traditions or approaches to critical theory discussed previously, or explicitly dealing with one of the four types of question discussed previously, might still be regarded as critical in the sense of focussing attention on a topic that is usually marginalised in the disciplines of international politics, philosophy, sociology, or history (geography is perhaps an exception here, being a discipline in which environmental studies are quite mainstream). I will not go this far – there are too many examples of narrow, technocratic, problem-solving, pseudo-objective and unreflective approaches to the study of environmental politics that are *uncritical* in the ways set out previously. But it is surely true that – especially evident in the work of the Frankfurt School – the environmental consequences of modernity have been a major spur in fermenting critical thinking, and the field of environmental politics is particularly suited to and in need of critical tools of analysis.

Environmental

If there are a shared critical theoretical literature, types of questions, and critical ethos that draw together the contributors to this volume, what is the field that they share? What is the 'environment' that this volume seeks to illuminate?

The environment is hard to define, but most people feel they know it when they see it. Two broad understandings tend to dominate: the environment as nature or 'the wild' and (as mentioned previously) the environment as where we all live. The former conjures up images of mountains and forests, rivers and lakes and the oceans, great plains and savannahs, jungles and marshes (Cronon 1996; Neumann 1998). The environment, in this sense, is the object of conservation and preservation: something 'natural' best found in the absence of humans and society. For John Muir, the great nineteenth- and early twentieth-century American author and conservationist, 'Nature as a poet, an enthusiastic workingman, becomes more and more visible the farther and higher we go; for the mountains are fountains – beginning places, however related to sources beyond mortal ken' (Muir 2003 [1911]: 211–12).

The second understanding draws on the origins of the word itself – *environ* – as surroundings.[1] Thus the environment is 'where we live, work, and play' (quoted in Schlosberg 2013: 39) – whether in towns and cities, villages, or rural farms. In a broader sense, as a species we live within a planetary system and an atmosphere that permits our particular oxygen- and carbon-based lifeforms: so this, too, is our environment. Drawing on a wide range of philosophical influences, many theorists accordingly talk about the social construction of nature, or the deconstruction of terms like *wilderness* and the *environment* (see, among many, Castree and Braun 1998, 2001; Demeritt 2002; Soper 1995).

Many chapters in this volume explore these terms in much more depth and with more sophistication (see particularly Büscher, Hobden, Igoe, McShane, and Rudy and White), and so they do not need more extensive elaboration here. Indeed, it is one of the defining features of *critical environmental* studies that there is some concern with the implications of various assumptions about what is natural, social, environmental, and so on (Barry 2001; Beck 1995; Blühdorn and Welsh 2007; Cudworth and Hobden 2011; Dalby 2009; Escobar 1995: 196; Peet et al. 2011: 29; Sachs 1992). For this reason, our volume does not start with a list of 'environmental' topics (water, land, forests, mountains) and discuss the problems they face; nor do any of the contributors subscribe to an unproblematic preservationist worldview of humans as stewards of external natures. Although Romantic visions of sublime and fragile nature can play a useful tactical role in unsettling prevailing economic and developmental assumptions, it is also a discourse that tends to reinscribe politically troubling assumptions about gender, class, race, knowledge and many other reified categories (Cronon 1996).

Of course, the various chapters in this volume do discuss a wide array of issues commonly thought of as 'environmental'. It will not be surprising that climate change features in many chapters (see particularly Okereke and Charlesworth; Paterson; Bond; Methmann and Oels; Price, Saunders and Olcese; Dalby; and Forsyth), as does biodiversity and species conservation (see particularly Büscher, Igoe, McShane, Hobden, and Whitehead). Issues related to the consumption of natural resources are widespread (see particularly Brooks and Bryant, Watts and Peluso, Kütting, Whitehead, Wapner, Litfin, and Dalby), and pollution is a recurring topic (see particularly Pellizzoni, Whitehead, Baker, and Hinton). Other topics include genetic modification (see particularly Rudy and White, and Forsyth), disasters (see particularly Grove, Pellizzoni, and Methmann and Oels), sustainable development (see particularly Whitehead, Baker, Death, and Kütting), agriculture and food (see particularly Kuehls, Watts and Peluso, Paterson, and Litfin), and population (see particularly Grove, Lövbrand and Stripple, Kütting, and Kuehls). There are also many others, including energy, fishing, migration, animal rights and so on. No restrictions have been placed on the type of issues or examples discussed – but all these issues are united by being usually or sometimes regarded as environmental issues by experts, concerned publics, activists, or governments. Beyond this, what many of the chapters share is a concern with the labels and frameworks we use to describe, understand and explain human and non-human relationships.

It is in such discussions over the role and meaning of nature and the environment that critical environmental studies often tends to distance itself from some aspects of the broader traditions of critical theory – particularly those associated with the Marxist and some elements of the Frankfurt school approaches.[2] Both these conceptions of critical theory insist on the place of emancipation at the centre of any critical theory or project, and for many key thinkers in these traditions, emancipation has been defined as the human domination of nature (see Harvey 1996: 133–5; Linklater 1990: 25; Wyn Jones 1999: 23–4). Marx and Engels comment with awe on the productive forces unleashed by the bourgeoisie: '[s]ubjection of Nature's forces to man, machinery, application of chemistry to industry and agriculture, steam-navigation, railways, electric telegraphs, clearing of whole continents for cultivation, canalisation of rivers, whole populations conjured out of the ground' (1848). Furthermore, Horkheimer 'equates emancipation with the increased domination of nature: Human beings are freer when they are less subject to the vicissitudes of nature' (in Wyn Jones 1999: 23–4). Many environmentalists, of whatever shade of green, retain some unease about such unapologetically and confidently anthropocentric visions of politics.

Many of the contributors to this volume, as a result, would therefore feel themselves more comfortable within the context of literatures on *critical political ecology* (see Bryant 1998; Castree and Braun 1998; Escobar 1995; Peet and Watts 1996a; Peet et al. 2011). Such literatures are concerned with the relationships among and between entities, and the politics of whether we term these entities social or natural. Indeed, *nature* has famously been described as one of the most complex words in the English language (see Demeritt 2002: 277) and can be deployed in reference to the essential quality or character of something, a universal and ahistorical force (the laws of nature), or the external material world (nature as a synonym for reality). Few would disagree, however, that our conceptions of natural landscapes or 'human nature' are socially, culturally and historically produced. Moreover, it is clear that we exist in complex interdependencies with animals, crops, the air and water cycle, microbes and so on. These relationships are not static, essential, or 'natural', but they are both productive of and produced by power relations in all their forms.

This was the great insight of the environmental justice activists and theorists of the 1980s and 1990s, who reframed contemporary environmentalism as more about 'where we all live' than about the preservation or conservation of an external wilderness (Harvey 1996; Schlosberg 1999, 2013), drawing on older syntheses of ecological and radical politics (e.g., Bookchin 1971, 1982; Illich 1973). For them, environmentalism concerned clean water, secure shelter, safe and appropriate food, less harmful and risky technologies and industry, as well as a less exploitative and violent relationship with the flora and fauna around us. Crucially, however, these relations are all imbued with power and politics. If they are produced through power relations, then it is possible to change them through practices of resistance. Thus Castree and Braun suggest that 'we need to fashion new – or refashion old – analytical and political tools, tools for making the future natures that we wish to inhabit' (1998: 35). And it is here that we come to the final term in this book's title: *politics*.

Politics

This volume is explicitly political in that it seeks to keep power relations in view at all times. This aspect is absolutely key to all that follows: it is not enough to simply say 'let's try to see things differently', or think things differently, and expect change to follow accordingly. A truly *political* perspective must be aware of the power relationships, interests, subjectivities and structures that produce forms of environmental harm around us. More accurately, we might say that a critical and political attitude is one that recognises making the familiar appear strange and bringing the unfamiliar into clearer focus as *political* acts, but acts that are also conditioned by prevailing power relationships.[3]

There are a number of ways to think about politics and the political – and these terms are no less complex or ambiguous than the two that have preceded it – but it is useful to begin by clarifying what is *not* meant by politics here. I do not equate politics solely with formal political processes, actors and institutions. Politics is much more than political parties, policy disputes, and the parliament or government (Barry 2001: 6–7; Edkins 1999; Magnusson 2003; Mouffe 2005; Walker 2003). Neither is politics a clearly delimited realm, distinct from 'economics', 'society', or 'nature'. Rather, the use of politics in this volume title is intended to convey a perspective and set of questions: an attention to power relationships and the presence of conflicts and antagonisms in society. Who gets what, how and why? Who or what are the most important actors, institutions, groups, movements, ideas and practices in a given situation or issue? What are the rules of the game, and who sets them and why (as well as who are the winners and losers in the game)? What are the pros and cons of particular ideas, structures, rationalities and programmes? Who is being silenced, excluded, marginalised, or harmed? What are the consequences of particular actions or ways of thinking? What values or principles should guide our action and thought? What are the conditions of possibility of change? Where can we identify resistance?

Many political thinkers have sought to broaden our conception of politics beyond the 'players in the game' to a wider perspective encompassing the rules of the game and the very existence of the game itself (Walker 2003). For Andrew Barry, 'an action is *political* . . . to the degree to which it opens up new sites and objects of contestation. And it is *anti-political* to the extent that is closes down the space of contestation' (2001: 194, emphasis in original). There is a resonance here with the Coxian definition of critical theory, which aims to identify feasible alternative formations of the existing world order and 'clarify this range of possible alternatives' (1981: 130). Being political is thus akin to resisting the status quo: for Edkins a political act 'would be to interrupt discourse, to challenge what have, through discursive practices, been constituted as normal, natural and accepted ways of carrying on' (1999: 12).

This, it will be evident, is a very broad conception of politics. It is strongly influenced by the Marxist emphasis on the presence of conflict, struggle and antagonism within society, and the Gramscian extension of struggle to the realm of common-sense and hegemonic structures (indeed eco-Marxists have been debating many of the political dilemmas facing the green movement for a long time: see, for example, Bahro 1984). It has much in common with a Frankfurt School conception of critical theory as orientated towards the potentiality for progressive change in a given situation. And it resonates strongly with the emphasis in much poststructuralist thought on a conception of 'the political' as an irreducible domain of undecidability and contingency, where the very boundaries that structure the rest of social life are instantiated, contested, dissolved and reinscribed (Edkins 1999). For Foucault (as indeed for Marx and Gramsci), critical thought and politics were closely linked: critique is 'the art of voluntary insubordination, that of reflected intractability' (Foucault 2007b: 47).

As with the terms *critical* and *environmental,* the contributors to this volume have interpreted the term *politics* in very different ways. For many it involved some engagement with the movements and groups outside the institutionalised and formalised processes of governance (see chapters by Bond; Cudworth; Hinton; Litfin; McShane; Price, Saunders and Olcese; and others). For some it involved an account of structures and deeply sedimented power relationships (see Brooks and Bryant, Dalby, Grove, Igoe, Kuehls, Lövbrand and Stripple, Luke, Paterson, Pellizzoni, Watts and Peluso, and others). For some it involved engagement in some form with policy debates and issues, how these are framed, and who are harmed by them (see Baker, Büscher, Okereke and Charlesworth, Death, Forsyth, Kütting, Methmann and Oels, Whitehead, and others). For some it involved more sustained reflection on how things might be otherwise or thought differently (see Hobden, McShane, Rudy and White, Wapner, and others). Most chapters included elements of all of these.

Most fundamentally, all the contributors would agree that the environmental issues discussed here are inherently political: whilst they may have technical and policy dimensions; whilst there might be elements of chance or fortune involved; and whilst there might be many issues that seem too difficult, complex, or intractable to change, they are all shaped and reshaped by existing politics and power relationships, and visions of alternative relationships. Thinking about, studying and acting upon the environmental crisis is therefore a quintessentially political task, and one that this volume hopes to show is well-suited for critical modes of thought.

This volume

As set out in the preceding sections, the interpretation of the terms *critical, environmental,* and *politics* in this volume are all broad and interdisciplinary. It is therefore a major strength of the following chapters that they include contributions from authors drawing upon a wide range of disciplines: including international relations, geography, sociology, history, philosophy, anthropology, and political science. The natural sciences also inform any discussion of environmental issues – and indeed the artificial distinction between arts, social science, and natural science is rendered problematic and unhelpful by many of the issues we face – and contributors draw upon biology, chemistry, physics, medicine, psychology, geology, and many others.

The range of concepts covered is also extensive, including terms that have been central to many of the social science disciplines for a long time (such as citizenship, commodification, consumption, feminism, justice, movements, science, security, the state, summits, and technology), terms that have been at the heart of environmental politics for many years (including biodiversity, climate change, conservation, ecocentrism, limits, localism, resources, sacrifice, and sustainability), and terms that have been introduced to these literatures and debates more recently (biopolitics, governance, governmentality, hybridity, posthumanism, risk, and vulnerability). There are of course many other concepts we could have included, and many readers will doubtlessly lament the omission of their particular favourite. Some concepts were intended to be here, but unfortunately did not make it into the final volume. There was an explicit decision, however, not to include a long list of 'issue-based' chapters on topics such as water, food, forests, minerals, fish, chemicals, nuclear power, and so on. Rather, the volume aims to take a more cross-cutting approach to the sorts of analytical concepts that will enable researchers to see these familiar issues in different ways. The chapters are therefore tools, rather than the 'problems' or issues on which the tools must work. The two partial exceptions to this are the chapters on biodiversity and climate change. These are only partial exceptions because, whilst both are frequently presented as self-evident 'problems' or issues requiring our attention, they are also particularly significant and hegemonic ways of constructing environmental issues more broadly, and thus can also be regarded as tools for comprehending a much wider range of problems. Both these chapters endeavour to make the familiar appear a little stranger.

The volume attempts to combine global and local studies and cases, and there is an impressive diversity of examples and contexts discussed in the following chapters. These range from the Cochabamba conference in Bolivia to climate camps in the UK; UN summits in Rio de Janeiro and Johannesburg to climate migrants from Pacific islands; forests in Indonesia to Dutch energy governance reform; indigenous communities in Namibia to oil extraction in the Niger Delta; survivalist militias in the United States to Maasai tribesmen in Kenya. Volumes on environmental politics have frequently ended up inadvertently portraying the United States and Western Europe as the most important arenas of study, and this volume explicitly tries to think more globally. Despite this, there are clearly many areas of the world relatively untouched in the chapters that follow; but again, this is a product of a volume that is intended to be primarily conceptual rather than an in-depth guide to global environmental politics in all its particularities. Examples and case studies are illustrative, therefore, and do not pretend to be comprehensive.

In each chapter the authors were asked to provide an introduction to the concept for those new to the field – including undergraduate and postgraduate students – as well as to draw connections between concepts and thinkers that might be provocative or illuminating for more established researchers in the field. They were also asked to reflect upon some of the following questions or issues: How has this concept commonly been used in the study of environmental politics? In what sense is this concept critical? What are some of the most significant ideas or arguments that this concept raises? What critical thinkers have deployed this concept? What are some of the most significant pieces of research that have used this concept? How might this concept be used to make a critical intervention into environmental politics? To what sorts of research agendas might such critical interventions lead?

To facilitate this reflection, and to provide a flexible framework around which to organise the volume as a whole as well as the chapters, each chapter considers these questions under some combination of the headings 'Core Ideas', 'Key Thinkers', and 'Critical Potential'. The chapters include suggested further reading, and most provide useful internet links. Connections between chapters have also been encouraged throughout; in the spirit of interconnected ecosystems and rhizome structures, no concept can really be understood in isolation. The pointers to other chapters that recur throughout the volume are exactly that – suggested additional chapters to pursue related lines of enquiry, or different perspectives on the concepts, thinkers, and cases discussed.

As such, it would be both impossible and meaningless to try to provide a summary of the chapters, or any kind of 'conclusion'. The aim of this book, by providing a set of conceptual tools drawn from critical theory (understood very broadly), is to open up questions and new problems and new research agendas, not to provide answers or conclusions. Of course, I hope that you will find some or all of the chapters useful and insightful in helping to make sense of the complex politics of global environmental change. Moreover, I hope that it will facilitate critical thinking about some of these seemingly 'self-evident' ideas, problems and practices. But, in the spirit of critical enquiry, I am comfortable and confident that this volume will elicit its own critiques: including those who think it is 'too critical' and hence of little 'real world' utility, as well as those who feel it doesn't go far enough in deconstructing established ways of thinking and power relations.

There is, of course, a tension at the heart of a volume such as this: what is presented here as critical may become system-reinforcing when viewed from another perspective, and most of the concepts here have the potential to be conservative as well as critical. This is true of environmentalism more broadly (see Harvey 1996: 172). In his classic collection entitled *The Development Dictionary* (which, although published more than 20 years ago, is in many respects the inspiration for this volume), Wolfgang Sachs noted the 'successful ambivalence' at the heart of the ecology movement (1992: 31). It is a movement that has drawn upon hard science as well as quasi-spiritual mysticism (Barry 2001; Beck 1995; Foucault 1997: 295). Environmentalism can act as a stimulus to radical system change, or conservation and precaution. It asserts the value of the small and the local and the traditional, as well as the global, the systemic and the macro. This ambivalence is doubtlessly reflected in the chapters that follow. Whether any of these concepts have the key to unlock the paradox in which modern society and the environmental movement finds itself is unclear, and perhaps ultimately doubtful. But they certainly demonstrate that there is considerable potential within the field of critical environmental politics to make the familiar appear strange and bring the unfamiliar into clearer focus.

Notes

1. Webster's English dictionary of 1913 gives the following definitions of environment: '(1) Act of environing; state of being environed; and (2) That which environs or surrounds; surrounding conditions, influences, or forces, by which living forms are influenced and modified in their growth and development'. See http://machaut.uchicago.edu/?resource=Webster%27s&word=environment&us e1913=on (accessed 21 March 2013).
2. Of course, there is much more nuance in many of these accounts of emancipation than is often given credit. Harvey (1996: 184) quotes Engels at some length on this: '[l]et us not, however, flatter ourselves overmuch on account of our human victories over nature. For each such victory nature takes its revenge on us. . . . Thus at every step we are reminded that we by no means rule over nature like a conqueror over a foreign people, like someone standing out of nature – but that we, with flesh, blood and brain, belong to nature and exist in its midst'. See also Peet and Watts (1996b: 1) for a similar quote from Marx; and Cox on how 'to think through the consequences of understanding ourselves as part of nature rather than as dominant over nature' (2001: 52).
3. A critical and political attitude, as set out briefly here, has some resonance with E. H. Carr's balance between utopianism and realism: '[t]he utopian is necessarily voluntarist: he believes in the possibility of more or less radically rejecting reality, and substituting his utopia for it by an act of will. The realist analyses a predetermined course of development which he is powerless to change. . . . The utopian, fixing his eyes on the future, thinks in terms of creative spontaneity: the realist, rooted in the past, in terms of causality. All healthy human action, and therefore all healthy thought, must establish a balance between utopia and reality, between free will and determinism' (Carr 2001 [1939]: 12).

2   Biodiversity

Bram Büscher

Introduction

At a first glance, the concept of 'biodiversity' as the short-hand for 'biological diversity' is rather straightforward. To most people and academics, including many studying environmental politics, it simply refers to the multitude of different species, organisms and variations of life on earth. This, however, does not mean that the concept is not political. On the contrary. Biodiversity, from its earliest introduction, has been highly political, and continues to be so (Sarkar 2005; Takacs 1996). Yet, this political content, and as a corollary the concept's critical potential, is not very often recognized or consciously employed in environmental politics or other academic fields. Of course, there are important exceptions, but on the whole these seem to be few and far between.

This, I will also argue, is unfortunate, because biodiversity has become nearly ubiquitous in environmental debates and is often used as a seemingly non-political shorthand for the much more contested concepts of 'nature', 'environment' and even 'wilderness'. As such, the *potential* for the concept to make critical interventions in environmental politics is considerable. *Critical,* in this chapter, is employed in a Coxian way, hence, contrary to *problem-solving* (Cox 1981; see also the introductory chapter by Death, this volume). Following Cox, Ford argues that 'a critical approach distinguishes critical theory from problem-solving theory, where the latter takes for granted the framework of existing power relations and institutions and is concerned with the smooth functioning of the system. By contrast, critical theory calls the very framework into question and seeks to analyse how it is maintained and changed' (Ford 2003: 121).

Emphasising this conceptualisation of critical theory, I will argue, is especially important in the light of current trends related to the rapid commodification and financialisation of biodiversity by many mainstream actors in environmental politics, including governments, international and non-governmental organizations and business (Büscher, Sullivan, Neves, Igoe and Brockington 2012; see also Igoe and Paterson this volume). I will therefore conclude that while biodiversity's *current* critical potential is limited, a long overdue reinterpretation – and, in Latour's (2010) words, 'recompositioning' – of the concept is highly necessary. Moreover, I will argue that a promising avenue for this reinterpretation could be to reemphasize biodiversity's *emerging properties,* namely the ecological properties that biodiversity acquires or maintains in their dynamic interaction *over time.* Before I get there, however, I will outline some of the core ideas and key thinkers associated with the concept in the context of the global environmental politics of biodiversity and its critical potential.

Core ideas

The concept of biodiversity originated in conservation biology and is attributed to Walter G. Rosen, who coined it for a conference in 1986 entitled 'The National Forum on Biodiversity', after which Edward O. Wilson popularized the concept by editing and publishing the proceedings of the meeting under the title 'Biodiversity' (Wilson 1988; see Takacs 1996: 37). This means that in a fairly short life-span the concept has rapidly gained popularity, to the extent, as stated previously, that it is nearly ubiquitous in how nature is referred to and explained, both in the contemporary biological sciences and in most international and national conservation policy and discourse. Yet, as stressed by Guyer and Richards (1996: 5), 'from the outset the term was political as well as biological. Wilson himself has explained that it was his attempt to try and protect a specific academic interest (in whole organisms) from the radical reductionist currents in molecular biology then threatening to rule the roost'. But, as stressed by many conservation biologists, biodiversity is more than 'whole organisms'; it refers also to the importance of emergent properties; indeed to the diversity of specific species *and* the dynamic interactions between habitats, ecosystems and species over time (Takacs 1996: 72–3). It is thus precise enough to convey what is being referred to, but broad enough to allow different interpretations to come together under the same term. And this, at least in part, explains its popularity. The concept is employed by many seemingly contradictory or even opposing agendas and interests that, as we shall see, have had major influences on the concept's critical potential.

David Takacs, who arguably wrote the definitive genealogy of the concept of biodiversity based on interviews with many key thinkers in conservation biology, summarizes these well:

> The term *biodiversity* makes concrete – and promotes action on behalf of – a way of being, a way of thinking, a way of feeling, and way of perceiving the world. It encompasses the multiplicity of scientists' factual, political, and emotional arguments in defense of nature, while simultaneously appearing as a purely scientific, objective entity. In the term *biodiversity,* subjective preferences are packaged with hard facts; eco-feelings are joined to economic commodities; deep ecology is sold as dollars and sense to more pragmatic, or more myopic, policy makers and members of the public. Biodiversity shines with the gloss of scientific respectability, while underneath it is kaleidoscopic and all-encompassing: we can find in it what we want, and can justify many courses of action in its name. It reflects the interrelatedness of all living beings, of humans with the rest of the living world, of our ideas of nature with nature itself. (Takacs 1996: 99)

Importantly, Takacs adds to this the role that biologists see for themselves in relation to the concept: 'by promoting and using the concept of biodiversity, biologists hope to preserve much of the biotic world, including the dynamic processes that shape the world, while simultaneously appropriating for themselves the authority to speak for it, to define and defend it' (Takacs 1996: 99). Here, clearly, the political content of the concept of biodiversity shines through. Conservation biologists, who invented and launched the concept, see for themselves a privileged role to 'define and defend' it (see also Forsyth, this volume).

Yet, while conservation biologists are still often seen as the 'natural' spokespersons for biodiversity, they are no longer as central to its defense and definition as Takacs assumed. This, I argue, is clear from how the concept has been taken up in international environmental politics and caught up in international neoliberal restructuring, especially since the mid-1990s.

However, in order to demonstrate this, we need to show how key thinkers started becoming frustrated with the concept itself.

Key thinkers

As it is impossible to include contributions of all key thinkers in one chapter, I will focus on some of the main contentions around the concept and draw out where key thinkers stand on these. We can arguably distinguish between several, interrelated types of contention. The first have to do with *defining* the concept itself. The second relate to the *use and purpose* of the concept, while the third and last are about who can *speak* for biodiversity.

First, the definition of the concept. Previously, I alluded to broad conceptualisations of biodiversity and how these have impacted on its use, purpose and who gets to speak for it. So far this has mainly related to the *biological* part of the concept: the species and the emergent properties of the habitats, ecosystems and landscapes they are part of (see also McShane, this volume). The other part of the term – *diversity* – is equally contentious. However, some key thinkers have argued that diversity as a simple, material fact is all that is needed to create biological value. David Ehrenfeld, a key thinker in conservation biology and the founding editor of the journal with the same name, argued that 'value is an intrinsic part of diversity; it does not depend on the properties of the species in question, the uses to which particular species may or may not be put, or their alleged role in the balance of global ecosystems. For biological diversity, value is' (Ehrenfeld 1988: 214). Diversity, thus, is often seen as (innately) good; a measure of robustness and resilience of ecosystems. Yet, how do we measure diversity in biological terms, and is mere 'diversity' good enough? What about ecosystem and biological integrity (Angermeier and Karr 1994)? Do we need to distinguish the different values of species, or will any type of diversity suffice? And how to link 'cultural diversity' to biological diversity in order to acknowledge the fact that different cultures value and conserve dissimilar types of biodiversity differently (Caillon and Degeorges 2007)? Lastly, how do these issues relate to and produce variegated effects on human welfare (Blaikie and Jeanrenaud 1997)?

These are questions at the heart of using biodiversity as a planning and management tool. This, according to another key thinker, Sahota Sarkar (2005: 153–9), leads to further, intricate problems and questions around *place prioritization* (how to prioritize places around biodiversity content?), *surrogacy* (how to select the features upon which biodiversity may be estimated?), *viability* (will the biodiversity in a place have long-term prospects?) and *feasibility* (how does biodiversity as a criterion weigh against (other) socioeconomic and political criteria in relation to the use of a particular place?). The point here is not to answer all these questions, or even to do justice to them. It is simply to posit them and so hint at the complexities that they are informed by and raise. Biodiversity, as mentioned previously, is a problematic concept and not easily defined and rendered operationalisable (Haila and Kouki 1994; see Brown 1998 for a political ecology approach). To this it should be added that the generally accepted categories by which biological diversity is normally measured (genuses, families, kingdoms, etc.) are contentious in terms of the scientific history underpinning them (see Bonneuil 2002). This history is anything but neutral and is closely associated to very particular political, cultural and epistemological interests and ideas. All of this ambiguity and uncertainty has further rendered problematic and frustrating the use of the concept (for a complaint about this, see Bowman 1998).

In terms of the purpose of, and who gets to speak for, the concept, this is clearly related to informing and aiding discussions about the global ecological crisis and what to do about this.

Biodiversity is directly related to the 'mission-drivenness' of the discipline of conservation biology (Meine, Soulé and Reed 2006), and one could argue that the ambiguity surrounding the definition and use of the concept has helped to mobilize people around this purpose. However, conservation biologists were very soon 'outflanked' as the designated experts 'authorized' to define and defend biodiversity, much to their dismay. Indeed, this is a reason why some key thinkers have become quite critical of how the concept is operationalized, such as Sanderson and Redford, who argue as follows:

> Biodiversity, a concept that originated in biology, has been wrested from its originators, first by conservationists, then by economic actors. Conservation activists are committed to a conservation agenda that is centred on 'sustainable use'. Economic actors, also advocating sustainable use, are interesting in forwarding a conservation agenda that generally does not interrupt the course or abridge the prerogatives of economic growth. (1997: 116)

This quotation comes from a chapter in the book *Last Stand: Protected Areas and the Defense of Tropical Biodiversity,* edited by Kramer, van Schaik and Johnson in 1997. The book is a 'classic' in the so-called *back-to-the-barriers* literature that heavily criticized 'integrated conservation and development programmes' for failing to meet conservation (*and* development) objectives (Hutton, Adams and Murombedzi 2005; see Igoe, this volume). These authors, and many other key thinkers in the back-to-the-barriers literature, such as John Oates and John Terborgh, complained that 'conservationists' and 'economic actors' have now appropriated (speaking for) biodiversity and turned it into a 'political term' so that 'its use now revolves around economic appropriation, not natural preservation' (Sanderson and Redford 1997: 116).

These sentiments, however, were around from the beginning of the concept. Paul Ehrenfeld, in his chapter in the 'original' edited collection *Biodiversity,* argued that

> In the long run, basing our conservation strategy on the economic value of diversity will only make things worse, because it keeps us from coping with the root cause of the loss of diversity. It makes us accept as givens the technological/socioeconomic premises that make biological impoverishment of the world inevitable. If I were one of the many exploiters and destroyers of biological diversity, I would like nothing better than for my opponents, the conservationists, to be bogged down over the issue of valuing. As shown by the example of the faltering search for new drugs in the tropics, economic criteria of value are shifting, fluid, and utterly opportunistic in their practical application. This is the opposite of the value system needed to conserve biological diversity over the course of decades and centuries. (Ehrenfeld 1988: 214; see also Ehrenfeld 2008)

Ehrenfeld makes an interesting point here, because many conservationists these days are indeed 'bogged down over the issue of valuing', especially the monetary valuation of 'ecosystem services'. While the origins of this 'neoliberalisation' of biodiversity conservation are outside of the purview of this chapter (see Arsel and Büscher 2012; Brockington and Duffy 2010; Igoe, Neves and Brockington 2010; MacDonald and Corson 2012), it is clear that it brought new key actors into the picture that have shaped some of the current contentions around the concept of biodiversity.

One of the most important of these is the Convention on Biological Diversity (CBD), a legal agreement between states, an institution, and an arena for debate that has deeply influenced the global politics and governance of biodiversity (see Death, this volume) and also the ideas of key thinkers such as Sanderson and Redford. According to the CBD website,

> The objectives of this Convention, to be pursued in accordance with its relevant provisions, are the conservation of biological diversity, the sustainable use of its components and the fair and equitable sharing of the benefits arising out of the utilization of genetic resources, including by appropriate access to genetic resources and by appropriate transfer of relevant technologies, taking into account all rights over those resources and to technologies, and by appropriate funding. (CBD 2012)

Reflecting on the convention, Swanson (1999: 308) argues that the 'CBD came into existence because there exists a common interest in the coordinated management of domestic resources, not on account of a joint interest in a common resource. The recognition of this more complicated form of commonality is an achievement in itself'. This, according to Moran, King and Carlson (2001: 505–6), is the 'grand-bargain' of the CBD: it gave nation-states sovereignty over their 'bioresources' and rights 'to regulate and charge outsiders for access to their biodiversity'.

Hence, the CBD transformed biodiversity from a global 'common heritage' to something that can be traded and privatized (see Paterson, this volume). And it is precisely this point that leads a more critical key thinker, Ken MacDonald, to argue that with the CBD, 'the devil is in the (bio)diversity'. He summarizes three main critiques of the CBD from a political economy perspective:

> [F]irst, it codifies a dominant perspective of nature as capital through its emphasis on sustainable use initiatives that, when translated into practice, means the use of *in situ* biodiversity to realize profit through the conversion of use value to exchange value; second, it positions biodiversity as genetic material available for exchange in a global market; and third, it explicitly recognizes that states have a sovereign right to determine access to genetic resources in their territories and to allocate the benefits from the use of those resources. (MacDonald 2010b: 526)

These three innovations brought in by the CBD were key in a broader process of the neoliberalisation of conservation: a trend that really took off in the mid-1990s and has since impacted heavily on the political content and contentiousness of the concept of biodiversity (Büscher 2008; Büscher et al. 2012; MacDonald 2010b; see also Igoe, this volume). This has serious consequences for environmental conservation and politics, but also for the critical potential of the concept of biodiversity and how it could relate to other key concepts discussed in this volume, such as justice and sustainability (see Bond and Whitehead, this volume). I will now turn to these issues.

Critical potential

The neoliberalisation of environmental politics since the 1990s, simply put, means that biodiversity must increasingly pay its way, and so 'legitimise itself', in economic terms (McAfee 1999). Biodiversity, in short, has become 'big business'.[1] The idea, according to the Business and Biodiversity Resource Centre, is that 'companies . . . depend on biodiversity. It helps to stabilise the climate and provide clean air and water, services vital for a stable operating environment. It provides raw materials, technology and business opportunities'. Hence: 'loss of biodiversity represents a business risk. As diversity disappears, so do the opportunities for new products, new technologies and new business opportunities' (Business and Biodiversity 2012). In turn, with this reoperationalisation come new spokespeople for biodiversity. Many nongovernmental organisations, governments, companies and scientists other than biologists have started to claim the right to 'define and defend' biodiversity, and in a distinctly neoliberal manner that subjects the concept's social, political and ecological dimensions to their value as determined by capitalist markets. While it is impossible to give an overview of all the new actors that have joined the neoliberal biodiversity boat, one particularly dominant and illustrative example is a set of actors behind 'TEEB' or 'The Economics of Ecosystems and Biodiversity' (MacDonald and Corson 2012): a broad coalition of scientists, economists, national and international policymakers from environmental and other ministries and organisations, and interested companies.

TEEB started as a 'study' in 2007, led by Pavan Sukhdev, a former banker with Deutsche Bank. The aim was to 'to sharpen awareness of the value of biodiversity and ecosystem services and facilitate the development of effective policy, as well as engaged business and citizen responses' (TEEB 2012). Since then, it has become much more than a 'study', and rather a loose movement of scientists, NGOs, business and policymakers interested in ending the 'invisibility of nature'.[2] They do so by subjecting nature and biodiversity to economic calculation and measurement and so turn them into 'natural capital'. According to the Bank of Natural Capital website, set up by TEEB, 'when talking about the value of the environment, it's quite usual to talk in wider social and ecological terms. What's different about The TEEB Study is that it makes the link between nature and economic value explicit'. The conclusion: 'only when we account for natural capital will we be able to see the invisible wealth we've been wasting all these years' (Bank of Natural Capital 2012a).

Obviously, these and similar initiatives have drastically changed the global environmental politics of biodiversity. Moreover, they have radically impacted on the way many people view biodiversity. While many of the outlets, publications, websites, brochures and other utterances of these new spokespeople still state that biodiversity is complex, hard to define and render operationalisable, at the same time they reinscribe a simplistic idea about biodiversity as 'all life on earth' that can easily be counted, in which the more species that exist within a particular area almost automatically make a place more valuable as a 'biodiversity hot spot' (see Ehrenfeld 2009: 106–20, for a critique). A brief animated film on the Bank of Natural Capital website, for example, explains biodiversity as follows: 'Biodiversity is a pretty neat idea. In a nutshell, it is all life on earth. Simple. And, you know, not just cute animals you see in nature films or more sophisticated animations by Disney; it's all life, including me and you' (Bank of Natural Capital 2012b). Biodiversity, it seems, *needs* to be communicated simplistically to convince audiences of its importance, even though – it is often immediately stressed – its actual valuation is something that only *experts* can do. It also needs to be subjected to quantitative measurement in order to monetize it. In sum, many actors in environmental politics are trying to transform biodiversity into a 'nature that capital can see' (Robertson 2006), hence the importance of the idea of 'natural capital'.

But this is no easy feat. Behind the stabilized neoliberal discourses of biodiversity, warns Robertson (2006: 367), the 'new round of the commodification of nature may overwhelm the capacity of science to provide stable representations of commodity value'. Robertson and others (Castree 2003a; Dressler 2011; Igoe et al. 2010; Sullivan 2013; see also Forsyth, this volume) show that such an 'uncontroversial measure' is not possible and that, as a result, a great deal of wishful thinking is necessary in order to make the link between 'business and biodiversity'. However, one can wonder whether this is really the key point. From a critical environmental politics perspective, the point might rather be that global capital has been trying to find a way to reduce its environmental footprint and increase its chances for profits and capital accumulation (Büscher et al. 2012; Sullivan 2013). Hence, one could argue that the business of biodiversity is not so much about its conservation but about reoperationalising the term so that biodiversity becomes part of a particular worldview. Phrased differently: many key actors in global environmental politics today are actively trying to ensure that biodiversity has little to no critical content or potential in order for it to play its role in a world defined by global capital. And this is exactly the point that MacDonald and Corson are making about the TEEB study: 'TEEB, then, is performative; a project that, even as it claims to be descriptive of the world, actively works to bring the world it describes into being by circulating and promoting its ostensibly descriptive models as the best basis for policy and action' (2012: 163).

Obviously, TEEB and other 'business and biodiversity' initiatives do not function in isolation; they are part of broader and contested structures of environmental politics, including international regimes, national and international institutions and actors, and different knowledge structures and discourses that intersect with, frame and relate to these (see Baker and Death, this volume). Moreover, as Blaikie and Jeanrenaud (1997: 47) emphasize, 'different actors create their own ideas about biodiversity, appropriate it and adapt others, and experience and use them in different ways in different arenas'. From a global environmental politics perspective, the link between developed and developing countries in international negotiations is especially important because much important global biodiversity is situated in developing countries, yet it is actors from developed countries who are mostly pushing for its commodification (Duffy 2010). One arena where this has played out in particular, and that has had important effects on broader debates, politics and practices related to biodiversity, is the aforementioned Convention on Biological Diversity.

One of the main issues around the CBD has been that it further codifies so-called bioprospecting, the 'arrangements to explore biological diversity for commercially valuable genetic and biochemical resources' (Moran et al 2001: 506). This has in turn led to a highly polarized debate in environmental politics, especially around the 'intellectual property rights' of different groups of people in relation to biodiversity. In particular, this has led to substantial developing country versus developed country divides because, with vast differences in resources, connections and power, companies from rich countries have often been able to wrestle the 'sovereignty' over resources away from developing countries in order to turn them into privatized profits (Duffy 2010; see also Brooks and Bryant, and Watts and Peluso, this volume). Yet, while acknowledging these and other problematic aspects of bioprospecting, Castree (2003b: 52) argues that 'rather than reject biological prospecting on grounds of principle, we need instead to ask: *what kind* of bioprospecting for *what kind* of benefits in *which* contexts?' This leaves the door open for understanding the ways (cultural, medicinal and other) in which indigenous peoples have long been and continue to make use of biodiversity resources, for example.

This, then, is perhaps also the key to evaluate the CBD and its impact on biodiversity. Taking my cue once again from MacDonald,

> The CBD, like all international agreements, is more than simply a document; it is an institution that calls into being an active political space – an arena in which rights and

interests may be negotiated and new social relations configured around those negotiations. . . . This arena can lead to creative opportunities for new, and previously
excluded, groups to claim authority, but it also creates a context in which privileged
positions and perspectives can be consolidated and codified in ways that structure
policy and practice. (2010b: 527)

This, I argue, is what has happened and is still ongoing: the critical potential of the concept
of biodiversity is (being) defused and appropriated into the larger frameworks of politics and
the power of neoliberal capitalism, a process in which institutions like TEEB and the CBD
play an important *part*. I emphasize 'part', as many other institutions, actors and initiatives
in global environmental politics are also currently trying to financialize and commoditize
biodiversity, among others through 'creative' new forms such as 'biodiversity derivatives',
'wetlands banking', 'species banking' and 'carbon credits' (Arsel and Büscher 2012; Sullivan
2013). With all this underway, a crucial question is whether there are other critical potentiali-
ties in the concept of biodiversity. I will explore these in the concluding section of this chapter.

Conclusion

As the loss of biodiversity continues apace and is even accelerating in some regions according to the 'Third Global Biodiversity Outlook' (CBD 2010), it seems more important than
ever to stimulate and rethink the concept's critical potential. Coming back to the conceptualization of critical theory with which I started the chapter, one that 'calls the very framework
into question and seeks to analyse how it is maintained and changed' (Ford 2003: 121), the
concept of biodiversity as operationalised in mainstream science and policy as the diversity
of life renders this ambition problematic. Indeed, the commodification of biodiversity is
partly made possibly through this simplistic (re)defining of the term which then leaves it to
(often self-proclaimed) experts to interpret what is valuable in terms of profits.

A more explicitly complex rendering of the term, I argue, could lead to more critical potential if – crucially – biodiversity is placed within a broader political-economic context. Sarkar
(2005: chapter 6) is one key thinker who provides a more complex rendering of biodiversity based on philosophical considerations, but here I want to emphasize Stahel's point that
'only within a mechanical time framework can the economic valuation of single species be
conceived. It is only within this framework, too, that the global value of an ecosystem's biodiversity can be expected to be obtained by simple summing-up of single values, *ignoring the
emergent properties which arise from the interrelations and interdependencies of the different
species within the whole*' (Stahel 1999: 124, emphasis added). What makes biodiversity complex, as also referred to previously, is not just understanding the taxa, but – more importantly,
the 'interrelations and interdependencies of the different species within the whole' *over time*.
Biodiversity is dynamic and changes over time; indeed, it could only have come into existence
due to dynamic emergent properties that develop and play out as time goes by. The quantification necessary in the commodification and financialisation of biodiversity is necessarily
a 'mechanical' exercise that disrupts these dynamic emergent properties and so castrates the
critical potential of the concept (see also Rudy and White, this volume).

Emphasizing the idea of emergent properties in the concept of biodiversity may, I argue,
help to stimulate the concept's neglected and seemingly forgotten critical potential (see also
Hobden and Grove, this volume). To make this credible, however, more research should be
done to understand the longitudinal impacts of the commodification and financialisation of

biodiversity's emergent properties. At the same time, future research needs to focus on the political processes and tactics employed, both on the global level through initiatives such as TEEB and the CBD, and on the local level in communities, private companies and other organisations and events, which make it seem as though the impacts of commodification and financialisation on biodiversity's emergent properties not only are not harmful, but indeed beneficial. By employing the concept of biodiversity with more awareness of its nuances, complexities and – crucially – its inherently political nature than has been done before, and stressing its ubiquity in environmental debates, research can further help to bring out its critical potential.

Finally, this same potential could be used to follow Latour (2010) and to 'recycle' critique and 'recompose' biodiversity (see Forsyth, this volume). While inherently political, biodiversity is not inherently neoliberal, commodified or financialised. In fact, as I have tried to show, this recomposition is incredibly hard. But it is here that we can perhaps find the 'compositionalist' quality of the concept; a way in which it can be used to hold both the 'larger framework of power' to account while building on its emerging properties to build emerging potentials.

Further reading

A key resource on the idea of and politics around biodiversity is David Takacs (1996) *The Idea of Biodiversity: Philosophies of Paradise,* Baltimore: The Johns Hopkins University Press. This book not only contains interesting discussions of the concept, but also many interviews with key thinkers. For a more philosophical approach to biodiversity, Sahota Sarkar's (2005) *Biodiversity and Environmental Philosophy: An Introduction,* Cambridge: Cambridge University Press, is a must-read. For those who want to get into the discussions that led to the birth of the concept, see E.O. Wilson (ed.) (1988) *Biodiversity,* Washington DC: National Academy Press. Beyond these key readings, there are many articles and books that touch on the concept but without necessarily conceptualising it (critically) in relation to global environmental politics. Interesting exceptions are articles by Angermeier and Karr (1994), Blaikie and Jeanrenaud (1997), Guyer and Richards (1996), Haila and Kouki (1994), and MacDonald (2010b), amongst others.

Useful websites

Convention on Biological Diversity: http://www.cbd.int/
The Guardian biodiversity website: http://www.guardian.co.uk/environment/biodiversity
Biodiversity Heritage Library: http://www.biodiversitylibrary.org/
Bioversity International: http://www.bioversityinternational.org/
International Institute for Environment and Development Biodiversity site: http://www.iied.org/ biodiversity

Notes

1. See, for example, the Global Business of Biodiversity Symposium, 13–17 July 2010, London, UK, http://www.businessofbiodiversity.co.uk/ (accessed 7 May 2012).
2. As witnessed at the TEEB Conference 2012, 'Mainstreaming the Economics of Nature: Challenges for Science and Implementation', March 19–22, 2012, Leipzig, Germany.

3 Biopolitics

Kevin Grove

Introduction

Few concepts have captured the imagination of critical theorists in recent years quite like biopolitics and its corollary, biopower. In a nutshell, *biopower* can be defined as a mode of power that takes life as its object, while *biopolitics* refers to techniques and rationalities of power mobilized in pursuit of the security, growth, and development of individual and collective life (Foucault 1979, 2003). Its current popularity is indebted to French historian Michel Foucault, who developed his understanding of biopolitics to study power relations in a way that did not privilege the state or sovereign models of power. Biopolitics acts in the interest of individual and collective life through producing knowledge of the processes that sustain or retard the optimization of various life processes. It therefore operates through, and directs analytical attention towards, shifting regimes of power/knowledge as well as governmental technologies and interventions that operate beyond the state (Dillon 2007a; Duffield 2007).

Foucault's work on biopolitics sparked an ongoing revolution in thought that creates a new political imaginary for analysing contemporary practices of power and politics. Critical scholars have deployed this concept to theorize the networked and decentralized practices of rule that structure global liberal order but exceed traditional concepts of power and politics centered on the state (e.g., Agamben 1998; Hardt and Negri 2000). The ability of biopolitics to envision seemingly technical, apolitical, and mundane activities as power-laden makes it particularly attractive to research on critical environmental politics. To take one example, Erik Swyngedouw (2010) provocatively argues that widespread calls to save humanity from impending climate catastrophe depoliticize climate change adaptation and curtail critical lines of questioning into what form of life 'we' are protecting and what form of life 'we' *should* protect. In this light, Andrew Baldwin suggests that the concept of biopolitics allows us to 'sharpen our understanding of political rule in an era in which climate change is framed as a security issue' (Baldwin 2013: 60). As I hope to show, biopolitics offers a new conceptual apparatus capable of critically analysing how power and environment intertwine in contemporary political practice. Through an analytical framework focused on, inter alia, strategies, techniques, and relations, biopolitics enables critical scholars to recognize how key categories of environmental practice – including risk, adaptation, vulnerability, sustainability, and resilience – can instantiate, legitimize, and reinforce uneven power relations when deployed in an uncritical manner.

Core ideas and key thinkers

There is a lively philosophical and political debate over biopolitics informed by a number of theorists, such as Giorgio Agamben, Antonio Negri, Roberto Esposito, and Peter Sloterdijk (see Campbell 2011; Lemke 2011). While their debates are pushing the theory of biopolitics in new directions, I have purposefully chosen not to include a discussion of their work here, given how much current research on biopolitics and the environment draws almost exclusively on Foucault.[1] This account of biopolitics is admittedly myopic, but provides a detailed overview of Foucauldian approaches that are currently more frequently utilized in critical environmental research (see also Kuehls, and Lövbrand and Stripple, this volume).

While the term *biopolitics* was coined in political philosophy in the early twentieth century (Esposito 2008), its contemporary usage emerged through Foucault's efforts to think power and resistance outside dominant models of power based on Hobbes's notion of the social contract. As he details throughout his 1975–1976 Collège de France lectures, entitled *Society Must be Defended* (Foucault 2003; hereafter *SMBD*), sovereign-juridical models account for power in terms of the sovereign's prohibitions and oppressions. This is a form of analysis largely concerned with the topography of power: where it is located; how it should be distributed, exercised, and limited; and so forth. Sovereign-juridical models sequester power in the political sphere; it does not bleed into other domains such as economy, society, or culture. For Foucault, this ignores how modern liberal societies are structured around far more pervasive relations of domination and repression that follow the mode of warfare. The genealogy of race war in France and England he offers in *SMBD* uncovers the bellicose foundations of liberal order. *Race war* here refers to the confrontations between competing factions within society – the bourgeoisie and the aristocracy, for example – whose stakes are the possibilities for social and political order. Foucault inverts Clausewitz's famous statement that war is politics by other means to suggest that liberalism involves a 'social warfare' that permeates all domains of life. His genealogy demonstrates how diverse techniques and strategies for improving the health, security, and productivity of populations operate outside the sovereign state to create and sustain what he calls a 'regulatory society'. Rather than establishing peace through the dissemination of universal values, liberal order is sustained through biopolitical techniques that continuously identify, sequester, and negate the internal enemy – the 'abnormal', the 'recalcitrant' – in the name of securing the population's essential life processes.

Thus, in his initial analysis of liberal biopolitics in *SMBD,* Foucault uses 'biopower' to signify a form of power concerned with the quality of life, both individual and collective. Key to this definition of biopower is how Foucault reworks a number of commonplace concepts. First, power is not a quantity to be held, but the effect of a relation between individuals. It is action on the action of another (Foucault 1982b). Second, government does not refer to an institutionalized organization that holds power, but refers instead to practices that attempt to modify the thoughts and actions of others. In his famous phrasing, government is concerned with the 'conduct of conduct' (Foucault 2007a). Third, power is productive. It is not the property of individual subjects, but instead produces both objects and subjects of government (Foucault 1991a). The former are those whose conduct is targeted for improvement; the latter are those who devise the mechanisms for targeting and transforming conduct. Fourth, freedom is no longer the antithesis of power but is rather a precondition of power relations. Power relies on freedom (Elden 2001), but this is not the freedom of individual choice. Rather, freedom refers to the capacity to transgress the limits of any social order: the potential to refuse to be governed as such (Foucault 1982b, 2007b).

As a result, Foucault is less concerned with identifying the topography of power than analysing the *techniques* or *mechanisms* through which power is exercised, and the underlying *strategies*. Strategies comprise set objectives – visions of proper forms of conduct or desired forms of order – and mechanisms of power deployed to realize these objectives (McWhorter 2011). A focus on strategies and mechanisms enables a topological analysis of power that recognizes how a variety of techniques may be re/combined in multiple ways to realize the same objective (see Collier 2009). Ladell McWhorter, commenting on Foucault's recently published lectures, suggests that 'when strategic operators encounter obstacles or resistance, they must develop tactics and deploy mechanisms to overcome those obstacles or break that resistance and deflect or absorb its energy' (McWhorter 2011: 95). Strategic efforts to shape the conduct of others are thus *responses* to the resistance of those targeted.

Foucault differentiates sovereignty and biopower in terms of relational strategies and tactics. Sovereignty is an anti-normative power, the power of appropriation, which he famously defines as the power to 'make die and let live' (Foucault 1979). Key techniques are the law and violence. Importantly, this understanding of sovereign power as a form of power exercised through techniques of prohibition and appropriation differs from conventional readings of *sovereignty* as the legitimate basis of state rule and the foundation of modern political life. Biopower, in contrast, refers to a normative power, the power to 'make live and let die'. In *SMBD*, Foucault disaggregates biopower into two components: disciplinary techniques that operate on individual bodies, and governmental techniques that operate on the population. Together, discipline and government create particular forms of order by bringing individual capacities and actions in line with normative visions of proper ways of being (see Lövbrand and Stripple, this volume). Recent analyses departing from Foucault's newly translated Collège de France lectures – 1977–1978's *Security, Territory, Population* (Foucault 2007a) and 1978–1979's *Birth of Biopolitics* (Foucault 2008) – have identified additional biopolitical techniques such as security and environmental power (Anderson 2012), which will be discussed later.

'Populations' and 'bodies' are not stable categories of knowledge: their meaning and significance changes in response to new understandings of life and security that are driven by the refusal of people and things to be governed as intended. Genealogies of security have detailed the transformations in these twin targets of biopolitics. The entry of life into politics was historically conditioned by new experiences of existential insecurity associated with the European Enlightenment. The 'death of God' brought about by, inter alia, the Reformation, the colonial encounter, and subsequent struggles against absolutist rule endowed European modernity and its subjects with a newfound freedom, the freedom of life in a world without deep or essential meaning. This freedom is also the source of insecurity about a future no longer determined by divine order and rigid hierarchies (Dillon 1996; Foucault 1970). This radically uncertain future forms a core problem of biopower. Suffering, loss, and even death are no longer part of a divinely ordained plan that culminates in salvation and eternal life; instead, they are contingencies to be avoided in order to prolong and improve the quality of life.

The problem of contingency – the problem of a finite life that carries with it the possibility of death – forms the backdrop against which 'modern Western societies took on board the fundamental biological fact that human beings are a species' (Foucault 2007a: 1). Life's contingencies became governmental problems during Europe's internecine wars of the seventeenth and eighteenth centuries. State agents developed two biopolitical techniques to maintain a population and economy capable of fueling monarchies' war efforts (Foucault

2007a; Pasquino 1978). First, an anatamo-politics of discipline utilized training exercises to exploit the body's open-ended potential for action to foster desired capabilities, such as skills associated with being an effective soldier. Disciplinary techniques spread to factories, schools, churches, hospitals, and other institutions vital to modern European life to form 'archipelagos of discipline' that fashioned subjects proper to emerging capitalist society (Foucault 1991a). Second, what Foucault calls a 'biopolitics of the population' deployed statistical techniques, such as accounting and demographic calculation, to visualize the life of its population as a series of regularities, such as birth rate, death rate, and economic growth (Foucault 1979). In his famous 'governmentality' lecture, Foucault demonstrates how governmental technologies strategically aligned with a biopolitics of the population to identify ideal economic and demographic targets and work on individuals' beliefs and practices to bring the population in line with these goals (Foucault 2007a: 87–114; see also Kuehls, this volume).

Liberal rationalities of government emerged in response to the biopolitical tendency towards greater state centralization and associated fears of resulting scarcity, most famously displayed in Malthus's critiques of the English Poor Laws (Dean 1999). Liberalism's defining characteristic is the introduction of economy into state practice, which maintains the biopolitical goals of ensuring the state's enrichment and the population's growth, but advances a new configuration of sovereignty, discipline, biopolitics, and mechanisms of security to pursue these goals. These techniques are reconfigured around an understanding of contingency in terms of everyday dangers: 'individuals are constantly exposed to danger, or rather, they are conditioned to experience their situation, their life, their present, and their future as containing danger' (Foucault 2008: 66). A qualitatively new form of biopower – security – emerges here to govern life through this interplay of freedom and danger (see Dalby, this volume). Danger implies an uncertain future that exceeds the state's attempts at direct control through biopolitical regulation. Instead, security 'anticipates possibilities and takes into account what might happen' (Foucault 2007a: 20). Actuarial techniques of prediction associated with insurance and risk management are examples of anticipatory security mechanisms. Actuarial techniques deploy statistics not simply to describe regularities within the population, but to project probable consequences and thus calculate risks for action taken in the present. Risk introduces a distinct rationality to the government of uncertain futures (see Pellizzoni, this volume). It instills fear and unease about the future, but charts a course for action in the face of paralyzing uncertainty. Specifically, it turns people into calculative subjects who measure their current situation against the possible future outcomes it could generate (O'Malley 2004). Because the prudent subject of liberalism freely and rationally acts in response to his or her surroundings, a population is now envisioned as a multiplicity of individuals *as it exists in relation to its milieu.* Foucault (2007a) uses the biological term *milieu* to indicate a space in which a series of aleatory events unfold. This vision of a population immersed in spaces of circulation, interaction, and exchange with its surroundings creates a new object for biopower, which intervenes on the 'naturalness' of species life in its milieu to maximize the 'transactional economy' of circulation (Dillon 2008).

The twentieth century was marked by a series of developments in war, economy, and the life sciences that introduced new experiences of insecurity and altered what it is to be a living being (Sloterdijk 2009). For example, military techniques associated with air and atomic warfare gave rise to a rationality of what Stephen Collier and Andrew Lakoff (2008) call 'vital systems security'. The object of vital systems security is not sovereignty or a population's well-being, but the physical, technological, and cybernetic infrastructure that sustains flows of goods, people, and information on which capitalist societies depend for growth and development. A qualitatively new form of insecurity emerges here: 'critical infrastructure' is vulnerable because society's reliance on it makes it an inviting target for air attacks; society is consequently vulnerable because its quality of life – indeed its very existence – depends on material and cybernetic networks supported by exposed infrastructure. This vision of insecurity drove the emergence of complex systems theory in the 1930s and 1940s (de Landa 1991; Duffield 2011; Hobden, this volume). Systems theory offers a vision of life as an interconnected and self-organizing system sustained by information flows. Self-organization occurs as systems automatically adapt to external stimuli in a dynamic and unstable milieu. The relations between different elements in a system and the quality of information flows between them topologically determine the types of adaptation that are possible. Proper adaptation is a matter of maintaining appropriate levels of 'diversity' within a system because maladaptations can occur from both a lack of information and resources and too much information and resources. In the extreme, maladaptation can result in system collapse (Dillon and Reid 2009).

Systems theory transforms the nature of risk, uncertainty, and security. Risk is no longer simply the threat of loss; it is now also an opportunity, the possibility of profit or positive change that results from good adaptations. Uncertainty is now thought in terms of emergence, radical contingency that exceeds actuarial prediction and threatens systemic transformation (Cooper 2008). Security is no longer a matter of engineering a milieu to ensure the population's optimal functioning because homeostasis is not possible in an emergent world (Anderson 2012). Instead, it now attempts to create resilience, a meta-stable condition in which the system maintains its basic function and coherence even as individual elements experience considerable disruptions and change as they circulate and interact with one another (Walker and Cooper 2011). Resilience is an essential component of neoliberal security initiatives in diverse fields such as military planning, economic policy, humanitarian intervention, and emergency management (Duffield 2011; Walker and Cooper 2011). Security becomes a matter of creating decentralized, self-organizing systems whose spontaneous adaptations sustain rather than threaten global political economic order (Dillon and Reid 2009).

Resilience mobilizes a distinct form of biopower that attempts to shape the possibilities for emergent life, what Ben Anderson (2012) refers to as 'environmental power', the power not simply to govern life but to produce life-worlds so as to govern the *possibilities* for emergent life (see also Massumi 2009). Like security, it targets a milieu, but environmental power focuses on the *relations* between people and things that constitute a milieu. In brief, it attempts to influence how the complex of people and things that form a milieu relate to one another. Two examples here include the U.S. government's color-coded terror alert system (Massumi 2005) and the design and architecture of airports (Adey 2008). Each attempts to influence information that circulates within a milieu and the affective hue of these information flows in order to foment certain relations. As environmental power instantiates specific relations between the people and things comprising a milieu, these elements become endowed with certain capacities for action in an emergent environment rather than others. A system's meta-stability, or resilience, is thus an emergent effect of environmental techniques that strategically activate desirable adaptive capacities and deactivate (or indifferently ignore) other, less desirable ones.

A genealogy of security illustrates how liberal order rests on nothing more or less than historically and geographically specific configurations of techniques of biopower and sovereignty (Dillon 1995). Seemingly apolitical and technical categories such as risk, vulnerability, and resilience are unstable sites of conflict where liberal order is produced and contested; each attempts to fold a recalcitrant life into calculative governmental rationalities. Their inevitable failures drive reconfigurations of these categories and the emergence of new understandings of life and security. We can thus refine our definition of biopolitics in strategic and topological terms: biopolitics signals a *problem space* in which life is made amenable to calculated programs of governmental intervention and improvement. The next section details how biopolitics as both a form of power and problem-space has informed critical approaches to environmental politics.

Critical potential

Even though Foucault's indifference to nature and the environment is well documented (see Darier 1999), biopolitics infuses many other concepts in critical environmental thought, such as governmentality (see Lövbrand and Stripple, this volume), risk (Pellizzoni, this volume), vulnerability (Methmann and Oels, this volume), and security (Dalby, this volume). Indeed, many field-defining studies in nature-society theory utilized biopolitics to critique how state programs render the environment an object of governmental intervention, often with unintended and potentially disastrous consequences (see, e.g., Braun 2002; Mitchell 2002; Scott 1998; Whitehead, Jones, and Jones 2007; see also Watts and Peluso, this volume).

Contemporary research on biopolitics and the environment has taken these arguments in two directions. The first examines how biopolitical techniques render 'climate change' an object of governmental intervention (see Okereke and Charlesworth, this volume). Research on climate change biopolitics deploys this concept to classify, categorize, and differentiate certain practices and ways of thinking from others, and thus produce a typology of power relations at play in climate change mitigation and adaptation initiatives (Methmann and Rothe 2012; Oels 2011). As such, it helps us understand how dominant state- and market-based responses to climate change reinforce existing political economic order. For example, Angela Oels (2005) argues that different approaches to climate change mitigation, such as international treaties, national emission reductions, or individual consumption changes, result from specific governmental rationalities such as sovereignty, biopolitics, and advanced liberal governmentality, respectively. Thus, even though global climate change exceeds the territorial boundaries of the state, various techniques of biopolitics, sovereignty, and governmentality enable it to be visualized and managed by modern institutions. Innovations such as carbon emissions accounting articulate the territorial assumptions of sovereignty with biopolitical techniques of calculation in climate science in order to territorialize the global carbon cycle and make it legible and manageable through the modern state's territorial logics, at both the national and local scales (Lövbrand and Stripple 2006; Rice 2010). Likewise, biopolitical techniques form the basis for state and non-state programs that attempt to reduce carbon emissions through fashioning responsible environmental subjects. Calculatory techniques create carbon footprints that represent the individual's contribution to climate change; governmental programs encourage individuals to reduce their footprint through, for example, purchasing personal carbon offsets or behavioral changes, such as taking public transportation (Paterson and Stripple 2010; Rutland and Aylett 2008).

A second slant on biopolitics and environment is found in research on governing uncertain futures. This work approaches biopolitics more as a problem-space and less a specific technique of power. It departs from the recognition that new experiences of uncertainty, such as terrorism, climate change, and biosecurity, transform contingent life into problems of socio-ecological interconnection and radical emergence (Braun 2007; Grove 2010). A variety of what Pat O'Malley (2010: 488) calls 'discursive security assemblages organized around imaginaries of increasingly uncertain and potentially traumatic futures' govern this emergent life. Ben Anderson (2010) usefully characterizes these assemblages as forms of 'anticipatory action', which include precaution, preparedness, preemption, and resilience. Each form of anticipatory action deploys imaginary and calculative mechanisms to visualize an uncertain future and bring this future to bear on life in the present.

Examples of preparedness, preemption, and resilience illustrate how anticipatory action relates to environmental politics. First, preparedness attempts to develop individuals' response capacities before an exceptional event occurs in order to ensure that, for example, a terrorist attack or hurricane does not lead to catastrophic social breakdown. Techniques of preparedness, such as scenario exercises and vulnerability analyses, enable emergency managers to visualize how a potentially catastrophic future might play out, and thus identify areas where preparedness is lacking (Anderson and Adey 2012; Collier and Lakoff 2008). The biopolitical effect of preparedness is to construct a distinct form of collective life that defends capitalist order against unpredictable threats to its vital infrastructure, what Julian Reid (2007) calls 'logistical life'. This is a networked and adaptable form of collective existence that organizes flows of people, goods, and information in strategic relation to an uncertain future that threatens liberal order. Although preparedness emerged through Cold War–era civil defense programs in the United States and the United Kingdom that sought to develop the population's capacities to survive a nuclear attack, contemporary concerns over climate change and disasters extend this biopolitics to human–environment relations. The fear now is that more frequent disasters will disrupt vital infrastructure and result in 'bad' circulations that undermine global political economic order and ignite social upheaval (Grove 2012a). Preparedness increasingly targets vulnerable populations' inherent adaptive capacities through community-based disaster management programming and financialized disaster management (Grove 2012a, 2012b).

Second, preemption seeks to manage an uncertain future by turning virtual threats into actual risks. The problem here is not to control bodies to eliminate surprise, but rather to shape the possibilities of future worlds so that surprises are acceptable and manageable (Massumi 2007). This biopolitical rationality features prominently in financialized disaster management instruments such as weather derivatives and catastrophe insurance (Cooper 2008, 2010). For example, catastrophe insurance initiatives in the Caribbean utilize computer simulations to visualize and price the risk disasters pose to a state's economy. These risks are then transferred to global capital markets through catastrophe insurance contracts and weather derivatives in order to provide member states with an alternative source of disaster response financing. At stake is the state's capacity to quickly repair and secure its vital infrastructure and thus preemptively negate the possibilities for non-liberal forms of adaptation. Catastrophe insurance articulates techniques of preemption and preparedness with those of sovereignty to intensify the ability of both capital and state agents to visualize, manage, and increasingly produce life in an emergent environment (Grove 2012a). Financialized disaster management may enable states to perform their sovereign responsibility of securing their populations against calamities (Lobo-Guerrero 2010), but this comes at the expense of marginalized peoples whose world-forming adaptive capacity is problematized as a threat to global order that must be preemptively managed or negated.

Third, techniques of resilience attempt to 'create a subjective and systematic state to enable each and all to live freely and with confidence in a world of potential risks' (Lentzos and Rose 2009: 243). Key techniques here include education and training programs designed to build confident and self-sufficient subjects capable of adapting to environmental surprise without external aid or intervention (Chandler 2012; O'Malley 2010). While *resilience* has become a buzzword in both applied and critical environmental research, a focus on how resilience governs uncertain futures draws out its biopolitical effects. For example, Julian Reid (2010, 2012) analyses how disaster resilience programming does not reduce exposure to danger, but rather strategically utilizes this exposure to produce subjects amenable to neoliberal governmental technologies – subjects who understand how risk and hazards are a permanent feature of the world and that security is a matter of properly embracing this uncertain future. The resilient subject is 'not a political subject which can conceive of changing the world, its structure and conditions of possibility with a view to securing itself' (Reid 2012: 74). Resilient subjects see their vulnerability and insecurity not as the result of uneven political economic relations that can and should be changed, but rather as unavoidable consequences of living in an emergent and interconnected world. Disaster resilience thus works against the political possibilities of adaptation: adaptation is not a matter of transforming life-worlds to remove vulnerability and insecurity; instead, it is depoliticized and individualized as a matter of 'surviving the after-effects of industrial modernization, the green revolution, and the Washington consensus' (Walker and Cooper 2011: 155).

Despite the differences between these three forms of anticipatory action, they illustrate how biopolitics-as-problem-space might contribute to critical environmental politics. This research draws attention to the complex and place-specific configurations of governmental techniques and strategies that attempt to govern emergent life. As such, it locates environmental forms of anticipatory action within a wider genealogy of liberal security. From this perspective, attempts to govern emergent socio-ecological futures are an extension of long-standing struggles to fold the totality of socio-ecological existence into liberalism's calculative rationality. New understandings of life enable power to operate on more intimate levels – the potentiality that inheres in everyday socio-ecological relations. At the same time, this slant on biopolitics also foregrounds new possibilities for resisting liberal order. Despite their refinement, techniques of security and environmental power never fully succeed in getting people and things to behave exactly as intended; documenting power's *failures* in the face of life can open new avenues for critical thought and practice. For example, research on critical infrastructure security is beginning to draw on the Deleuzian-inspired work of Jane Bennett (2007) to study how the lively 'materiality' of critical infrastructure disrupts attempts to secure it. This work demonstrates how critical infrastructure security is never as unified or unproblematic as the literature makes it appear to be; instead, its attempts to produce resilient societies are complicated by iron that unexpectedly corrodes, data monitoring programs that don't work as planned, or power point scenario exercises that fail to properly function (Adey and Anderson 2012; Aradau 2010; Lundborg and Vaughan-Williams 2011). Likewise, it also recognizes the critical potential of marginalized groups' immanent adaptive capacities. The inherent self-organization capacities and adaptive self-reliance of peoples marginalized for centuries by the global political economy continues to escape development and resilience programming (Duffield 2010; Grove 2012a). The recognition that life always exceeds power opens new ethical and political questions about what kind of life should be secured, and how we should pursue this security, against social and ecological uncertainty (see Hobden, and Rudy and White, this volume).

Conclusion

As the previous examples of climate change biopolitics and anticipatory action show, biopolitics offers a set of analytical tools and a new vocabulary for critical thought on environmental politics. Recognizing how power operates through seemingly benign projects designed to secure and improve collective life clears a space for rethinking *whose lives* are ultimately secured, and for what purpose, through environmental initiatives of all political and economic leanings. These kinds of questions enable critical thought to reappropriate a foundational category of modern political life – security (see Dalby, this volume) – and direct it towards radical programs of social and ecological change set against what Mark Duffield (2011) calls the 'fabricated uncertainty' of global neoliberal development.

As such, biopolitics introduces new political possibilities *for* critical research and the researcher. Recognizing how biopower responds to an inventive life that exceeds governmental control creates a new terrain of political possibility that can enable researchers, in the words of Melinda Cooper, to 'creative[ly] sabotage . . . the future' (Cooper 2006: 129): to turn neoliberal security's anticipatory mechanisms and governmental techniques against its efforts to secure a meta-stable future for global liberal order. As one component of socio-ecological apparatuses among many, the researcher can shape the efficacy of biopolitical techniques and potentially direct them towards new purposes. For instance, the work of Sarah Whatmore and colleagues on participatory risk management planning in the UK highlights how techniques commonly associated with neoliberal security, such as vulnerability mapping and computerized simulations, can be reconfigured to visualize and realize alternative social and political outcomes (Landström et al. 2011; Lane et al. 2011). To paraphrase Matthew Hannah's (2011) discussion of left politics and biopower, the challenge moving forward for critical environmental scholars is to creatively utilize the research process itself to devise and deploy biopolitical techniques configured around the imperative to relieve actually existing suffering and insecurity, rather than build the resilience of existing liberal order and its manifold inequalities.

Further reading

Along with Foucault's books and lectures referenced throughout the text, foundational readings on biopolitics include the following: Michael Hardt and Antonio Negri's trilogy of *Empire* (2000), *Multitude* (2004), and *Commonwealth* (2009); Giorgio Agamben's trilogy of *Homo Sacer* (1998), *Remnants of Auschwitz* (1999), and *State of Exception* (2005), as well as *The Coming Community* (1993); and Roberto Esposito's recently translated trilogy of *Communitas* (2009), *Immunitas* (2011), and *Bios* (2008). Excellent overviews of the political and philosophical debates in these foundational texts are found in Timothy Campbell's (2011) *Improper Life: Technology and Biopolitics from Heidegger to Agamben* and Thomas Lemke's (2011) *Biopolitics: An Advanced Introduction.* The English-language publications of *Security, Territory, Population* (Foucault 2007a) and *The Birth of Biopolitics* (2008) have sparked new appraisals of Foucault's understanding of biopolitics. The special issue of *Theory, Culture & Society* published in 2009 (volume 26, issue 6) offers a number of essays that discuss these lectures' impacts, as do recent articles by Ben Anderson (2012) and Chris Philo (2012). Finally, generation-online.org contains a large online collection of writings by leading thinkers on biopolitics (and critical thought in general), as well as a number of helpful interpretive essays.

Note

1. However, readers are encouraged to explore Mick Smith's (2011) Agambenian analysis of environmental governance and environmental sovereignty, as well as Melinda Cooper's (2008, 2010) engagements with Negri's philosophy in her studies of climate security and weather derivatives.

4 Citizenship

Emma Hinton

Introduction

What does it mean to be a citizen? Who can be a citizen, what should a citizen do, and what can citizens expect in return? Broadly speaking, *citizenship* is 'a socio-legal status defined by specific sets of rights', or put another way, it 'is concerned with a diverse set of practices and cultures that structure complex patterns of inclusion and exclusion within modern society' (Stevenson 2006). The concept has a long history – it can be traced back to ancient Greece, but modern conceptualisations have developed since the seventeenth century, in tandem with capitalism (Dean 2001) – and in that time, multiple approaches to citizenship have developed. They vary in terms of what citizenly action entails, the extent to which this requires interactions with the state (and what forms that might take) and associated rights and duties. In recognition of this volume's focus on critical environmental politics, this chapter will focus on some of the key ways that environmental citizenship has been understood. Broadly speaking, there are three main approaches to understanding this kind of citizenship – republican, liberal and post-cosmopolitan – which will be discussed in more detail in the section on 'key thinkers' (see Dobson 2003 for a detailed discussion of these differences).

The concept of environmental citizenship was born in the early 1990s. In 1992 at the United Nations Conference on Environment and Development, citizen participation in environmental democracy formally became a concern of signatories to the Rio Declaration on Environment and Development (UN 1992b), which set out the rights of citizens to environmental information, participation in democratic processes and environmental justice. This commitment was reaffirmed 20 years later at the United Nations Conference on Sustainable Development, also held in Rio, in 'The future we want' document (UN 2012; for more on summits like these, see Death, this volume). In addition to establishing state commitment to a particular understanding of the rights and duties associated with environmental citizenship, these two summits had something else in common: the majority of citizens were not invited, re-establishing the boundary between political representatives and citizens. Instead, many citizens organised their own parallel summits in order to provide an opportunity for people and groups with diverse interests, concerns and politics to discuss their take on sustainable development and how best to achieve it, providing a forum for voicing their discontent at the collective failure of governments to deliver sustainability. The official and counter conferences had little formal interaction with each other.

In this example, what does environmental citizenship entail? Should environmental citizens endeavour to participate in formal democratic processes, where elites define the issues and appropriate actions, as well as who can participate and how? Or should environmental citizens define appropriate problems and solutions themselves, organising as they see fit and operating outside the mainstream? Perhaps both forms of activity count. As Dobson and Bell put it,

> There is no determinate thing called 'environmental citizenship' [. . .] Within the broadest possible compass, such citizenship will/can/may surely have something to do with the relationship between individuals and the common good. (Whatever the common good, in the context of sustainability, might mean. And we take it that part of what being an environmental citizen might mean is to participate in the never-ending process of defining what sustainability does mean.) (Dobson and Bell 2006: 4)

Rather than there being one vision of 'environmental citizenship', there are many, which I term *environmentally oriented*. In the rest of this chapter, I begin by discussing some core ideas, notably that understandings of environmentally oriented citizenship vary in terms of their emphasis on and definitions of rights and responsibilities, on who (or what) counts as an environmental citizen, on what forms citizenly action can take and in which spaces. I then discuss some key thinkers associated with three distinct formulations of environmentally oriented citizenship (post-cosmopolitan, liberal and republican) before going on to consider the critical potential of environmentally oriented citizenship in the round, drawing from ideas of governmentality and post-politics.

Core questions

Do environmental citizens have rights or responsibilities?

Each of the three broad approaches to environmentally oriented citizenship – liberal, republican and post-cosmopolitan – include ideas of appropriate rights and responsibilities, but differ in where they place the emphasis. Liberal forms of environmental citizenship might focus on 'the right to a liveable and sustainable environment' (Dobson 2003: 68) as a 'precondition for the enjoyment of other political, civic and social rights', where it is the duty of the state to protect environmental goods and limit environmental harm (Dobson 2009: 131). Responsibilities are less important than rights here. In contrast, republican forms of environmental citizenship emphasise responsibilities over rights; here, the environment may be framed as a common good that citizens have a responsibility to take action to protect, linked to political virtues of justice, care and compassion (Dobson 2003, 2007). In both liberal and republican citizenship, rights and responsibilities are contractual; in contrast, in post-cosmopolitan ecological citizenship, they are cast as non-contractual (Dobson 2003). Here, responsibility to act is related to environmental rights through environmental justice (Dobson 2007).

Who can be an environmental citizen?

Just who has these rights and responsibilities can be identified in terms of membership of a polity, but there are different ways in which 'polity', 'membership' and their relationship to 'politics' can be understood (Dobson 2006: 447). In a more traditional sense, membership relates to residence in a territory, where rights and obligations are associated with the citizen's relationship with the state. Alternatively, membership may be conceptualised in terms of affiliation, where responsibilities are associated with the citizen's relation to various communities or publics – associated with a cause, a social group or even life as a whole. In post-cosmopolitan ecological citizenship, transnational civil society is considered an appropriate political community, since production and consumption, environmental problems and political processes are increasingly globalised. Some argue for consideration of organisations and social movements (see Price, Saunders and Olcese, this volume) as citizens in recognition of their involvement in civic engagement around the environment (Smith and Pangsapa 2008: 25); Barnett, Cloke, Clarke and Malpass (2010) illustrate this by describing the ways in which civil society organisations and movements, with individuals, collectively alter demands for ethical products, shape systems of provision and engage in lobbying. Furthermore, it is not only humans – individually or collectively – that may be environmental citizens; according to an ecocentric orientation (see McShane, this volume), such citizenship may be trans-species, where rights and entitlements may be understood as being held by both human and non-human natures (Smith and Pangsapa 2008).

What forms can citizenly action take, and where?

Approaches to citizenship also differ in terms of their stance on what counts as citizenly action and where this should take place. This can be understood in terms of 'political space', which is 'the space in which citizens move, and which constitutes the arena in which citizens' rights and obligations are exercised' (Dobson 2009: 135).

Generally speaking, citizenship involves some kind of private action (i.e., taken by citizens) for the common good, or 'activity with public implications' (Dobson 2007: 281). Traditional understandings of citizenship might emphasise reciprocity and the distinction between the public and the private sphere; this differs from environmentally oriented approaches, some of which may consider duties and obligations to be shared between the public and private sphere and do not always consider rights and entitlements to be reciprocal (Smith and Pangsapa 2008). The political spaces of liberal forms of citizenship tend to be in the public sphere, emphasising procedural legitimacy and focused on political configurations modelled on the nation-state (Dobson 2003: 89). In republican forms, political spaces may be in both the public and the private sphere: citizens are obliged to take responsibility for taking personal action for environmental benefit in the private sphere, but also to actively participate in governance mechanisms and democratic institutions (Dobson 2003). In Dobson's post-cosmopolitan ecological citizenship, everyday consumption is a valid political space.

Whereas in traditional forms of citizenship political spaces were always physical spaces, contemporary environmental citizenship increasingly utilises virtual spaces. New social movements – including the environmental movement – use the Internet to mobilise environmental citizens at different scales, supporting the flow of non-authorised information and alternative conceptualisations of what constitutes right action for the environment (Castells 1997). In contrast to early web-based communication, in 'web 2.0' virtual spaces have become increasingly participatory and facilitate the performance of environmentally oriented citizenship in very particular ways (see Hinton 2011 for a discussion of some of the ways that environmental third sector organisations utilise the Internet in their sustainable consumption advocacy). Online environmentally oriented citizenly action may be diverse, including signing online petitions, discussing issues, organising protests or using online tools to judge or offset personal environmental impact (see, for example, Barr 2011; Paterson and Stripple 2010). For some, valid citizenly action can only take place in physical spaces and not in virtual alternatives (as argued by Paul Virilio, as discussed in Stevenson 2006). Although online political participation – sometimes referred to as 'slacktivism' or 'clicktivism' – has been criticised for achieving little in physical spaces and having minimal impact on formal democratic processes, it does not (necessarily) substitute for political participation in physical spaces, nor does it always have limited impact (Christensen 2011).

Key thinkers

Arguably one of the most important theorists of environmentally oriented citizenship is Andrew Dobson, whose work on the topic has been the subject of much subsequent academic engagement. In this section, Dobson's novel conceptualisation of citizenship – post-cosmopolitan ecological citizenship – is discussed first, followed by brief discussion of a liberal and then republican alternative.

Post-cosmopolitan ecological citizenship

Although Dobson has written about environmentally oriented citizenship since at least the 1990s, he established his position as a key thinker in this field when he published the seminal *Citizenship and the Environment* in 2003. In this, he developed the concept of post-cosmopolitan ecological citizenship as an alternative to liberal and republican approaches.

Dobson's approach aligns more with post-rather than dialogic-or distributive-cosmopolitanism. For him, dialogic cosmopolitanism under-develops obligations and lacks mechanisms for addressing environmental harms, and distributive cosmopolitanism under-develops the reasons for citizens to take action (noted in Smith and Pangsapa 2008). Post-cosmopolitanism emphasises responsibilities, which are considered non-reciprocal; and virtues, which are considered relevant in both the private and public spheres (Dobson 2003: 139). Whereas cosmopolitanism considers political communities to be held together by social bonds, Dobson argues instead that such communities are bound by obligation; in the context of globalisation, these obligations are transnational and asymmetrical, where the positive and negative effects of globalisation are inequitably distributed between globalisers and the globalised, and where those experiencing net negative effects have no duties of ecological citizenship.

Working with the feminist idea that the private sphere is a valid political space, he argues that it can be the site for enactment of such obligations to transnational others. If we accept that the environment's capacity to act as a source and a sink is limited, he argues, then globalised production and consumption regimes implicate everyone in such relations of transnational obligation (see Brooks and Bryant, this volume). Here, 'the duty of the environmental citizen is to live sustainably so that others may live well' (Dobson 2007: 282). He argues that the extent of these obligations can be discerned from the size of an individual's ecological footprint, which quantifies the amount of ecological space they occupy (Dobson 2003: 139). If a citizen is in 'ecological space debt' (i.e., they occupy more than their fair share), then the just course of action is to take action to address this imbalance (Dobson 2006: 449). Although justice is the primary citizenly virtue, care and compassion are also considered important.

Dobson's conceptualisation of ecological citizenship has been praised for its 'more rigorous treatment of the notion of rights, a definition of the space of ecological citizenship that takes better account of the globalisation of environmental problems, and finally a broader treatment of the virtues of citizenship that puts the ethic of care and/or compassion in a less central position than in his earlier work' (Sáiz 2005: 176). Whereas *environmental* citizenship separates out morals from politics, *ecological* citizenship here brings environmental ethics in (Smith and Pangsapa 2008: 51). Post-cosmopolitan ecological citizenship is also vulnerable to critique, as I shall show, in its conceptualisation of political community, its use of ecological footprinting, its emphasis on consumption and its understanding of agency. I will discuss each in turn before moving on to consider liberal and republican alternatives to environmentally oriented citizenship.

First, post-cosmopolitan ecological citizenship's focus on global civil society as a political community has been critiqued by Hayward (2006), who takes a more traditional view of what constitutes political community. For Hayward, the closest thing to a political community within global civil society is international non-governmental organisations; he argues that their efforts to influence political processes are not analogous to the 'properly political bonds' and political power associated with traditional understandings of a polity (Hayward 2006: 437). Dobson (2006) counters that his conceptualisation of political community is not problematic because it 'gives a political account of the ties that bind and the obligations that are at work in the space of the ecological footprint' where 'the community created by the material relations of cause and effect in the guise of the ecological footprint is a political community rather than a community of friends or family, and this community is a space in which political obligation operates' (447).

Second, post-cosmopolitan ecological citizenship's reliance on ecological footprinting may be problematic. As Marres (2008) argues, such tools work to dematerialise and virtualise by focusing on abstractions of complexity arrived at through processes of simplification and transformation into particular kinds of data points. Since the creation of the earliest footprinting tools (e.g., Rees 1992; Wackernagel and Rees 1996), many more have been produced, with different authors, variously associated with different governmental programmes. These tools are not neutral, they are socially constructed: power relations are involved in decisions about what to count and what (numerical or moral) values to attach to it (see Forsyth, this volume). Whilst they all share roots in ecological economics and rely on the concept of environmental limits and justice based on equal per capita entitlements to environmental resources, there is variation relating to a host of other assumptions relating to environmental risk, how commodities are included in assessments, duties to non-humans, and which environmental issues can be represented in terms of environmental absorptive capacity (Collins, Cowell and Flynn 2009). Ecological footprinting implies a degree of certainty about knowing the impact of our actions on the environment and what environmental systems will tolerate before changing, yet there is inevitably at least some scientific uncertainty involved – not least in the context of a changing climate (as Charlesworth and Okereke 2010 note in the context of policy responses to climate change). Footprinting tools also fail to adequately take pollution into account, especially persistent organic pollutants that cannot be ameliorated. Despite these issues, ecological footprinting may be one of the best available tools for attempting to determine the public implications of our individual consumption.

Third, whether or not consumption constitutes a valid political space has been the subject of much debate (see, for example, Barnett, Cloke, Clarke and Malpass 2005; Brooks and Bryant, this volume; Clarke, Barnett, Cloke, and Malpass 2007; Hobson 2002; Johnston 2008). Accompanying the roll-back of the state, individuals became cast in the role of citizen-consumer in UK and EU policy (Barr 2011; Slocum 2004). The political space conferred by market-mediated consumption may be problematic because our consumption choices are dependent on those products and services made available by the market (Seyfang 2005; Smith 2000); it is important to note, however, that not all consumption is market-mediated. Even when market-mediated, consumption politics has led to some social and political change (e.g., around ethical consumption and fair trade), and consumer-citizens do not inevitably reinforce the neoliberal norm that is often the target of critiques of consumption as a political space (Clarke et al. 2007; Seyfang 2005; Slocum 2004).

A related problem concerns citizenly agency. Citizens are required to passively accept the validity of ecological footprinting and its judgements of the effects of our consumption choices on the environment, and to alter their consumption as a result. This implies, and takes for granted, that citizens have sufficient agency to do so (Barr 2011). However, citizen-consumer agency is not (always) a given; we live complex lives that blend habitual and rational action, where our consumer choices may be influenced by a plethora of structural, psychological, cultural, social and economic factors (e.g., Seyfang 2005). Dobson acknowledges that living within contemporary advanced industrial societies limits the extent to which change is possible (2009: 136) and recommends that personal action to limit the size of our ecological footprints is combined with active engagement with democratic political processes to attempt to reform those limiting societal and political structures (Dobson 2007: 281). However, central to Dobson's approach is the belief that citizens must have the 'right' attitudes and values in order to take citizenly action, such that they will take this action even when supportive structures (such as infrastructure or financial incentives) are not in place (see, for example, Dobson and Sáiz 2005; Dobson and Bell 2006; Dobson 2007, 2009). In contrast to this rather psychological understanding of change, sociological understandings emphasise the influence of other factors on action. One such view that has become popular in recent years understands agency in terms of social practices: attention is shifted from an individual's psychological characteristics to the range of sociocultural and material factors that constrain or enable the performance of particular practices. There are some examples of working with these ideas in the context of environmentally oriented citizenship (e.g., Evans 2011; Spaargaren and Oosterveer 2010).

One noteworthy and related example is Noortje Marres's conceptualisation of 'socio-material ecological citizenship'. Here, citizenly agency in the private spaces of the home may be at least partially located in 'the world of things' (Marres 2008: 27), where 'publics are also held together by material and physical associations' (28) and 'by virtue of their habits and habitats' (36). Socio-technical context is considered here to be an important factor mediating citizenly action. Through various government and civil society campaigns, new material artefacts may be introduced into the home (such as various eco technologies), or citizens may be encouraged to interact with existing artefacts in new ways once these interactions have been invested with particular meanings around the environmental significance of such interactions (see Luke, this volume). If ecological citizenship is understood in terms of reducing a citizen's ecological footprint within specified limits, then in some cases, such artefacts may effectively perform citizenship on occupants' behalf (e.g., through minimising resource consumption), leading to the production of 'material publics'. When individuals open their homes to others and talk about the various material artefacts that are implicated in this performance of ecological citizenship, particular kinds of 'climate publics' are produced (Marres 2008: 27); socio-material ecological citizenship, though it takes place in the private sphere, also therefore has public dimensions. Marres argues that this may work to 'de-citizenise' individuals, who can seem almost incidental in some campaigns promoting the uptake of, for example, domestic energy efficiency improvements (2008: 29).

Cosmopolitan liberal environmental citizenship

Derek Bell has engaged with Dobson's work to advance an argument for cosmopolitan liberal environmental citizenship (Bell 2003, 2005). He argues for an extension of liberal understandings of the environment as property to reconceptualise it as a provider of basic needs, a core tenet both of liberalism and of sustainability. The state, here, is a duty-bearer (although this may be delegated to intermediaries), and the citizen is a rights-holder. The 'reasonable pluralism' associated with liberalism – that is, where there is no commitment to one set of morals or values – is considered by Bell to be a useful way to approach the environment, since there already exist a multiplicity of ways of understanding and relating to it. Citizens have the substantive right to have their basic needs met via the environment, procedural rights to defend this substantive right and to engage in related decision-making and policy-making, and personal rights to make their own choices about what to do in relation to the environment. Although there is no duty to take action in our private lives (unless this supports some political system, such as the use of local authority recycling services supports its continued provision), there is a duty to engage in democratic systems and to attempt to persuade others of the merits of a particular understanding or approach to the environment. As Bell notes, this can mean that those who do not hold 'green' values could still be considered liberal environmental citizens (2005: 187).

Bell's conceptualisation of citizenship takes a more positive reading of power than Dobson's. For Bell, the emphasis is on using power positively and proactively: citizens have a duty to secure the right to a fair share of ecological space through formal democratic processes in order to avoid injustice. In contrast, Dobson focuses on responding to negative aspects of the exercise of power: citizens have a duty to not violate someone else's right to this space by taking up too much of it. Bell's approach extends political activity beyond consumption and the individualisation of responsibility and overcomes the problem of objectively identifying causality (a problem discussed earlier in the context of footprinting). However, as Bell notes, this is not without its own problems: there may be limits in the extent to which democratic processes produce environmentally just outcomes.

Sustainability citizenship (or green civic republicanism)

John Barry (2006b) draws from civic republicanism to theorise sustainability citizenship, which sees a more active and even radical role for citizens. Like Bell's articulation of citizenship, this is committed to plurality and non-domination, where citizens accepting a particular argument for sustainability have the obligation, rather than the right, to demand related changes (Barry 2006b: 33). Barry considers this vision of citizenship to be more ambitious and challenging, integrating political, economic, cultural and social concerns and 'focus[ing] on the underlying structural causes of environmental degradation and other infringements of sustainable development such as human rights abuses or social injustice' (23–24). He considers liberal environmental citizenship – with its focus on the environment – to be lacking in the 'transformative, oppositional, and radical political dimensions' of sustainability citizenship (24). In contrast to cosmopolitan liberal environmental citizenship, sustainability citizenship considers lifestyle change to be a valid form of citizenly action; in contrast to post-cosmopolitan ecological citizenship, it also includes action in the public domain. Sustainability citizens carry out their citizenly obligations across all areas of their life – from the home to the workplace – and engage in the public sphere, participating in or defending their collective way of life but only up until the point that this entails sacrificing self-interest. In green civic republican citizenship, the state would actively create structural conditions to support the development of citizenly virtues and behaviours (Barry 2006b: 28). Whereas Dobson considers all consumption to be implicated in citizenship, for Barry, only active and 'mindful' consumption connected with some form of political struggle around sustainability (such as consumption targeted at 'market and state-based forms of inequality, injustice and ecological unsustainability' (2006b: 38)) is considered valid citizenly action. In critical sustainability citizenship, valid citizenly action also includes challenging established ideas of environmental rights and obligations, comprising a form of 'resistance citizenship' that challenges the underlying causes of unsustainability (Barry 2006b: 32). Barry acknowledges that a range of factors may limit participation in formal democratic procedures – including alienation and socioeconomic factors – and argues that by considering action in both the private and public spheres (rather than just the latter) to be valid, the notion that citizenship is in decline can be challenged.

Critical potential

What critical potential might environmentally oriented forms of citizenship have, if we understand this in terms of emancipation from systems of domination or dependence and expanding the scope of autonomy? No conceptualisation of citizenship is neutral: all are historically situated, internally malleable and inherently political, as Dobson notes:

> Definitions cannot stand outside the relationships of political power that they are intended to describe. They stand in a complex relationship to this power: neither simply reflecting it nor uncomplicatedly calling it into question. To this degree, citizenship is a site of political struggle. (2009: 134)

What is understood as an appropriate manifestation of citizenship should be 'acknowledged as provisional, open to contestation and subject to deliberation' (Smith and Pangsapa 2008: 62). A critical approach to environmentally oriented citizenship might involve taking Foucault's lead and setting out to 'detach the power of truth' from systems of power (Foucault 1980b: 133). The neo-Foucauldian concept of governmentality provides one set of tools with which to attempt this emancipatory project, primarily by facilitating the recognition of the ways in which these flows of power operate (see Lövbrand and Stripple, this volume). Briefly, governmentality allows for 'government at a distance' via indirect mechanisms of rule that operate through governmental networks involving heterogeneous constellations of actors and that translate governmental objectives and so shape the 'conduct of conduct' (Miller and Rose 2008: 33). These indirect mechanisms include the discursive construction of citizenly subjectivities and appropriate ways of performing citizenship linked to particular problematisations of the world. The category of civil society and the figure of the citizen, according to this view, work to both legitimise government, at the same time as constituting the object of government (e.g., Miller and Rose 2008; Swyngedouw 2005): individuals are encouraged to recognise themselves as citizens and to consequently govern their conduct in line with wider socio-political goals. Where action is focused on taking action in the private sphere, this individualisation of responsibility has been criticised for apportioning responsibility in the wrong place: it may be more appropriately targeted at the rich and powerful, who make a proportionately greater contribution to problems of the environment and sustainability (Luke 1997). It may also distract us from the political and social dimensions of environmental problems and fail to fully tackle these problems since wider change is often required (Maniates 2002). Governance beyond the state offers some opportunities for citizen involvement in more horizontal forms of organisation and so with potentially greater opportunities to reshape existing social and political arrangements, but access to these opportunities is uneven, and citizen empowerment may be subsumed within undemocratic and authoritarian arrangements that are vulnerable to market forces (Swyngedouw 2005).

Governmentality also points to the flows of power involved in problematising aspects of the world in order to drive particular forms of action. A key element of Foucauldian understandings of power is that it only works where there is some freedom; where free subjects may engage in 'agonistic' struggle, actively resisting or submitting to flows of power (or choosing to respond passively); where power relations may be reciprocal, unstable and reversible (Dean 2007; Gordon 2001; Morris and Patton 1979; Miller and Rose 2008; Mills 2003). Although some articulations of environmentally oriented citizenship require citizens to accept expert problematisations of the environment and solutions to these problems in attempts to normalise particular forms of action, others – such as Barry's 'resistance citizenship', or liberal approaches with some commitment to pluralism – do not. The success of those approaches to environmentally oriented citizenship that depend upon citizens accepting top-down problematisations of the environment and appropriate actions may encounter a different form of resistance, where citizens may simply resist this information and so take no action. Information may be rearticulated, resisted or altered in the process of sense-making (Smith and Pangsapa 2008), or individuals may resist top-down information because it contradicts vernacular knowledges, or because lay publics recognise uncertainty, or they may mistrust the source of the information, or they may be sceptical about the potential change that individuals can make within systems (Burgess, Harrison and Filius 1998; Slocum 2004). Approaches that recognise the validity of lay understandings of issues and that balance these with 'objective' truths from 'experts' – such as community-based, participatory, inclusionary, deliberative 'civic' models of public engagement – may be more successful in generating pro-environmental behaviour than those channelling top-down 'expert' information (Burgess et al. 1998; Dobson 2007; Owens 2000). Citizen science may also provide a means for individuals to participate in knowledge production about problems of and solutions to the environment and sustainability (see Forsyth, this volume; Irwin 1995). Web 2.0 can also facilitate this more democratic politics of knowledge production and can constitute a valid political space for citizenly action and dissensus, as Barr (2011) argues.

Those articulations of environmentally oriented citizenship that encourage agonistic struggle through advocating critical engagement with existing systems of thought, provision and politics (e.g., cosmopolitan liberal environmental citizenship and sustainability citizenship), and those that consider appropriate action as working within and not challenging existing socio-cultural, socio-political and socio-material discursive and political frameworks (e.g., post-cosmopolitan and socio-material ecological citizenship), might be viewed as 'properly-' and 'post-' political, respectively, according to the nascent literature on 'post-politics' (see, for example, Mouffe 2005; Swyngedouw 2005, 2007b, 2009, 2010). This theoretical orientation considers much contemporary politics to take a 'post-political' form, where consensus (typically established with reference to scientific and moral arguments that establish the truth of discursive constructions of 'sustainability', for example) is prized and there is little room for agonistic debate or 'dissensus'. Radical points of view – those diverging from the mainstream consensus position – are silenced, and the interests of different stakeholders involved in establishing the consensus position are concealed. In contrast, 'properly political' action is directed towards engaging critically with, and even radically reshaping, the socio-political system, constituting a challenge to the liberal-capitalist order. As Smith and Pangsapa (2008) note, properly political environmentally oriented forms of citizenship should provide space for agonistic struggle over what constitutes the common good, appropriate configurations of entitlements and obligations, right courses of action, and desirable virtues. I would argue that environmental citizens can engage in properly political action not just through interactions within democratic processes (a political space that seems privileged in the literature on post-politics), but also in other ways, such as in changing our performance of everyday social practices, which may contribute to a societal transition in how things are done (e.g., Shove 2010: 1279), or by engaging in consumption and production outside mainstream market relations, or by arguing for our own interpretation of right understandings and action for environmental sustainability in public fora.

Conclusion

In this chapter, I have shown that environmentally oriented citizenship can take many forms, depending on how it is theorised, which may provide different opportunities for critical citizenly engagement in environmental politics. It is often acknowledged that there has been limited progress to date in meeting the kinds of sustainability goals articulated at the various UN summits (as noted by Barry 2006b; Hargreaves 2012). Environmental citizenship could constitute one way of plugging the gaps left by intergovernmental treaties and policies (Smith and Pangsapa 2008), and arguably, the role of the environmental citizen may increase in forthcoming years in tandem with climate change and its social, environmental and political effects (Spaargaren and Oosterveer 2010; see also Okereke and Charlesworth, this volume).

There is much room for further research. The potential for the internet to facilitate particular articulations of environmentally oriented citizenship is, as yet, relatively under-explored. It would also be worthwhile to study in detail the various understandings of what it is to perform environmentally oriented citizenship in terms of social practices, and to seek to develop a more nuanced understanding of how it is that these practices change, for better or worse. Psychological and sociological research into action tends to be compartmentalised: it would be worth doing more to unite these two approaches to develop a more nuanced understanding of how a range of internal and external factors work together to shape the performance of citizenship in particular spaces.

Further reading

Key texts on environmentally oriented citizenship, which consider a range of conceptualisations, include *Citizenship and the Environment* by Andrew Dobson (2003), 'Citizenship, environment, economy' (2005) by Andrew Dobson and Ángel Valencia Sáiz, *Environmental Citizenship* by Andrew Dobson and Derek Bell (2006) and *Environment & Citizenship* (2008) by Mark Smith and Piya Pangsapa. For further discussion of environmentally oriented forms of citizenship through the lens of governmentality, see Slocum's (2004) discussion of a top-down sustainable consumption campaign, Clarke et al.'s (2007) study of ethical consumption mediated by third sector organisations and Paterson and Stripple's (2010) examination of online carbon calculative practices.

Useful websites

The Access Initiative: www.accessinitiative.org
Aarhus Convention: http://ec.europa.eu/environment/aarhus/
Green Mountain Institute for Environmental Democracy: http://www.gmied.org
Green 10: http://green10.org
Rising Tide: http://risingtide.org.uk/
The Earth Charter Initiative: http://www.earthcharterinaction.org

5   Climate change

Chukwumerije Okereke and Mark Charlesworth

Introduction

Climate change is clearly a quintessential environmental issue of the late twentieth century and the twenty-first century. It is in many ways the most significant concept to permeate environmental politics, raising 'critical' questions and challenges in all types of ways. The significance of climate change as a scientific and socio-political challenge lies in its key attributes as follows: First, the causes are global and implicated in virtually every human activity, even breathing. Second, the impacts are equally global and wide reaching with no jurisdiction exempted from its potential negative consequences. The ubiquity of climate change causing activities entails that a huge effort in technical, social and economic terms is needed in order to achieve meaningful reduction in greenhouse gas (GHG) emissions. Indeed, the structural and social reorganization required by societies to effectively mitigate and adapt to climate change has been described as unprecedented in human history (Newell and Paterson 2010). The third unique attribute of climate change is the massive inequity in its causes and impacts both within and across states. Essentially, the poor, who have been least responsible for causing climate change, are the ones most affected by its negative impacts (Okereke 2008, 2010a, 2010b, 2011). Fourthly, the problem is long term but also could be abrupt, at least regionally. This not only complicates questions of responsibility, but also means that there are few, if any, solutions with immediately evident effects. If tipping points are excluded from analysis, the long time span between action and results creates a disincentive for action and raises difficult moral questions about responsibility to future generations. To wit, what moral status should we accord future generations, and to what extent should moderation or sacrifice be expected of current generations when they will not be alive to reap all the material benefits of their actions? These challenges are further compounded by the fifth unique attribute of climate change: the fact that there remains so much uncertainty about the effects, if less so the causes – a fact that can be used as a basis for more precaution and radical action or, conversely, an excuse for delay or inaction (Charlesworth and Okereke 2009).

It is easy to see from these reasons why climate change has been described as a super-wicked problem (Levin, Cashore, Bernstein and Auld et al. 2012) – one that poses significant challenges to environmental public policy making. At the same time, climate change has also resulted in some of the most significant challenges but also important new concepts, policies and institutions in environmental co-operation at the international level (Okereke, Wittneben and Bowen 2012). For these reasons, it will be difficult to imagine any discussion on critical environmental politics that would not place climate change at the centre of analysis.

Climate change challenges business-as-usual politics and poses intractable problems for long-standing approaches to economic management, regulation, commerce, ethics and international co-operation. We trace the transformation of climate change from purely an objective phenomenon to an idea interpreted and contested through a variety of political, economic, cultural and ethical prisms. While climate change may have provided the best inspiration and platform for critical environmental politics yet, it has also revealed the considerable embeddedness of prevailing managerialist socio-economic ideologies and practices. Building in particular on the analysis of MacIntyre (1990) on virtue ethics, we indicate a way for research and real climate politics to go beyond the sterility that has beset climate governance and negotiations.

Core ideas

As stated, climate change implicates a large number of different concepts. A few of these are relatively new, but the majority are pre-existing ideas that are amplified. Later, we elaborate on some of these concepts, indicating the contestations associated with them and how these have been used in relation to climate politics.

A key concept in climate politics is *attribution*. The central question is how much of climate change can be attributed to human activities rather than being 'natural' variation? This question is significant and has implications for other dimensions of climate change, not the least because if climate change is mostly naturally induced rather than anthropogenic, then both response strategies and politics are principally around adaptation, rather than reducing emissions.

Experiments demonstrate that more greenhouse gases such as CO_2 and methane increase the greenhouse effect already present in the atmosphere (Intergovernmental Panel on Climate Change Working Group 1 (IPCCWG1) 2007). Direct measurements since the 1950s demonstrate the amounts of greenhouse gases have been increasing (IPCCWG1 2007). There is little controversy until this point. The controversy of climate science centres on the wider consequences of these increases in gas concentrations, including on the global temperature. Broadly, two approaches are taken to resolve this question. The first is to look at records such as the concentrations of gases trapped in air bubbles in ice cores and correlating these to data that indicate temperatures at these times in the past (IPCCWG1 2007). Some of this research indicates perhaps as much as an 18 degree Celsius change in average temperature in as little as 10 years regionally, when a tipping point is crossed to a new state that then persists for thousands of years (Steffensen et al. 2008). This is less controversial, though interpretation of the data is not without its difficulties (e.g., Tingley et al. 2012). The second, more controversial approach is using models of the climate or planet to predict what temperatures will be in the future (IPCCWG1 2007). Some of this research suggests that existing emissions already commit the climate system to perhaps thousands of years of human created change (inertia) (Intergovernmental Panel on Climate Change Synthesis Report (IPCCSR) 2001, 16–21; Armour and Roe 2011) with unimagined tipping points (Charlesworth and Okereke 2010) potentially being crossed at any moment. The two approaches combined have so far provided the basis for much of the climate stabilization targets at the various regimes of climate governance, across geographical scales.

Both climate sceptics and believers in man-made climate change recognize the ultimate importance of the debate around attribution and have made it a key focus in advancing their arguments for and against climate action. Years of painstaking work has been done by independent researchers, national academies of science and international scientific bodies to establish exactly how much of global warming and climate change is due to human activity. The results of these works are scrupulously scrutinized and regularly deployed in the debate about climate change. These works have caused an overwhelming consensus among the scientific community that man-made climate change is a reality. However, climate sceptics continue to contest the methodology and validity of dominant scientific opinion about attribution. They argue that natural sources of change, including changes in energy from the sun, have far more influence on climate change than mainstream climate science indicates (Booker 2009; Durkin 2007; Meyer 2012). They also argue that climate change is within normal climatic variation and that talk of catastrophic climate change is fictional and unjustified (Booker 2009; Durkin 2007; Meyer 2012). It should be noted that tipping points and their policy implications are typically barely considered by sceptics – indeed even in mainstream climate literature the consideration of tipping points is minimal.

Many people in Europe believe that climate change is man-made, signifying that the climate sceptics have lost the debate in these countries. In North America, however, these 'Merchants of Doubt' have had more success as perhaps up to half of the population does not believe in anthropogenic climate change (Oreskes and Conway 2010). Even in Europe, climate scepticism was temporarily revived in the wake of 'climategate', which involved the hacking of emails of the Climate Research Unit at the University of East Anglia and the allegation that scientists manipulated climate data and attempted to suppress critics (Scruggs and Benegal 2012). Although hardly any credible science now denies man-made climate change, raising doubt about attribution remains the key point of attack in popular media and political circles by those wishing to challenge radical and urgent action against climate change (Latour 2004b; Oreskes and Conway 2010; Scruggs and Benegal 2012).

Next in the discussion we turn to two other concepts – *robustness* and *prediction* – both of which are closely linked to attribution. Here, the first key question is how robust is the Earth System; to what extent can it withstand stress from human activities, and can science effectively predict the limits of stress that the Earth will withstand? There is a lot of literature that questions the extent to which climate modelling can be relied on to provide an accurate account of the complex global climate system with all its feedback mechanisms (Knutti 2008; Myanna 2005). Drawing from this literature, some climate sceptics argue that the Earth System is far more robust and able to cope with climate variations than is suggested by mainstream science (Goklany 2008). But while climate sceptics criticize dominant climate science for going too far, there are others who argue that mainstream science does not go nearly far enough (Anderson and Bows 2008; Schneider 2008). These scholars argue that mainstream prediction and probabilistic science makes unwarranted optimistic assumptions about the robustness of the Earth System, for example, in presuming that the Earth System will continue to absorb the large amounts of greenhouse gas emissions provided for in the lax stabilization targets agreed within institutions of global climate policy making, such as the Kyoto Protocol and the United Nations Framework Convention on Climate Change (UNFCCC) (Anderson and Bows 2008; Harvey 2007; Oppenheimer 2005).

One of the main reasons for establishing the Intergovernmental Panel on Climate Change (IPCC) in the late 1980s had been to provide conclusive scientific statements about these controversial issues and serve as a definitive voice in communicating the science of climate change (Agrawala 1998). The basic process that the IPCC has followed is reviewing the vast body of published evidence in five-year cycles. Because of the political sensitivity of IPCC documents, painstaking care is taken to calibrate the language of the reports. But while the IPCC has indeed become the authoritative voice in defining the standard view of climate science, controversy remains over its findings and recommendations (see Forsyth, this volume). Some continue to insist that the IPCC is nearly as much a political as it is a scientific body (Gough and Shackley 2001; Grundmann 2007). A frequent point of attack is usually the Synthesis Reports or Summaries for Policy Makers (SPM), the wording of which many argue are determined by politicians rather than scientists (Grundmann 2007; Miller and Edwards 2001). It is indeed a fact that some governments such as Saudi Arabia have in the past been known to engage in 'wording wars': tactics aimed at watering-down the tone of urgency in the SPM (Depledge 2005; Paterson 1996). Yet even the IPCC itself admits that many of its recommendations are based on probabilistic evidence and that many important questions about climate change may never be conclusively answered.

A key concept that emerges in the context of the impossibility of absolute certainty about the robustness of the Earth System is that of *risk* (Oppenheimer 2005; see also Pellizzoni, this volume). If indeed science is unable to determine precisely the capacity or limits of the Earth System, then what is the safe level of risk that should be permitted in climate policy making, and on what basis should such a decision be made? Many economic libertarians have argued that the negative economic implications of huge cuts in carbon emissions far outweigh potential environmental benefits (Goklany 2008; Michaels 2012). They point to the strong links between carbon emissions and economic development and argue that the inconvenience of climate change is a rational price to pay for continued economic success and the improvement of the material quality of life for millions around the world (Goklany 2008). As the argument goes, even if global warming is caused solely by the burning of fossil fuels, restricting their use would have more damaging effects on the world economy than the increases in global temperature. Of course this argument is opposed by many who argue that early action to reduce emissions would help avoid much greater economic costs later and would reduce the risk of catastrophic, irreversible change (Stern 2007). Governments have tended to rely on economists, with their standard techniques such as cost benefit analysis and contingent valuation, to work out the economic risks and benefits of tackling climate change now as opposed to deferring action to the future. But among economists, there is serious disagreement about what scale of effort is needed, the time for deployment of actions that makes the most economic sense, and how to allocate resources for climate mitigation and adaptation. The key issue in this debate is about the discount rate that should be used in economic and contingent valuation of climate change, which in ordinary terms quite simply boils down to differing views about the costs, risks and benefits of taking early action versus delaying action to a future date (Ackerman, Stanton, Hope and Alberth 2009; Barker 2008; Nordhaus 2007; Pielke 2007; Stern 2007; Tol and Yohe 2009).

It turns out then that debates about risk, regardless of the technical jargon involved, are essentially managerialist disputes about how to resolve different conceptions of value (Adger, Barnett, Chapin III and Ellemor et al. 2011; Neumayer 2007). It is basically about how much of climate and broader environmental governance should be predicated on precaution or utility; the basis on which utility should be calculated and how to reconcile different notions of utility. As stated, these are fundamental normative questions that neither climate science nor economic valuation can answer (see Wapner, this volume). As a no less eminent person than the IPCC chief scientist, Dr Pachauri, admits, 'dangerous climate change is no doubt a question that must be decided on the basis of value judgment'. 'What is dangerous', he says, 'is essentially a matter of what society decides' (Pachauri 2006: 3). Hence, even among believers in man-made climate change, there are deep disagreements about what scale of effort is needed and the best approach to addressing the risks imposed by climate change. One manifestation of this disagreement at the international regime level is the politics around stabilization targets. The Small Island States are aggressively pushing for a 1.5°C target as the official goal of international climate policy (Farbotko and McGregor 2010). The EU supports a 2°C target (which some argue is actually a political rather than scientific target) (Anderson and Bows 2008). Meanwhile, many of the climate laggards and their demagogues would prefer that international climate policy documents make no reference at all to stabilization targets (Cato Institute 2009).

Differences of this nature, which are underpinned by different perceptions of risk, account for much of the misunderstanding, wrangling and recrimination in international climate politics (Bodansky 2010, 2011; Okereke and Dooley 2010; Okereke 2008; Rajamani 2011; see also Death, this volume). For example, on Saturday, 17 October 2009, in the run up to the Copenhagen meeting, the government of the small island of Maldives stunned the world by holding a cabinet meeting underwater to highlight the threat of global warming to the low-lying Indian Ocean nation (BBC News 2009). Soon after the meeting, the president accused the West of looking idly on while the Maldives and other Small Island States faced extinction as a result of climate change. Many other poor and climate-vulnerable countries have also consistently argued that whilst they are already suffering massive impacts of climate change, much of the population and governments of the rich West continue to treat climate change as a future threat (see Methmann and Oels, this volume).

A fundamental weakness of the climate regime frequently noted by scholars is that mainstream policy 'underemphasizes, or more often ignores completely, the symbolic aspects of settlements, places and risks to them' (Adger et al. 2011: 2). The mainstream approach also 'discounts the ethics of intergenerational equity' (Barker 2008: 173) and tends to 'reduce all risks to aggregate measures of human welfare' (Adger et al. 2011: 2). This approach, moreover, it is argued, cannot deal with the risk of irreversible changes nor the incommensurability of market and non-instrumental aspects of environmental and social change (Ackerman et al. 2009; Neumayer 2007).

But it is not, strictly speaking, correct to say that climate policy ignores non-instrumental components of the environment. Rather, it would be more accurate to say that mainstream frameworks ignore these components and risks, so long as they are being borne by the poor and underprivileged groups in the global community (see Bond, this volume). These are mostly the ones that have no power to press their claims in national and international policymaking arenas. Norms and rules about what and how to conserve are, after all, not pre-ordained choices governed by rigid technical science. They are ultimately political decisions over which the powerful regularly exert influence at both national and international levels (Roberts and Parks 2007). In the final analysis, then, climate change is about fairness, justice and equity (Okereke 2008). These concepts are more pertinent to climate politics when one recalls that the people who are primarily responsible for causing the problem are not the ones that are bearing much of the negative impacts of the change.

Key thinkers

The first important set of thinkers are those who highlighted the anthropogenic nature of climate change and took the call for urgent action into the mainstream political space, popular media and public consciousness. Here, a leading figure is NASA scientist James Hansen. Hansen helped to raise the profile of climate change and catalyse political action when he testified to a committee of the U.S. Senate in 1988 (Pielke 2000: 9). Another leading voice was the then-Prime Minister of the United Kingdom, Margaret Thatcher, who, in her address to the UN General Assembly, long before climate change became an issue fought from behind fixed ideological lines, described climate change as a challenge that in 'future is likely to be more fundamental and more widespread than anything we have known hitherto' (Thatcher 1989). The prospect, she said, 'is a new factor in human affairs... comparable in its implications to the discovery of how to split the atom. Indeed, its results could be even more far-reaching'.

Thatcher's speech helped galvanize action in the United Nations, including the establishment of the IPCC and the UNFCCC. Other advocates who helped embed the notion of anthropogenic climate change into public consciousness include Sir John Houghton, who was the co-chair of the IPCC scientific assessment working group and the lead editor of the first three IPCC reports. Sir David King, then the Chief Scientific Adviser to the UK government, attracted widespread attention to the issue when he said that climate change was a more serious threat than terrorism (King 2004). He continues to be a powerful voice, galvanizing action on climate change at national and international levels. Professor Mike Hulme was one of the first to highlight the impact of climate change on the social and agricultural systems in Africa. His work (Hulme, Doherty, Ngara, New and Lister et al. 2001) showed that climate change was probably already having a far-reaching impact and increasing the vulnerability of those exposed to a host of other socioeconomic problems.

But the works of these scholars have not gone unchallenged. A leading climate sceptic was Bjørn Lomborg. His argument was that climate change was a real problem but that others are more important on the basis of his cost-benefit analyses (CBAs) (Lomborg 2001; c.f. Goklany 2008). Lomborg campaigned against the Kyoto Protocol and other measures to cut carbon emissions in the short-term, and he argued that money should instead be spent on research and development for longer-term environmental solutions and on other important world problems such as AIDS, malaria and malnutrition. His limited treatment of how CBA handles thresholds in the Earth System, and the fact that other CBAs reach different conclusions, limits the usefulness of this research. However, this and similar CBAs have been influential in affecting the views of public figures such as Nigel Lawson (2009), George W. Bush, and companies that oppose action to reduce CO_2 emissions (Friel 2010).

Although, as stated, there remain some voices against the need for global action on climate change, in fact the vast majority of academic discourse has long moved beyond questioning climate change to focusing on what the best approaches are for addressing the challenge. One can therefore organize the key thinking around the three main broad approaches or areas of focus: (i) institutionalism, (ii) critical perspectives and (iii) ethical approaches. The rest of the section discusses these perspectives and highlights the works of key scholars.

The first is the institutionalist or managerialist approach, which focuses on the mechanisms and procedures through which nation states and other key actors (e.g., corporations) in the absence of a world government can best co-operate to address the problem of climate change. Two leading thinkers on the institutional dimensions of climate change are Frank Biermann (2001, 2007, 2012; Biermann and Bauer 2005) and David Victor (2001).

Institutional scholars view climate change as an international problem that is best tackled through inter-state co-operation. They take the view that climate change is a collective action problem and that the most rational course of action is, therefore, for states to collaborate to share the burdens and benefits of the cooperation entailed in addressing the problem. Institutionalists emphasize the prevalence of inter-state co-operative arrangements and the tendencies of states to regulate their practices in a fairly well co-coordinated manner given the right incentive structure (Keohane and Victor 2011; Young 1994). The focus, therefore, is mainly on exploring ways to make international institutions for climate governance more effective both in terms of emission reduction and the allocation of costs (Keohane and Victor 2011; Oberthür and Gehring 2006; Victor 2001). Because states are seen as the main actors or agency for governance as well as the primary locus of authority, there is less emphasis on the needs and potential agency of individuals, communities and other sub-national entities.

Critically, the managerialist approach emphasizes the preeminence of economic efficiency as the central guiding principle in climate policy making (Victor 2001). Economic efficiency is in turn mostly sought through reliance on the capitalist free market system. Biermann (2001, 2007, 2012; Biermann and Bauer 2005) has authored several highly influential contributions focusing on various aspects of institutions for international climate governance. He is well known for pioneering the concept of 'earth system governance' in 2005, which has evolved into a major global research programme in this field. His research identifies issues of architecture, regime interplay and fragmentation, allocation and regime stability as some of the key aspects needing more attention in order to advance effective international cooperation on climate change and other environmental problems. Some of his more practical recommendations that have inspired much debate in the literature include strengthening the UN system through the creation of a UN or world environmental organization, the creation of a UN Parliamentary Assembly and empowering existing bodies like the United Nations Environmental Programme with monitoring and sanctioning abilities (cf. Ivanova 2012; see also Death, this volume).

David Victor is renowned for his argument that the best way for nation states to deal with climate change is through the use of market instruments, especially emission trading (Victor 2001). This view, supported by many liberal economic scholars, has been heavily influential in climate policy making at global, regional and national levels with a lot of focus given to market instruments such as cap and trade (taken up in places like the EU, Australia and groups of states in the United States), the clean development mechanism and international carbon offset (Barker 2008; Nordhaus 2007; Pielke 2007; Stern 2007; see also Paterson, this volume). More recently, and especially following the perception that the Kyoto Protocol has not been effective in helping states reduce emissions, some institutionalists have begun to call for less 'top down' and more 'bottom up' approaches to global climate policy (Rayner 2010; Verweij et al. 2006). The idea here is not to abandon states and the market as the key institutions for climate action. Rather, it is to de-emphasize target-setting at the UN level and to encourage a raft of voluntary actions at the state level, including especially green technology innovation and emission trading.

The managerialist approach to climate change governance is criticized by scholars from the Marxist-inspired critical perspectives with Matthew Paterson (2000), Peter Newell (2001) and Larry Lohmann (2006, 2010) as some of the key thinkers. Here, the starting point is to highlight the relationship between the dominant capitalist economic system and climate change. Furthermore, critical scholars question the suitability of the state-based system as the main platform for addressing the problem of climate change. Paterson and Newell have argued in several places that 'a perspective which starts from the role of the state in promoting capital accumulation can much better explain the content both of state policies and of particular international agreements' on climate change (Newell and Paterson 1998: 679; cf. Paterson 2000; 2007; Newell 2001; Newell and Paterson 2010). Critical voices also emphasize the structural power of capital, the role of historical materialism and the incredible ability of business to influence prevailing approaches to climate governance at both state and the international levels (Clapp 2005; Levy and Egan 2003). In addition to pointing out that a capitalist or market-oriented approach to climate change is ineffective in achieving realisable emission reduction and addressing the long-term challenge of climate change, Larry Lohmann is noted for his emphasis that the core market instruments for climate governance such as carbon trading results in the further dispossession of the poor and the transfer of wealth from the global South to the richer global North (Lohmann 2006, 2008, 2009, 2010). The conclusion is that climate change is caused by the competition for resources engendered by the interstate system and the values underpinning the consumer capitalist economy. Hence, that it is futile to expect that climate change can be solved through the same system and processes and that caused it. But while critical scholars are very insightful in their critique of 'climate capitalism' and the managerialist approach, they are less clear about the alternatives for addressing climate change.

An important apparent shift of emphasis has been made by key authors Newell and Paterson in their book entitled *Climate Capitalism* (2010). While acknowledging the problematic relationship between capitalism and climate change, they nonetheless suggest the dominance of capitalism makes it difficult to see how else to deal with climate change. They argue that the best chance to address climate change lies in mobilising and greening capitalist institutions and instruments such as the carbon market, and they conclude that '[c]apitalism of one form or another will provide the context in which near-term solutions to climate change will have to be found' (2010: 161). In contrast, authors like Larry Lohmann (2010) remain adamant that it is inherently impossible to reorganize capitalism to accommodate genuine environmental solutions because capitalism depends for its survival on primitive accumulation and in externalizing the environmental cost of production.

The third main approach is the more overt discussions of the distributive and ethical aspects of climate change. Leading thinkers here include Andrew Dobson (1998), Benito Muller (2001, 2002) and Dale Jamieson (1992). Authors on the distributive dimensions of climate change focus on the differentiation in the cause and impact of climate change both within and across states. As stated in the previous sections, the core argument is that climate change is essentially a justice problem because it involves the rich imposing their burden on the poor. Following, it is argued that questions of justice are imperative both in finding effective solutions to climate change and in getting an agreement that will be widely acceptable internationally. The works of Andy Dobson (1998, 1999) on the relationship between various notions of sustainability and different conceptions of justice have inspired a generation of scholars to explore equity implications of prevailing climate policy and alternative arrangements for achieving climate justice at the domestic level at the realm of global climate regime, with emphasis on North–South climate justice (Garvey 2008; Okereke 2008, 2010a, 2010b; Gardiner 2011).

While a lot of work focuses on temporal and inter-temporal distributional implications of climate change, others highlight the general limitations of the dominant utilitarian economic philosophy and values that underpin conventional climate policy (Attfield 2003; Earth Charter 2000; Engel and Engel 1990; Palmer and Finlay 2003; Sandler and Cafaro 2005). The core argument is that drastic changes in the global environment raise fundamental questions about the dominant modes of relationship between human beings as well as their relationship to the environment and its non-human content. Specifically, it is argued that climate change is fundamentally caused by the quest for economic growth and associated values, such as greed, consumerism, competition and man's intent to dominate nature. The suggestion is to replace these utilitarian ethics with a broad range of other cultural and spiritual perspectives, especially those that privilege precaution, moderation and sacrifice (Shaw 2009; see also Wapner, this volume).

To be clear, climate ethics scholars do not contest the importance of economic information or effective legal frameworks in environmental decision-making. Nor is it suggested that rational self-interest is not a strong motivation for individual and public action. What is contested is the 'more grandiose claim' (Jamieson 1992: 143) that utilitarian economics provides the most important benchmark for environmental policy decision-making. In other words, that an exclusively managerialist approach to climate change is bound to fail in that such an approach avoids a critical engagement with the underlying values and systems – e.g., greed, consumerism, unequal resource distribution, unfettered capitalism and economic liberal individualism, etc. – that are at the heart of current drastic changes in the environment.

Critical potential

Climate change offers much in the way of critical potential. Conceptually, it is perhaps the paradigm case that challenges the prevailing view of 'nature' as something that can and should be dominated to provide maximum material comfort. It presses the case for a more humble outlook or enlightened anthropocentrism that was dominant in society before *New Atlantis*. This view recognizes the need for moderation, humility and precaution (Charlesworth and Okereke 2010). Climate change has raised serious questions about the extent to which humans can externalize the cost of economic production and consumption without undermining the very basis of human existence itself.

Unimagined tipping points in the Earth System and climate system raise profound questions about the notion of risk. Where there is not actuarial data from experience (and perhaps even where there is), basing policy decisions entirely on utilitarian cost benefit analyses entails a significant leap of faith. Although nearly all political decisions entail some form of uncertainty and risk calculation, the prevailing approach that privileges market economics over intrinsic value of nature constitutes a major hindrance to addressing long-term climate change.

In general, contemporary policy processes tend to have very short time horizons related to elections, media attention and, perhaps most importantly, the quarterly financial returns of stock-market listed companies and the instantaneous whims of financial speculation. It is instructive that calls for urgent action on climate change have all but been put on the back burner since the onset of the global economic crisis in late 2008. Recent events in Canada, Australia and the United States demonstrate clearly that government policies and action on climate change is contingent on political expediency. Canada pulled out of the Kyoto Protocol and has aggressively encouraged oil mining from tar sand in a bid to boost its flagging economy. The Australian government had its proposals for a carbon tax drastically altered following campaigns and threats from the coal industry. The first Obama administration had to 'park' proposed legislation on climate change to secure the support of the Republican-dominated senate for President Obama's financial and economic reforms. The long-term nature of climate change makes short-term approach to policy very unsuitable and ineffective (Anderson and Bows 2008). Even if an assumption is made that there will be no abrupt climate changes, it should be noted that the burdens of increases in global mean temperature, droughts, floods and other extreme weather events are already on many of the current global poor who have contributed the least to climate change (Oppenheimer 2005; Sundaraman 1995). Given the actual harm occurring now, which is attributed to climate change, the wealth of literature that discusses questions around climate change and future generations is perhaps intrinsically 'academic' and is even more so when the literature tends to use lack of knowledge of future generations' preferences almost as an excuse to maintain their own ideological positions – often little more than business as usual (c.f. Böhm and Dabhi 2011; Harvey 2006, 2010; Lohmann 2006, 2008).

As we have already seen, the conceptual questions raised by climate change immediately raise ideological questions. In particular, difficulties in framing markets make the marketization of carbon difficult to justify unless substantial emission reductions can be unquestionably demonstrated prior to that marketization (Böhm and Dabhi 2009, 2011; Bumpus and Liverman 2008). The experience of carbon marketization only reinforces these issues (see Paterson, this volume). There are indications that existing carbon markets have made rich people richer and not reduced emissions (Böhm and Dabhi 2009, 2011; Lohmann 2006, 2010). Questions related to other markets are more complex, but unless they are local exchange subsistence markets, there is a likelihood they end up promoting increased resource consumption and associated emissions (Lohmann 2008, 2009). These observations further reinforce the importance of questions of justice (see Bond, this volume). If justice is not seen as to each according to what the capitalist market dictates, then the rich getting richer through relatively little work, whilst the poor and vulnerable get more exposed to climate risks, must surely be unjust (Okereke and Schroeder 2009; Okereke 2011). Henry Shue put it aptly when he said, 'whatever justice entails, it is clearly not justice to ask the poor to sell their blankets so that the rich can keep their jewelleries' (1992: 453). Yet it needs to be acknowledged that while the intuitive appeal to climate justice at the global level is strong, outlining what exactly it entails and how that might be achieved in the anarchical inter-state system is a very challenging task.

Arising from all of this, there has been much discussion of how relevant states are for a global issue such as climate change (Okereke, Bulkeley and Schroeder 2009; Paterson 2000; see Kuehls, this volume). As stated, the competition for resource accumulation engendered by the logic of the state and the related imperative to protect domiciled companies has been identified as a major cause of global environmental degradation (Paterson 2000). However, states can set a legal (soft or hard law) framework in which companies and capitalism work, in a way that no other actor can (Barry and Eckersley 2005; Eckersley 2004). Yet, since state authorities achieve their mandates to govern through democratic elections and are mostly interested in their re-election, it is evident that states' ability and willingness to challenge vested interests will depend to a large degree on the measure of support they get from citizens. Hence, a critical question is really to what extent climate change can serve as a mobilizing force for global citizens to press for fundamental changes in the structure and functioning of the prevalent economic order (see Price, Saunders and Olcese, this volume).

If the underpinnings of such utilitarian economics struggle to provide a basis for effective climate policy, to what else can we look? MacIntyre (1990) powerfully argues that virtue provides a better approach to dealing with complex political and environmental problems than dominant free market capitalism and associated economic cost benefit analysis. Developing from MacIntyre, one approach could be the elevation of virtue ethics, which emphasizes precaution, moderation and sacrifice (Shaw 2009). One common criticism is that ideas of virtue vary widely between cultures (e.g., Statman 1997: 20–23; Louden 1984). However, for environment and development questions, the Earth Charter (2000), Engel and Engel (1990), Palmer and Finlay (2003) among others suggest sufficient similarity to enable talk of a global virtue tradition. This tradition sees greed, selfishness and gluttony as vices, and justice, wisdom, courage and moderation as cardinal virtues that resonate across cultures (cf. Sandler and Cafaro 2005). Yet, even on a broad level, translating these virtues into practical policy making at the global level cannot by any means be seen as an easy task.

Conclusion

Climate change raises critical questions that much theoretical and practical (environmental) politics tends to ignore or under emphasize. Firstly, despite widely appreciated shortcomings, much of climate discourse and policy continues to elevate probabilistic prediction science as the basis for global climate public policy (see Forsyth, this volume). To worsen matters, the blind faith in prediction is matched by a strong ideological commitment to utilitarian economic tools as the basis for deciding environmental value and actions that are worthwhile in saving the planet. Despite ample evidence of poor performance, governments are fixed on the idea of commodifying carbon and constructing different types of carbon market as inevitable tools in solving climate change (see Paterson, this volume). As ever, conventional wisdom remains that there is no alternative to markets. The result appears to be little more than business as usual with plenty of rhetoric and little in the form of adequate action.

Moreover, the four- or five-year perspectives promoted by electoral cycles means that representative democracy has difficulty taking a long-term perspective, particularly when the purchase of media coverage to engage voters means that candidates literally owe a debt to the large corporations that tend to have sufficient disposable income. Thus, forms of democracy that can take a longer view and are also better able to deal with difficulties in predicting climate change appear to be needed. Such forms of directly democratic policy making have received extensive attention (Dryzek 1987, 1990; see also Hinton, this volume). That participative policy processes are mandated by international agreements, including *Agenda 21* (UN 1992a), adds to the impetus for these processes to complement existing representative (electoral) democratic processes.

But in the absence of strong global institutions for governing sustainability (see Baker and Death, this volume), the burden of climate change continues to fall disproportionately on those that have least caused it. Climate change thus brings questions of global justice to the fore (see Bond, this volume); it also suggests the need to go beyond utilitarian ethics and unbridled anthropocentrism (see McShane, this volume). While the suggestion to accord non-human nature moral rights as implied in ecocentrism may be going too far, there is certainly the need to embrace ethical approaches that emphasize the unity of all beings. Some form of cautious anthropocentrism, or of what Welchman (1999) calls 'enlightened anthropocentrism', should be sufficient to promote more care and prudence in our dealings with nature (see Wapner, this volume). In any case, it is clear that the challenge climate change poses is fundamental, wide-ranging and at the heart of contemporary critical environmental politics.

Further reading

Key texts include Mike Hulme (2009) *Why We Disagree About Climate Change Understanding Controversy, Inaction and Opportunity*, Cambridge: Cambridge University Press; Pete Newell and Matthew Paterson (2010) *Climate Capitalism: Global Warming and the Transformation of the Global Economy*, Cambridge: Cambridge University Press; John Dryzek, Richard Norgaard and David Schlosberg (2011) *The Oxford Handbook of Climate Change and Society*, Oxford: Oxford University Press; Frank Biermann and Philipp Pattberg (2012) *Global Environmental Governance Reconsidered* (Earth System Governance), Cambridge, MA: MIT Press; David Victor (2001) *The Collapse of the Kyoto Protocol and the Struggle to Slow Global Warming*, Princeton: Princeton University Press; and Anthony Giddens (2011) *The Politics of Climate Change*, Second edition, Cambridge: Polity.

Useful websites

Intergovernmental Panel on Climate Change: http://www.ipcc.ch/
United Nations Framework Convention on Climate Change: http://unfccc.int/
The 350 campaign: http://www.350.org/
A commentary site on climate science by working climate scientists: http://www.realclimate.org/
Global Governance Project: http://www.glogov.org/
Earth System Governance Project: http://www.earthsystemgovernance.org/
Climate Ethics blog: http://rockblogs.psu.edu/climate/

6 Commodification

Matthew Paterson

Introduction

Commodification has become a key concept underpinning critiques of how (neoliberal) capitalist societies have responded to a range of environmental problems. Critics have used the concept to highlight the political-economic dynamics underpinning environmental degradation. They have also used it to show how the articulation of such problems has been appropriated by capitalists to generate novel forms of market exchange that simultaneously fail to address the original problem effectively, that generate ideological obfuscations over how to respond to environmental degradation, and that generate novel forms of socio-ecological inequality and exploitation (see Bond, this volume). Understanding the character of commodification and its deployment in relation to environmental problems is therefore a crucial component in a critical approach to environmental politics.

Core ideas

Within capitalist societies, commodification is the central process by which the bundle of things human societies conventionally but problematically call *nature* (see Latour 2004a on the problems of the term) are transformed into the myriad products that appear magically in shops and markets. It is that aspect of capitalist social relations that involves turning the products of human labour as it transforms nature into something for exchange in markets. A commodity is precisely a thing produced by its producer purely because it has some exchange value – it has no direct use value for the producer herself. Or rather, and more precisely, even if it might have such use value, the direct producer in capitalist societies has little or no control over what is produced and for what purpose it is put – it is produced purely for the purposes of sale in markets.

Commodification is thus key to ecological politics because it sets in train the abstraction of the economy from its socio-ecological contexts. It enables the vast array of objects that we use in daily life to be considered as somehow separate from flows of carbon, water, and nitrogen, or lead, mercury, and gold, and the various social and ecological degradations generated by the flows of these chemicals. Prior to an economy organised around commodity production (without wanting to idealise those societies, which had their own contradictions), most things consumed were produced by the consumer themselves or by someone physically close to them (see Brooks and Bryant, this volume). As a consequence, the various dependencies and consequences of the production and consumption – where resources are taken from the ground, where the waste and by-products go, and who benefits and loses from this process – are normally visible to all concerned. If a stream becomes polluted and unusable for fishing or drinking water, you know who is dumping mining residues or letting their sheep get too close to it.

But with commodification, these links get radically broken. The abstracted exchange of goods means that these dependencies and consequences are often virtually impossible to trace and certainly impossible to experience directly. The laptop on which I write this contains all sorts of resources – aluminium, plastics (from oil), various metals in the circuit boards, and so on – of whose origins I am completely ignorant and whose destination when I get rid of the laptop I have only very limited control over and a vague general sense that it may end up in a toxic 'recycling' site in China (Iles 2004; Lepawsky and Mather 2011). While this may be the extreme example, it is the logical outcome of an economy organised principally around commodification. The same is still true for much simpler processes – the bread we eat in a sandwich contains wheat that comes from more or less anywhere, likely to have been produced in a way that depletes soil of its nutrients, depletes the earth's surface of topsoil, entails very significant greenhouse gas emissions, and pollutes local watercourses with nitrate residues. Where it does this, and to whose benefit and detriment, we can normally only guess.

So commodification creates a radical distanciation (Dryzek 1987; Giddens 1990; Saurin 1994) between the commodity and its socio-ecological consequences. But commodification is also central to ecological politics in another way, connected to but distinct from the former. This is that commodification is central to a capitalist economy that is oriented structurally towards endless accumulation and thus to the growth-related character of environmental problems. Central to capitalist social relations is the commodity form, which becomes the overarching form of social relation. Particularly important is that human labour itself becomes commodified – organised around the payment of wages rather than, for example, tithes or slavery.

The wage-labour relation generates a particular sort of class dynamic that engenders a growth-oriented, and indeed growth-dependent, economy, in a number of ways (for a fuller account than I give here, see Paterson (2007: chapter 4), which draws mainly on Held (1987) and Harvey (1990). First, it means that employers (capitalists) see labour as a burden (as they need to be paid) rather than benefit (as a source of tithe income, for example) and thus have incentives to find ways to reduce labour costs. This is a key origin of technological innovation in capitalist societies, as capitalists generate novel machinery to displace labour, thus increasing overall productivity (see Luke, this volume). Second, employers face each other in the marketplace in ever-more ruthless competition (in part stimulated by the search for new technologies) and thus develop a sort of 'grow or die' mentality. Third, the direct confrontation of workers and capitalists over the distribution of the surplus labour produced (i.e., over wages and working conditions) is recurrent throughout capitalist history, meaning that capital feels insecure in its capacity to realise profits and turns to the State to get that institution (which evolves as a consequence – see Kuehls, this volume) to discipline labour and secure its conditions for accumulation. Fourth, one of the main contradictions to the system based on the commodification of labour is recurrent cycles of boom and slump as capital fails periodically to realise profits, often because of a lack of 'effective demand', that is, not enough money in workers' pockets for them to become effective consumers. These periodic crises also generate pressures for the State to develop strategies and institutions to promote growth.

So while in classical accounts going back to Marx the commodification of labour is the key social innovation that starts in England in the seventeenth century and becomes globalised through various means (mercantilism, mimicry, imperialism, corporate domination, etc.) over the next few centuries, there is also a very specific set of commodifications that are crucial to both the dynamism of capitalist growth and to its ecologically destructive character. This is the development of technologies in the eighteenth century, again first in England, that enable and generate the deployment of fossil fuel resources (initially, coal, then later oil and natural gas) in great and growing quantity. The development of the steam engine, of canals that enable the shipment of coal across a country, and later of railways were crucial technologies that made coal the central resource to the nineteenth-century economy and to its rapid growth. The internal combustion engine, combustion for electrical generation, and later the jet engine did the same for oil and gas in the twentieth century. Many scholars in environmental history and sociology refer to this as the 'metabolic rift' (Clark and York 2005) – that the late eighteenth century sees the shift from an essentially cyclical economy, powered by human and animal labour and by renewable resources (wood, water), to a linear economy powered by the 'ancient sunlight' (Mumford 1932) contained in coal. This shift is crucial to the sorts of throughput of resources and pollution conventionally identified by environmentalists of all stripes – an acceleration of the take of resources from the earth and of pollution into it (Dalby, Katz-Rosene, and Paterson 2013; Daly 1973; Georgescu-Roegen 1971; see also Kütting, this volume).

Two types of commodification of nature are worth distinguishing at this point (see also Castree 2003a for further elaboration of the plural character of commodifications of nature). The first refers to the original appropriation of nature discussed previously, including both long-standing forms such as in agriculture, to the novel commodifications of animal and plant (including human) genes, bacteria, and so on that have developed more recently. Here commodification enables us to understand much of the dynamic behind the accelerated throughput of resources and pollution, the shifts in economic and socio-ecological metabolism that capitalism engenders, and the politically charged character of claims to 'limits to growth' (on which more in the 'Critical Potential' section below).

But commodification has also taken on a second significance in relation to contemporary responses to environmental problems. Many responses, starting in the 1970s and accelerating in the 1990s and since, have been organised around novel commodifications as means to 'internalise the external costs' of pollution (see, e.g., Smith 2006). The most visible is in the development of carbon markets, but there are or have been such markets, notably but not only in the United States, for wetlands management, sulphur dioxide emissions, chlorofluorocarbons (CFCs), and more general 'payments for ecosystem services' (see Büscher, this volume). These entail the generation of property rights to emissions, which then become tradable, that is, they become commodities.

Key thinkers

Marx is clearly the central theorist on whom debates about commodification have drawn in environmental debates. The earlier discussion of the concept draws directly on Marx's account of the central institutions of capitalist society and their contradictory dynamics. Some of the environmental implications can also be seen in Marx's work (see, e.g., Foster 2002; Smith 2006), but much of this literature gets caught up in the (not very interesting) question of whether Marx was 'really' an ecologist, and it is more in the extension of the logic of commodification in Marx's thought that we see the potential of the idea to enable our understanding of key dynamics in environmental politics.

The other thinker whose work has inspired work on commodification is Karl Polanyi (especially 1944). Central to Polanyi's account of contemporary life was a pressure from 'market society' to liberate itself from social constraints – norms, rules, and traditions that put constraints on what market actors could do. In effect these are principally constraints on what can be commodified – produced for sale in the marketplace for a profit. But while capital seeks to 'disembed' itself from such social norms, other social actors react to this and, particularly for Polanyi, to the attempt to commodify land and labour. There is particular resistance to the commodification of these things as they are 'fictitious commodities' for Polanyi. By this he means that they are not and cannot be produced by the market itself, unlike say the laptop I write this on or the book (or laptop) you read it in, which has been produced more or less entirely by human labour in order to be sold in the market. Resistance thus arises because this is thus an act of appropriation by market actors of things they cannot claim to have produced. This notion of fictitious commodities has become particularly important in critiques of the second form of environmental commodification discussed previously.

There are four sets of literatures worth highlighting that have developed Marx and Polanyi's ideas in environmental debates. First is the engagement with animal rights debates by writers from these traditions. These focus on explaining how the exploitation of animals co-evolves with social relations, and thus commodification transforms those sorts of relations (see, for example, Dickens 1996; Nibert 2002; Rudy and White, this volume). Part of the story here is about distanciation: that commodification enables greater scales and intensities of animal exploitation and violence. But part of the story is also that commodification of animals has particular qualities because of their live, self-reproducing characteristics, which conditions and, to an extent, limits the forms that commodification takes.

Second are the theorists in what has come to be called ecological Marxism, such as John Bellamy Foster or James O'Connor (for a selection, see, for example, Benton 1996; O'Connor 1994; Schnaiberg, Pellow, and Weinberg 2002). Their work is most closely associated with the journals *Capitalism Nature Socialism* and *Monthly Review.* While commodification is not always made absolutely central to these analyses, it is part of the bundle of concepts that explain the unsustainability of capitalist societies. Central to their analyses (see in particular O'Connor 1991) is the concept of the 'second contradiction of capitalism'. While capitalism's first contradiction is that between the forces and relations of production, as analysed classically by Marx, the second contradiction is between the combined forces/relations of production and the conditions of production, which is understood as the socio-ecological conditions on which capitalist production is based but which it systematically undermines. Commodification is part of this process, but it is capital's endless search for accumulation that is perhaps the central problem for these writers. The exception is perhaps Neil Smith, whose article 'Nature as Accumulation Strategy' (2006) elaborates in detail the centrality of commodification to the social production of nature.

Third, and more tightly focused on commodification itself, is a more recent literature amongst environmental geographers, such as Noel Castree, Scott Prudham, and Karen Bakker, associated with the notion of 'neoliberal environments', the title of an edited book that exemplifies this approach (Heynen, McCarthy, Prudham, and Robbins 2007). Here the analysis, while still drawing on a general Marxist account of commodification, tends to be more historically specific in arguing that the emergence of neoliberalism from the early 1980s onwards has shaped a particular form of response to environmental problems centred on the deregulation of environmental controls, but more precisely also a privatisation of resources and the establishment of markets for environmental resources. The second form of environmental commodification is thus central to these analyses. Many of these authors engage in highly detailed analyses of a specific sort of environmental commodification, such as water (Bakker 2005; Swyngedouw 2007a), wetlands (Robertson 2004), and various specific resources (Bridge 2007; Robbins and Luginbuhl 2007; St. Martin 2008). Meanwhile, Noel Castree (2003a, 2008) in particular has interrogated and developed the notion of commodification of nature in all its complexity, drawing our attention to the plurality of forms of commodifications of nature produced in good measure by the specificities of different sorts of natural objects being commodified – from traditional commodities such as agricultural crops or timber, to genes, or CO_2 emissions rights.

Fourth is the large literature that has emerged as a critical response to the commodification of the atmosphere as a response to climate change (see Okereke and Charlesworth, this volume). Carbon markets of two different types – cap and trade (or emissions trading) and offset – have become central to such responses. The UN's Kyoto Protocol establishes both types of market, and cap and trade systems have been established in the European Union, New Zealand, New South Wales, the northeastern United States (the Regional Greenhouse Gas Initiative), as well as internally by BP and Shell, and are in various stages of implementation in another regional scheme in North America (the Western Climate Initiative), Australia, South Korea, and, less certainly, China (for a comprehensive review, see Betsill and Hoffmann 2011). Many have provisions for regulated companies to use offsets as a means of compliance, and the largest such provision, in the EU Emissions Trading Scheme (ETS), drives the investment in the Kyoto offset systems, the Clean Development Mechanism (CDM) and Joint Implementation. The combined 'value' of these markets in 2011 was $176bn (World Bank 2012), comfortably the largest of existing environmental markets.

The emergence of carbon markets has stimulated a trenchant critique. While legitimised by its proponents (e.g., Ellerman, Convery, and de Perthuis 2010) as a means of giving carbon a 'price' and stimulating emissions reductions in a cost-effective and economically efficient manner, it is widely argued to engender a series of consequences that need to be resisted. Central to the generation of these problems is the commodification at the heart of the phenomenon (Bumpus and Liverman 2008; Brunnengräber 2006; Newell and Paterson 2010; see also Figure 6.1).

Carbon markets establish either a set of rights to emit carbon (in cap and trade systems) or a set of rights to issue credits based on promises not to emit carbon (in offset systems) (Hoffmann 2011). These rights are tradable and thus function as property rights just as in other forms of property ownership. These carbon emission rights thus become commodities for abstracted sale in markets. For some, this is a sufficient critique, redolent of the Polanyian account of resistance: the atmosphere is a 'fictitious commodity' and should not be subject to the laws of the market and private property. It should be regarded rather as a commons to be collectively managed for the good of all.

Larry Lohmann (e.g., 2005, 2006) has emerged as the most articulate and theoretically sophisticated of these critics of carbon markets. Lohmann draws not only on Marx and Polanyi in the ways suggested previously, but on economic sociologists, notably Michel Callon, to draw attention to the messy construction of carbon markets through a series of devices that both enable the markets to operate but also to obscure their failure in dealing adequately with climate change. Lohmann pays considerable attention to the means by which different sorts of socio-ecological practices (from power stations to forests or agricultural practices) are commensurated via the means of a whole series of institutionalised processes to generate the commodities that can be sold in carbon markets. He also shows in great detail the problems that such markets entail.

Figure 6.1 The carbon supermarket
Reproduced with kind permission of Kate Evans.

Critical potential

The concept of commodification is intrinsically critical in its focus on one of the central processes through which environmental degradation is organised socially. It enables scholars and activists to understand why, at a fundamental level of social organisation, environmental degradation occurs, why it tends to take the forms it does, and why the politics of responses to environmental degradation play out in the way they do. While similar sorts of critique have been addressed to other sorts of environmental markets, exploring this in relation to the critical literature on carbon markets is a useful way to exemplify this critical potential. Building on the central insight about the problem of commodification, a number of specific problems flow from the initial commodification of climate.

First, it constitutes a question of 'climate fraud' (Bachram 2004). Carbon markets constitute in this view an inevitable evasion of the responsibility and need to reduce emissions. They enable corporations and countries to engage in complicated accounting scams that present the appearance of emissions reductions without this in fact being the case. For example, in many cap and trade systems companies are allocated a certain number of allowances based on data about past emissions and projections of future emissions. But companies have significantly better information about this data than regulators and are thus able to inflate baselines to their advantage. Offset systems are even more vulnerable to the problem of the counterfactual – it is necessary to project what emissions would have been if a project had not gone ahead, but the number of credits awarded is extremely sensitive to this initial baseline projection, which of course cannot be directly measured since the project does go ahead. The incentives to massage the baseline projections to generate more credits are huge.

Second, carbon markets entail a form of 'carbon colonialism' (Bachram 2004; Lohmann 2006). There are two aspects here. First is the initial act of appropriation. Effectively, in establishing an emissions trading system in the Kyoto Protocol, industrialised countries transformed their obligations to reduce carbon emissions into a property right to emit carbon up to that level. Given that successful responses to climate change involve a limited overall 'carbon budget', this constitutes an effective appropriation of the rights of peoples elsewhere in the world. Second, however, is the colonialism involved in offset projects themselves. On the one hand this is a displacement of the obligation to reduce emissions by the rich; by purchasing offsets in the developing world they entrench a division of the world into the 'carbon rich' and 'carbon poor'. On the other hand, the projects themselves involve significant monitoring and control within the developing countries where the projects take place – an extension of direct control over energy, agriculture, and forestry in the South by or on behalf of actors in the North.

Third, carbon markets operate as a sort of 'indulgence' system (Smith 2007), much like the Catholic Church operated in the medieval period. The rich (individuals, companies, and countries) are able to buy a clean conscience via carbon offsetting, thus obviating the need for the structural transformation of their own economies and daily lives. These markets thus enable novel sorts of competition amongst consumers, as offsetters attempt to position themselves as 'virtuous' through their offsetting practices. But whether offsetting in fact leads to substantial shifts in emissions towards sustainability is far from clear (e.g., Lovell, Bulkeley, and Liverman 2009; Whitehead, this volume).

Fourth, and in the context of the financial crisis from 2007 onwards, carbon markets became seen as vulnerable to financial manipulation similar to that which triggered the financial crisis. Alongside the direct exchanges of emissions allowances and credits, a thriving, if still relatively simple, derivatives market has emerged. Futures, forward contracts, options, and swaps all have become integral to these markets, enabling regulated companies to hedge against price volatility and enabling speculators to profit from short-term price movements. The U.S. Friends of the Earth coined the term *subprime carbon* (Chan 2009) to suggest that this reliance on derivative markets, as well as some of the climate fraud problems outlined previously, meant that carbon markets were similarly likely to generate bubbles that would render the entire system vulnerable to collapse (see Pellizzoni, this volume). Most worrying perhaps was the emergence of contracts that bundled together different 'carbon commodities' and then repackaged them again for investors, making the risks attached to each investment (for example, the risk that a CDM project would not be approved and the underlying credit therefore not issued) obscure to the investor.

A core question here concerns how to understand the character of this problematic nature of such environmental commodifications. For most critics (Bachram 2004; Böhm and Dabhi 2009; Gilbertson and Reyes 2009; Lohmann 2006; Smith 2007), a very strong ontological claim is made about these markets. The commodification involved is understood as fundamentally impossible to articulate with principles of justice or sustainability and needs to be radically opposed. While Lohmann in particular (2005) pays a good deal of attention to the assembled character of such markets, drawing on Callon and MacKenzie (see, e.g., Callon 2008; MacKenzie 2009), this stands in tension (an interesting tension, but a tension nonetheless) with his insistence on the fundamental inacceptability of such markets – that they *must* operate in a singular manner undermining sustainability and social justice and can neither be reformed, nor have messy or contradictory consequences.

However, some within this literature (notably Newell and Paterson 2010), while accepting the highly problematic character of such markets, do not start with such strong ontological assumptions about the inevitable and singular character of commodification. Rather, given that any specific market (and thus commodity) is the result of particular political contexts and processes, and especially because environmental markets such as carbon markets are always highly contested politically, the socio-ecological character of such commodification may have various qualities depending on the outcome of these political struggles. For example, carbon markets have been shaped in various ways. Forestry projects have to date (but the struggle is on-going) been almost entirely excluded from the main offset market, the CDM, because of successful struggles by NGOs in the late 1990s (Bäckstrand and Lövbrand 2006). In the light of worries about financial speculation and price volatility, many of the proposed (but as yet unsuccessful) legislation to create cap and trade systems at the federal level in the United States specifically excluded participation by financiers, and regulatory measures for carbon markets have already been introduced in the United States in advance of a federal cap and trade system (Helleiner and Thistlethwaite 2012). The socio-ecological consequences of these markets depend on these types of regulatory variation (which are the outcomes of political struggles) and the sort of commodities and commodification processes that result.

The second critical insight that can be drawn out of the notion of commodification concerns the question of limits to growth (see Kütting, this volume). The importance of the concept here is to draw our attention to the core dynamics of capitalism and thus why to argue for limits to growth is to make a much more radical challenge to capitalism than most of its proponents, from Meadows, Meadows, Randers, and Behrens III (1972) onwards, accept (for interesting recent accounts of this position, see Jackson 2009; Princen 2005; or Victor 2008). In effect, it is a core part of an overall theoretical perspective that demonstrates that growth is not best understood as a 'choice', nor as the result of some naturalised notion of human ambition or desire, but rather as an aspect of the specific features of capitalist social relations. This is alluded to previously but worth elaborating further.

The specificities of capitalism are usually taken to be the combination of wage-labour relations and competitive markets. These set in train the sorts of dynamics elaborated previously – class conflict, technological innovation, crisis tendencies, and globalisation (via imperialism or a more 'benign' set of transnational processes). But the relevant point regarding limits to growth is that such a system cannot countenance these limits. It is a system whose very survival depends on continuous growth. That this is the case can be amply illustrated by the fact that a recession – the temporary lack of growth or contraction of an economy – is more or less the definition of an economic crisis. If a steady-state economy were to come into being, this would necessarily result in recurrent crises of profitability as firms found it progressively more difficult to find profitable investments (see Whitehead, this volume). It would also result in legitimacy crises for capitalist states both because capital would find limits on its accumulation intolerable but also because growth has, at least since the inception of the welfare state, been consciously pursued by many governments in order to displace concern and protest about inequalities.

There are of course questions to be asked of this argument. In particular, economic growth in monetary terms is not the same as limits to growth that are biophysical. But to the extent that economic growth can continue while biophysical appropriations of 'nature' decline, this would entail the progressive commodification of everything as capital sought to find new ways of investing and growing. Environmental markets may indeed be seen precisely as one sort of search for novel commodification processes in situations where growth has been relatively slow, at least in 'advanced' industrialised countries, since the 1970s.

Conclusion

Given the previous argument about the key role that commodification plays in the generation of environmental degradation, in the politics of who wins and loses from this degradation and from responses to it, and in the generation of types of policies and practices to address environmental change, commodification has a great many connections to other concepts in this book. It is key to the structuring of responses to particular problems, notably climate change, biodiversity, and various aspects of conservation (see respectively Okereke and Charlesworth, Büscher, and Igoe, this volume). Responses to each of these have in many places been structured around novel forms of commodification. It has engendered novel forms of colonialism and injustice (see Bond, and Watts and Peluso, this volume). Environmental commodification can also be seen to operate as a distinct form of governmentality, structuring agents to operate in relation to environmental degradation via modes of subjectivity centred on market calculation, the internalisation of economistic notions of 'efficiency', and highly individualised responses to environmental degradation (see Lövbrand and Stripple, this volume; also Bäckstrand and Lövbrand 2006; Lövbrand and Stripple 2011; Oels 2005; Paterson and Stripple 2010). Finally, as suggested previously, understanding the dynamics and politics of commodification is central to explaining the politics of limits, since it shows how the capitalist economy and the political institutions that sustain it materially and ideologically cannot countenance such limits, and thus claims about limits operate as a profound challenge to the existing order.

One key remaining debate, however, is about the character of this challenge and the relationship of commodification to it. On the one hand, most of those working in the Marxian-Polanyian traditions regard the dynamic of commodification as inevitably producing a range of socio-ecological degradations and, thus, to be fundamentally unsustainable. On the other hand, the notions of commodification developed by writers like Callon and MacKenzie are suggestive of a greater messiness in the ways that commodities are created and regulated and, thus, of their social and ecological consequences. Commodities in this view are regarded as assemblages – put together by a range of specific techniques, rules, actors, and contexts with specific effects that cannot be reduced to the generic term *commodity*. As noted previously regarding Lohmann's work, this generates a significant tension when both traditions are used. If this is the case, then the character of the critique of environmental commodification needs to pay considerable attention to the nuances and specificities of how such commodities are put together and the role of political activism (including resistance) in shaping their character and effects.

Further reading

An excellent overview of the question of commodification of nature can be found in Castree's 'Commodifying what nature?' (2003a), and an excellent account of how commodification connects to broader processes of capital accumulation and ecological degradation is provided by Saurin (1994), in Smith's 'Nature as accumulation strategy' (2006), and in various essays in Benton's *The Greening of Marxism* (1996). Heynen et al.'s *Neoliberal Environments* (2007) provides a large number of cases of environmental commodification as well as an argument connecting the rise of novel forms of such commodification to neoliberalism. Lohmann's various works (2005, 2006) provide a particularly rich critique of the commodification of climate change, while Newell and Paterson's *Climate Capitalism* (2010) provides a broad overview of climate politics focused on capital's search for novel commodities to produce and sell.

Useful websites

Carbon trade watch: http://www.carbontradewatch.org/
Carbon market watch: http://carbonmarketwatch.org/
Ecosystem marketplace: http://www.ecosystemmarketplace.com/
IETA: http://www.ieta.org/

7 Conservation

James Igoe

Introduction

In my book *Conservation and Globalization* (2004), I relate a conversation with a Maasai elder in Tanzania in which I asked, 'Do Maasai do conservation?' 'Of course not,' the elder replied, 'why would we do anything so stupid?' As the conversation continued, I posed a series of questions about whether Maasai set aside and protected natural resources, or otherwise managed them in ways designed to ensure their continued availability for future generations. My informant responded enthusiastically in the affirmative and proceeded to provide elaborate and detailed accounts of precisely these kinds of practices. Such accounts inform the Maasai resource management model I present in the book, the viability of which depends entirely on resource conservation at multiple temporal and geographic scales.

For my informant, however, the word *conservation* had entirely different connotations. For him conservation was a system of ideas and technical interventions, brought to Tanzania by Europeans, and that entailed enclosing traditional Maasai grazing land in parks for the exclusive enjoyment of Western researchers and tourists. Investigative journalist Mark Dowie (2009) has recorded similar sentiments from local and indigenous people around the world.

This assessment of conservation is consistent with the observations and analyses of a growing network of social scientists and concerned conservationists. In his article 'A Challenge to Conservationists' (2004), anthropologist Mac Chapin noted that a small group of large conservation organizations was capturing the bulk of global conservation funding. These organizations have come to dominate the field in terms of ideology, visibility, practice, and resources brought to bear on conservation interventions. They in fact appear to have become part of a hegemonic bloc that Brockington, Duffy, and Igoe (2008: 9) have termed 'mainstream conservation' (also see Igoe, Neves, and Brockington 2010). This bloc tends to drown out the full diversity of conservation perspectives and practices and, consequently, is often represented, understood, and responded to as conservation tout court.

Relative to all this, conservation politics can be understood from at least three perspectives. The first is related to pervasive conflicts between protected areas and local livelihoods, which pits conservation against local and indigenous communities around the world. The second is a conservation anti-politics, in which political struggles inherent to resource conservation are recast as essentially a-political problems amenable to technical intervention. This trend, as we shall see has intensified with the recent rise of neoliberal conservation, under which conservation has been transformed from a project of 'saving the world from the broader excesses of human impacts under capitalism [to one dedicated to] entraining nature to capitalism, while simultaneously creating broader economic possibilities for capitalist expansion' (Büscher, Sullivan, Neves, Igoe, and Brockington 2012: 7). Finally we have struggles to move conservation away from these definitions and trajectories and the formation of popular and quotidian conservation politics.

Core ideas

Conservation politics over the first decade of the new millennium have been fascinating, worrisome, and rapidly changing. In the early millennium there was a great deal of talk about community conservation, conservation and poverty reduction, and potential partnerships between indigenous communities and conservation initiatives. These conversations led to questions of whether indigenous peoples were good conservationists (Hunn, Johnson, Russell, and Thornton 2003; Redford 1990). They also were associated with the rise of the idea of biocultural diversity, a measurable correlation between biodiversity and cultural diversity on a planetary scale.

These conversations became particularly intense following the 2004 World Parks Congress in Durban, South Africa. Strategic alliances of indigenous activists and their supporters made sure that indigenous issues were on the agenda, particularly through the themes of protected area governance and communities and equity. Throughout the Congress they repeatedly sought to call conservationists to account for displacements and inequities associated with conservation in both the nineteenth and twentieth centuries (Bonner 1994; Neumann 1998; Spence 1999; Dowie 2009). A key precursor to this event, explains Brosius (2004: 609), was the creation of the Theme of Indigenous and Local Communities, Equity and Protected Areas (TILCEPA) and the Commission on Environmental, Economic, and Social Policy (CEESP), both within the World Conservation Union. These institutions remain actively involved in global conservation.

Similarly vibrant confrontations have not been repeated, in part due to intentional restructuring of global conservation events (see MacDonald 2010a). However, the events of the 2004 World Parks Congress continued to reverberate in conservation politics. On the one hand they iconified and amplified concerns of a backlash called 'the Back to the Barriers Movement', conservation traditionalists who felt that far too many concessions were being made to indigenous peoples (Igoe 2005), or even that indigenous peoples had hijacked conservations agendas (Terborgh 2004). Indigenous activists and their supporters, for their part, have continued to point to their continued marginalization in the global conservation movement. Two important concerns are that they are being held to unrealistic expectations of 'staying primitive' if they wish to be recognized as legitimate inhabitants of key conservation spaces (Holt 2005; Igoe 2005) and that indigenous people and conservation scientists often talk across very different cultural understandings of nature and what constitutes good conservation. When they disagree, Western science consistently trumps local knowledge (Ross, Sherman, Snodgrass, and Delcore 2011; see also Forsyth, this volume).

Most recently social scientists and conservationists have grown concerned about the emergence and proliferation of 'neoliberal conservation' (Igoe and Brockington 2007), dedicated to harnessing market forces and private enterprise in the service of protecting nature. Partnerships between conservation non-governmental organizations (NGOs) and corporations, which caused such a stir when Chapin wrote about them in 2004, are now commonplace and openly celebrated (MacDonald 2010a; MacDonald and Corson 2012). Some conservationists have warned of the need to be mindful of the nature of these relationships. Under what conditions might they be worthwhile and actually further conservation goals? Under what conditions might they have negative effects and harm the reputation of conservation NGOs (Robinson

2012)? More critical observers argue that such arrangements are less about putting capital in the service of nature, and more about putting nature in the service of capital (Ehrenfeld 2009; Sullivan 2009; Igoe in press).

The critical potential of these concerns is significant. However, as we shall see the realization of this critical potential depends in large part on how these concerns are articulated. In a recent assessment of social science critiques of conservation, Kent Redford (2011) has argued that social scientists have perpetuated limited stereotypes of conservation while failing to offer viable alternatives. While Redford's assessment provides a limited account of conservation critiques, failing, for instance, to account for much of the analysis presented in the present essay, it does point to a fundamental danger of conservation critique and the possibility of more effective and meaningful conservation politics. The danger is that by fixating on the hegemonic elements of neoliberal conservation, conservation critics will unwittingly contribute to the reproduction of those very elements by ignoring the diversity and interconnection of conservation movements around the world (Adams 2004). The possibility of a more effective conservation politics almost certainly depends on the revitalization of a vibrant diversity of these movements, which, while mindful of the effects of neoliberal conservation raised in this essay, are primarily concerned with making a world according to their own desires and values.

Key thinkers

The history of contemporary 'mainstream conservation' is closely associated with the production of a certain kind of nature, one that is putatively timeless and pristine, a wilderness free of human beings and any evidence of human labour (see Price, Saunders, and Olcese, and Wapner, this volume). William Cronon's essay 'The Trouble with Wilderness' (1996) is the key work here. Cronon makes three key points in this essay that have informed a significant body of conservation literature. The first is that the production of wilderness, beginning in the nineteenth century, was actually made possible by the emergent conditions of industrial capitalism to which it was putatively the antidote. The second is that the creation of wilderness consistently entailed the forced removal of indigenous and local people and the subsequent concealment of those removals. The third is that wilderness is consistently presented as the only nature worth saving and existing at locales that are distant and exotic from the point of view of Western consumers.

Thus, Cronon (1996) concludes, nature-as-wilderness paradoxically works against meaningful connections to environments that are more proximate and mundane, and thus against quotidian environmental ethics essential to sustained engagement with pressing environmental problems.

Key thinkers influenced by these insights have engaged with the ways in which established ways of imaging nature have been imposed on landscapes and people at different times and places. Paige West and James Carrier (2004) describe the wilderness paradigm as a virtualism: a model that does not change in response to the realities it encounters, but rather seeks to change those realities in accordance with its prescriptive visions (also see West, Igoe, and Brockington 2006). In *Imposing Wilderness,* Neumann (1998) traces the wilderness paradigm to the European enclosures of the eighteenth and nineteenth centuries and the creation of country estates built around spectacular views known as 'pleasing prospects'. Spence's *Dispossessing the Wilderness* (1999) chronicles the influence of the European country estate and aristocratic appreciation of nature on Eastern elites in nineteenth-century

North America, many of whom championed the creation of national parks. Adams and McShane's *The Myth of Wild Africa* (1996) traces wilderness fantasies to colonial conservation interventions in Eastern and Southern Africa, as well as the continued problems that this legacy presented to African conservation at the end of the twentieth century (also see Bonner 1994; Brockington 2002; Igoe 2004; Neumann 1998). West's *Conservation is Our Government Now* (2006) adds additional complexity to these insights by illuminating how culturally and historically informed visions of society and the environment are socially and materially produced and reproduced in ongoing encounters between conservationists and local people in Papua New Guinea. Dowie's (2009) *Conservation Refugees* provides the first comparative survey of historical and contemporary encounters between transnational conservation and indigenous communities on every continent (also see Brockington and Igoe 2006).

With the emergence of neoliberal forms of conservation (Igoe and Brockington 2007), visions of nature as wilderness are overshadowed by visions of nature more amenable to capitalist value production. The production of this kind of nature still turns on the spectacular beauty of wilderness, but requires much more complex kinds of mediation and presentation. Research that addresses the role of conservation in neoliberalism and anti-politics is being produced by a global network of scholars, many of whom are associated with a series of meetings and workshops, the most recent being Nature Inc. (2011). Brockington (2009) describes and analyses intensifying connections between celebrities and conservation, and particularly the role of celebrities in producing a 'mediagenic world'. Sullivan (2009, 2013, in press a) and Büscher (in press) both engage the abstractions and mediations involved in translating ecosystem functions into financial values and services. Igoe (2010, 2013) examines how these ways of imagining nature figure in marketing campaigns claiming to connect consumer choices with positive conservation outcomes at distant and exotic locations. MacDonald and Corson (2012) document the rapid realignments of conservation and capital that have accompanied and facilitated these new productions of nature. Fletcher (2010), MacDonald (2010a), and Büscher (2013) demonstrate the anti-political effects of these realignments, as complex political struggles are recast in terms of impersonal market forces and technical interventions, overseen and orchestrated by competent and rational experts.

The thinkers and works outlined in the previous paragraph reveal the hegemonic aspects of neoliberal conservation, presented as a *fait accompli* and apparently without viable alternatives (Igoe et al. 2010). While such analysis is important, its fixation on hegemonic effects risks inadvertently reinforcing those effects by downplaying thinkers who are already pointing to alternative possibilities. Adams's (2004) *Against Extinction* points to the failures of global conservation in the twentieth century, while also highlighting the possibilities inherent in the diversity of the movement and its concern with globally important issues such as species extinction and sustainable development. Ehrenfeld's (2009) *Becoming Good Ancestors* raises concerns about conservation's neoliberal turn, while exploring possibilities for a quotidian conservation ethic, woven into the fabric of culture and people's everyday lives. Johns's (2009) *A New Conservation Politics* warns against the dangers of conservation as a technical enterprise. To really make a difference, he argues, conservation will have to become a social struggle comparable to the civil rights movements of the 1960s. Sullivan (in press b) and West (2006) both point to the salutary potential of non-Western/non-capitalist ways of knowing and being for conservation politics that are more equitable, liberating, and grounded in place-based ecologies.

Critical potential

It is important to note that recent developments in neoliberal conservation have significant connections to and continuities with the history of mainstream conservation. Mainstream conservation has been associated with capitalist expansion since its inception in the nineteenth century (Bonner 1993; Brockington, Duffy, and Igoe 2008: 9). What is new today is a remarkable presence of corporate actors on NGO boards (Chapin 2004) and an increasingly visible orientation of 'mainstream conservation' to corporate agendas (MacDonald and Corson 2012).

Another notable element of these transformations is an increasing association of extractive enterprise and conservation, which sometimes entails revenues from a particular enterprise paying for the protection of nature. Early examples include hydroelectric dams in Laos (Goldman 2005) and the Chad-Cameroon Oil Pipeline (Brockington et al. 2009: 3). Büscher and Davidov (in press) are now positing an 'ecotourism/extraction nexus'. A panel they organized at the 2012 meetings of the European Association of Social Anthropologists featured papers on ecotourism, conservation, and bauxite mines in the Dominican Republic, oil extraction and copper mining in Ecuador, Diamond mines in Northwest Canada, hydroelectricity in Lapland, rubber tapping in Laos, and quarry mining in Karelia (Davidov 2012).[1] Other examples include cobalt in Congo (Duffy 2010), sapphires and ilemite in Madagascar (Walsh 2012; Seagle 2012), and uranium in Namibia (Sullivan 2013). For a discussion of forestry in Indonesia and oil extraction in Nigeria, see Watts and Peluso (this volume).

It is in light of these types of developments that former constructions of pristine and priceless nature are being overwhelmed by a seemingly omnipresent imperative of pricing nature's components and functions (see Büscher, this volume). These developments also complicate ongoing struggles over conservation displacement by local and indigenous peoples. Local communities are finding themselves doubly squeezed between conservation and extractive enterprise. Alignments between conservationists and local communities against extractive enterprise, such as resistance to hydroelectric dams on Brazil's Xingu River (Dowie 2009), appear to be increasingly overshadowed by a possible conservation/extraction nexus. Much more work will need to be done before the diversity of these complex relationships is fully understood.

What these examples seem to share in common, however, is the way in which presentations of these relationships, either by tour companies or conservation organizations, smooth over the complexity and/or contradictions of these relationships, while at the same time often infusing them with an aura of authenticity. Such arrangements are greatly illuminated by the Marxian concept of fetishization, which describes situations in which objects circulate and are encountered without reference to the conditions and relationships that produced them (see Paterson, this volume). This brings us full circle back to Cronon's (1996) discussion of wilderness, conservation's foundational fetishized object. The creation of timeless wilderness has paradoxically entailed the removal of resident people. Moreover, in order to be experienced as authentic, this process of erasure had to erase itself, as evidence of removals itself disrupts experiences of timelessness. Vast areas of the world have been remade in order to conform to Western tourist fantasies of a place without people (West and Carrier 2004). By controlling where tourists go, which way they gaze, and who they encounter, the contradictions of this authenticity can artfully be hidden from view (Carrier and Macleod 2005).

By similar techniques, contradictions between mining and conservation can be hidden and/or smoothed over, while both the gemstones and the green holidays can be experienced as authentic (Walsh 2012). But this potential can be taken further via Debord's (1995 [1967]) concept of spectacle, which is concerned with the ways in which fetishization becomes a generalized cultural phenomenon. Writing in the 1960s, Debord was fascinated by the ubiquity of images and the speed with which they circulated, a reality that has only intensified over the intervening decades. Thus, we continuously encounter images that confront us without reference to their original context. Debord (1995 [1967]: thesis 4) accordingly defined *spectacle* not as 'mere image, but social relations between people mediated by image'. As Marx wrote of money, spectacle mediates relationships while mystifying the nature of its own mediation. Unlike money, however, spectacle can trick our senses into experiencing it as reality itself. Debord described it as a 'pseudo-reality', in which the human is continuously bombarded by endless exchangeability.

In my latest work (Igoe in press), I argue that the circulating spectacle of nature cannot only smooth over paradox, but forge imaginary connections that would previously have been impossible. On Earth Day 2011, for instance, a person standing in Times Square could use their cell phone to text 'tree' and see their name appear on towering digital billboards known as jumbotrons. They simultaneously helped make a 'virtual forest' grow on neighboring jumbotrons, corresponding to actual forests being planted in Kenya, Mexico, and the Philippines. The person would also be helping grow those forests with a $5 donation s/he made the moment she texted 'tree'. While it is almost impossible for someone who texts 'tree' to know if trees were actually planted anywhere, it is reasonable to believe that some were. More problematic is the contradiction of depending on a technology with such a deep ecological footprint – a soon to be landfilled cell phone – as the means for solving environmental problems. Most paradoxically with respect to the present discussion, the tantalum capacitors used in cell phones are made from coltan. Duffy (2010: chapter 5) explains that coltan is a conflict mineral at the center of armed confrontations in Eastern Congo that have claimed the lives of thousands of people, as well as endangered gorillas.

While further examples are beyond the scope of this chapter, research is documenting a proliferating array of spectacularly mediated interventions that imply that the push of a virtual button appears to instantaneously affect positive socio-environmental effects at distant and exotic locations (Büscher and Igoe in press; Igoe 2010, 2013). While these mediations are related to conservation fundraising, they are also often connected to consumptive choices and participatory brand making for NGOs and corporations (Büscher and Igoe in press). They also systematically conceal myriad contradictions and paradoxes involved in harnessing consumption to fix environmental problems caused in large part by consumerism.

But this is only part of the story. Conservation spectacle, I argue, is also essential to the production of values from nature, associated with eco-system services (Igoe in press; see also Büscher, this volume). Most simply, this idea asserts that we need to get better at valuing things like clean water, clean air, and places where human beings can go to relax and renew our spirits away from the stress of everyday life. These of course are fine ideas and not something that anyone is likely to readily oppose. The reality, of course, is more complex. In order to work by capitalist logics, ecosystem services must be quickly and significantly profitable. Sullivan (2009, 2013) and Büscher (in press) have both argued that ecosystem services in which nature operates as fixed capital (e.g., a clean water or fresh fish producing machine) are often not profitable enough. Consequently, as both scholars have shown, capitalists and conservationists have devoted their energy to generating new kinds of nature as liquid capital, such as carbon credits, habitat credits, and species derivatives. These forms of capital gain value by virtue of their circulation and are more amenable to speculation on their potential future values. Unfortunately, their relationships to the underlying assets from which they putatively derive their value is not always clear. Thus it is also not clear how investment in these reified derivative forms will actually save nature (see Paterson, this volume).

Spectacle makes such possibilities visible and, therefore, more comfortingly compelling in a variety of ways. First, as MacDonald (2010a) has shown, the use of spectacle at high-profile conservation events helps create an appearance of consensus around conservation's financial trajectories. Also, through the use of spectacle conservation, organizations are able to 'visibly and generally align their activities, capacities, and objectives with (the) logics and mechanisms of market actors' (MacDonald and Corson 2012: 162). They are able to signal their affinity to corporate interests, thus gaining access to resources to support their continued conservation work.

More generally, and following Debord (1995 [1967]: thesis 15), I see nature spectacle as the 'indispensable decoration' and 'general gloss' of the increasingly financialized logic of the neoliberal forms of conservation that produce it. As Žižek (2009) explains, it is difficult for human beings to empathize or fall in love with an idea. It is even more difficult, I believe, to relate to numbers, especially big ones. Financial futures and derivatives baffle the imaginations of most non-experts. For people to imagine that such mechanisms can actually translate into actual conservation, certain visual embellishments are almost certainly required.

Two places where this kind of visual embellishment can be clearly seen are the web sites of TEEB (The Economics of Ecosystems and Biodiversity) (see Büscher, this volume) and ARIES (Artificial Intelligence for Ecosystem Services). Both TEEB and ARIES are bundles of institutional mechanisms, technologies, and procedures for valuing nature at multiple and interconnected scales (for details on TEEB, see MacDonald and Corson 2012; for ARIES, see Sullivan 2013). TEEB's dual taglines appropriately read, 'You Cannot Manage What You Do Not Measure' and 'Making Nature's Values Visible'. The TEEB page accordingly features a montage of endangered species, stock market trading screens, pristine landscapes, bar charts, and local people. A video promoting ARIES (Artificial Intelligence for Ecosystem Services) intersperses images of wildlife and satellite maps with illustrated explanations of how the technology operates to calculate values of environmental assets.

Critiques of these and similar initiatives do not take issue with their intended effect of saving nature, but with their faith in markets and money and the potential effects of their larger cultural logics. The kinds of widely circulating visual presentations associated with all the initiatives I have outlined here still incorporate fetishized nature but are turning it into something new. The nature they present is still beautiful and entertaining, but no longer pristine and best left to its own devices. I call this new nature 'Eco-Functional Nature' (Igoe in press). Its distinguishing feature is appearing eminently reconfigurable, open to technical interventions that will putatively optimize economic growth and ecosystem health (see Hobden, and Rudy and White, this volume). This reconfigurable nature illuminates the logics of ecosystem services, at least those that depend on environmental damage in one context being offset by nature conservation in another.

In her survey of ecosystem service mechanisms, Sullivan (in press b) found that the mechanisms and logic of mitigation are becoming increasingly prominent. Indeed Fairhead, Leach, and Scoones (2012) argue that we are seeing the emergence of a global economy of repair in which fixing ecological damage has become a growth industry, making environmental harm a profitable problem. These developments become most concerning when cultural logics that conservationists helped create get out of their hands. Thus, for instance, Sullivan (in press b) has traced the supply chain of uranium from Namibia to the UK to show how biodiversity offsetting services are becoming incorporated into industry discourses of uranium as a green fuel source. The key question, of course, is whether the quantitatively defined biodiversity offsets can really mitigate the qualitative environmental effects of uranium mining, processing, and waste disposal. Similar questions can be posed and explored for the other extractive enterprises noted previously.

Beyond this, Fairhead et al. point to recent financial catastrophes to question the wisdom of a worldview that holds that turning nature into a giant bundle of assets will automatically result in the global spread of holistic stewardship practices:

> Logic might suggest that this would inevitably value ecosystems over and above the sum of its parts. And yet that is what employees often think of viable businesses they work for when they are sold – before they are asset-stripped. The perversities of the financialized world are legion, and once there are markets for nature's assets, so nature's assets can be stripped. (2012: 244)

Sullivan puts it more basically still: 'we are critically impoverished as human beings if the best we can come up with is money [and to this I would add images] as the mediator of our relationships to the non-human world' (2009: 26).

Conclusion

It appears that conservation, at least mainstream conservation, is a poor catalyst for critical environmental politics. But the picture may be more promising than it first appears. As Adams (2004) reminds us, conservation is a diverse movement, and we need not become overly fascinated by its mainstream or hegemonic strain. For example, uranium-network. org's press release on uranium mining and Tanzania's Selous Game Reserve are endorsed by organizations like Econature for People and Nature, and Friends of Serengeti, in cooperation with anti-nuclear and human rights groups, as well as indigenous communities and organizations (Uranium-network 2012). Such alliances and their constituent organizations may well be the basis of a critical environmental politics, along the lines of alter-globalization, but one that has yet to be fully articulated. As Deleuze and Foucault opined, 'it is possible that [in] the struggles now underway, the local, the regional, [and we can add the transnational], discontinuous theories being elaborated in the course of these struggles, and which are absolutely of a piece with them, are just beginning to discover the ways in which power is exercised' (2004: 212). Thus, the kinds of knowledge essential to critical environmental politics may well be emerging from the experiences and practices of people in these kinds of network formations (cf. West 2006).

Some emergent key insights are already evident in the scholars I have cited previously. The first is that distance, fetishization, marketization, and 'push button care' cut some humans off from a sense of being part of animate ecology (Cronon 1996; Ehrenfeld 2009; Sullivan in press a; also cf. Latour 2010). At the same time, without fetishizing or romanticizing indigenous communities, people whose experiences and practices have fostered more animate and ecologically embedded understandings of the world are precisely those whose lives and livelihoods are most often displaced by mainstream conservation and extractive enterprise, increasingly in (at least geographical) association with one another (Fairhead et al. 2012; Sullivan 2009). Costs include impoverishment and inequity, as well as a massive loss in human ways of living, knowing the world, and doing conservation.

Diverse voices emerging from conservation encounters, and concerned with critical environmental politics, consistently point to the critical importance of cultivating conservation ethics that are derived from active, reciprocal, and intersubjective relationships to other people and the more-than-human world (see Hobden, this volume). Such ethics are essential to 'new conservation politics' (Johns 2009), whereby people become willing to make economic and political sacrifices over extended periods of time in order to achieve more equitable and ecologically sound ways of living. While such movements may oppose and raise questions about the costs of mainstream politics and the financialization of nature, their main strength would be in modeling the change that they wish to effect in the wider world. This will turn primarily on fostering conservation ethics and value practices that put ecology (including human beings) ahead of profit and are woven in the quotidian fabric of people's everyday lives. Such transformations, Ehrenfeld (2009) asserts, are essential to any hopes we may have of *Becoming Good Ancestors.*

Further reading

For a historical overview of conservation and its developments in the late twentieth century, see Borgerhoff Mulder and Coppolillo, *Conservation: Linking Ecology, Economics, and Culture* (2004). For a collection of recent engagements with conservation's neoliberal turn, see Brockington and Duffy's edited collection called *Capitalism and Conservation* (2011). Fairhead et al. (2012), and the special issue of the *Journal of Peasant Studies* that it introduces, situates conservation's neoliberal turn in a broader context.

Useful websites

The BBC Series *Unnatural Histories* (part 1. Serengeti; part 2. Yellowstone; part 3. Amazonia): http://www.bbc.co.uk/programmes/b011wd41
Native Solutions to Conservation Refugees: http://www.conservationrefugees.org/
Conservation Refugees: Expelled from Paradise (film): http://intercontinentalcry.org/conservation-refugees-expelled-from-paradise/
Suits and Savages (film): http://www.cultureunplugged.com/play/6216/Suits-and-Savages – Why-the-World-Bank-Won-t-Save-the-World
Place without People (film): http://www.anemon.gr/place.html
Milking the Rhino (film): http://milkingtherhino.org/film.php
Terra Lingua: http://www.terralingua.org/overview-bcd/
The IUCN: http://www.iucn.org
The Facebook Forum *Just Conservation:* http://www.facebook.com/JustConservation
Rainforest Action Network: http://ran.org/
TEEB @ Yale: http://environment.yale.edu/TEEB
The ARIES Web Site: http://www.ariesonline.org/

Note

1. For all the citations included in Davidov and Büscher's panel, visit http://www.nomadit.co.uk/easa/easa2012/panels.php5?PanelID=1085, (accessed 30 November 2012). All author e-mails are available also on the site.

8   Consumption

Andrew Brooks and Raymond Bryant

Introduction

The subject of this chapter, consumption, is a most paradoxical of concepts. It is intimately and inescapably individual even as it is quintessentially social. Some see it as a celebrated arena of human agency, while others consider it a disingenuous guise for powerful structural forces that crush or manipulate agency. It is simultaneously an exemplar of human ingenuity in transcending nature while being a testament to human folly in despoiling nature. In short, consumption is a concept central to understanding critical environmental politics.

Yet it is a sorely contested one. It has long been defined in popular and physiological terms as a matter of life and death. Thus, in everyday conversation, consumption (usually) implies imbibing life-giving substances, while, more darkly, it is an archaic name for pulmonary tuberculosis. Here is a 'Change embodied' concept irreducibly associated with rhythms of individual life. Within ecological economics consumption is conceptualised as a measure of the aggregate throughput and the 'using up' of natural resources such as oil, soils or fossil water frequently measured at the planetary scale and categorised as a threat to all life (Royal Society 2012; see Kütting, this volume). This formulation of consumption considers both the commoditised constituents of the natural environment (see Paterson, this volume) as well as all human usage outside of market exchange. More narrowly, political economists describe it as the moment of exchange between vender and buyer in capitalist relations – a society-centred definition, which we broadly follow in this chapter.

Scale is important to consider in definitions of consumption, and we privilege individual consumption for discussion and the role of the consumer, rather than considering the consumptive activities of businesses or states (see Hinton and Kuehls, this volume). Of particular interest is how shopping, hiring or renting connects people to environmental politics, as consumption-based relationships interweave nature, culture and political economy. Two key insights emerge: (1) consumption is a critical pathway connecting people directly and indirectly to human modification of the environment – buying things changes nature; and (2) in a world in which most people are embedded in the market, we are nearly all consumers now as consumption is a foundational and 'normal' part of everyday life – I consume, therefore I am. For many environmental writers who aggregate individual acts and discuss societal level consumption, this combination has been lethal for the planet, such that they view consumption negatively – equating it with excessive and unsustainable living in the global North (Stiegler 2011; Wackernagel and Rees 1996; see also Kütting, Whitehead and Wapner, this volume). Yet this argument is easily overegged. We can no more choose to stop consuming than elect to live without eating, drinking or finding shelter – essential life requirements presently subject to market exchange. The practices that operate across the social system can also be characterised as *infrastructures of consumption,* as non-individual actors like banks, corporations or militaries both directly consume and structure the consumption of individuals and institutions, for example, through the provision of consumable credit or the building of road infrastructures (Fine 2002; Paterson 2007; van Vilet, Chappells and Shove 2005). At the same time, and as the sorts of social science literature discussed in this chapter underscore, *how* consumption is to be understood is as important in many ways as ascertaining *what* impacts this process has on society and nature. While our approach herein is critical in tone, even as it is broadly sympathetic to a political economy perspective, we seek to provide a selective survey of multifaceted academic understanding of this much-debated concept.

The chapter begins by discussing key thinkers in and/or inspirations for consumption studies. Here, two overarching approaches (and associated figures) are identified. The one is structural in tone, drawing inspiration notably from Karl Marx's theory of commodity fetishism, while the other is post-structural in outlook, emphasising the role of the individual and cultural perception in the meaning and practice of consumption. The discussion then considers selected core facets of the 'consumption problem' (Maniates 2001: 50). This is done with an eye to the ethical consumption of socio-environmental goods that holds particular implications for environmental politics occurring as it does against a backdrop of intensifying ecological crises and a new global politics of 'foreboding' (Abélès 2010). The shortcomings of ethical consumption as a neo-liberal and individualized form of politics are canvassed before the need for a post-consumption agenda is asserted that re-integrates consumption with production as part of de-fetishist radical politics (Soper 2000). We end by underscoring the importance of consumption to other processes in critical environmental politics.

Key thinkers

The study of consumption did not begin with the birth of consumption studies but rather has been a recurrent feature of scholarship going back at least to the late nineteenth century and early twentieth century. Thinkers like Karl Marx and Walter Benjamin tackled its social and economic import, especially as the stirrings of modern consumer society – mass produced goods, elaborate retailing outlets (arcades, department stores), consumer 'education' notably via advertising – became visible, underpinning the very idea of progress itself. Since the 1980s though, multi-disciplinary consumption studies has taken off with an array of topics, debates and scholars. Thinkers such as Ben Fine, Daniel Miller and Rick Wilk have pushed the field forward in various ways.

The role of consumption certainly figures in work by Karl Marx, being integral to his path-breaking analyses of capitalism. Above all, and central to critical studies of consumption ever since, is his work on commodity fetishism (Fine 2002). Notably in *Capital,* Marx (1976) illuminated how consumers are distanced from the social and environmental relations that constitute production by the veil of market-exchange. Both producers and consumers are thereby alienated. As Fine (1976: 25) succinctly puts it, 'whilst capitalism organises production in definite social relationships between men, these relationships are expressed and appear as relationships between things'. Because consumers buy things ignorant of conditions of production, the fetishism of the commodity is such that it even appears as if things exert control over people and environments rather than control being central to social relations under capitalism (see Paterson, this volume).

Two implications are of interest here. First, commodity fetishism is ideally suited to the concealment of unsavoury relationships of exploitation of both people and environments, especially when allied to the doctrine of freedom of exchange: a license to exploit. Second, it facilitates the production of goods well beyond base necessities by inculcating in the consumer via advertising 'false needs' (Marcuse 1964): a license to over-produce. The combination of these two processes has been simply catastrophic – encouraging a 'fast capitalism' (Agger 2004) based on a turbo-charged consumerism (Schor 2008) that is 'wasting' the environment across the planet (Dauvergne 2008; Redclift 2000) – reflecting what the ecological Marxist James O'Connor (1996) dubs the 'second contradiction of capitalism'.

Not surprisingly, critical scholars have pursued a de-fetishism agenda in their work, thereby heeding the call of David Harvey (1990: 422) to investigate connections between consumers and producers so as to 'get behind the veil, the fetishism of the market'. For example, research by Hartwick (1998) on gold, Le Billon (2006) on diamonds, and Bryant (2010) on teak, travels along the commodity chain exploring the bloody conflict and ecological devastation that connects production, consumption, politics and ecology (see also Watts and Peluso, this volume). Such research reflects diverse influences, including work in sociology on commodity chains (e.g., Gereffi 1999; Hopkins and Wallerstein 1986), in political ecology on chains of explanation (Blaikie 1995), via political science on consumption and environment (Princen, Maniates and Conca 2002), and in anthropology on multi-sited ethnography (Marcus 1995; Mintz 1986).

The study of global chains has proliferated, becoming notably a preoccupation in business studies and economic geography alike. Ever more sophisticated and quantitative analyses trace precise economic and material flows over time and space (Dicken 2011). Case studies often stretch between the developing and developed economies explaining globalisation in terms of Global Commodity Chains, Global Value Chains and Global Production Networks (Coe, Dicken and Hess 2008; Gereffi 1999; Kaplinsky 2000). Yet such work often tends to be Eurocentric insofar as consumption in the global North is the entry-point for most research, thereby rendering marginal the consumer in the global South and associated environmental impacts (Brooks 2013; Hassler 2003). Furthermore, Fine broadens this vein of research and argues for a *systems of provision* approach that explores 'the inclusive chain of activity that attaches consumption to the production that makes it possible' (2002: 79). The spheres of production and consumption influence one another and the provision of what is socially useful, rather than all consumption occurring through the market. Individual consumption is shaped by cultures and a 'variety of institutional, organisational and technical regimes that may potentially influence the way demand is constructed and managed' (Chappelles 2008: 263).

Missing from much of this research on commodities has been the role of culture and language as diffuse yet powerful forces that surround the production of distinctive textures of value in different commodities and acts of consumption. Richard Wilk (2010) has explored how the linguistic definitions of consumption are based on the use of metaphors as consumption is variously analogous to fire or eating, and includes disparate activities that may or may not be environmentally destructive. For Wilk, consumption is an unbounded category performed not for its own sake, rather 'to achieve some other end, but those ends are not necessarily connected to one another except in a metaphorical way' (2010: 9). To appreciate the full implications of consumption, then, is to investigate what Arjun Appadurai (1986) dubs 'the social life of things' – and specifically, the changing nature of consumer culture and associated identity politics. Pioneering work in the early twentieth century by the German cultural philosopher Walter Benjamin that culminated in his fragmentary magnum opus *The Arcades Project* (posthumously published in English in 1999) explored the cultural meanings and transformations associated with the development of the Paris shopping arcades in the nineteenth century as centres of the luxury-goods trade. Such analysis has become de rigueur in recent post-structural times with social science research, notably in cultural geography and social anthropology, privileging the realm of the individual consumer (Cook and Crang 1996; Crang, Jackson and Dwyer 2003; Miller, Jackson, Thrift, Holbrook and Rowlands 1998). Thus, scholars such as Ian Cook (2004), Peter Jackson (1999) and Daniel Miller (2008) 'follow things' and trace commodity cultures exploring the shifting cultural and personal meanings of commodities as well as experiences of shopping.

This cultural turn in consumption studies shares with postmodern thinkers such as Jean Baudrillard a fascination with signs. Social relations are mediated through 'signifying culture'; as such, the signs of commodities and what they represent within society have frequently attracted more attention than the matter of material goods (Featherstone 1991: 6; see also Luke, this volume). Other strands of work have investigated if, or how, global flows of commodities transmit culture(s) across space and supplant local forms of culture (Miller 1998). Debate here assesses whether the spread of standardised goods to different localities erodes local norms, or if the broadening of consumption opportunities allows for re-imagined cultures in diverse places (Mansvelt 2005). For some, such as Baudrillard (1998), this process entails a nightmarish version of consumption, relating notably to cultural currents in the global North. Such processes feed through complexly to the representation of peoples and environments in the global South – for example, in the use of representations of indigenous people and tropical forests to sell breakfast cereal and sorbet to affluent Northerners (Bryant and Goodman 2004).

Whether dissecting commodity fetishism or unpacking commodity cultures, key thinkers past and present have oscillated between cultural and political economy explanations in understanding consumption. In the process, they have generated much debate as to what trends and ideas are and ought to be central to its appreciation.

Core ideas

Consumption has been a rather slippery concept in practice, belying its ostensibly obvious meaning. Scholars have sought to render it tangible by examining its socio-ecological impacts, main driving forces and uses of place. Such concerns have crystallised of late around the notion of ethical consumption – where debate over its critical potential as a force for political and environmental change is fierce (Carrier and Luetchford 2012).

The idea that turbo-charged consumption today reflects and reinforces socio-economic inequality even as it degrades the environment is an axiom in consumption studies (Redclift 2000). For one thing, such consumption – and its intertwining with social aspiration and class advancement through the distinction-making strategies of individuals – has prompted an array of practices that drive inequality (see Bond, this volume). Thus, the quest for 'cheap' but serviceable commodities by consumers has led to the migration of industries from (more expensive) North to (less expensive) South and/or the inexorable depression of inflation-adjusted wage rates for many workers (Shell 2009) – with the result that inequality in the 'developed world' has sharply widened (Wilkinson and Pickett 2009). At the same time, a growing premium on consumption as *the* defining trait of modern social identity has placed enormous (financial and psychological) pressure on individuals to participate in a 'consumption arms race' – more distinction-making consumption notably via ubiquitous brands (Lury 2004), including in the environmental sector where 'going green to be seen' is a growing phenomenon (Griskevicius, Tybur and Van den Bergh 2010).

For another thing, frenetic consumption directly underpins the rapid despoiling of the Earth's environmental systems. Much evidence is now available charting the myriad ways in which consumption destroys the environment (see Kütting, Wapner and Whitehead, this volume). For example, a recent report by the Royal Society (2012) gives ample quantitative evidence of how such key things as fresh water, food and mineral usage have grown exponentially since the Industrial Revolution – much of that time linked to development in the global North but increasingly in recent decades reflective of accelerated growth in the global South, too. Here we see the aggregate effects of countless practices of consumption around the world – giving rise to strident calls for 'sustainable development' and a 'sustainability' agenda on the international stage (see Death and Whitehead, this volume). Yet often the very complexity of consumption today, reflective of a global marketplace that is inhabited by myriad goods – all of which have different 'biographies' and that involve a near infinite array of ecological impacts – stymies effective collective action. Thus, efforts to chart consumption patterns through the 'ecological footprints' of individual consumers have been ineffectual (Wackernagel and Rees 1996; also see Hinton, this volume). In the penultimate section of this chapter, we introduce the idea of 'post-consumption', which seeks to stretch environmental politics beyond this impasse.

Scholars find that attributing causation has proved just as difficult as untangling and measuring the socio-natural impacts of consumption. What drives consumption? Two views stand out: (1) production-stimulated demand, and (2) consumer-led demand (Fine 2002). The former stresses the role of the capitalist in not only anticipating but even creating the bases for consumption. Thus, Henry Ford's infamous (and possibly misattributed) quip that 'If I'd asked my customers what they wanted, they'd have said a faster horse' illuminates how capitalist production could bring new types of commodities to the market, thereby driving forward consumption while transforming human–environmental relations. The automobile is indeed the iconic example – a case of 'creative destruction' (Schumpeter 1975 [1942]) resulting in the creation of new patterns of consumption and associated environmental politics and establishing new infrastructures of consumption (van Vilet et al. 2005). The rise of what Paterson (2007) terms *automobility* prompts the spread of a car culture with manifold implications – ranging from massive ecological destruction to create infrastructure, to rapid suburbanisation and associated commuter living; from the accelerated and wider circulation of goods and services to the easier extraction of natural resources; and from the nurtured imaginaries of the car-fixated consumer to the ironic rise of car-enabled nature tourism (Sutter 2002). Automobility is directly linked to toxic political ecologies along the commodity chain – to take one example, rubber plantations that degrade tropical landscapes due to demand for tyres (Hecht and Cockburn 1989; Peluso 2012) – even as it is central to wider processes of capitalist accumulation and pollution (Paterson 2007).

In a contrasting view, consumer-led demand through the market is largely deemed responsible for consumption trends. With roots in economic liberal doctrine on freedom and choice in society, the consumer here is viewed as a rational individual who freely chooses what s/he wants to buy in the marketplace subject to available resources (Bauman 1992). While reflecting differing intellectual lineages, much post-structural research also tends to privilege the autonomous role of the individual, whereby the production of the 'self' continues to be prioritised and the desire for 'signs' (linked notably to advertising) catalyses consumption.

As Stuart Hall characterises it, '[e]verybody . . . knows that today's "goods" double up as social signs and produce meanings as well as energy' (1989: 131). This explanation, which Lodziak critically defines as a false 'ideology of consumerism' (2000: 112), also casts the individual consumer as being responsible for the environmental impacts of their shopping, rather than corporations. 'Everybody' is primarily motivated to consume without accounting for the ecological impacts. For instance, when buying a child a gift of replica British Olympic sportswear, the giver is not only expressing their emotional attachment, but also acknowledging how the recipient can build their identity through establishing a shared and symbolic solidarity with other 'Team GB' supporters. The emotional connection with the child and nation overrides concerns for the environmental and social impacts of the production of sports goods, such as controversy over GB-branded Adidas products (ITGLWF 2012). Even in the niche market for ethical clothing, individual desires for 'style and image' as well as 'value for money' compete with environmental and ethical concerns (Jägel, Keeling, Reppel and Gruber 2012: 386).

In reality, these two views represent extremes, prompting calls for greater nuance (Trentmann 2006). For instance, it is well known that industrial production and the generation of markets through advertisers' manipulation of consumer behaviour is notably associated with producer-stimulated demand. However, advertising practise is itself influenced by broader societal and geo-political changes (Domosh 2006). Hence, adverts themselves may be thought of to some extent at least as mirrors of shifting popular cultures. Ben Fine is amongst those who reject the two poles noted previously. Thus, in discussing the fashion industry and clothing consumption, he illuminates how the construction of identity is indeed manipulated by enterprises that bring products with a stimulated demand to market, whilst also acknowledging the role of choices made by consumers as well as the complex impact of broader social change on demand for commodities (Fine 2002; also Lodziak 2000) – including pressure for a 'sustainable' political ecology of design and technology in consumer products (Petrina 2000).

Scholars have also sought to explore consumption empirically through attention to the role of place as a key generator of ideas and site of retailing. Geographers have been particularly prominent here (Gregson 1995). One focus is the shopping mall – in an elaboration of pioneering work by Walter Benjamin – those mega-cathedrals to contemporary consumption (Staeheli and Mitchell 2006). Shopping malls are located in the context of a retailing history of the twentieth century that broadly reflects and reinforces both Fordist and post-Fordist political and cultural economies (Harvey 1990; Shell 2009). As Goss (1999) illustrates, the mall (like the automobile to which it is connected) is at the heart of modern capitalism being a prime site where globalisation, consumption, identity and cultural politics collide. These distinctive places of and for consumption are simultaneously prime examples of how place is a source of potent imagery imbuing commodities with imagined values (cf. Cosgrove 2008). Nature has been one such prominent value in what Bryant and Goodman (2004: 355) term a 'conservation-seeking commodity culture' – a commercialised environment in which 'nature' is literally and figuratively consumed and market logic and economic growth are promoted as means of preserving the environment within tourist-friendly landscapes (Goss 1999; Igoe 2010; Igoe, Neves and Brockington 2010; Kaplan 2007; Price 1995). Such individualised behaviour sometimes feeds into the view that consumer choice in the marketplace is *the* contemporary form of environmental politics – a point considered further in the following analysis of ethical consumption.

Ethical consumption

For some, to consume ethically is to promote social and ecological justice, while for others it is simply a new form of ineffectual feel-good politics that aspires to save the planet one step at a time. Yet the emergence of ethical consumption as one response to gathering social and ecological crises has sparked much scholarly analysis notably focused on gauging whether, if at all, it represents a critical form of environmental and political engagement (Barnett, Cloke, Clarke and Malpass 2010; Carrier and Luetchford 2012; see also Wapner, this volume).

One thing is clear: there is more at stake here than advertising sophistry. That advertising can shape perceptions that stimulate in turn consumption is not new. As Marx long ago noted, 'The need which consumption feels for the object is created by the perception of it. The object of art – like every other product – creates a public which is sensitive to art and enjoys beauty' (1857: 92). What is important to note here is that the material culture that surrounds consumption is sustained by acts and aesthetics that extend beyond production/consumption relations, with implications for how environmental and political narratives and practices occur. The rise of ethical consumption epitomises this such that a narrow reading of consumers responding to advertising signs does not account for its growth. As Barnett et al. (2005) argue, such consumption is marked by activities and motivations complexly associated with ethics, morality and the politics of responsibility – through consumption, 'moral selves' are co-constructed, alongside other ethical and political activities.

Five points stand out in assessing the critical environmental political import of ethical consumption. First, ethical consumption may be a performance mediated by different 'kinds of cultural-semiotic codes and values' (Popke 2006: 509), but it does not remove the veils of the commodity fetish. Instead, as Goodman (2004) notes, it re-works the fetish in new forms, as 'caring at a distance' consumers draw on fresh imaginaries. Thus, a 'fair trade' cotton t-shirt may be manufactured by 'fairly' paid labour in poor developing countries, but these workers could be stitching together monocropped non-organic cotton produced on ecologically degraded farms in Texas (Rivoli 2009). Worse, ethical consumption feeds off images of pristine nature and worker contentment, but these codes and values are a new fetish rather than an objective record of relations between capital, labour and the environment. In turn, the new fetish simultaneously proclaims an ethos of caring at a distance while in practice often perpetuating production practices that, on balance, undermine other efforts (such as organised movements; see Price, Saunders and Olcese, this volume) to promote political and ecological justice in producer countries, thereby affirming the adage 'distance leads to indifference' (Smith 2000: 93). Indeed, what some political scientists call the process of 'distancing' – whereby consumers remain cut off from crucial information about the conditions of production and distribution associated with their purchases – seems to be alive and well here (Princen et al. 2002).

Secondly, ethical consumption taps into and reinforces an emotional politics that at the same time serves to promote individual distinction-making and class positioning. Just as middle-class social and environmental activism through social movements and NGOs has long been seen in part as a manifestation of class-based status anxiety (e.g., Eder 1993), so ethical consumption can be seen to serve a similar purpose as the 'personal becomes political' via discrete and repeated consumption acts. Yet the ability to 'save' something – rainforest, polar icecaps, whales, indigenous peoples, etc. – via consumption is not universal. Premium prices on ethical goods exclude poor consumers. Nonetheless, such brutal class dynamics are firmly glossed over through an emotional politics that carefully aligns *some* people with selected objects worthy of an ethical gaze. As Ahmed (2004: 119) notes, 'In such affective economies, emotions *do things,* and they align individuals with communities – or bodily space with social space – through the very intensity of their attachments'. Here ethical consumption is precisely conspicuous as part of a wider public process of class-based identity formation (Griskevicius et al. 2010).

Thirdly, ethical consumption simultaneously helps to create a shared but more diffuse consumer identity in the market-place that may transcend class divisions. Here is a pattern of behaviour akin to some other types of contemporary consumption – think of 'devoted' Apple consumers, pop music fans or football supporters. People can be mobilised in support of an ideal or product such that shared values are formed through buying things and publicly performing the act of consumption. Of course, some consumer identities may come to be viewed negatively by much of the public inasmuch as they are linked to socially or environmentally harmful outcomes – as with, for example, SUV drivers or pornography consumers (Mitchell 2005). In contrast, ethical consumption tends to have a more positive popular reception. Fair trade is exemplary in this regard – standing out for many as signs of a progressive individualised politics that is seen to add up to social and/or environmental improvements. The appeal of this sort of fairly instantaneous and hopeful politics that individuals can 'control' is not to be gainsaid at a time of widespread disenchantment with conventional political processes (Warrier 2011).

And yet, fourthly, ethical consumption is increasingly seen to be quite compatible with if not outright supportive of neo-liberal social and environmental governance today. Indeed, despite its professed 'alternative' status to mainstream capitalism, its form and content tends to be broadly supportive of the status quo. Thus, the individualised and optional nature of this consumption process fits hand-in-glove with neoliberal doctrines about individual responsibility and voluntary action via the market, even as it helps to dismantle a sense and praxis of collective responsibility and action (Goodman 2004). As noted, ethical consumption is ultimately in the business of re-fetishism and increasingly reflects the business models and ethos of the mainstream corporate world with which it is more and more intertwined (Barnett et al. 2010; Warrier 2011). The result is, at best, politically minute change. Thus, for instance, the fair trade network 'rather than presenting a radical challenge to conventional trade . . . [only] appears to be assisting certain groups to enter the global capitalist market on better terms' (Fridell 2006: 24). Such action helps to erode support for more radical forms of environmental political action by encouraging producers and consumers to 'buy into' a capitalist system that will set to rights existing inequities. At the same time, ethical consumption represents a new form of capital accumulation – here 'consumption, ironically, could continue to expand as the privatization of the environmental crisis encourages upwardly spiralling consumption, so long as this consumption is "green"' (Maniates 2001: 50).

Fifthly, and for the kinds of reasons noted previously, ethical consumption has become the focus of growing critique and resistance in recent years. Thus, and insofar as ethical consumption increasingly becomes a branded phenomenon (for example, see Dolan 2011 on the branding of fair-trade), then the option of an anti-brand consumer boycott campaign has been put on the table. Brands are indeed influential in helping to construct consumer identity thereby allowing people to express themselves, but people then also avoid companies precisely in order to define themselves in opposition to the values associated with a particular product (Klein 2000). Thus, for example, Thompson and Arsel (2004) dissect the fair-trade inflected Starbucks' 'brand-scape' and the anti-Starbucks discourse and movement that emerged in response, which has more recently extended to popular protests over tax-avoidance in the UK and elsewhere. Yet consumer boycotts are scarcely radical in that they are, by nature, usually temporary phenomenon – implying a commitment to return to buying a product once production conditions have improved. In contrast, what Lee, Moron and Conroy (2008: 178) term 'anti-consumption' is a permanent expression of dissatisfaction with a brand emerging from 'unmet expectations', 'symbolic incongruity' or even 'ideological incompatibility'. Here, there is a movement towards a more powerful political response, albeit one still framed in a consumption idiom.

It would seem that ethical consumption does not ever really confront the 'consumption problem' bedevilling the contemporary world. Its utility as a critical source of environmental politics has thus been found wanting – such consumption represents a process that scarcely confronts, and may indeed even reinforce, a business-as-usual approach marked by a 'consumer arms race'. In the next section, we posit how a *post-consumption* agenda can look beyond people's relationships with individual brands and corporations to understand how the provision of goods and services can exist outside of contemporary capitalist nature/social relations deeply branded by unfettered consumption.

Critical potential

Before turning to post-consumption, we should acknowledge that *sustainable consumption* has previously been offered as a way of forward thinking about the environmental dimensions of consumption at a systemic level, rather than individualistic ethical consumption (Cohen and Murphy 2001). Yet this notion is associated with a contested, uncritical and conformist politics of sustainability that has become a mainstay of market friendly environmental liberalism (see Whitehead, this volume). In the end, the nature of consumption seems ill-suited to serving as a focus for critical political and environmental action. Žižek (quoted by Aitkenhead 2012) captures the problem: 'Like when you buy an organic apple, you're doing it for ideological reasons, it makes you feel good: "I'm doing something for Mother Earth," and so on. But in what sense are we engaged? It's a false engagement. Paradoxically, we do these things to avoid really doing things. It makes you feel good'. And yet consumption will not go away since to be a (post)modern human *is* to consume – and the consuming human is inescapably involved in political and environmental action. Consumption has become standardised as behaviour that is formatted to manufacture desire (Stiegler 2011). For us, then, the challenge is for scholars to develop a post-consumption agenda that takes consumption seriously while critically embedding it in wider political, economic and cultural currents.

The kernels of a post-consumption idea have previously been engaged with in various ways by Kate Soper (2000), but much work still needs to be done, and for us such an agenda would likely involve at least three interconnected elements. First, there is the need to elaborate de-fetishism scholarship – that is, research that dissects complex commodity chains and cultures. Such work integrates insights from the study of everyday consumer practices and perceptions with attention to how 'the generalized compulsion to consume' is based in 'the general alienation of labour and the complex phenomenon of the fetishism of commodities under contemporary capitalism' (Goss 2004: 376). This step re-integrates consumption with production even as it acknowledges the wider totalising nature of capitalism in the regulation of people's everyday lives.

Second, a post-consumption agenda ought to feature space for 'spirited debate and animated conversation' (Maniates 2001: 50) by concerned citizens and social justice organisations about both the causes and implications of contemporary consumption (be it ethical or not) as it relates to social and environmental practices. Following the 'deliberative turn' in theorising on democracy (Dryzek 1990), there is scope here for 'deliberative environmental politics' (Baber and Bartlett 2005; see also Hinton, this volume) in which calculations on environmental sustainability move to the political centre-stage. While such a scenario seems remote in these austere times, widespread pressure on household budgets in the global North in particular might provide an opportunity to ratchet up the debate on over-consumption, thereby promoting a more collective sense of understanding as to how to proceed in challenging the status quo: consuming less, consuming differently, consuming reflectively.

Third, the post-consumption agenda must use such deliberative efforts to leverage concrete political gains at local, national and international levels. The goal needs to be promoting action in the form of stricter regulation and legal protection to enforce the production of commodities in socially and environmentally responsible ways. No longer left to voluntary interventionism, such regulation would form part of a move towards the 'green state' model based on principles and practices of deliberative ecological democracy (Eckersley 2004) rather than the authoritarianism of earlier 'ecological Leviathan' proposals (e.g., Ophuls 1977; see Baker and Kuehls, this volume).

Stated thus, the elements of a post-consumption agenda may sound incommensurate to the immense task at hand. Yet when seen as concurrent and interweaving phenomenon that build political synergies, they may nonetheless be seen one day as ingredients for a 'post-capitalist *nébuleuse*' (to modify Cox 1997: 59–61): a loose, multi-scale and consensual network of actors and individuals sharing common ideas on political economy, governance, production, consumption and ecology.

Conclusion

The concept of consumption is today at the heart of understanding of both contemporary capitalism and the often toxic human–environmental relations that are its essential attribute. Yet consumption is a rather slippery phenomenon – one superbly adapted to the creative and destructive practices of capital but less so to efforts to build a critical environmental politics. Research in both the political-economic and cultural traditions in consumption studies has amply documented this, thereby raising questions about the need for a post-consumption agenda of scholarship and action.

In pushing this concept beyond the confines of consumption studies, a post-consumption agenda inevitably engages with other concepts central to critical environmental politics. Thus, for example, the study of consumption sheds light on the contemporary workings of capitalism (see Paterson, this volume). It emphasises the ongoing role of the commodity fetish including its discursive malleability in the face of 'alternative' projects such as ethical consumption. At the same time, consumption has become a focus of public and private efforts to promote sustainability (see Baker; Price, Saunders and Olcese; and Whitehead, this volume), even as those efforts are often articulated in a neo-liberal idiom. While the inescapable human need to consume puts limits on how sustainable we can become, the very contingency of consumption may nonetheless offer encouragement to those who believe that quick but socially diffuse action is the only answer. Finally, work on consumption tends to affirm calls for a deliberative democracy in which citizens engage in debate, reflection, political action, and consumption (see Hinton, this volume). Indeed, the democratisation of consumption (with an eye to social and ecological justice) requires the consumption of democracy by a wider citizen base than under many 'liberal democracies'. Here then, perhaps, resides hope for an effective critical environmental politics.

Further reading

For invaluable overviews on consumption, politics, geography and the environment, see Peter Dauvergne (2008) *The Shadows of Consumption: Consequences for the Global Environment*, Michael Redclift (2000) *Wasted: Counting the Cost of Global Consumption*, and Juliana Mansvelt (2005) *Geographies of Consumption*, while Thomas Princen, Michael Maniates and Ken Conca's (2002) edited collection *Confronting Consumption* remains a landmark. On the tensions within ethical consumption, the edited collection *Ethical Consumption: Social Value and Economic Practice* by James Carrier and Peter Luetchford (2012) provides insightful discussion and *The Politics of Fair Trade: A Survey* edited by Meera Warrier (2011) offers a superior analysis of one of the main ethical consumption projects. For contrasting political economy and cultural explanations of modern consumption, see Ben Fine (2002) *The World of Consumption: The Material and Cultural Revisited* and Daniel Miller (2008) *The Comfort of Things*, respectively. Frank Trentmann's (2006) edited collection *The Making of the Consumer* offers an excellent historical introduction.

Useful websites

Adbusters: http://www.adbusters.org
Brandalism: http://www.brandilsim.org.uk
Fairtrade Foundation: http://www.fairtrade.org.uk
Follow The Things: http://www.followthethings.com
Source Map: http://www.sourcemap.com
The Story of Stuff Project: http://www.storyofstuff.org

9   Ecocentrism

Katie McShane

Introduction

Aldo Leopold famously recommended a shift in the way that humans think of themselves, 'from conqueror of the land-community to plain member and citizen of it' (1970: 240). What implications would thinking of ourselves this way have for our ethical and political lives? This chapter describes one approach to answering this question within environmental philosophy: ecocentrism. *Ecocentrism* involves a reorientation of our moral perspective away from a view of the nonhuman natural world as merely a means for satisfying human interests and towards a view of it as something to which we have moral responsibilities. While not traditionally thought of as part of Critical Theory (see the introduction to this volume), ecocentrism is a critical attitude in the sense that it raises questions about the moral presuppositions that guide (sometimes surreptitiously) many contemporary approaches to environmental problems. Thus, ecocentrism offers an alternative moral framework from which we can see the inadequacy of technocratic and instrumentalist approaches to the nonhuman natural world.

Core ideas

Ecocentrism is the view that the interests of ecosystems (or other ecological wholes) are of direct moral importance. That is to say, the welfare of these systems matters directly, in a way that is independent of its importance to human interests. This is in contrast to views such as anthropocentrism, which claims that only human interests are of direct moral importance and that the interests of other things matter only insofar as they affect human interests. Ecocentrists often present their views as a response to anthropocentric approaches; in fact, arguments for ecocentrism often begin with a critique of anthropocentrism (Callicott 1984; Johnson 1991; Leopold 1970; Routley and Routley 1979).

Ecocentrists argue that anthropocentrism encourages an instrumentalist attitude towards the nonhuman natural world (though this claim has been controversial; see Norton 1984). That is to say, in thinking of the nonhuman natural world as valuable only insofar as it serves our interests, we view nature as a mere resource for human beings. This kind of attitude would be objectionable if one group of humans took it towards other groups of humans or towards humanity as a whole – e.g., if Americans viewed non-Americans as having value only insofar as they served American interests, or if Americans viewed humanity as a mere resource for satisfying the interests of Americans. Ecocentrists claim that we should think the attitude equally objectionable when taken by humans towards nonhuman members of our ecological communities or towards the communities themselves. To think that all other forms of life matter only insofar as they serve human interests, or to think that the whole ecological community is nothing more than a resource for meeting our needs, evinces an attitude of 'human chauvinism' or 'speciesism' (Routley and Routley 1979; Singer 1990). The ecocentrist claim is that this kind of chauvinistic or speciesist attitude presents nonhuman nature as something we use, not as something to which we are responsible. Since failure to use our resources well is a failure of prudence, while failure to meet our responsibilities is a failure of morality, anthropocentrism puts our treatment of nonhuman nature outside the realm of morality except insofar as it has an effect on our fellow humans. Ecocentrists argue that while we are right to oppose harming our fellow humans, we would be wrong to think that ecological destruction is morally acceptable so long as it avoids harming humans.

While many early ecocentrists were motivated by opposition to anthropocentrism, a rejection of anthropocentrism is not yet a justification for ecocentrism. Ecocentrism is a holist view: it says that we ought to have as our goal the welfare of the ecological community as such. However, one could instead adopt an individualist version of nonanthropocentrism: one might claim that we should have as our goal the welfare of individual sentient animals (sentientism) or the welfare of individual living organisms (biocentrism). Ecocentrists, then, must argue not only against anthropocentrism but also for the superiority of holist nonanthropocentrism to individualist nonanthropocentrism.

Most arguments for the holist claims of ecocentrism have been pragmatic in that they evaluate individualism and holism by their helpfulness for formulating sensible environmental goals. Holists have argued that most of our environmental goals are really about the welfare of ecological wholes rather than individuals, and rightly so (Callicott 1980; Johnson 1991; Rolston 1988). If the only way to preserve an ecosystem would be to sacrifice the lives of its current members (by allowing a fire to burn, perhaps), most conservationists would accept that sacrifice (see Igoe, this volume). When we think about extinction and habitat loss, we tend to take the long view as well: it is not preserving the lives of currently existing individuals that is our first concern, but preserving whole evolutionary branches and ecological systems (see Büscher, this volume). To focus on individuals in these cases would lead to bad policy choices: preserving individual organisms at the cost of losing whole species or ecotypes.

Other arguments for holism are less policy-oriented in nature. Some theorists oppose individualism on principle, on the grounds that it produces an atomistic picture of ethics as a matter of individuals in competition with one another and ignores the interrelatedness of life on earth (Morito 2003; Rolston 1988). If ecological science has taught us anything, it is that living things are highly interrelated and interdependent (see Hobden and Forsyth, this volume). An ethics that takes this fact seriously, it is argued, should not operate by dividing up the world into discrete units, asking what features each unit possesses in its own right, and then deciding how the unit ought to be treated on the basis of those features (Weston 1996). Rather, an ethic that takes seriously the lessons of ecology should start from a conception of the ecological common good and set about trying to protect the relationships and processes that contribute to that good (Rolston 1988).

This is a picture that other ethicists have found very troubling. This holist aspect of ecocentrism has been labeled 'ecofascism' by some critics for its implication that the value of individuals is dependent on their contribution to the good of the whole (Regan 1983; Shrader-Frechette 2002). Their argument has been that just as the only way to respect the value of persons is to adopt an individualism according to which the good of the whole just is the good of its constituent individuals, so the only way to respect the value of other individuals is to reduce the good of the whole to their individual goods. Fraught as this debate has been, more recent ecocentrists have tried to circumvent the problems raised in it by adopting a pluralist version of ecocentrism, i.e., the view that the good of individual organisms and ecological wholes both matter and that neither is reducible to the other (Callicott 1999; Eckersley 1992; Norton 2005; Varner 1991).

Ecocentrists thus claim that we ought to broaden our sense of morality to value not merely the good of human beings, but the good of the ecological community as a whole. From an ecological point of view, what matters is not the flourishing of any particular individual or set of individuals but rather the flourishing of the system that they comprise, the system by which all individuals enable and sustain one another's lives. An ecocentric view takes this ecological perspective and makes it central to morality.

Key thinkers

One finds ecocentric views in philosophical and religious traditions that long predate the contemporary discussions within environmental philosophy. In contrast to the contemporary 'ecosystem services' approach to environmental policy (see Büscher and Igoe, this volume), which represents the natural world as a resource that functions to serve human beings ('nature in the service of culture'), Sian Sullivan has argued that many people, especially those outside of the mainstream cultures of Western industrialized nations, view nature instead as an ongoing set of reciprocal relationships among living things, including but not limited to humans, in which humans must be givers as well as takers (Sullivan 2009: 23). Sullivan, in work on Namibia, describes the ≠Nū Khoen (Damara) people's view: 'Non-human worlds were alive to be spoken to, and variously remonstrated with and celebrated through words, song, dance, and gift-giving. People were not separate and alienated from the non-human world; they were co-creators with it' (2009: 24). The ≠Nū Khoen ethos is an ethos of reciprocity. It is a view of beings cooperating in a shared endeavor, as opposed to a view of human agents extracting value from a passive resource. As Sullivan points out, the ecosystem never gets paid for the 'ecosystem services' it provides to us; on the ecosystem services approach the relationship is never really seen as a reciprocal one. The success of the shared endeavor is what matters morally on the ≠Nū Khoen view, not maximizing the benefits that accrue only to certain participants.

In addition to this type of ecocentric view, and sometimes as a part of it, many people also appear to reject any kind of categorical distinction between humans and nature (see Hobden, and Rudy and White, this volume). Tim Ingold, for example, notes that the Western assumption 'that personhood as a state of being is not open to non-human animal kinds' (such that it would make sense to speak of the animality of humans but not the humanity of animals) is not an assumption accepted by many northern hunter-gatherer groups, including the Waswanipi Cree in Canada (Ingold 2000: 48). Western interpreters of the Cree have tended to assume that Cree ascriptions of animal traits to humans are literal, while their ascriptions of human traits to animals are metaphorical or mythical. But the duality of animality and humanity, Ingold argues, is an assumption that Westerners import from their own cultural ontologies, not one that the Cree themselves accept. Ingold argues that on the Cree view,

> [A]nimals do not participate with humans only in a domain of virtual reality, as represented within culturally constructed, intentional worlds, superimposed upon the naturally given substratum of organism-environment interactions. They participate as real-world creatures, endowed with powers of feeling and autonomous action, whose

characteristic behaviours, temperaments, and sensibilities one gets to know in the course of one's everyday practical dealings with them. (2000: 52)

That is to say, one gets to know animals the same way that one gets to know people: by learning their personalities, by thinking about the world from their point of view. One works together with animals in the same way that one works together with people: by forming relationships of reciprocity and respect. Ecological communities among animals and other organisms succeed for the same reasons that communities among humans succeed: because of the formation of reciprocal, mutually beneficial ways of life that sustain individuals and the functions of the community over the long run.

In Anglo-American philosophy, Aldo Leopold's *A Sand County Almanac* (1970) is typically regarded as the classic formulation of ecocentrism. Leopold took as his starting point the then-emerging science of ecology. He wrote of the 'biotic community' and 'the land' rather than 'the ecosystem', as the term 'ecosystem' was not yet widely used (Golley 1996). Leopold articulated an ethical view that he named 'the land ethic', and he described its central principle as follows: 'A thing is right when it tends to preserve the integrity, stability and beauty of the biotic community. It is wrong when it tends otherwise' (Leopold 1970: 262).

Leopold's writings seem to presuppose Frederic Clements's model of ecological communities as superorganisms: entities that have a structure and functioning parts just as organisms do but on a larger scale (Clements 1916). On this model, it is not difficult to see how ecosystems could be harmed or benefited by one's actions; if one can harm an organism, then one can harm a superorganism. If ecosystems can be harmed or benefited, it does not take a great conceptual leap to see them as having interests that could make a moral claim on us. Since Leopold's time, however, the organismic model of ecosystems has been abandoned by ecologists in favor of models that represent ecosystems as more loosely and contingently defined systems (Golley 1996; McIntosh 1985). This has raised the question of whether ecosystems, or other ecological wholes (biomes, etc.), are the kind of thing that can count as having interests of their own. A debate about this issue is still ongoing today. Some theorists claim that to be a bearer of interests, a thing must be sufficiently bounded, unified, enduring, and organized enough for us to characterize its behaviour as goal-directed. While its goals needn't be conscious goals, it must have something worth calling 'goals' (biological goals, perhaps, such as reproduction or metabolism) for us to be able to ground our claims about which states of the world further its interests and which states of the world frustrate its interests. Furthermore, on some prominent analyses of 'goal-direction' within philosophy of biology, for an ecosystem's behaviour to count as goal-directed, the ecosystem itself must be a unit of selection (i.e., it must be the entity whose traits are selected for by natural selection). Since ecosystems are generally not considered units of selection, they cannot possess interests (Cahen 1988; Varner 1998). Others have criticized this line of reasoning, questioning the conceptual connection between having interests and having goals and/or the connection between having goals and being a unit of selection (Landen 2003; McShane 2004).

Deep ecology is another philosophical approach that can be considered broadly ecocentric. Deep ecology began with the work of Arne Naess in the 1970s (Naess 1973). Deep ecologists argue that human beings can achieve a deeper environmental ethic by changing the way that they think of themselves as selves. By thinking of the ecological communities to which one belongs as literally part of oneself, humans can transcend the limitations of both anthropocentrism and individualism and see the ecological community's good as constitutive of one's own good (Fox 1995; Naess 2009). One appeal of this approach is that it offers a way around the debate between individualism and holism: on this 'extended self' model, there is no ethically important distinction between individuals and communities. Other deep ecologists have focused less on the metaphysics of the extended self, and more on the goal of wilderness preservation, an activism of direct action, or the claim that the nonhuman natural world has intrinsic worth (Devall and Sessions 1985; see Igoe, this volume).

Many contemporary versions of ecocentrism have echoed Leopold in trying to construct an ethical perspective that takes seriously the relationships among and interdependence of organisms that ecological science has revealed. As ecology has developed, some versions of ecocentrism have been modified and adapted to it (Hettinger and Throop 1999). Ecocentrists no longer claim that ecosystems are analogous to organisms, but they do maintain that ecological wholes can be made better or worse off and that part of morality is to avoid behaviors that make them worse off. This is a controversial philosophical claim: ecological wholes as such do not have a subjective point of view on the world; they do not have preferences; they do not feel pain; they cannot communicate; they cannot reason; they cannot empathize or reciprocate care; they are not alive. Standard Western philosophical conceptions of moral and political philosophy typically consider at least one of the previous criteria to be a necessary condition for moral considerability, and this is what critics often argue recommends individualism over holism. However, it is an open question whether such criteria should be thought of as justifying individualism, or whether they follow from a prior commitment to individualism. If the badness of suffering can be taken as a first principle by individualists (Bentham 1948: 4; Mill 1962: 254–5), it is unclear why the badness of ecological destruction could not be so taken by holists. Whether one has to model ecosystems as analogous to individuals in order to think of them as entities to which we bear moral responsibilities, then, is still an open question.

Contemporary biology has also given us reason to question the coherence of the distinction between wholes and individuals. As research into the human biome continues, it has become clear that the human body is more of an ecosystem than it is a single, self-contained organism. Approximately 90 per cent of our weight is made of bacterial rather than human cells; these nonhuman cells within us are crucial for performing many of our bodily functions (Gill et al. 2006; Pflughoeft and Versalovic 2012). Medical researchers now urge the study of human health as a kind of ecosystemic health – a healthy biome as opposed to a healthy discrete individual. Advances in genetics have also made it clear that the human genome has within it the genetic material of many microbes that have been part of our environment in the evolutionary past (Feschotte 2010). Humans, then, cannot be cleanly distinguished from nonhuman forms of life (see Hobden, this volume). The more we come to understand our biome and our evolutionary history, the more individuals start to look like holistic entities. If that is right, then individualism may well collapse into holism rather than the other way around.

Critical potential

Ecocentrism is a radical departure from much of mainstream ethical theory and social science because it asks us to evaluate the adequacy of our attitudes, actions, principles, policies, and institutions by looking at their effects on the well-being of ecological communities, communities of which we are often members. In asking us to evaluate our practices by this standard, ecocentrism offers a novel critical perspective on politics: when we think about how well various systems of government or civil society work, we tend not to answer these questions by looking at what effects they have on the earth's ecosystems. To evaluate our political systems by their impact on our ecological communities is to reject a view of community life as an intraspecies affair.

If we adopt the ecological good as our evaluative standard, we get a number of fundamental challenges to contemporary political institutions. Among these are criticisms of democratic decision-making, neoclassical economics, and the nation-state system (see Baker and Kuehls, this volume). The criticism of democratic decision-making comes from noticing that democratic decision-making does not always lead to ecologically wise decisions (Dobson 1996; Goodin 1992; Ophuls 1992). From the perspective of ecocentrism, this should be considered a problem for democratic decision-making. The political imperative, then, is to find the types of democratic decision-making, or constraints on democratic decision-making, or alternatives to democratic decision-making, that are best for our ecological communities (see Doherty and de Geus 1996).

Similarly, neoclassical economics might describe efficient systems for maximizing the satisfaction of human preferences, but from an ecological point of view this doesn't necessarily recommend it. If human preferences turn out to be preferences for ecologically destructive acts and outcomes, then ecocentrism will not deem their satisfaction to be a good thing (see Okereke and Charlesworth, this volume). Insofar as the 'value' produced by market exchanges is ecologically disvaluable (e.g., economic growth that is bad for the ecological community), markets will be highly efficient in producing disvalue (Daly and Townsend 1993). The field of ecological economics has emerged recently as an attempt to model economic interactions using a conception of value such that what is valuable is by definition what is good for the ecological community. While the development of this approach is still in its early stages, seeking to maximize the production of this kind of value would be much more in line with ecocentric goals.

Ecocentrists would evaluate the current nation-state system, including the Westphalian model of state sovereignty, in a similar manner. Whatever one thinks about this system's success in promoting human well-being (Frank, Hironaka and Schofer 2000), its failure to address climate change in any meaningful way is reason enough for an ecocentrist to find it deeply flawed (see Death, and Okereke and Charlesworth, this volume). Thus, ecocentrists often express a desire for a way to regulate self-interested behaviour of nation-states, for example, by advocating the strengthening of international institutions, the creation of global governmental institutions, and/or limitations on state sovereignty (see Baker and Kuehls, this volume).

An ecocentric perspective also requires the revision of some philosophical concepts that play an important role in political discourse. For example, thinking of property rights simply as rights of exclusion might make sense on an anthropocentric understanding of the nonhuman nature on one's property as simply a resource. But once one thinks of other organisms as fellow citizens in the biotic community, the question of their exclusion becomes more complicated. Some fellow citizens (coyotes, bears) we might be able to exclude; others (microbes, insects) might be more difficult. Furthermore, one of the rationales for systems of private property over communal property, that privatizing land internalizes externalities and thus prevents tragedies of the commons (see Kütting, this volume), makes less sense once we take a broader view of the morally relevant interests involved. When I allow overgrazing on my own land, I never bear all of the costs of doing so. Even if I could somehow prevent my fellow humans from bearing such costs, other organisms in the ecological community would still be affected (the fish who live in the rivers now filling up with eroded soil; the microorganisms living in the soil that now blows away as dust, etc.), as would the community itself (nitrogen and carbon cycles are disrupted, etc.). Privatization, then, might prevent a person from shifting the costs of her bad environmental behaviour to other persons, but it does not prevent her from shifting those costs to other members of the biotic community. If that is right, an eco-centrist might well think it unethical to allow a system that allows persons to have property rights without any attached property responsibilities.

Another philosophical view challenged by ecocentrism is the idea of political communities as fundamentally about reciprocal agreements among autonomous individuals (see Hinton, this volume). This idea has long been criticized by feminists and communitarians, but eco-centrists have a different kind of complaint about it (see Cudworth, this volume). Even if our citizenship in cities or nation-states is autonomously chosen, our ecological citizenship is not. As all animals do, we inhabit an ecological niche, and we must depend on other members of our ecological community for our survival. Rather than think that all limitations on our liberty must be ones we consent to, rather than think that one can accept these constraints or not as one sees fit, ecocentrism views ecological constraints as a basic and inescapable fact of human life and views living within them as a fundamental moral obligation (see Kütting and Litfin, this volume).

Finally, ecocentrism changes our sense of what makes a community a community. Our eco-logical communities are not communities made up of members who can reason together, who have a shared culture, or who are capable of intersubjective agreement. In our ecological com-munities, we must interact as fellow citizens with organisms that are radically different from us. Our theories about what it is that prompts the ethical response to other humans – whether we empathize with their suffering, or see that they have a face, or realize that they possess rational agency – are unlikely to be helpful in guiding our behaviour towards things that are very unlike us – plants, bogs, beehives, etc. The moral psychology of an ecocentric ethic, then, requires modes of recognition (i.e., recognizing another as making a moral claim on us) that do not depend on noticing a resemblance to us (i.e., a way in which the other is 'just like us'). Likewise, the politics of an ecocentric ethic requires ways of representing the interests of our fellow citizens and of the community itself within human decision-making processes.

Some of ecocentrism's critical potential is starting to be actualized by global movements that insist on the formation of laws and policies with an explicitly ecocentric orientation (see Price, Saunders and Olcese, this volume). Probably the most well-known recent successes of such movements are in Latin America. Both the Constitution of Ecuador, passed in 2008, and Bolivia's Framework Law for Mother Earth and Integrated Development to Live Well [Ley Marco de la Madre Tierra y Desarrollo Integral para Vivir Bien], passed in 2012, explicitly grant rights to nature. The Ecuadorian constitution's preamble refers to 'celebrating nature, the Pacha Mama (Mother Earth), of which we are a part and which is vital to our existence', and Chapter 7 (entitled 'Right of Nature') describes Pacha Mama as having explicit rights:

> Nature, or Pacha Mama, where life is reproduced and occurs, has the right to integral respect for its existence and for the maintenance and regeneration of its life cycles, structure, func-tions and evolutionary processes. All persons, communities, peoples and nations can call upon public authorities to enforce the rights of nature. (Constitution of Ecuador 2008)

Bolivia's Framework Law, a more detailed version of the 2010 Law of the Rights of Mother Earth, states that

> Mother Earth is the living dynamic system made up of the indivisible community of all living systems and living beings, interrelated, interdependent and complementary, which share a common destiny. Mother Earth is considered sacred; it feeds and is a

home that contains, sustains and reproduces all living things, ecosystems, biodiversity, societies and the individuals that compose them. (Shahriari 2012)

Note that in both cases, people are described as part of the natural world, not separate from it. And in both cases, the whole (Pacha Mama/Mother Earth) is considered not only to have moral status, but a highly important moral status ('sacred', 'vital'), which justifies the conferral of independent rights on it. Ecuador and Bolivia both have large indigenous populations, and both countries' laws were enacted as the result of pressure from indigenous groups. Both were enacted by left-leaning governments as an effort to offer legal protections against the harms that environmental commodification, exploitation, and degradation have brought to people and the natural environment in each country (Arsel 2012; Shahriari 2012). Both also aim to keep environmental protections from being at the mercy of market forces, corporate powers, international NGOs, or foreign countries. It remains to be seen whether legal protections with an explicitly ecocentric basis will be any more successful in achieving environmental protections than their more anthropocentric predecessors.

Conclusion

The most important contribution of ecocentrism, then, is that it adopts an evaluative perspective that takes seriously our membership in ecological, not just human, communities. In the same way that ethics tells us not just to ask 'what is good for me?' but also 'what is good for all of us?', ecocentrism tells us not just to ask 'what is good for people?' but also 'what is good for the ecological community as a whole?' To think of ourselves as members of ecological communities and to ask what good ecological citizenship would consist of is to ask a different question than we typically ask about our political institutions, but it is a question that is long overdue. What might someday surprise us is that we ever allowed ourselves to evaluate our political systems independently of their effect on the earth's ecological systems.

Further reading

A more detailed philosophical analysis of Leopold's environmental ethics can be found in J. Baird Callicott (ed.) (1987) *Companion to A Sand County Almanac: Interpretive and Critical Essays*, Madison: University of Wisconsin Press. For an overview of the many forms that contemporary deep ecology takes, see Alan Drengson and Yuichi Inoue (eds) (1995) *The Deep Ecology Movement: An Introductory Anthology*, Berkeley: North Atlantic Books. Contemporary arguments for holism over individualism can be found in Eric Katz (1997) *Nature as Subject: Human Obligation and Natural Community*, Lanham, MD: Rowman & Littlefield. For a broader critique of the use of individualist and instrumentalist frameworks in addressing environmental problems, see Sian Sullivan (2011) 'On bioculturalism, shamanism and unlearning the creed of growth' *Geography and You*, March–April 2011: 15–19.

Useful websites

Foundation for Deep Ecology: http://www.deepecology.org/index.htm
The Pachamama Alliance: http://www.pachamama.org/
Global Alliance for the Rights of Nature: http://therightsofnature.org/
The Aldo Leopold Foundation: http://www.aldoleopold.org/

10 Feminism

Erika Cudworth

Introduction

Since the early 1970s, a distinct strand of feminist theorizing and activism has explicitly linked human relations with the 'environment' to gender (and other) inequalities. Ecofeminism emerged from a critique of both sexism in the green movement (Doubiago 1989) and an absence of awareness about 'environmental' questions in feminist politics (Plumwood 2004: 43; Salleh 1984). Ecofeminists draw on and develop various elements of both ecological and feminist politics however. For example, like deep ecologism (see McShane, this volume), most ecofeminists conceptualise human relations with 'nature' as a form of domination. They also can be understood to provide a version of social ecology in which the domination of nature is interrelated to intra-human social hierarchy and difference based on gender, race and class amongst other formations. Here, they are influenced by the work of ecosocialists and postcolonial scholarship. The influence of feminist politics is perhaps the strongest, however, as ecofeminists deploy concepts of gender domination and inequality in thinking about labour, production, knowledge and power and interrogate our ideas of what it means to be human.

This chapter focuses on the concepts and theories of ecofeminism, or ecological feminism, and its influence on environmental politics. It proceeds through three sections. First, the core ideas section considers various influences and approaches in ecofeminist analysis; the use of 'patriarchy' to explain the domination of 'otherised' groups (including women, non-human animals and non-human life), and ideas of 'linked dualisms' and 'multiple oppressions', which have been used to explain how the human treatment of the environment is bound up with (or 'intersectionalised' by) social inequalities. The section on key thinkers maps the different strands of ecofeminist thinking in focusing on some influential thinkers from different geographic and disciplinary locations. The final section will consider the critical potential of ecofeminism and argue that in emphasizing the intersectionalised qualities of exploitation and exclusion, ecofeminism has provided an important critique of other kinds of political ecologism.

Core ideas

Ecofeminism draws conceptually on both the critical politics of feminism and political ecologism. On the one hand, political ecologism provides a range of explanations for the problematic relationships human communities have with non-human species and scapes. Deep ecologists speak of our humancentric ('anthropocentric') social order in which we have social and economic practices that systematically deplete natural resources and exploit and destroy 'nature' (Devall 1990; see McShane, this volume). Others consider the ways different groups of human beings are variously placed in relation to environmental exploitation. A range of leftist approaches (drawing on Marxist, socialist, anarchist and postcolonial perspectives) have explained human relations with the 'environment' as constituted by exploitative relations of capitalism and/or colonialism (Bookchin 1982; Dalby 2009; Dickens 1996; see also Bond, Brooks and Bryant, Watts and Peluso, and Paterson, this volume). Feminism, on the other hand, has developed explanations for patterns of gender inequalities and exclusions and interrogated the validity of gender as a social category. Whilst eclectic, all varieties of feminist thinking have seen gender relations as socially constituted, problematic and inherently political. From the early years of the 'second wave', some feminists were suggesting that environmental degradation was a matter for feminist theory and political activism (Caldecott and Leyland 1983; Collard 1988; Plant 1989).

Ecofeminism is characterised by various preoccupations and analyses, and these are usually seen as falling into two distinct strands. Victoria Davion (1994: 8) suggests that one strand is 'eco-feminine', rather than feminist, because it celebrates traditional feminine roles and the 'values' associated with them. Chris Cuomo distinguishes 'eco-feminism' – primarily concerned with the similarities among the 'objects' of oppressive thought and action (women, animals etc.) – and 'ecological feminism' – focused on links between forms and instances of oppression (1998: 6–7). Mary Mellor describes the difference in terms of 'social' and 'affinity' explanations of women's relationship to nature (1992: 51–2), and this best captures a substantive difference in concerns and approach. Affinity approaches are more likely to consider issues of spirituality (Adams 1993; Daly 1988; Starhawk 1990) and the material experiences of women (Griffin 1984), both of which are seen to encourage identification with 'nature'. Affinity approaches are related to radical feminism, and this has meant ecofeminism, often in its entirety, has been perceived to be a reflection of (some of) the ideas of some particularly controversial radical feminist figures and criticized as essentialist for apparent allusion to the particular knowledge, emotion, sensuality, thought and morality of women (Balsamo 1996; Carlassare 1994; Segal 1987; Spelman 1990). Some social ecofeminists deploy the radical feminist-influenced conception of patriarchy (Cudworth 2005; Plumwood 1993), but they also share interests, concepts and approaches with scholarship on (post)colonialism (Shiva 2009) and left critiques of capitalism (Mellor 1997), and they reflect the influence of the 'post-modern turn' (Salleh 1997). Whilst the ideas of both 'affinity' and 'social' ecofeminists can be found in this chapter, the emphasis is on common themes. This section will focus now on common concepts (patriarchy, dualism) and issues of debate (social relations with non-human animals, gender roles and the ethics of care).

Many ecofeminists have deployed a concept of *patriarchy* in their work. Patriarchy is associated with the division between public and private spheres of life in which the private sphere is associated with nurturance and the reproduction of everyday life and is devalued and associated with women. In addition, this is seen to be environmentally problematic, as men are further away than most women from the reproduction of the material conditions of life. Some have suggested that patriarchal discourses carry gender dichotomous normalizations, which feminize the environment and naturalize women, constructing a dichotomy between women and nature on the one hand, and male-dominated human culture and the 'public' on the other (Griffin 1984; Plumwood 1993). The arguments presented often also draw on a form of standpoint epistemology – gender roles constituted through such discourses render women in closer material proximity and relation to the environment than men. Some further suggest this means a greater concern with preservation and the avoidance of harm for living things, and potential to develop an ecologically sensitive value system (Elshtain 1987; Ruddick 1990). According to Griffin (1994) and Daly (1988), patriarchal culture venerates death and violence and is preoccupied with dominance and control over women and the non-human lifeworld. Thus, the specific application of patriarchy associated with ecofeminism is that it is responsible for environmental devastation as well as the oppression of women because of a denial of human embodiment and corporeal vulnerability.

However, the use of patriarchy in some ecofeminist accounts has a tendency to underestimate the cross-cutting influences of oppressions based on race and class (and various other forms of difference) as qualitatively and quantitatively affecting the form and degree of women's oppression. For example, Adams and Donovan (1995: 3) have contended that patriarchy is 'prototypical for many other forms of abuse', and Suzanne Kappeler (1995: 348; also Collard 1988; Gaard 1993) has echoed Daly and Griffin in asserting that patriarchy is 'the pivot of all speciesism, racism, ethnicism, and nationalism'. Yet patriarchy alone cannot explain other forms of oppression, exploitation and domination or account for differences in forms and degrees of domination. The reduction of multiple forms of oppression/exclusion/domination to an explanation focused on patriarchy has led to charges of over-generalisation (Walby 1990) and an insensitivity to differently constituted sets of oppressive relations with their own histories, conceptual repertoire and social forms (Cudworth 2011: 41–6).

Conceptually related to the use of patriarchy in ecofeminist work is the critique of *dualism*. In works from the 1970s onwards, the dominant worldview of Western modernity was characterised as problematic in that it was based on dualistic categories such as man/woman, culture/nature, mind/body, human/animal, rationality/emotion. What is 'essentially human' in such a dualistic world view is separate from 'nature'. This notion of a dualistic worldview is embedded in all ecofeminist writing, whether looking at the linking of oppression of animals and women (Adams 1990), or disturbing the boundaries between the dualist categories themselves (Haraway 1989, 2008; see Hobden, and Rudy and White, this volume). The critique of dualism has been an important way in which ecofeminist thinking has contributed to debates on the *interlinking of different forms of oppression*. In Plumwood's words, 'inferior orders' of humanity (colonized, native, female) are categorically separated from the 'order of reason' and fail to come up to the dominant Western ideal of the human (1993). The ways in which these categories are discursively constituted may be overlapping; for example, native peoples specifically, and those more generally gendered female, may be more strongly naturalised.

Closely linked to the debates on linked dualisms and overlapping oppressions are ecofeminist contributions to our understanding of *human relations with non-human animals,* which has constituted a prolific and important body of work. In early works, Connie Salamone (1982) claimed that women's social practices of care mean they are more likely than men to oppose practices of harm against animals. Norma Benny made the rather different case that women may empathize with the sufferings of animals as they have some common experiences; for example, female domestic animals are most likely to be 'oppressed' via control of their sexuality and reproductive powers (Benny 1983: 142). Joan Dunayer (1995) has examined the speciesism of linguistic practices and the links between this and our gendered and racialized use of language, whilst others have looked at the interrelations between gender and the environmental and species impact of colonial practices (Lee-Sanchez 1993; Shantu Riley 1993). Carol Adams (1990, 2003) argues that social practices such as meat eating are gendered and sexualised and that popular culture is saturated with interpolations of gendered nature and natured gender. There have been disputes, however. Val Plumwood (2004) has critiqued the 'ontological veganism' of Adams (and others, see Kheel 2008), which advocates individual abstention from all use of animals, as universalist and ethnocentric. Plumwood also argues that ontological veganism confirms the view that, unlike other species, humans can place themselves outside or above nature in avoiding the use of animals that is part of the human condition as ecologically embedded beings. As an alternative, Plumwood (2004) proposes 'ecological animalism', wherein a critique of the human exploitation of animals is combined with respect for different cultural meanings of certain practices (such as the hunting of animals and the eating of 'meat'). Whatever the differences, this work has been influential in problematising human relations with non-human animals and alerting us to the intersectionalised qualities of oppression. These approaches provide a powerful analysis of the ways the social system of gender relations is co-constituted through ideas and practices around 'nature' and species relations.

Feminist influence is particularly evident in the wealth of ecofeminist writing on *gender roles* and the link between this and an '*ethic of care*'. A key theme is that female values are a product of a different socialisation process and a different placement in the public and private division of labour. In ecofeminist writings in the 1980s, this involved the claim that socialisation into feminine roles inculcates characteristics of care, nurturance, sympathy, empathy and 'feeling the life of the other' (Plant 1989: 1). One of the most controversial early examples is the poetic piece *Woman and Nature* (1984) by Susan Griffin, which juxtaposes two sets of discourses. One set contains dominant Western narratives on women and nature, exemplified by the teachings of Judeo Christianity and the understandings of mechanistic science. The other set are 'voices' of the marginalised and exploited – women (as housekeepers, mothers and carers) and 'nature' (domesticated and wild animals, various other non-human natures). Underpinning Griffin's writing is the idea that there is an authenticity in the voices of 'woman and nature', and in women's caring labour. Furthermore, that the standpoints of those who care must be valued and reclaimed.

There are difficulties inherent in a 'reversal strategy' of social change in which the dominant culture is subverted by giving positive value to what has been previously despised. The 'care ethic' has been highly controversial within ecofeminism (Plumwood 1993: 30–3), and feminism more widely (Segal 1987), for reinforcing rather than problematising gender role stereotypes. Griffin is seen to glorify patriarchal gender roles (Alaimo 2000), draw 'a stereotypical rendering of femininity' (Stabile 1994: 60), deny the variety of women's experience (Segal 1987) and sentimentalise domesticity (Soper 1995). Rather, critics have maintained that the domestic sphere remains a site of exploitation of women's labour, and it is this that leads to the devaluation of women and the values associated with femininity (Cuomo 1998: 127–30). Some of these critiques are not entirely fair. Griffin (1994: 167) is clear that it is gendered discourses that normalize women's caring labour, and a positive reading of female domesticity is but one amongst many themes in her work. In addition, Griffin is highly critical of the impact of patriarchal femininity on women, and Cuomo (1998: 120) rightly suggests that she articulates 'unimaginable' ontological possibilities within patriarchal normativity. Key to Griffin's work is the materialist notion of our embodied and embedded existence, the interlinked oppressions of gender, of 'race' of nature, and of the dichotomous spheres of public and private in Western social and political thought and practice (Griffin 1988: 7–17).

These concepts of gender role differences, of linked dualisms and overlapping oppressive and exploitative relations come through in the writing of all the theorists we consider in the next section, albeit in rather different ways.

Key thinkers

In this section, we look in detail at the work of four ecofeminists who have contributed to the analysis of intersectionality in terms of overlapping and interlinked patterns of exploitation and domination.

In *The Death of Nature* (1980), U.S. environmental historian Carolyn Merchant identifies the development of mechanistic science as a key facilitator of the exploitation of women and nature. The scientific revolution of seventeenth-century Europe saw the establishment of a dominant discourse in which women and the natural environment were objectified and characterized as possessing similar subordinate inherent qualities (also see Forsyth, this volume). Modern Western philosophy, she contends, constructed a dichotomy between nature and 'civilization', and mechanistic science sanctioned the exploitation of nature, unrestrained commercial expansion, and a new socio-economic order subordinating women. She traces the decline of an older, animistic and gynocentric European worldview based on co-operation between humans and nature and claims we need to rediscover such pre-modern ideas as a solution to the present environmental crisis and as a means of patriarchal contestation. The relationship between social exclusion and commercial exploitation is later elaborated in her work (Merchant 1985) to focus more closely on the development of capitalism and its relation to the sexual division of labour. Men become associated with commercial production and women with unpaid labour and reproduction, and commercial production is also 'alienated' from the natural world, which it pollutes and exploits.

Well-known Indian writer and activist Vandana Shiva (1988) examines the impact of Western modernity on colonised countries. Shiva's solution to the oppression of women and nature is similar to Merchant's: we must rediscover pre-modern, and in particular, non-Western, conceptions of nature and gender. Poor women in the rural Indian context already have such a conception, she argues: the holistic 'feminine principle' that emerges from their daily practices as partners with the environment in food production. Shiva links the historical development of social, political and economic structures of colonialism to those of patriarchy and environmental exploitation. The West has imposed its model of modernity on the rest of the globe through an ideology of scientific knowledge and the material institutions and practices of industrial capitalism. This has been ecologically destructive (particularly in terms of unsustainable agricultural practices) and has a gendered impact, excluding women in developing countries from their traditional roles in food production and subjecting them to invasive and inappropriate reproductive technologies. Thus, for Shiva (1988), the domination of colonized peoples, of humans over the environment, and of men over women are all linked.

Merchant and Shiva prioritize patriarchal relations in accounting for human domination of the environment. Shiva (1988: 82) goes as far as to assert that 'gender subordination and patriarchy are the oldest of oppressions' and argues that these structures of power gain strength through the process of development or, rather, 'maldevelopment'. An important strength of Shiva and Merchant's work, however, is an implicit notion of systemic domination and the use of discursive analysis to reveal the content and patterning of such domination and the shifts in pattern over time. They both make intersectional links in terms of the role of Western scientific knowledge, institutions and practices as key to the structuring of gendered, racialised, natured and postcolonial social formations of domination and have drawn on feminist epistemology in doing so. For Shiva (1993, 1998), for example, traditional ways of knowing are undermined by the Western rationalist paradigm, establishing a 'monoculture of the mind', which is both an aspect of colonialism and a form of violence against nature.

Australian philosopher Val Plumwood (1993) focuses on how we might think in more detail about these linked discourses of domination. Plumwood argues that 'reason' is a master narrative of Western culture and key to the construction and maintenance of oppressive relations around gender, nature, race and class. Western social thought is based on dualistic concepts: culture/nature, male/female, mind/body, master/slave, civilized/primitive, production/reproduction, public/private, human/nature (Plumwood 1993: 43). This constructs difference in terms of power relations of domination and subordination. Plumwood brings together the insights of a range of -isms in order to understand the interlocking of domination(s). Plumwood understands gender, nature, race, colonialism and class as interfacing in a 'network' of oppressive 'dualisms' (1993: 2). They exist as autonomous entities but are also mutually reinforcing in a 'web' of complex relations (1993: 194). Although Plumwood argues oppressions within the web have 'distinct foci and strands' and 'some independent movement', she adopts a conflationary approach in arguing that, 'ultimately', forms of domination have 'a unified overall mode of operation, forming a *single system*' (1994: 79, my emphasis).

In later work, Plumwood suggests a 'common centric structure' (1997: 336) that places an 'omnipotent' subject at the center and constructs non-subjects as having various negative qualities. This structure underlies racism, sexism, colonialism and 'naturism'. In her three examples (Eurocentrism, androcentrism and anthropocentrism), two questions emerge. First is the question as to whether these are anything more than ideological frameworks, rather than discursive regimes embedded in the material world of institutions, processes and practices. This is reflected in how Plumwood envisages political change. She urges us to replace dualist concepts with a non-hierarchical concept of 'difference' (1993: 59). Here, Plumwood's position is not so far from the postmodern theories of which she is so critical: we dissolve the dualisms by re-conceptualising them as non-hierarchical difference. Deep-seated forms of inequality and structures and practices of domination cannot be altered ideationally. A second problem is that the elements of the centrisms in Plumwood's model are parallel, yet sets of oppressive relations (based on ethnicity, gender etc.) may not be identical given their specific patterns of historical and geographical emergence and the kind of difference they primarily construct.

A more sociologically satisfying account comes from British political economist Mary Mellor (1992), who argues that we need to integrate an analysis of capitalism and patriarchy into an analysis of human relations with the environment. Mellor considers the limits of Marx and draws on the arguments of some eco-socialists in arguing that an adequate theory of capitalism must acknowledge the concepts of natural capital and natural limits (see also Bond, Paterson, and Kütting, this volume). When we consider such natural boundaries, capitalism is incapable of meeting the basic needs of the 'world community'. Mellor sees patriarchy as a system of gender relations that has divided the human world into feminized private and masculinised public spheres, 'placing on women the major responsibility for nurturing and caring values and activities' (1992: 251). This is an 'imposed altruism' and does not foster a particular relationship to the environment by extension of empathy beyond family members. Whilst the public face of capitalist production takes as its premise an autonomous individual, the nurturing private world 'which has its material base in women's time and work', remains invisible (Mellor 1992: 174). Women's imposed altruism means that they are not so embedded within advanced capitalist time – 'a sphere of false freedom that ignores biological and ecological parameters' (1992: 173) – as most men are. Rather, in their closer links to reproductive labour, women are influenced by biological time.

All these accounts have weaknesses: in some cases, an emphasis on the ideational at the expense of the material, or an under- or over- prioritisation of one element of an intersectional analysis. Despite their diverse political and disciplinary positions, however, all these writers emphasise the ways women's lives are crucially located at the boundaries between the public and private, society and nature and the intersections of multiple inequalities.

Critical potential

For Niamh Moore (2004), the backlash against ecofeminism and its writing-off as 'essentialist' or 'dated' are inaccurate and underestimate the vibrancy of both ecofeminist writing and activism. I very much concur, and in considering the potential of ecofeminism, I will take on both criticisms.

Ecofeminist work is certainly not 'dated'. Rather, it has been increasingly influential in various academic disciplines. For example, the extent to which gender inequalities differentiate human causes of environmental changes and their effects is at last making inroads into the study of International Relations, Politics and Development Studies. Here, Ariel Salleh has provided an ecofeminist critique of the notion of ecological footprint that has been used in studies of environmental problems across these disciplines often in an essentialist way, as it differentiates humanity only in terms of Northern or Southern location (Salleh 2009: 11; see also Hinton, this volume). This ignores the gendered qualities of paid and unpaid work and of transport and energy use and the feminisation of poverty. Collectively, as Meike Spitzner notes, these inequalities mean that both the causes and consequences of global warming are gendered (2009: 218–22). An exception here is the work of Úrsula Oswald Spring (2007, 2008a, 2008b) who has suggested a conceptualisation in terms of 'human, gender and environmental security' or HUGE. Oswald Spring combines a 'broad' understanding of gender in terms of vulnerability rather than, as she suggests (somewhat simply), the more traditional approach of inequality. A key strength of this work is the placing of gender on environmental security agendas and, of equal significance, an attempt to mainstream issues of intra-personal violence as systemic and structural in terms of the vulnerability (of elders, woman and children) in situations of environmental and other conflict (see Dalby, this volume).

In examining the intersections of domination, and deconstructing our presumptions about women and nature, ecofeminism is unlikely to be essentialist. However, there is a tendency to prioritize gender as an explanation for various kinds of social inequality and power relations of domination, which can invite criticism for an under-theorization of difference and, therefore, of homogenization. As Warren suggests, perhaps the crux of the ecofeminist project is,

> '(e)stablishing the nature of the connections . . . between the treatment of women, people of colour, and the underclass on one hand and the treatment of non-human nature on the other'. (1997: 3)'

In my view, this must involve consideration of separate processes and systematic relations of domination and not conflate these into a gender-based account.

The theorization of multiple, intersecting social inequalities has now become a preoccupation in critical social theory (Walby 2009). Theorists within feminism, postcolonial studies and Marxism/post Marxism have been concerned with the impacts and effects of various forms of social inequality – from the well-established concerns around the intersections of class, race and gender to newer interests in region and locality, nation, religion and ethnicities. In feminism, the theorization of multiple differences and inequalities has been difficult and contested. Some of those attempting to understand the cross cutting of multiple social inequalities with gender have used the term *intersectionality* to emphasize the ways social differences and dominations are mutually constitutive. The effects of, for example, 'race' for gender are not simply an overlapping of inequalities. Gender relations, through intersection, change the properties of 'race' (McCall 2005; Phoenix and Pattynama 2006). Whilst the term 'intersectionality' emerged from black feminism in the United States (Crenshaw 1991), this focus on multiple inequalities and forms of social domination was a characteristic of socialist feminist writing (Walby 1990, 2009), work with postcolonial feminisms (Yuval-Davis 1997, 2010) as well as ecofeminism (Cudworth 2005; Sturgeon 2009).

Conclusion

This is what, in my view, is the most pertinent critical potential of ecofeminism: working towards more fully intersectionalised understandings of the world – including the world beyond the human – that might best inform practical political projects. Human relations with 'the environment' are socially intersectionalised, that is, they exist in a context of overlapping relations with other systems of social relations, such as those based on class, gender and ethnic hierarchy (see Hobden, this volume). Social ecology, ecosocialism and postcolonial ecologisms have accounted for the interplay between human domination of nature and our various kinds of systemic domination of each other (Bookchin 1990; Dalby 2009; Dickens 1996; Peet and Watts 1996b). However, such scholarship still has little to say of gender inequalities and the complicated ways in which these intersect with those of capital and place. Whereas postcolonial and socialist ecologism is not fully intersectionalised in its analysis, ecofeminism can provide a version of political ecologism in which the domination of nature is interrelated, particularly with gender, but also with a range of other forms of systemic inequalities. As Salleh has emphasised, a 'triangulated' political ecologism would need to integrate the analysis of gender relations, north–south relations and those of capital into an understanding of human relations with 'nature' (2009: 3–5).

Across the range of ecofeminist work, understanding and resisting linked forms of domination is absolutely key to responding to environmental crises and remaking relationships with the non-human world. This requires a theoretically wide-ranging, empirically tested analysis of social intersectionality, and I would suggest that developments drawing on the insights of ecofeminism are best placed to deliver this.

Further reading

A good place to start is with an engaging and provocative introduction to some of the ideas informing ecofeminist engagements on environmental questions such as Vandana Shiva's (2009) *Soil Not Oil: Climate Change, Peak Oil and Food Insecurity*, London: Zed. In order to get a fuller picture of the range of ecofeminist ideas, Mary Mellor's (1997) *Feminism and Ecology*, Cambridge: Polity, is very useful; and Mellor's own innovative contribution to the development of links between feminism, political ecology and socialist ideas and projects can be found in Mellor (1992) *Breaking the Boundaries: Towards a Feminist Green Socialism*, London: Virago Press. For other examples of theoretical work on ecologism, feminism and various forms of inequality and difference see Erika Cudworth (2005) *Developing Ecofeminist Theory: the Complexity of Difference*, Basingstoke: Palgrave; Val Plumwood (1993) *Feminism and the Mastery of Nature*, London: Routledge; and Nöel Sturgeon (2009) *Environmentalism and Popular Culture: Gender, Race, Sexuality and the Politics of the Natural*,

Tempe: University of Arizona Press. Chris Cuomo (1998) *Feminism and Ecological Communities: An Ethic of Flourishing*, London: Routledge, links intersectionality and feminism to political organisations and projects in an interesting way. For examples of critiques of ecofeminist work see Stacy Alaimo (2000) *Undomesticated Ground: Recasting Nature as Feminist Space*, New York: Cornell University Press; Ann Balsamo (1996) *Technologies of the Gendered Body: Reading Cyborg Women*, London: Duke University Press; and Elizabeth Carlassare (1994) 'Essentialism in ecofeminist discourse', in C. Merchant (ed.) *Ecology: Key Concepts in Cultural Theory*, Atlantic Highlands, NJ: Humanities Press. For a strong defence against such criticisms, see Niamh Moore (2004) 'Ecofeminism as third wave feminism: Essentialism, activism and the academy', in S. Gills, G. Howie and R. Munford (eds), *Third Wave Feminism: A Critical Exploration*, Basingstoke: Palgrave.

Useful websites

For an idea of practical ecofeminist political projects see: Women's Earth Alliance (global projects and interests – India, East Africa etc.): http://www.womensearthalliance.org/
Women's Environmental Network (UK based): http://www.wen.org.uk/
Women's Voices (U.S. based): http://www.womensvoices.org/
For general/reading material, see: Ecofeminist and Ecology Resources: http://www.ecofeminism.net/
ENVIROETHICS home page: http://www.jiscmail.ac.uk/lists/ENVIROETHICS.html
http://richard.twine.com/ecofem/ecofembiblio.htm/

11 Governance

Susan Baker

Introduction

Broadly speaking, 'governance' deals with managing, steering and guiding actions in the realm of public affairs (Pierre 2000). As such, the term *governance* is usefully employed in a wide range of discussions about the responsibilities of public authorities in modern society (Meadowcroft 2007a). Governance is typically grouped into three 'ideal types': hierarchies, markets and networks. Hierarchy involves top-down control and regulation by the state through the use of legal rules backed by (often criminal) sanctions (Black 2008). Market governance involves the use of a range of markets tools, such as prices, taxes, subsidies or permits, to provide incentives for action (see Paterson, this volume). Finally, governance can occur through networks involving various forms of public–private collaboration (Pierre and Peters 2000). Analysis of state steering through these ideal types focuses on the extent to which a particular state or international agency has the political and institutional capacity to steer, the tools that it uses and whether the interests of different stakeholders are taken into account in policy decisions (Pierre 2000: 3).

Traditionally, governments have drawn heavily upon regulations and sanctions as steering instruments, so-called 'command and control' steering. In the environmental arena, this sees the state pass legislation governing the environmental consequences of economic activity (see Kuehls and Whitehead, this volume). They ensure compliance with international agreements, set regulatory standards in relation to pollution prevention and control, oversee the application of environmental law, negotiate voluntary agreements with industry, monitor the impacts of its policies and address the relationship between environmental and other policy fields, such as transport, energy and trade. However, traditional methods of governance have come under pressure (Kooiman 2000). This has been attributed to a variety of factors, including the complexity of problems facing society, and so called problems of 'ungovernability', including the claim that command and control regulation produces unintended consequences that are not contained with a national territory but extend beyond to the global level (Black 2008). As a result of these factors, researchers into governance have been forced to rethink the role of formal authority, and thus of hierarchal governance, in public policy processes.

Claims as to the emergence of new patterns of governance are, at least in part, based on observations on the changing role of the state in the mid-1980s, particularly in Western Europe. These changes formed part of the neo-liberal wave of reforms that swept many European states in the latter half of the twentieth century, designed to improve efficiency, effectiveness and accountability of public service provision (Kooiman 2000). While such claims are primarily ideological in nature, they were also strengthened by reference to evidence of policy failure.

The state's capacity to intervene was also seen to be restricted by a questioning public and their scepticism about the scientific base and technocratic nature of state-centred approaches to environmental risk regulation and management (Gunningham 2009). This often erupted into civil action to overturn public policy decisions, for example, in relation to nuclear power, road building and airport extensions, or to ensure more environmentally sensitive regulation of toxic by-products of industrial production (see Price, Saunders and Olcese, this volume).

As a result of these changes, the term *governance* is employed in contemporary discussions to capture the use of governing mechanisms that do not rest on the authority and sanctions of government alone (Gouldson and Bebbington 2007: 7). This 'decentred' form of state engagement sees governance become a multi-level, multi actor process that is varied, complex and fragmented (Black 2008). Growing international engagement in environmental policy has a role to play here, also.

Core ideas

The concept of governance has proved very important for understanding how society addresses environmental issues and has been applied to the study of environmental policy primarily in two ways. First, it has been applied to investigate the use of different styles of governance, in particular, market and network governance, for the delivery of environmental policy objectives (Jordan 2008). Second, it has been used to identify how society ought to be governed in pursuit of sustainable development (see Whitehead, this volume). The application of the concept for investigating the normative goal of sustainable development has produced the most critical insights.

Styles of environmental governance

Here we point to work on the use of both market-based policy instruments and network governance processes in addressing environmental problems. Research on the use of so-called 'new environmental policy instruments' (NEPIs) has focused in particular upon their use in the EU and its member states.

The latter half of the twentieth century has seen the EU and its member states significantly increase the range of instruments involved in environmental management (Jordan, Wurzel and Zito 2003). These include environmental taxes, tradable permits, such as carbon trading, and voluntary agreements, for example, within the car industry. These developments were supported by several arguments. The European Commission, for example, believed that the use of market instruments could relieve regulatory burden by reducing the overall volume of legislation, while at the same time fostering responsibility among key economic actors. It was also hoped that their use would reduce the implementation deficit, thereby helping to achieve more effective implementation of EU regulatory and sustainable development goals. Here, the overlap between, on the one hand, the rise of neo-liberalism, which emphasised belief in the efficiency of markets and their associated economic instruments, compared to interventionist measures and, on the other hand, the growth in use of new forms of market governance, can be clearly seen (Lenschow 1999: 40–1).

Europeanization has also promoted the rise of network governance arrangements at both the EU level and among the member states. These are seen as better able to transcend jurisdictional boundaries compared to traditional approaches and as particularly apt for addressing environmental problems within the framework of the EU's multi-level governance system.

Investigation into network governance points to the rise in use of public/private partnership agreements, especially for policy delivery. Research has also shown how network governance can weaken the role of environmental administrators, especially when the administration loses competence over implementation (Holzinger, Knill and Schäfer 2006), as seen for example in the waste management sector in Ireland (Connaughton, Quinn and Rees 2008). Their use has also been shown to pose problems for the democratic character and thus the legitimacy of governance arrangements. Arguments abound for the state to carry the mantle for ensuring the legitimacy of network arrangements and for overseeing the inclusion of broad societal interests in the policy-making process (Baker and Eckerberg 2008; Black 2008; French 2002; Gouldson 2009).

Empirical research on the use of different policy styles for environmental governance has pointed out that markets and networks do not in practice replace but *co-mingle* with traditional, hierarchical governance (Baker and Eckerberg 2008). For example, at least up until the late 1990s, almost eighty per cent of EU directives and regulations were still of the 'command and control' variety (Holzinger et al. 2006). The rise of global environmental problems, such as biodiversity loss (see Büscher and Igoe, this volume) and climate change (see Okereke and Charlesworth, this volume), also gives a heightened role for the state in global environmental governance regimes, such as those emerging through the UN (see Death, this volume). In addition, most environmental agreements are only semi-voluntary, and there is typically some 'carrot and stick' involved in the form, for example, of tax reductions, retroactive penalties, threats of future regulation, or license requirements. There are also good reasons for believing that the state *should* continue to play a strong role in initiating actions, co-ordinating responses, legitimising decisions and monitoring performance and addressing the unintended consequences of policy (Baker and Eckerberg 2008). Otherwise, gains from 'standalone' environmental initiatives could be outweighed by the negative environmental consequences of other developments, particular in the areas of energy, transport, industry and agriculture. Furthermore, in the face of market failure, where environmental goods are public goods that do not command a price, the state must remain a central component of governance if we are successfully to steer society along more sustainable development trajectories (Bleischwitz 2003; Gouldson 2009; Stiglitz 1988).

Global environmental governance

Seeing the promotion of sustainable development as a quintessential *global* project, the UN-sponsored Brundtland Report (WCED 1987) set an international, political agenda for the promotion of sustainable development built upon the construction of effective, international co-operation to manage ecological and economic interdependences. Brundtland called for both new international institutions for global environmental governance and for changes in existing international agencies concerned with development, trade regulations and agriculture. This internationalisation of environmental governance is primarily built upon negotiations and agreements between states, but non-state actors, including environmental non-governmental organisations (NGOs), and economic actors play an increasingly significant role. This collective activity, termed *global environmental governance,* can be defined as the establishment and operation of a set of rules of conduct that define practice, assign roles and guide interaction so as to enable state and non-state actors to grapple with collective environmental problems within and across state boundaries (Stokke 1997: 28).

At the international level, governance can also be a tool for the promotion of democratic pluralism, that is, to establish structures and means to accommodate the divergent preferences of different social, economic and political actors and to enable these preferences to be translated into co-ordinated action (Kemp, Parto and Gibson 2005: 17). This idea of 'good governance' has particular salience within international efforts to promote sustainable development. The Brundtland Report provided an important rationale for this by arguing that reconciling environmental and development goals hinges upon the fair and equitable distribution of bargaining power so as to ensure that the influence and voice of the world's poor is heard and indeed reflected in international decisions and outcomes. UN summits have also led to a set of expectations about the conduct of global environmental governance regimes (see Death, this volume). Within the UN, 'good governance' now refers to a diverse array of criteria including effectiveness and efficiency, rule of law, participation, accountability, transparency, respect for human rights, absence of corruption, tolerance and gender equality. Many other international organisations and institutions use the term *governance* in this normative sense of 'good governance', including the OECD as well as the World Bank, albeit with different emphases on key components (Esty, 2006; see also Lövbrand and Stripple, this volume). Mention should be made of the Earth System Governance Project, a social science research network in the area of governance and global environmental change. The research explores political solutions and novel, more effective governance systems to cope with the current transitions in the biogeochemical systems of our planet. The research is driven by the normative goal of promoting sustainable development that links earth system governance not merely to questions of governance effectiveness, but also to issue of political legitimacy and social justice (Biermann 2007; http://www.earthsystemgovernance.org/).

Key thinkers

These developments at the international level bring our attention to the fact that, as well as the use of the term *governance* to capture important changes in contemporary policy-making processes, the concept of governance is also used as a normative prescription to describe the type and style of steering that ought to be adopted to achieve a preferred societal value (Kohler-Koch and Rittberger 2006). The concept has been used most critically to investigate how best to govern *for* sustainable development, with a strong focus on both clarifying the role of the state and investigating participatory governance processes (Farrell, Kemp, Hinterberg, Rammel and Ziegler 2005; Lafferty 2004; Meadowcroft 2007b). The contributions of Farrell et al., Lafferty and Meadowcroft are central and are where the focus overlaps with, but is not limited to, the use of the concept of 'good governance'.

As an agent of social change, the state is seen to have a particularly important role in the pursuit of sustainable development. This pursuit involves tasks with broad reaching and long-term horizons, necessitating in turn a radical re-ordering of social institutions. Furthermore, the pursuit can be understood as presenting society with a 'wicked problem', that is a problem of social values that are not amenable to simple solutions (see also Okereke and Charlesworth, this volume). Indeed, it has been argued that the continued existence, even pre-eminence, of a pro-active state is essential if the intergenerational and intra-generational aspects of sustainable development are to be respected (French 2002). This would include, for example, undertaking welfare functions, such as supporting groups in society that are particularly vulnerable in the face of climate change.

At the same time, the participation of social actors has come to be seen as a necessary quality of sustainable development governance (see Hinton and Whitehead, this volume). Participation occurs through institutional settings that bring together various actors at some stage in the policy-making process (van de Hove 2000). They are best seen as located along a continuum, ranging at their extremes from allowing only a minor, consultative role for non-state actors to more deliberative processes in which actors have a major say in shaping policy goals through dialogue and social learning (van Zeijl-Rozema, Cörvers, Kemp and Martens 2008).

All manner of arguments have been put forward in support of participation. These can be grouped into instrumental arguments, such as the claim that participation increases the range of policy solutions available to policy makers; results in policy responses that better take account of local circumstances, local knowledge and capacities; produces greater stakeholder 'buy in'; and reduces the risk of policy failure (Gunningham 2009: 146). The second group of arguments relates to democratic considerations. Approaches to governance that draw upon participatory practices are seen as more responsive to societal needs as well as more legitimate. These arguments draw upon the claim that deliberation, co-operation and learning – all of which are purported to be stimulated and facilitated by participatory practice – leads to better policy outcomes. Participation is also purported to give a voice to marginalised social groups that might otherwise be excluded from influencing policy-making processes (Gouldson and Bebbington 2007: 6). Furthermore, they are seen as having the potential to move beyond an adversarial approach to environmental problems by facilitating partners to better understand the interests of others, to develop an integrated vision and thus a shared agenda for the future (Gunningham 2009: 161). The development of more open, inclusive and participatory approaches to public policy making can also be seen to promote deliberative forms of democracy (Dryzek 2005; Fischer 2003) and help develop active environmental citizenship (Dobson 2003; see also Hinton, this volume).

However, empirical research into the use of participatory governance has revealed that the extent of genuine devolution of power to civil society actors is limited (Baker and Eckerberg 2008; Gouldson and Bebbington 2007; Gunningham 2009). Here the state has been shown to retain 'a very high degree of discretionary intervention and direct control' over these processes (Gunningham 2009: 160). Furthermore, there is also evidence to suggest that participatory processes can paradoxically enhance the role of hierarchical steering. This is not least because promoting participation itself needs additional administrative capacity within state agencies (Jordan et al. 2003: 222). Of course, that is not to suggest that the state fully embraces the sustainable development agenda. Neither is it to forget that the prioritisation of traditional goals of economic growth by many states continues to act as a barrier to effective governance for the promotion of sustainable development.

Research has also revealed problems arising as a result of skewed distributions of power within participatory processes, which bias in favour of economic, as opposed to social, interests. The capacity for participatory processes to provide a meaningful forum for deliberations is heavily dependent upon the type of formal access to policy making that is given; the stage in the policy making-process in which participation is allowed; the 'opportunity structures' that exist within the policy process to influence policy making; and the institutional constrains that are placed both on them and that are present more generally (Hallstrom 2004). Participatory practices are often weak in terms of traditional political accountability and representation. As power to influence outcomes is unevenly distributed, this means that such processes can become arenas for the expression of narrow, vested interests (see Bond, this volume). This can weaken their ability to reflect wider, collective interests that can, in turn, undermine their credibility. In addition, there are also no *a priori* reasons to believe that participation leads to better environmental decisions, especially with respect to long-term, strategic planning (see McShane, this volume).

Mention also needs to be made of the concept of 'metagovernance', which can be understood as the 'governing of governing' (Sørensen 2006). It represents the established ethical principles, or norms, that shape and steer the governing process, such as the norm of 'good governance'. The fact that norms can be used to shape governance means that metagovernance is part of both the input into, and the output of, a governing system. Many key, international organisations and institutions endorse good governance practices, including the UN, OECD as well as the World Bank, and often use this as a conditionality clause for aid and trade. During the 1980s, the notion of good governance gained prominence in development discourse, especially among donor countries. However, it was soon used in a broader political manner and, by the 1990s, the benchmark of good governance had expanded to include governance practices whose legitimacy is derived from a democratic mandate, which follows the rule of law, promotes free market competition and encourages greater participation of civil society in policy-making processes (Kohler-Koch and Rittberger 2006). Applied to the environmental arena, this has led to calls for local people to have a greater say in shaping how their natural resource base is used; for the inclusion of different forms of knowledge, especially traditional and experiential knowledge in policy making, in particular as they relate to access to and benefit sharing from plant and animal genetic resources; and calls for more open and transparent planning processes, especially as they relate to land use and large infrastructure projects (see Igoe, this volume). Indigenous peoples are often heavily affected by dam building projects, such as the controversial Belo Monte dam complex now under construction along the Xingu River in the Brazilian Amazon (Amazon Watch, International Rivers, Movimento Xingu Vivo 2012).

Critical potential

The critical potential of the concept of governance has been highlighted in research on how to steer society when the pursuit of sustainable development is the key steering objective. Promoting sustainable development presents very wide-ranging governance challenges that stem from the scale of social transformation it requires and the character of the steering logic involved in promotion efforts.

Sustainable development is a form of development that mutually reinforces societal, economic and ecological well-being over time (see Whitehead, this volume). It requires action across a variety of temporal and spatial scales, for example, taking account of future generations in present policy and taking action at both the local and global levels in both designing and implementing policies. In addition, it is a very ambitious project as it requires decoupling economic development from both environmental harm and social exclusion and inequality (Baker 2006). In turn, this necessitates transformation of key economic sectors, including energy, transport, agriculture, manufacturing and construction and trade. This transformation is also premised upon changes in cultural values, particularly those related to consumerism (see Brooks and Bryant, this volume). All of these changes have to be underpinned by technological advances taking place alongside profound shifts in the organisation of society (see Luke, this volume). These characteristics present challenges that go beyond the need to promote sound practices of environmental and resource management.

Added to this complexity, there is also a very distinctive steering logic involved in the promotion of sustainable development. First, it requires steering in the context of uncertainty and ambivalence, as it is an open-ended process, one that is not usefully conceived of as aiming towards a specified or specifiable target (Kemp et al. 2005: 16). Thus, governance has to cope with the complexity and the indeterminacy of sustainable development as a steering objective. Promoting sustainable development also has to take place amidst a profound lack of knowledge about the complex and dynamic interactions between society, economic development, technology and nature. This has consequences for governance because traditionally policy making has started from the basis that effective steering requires clear goals. Indeed, the modernist, 'linear' attempts to engineer social and environmental change have focused on the realisation of clearly defined 'end states' or goals. In this context, uncertainty or disputes about these 'end states' come to be seen as problems that have to be contained and minimized (Walker and Shove 2007: 214). In addition, policy making is typically premised on the belief that a good understanding of the relevant causal relationships is a prerequisite for effective steering. In contrast, governance for sustainable development has to acknowledge that efforts to promote sustainable development are characterised by inherent policy ambivalence and uncertainty (Voβ and Kemp 2006). Finally, given its strong intergenerational element, the promotion of sustainable development requires steering for the long-term (Meuleman and in't Veld 2009). However, adopting long-term horizons in decision-making presents steering problems as it adds to uncertainty, and the further into the future we project, the weaker our knowledge base becomes.

How does the nature of the task and the steering logic involved impact upon governance for sustainable development? This question brings our attention to new efforts to promote sustainable development through 'reflexive' modes of governance.

Reflexive governance for sustainable development

Reflexive governance is believed by many researchers to offer the best way to deal with adopting sustainable development as a steering objective (Voβ, Bauknecht and Kemp 2006). The literature on reflexive governance draws from systems theory, in particular, the latter's focus on complexity, uncertainties, nonlinear processes of change and innovation (Loorbach 2010; see also Hobden, this volume). This research starts from the realisation that governments are increasingly devoting time and resources to dealing with problems that are themselves a result of governing. As such, governance becomes ever more preoccupied with repairing the unintended consequences of prior attempts at shaping societal development. Reflexive governance is an approach to governance that acknowledges that governing activities are entangled in wider societal feedback loops that are partly shaped by unintended side effects stemming from its own working (Voβ and Kemp 2006). Reflections seek to identify these side effects and either pre-empt them or address them at an early stage in policy making. Reflexive governance involves not just societal self-reflection, but also the development of new kinds of strategies, processes and institutions that emerge under this condition of 'self-confrontation' (Voβ et al. 2006: 421).

Voβ et al. (2006) distinguish between what they term 'first-order reflexivity' and 'second-order reflexivity'. The first refers to how modernity deals with its own implications and side effects, the mechanisms by which modern societies grow in cycles of producing problems and solutions to these problems that then produce new problems. Second order reflexivity interrupts the automatism of executing 'problem solving routines' by cognitive reconstruction of this cycle and through critical reassessments of rational problem solving methods. In its place it develops alternative methods and processes of problem handling that are more open, experimental and learning-orientated. This involves more conscious re-ordering of social life.

In the reflexive governance literature sustainable development is understood as a particular kind of problem framing, one that emphasises the interconnectedness of different problems and scales, as well as the long-term and indirect effects of actions (Voβ and Kemp 2006). Rather than attempting to ignore or minimize the ambiguity of goals, uncertainty about cause and effect relations and the feedbacks that occur between sustainable development steering activities, reflexive governance seeks to find ways to address and handle this ambiguity. In doing this, sustainable development comes to be seen to be more about the organisation of processes rather than about particular outcomes. Thus the approach recognises the limitations of rigid methods aimed at achieving predetermined outcomes and of steering efforts that delimit problems and treat them in linear ways (Kemp and Martens 2007). In this view, the promotion of sustainable development becomes a constant process in which further adjustments are made as environmental, social and economic conditions change, changes that are, in part, the outcome of previous interventions (Walker and Shove 2007: 219). Voβ and Kemp have gone on to derive cornerstone strategies to handle governance problems of sustainable development. A compilation of these strategies has been presented as a practically-orientated framework for reflexive governance. This has given rise to the development of new reflexive models of steering that take into account the need for governance to be more anticipatory, orientated towards the long-term, to make use of visions of sustainability and to be more concerned with learning, innovation and adaptation (Kemp et al. 2005: 22). Reflexive governance also links well with the democratic and participatory dimensions of policy making discussed previously, as it requires interactive participatory goal formulation and interactive strategy development (Voβ and Kemp 2006: 17–20).

Transition management in the Netherlands is seen as an example of reflexive governance for sustainable development, particularly as applied in the energy sector (Kemp and Martens 2007). The Netherlands has developed an approach to energy policy that involves exploring different policy options and trajectories and employing steering methods that maintain flexibility, especially through variation and selection, instead of rigid planning. This transition management is seen as innovative in two ways. First, it offers a prescriptive approach towards governance that can be used as a basis for operational policy models, and, second, it explicitly adopts a normative model by taking sustainable development as its long-term goal (Loorbach 2010).

However, reflexive governance, as both a model of governance and as a policy practice, is not without its critiques. The idea that we can actively manage moves towards sustainable development could be seen to represent a reassertion of the intent to 'socially engineer' (Walker and Shove 2007: 218). In defence of reflexive governance, it could be argued that this approach differs from the modernist project in that its methods of engineering are no longer, at least not exclusively, conceived of in modernist terms. Meadowcroft (2007b) has argued that this new theorising on reflexive governance is resulting in the emergence of social theorists that are pushing the implications of second-order reflexivity further, suggesting the need to reassess the place of instrumental reason in public life and to abandon linear models of planning and reductionist science. As such, it moves beyond the modernist modes of rationality towards more self-conscious, holistic and communicative forms of reason. But Meadowcroft also argues that the key elements of this second-order reflexivity, in particular as they relate to reconsidering existing practices, critically appraising current institutions and exploring alternative futures, was embedded in the concept of sustainable development *from the outset* (2007b: 160).

In addition, the reflexive governance literature has been criticised for downplaying the political dimensions of reflexive processes and the politics that they generated (see Grove, and Lövbrand and Stripple, this volume). The literature has been largely silent on issues of power and the ways in which the distribution of power shapes steering outcomes. Assumptions that the world can be characterised by co-operation, collaboration, consensus building and what has been referred to as 'the post-political' claim of common interest have also been questioned (see Hinton, this volume). This questioning points to the tendency of the reflexive governance literature to obscure the politics and dynamics of power involved and gloss over the related, potentially contentious question about how systems are specified and managed (Walker and Shove 2007: 222). It also leaves unaddressed the question of who wins and who loses out as transitions are steered and managed in one direction but not another (Walker and Shove 2007: 221; see also Bond, this volume). The research has also been criticised for holding questionable assumptions about the way contemporary policy making is undertaken, in particular, its tendency to downplay the role of the state in policy making and for ignoring how institutional configurations often hinder the capacity of actors to engage in reflexive steering (Hendriks and Grin 2010). Green theorising, in particular, the pioneering work of Robyn Eckersley, has shown that the state is still the preeminent political institution for addressing environmental problems. States remain the gatekeepers of the global order, and greening the state is a necessary step, Eckersley argues, towards greening domestic and international policy and law (Eckersley 2004; see also Kuehls, this volume). There are also divisions within green theory over whether capitalist economies, states or the state system are indeed capable of becoming ecologically reflexive (see Barry 2006a for further discussion). In addition, there are concerns that the links between the emergence of new governance practices and neo-liberalism, as mentioned in the opening sections of this chapter, remain strong, reducing the potential for existing governance processes to promote sustainable development in practice.

Coupled social-ecological systems analysis

Systems theory has also given rise to a different treatment of environmental governance (see Hobden, this volume). This is one that sees governance as the institutional interface operating between ecological and human systems (Paavola, Gouldson and Kluvánková-Oravská 2009: 149). This approach owes much to the original work of Holling on resilience and the adaptive cycle (Holling 1973). Holling's work has deepened our understanding of the dynamics that drive both continuity and change, including at the societal level. Subsequent work has explored renewal, innovation and reorganisation in system development and how they interact across scales. These theoretical developments have come to see the dynamics of the relationship between periods of change and the capacity to adapt and transform for persistence as lying at the core of the resilience of coupled social-ecological systems (Berkes, Colding and Folke 2003; Folke et al. 2010; see Methmann and Oels, this volume). This work has also shown how the dynamics of this coupled system can generate non-linear processes of change, tipping points and emergent properties that have far-reaching consequences for human–environment interactions (Folke 2006; Adger, Arnell and Tompkins 2005; see also Okereke and Charlesworth, this volume). Recent research that situates climate change in the context of more widespread breaches of planetary boundaries has highlighted the urgency of putting in place governance arrangements to ensure that development moves along trajectories where societal needs are met in ways that maintains a safe operating space for humanity (Rockström et al. 2009).

This view of coupled social-ecological systems highlights human dependence on the capacity of ecosystems to generate essential services (or ecosystem services) and the importance of ecological feedbacks for societal development. From a governance perspective, this means that institutions should 'fit' environmental conditions so that there is a possibility of a co-evolutionary relationship between nature and society (Paavola et al. 2009: 152). In this context, the pursuit of sustainable development has enhanced policy resonance because it can act as an organising principle to underpin the steering of society within safe ecological limits (see Büscher and Kütting, this volume).

Research on the governance of coupled social-ecological systems uses three analytical lenses: scale, interplay and fit. The problem of fit relates to the match between the key physical attributes of ecological systems and the design of institutions used for their governance (Ostrom 2009). Attention is thus focused on the relevance of multiples scales in environmental governance, scales operating across both space (including multi-levels of political scales, ranging from the international, to the national and down to the regional and local levels) and time. The focus on time draws attention to the importance of inter-generational matters in the governance of sustainable development. Taking account of the multiple spatial and temporal scales is important to ensure 'fit' between governance institutions and the coupled socio-ecological system (Loorbach 2010: 167–8).

However, within the political science literature, the dominant focus has been on the 'fit' between specific institutional frameworks and the broader institutional setting. The systems approach goes beyond this by focusing on the fit that institutions provide between ecological and social systems. Given the limitations of political science engagement, there remains the need to investigate how disturbances and crisis may instigate institutional learning and creative re-organisation. This is especially important given concerns that the over-emphasis within the literature on coupled social-ecological systems on adaptation within complex systems, and on showing how these systems are capable of internalising challenges to their existence, could function to neutralize critical inquiry about the underlying causes of disturbance arising from unsustainable behaviour (Walker and Cooper 2011; see Grove, this volume). It is here that the literature on reflexive governance in the pursuit of sustainable development could come to the fore and where insights from this literature could fruitfully be applied.

Conclusion

Recent years have seen the publication of a diverse body of literature, within social and political science, planning, public administration and policy studies and economics, that examines whether and to what extent existing governance structures help to promote better environmental outcomes and also more sustainable futures. Empirically, this research has focused on the growing array of practices used to steer society's future, and the most critical reflections come in this literature when attention is paid to governance in pursuit of sustainable development. It is clear that the governance of sustainable development gives a heightened and positive role for the state in directing societal change, even if this steering remains open-ended and increasingly needs to be collaborative in nature. Discussion has also focused on the specific characteristics of sustainable development as a steering objective and how these characteristics add both complexity and ambiguity to governance. This literature has also taken a normative approach, exploring what adjustments ought to be made to governance structures and processes so as to help society in its pursuit of sustainable development. This has pointed discussion in the direction of reflexive governance for sustainable development and for the need to ensure fit between governance processes and ecological systems. These approaches share in common the belief that intervention in pursuit of normative goals, like those of sustainable development, is possible and potentially effective (Walker and Shove 2007: 219).

Gouldson and Bebbington (2007) argue that we can look at the potential influence of new and emerging forms of governance in an optimistic or a pessimistic manner. The optimistic view sees new forms of governance as providing opportunities or spaces for communicative action and social learning. This is achieved by enhancing transparency and creating opportunities for engagement and accountability, which can, in turn, lead to more legitimate decision-making processes and more socially desirable outcomes. As such, new approaches to governance have transformative potential. The challenge is to ensure that this potential can be realised. The more pessimistic view on governance points to the prevailing power relations and the ways in which particular roles, responsibilities and levels of influences are assigned, which enables the more powerful actors to use governance processes to legitimise, without obliging them to transform, their activities (Gouldson and Bebbington 2007: 10–11).

Further reading

A comprehensive treatment of governance as it relates to the promotion of sustainable development can be found in Baker (2012) 'The governance of sustainable development', in Bitzer et al. (eds) *European Union, Governance and Sustainability*, Den Haag: Open University Press. A review of the academic literature and how it has treated the interrelationship between governance and sustainable development is provided by Jordan (2008). The paper also identifies a number of key themes and explores future research needs. A path for future research that describes not only governance and sustainable development but also how governance can be 'for' sustainable development is provided by Farrell et al. (2005).This paper also explores the use of objectives and indicators so as to make useful policy recommendations possible. A more specific focus on the extent to which governance arrangements in high consumption societies have been adapted to promote sustainable development is provided by William Lafferty (2004) *Governance for Sustainable Development: The Challenge of Adapting Form to Function*, Cheltenham: Edward Elgar. One of the major challenges associated with governance for sustainable development is that of managing change in a context where power is distributed across diverse societal subsystems and among many societal actors. This issue is taken up by Meadowcroft (2007a). The paper also advances some approaches to governing for sustainable development in a radically 'decentred' societal context.

Useful websites

European Union, Research and Innovation: Sustainable Development: http://ec.europa.eu/research/sd/index_en.cfm
International Institute for Sustainable Development: http://www.iisd.org/
Sustainable Development Group International (SDGI): http://www.sdg-int.org/index.php
United Nations Sustainable Development Knowledge Platform: http://sustainabledevelopment.un.org/
Rio+20: United Nations Conference on Sustainable Development: http://www.uncsd2012.org/index.html
UN Sustainable Development Solutions Network: http://unsdsn.org/

12 Governmentality

Eva Lövbrand and Johannes Stripple

Introduction

More than ten years ago, Paul R. Brass wrote an article in the journal *Annual Review of Political Science* entitled 'Foucault Steals Political Science' (Brass 2000). By 'stealing' Brass had in mind the way in which power, government and governance – themes traditionally understood as central to political science – have been approached in original ways by Michel Foucault and scholars working in the analytical space opened up by this influential French thinker. Brass argued that a Foucauldian approach to power and government is not a kind of theorising on the margin, dealing with esoteric phenomena unimportant for the discipline at large. Rather, Foucault's work 'ought by now to have become a focal point for the resurrection of these topics and their restoration to centrality in the discipline' (Brass 2000: 1). While it is not possible (yet) to speak of a widespread Foucauldian turn in political science, not the least in the United States, vibrant research on the 'art of governing' has emerged across disciplines such as sociology, geography, history, gender studies and science and technology studies. For students of environmental politics, Foucault's ideas on how thought and knowledge are linked to the government of human conduct have advanced new perspectives on the forms and operations of power in the environmental domain. How did, for example, tropical rainforests, carbon markets and waste become domains amenable to governmental intervention? What kinds of subjectivities are established when individuals seek to shape their environmental conduct in various ways?

Looking back at thirty years of work, Rose, O'Malley and Velverde (2006) are happy to note that the language and analytics of governmentality has dispersed, become mixed with other approaches and gone off in many different directions. What remains salient and challenging, however, is the insistence on moving away from grand theories (e.g., globalization, modernization, risk society) and instead investigating the practices through which we govern, and are governed, in our everyday lives. Scholars in this field thus urge us to look in to the gray sciences, the minor professions and the mundane practices through which objects and subjects of governance are constituted and stabilized at particular times in history. In this chapter we seek to illustrate how this analytical approach may speak to scholars of environmental politics and governance. We begin by outlining what we think represent important and useful analytical traits in Foucauldian governmentality studies. Secondly, we offer some examples of how environmental scholars have interpreted and employed the governmentality concept in the social study of nature and environmental politics. Finally, we reflect upon the critical potential of Foucault-inspired governmentality studies and discuss how this field of inquiry may help us to rethink the nature and limits of environmental politics and statehood in the years to come.

Core ideas

Foucault was in 1970 offered a chair in 'The History of Systems of Thought' at the pres-
tigious French institution *Collège de France,* where he began teaching the following year.
Foucault had himself chosen the name of the chair, which exemplifies how he described his
academic oeuvre. In his fourth and fifth lectures in 1978, Foucault launched the neologism
'governmentality' to describe a particular art of government that emerged in eighteenth-
century Europe and concerned the regulation and administration of life at the level of populations (Foucault 2008). However, later in the course the word no longer only designated
governmental practices constitutive of a particular regime of power, but denoted, in a much
broader sense, the heterogeneous assemblage of techniques, mechanisms and knowledges
that conduct people's conduct (Senellart 2007: 388). This more open definition of government as 'the conduct of conduct' refers to any 'form of activity aiming to shape, guide or
affect the conduct of some person or persons' (Gordon 1991: 2). To govern, in this sense,
claimed Foucault 'is to shape the field of possible action of others' (Foucault 1982a: 221).

When Miller and Rose wrote a retrospective on what they cautiously termed *governmentality studies,* they described their Foucauldian analytics of government as one concerned with
questions about how, and to what ends, socially legitimated authorities seek to intervene in the
lives of individuals in sites as diverse as the school, the home, the workplace, the courtroom
etc. (Miller and Rose 2008:1). Inspired by Foucault's (1991a) *Discipline and Punish,* which
brought about a widespread shift in ways of thinking about power and the 'micro-physical'
effects of disciplining the individual body, Rose and Miller have followed the 'birth and the
activities of many of these little engineers of the human soul, and their mundane knowledges,
techniques and procedures – psychologists, psychiatrists, medics, accountants, social workers, factory managers, town planners and others' (Miller and Rose 2008: 5). In their work they
have taken an interest in the conceptions of the human being that are held at particular times
(as citizen, schoolchild, customer, worker, manager) and, particularly, how such conceptions
are problematized and how interventions are devised (Miller and Rose 2008: 7).

For students of environmental politics and governance, the analytical direction pointed
out by governmentality scholars such as Rose and Miller is useful. In an age when softer
and more horizontal forms of steering have proliferated in the environmental domain,
a growing literature has asked questions about the *who* and the *locus* of political power
and rule (see, for instance, Bäckstrand, Khan, Kronsell and Lövbrand 2010; Bulkeley
et al. 2012). For students of governmentality, by contrast, attention is drawn to the *how*
of environmental governance; *how* is the environment conceptualised and construed as
a domain of government; *how* is environmental governance accomplished in practical
and technical terms; *how* are agent categories and subjectivities constituted through the
practices of environmental governance? For Dean the identification of 'problematizations'
is a key starting point for such investigations into 'the how of government'. The calling
into question of aspects of the conduct of conduct has particular dates and places, i.e., it
occurs at particular locales or within specific institutions (Dean 1999: 27). A Foucauldian
analytics of government is thus not derived from general principles or theories about, for
example, capitalism, the working class or the bureaucratic state, but through identifying
those moments and practices where our own conduct, and that of others, is called into
question (Dean 1999: 28).

Central to such problematizations are particular forms of knowledge and expertise that
define the 'right disposition of things' and thereby constitute and make visible problems of

government. Foucault himself was particularly concerned with the social forms of knowledge that emerged with the constitution of the population as a domain of regulation and action in late eighteenth-century Europe (Foucault 1991a, 1991b; see also Kuehls, this volume). His account of biopolitics, or the politics of life (Foucault 1979), refers to a set of governmental practices 'concerned with matters of life and death, with birth and propagation, with health and illness, both physical and mental, and with the process that sustain or retard the opti-mization of the life of a population' (Dean 1999: 99; see also Grove, this volume). In order to constitute the population as an intelligible object of government, biopolitics draws upon detailed knowledge of the social, cultural, economic, geographic conditions under which humans live, procreate, become ill, maintain health and die (Dean 1999: 99). Against this background, Rose and Miller have suggested that problematics of government should be studied in relation to their 'political rationalities'; i.e., how they represent the nature of the objects and subjects over which government is to be exercised, the moral principles they draw upon to justify certain ends of government, and the language they use to codify and contest the nature and limits of political power (Rose and Miller 1992: 179).

However, for Foucault and his followers, government is not only a matter of representa-tion. It is also a matter of intervention. Accordingly, Rose and Miller have proposed that governmentalities also should be analysed in terms of their 'governmental technologies'; i.e., the humble and mundane mechanisms (e.g., techniques of notation, calculation, examination) through which authorities of various sorts seek to shape and normalise the conduct, thought and decisions of others (Miller and Rose 2008: 32). Although such 'regimes of practices' function as mediums of thought that translate political rationalities into reality and hereby make government possible, we should not think of them as the extension of control from the seat of power (Dean 1999). Following Foucault's interest in the non-subjective 'micro-physics of power' (Foucault 1979, 1991a), the analysis of technologies of government draws attention to the complex relays and interdependencies that enable 'regimes of practices' to act upon those places, people and populations that are their concern (Miller and Rose 2008: 33). In the field of environmental governance, we may think of routinized ways of eating, flying, driving, shopping or heating our homes as 'regimes of practices' within which our carbon emissions and environmental conduct are generated, problematized and corrected.

If rationalities and technologies of government represent analytical categories that can help us to uncover the different ways in which the activity of government has been made thinkable and practicable as an art, they may also tell us something about the forms of individual and collective identity that problematizations of government seek to promote, facilitate and foster. Dean (1999), therefore, asks students of governmentality to be atten-tive to the forms of person, self and identity that are presupposed by different practices of government and to identify what sorts of transformation these practices seek. But, as Dean argues, 'the forms of identity promoted through governmental practices should, however, not be confused with a *real* subject or subjectivity' (1999: 32). In Foucault-inspired govern-mentality studies there is neither a foundational, pre-existing starting point nor an endpoint in the constitution of subjectivities. The subject has no essence. In the afterword to Dreyfus and Rabinow's critical engagement with Foucault's work, Foucault himself explains that the objective of his intellectual inquiry has been to 'create a history of the different modes by which, in our culture, human beings *are made subjects*' (Foucault 1982a: 208, our emphasis). His own work did not point to a continuous narrative or a single time of history that has made human beings what they have become. Rather, Foucault and his followers have highlighted how subject formations are bound up with 'multiple times, moving at different speeds and according to their own trajectories, multiple forms of reason, formed in specific locales in relation to particular problems' (Miller and Rose 2008: 16).

Key thinkers

When Éric Darier edited the influential volume *Discourses of the Environment* in 1999, he noted that there had been a tendency to omit Foucault from most critical studies in environmental theory. Up until then there had been no systematic work aimed at exploring the possible connections and relevance of Foucault's analytics of government to environmental thinking (Darier 1999: 5). In the years to come, however, we have seen numerous efforts to make Foucault's governmentality concept useful in the social study of nature (see Hinton and Kuehls, this volume). Although Foucault himself never addressed the environment as a problem of government, his analytical legacy is today regularly found in fields such as political geography, environmental history and environmental politics. It may still be premature to speak of 'environmental governmentality studies' as a distinct analytical field, however. Critical engagements with Foucault's work in the study of environmental politics and governance have to date produced dispersed and heterogeneous results. Yet there is no lack of Foucauldian contributions to environmental theory. In the following sections we exemplify some of the directions taken in this literature thus far.

Historical productions of nature

In 2007–2008, Foucault's full lecture series from *Collège de France* in 1978–1979, previously only available as audio recordings, was published in the two edited volumes entitled *Security, Territory and Population* (2007a) and *The Birth of Biopolitics* (2008). Reflecting upon the full content of the lecture series, Elden (2007) notes that it has much to say about the organisation and politics of space and hereby is of highest relevance to the discipline of geography. It is therefore not surprising that political geographers have led the way in the analysis of how nature has been constituted as a social and political object. In this literature, graphical inscriptions such as surveys, inventories, maps and accounting schemes emerge as powerful and productive 'regimes of practices' that constitute particular ways of seeing, knowing and acting upon nature at particular times in history. Murdoch and Ward (1997) and Braun (2000) have, for instance, illustrated how mundane spatial and historical practices, such as the invention of agricultural statistics and geological surveys in eighteenth- and nineteenth-century Britain and Canada, are bound up with the constitution of national nature(s). By rendering domains of life visible that were once invisible, statistical representations helped to make agricultural and geological territories thinkable as discrete sectors of the British and Canadian national economies (see Kuehls, this volume). Scott (1998) and Agrawal (2005) have, in turn, detailed how the introduction of scientific forestry in early modern Europe and colonial India constituted forests as a natural resource to be systematized, ordered and controlled. New procedures for measuring, aggregating, differentiating and analysing landscapes, vegetation types and species created a legible natural terrain that made possible the reworking of existing vegetation in terms of sustainable yields and profit maximization (see Whitehead, this volume).

Central to all these engagements with Foucault's governmentality concept is the assumption that natures do not come ready made. As suggested by Baldwin (2003), nature must first and foremost be understood as a political space, or a technological artefact, that is brought into being and gains meaning through representational practices and technologies. Hence, rather than looking for any presumed essence – a pristine, absolute nature – work in this field has drawn attention to the contingent knowledge practices through which representations of nature as an object of political concern are stabilised and transformed (Baldwin 2003). While these historical productions of nature constantly recreate the meaning of space, they are by no means innocent. Most studies in this field have detailed how 'nature's ordering in and through modern forms of knowledge is related to, and in part constitutive of, the ways in which nature is integrated into forms of economic and political rationality' (Braun 2000: 14; see also Büscher, this volume). These 'histories of nature's production' have also been analysed in terms of how they work upon the actions of individuals and hereby produce certain subjectivities and conceptions of the self. Whitehead (2009), for instance, examines the constitutive effects of clean air exhibitions and information campaigns in nineteenth-century England. Through charts, maps and graphic representations, British citizens were confronted with the collective atmospheric consequences of their personal choices and hereby fostered to develop a scientifically informed 'atmospheric self'. Along similar lines, Braun (2000) outlines how museum exhibits and the distribution of mineral kits and geological maps to schools in late nineteenth-century Canada worked to produce 'geological subjects' ready to align their behaviour with the new objective of the state; i.e., the optimisation of the nation's geological resources.

These different spatial and historical engagements with Foucault's governmentality concept have helped us to understand 'how natures and bodily behaviours are drawn into existence through the generation of knowledge, and why such practices should be theorized as exercises of power' (Baldwin 2003: 417). By investigating the meanings attached to nature and space in early industrial society, this literature offers an important historical background to parallel writings on ecopolitics and green governmentality.

Ecopolitics and green governmentality

Ecological or green governmentality are concepts coined by Rutherford (1999) and Luke (1995b, 1999b) to denote a particular art of government tied to the rise of modern environmentalism in the 1960s and 1970s. Drawing upon influential environmental texts from the time such as Rachel Carson's *Silent Spring* (1962), Paul Ehrlich's *Population Bomb* (1968) and the Club of Rome's *Limits to Growth* (Meadows *et al.* 1972), these authors have identified a political rationality that extends the biopolitical concern with human life to the entire biosphere and the environmental resource base upon which human populations depend (see Grove, this volume). As suggested by Rutherford, the knowledge systems that have constituted the environment as an environmental resource problem 'can be regarded as expressions of biopolitics, as these originate in, and operate upon, the same basic concerns for managing the 'continuous and multiple relations' between the population, its resources and the environment' (1999: 45). As implied by the concept of 'eco-politics', this literature assumes that the same governmental practices that once constituted the population as a domain of regulation now is constituting the environment as a problem of government. The horizon for government is no longer restricted to what Foucault termed 'the social body', but extends to all the conditions of life represented by 'the biological species body' (Rutherford 1999).

Luke's work directs our attention to the 'eco-knowledges' that have made the environment thinkable as 'the human race's ecological life support system' (Luke 1999b: 146). Here master concepts such as *carrying capacity, scarcity, survival* and *sustainability* (see Kütting and Whitehead, this volume), born out of the ecological sciences, global change research and natural resources management, emerge as important discursive traits that have inscribed a particular biological/economic/cultural order on the Earth's territories and hereby come to justify new regimes of 'enviro-discipline' that seek to normalise bodily behaviour in accordance with the principles of nature (Luke 1995b). In *History of Sexuality,* Foucault (1979) outlined how biopolitics simultaneously operates through disciplinary practices at the micro-level of the individual and through the administration of life at the level of populations. In the literature on ecological/green governmentality, ecopolitics rests upon similar power configurations. Sandilands (1999) details how modern environmentalism as a system of rule relies, on the one hand, on disciplinary mechanisms of self-limitation and denial. In the face of natural limits, the good ecological citizen will exercise self-restraint and control and hereby adjust his/her consumption patterns, dietary preferences and sexual habits to the common environmental good (see Wapner, this volume). On the other hand, ecopolitics also relies on a detailed administration of the complex biogeochemical processes that set the limits for human life on this planet (see Baker, this volume). To that end it relies heavily on a broad set of environmental expert practices 'that does not so much describe the environment as both actively constitute it as an object of knowledge and, through various modes of positive intervention, manage and police it' (Rutherford 1999: 56).

The literature on ecological/green governmentality is in this respect rooted in a strong biopolitical rationale. It speaks to an art of government that assumes that 'humans must manage themselves effectively – that is, in respect for nature's limits – if modernity is to be genuinely achieved' (Sandilands 1999: 85). Hence, the government of human nature is now intimately tied to that of resources (Sandilands 1999). Luke (1995b) suggests that the simultaneous disciplining of space, populations and individuals central to green governmentality may be interpreted as an effort to generate systems of 'geopower' that reduce the environment into a 'terrestrial infrastructure for global capital' that requires techno-scientific management on global scales. 'To save the planet, it becomes necessary to environmentalize it, enveloping its system of systems in new disciplinary discourses to regulate population growth, economic development, and resource exploitation on a global scale with continual managerial intervention' (Luke 1995b: 77). Green governmentality hereby emerges as a problematics of government that reinforces the power of the administrative state in the name of responsible environmental stewardship (Oels 2005: 195). While this interpretation of how the environment is governmentalized speaks to contemporary efforts to define the 'safe operating space for humanity' (Rockström et al. 2009), it is, interestingly, seldom reproduced in more recent engagements with Foucault's analytics of government. Rather than tracing a particular political rationality of the environment, recent work in this field has more often begun the analysis from below in the everyday practices of environmental statehood (see Kuehls, this volume).

Technologies of liberal environmentalism

In the new millennium the scholarship of environmental politics and governance has been preoccupied with the rise of softer and more participatory forms of steering. Public–private partnerships, carbon markets, product standards, city networks, and stakeholder dialogues are some examples of the manifold practical means by which the environment currently is governed (Bäckstrand et al. 2010; Bulkeley et al. 2012). Global governance studies have provided an influential analytical template through which students of environmental politics have tried to make sense of this new environmental order (see Baker, this volume). This is a literature that interprets the proliferation of 'new modes of environmental governance' as an expression of a more complex governance order marked by a retreat of the state in favour of hybrid or private forms of authority and regulation (Biermann and Pattberg 2008). Recent engagements with Foucault's governmentality concept in the study of environmental politics and governance speak to this scholarly interest in post-sovereign forms of environmental steering. However, rather than starting from an *a priori* assumption about the distribution of power in world politics, a certain location of government (the state), or a certain understanding of the locus of the political (local, national, international) with regard to the environment, this Foucauldian literature has sought to elucidate 'how different locales are constituted as authoritative and powerful, how different agents are assembled with specific powers, and how different domains are constituted as governable and administrable' (Dean 1999: 29). To that end the analysis typically starts from the constitutive processes of governing themselves (e.g., forms of calculation, ways of categorizing, standard-setting practices) rather than with the entities (e.g., public or private authorities) that set out to govern the environment (Stripple and Lövbrand 2010).

In recent years we have thus seen detailed empirical accounts of the dispersed and heterogeneous practices by which discrete environmental domains such as 'the urban environment', 'the carbon economy' or 'climate risks' are constituted and governed (see, for instance, Bulkeley and Schroeder 2012; Lövbrand and Stripple 2012; Oels 2011). Informed by the analytical trajectory set out by Rose, Miller and Dean, this is a literature that has drawn attention to the productive effects of seemingly mundane and everyday practices such as risk assessments, environmental accounting, voluntary codes of conduct, and corporate standards and benchmarks. Detailing how these 'regimes of practices' produce particular fields of visibility and agent categories, work in this field has sought to understand the distinct ways by which the environment is 'rendered governable' in an increasingly globalized world order(Oels 2005). In several of these studies the individual emerges as a central site of contemporary governmental action. In Rutland's and Aylett's (2008) study of climate policy making in the city of Portland, for instance, local emission inventories are approached as central technologies of government that encourage citizens to see themselves as carbon-calculating subjects actively engaged in the government of climate change. Paterson and Stripple (2010), in turn, outline how new carbon footprinting, dieting, rationing and offsetting schemes work to render individual carbon conduct problematic. In both these studies environmental governance is practiced *through* the individual in various part of his/her daily life as consumer, community member or homeowner.

From all these detailed accounts of how contemporary environmental governance is enacted emerge an empirically dense understanding of liberal forms of environmentalism. In Foucault's work liberalism was not approached as a theory, an ideology or a judicial philosophy of individual freedom, but as a particular way in which the activity of government has been made thinkable and practicable as an art (Burchell 1996: 21). As an art of government, liberalism, and in particular neoliberalism as it has been established in many Anglo-American countries in the second half of the twentieth century, is sceptical about the excess, inefficiencies and injustices of the welfare state and instead articulates ideas about a 'free market' and a 'civil society' in which a plurality of groups, organisations and individuals interact in liberty. The technologies of government that give shape to liberal arts of government typically seek to deploy the 'free subject' as an instrument in the achievement of governmental purposes and objectives (Dean 1999: 155). Although far from all engagements with Foucault's work in the environmental domain relate to this particular interpretation of advanced liberal government, they jointly offer a compelling story of how partnerships, accounting schemes and performance indicators are reconstituting environmental statehood.

In contemporary environmental governance the state is not governing less, but differently *through* new agent categories and indirect means of regulation and action (see Baker, this volume).

Critical potential

What sort of critique do governmentality studies foster? Dean understands Foucauldian analytics of government as a critical practice that seeks to 'gain clarity about the conditions under which we think and act in the present' (2010: 48). By problematizing what is given to us as necessary to think and do, this analytical tradition sets out to open up new fields of experience that allow us to do things differently. In this sense, Foucauldian governmentality studies both produce a critical and positive effect. It is a field of inquiry that seeks to disturb accustomed ways of thinking and clear a space for thinking and being otherwise (Burchell 1996: 33). While governmentality studies hereby emerges as a transformational practice, Walters (2012) notes that this school of thought does not tell us what to struggle for or against. While the objective is critical, the governmentality concept does not produce critique in the conventional sense of the term. Much of social theory assumes a particular ground from which critique can be leveraged. This assumed (and hence privileged) ground could be a certain subject of history (e.g., classes, civilizations), a certain ethics (e.g., Habermasian discourse ethics, Rawlsian veil of ignorance) or a certain ontological condition (e.g., utilitarian rationality, eternal anarchy). While Foucault used the term *critique* to describe his own analytical practice, his usage is different from the social theoretical positions alluded to previously.

According to Dean, Foucault's critique denotes 'the exposure and contestation of assumptions rather than to express a general oppositional stance to the putatively pathological character of a social or cultural totality' (Dean 1994: 119). Since there are no universal grounds from which criticism is undertaken, students of governmentality instead have to produce critique that is reflexive of its value positions and the ends it seeks. '[B]y being explicit about its perspective criticism itself enters into the space of the contestation and evaluation of arguments and ideas' (Dean 1994: 119). This analytical position produces a certain 'ethos of investigation'. As explained by Rose et al. (2006), governmentality studies offer a way of asking questions that does not lay claims to totality – it does not seek to explain why things happened, but how they happened and how they differ from what has been going on before. From this vantage point, the present time is not presumed to be the bearer of, or culmination of, some grand historical process. It has no inevitability, no spirit, no essence or underlying cause. 'The 'present', in Foucault's work, is less an epoch than an array of questions' (Barry, Osborne and Rose 1996: 5) and hereby something to be acted upon, cut up and decomposed by historical investigation.

Given the critical orientation described previously, Walters notes that students of governmentality have tended to eschew political prescriptions and instead 'been more comfortable playing the somewhat detached role of the sceptical commentator' (Walters 2012: 148). In order to offer scholars in this field a more invested role in political debates, Walter suggests two possible modes of critical engagement. The first role is that of the 'political amplifier'. While much social theory is drawn to the big controversies and grand debates, governmentality studies typically focus on the minor currents in contemporary politics. According to Walters, scholars in this field should write so that these minor energies are amplified, not because they might turn into something bigger but 'because of their potential to complicate political and intellectual space'(Walters 2012: 148). The second mode of critical engagement suggested by Walters is that of the 'political genealogist'. By investigating the 'historically tested but perhaps long forgotten practices' (Walters 2012: 148), students of governmentality may identify techniques of government that can be reactivated and fruitfully be put to use in the present.

Conclusion

We began this chapter with Brass's (2000) suggestion that Foucauldian studies may resurrect and revitalise the academic study of politics. In the same vein, we have in this chapter illustrated how the concept of governmentality can advance new perspectives on the nature of power and government in the environmental domain. If it is at all possible to define Foucault-inspired analyses of environmental politics and governance as a school of thought, we may think of it as an effort to redirect empirical analysis and ask new sets of questions. Whereas students of global governance in recent years have raised questions about the *who* and *locus* of environmental politics and steering students of environmental governmentality typically draw attention to the *how* of governance; how nature is conceptualised and construed as a domain of government; how environmental governance is accomplished in practical and technical terms; what forms of agent categories and subjectivities are constituted through the practices of environmental government. To date this intellectual inquiry has not resulted in a new theory of environmental politics or of the driving forces of environmental degradation. Environmental governmentality studies remain an analytically fragmented and unfinished project. As students of governmentality we do not, however, find this fragmentation problematic. We would rather approach it as a distinct, and even necessary, feature of Foucault's analytical legacy.

When Foucault first outlined his governmentality approach in the late 1970s, he was not applying the concept in any systematic way. As noted by Joseph (2009: 53), Foucault was instead thinking through his ideas during the lectures, offering very general definitions and applying the concept in different ways and in different contexts. This experimental attitude has been adopted by his followers and today informs governmentality studies as intellectual approach. The analytical tools developed in this field have thus far been open-ended and flexible. They are not tied to any particular political perspective and should as such inspire creativity. Foucault himself suggested that his work takes place 'between unfinished abutments and anticipatory strings of dots. I like to open up a space of research, try it out, and then if it does not work, try again somewhere else' (Foucault 1991c: 74). If governmentality becomes a well-institutionalised paradigm in the social science – an academic machine that yields predictable results and where 'settlement wins out over the unsettlement of the familiar and the self-evident' (Walters 2012: 142) – this methodological ethos may be lost. Hence, it is through continuous experimentation that governmentality studies will maintain its critical potential and keep an analytical space open that allows us to test the limits of our political rationalities and 'investigate how we might think in different ways about the action on the actions of self and others' (Dean 2010: 49).

Further reading

Full translations of Michel Foucault's governmentality lectures have recently been made available as *Security, Territory, Population: Lectures at the Collège De France, 1977–1978* (Foucault 2007a), and *The Birth of Biopolitics: Lectures at the Collège De France, 1978–1979* (Foucault 2008). For additional lecture material and influential reflections, see also

Burchell, Gordon and Miller (1991) *The Foucault Effect: Studies in Governmentality.* Useful interpretations and overviews of governmentality studies as academic field and practice are offered by Dean (1999) *Governmentality: Power and Rule in Modern Society*, and Miller and Rose (2008) *Governing the Present: Administering Economic, Social and Personal Life.* For innovative treatments and applications of the governmentality concept in the field of environmental politics and governance, see Death (2010) *Governing Sustainable Development. Partnerships, Protests and Power at the World Summit*, and Whitehead (2009) *State, Science and the Skies: Governmentalities of the British Atmosphere.*

Useful websites

Michel Foucault, info. Repository of texts, resources for research: http://foucault.info/
Welcome to the world of Michel Foucault: http://www.csun.edu/~hfspc002/foucault.home.html
Progressive Geographies: http://progressivegeographies.com/
William Walters homepage: http://williamwalters.net/

13 Hybridity

Alan P. Rudy and Damian White

Introduction

The idea that 'society' and 'nature' are interrelated but separate domains of reality is a central tenet of modernity. It has helped structure the intellectual division of labour between the social and natural sciences and has powerfully influenced modernist politics whether liberal, conservative, socialist, nationalist or fascist (see Barad 1996; Bookchin 1982; Harvey 1996; Latour 1993, 2004a; Merchant 1980; Smith 1984). Environmental politics has had a compli-cated relationship with this worldview. Many manifestations of twentieth-century environ-mentalism have understood themselves to be moving beyond these kinds of modernist and dualist perspectives (see Hobden and McShane, this volume). At the same time, a great deal of environmental rhetoric in the affluent world (from early twentieth-century conservation and preservation movements to late European Green parties) has been premised on dualistic assumptions, notably, the idea that the aim of environmental politics is to protect something called 'Nature' from something called 'Society'.

Dualistic framings of environmental politics have at times been very successful – par-ticularly in North America and certain parts of Western Europe – in bringing to public consciousness the need to protect natural resources from economic over-exploitation, spec-tacular landscapes from environmental degradation and endangered species from a wide range of social activities (see Igoe, this volume). However, many critics have argued of late that dualist understandings of society–nature relations can also be quite disabling for gain-ing a full understanding of socio-ecological processes and relations. The ideas that we can best study 'Nature' by taking humans out of the picture, that 'Nature' left to itself is optimal, self-regulating and in balance and, even, that this 'Nature' when mixed with humans is nec-essarily degraded are ideas that many natural scientists (Botkin 1990) as well as philosophers (Soper 1995) have suggested are incoherent in a world made up of dynamic ecologies that have mixed with humans across centuries. It has been argued that the dualist worldview, far from defending cultural universals, is actually defending very culturally, socially and histori-cally specific ideas and relationships about society and nature. Critics have suggested that when such culturally specific modern ideas are transposed onto the people and ecosystems of the Global South, the results often produce and legitimate forms of coercive conservation (see Forsyth 2003).

In a world where the basic building blocks of 'Society' and 'Nature' are harder and harder to disentangle, the concept of 'hybridity' – notably the idea that 'things' and specifically, 'societies', 'natures' and 'technologies' are mixed up and mingled – represents an ever more common way of thinking about society-nature relations. In this chapter, we explore the ways in which the concept of hybridity has emerged and been deployed in the environmental social sciences. In our first section we provide some historical backdrop to the concept of hybridity. We then move on to explore how Bruno Latour and Donna Haraway have pioneered discussions of hybridity in the natural and social sciences over the last few decades. We briefly appraise how some of these ideas have informed discussions of environmental politics as scholars explore the ideas of social natures and techno-natures. Finally, we sketch how ideas of hybridity presently inform a range of variously critical post-environmental thought.

Core ideas

The word *hybrid* is derived from the Latin word *hybridia* and has a complex history. Used rarely for most of its history, the term has most often referred to animal and plant half-breeds. In English, the most frequent traditional reference was to swine where the piglet was the offspring of a domesticated sow and a wild boar. It is, furthermore, a word possibly related to the Greek *hubris,* which can mean excessive pride but can also refer to an 'outrage against nature' (Kingsbury 2009: 75; Hinchliffe 2007: 50). Kingsbury notes that the word draws on a historical belief sometimes rooted in the Old Testament that sexual intercourse between different breeds was 'an immoral perversion'. From Shakespeare onward, a growing renaissance sense that plants might cross natural boundaries was used alongside ideas of gardening to generate suggestive and humorous literary metaphors for transgressive sexual behaviour (Kingsbury 2009: 77). Early plant breeders such as Joseph Gottlieb Kölreuter (1733–1806) nervously sought to experimentally challenge the dogma of the constancy of species, declaring in 1766, 'I could wish that I, or someone else, might one day be lucky enough to produce hybrids of trees, the use of whose timber might have great economic effect' (in Kingsbury 2009: 76).

From the late eighteenth century onwards, hybridity was increasingly used to refer to social phenomena that mix elements of society previously understood to be 'naturally' separate, from combinations of ancient and contemporary language to amalgamations of the public and private spheres. In both cases, the term is used to refer to problematic, inauthentic or unnatural combinations of genuine or natural types – plant, animal, human or social. This situation, of course, had ramifications relative to race mixing, and synonyms used for hybrid in the early nineteenth century included the terms *mulatto, quadroon* and *half-breed.* This pejorative use of the term *hybrid* is obviously connected to forms of modern ethnocentricity and Orientalism. Edward Said (1978) has defined Orientalism as a worldview that ranks individuals, cultures and nations according to scales measuring their closeness to – rather than their separation from – nature. Under these conditions, a clear connection is made between the unnatural mixing of plant and animal species, the blending of naturally discrete social institutions and social and sexual relations mixing exotic yet backwards men and women (so often of color) with civilized and progressive men and women (so often 'white'). Furthermore, such a discursive terrain also rejects mixing women, whose natural talents are assumed to be reproductive and domestic, with men's, assumed to be naturally productive and public, in either gender's 'natural' sphere (see Cudworth, this volume).

While the dominant use of the term *hybrid* has been deeply pejorative, it also possesses a more playful tradition relative to the strange nature of tangled connections. Charles Darwin, for example, in a joking letter to Asa Gray, observed, 'I will tell you what you are, a hybrid, a complex cross of lawyer, poet, naturalist, and theologian! Was there ever such a monster seen before?' (Darwin 1911 [1887]: 338). W.E.B. Du Bois implicitly anticipates themes of hybridity in his discussions of the dual consciousness of African Americans in *The Souls of Black*

Folk (1903), where African-Americans are made hybrid by cultural and political denial of their full humanity and citizenship. Much more recently, key figures in the development of post-colonial discourse, most notably Homi Bhabha (1994), have used the term *hybridization* in a more positive light to understand the long-standing historical entanglements of human cultures, languages and politics. Post-colonial approaches to hybridity problematize historical narratives focused purely on the nation state to open up and map the diverse mixings and movements of people across history and culture (see Kuehls, this volume). Salman Rushdie draws from and echoes Bhabha when he regularly argues that it is liminal in-betweenness (in Rushdie's own case never fully Indian, British or American) that generates the conditions for literary insights rather than genre writing. Ideas of cultural hybridity have also been used more recently in globalization literatures to think about the cultural mixings that are persistently produced by global interactions: from fusion cooking to hip-hop, Bollywood to hyphenated identities (Nederveen Pieterse 2004).

Key thinkers

Bruno Latour

Bruno Latour is a French sociologist, anthropologist and philosopher who currently teaches at Sciences Po in Paris. He is one of the key contemporary figures for introducing the term *hybridity* into science, cultural and environmental studies and latterly political theory (see Latour 1993, 2004a; see also Forsyth, this volume). Latour's core argument is expressed most famously in his now classic work *We Have Never Been Modern* (1993). In this text Latour argues that hybridity is explicitly *a problem* for modernity because the modern world was founded on an implicit agreement to separate nature and the practice of science from society and the practice of politics. Latour indeed refers to the dynamics of the separation between nature and society as 'the modern constitution'.

For Latour, the modern constitution and its guarantees are, however, paradoxical. The first element of the constitution is that nature is assumed to pre-exist and transcend us, while society is wholly the product of our actions. The second element – held simultaneously – is that we produce nature in the form of our understanding of natural laws as the product of our actions in scientific laboratories, while society is assumed to pre-exist and transcend us, since no one can survive without or outside of it.

The constitutional tension lies, Latour maintains, in the fact that we produce nature and our knowledge of it but deny our role in that process, *and* the fact that we do not produce society but rather inherit the knowledge and practices it imparts on us while acting as if we *do* produce society. Latour argues that what holds modernity together is, paradoxically, never letting the fact that we've been active in the production of ecologies and sciences come into contact with our efforts to produce or change the nature of society and politics.

The greatest contradiction for Latour is, however, that the constant effort to hold nature and science separate from society and politics necessitates constantly mixing the two together. This occurs very clearly in efforts to establish science-based ecological, health and social policies, but equally obviously in productive economic activities and reproductive domestic ones. *We Have Never Been Modern* suggests that despite two hundred or more years of mixing natures, sciences, societies and politics while treating the products of those mixings as either natural or social, what the natural sciences, social sciences and humanities have all clearly shown is that our bodies, our technologies, our selves, our knowledges, our infrastructures and our values are all products of sociotechnical activity. At the same time, lived experience and scholarship also shows that the landscapes, flora, fauna, resources and processes we treat as natural are, in extremely important and often robust ways, the outcome of prior rounds of socionatural engagement.

The heart and soul of hybrid scholarship and activism is, therefore, to reject the modern constitution whereby nature is over there and society is around here and never the twain shall meet. The effort, at all times, is to denature both society and nature where denaturing means both rejecting the idea that the reality of either and the separation of both is Natural, and adding elements that make digesting naturalized conceptions and actions impossible, at best, and unhealthy, at worst (see Braun and Castree 1998; Castree and Braun 2001; and White and Wilbert 2009 for examples of this research).

For Latour, even mainstream accounts of contemporary social problems, like those in newspapers, fail or find it impossible to hold the natural and the social separate. For example, he observes in *We Have Never Been Modern,*

> The smallest AIDS virus takes you from sex to the unconscious, then to Africa, tissue cultures, DNA and San Francisco, but the analysts, thinkers, journalists and decision-makers will slice the delicate network traced by the virus for you into tidy compartments. Where you will find only science, only economy, only social phenomena, only local news, only sentiment, only sex. Press the most innocent aerosol button and you'll be heading for the Antarctic, and from there to the University of California at Irvine, the mountain ranges of Lyon, the chemistry of inert gases, and then maybe to the United Nations. (Latour 1993: 2–3)

According to Latour, we live in worlds of multiple hybrid objects from ozone layers to GM crops and prosthetic implants. This means that attempts to understand the world through the purification of hybrids into boxes labeled 'Society' or 'Nature' have limited utility, whether because they are too partial to be effective in policy terms or because they simply displace problems from one element of a hybrid phenomena onto others, possibly making situations worse.

A clear example of this kind of issue lies in the resistance to genetically modified crops in the EU over the last decade and a half. University, corporate and government scientists have often responded to public resistance in one of two ways. First, scientists accuse the public of hysterical anti-scientism based on popular know-nothingness. These claims are made by the scientists based on their perspective on scientific evidence pointing to the ecological and health safety of genetically modified crops. Second, and usually afterward, scientists seek out social scientists to help with scientific communication to enhance public understanding of science. What the biotechnologists and their representatives generally do not understand is that the resistance to genetically modified crops most often represents a hybrid politics itself! Notably, opponents draw on a mixture of ecological, health, cultural and political economic concerns, and these concerns have been shown in repeated surveys to be weakly correlated at best and sometimes negatively so the more they know about genetically modified crops (Durant, Bauer and Gaskell 2008; Gaskell et al. 2003, 2010). There are two reasons for this latter development. First, oftentimes, the more opponents know about the science, the more questions they have about who did the testing, its quality and its limits. Second, the more activists know about the science, the more questions they have about the social interests expressed in the technology (Schurman and Munro 2003; Schurman 2004). For example, why was the insertion of genes that express resistance to commercial herbicides or 'natural' insecticides prioritized over the genetic promotion of ecological or nutritional benefits? Last, a great deal of the resistance to genetically modified crops in Europe derives from concerns about the concentration of power within the agri-food system, the homogenization of regional diets and the consequences for rural landscapes identified with national cultures (Lezaun 2011; FoEI-CFS 2008; Wynne 2001).

In line with this kind of analysis, Latour has proposed new metaphors and approaches more suitable for thinking about and across social, ecological and technological relations. Most clearly starting with his work in *Science in Action* (1987), but then more intensely across the 1990s with *We Have Never Been Modern* (1993) and *Pandora's Hope* (1999), Latour advanced the concept of 'networks' (Latour 1987, 1993, 1999) and 'assemblages' (Latour 1992, 1996, 2007) to provide more dynamic and fluid means of capturing our hybrid relations. Rather than see separate elements of society and nature, the argument is that the world is better understood in terms of variously larger or smaller connections, nodes or composites that draw together people, objects, measuring devices, non-humans, technologies and so on for longer or shorter periods of time. We can more productively think and explore the world if we see it in terms of a multitude of variously stable and unevenly shifting technological, scientific, cultural, political, urban and other kinds of networks – stretching near and far, more or less permanently across the globe (see also Luke, this volume).

This kind of approach emphasizes empirically discernible connections explicitly rejecting appeals to not only nature or society, but also to science, or technology, or politics, or capitalism, or bureaucracy, or even banks, climate change or extinction. All meso- and meta-terms are rejected in favor of an empirical focus on the strength and durability of connections between particular humans and non-humans. A central element of this approach is that, by rejecting the idea of a nature separate from society, Latour also rejects the idea that society and people tend strongly to be active while nature and objects tend strongly to be passive. He wants to recover a sense that human action can only occur with and when enabled by many other lively and active non-humans: including animals, ecosystems, microbes, bodily capacities, weather patterns and technological artifacts, all of which may enable, facilitate or resist plans and projects (see also McShane, this volume).

Just consider, for example, the ways in which we move through everyday life. From the moment we wake up in the morning, a Latourian worldview wants to emphasize how we, and our forms of social action, are 'lashed up' with a whole set of technologies, processes, energy systems, non-humans, all of which have to be successfully brought together or stabilized in a network for us to successfully get out of bed, turn off the alarm clock, use the bathroom and make some toast. In his wry and amusing essay 'Where Are the Missing Masses: A Sociology of Mundane Objects' (1992), Latour, for example, encourages us to think about all the objects we encounter in everyday life, from key fobs to door openers, seatbelt alarms to the dog that needs to be walked, hands-free digital devices to the surgical implants and on to the hills, rivers, parks and buildings that affect our movements, intentions and feelings. Action and agency are distributed and occur in and through multiple assemblages such that agency can never be adequately thought of as a purely human affair (see Hobden, this volume). As he sees it, things are best thought of as quasi-objects or 'actants' (not quite actors, or agents, but close) given the richness of their material activity when associated with people. He wants to additionally suggest that humans are best thought of as quasi-subjects given how non-human 'actants' persistently mediate human being and action, however much we are unaware of those mediations having accepted them as normal, black-boxed and deproblematized.

Donna Haraway

Donna Haraway is an American feminist, social theorist, biologist and key figure in the development of science and technology studies. With a background in biology and philosophy, she has played a key role in the development of feminist science studies drawing together Whitehead, Foucault and socialist feminism with her own concrete and grounded explorations of nature-cultures (as she refers to them; see Hobden, this volume). In terms of the rejection of modern dualisms and the embrace of an active material world, Haraway's writings have many resonances with Latour. Politically, however, Haraway's writing contains a rather more explicit commitment to a hybrid mode of socialist feminism (see Cudworth, this volume).

Haraway's work has never embraced disciplinary boundaries, and her dissertation, 'The Search for Organizing Relations: An Organismic Paradigm in 20th-Century Developmental Biology', while granted by Yale University's Biology Department, was coordinated between the Biology, Philosophy and History of Science and Medicine departments. Published in book form as *Crystals, Fabrics, and Fields: Metaphors of Organicism in Twentieth-Century Developmental Biology* (1976), the dissertation explored the interplay of scientific practice, Kuhnian gaps in paradigmatic coherence and the evolution of metaphoric representation in the generation of new theories of embryology and developmental biology. A related mid-career project, *Primate Visions: Gender, Race, and Nature in the World of Modern Science* (1989), went on to show how research programs and scientific accounts by primatologists focused on the reality and meaning of primate sociality, and human nature was always – in simplified form – a triangulation between (a) systematic but socially conditioned data collection, (b) the gender and scientific socialization and politics of the data collectors and (c) the diverse ecologically and historically situated practices of non-human primates. Most dramatically, Haraway showed how deeply primatology is embedded in contestation over the stories we tell ourselves about the meaning of race, gender and who 'we' are as human beings.

During the decade of research for *Primate Visions,* Haraway intervened in socialist feminist debates and nature, science, technology and subjectivity, writing what are certainly her two most famous articles: 'A Manifesto for Cyborgs: Science, Technology, and Socialist Feminism in the 1980s' (1985), and 'Situated Knowledges: The Science Question in Feminism and the Privilege of Partial Perspective' (1988). In 'A Manifesto for Cyborgs', an argument much like Latour's is made that the modernist separation of human beings from animals, and human beings from technology, is no longer sustainable given natural scientific knowledge and the lived experience of everyday life in contemporary times. In this light, Haraway appropriates the image of the cyborg from the patriarchal and militarist terrain of science fiction to theorize late-twentieth-century selves as cyborg subjects. A socialist feminist cyborg rejects romantic feminist identifications with nature and finds pleasure in engagements with the traditionally masculine realms of science and technology, while simultaneously rejecting the claims of normative neutrality associated with masculine technophilia.

Additionally, and perhaps more importantly, these variously pleasurable hybrid connections pose immediate questions for cyborg subjects about the many boundary interfaces and regulated flows that undermine previously essentialized animal, human, technological separations. As she puts it in a 1991 reprint,

> In so far as we know ourselves in both formal discourse (for example, biology) and in daily practice (for example, the homework economy in the integrated circuit), we find ourselves to be cyborgs, hybrids, mosaics, chimeras. Biological organisms have

become biotic systems, communications devices like others. There is no fundamental, ontological separation in our formal knowledge of machine and organism, of technical and organic. (1991: 177–8)

Haraway's commitment to illuminating the ways in which the hybridity of the world demands non-modern engagements lies at the core of her subsequent exploration of the meaning and power of metaphoric kinship with cyborgs in the form of 'coyote natures', 'vampiric races' and 'companion species'.

The argument in 'A Manifesto for Cyborgs' is deepened in her discussion of 'Situated Knowledges'. If the problematic necessity for cyborg subjects is to pay close attention to one's own boundary practices and sociotechnical connections – as well as the boundaries and connections generated and reproduced by others – then it becomes effectively impossible to continue the modern pursuit of disembodied knowledge about discrete objects. In this way, all knowledge is the product of regulated, bounded and embodied connections; all knowledge is situated and comprised by particular engagements. This, of course, raises the question as to whether anything can be reliably known – whether objective knowledge is possible. She writes,

> So, I think my problem and 'our' problem is how to have, *simultaneously* an account of radical historical contingency for all knowledge claims and knowing subjects, a critical practice for recognizing our own 'semiotic technologies' for making meanings, *and* a no-nonsense commitment to faithful accounts of a 'real' world, one that can be partially shared and friendly to earth-wide projects of finite freedom, adequate material abundance, modest meaning in suffering, and limited happiness. (Haraway 1991: 187)

Committed to hybridity at the most basic level, Haraway is insisting that our selves and our knowledges be generated in non-innocent (or we might say critical and reflexive) ways. Situated knowledges are never heroic or individual; they are never disembodied visions from nowhere. At the same time, however, Haraway aggressively rejects relativism: 'Relativism is the perfect mirror twin of totalization in the ideologies of objectivity; both deny the stakes in location, embodiment, and partial perspective; both make it impossible to see well' (Haraway 1991: 191).

Part of the non-innocence in cyborg connection lies in acknowledging the role of the entities, machines and objects that actively contribute, that negotiate, that converse, that pursue disengagement in the process of knowledge construction. The point is,

> to highlight the object of knowledge as an active, meaning-generating axis of the apparatus of bodily production, without *ever* implying immediate presence of such objects or, what is the same thing, their final or unique determination of what can count as objective knowledge at a particular historical juncture. (Haraway 1991: 200)

Scientific practice, then, represents the process whereby the boundaries that define an object of study are mapped through practical engagement with tricky materials, variously cooperative machines, limited metaphorical arsenals and other people variously committed or resistant to emergent boundary projects. The point of this work though is not to display that things are merely social, merely cultural, merely discursive; rather it is to get closer to objects, to get more worldly, to get more material but in doing so, demonstrate (1) the material semiotic complexities and layers that we can see as we get more material and (2) to advance human and non-human flourishing. As she notes,

> Instructed by companion species of the myriad terran kingdoms in all their placetimes, we need to reseed our souls and our home worlds in order to flourish – again, or maybe just for the first time – on a vulnerable planet that is not yet murdered. We need not just reseeding, but also re-inoculating with all the fermenting, fomenting, and nutrient-fixing associates that seeds need to thrive. Recuperation is still possible, but only in multispecies alliance, across the killing divisions of nature, culture, and technology and of organism, language, and machine. (Haraway 2013)

Unlike Latour, Haraway's writings have always combined her investigation of 'technoscience' and broader 'technocultures' with a critique of the ongoing power of stabilized – and naturalized – modern hierarchies relative to gender, race, class, compulsory heterosexuality and scientific, political and economic expertise. Here is an example of the extraordinary (if not always easy) way Haraway writes, in this case about nature:

> [n]ature is for me, and I venture for many of us who are planetary fetuses gestating in the amniotic effluvia of terminal industrialism, one of those impossible things characterized by Gayatri Spivak as that which we cannot not desire. Excruciatingly conscious of nature's discursive constitution as 'other' in the histories of colonialism, racism, sexism, and class domination of many kinds, we nonetheless find in this problematic, ethno-specific, long-lived, and mobile concept something we cannot do without, but can never 'have.' We must find another relationship to nature besides reification and possession. (Haraway 1992: 296)

Haraway is here making the point that despite the claim that moderns make about the purity and prior-ity of nature, the concept itself and the practices grounded in assumptions about that purity and prior-ity are bound up in historical relations directly connected with and constitutive of 'colonialism, racism, sexism, and class domination of many kinds'. It is this attention to the connections between modern efforts to stabilize the concept of nature and practices of naturalization and the structure of modern oppression that differentiates Haraway from Latour. On this terrain, it is incumbent on political people and scientific researchers to be socially self-aware of not only their own inescapably composite constitution as cyborgs but also concerned, clear and transparent about the specific embodiment and partiality of their perspectives.

Critical potential I: Hybrid environmental social and natural sciences?

Perhaps the most influential attempt in the environmental social sciences to think 'hybridity' informed by Science and Technology Studies (STS), Latour, and Haraway, as well as broader currents in post-structuralism, animal studies and feminist theory, has emerged from the work of the geographers Sarah Whatmore (2002) and Steve Hinchliffe (2007). Whatmore and Hinchliffe have used the terms *a-modern* and *more than human* to describe their particular vision of a hybrid environmental analysis. 'A-modern' work suggests that we need new 'hybrid' modes of social science that are neither modernist nor postmodern. A-modern social science denotes approaches that recognize the porous and unstable relations between technologies, ecologies, humans, animals and others and draws Latour and Haraway into engagement with Giles Deleuze, Isabella Stengers and neo-vitalist philosophies more generally. Emphasis is placed in this work on the notion that we live in lively, unstable worlds that are always 'a commotion', to use Sarah Whatmore's phrase, always surprising, always in a state of becoming.

Hinchliffe and Whatmore's work has focused on very specific moments when the liveliness and blurring boundaries of our worlds are revealed, such as when there are disputes in the governance of planetary genetic resources or urban ecological struggles in the UK around the protection of endangered species. Their work has sought to demonstrate how it can be productive to think of our worlds as mutually co-constituted by many human but also more than human elements and recalcitrant objects, ecologies and technologies at many different spatial scales. The general emphasis of Whatmore's work in particular stresses that the world is never stable or fixed.

At a more general level, it could be observed that a hybrid understanding of society–nature relations has increasingly dispersed well beyond poststructuralist influenced moments in the environmental social sciences and STS (see Forsyth, this volume). Thus, in the natural sciences, Crutzen and Stoermer's (2000) claim that our current geological era is best understood as 'the anthropocene' have strong resonances with discussions of hybridity in the social sciences (see Dalby, this volume). The anthropocene not only seeks to capture the idea that the impact of modern society, through agriculture and urbanization, population growth and CO_2 emissions, is so great that humans can now be viewed as a geological force on the planet, but that with the widespread and uneven social transformation of the planet there is no nature that is in any way straightforwardly 'Natural'. From the top of the Himalayas to the ocean floor we now find traces of humanity, whether in terms of garbage, wholesale land forming or chemical residues (Crutzen and Stoermer 2000).

Much work in environmental history, historical geography, political ecology and 'new' or non-equilibrium ecology over the last two decades has taken 'hybrid' directions. Such work shows that the history of society–nature mixing is much more dynamic and expansive than we previously thought. The idea that early humans or non-modern peoples had static, balanced relations to an external nature is seen as widely off the mark. By hunting and gardening, plant and animal breeding, irrigating and farming and the building of settlements, early humans transformed vast landscapes using relatively simple technologies such as stone axes or fire (see Denevan 1992; Botkin 1990; Mann 2005, 2011). The intensification of the movement of people and goods over the last 3,000 years, a process accelerated greatly by European circumnavigation of the globe in the 1500s, spread and broadened the trans-continental exchange of plants and animals, pathogens and microbes across the planet (Crosby 1986).

Critical potential II: Hybrid politics?

While the ontological case for thinking about the world in hybrid terms would seem very strong, the politics, and specifically the environmental politics, that follow from a hybrid ontology are much more contested. All forms of hybrid environmental politics reject modernist and dualist environmental politics in their neo-Malthusian, romantic and ecocentric forms (see Kütting, McShane, and Wapner this volume). However, beyond this, the types of critiques made by hybrid environmentalisms are quite varied. The extent of the necessity to move towards 'post-environmentalism' or a 'post-ecological' politics, is a matter of considerable contestation. This chapter can merely point to a number of interesting questions and directions, under the headings of critical hybrid environmental politics and post-environmental hybrid politics.

Critical hybrid environmental politics

Discussions of the politics of hybridity in the environmental social sciences, while critical of classic forms of environmentalism, are often sympathetic with (some) more conventionally green social movements (see Price, Saunders and Olcese, this volume). Most of these currents follow Haraway and Latour in arguing that future hybrid environmentalisms nevertheless need to try and democratize the processes of environmental knowledge production and expand the idea of the environment well beyond 'nature' understood in classic dualistic terms. We can distinguish two different schools of thought at present within critical hybrid approaches.

The first could be termed cosmopolitical approaches to hybridity. Here, Latour's work has framed the hybrid politics as the challenge to bring into democratic networks previously excluded voices, objects and agencies. As such, he has long argued we need a 'parliament of things' (1993, 2004a). Many others, such as Whatmore (2002), Hinchliffe (2007) and Braun and Castree (1998), have followed up this vision to advocate a 'cosmopolitics' or an 'ecology of practices'. In short, the argument made is that in a world of lively objects and hybrid processes, we need an environmental politics that can move beyond the apocalypticism, scientism and moral absolutism of much classic environmentalism.

The second might be termed a critical political economy of hybrid worlds. This more explicitly leftist approach to a critical politics of hybridity connects as much to Latour and Haraway as to critical theories of environmental justice and political ecology (see Peluso and Watts, this volume). Thinkers such as Erik Swyngedouw, Noel Castree, Tim Luke and Julie Sze – alongside a range of activists emerging from environmental and global justice efforts – have suggested that questions of power and capitalism need to have much greater centrality to a critical hybrid politics. These currents seek to give voice to the very different views of environmental degradation that emerge from communities of color, working class movements and indigenous cultures across the global south. This vision of hybridity seeks to explore the ways that ecological, health, cultural and political economic justice are irreducibly bound up together and entangled (see Bond and Cudworth, this volume). As such, it is argued that we need forms of hybrid analysis that demonstrate how environmental problems in the workplace are bound up with environmental problems in the community and how these broader concerns often directly link to global environmental concerns across rural, urban and global worlds. The ultimate aim of these critical hybrid environmentalisms then is to search for public ecologies that open up the production of natures to more democratic control (see Braun and Castree 1998; Luke 1997, 1999b, 2009; White and Wilbert 2009).

Post-environmental hybrid politics

Hybridity is not only deployed within leftist, radical or critical environmentalisms, as such perspectives also reside within perspectives skeptical of or hostile to environmentalism. Three currents stand out. The first is trans-humanist post-environmentalism. Left- and right-wing trans-humanist currents (see Hughes 2004) increasingly make use of hybrid arguments to advocate for the maximization of human augmentation technologies. Most currents of trans-humanism have been more focused on the potential implications of hybrid ideas for the human body than the broader environment. However, when environmental ideas are discussed, trans-humanist literatures have often emphasized the virtuous role that biotechnology, nuclear technology, geo-engineering and various other large scale technological fixes may play in overcoming environmental challenges (see Luke, this volume).

The second current is neo-liberal and contrarian hybrid politics. Hybrid ontological arguments have also been used by a range of contrarians, conservatives and neo-liberals, such as Virginia Postrel (1998) and Ron Bailey (2005), who are actively hostile to environmentalism in virtually all of its forms. They have used hybrid and trans-humanist ideas to systematically undercut traditional romantic environmentalism and, with that, to reject environmentalism tout court. Hybridity in this case is used to argue for the infinite plasticity of ecosystems and humanity and to celebrate the infinite sustainabilities that neo-liberal transformations of the natural world might produce. Along these lines, forestry companies in the Western United States have used the broad hybrid work of environmental historians such as William Denevan (1992) and non-equilibrium ecologists such as Daniel Botkin (1990) to push back against restrictions on forest cutting and more generally justify productivist approaches to landscape.

A third current of hybrid thinking has emerged as post environmentalist neo-modernization theory, as epitomized by The Breakthrough Institute (e.g., Nordhaus and Shellenberger 2007). Here, the hybrid ontological worldview is again used to undercut romantic versions of American environmentalism, classic conservation policy and global Malthusian thinking (see Igoe and Wapner, this volume). However, the emphasis shifts to linking ideas of hybridity to a reinvented 'muscular American liberalism'. In this particular version of hybrid thinking, the interventionist state is reclaimed as a critical force for envisaging large-scale, environmentally friendly technological innovations. Much of this work has drawn together an ecologically informed modernization theory with 'hyberbolic post-humanism' (to use the phrase of Lorimer 2009) to argue explicitly for a post-environmental politics. Drawing from Latour, it is argued a hybrid world invites a hybrid humanity to systematically reorganize itself.

Conclusion

In this chapter, we have reviewed elements of the concept of hybridity in environmental politics and the environmental social sciences. In a relatively short period of time the concept has made significant inroads into environmental debates, though its politics is clearly indeterminate and various. These ambiguities are tied to the loose fit between ontological positions, epistemological arguments and political and ethical standpoints. It has long been recognized, after all, that romantic environmentalism and equilibrium ecology have political associations varying from eco-fascism to eco-anarchism, eco-socialism to green conservatism. As such, it is not surprising that a similar plurality is emergent in current discussions on hybridity.

That there is nothing necessarily progressive or regressive about hybrid accounts of the world does draw into sharp focus the fact that a *critical* and *progressive* hybrid environmental politics is not something that simply follows from ontological or epistemological positions. Rather, it is a discourse that has to be constructed and argued for. A viable critical theory of hybridity *must* contain sophisticated theories of economic, political and cultural power. In order to do so, it must attend to its own hybrid productions and boundary practices so as to address socio-natures and techno-natures in a manner that does not fall back on modernist conceptions of economics, politics and culture. The risk of the rise of uncritical hybrid politics lies in their disinterest in mapping and investigating the ways in which highly uneven networks of inequality, degradation and destruction are actively making our contemporary world in a way that serves some interests rather than others. A critical hybridity acknowledges that we cannot 'save' 'Nature' from 'Society' or envisage environmental politics as seeking a simple return to purity and balance, but we can rigorously contest the current production of our hybrid natures and insist there are other ways – more equitable, democratic and sustainable ways – for producing future hybrid worlds.

Further reading

In addition to the wider work of Latour and Haraway, those interested in an early interrogation of the relation between nature, science and labour processes should read two articles by Robert M. Young: 'Science is a labour process' *Science for People,* 43/44 (1979), 31–7; and, 1985's 'Is nature a labour process?' in Levidow and Young (eds) (1985) *Science, Technology and the Labour Process: Marxist Studies, Vol. 2*, Free Association Books: London. There are a good number of excellent collections connected to issues of hybridity. In the late 1990s, an early set of synthetic chapters melding political economy, feminism, science studies and environmental politics set the stage for future efforts. See Braun and Castree (eds) (1998) *Remaking Reality: Nature at the Millennium*, London: Routledge. In the early twenty-first century, a series of interdisciplinary conferences were held under the Technonatures moniker and an excellent collection, *Technonatures: Technologies, Spaces and Places in the 21st Century*, Waterloo: Wilfrid Laurier Press, was subsequently produced by Damian F. White and Chris Wilbert in 2009. A few selected and exemplary articles that address issues of urbanization, humanism, naturalism and resources, respectively, include Matthew Gandy (2005), David Lulka (2009), Myra J. Hird (2010) and Patrick Carroll (2012). This area of scholarship overlaps at times with theories committed to queering conventional categories and practices relative to the non-human world, as well. One provocative collection in this area is Noreen Giffney and Myra J. Hird (eds) (2008) *Queering the Non/Human*, London, Ashgate. A review of the sociology of hybridity can be found in Damian White, Alan P. Rudy and Brian Gareau (forthcoming) *The Environment, Nature and Social Theory: Hybrid Approaches*, London: Macmillan.

Useful websites

Paris: Ville Invisible: http://www.bruno-latour.fr/virtual/index.html
Town Meeting Television: http://www.cctv.org/watch-tv/programs/donna-haraway-reads-national-geographic-primates-ted-koppels-long-march-viewed-dan
The Nature of Cities: http://www.thenatureofcities.com/
Ecology Without Nature: http://ecologywithoutnature.blogspot.com/
Larval Subjects: http://larvalsubjects.wordpress.com/
After Nature: http://afterxnature.blogspot.com/
Critical Animal: http://criticalanimal.blogspot.com/

14 Justice

Patrick Bond

Introduction

The 'Climate Justice' movement emerged from within the environmental movement during the early 2000s, fusing a variety of progressive political-economic and political-ecological currents in order to combat the most serious threat humanity and most other species face in the twenty-first century. The concept of climate justice addresses the intersections of 'green' ecological concerns and 'red' socio-economic ethical considerations, ranging from public policy deliberations to political practices. Climate justice follows directly from the much older 'Environmental Justice' movement that especially emphasised the racial and class injustices of pollution in the United States (Bullard 1990; Schlosberg 1999). This chapter will focus specifically on climate justice as a particularly important and prominent current manifestation of the broader environmental justice struggle.

The first known conference based on the term *climate justice* was a 2000 event in The Hague sponsored by the New York group CorpWatch (Karliner 2000). Four years later, the Durban Group for Climate Justice was launched, and for many years remained an important strategic listserve for those opposed to carbon trading and other 'false solutions' to the climate crisis (http://www.durbanclimatejustice.org/). The sometimes inchoate advocacy movement known as Climate Justice Now! (CJN!) began in 2007 and played a role in grassroots environmental advocacy as well as global-scale United Nations climate summits (http://www.climate-justice-now.org/; see also Kaara 2010). The highest-profile of these, with 100,000 protesters demanding a strong agreement from negotiators, was in Copenhagen in 2009 (see Death, this volume). In contesting mainstream environmentalists, Danes and other Europeans formed a Climate Justice Alliance (CJA) whose 'Reclaiming Power' protest was severely repressed by Danish police protecting the United Nations Framework Convention on Climate Change Conference of the Parties (COP) 15 (http://www.climate-justice-action.org/).

Shortly after the Copenhagen summit's well-recognised failure, the Bolivian government, led by Evo Morales and his then UN Ambassador Pablo Solon, hosted a 2010 conference in Cochabamba, attended by 35,000 activists, including 10,000 from outside the country (http://pwccc.wordpress.com/). This was important partly because of attempts to more deeply incorporate within mainstream climate politics a commitment to carbon markets and offset payments, especially through the Reducing Emissions from Deforestation and Forest Degradation (REDD) projects (see Okereke and Charlesworth, and Paterson, this volume). The Cochabamba conference adopted several demands that were anathema to mainstream climate politics. The Bolivian government struggled to put these (and a few others) into official UN texts:

- 50 per cent reduction of greenhouse gas emissions by 2017;
- stabilising temperature rises to 1°C and 300 parts per million;
- acknowledging the climate debt owed by developed countries;
- full respect for human rights and the inherent rights of indigenous people;
- universal declaration of rights of Mother Earth to ensure harmony with nature;
- establishment of an International Court of Climate Justice;
- rejection of carbon markets and commodification of nature and forests through the REDD programme;
- promotion of measures that change the consumption patterns of developed countries;
- end of intellectual property rights for technologies useful for mitigating climate change; and
- payment of 6 per cent of developed countries' GDP to addressing climate change (http://cochabamba2010.typepad.com/blog/2010/08/the-proposals-of-peoples-agreement-in-the-texts-for-united-nations-negotiation-on-climate-change.html).

As Edgardo Lander (2010) explained in his review of the Cochabamba conference,

> [s]truggles for environmental or climate justice have managed to bring together most of the most important issues/struggles of the last decades (justice/equality, war/militarization, free trade, food sovereignty, agribusiness, peasants' rights, struggles against patriarchy, defense of indigenous peoples' rights, migration, the critique of the dominant Eurocentric/colonial patterns of knowledge, as well as struggles for democracy, etc., etc.). All these issues were debated in Cochabamba and, to some degree, present in the Cochabamba Peoples' Agreement.

Cochabamba was a critical moment for generating positions and a Climate Justice manifesto, in part because several other uses of the term soon emerged. Grassroots social justice activists continued to radicalise these traditions when it became apparent, in the aftermath of the Copenhagen Accord between leaders from Washington, Pretoria, Brasilia, Beijing and New Delhi (followed by the Obama Administration's bribery and bullying to gain more support, unveiled by WikiLeaks), that global-scale advocacy would not succeed (Bond 2012).

However, the Climate Justice movement has not been without internal tensions, divisions and politics. The REDD mechanism proved amongst the most important wedge issues within the Climate Justice community, for late in 2010 sharp controversies emerged at the Cancun COP16 over forest preservation as major U.S. environmental foundations attempted to resurrect market strategies. In 2013 at the World Social Forum, such pressure led to a 'No REDD in Africa' network accusing proponents of contributing to a potential 'genocide' (http://climatespace2013.wordpress.com/2013/04/08/launch-of-no-redd-in-africa-network-redd-could-cause-genocide/). In the United States, tensions between the Climate Justice approach and the group of NGOs comprising the Climate Action Network and 1Sky continued over whether legislative lobbying, social marketing and top-down co-ordination of consciousness-raising activities without further strategic substance (for example, TckTckTck in 2009) are more appropriate advocacy methodologies than bottom-up linkage of organic climate activism. In a letter to 1Sky in October 2010, a coalition self-described as 'grassroots' and allied organisations representing racial justice, indigenous rights, economic justice, immigrant rights, youth organising and environmental justice communities criticised the vast expenditures on congressional lobbying (estimated at more than $200 million), at the expense of movement building:

> [a] decade of advocacy work, however well intentioned, migrated towards false solutions that hurt communities and compromised on key issues such as carbon markets and giveaways to polluters. These compromises sold out poor communities in exchange for weak targets and more smokestacks that actually prevent us from getting anywhere close to what the science – and common sense – tells us is required (Movement Generation 2010).

In short, from the realisation that 'neoliberalized nature' was the new global-governance approach for environmental (and social) management (see Büscher, this volume), there emerged, in direct response, a new Climate Justice philosophy and ideology, principles, strategies and tactics. However, contradictions and gaps marked at least the first period of climate justice advocacy, and these deserve explicit mention especially in their manifestations at the annual COPs, but more generally in the failure to broaden the climate justice movement to new constituencies.

Core ideas

The concept of environmental justice has generated a core lineage of ideas, bringing together a number of important intellectual traditions and movements. Four key aspects include, firstly, anti-racist environmentalism in the 1980s–90s, which first conclusively linked social justice to geographically discrete ecological problems, but which transcended 'Not in My Backyard' arguments in favour of a system-transforming narrative (see Pellizzoni, this volume). Secondly, there were global-scale demands in the 1990s to recognise the 'ecological debt' owed by the North to the South, made by groups such as Acción Ecológica (based in Quito, Ecuador), as well as for much wider-ranging considerations of climate politics, leading up to the Kyoto Protocol negotiations. Thirdly, the late 1990s Jubilee campaign against Northern financial domination of the South added ecological debt to financial debt and soon compelled consideration of climate from a radical standpoint within the World Council of Churches and other faith movements. Finally, these strands were reinforced in the 2000s by the global justice movement, which came to the fore with the December 1999 Seattle World Trade Organisation (WTO) protest and challenged corporations and multilateral institutions with much greater force than in previous years (see Agyeman, Bullard and Evans 2003; Bullard 2013; Camacho 1998; see also Price, Saunders and Olcese, this volume).

Since the 2000s, the climate justice manifestation has grown in strength and prominence. At the time of the Reclaim Power CJA/CJN protest at the Copenhagen COP17, which was the high point of the climate justice movement's global-scale advocacy, Anne Petermann (2009) of the Global Justice Ecology Project defined the concept as follows:

> Climate Justice is the recognition that the historical responsibility for the vast majority of greenhouse gas emissions lies with the industrialized countries of the global north. It is the understanding that peasants, indigenous peoples, fisher-folk, women and local communities have been disproportionately affected by climate change, also by the fossil

fuel industry and by false solutions to climate change, including tree plantations, genetically modified organisms like crops, large scale hydro projects and agro-fuels. These are also the people least responsible for climate change. Climate Justice recognizes that instead of market based solutions, the sustainable practices of these peoples and communities should be seen as offering the real solutions to climate change. Climate Justice is the fundamental knowledge that climate change cannot be addressed through corporations and the market as these are the entities that caused the problem in the first place.

The development of climate justice politics has been built around an orientation to questioning the for-profit economy as the underlying cause of the climate crisis and an uncompromising opposition to market-based strategies (see Paterson, this volume). There is also an ambitious emphasis on emissions cuts (far greater than those proposed by UN negotiators) and a marked disdain for the inadequacy of official global-scale and most national climate mitigation efforts. In a rejection of technocratic and tinkering responses to climate change, there is a hostility to technological fixes and geo-engineering and, instead, a search for prefigurative post-carbon lifestyles and production systems (see Luke, this volume). Climate Justice activists seek explicit alliances with activists specialising in food sovereignty and land access (Via Campesina is typically central within Climate Justice mobilisations), decommodified water, renewable energy, economic justice and other overlapping struggles – given how many issues have climate implications. This is a feature of a broader orientation to the politics of the 'Global South' (not just North–South power adjustments) and an openness to fusing traditional Left and radical environmental politics with new 'Rights of Nature' strategies, ecofeminist and ecosocialist philosophies, and horizontalist political strategies and tactics, especially in concrete sites of struggle (see also Cudworth and McShane, this volume).

These ideas emerged from the early 2000s as the limits of prior climate advocacy efforts became clear. For many, the replacement of the phrase 'Climate Action' as a late 1990s slogan mobilising civil society with 'Climate Justice' occurred because of the ongoing failure of elite power deal-making in the COPs and acquiescence to the dominant mode of neoliberal public policy within the UN negotiating framework – especially the 1997 Kyoto Protocol – by the large environmental NGOs that for many years set the activist agenda. This acquiescence followed the persuasiveness of U.S. Vice President Al Gore's pledge that in exchange for adding carbon trading to the Kyoto Protocol, it would receive U.S. Senate endorsement – when in fact a few months earlier the vote *against* was 95–0 (in the Byrd-Hagel Global Warming/Climate Change Sense of the U.S. Senate Resolution). Those in Chicago who attempted to mimic Kyoto by establishing a voluntary carbon market were rewarded with bankruptcy in 2010, in part because neoconservative forces funded by petroleum and coal industry interests swayed public opinion towards a climate denialist perspective, fatally denting demand for emissions trading within the national economy that over the prior century was by far the world's largest greenhouse gas polluter (Lohmann 2006). Attempts by the Obama Administration to generate carbon trading legislation in 2009–10 simply failed in this context, although after Superstorm Sandy in October 2012 assisted Obama's re-election campaign against climate-denialist Mitt Romney, there was talk of reviving the neoliberal strategy in 2013 (Skocpol 2013).

The climate justice advocacy challenge to orthodox market-oriented environmentalism and failed insider deal-making surfaced as a formal movement beginning in 2007 at the UN COP13 climate summit in Bali, Indonesia. By then it was obvious that the era of extreme global state failure and market failure – i.e., because the 'externality' of pollution remained unaccounted for within capitalist production, trade, consumption and disposal – would continue unabated. Within months, these failures were amplified by a world capitalist crisis that had broken out in East Asia and soon threatened the world economy. The basic dilemma was the inability of global leaders to solve major environmental, geopolitical, social and economic problems; none of significance were properly addressed in world summits after 1987, the year that the Montreal Protocol on the ozone hole banned chlorofluorocarbons (see Death, this volume). The inadequacy of global climate negotiations, and the turn by the United Nations towards 'Type Two Partnerships' involving corporations, together generated enormous frustration in civil society. Indeed, by the time of the 2002 World Summit on Sustainable Development in Johannesburg, many activists had come to the conclusion that the UN was part of the problem, not the solution. This frustration was dramatized by a march of 30,000 against that UN summit in Johannesburg, from a poor neighbourhood in Alexandra across to Sandton (the wealthiest suburb in Africa) where the convention was held (Death 2010). This was at a time when South Africa had become the world's most unequal major country, Johannesburg had become a major site of conflict over water privatisation and carbon trading experimentation had begun in nearby Durban (Bond 2002, 2012; McDonald 2002).

In short, climate justice only arrived on the international scene as a coherent political approach in the wake of the failure of a more collaborative strategy between major environmental NGOs and the global managerial class. The first effort to generate a global climate advocacy movement in civil society was the Climate Action Network (CAN). But from 1997 in Kyoto, CAN adopted as its core strategy an emphasis on regular UN interstate negotiations aiming at minor, incremental emissions reductions augmented by carbon trading and related offsets. The cul-de-sac of CAN's commitment to carbon trading was confirmed when Friends of the Earth International broke away in 2010. But even before this, at the time of the December 2009 COP15, CAN's critics from the climate justice movement made the case for an alternative strategy with such force that they gained half the space reserved for non-governmental delegations in Copenhagen's Bella Centre.

Climate justice activists entered this terrain with a programme that was beyond the capacity of the global establishment to meet, even if 'science required' roughly a 50 per cent greenhouse gas emissions cut by 2020 and 90 per cent commitment for 2050, simply so as to prevent runaway climate change and keep temperature rises within reason (see Okereke and Charlesworth, this volume). But there was a broader agenda, and the CJN! network made the following five core demands at its founding meeting in Bali, in December 2007:

- reduced consumption;
- huge financial transfers from North to South based on historical responsibility and ecological debt for adaptation and mitigation costs paid for by redirecting military budgets, innovative taxes and debt cancellation;
- leaving fossil fuels in the ground and investing in appropriate energy-efficiency and safe, clean and community-led renewable energy;
- rights-based resource conservation that enforces indigenous land rights and promotes peoples' sovereignty over energy, forests, land and water; and
- sustainable family farming, fishing and peoples' food sovereignty.

To these ends, core concerns of climate justice activists included the decommissioning of the carbon markets so favoured by elites, massive investments in renewable energy, a thoroughly reformed agricultural system, public transport and other transformative infrastructure, production and disposal technologies. Strategically, however, it soon became evident that the next stage of the climate justice struggle was necessarily to retreat from a naively over-ambitious reform agenda at the global scale, given the adverse power balance. Instead of politely asking UNFCCC delegates to save the planet, the challenge for climate justice activists from Copenhagen in 2009 into the future would be to whistle-blow and prevent further deterioration in global environmental governance at the annual COPs, but in the meantime to intensify both local and national activism.

Key thinkers

One reason for the turn to local processes was the strongly autonomist orientation of some leading strategists for climate justice. They brought to the movement a conviction, first, that the prevailing global and national balance of forces favoured micro-level interventions in most settings, and second, that even where a few national states were run by self-described socialist leaders – especially Venezuela, Ecuador and Bolivia – there were nevertheless major contradictions between ecological ambitions and their economies' addiction to extractive industries, especially hydrocarbons. Thus, whereas 'Climate Justice' was occasionally declared as policy in such states, the reality was that sharp challenges to oil extraction were emerging from radical environmentalists and indigenous peoples in Amazon jungle sites, such as Ecuador's Yasuni Park and Bolivia's TIPNIS.

Still, the 2010 Cochabamba people's summit was a site for a few state elites, formal academics, NGO workers and organic activist intellectuals to mull over the nature of their demands. The conference reflected both activist experience and influences from key thinkers in the field. Since the climate justice perspective is a relatively new one, given that climate itself only gradually became a concern for environmentalists during the 1990s, the mix of formal analysis and activism only gradually created a cadreship of strategists. Strategic reflection within the Climate Justice movement has been largely based upon site-specific struggles, which began reaching critical mass in some of the hot-spots.

But the bigger challenge awaits a connecting-of-the-dots between such sites. The single biggest movement with the potential to generate such links is probably 350.org, whose visionary founder Bill McKibben – an economics professor from a small U.S. university – long avoided an explicit identification with Climate Justice so as to continue building a big tent of activists from across the spectrum. The tactical graduation of 350.org from publicity-oriented consciousness-raising to civil disobedience at the White House in 2012, to a 2013 divestment campaign – with more than 200 campaigning groups mainly at universities – aiming to defund fossil fuel corporations is a trajectory reflecting the necessity of growing militancy, more concrete local activities, and common campaigning strategies, tactics and targets.

Some of the other best-known names in environmental advocacy are firmly within the Climate Justice camp, having produced influential books, films and high-profile statements. These include Nnimmo Bassey (2011), Tom Goldtooth, Martin Khor, Kok Peng, Naomi Klein (2008), Avi Lewis, Annie Leonard (2009, 2010), Joan Martinez-Alier (2005), George Monbiot (2006), Sunita Narain (1990), Vandana Shiva (2009) and Pablo Solon and Walden Bello (2012). Other scholar-activists and critical academics have written specialist books about climate justice, including critiques of carbon trading, led by Larry Lohmann's seminal analyses and a special issue of *Development Dialogue* journal (2006); other authors or editors of important climate justice books include Praful Bidwai (2011), Steffen Böhm and Siddhartha Dabhi (2009), Gar Lipow (2012), Hilary Moore and Joshua Kahn Russell (2011),

Ted Nace (2009), Jonathan Neale (2008), Christian Parenti (2012), Brian Tokar (2010) and Chris Williams (2011). Those green-left intellectuals who are best known for promoting ecosocialism – e.g., Ian Angus (2010), David Barkin (2002), Uli Brand (2012), John Bellamy Foster (2002), Joel Kovel (2007), Michael Lowy (2001), Ariel Salleh (1997) and Derek Wall (2010) – typically utilise the climate justice movement's arguments as much as they rely upon the core insights from founders of the eco-feminism and environmental justice intellectual currents, e.g., Maria Mies (1997) and Robert Bullard (1990, 2013).

But beyond academia, there is no doubt that civil society organisations have done the most to contest the terrain of ideas about climate, simply by driving forward practical and political challenges to state and corporate power, ranging from the UN COPs to local emitters. As an illustration (with an English-language bias), some of the leading organisations and highest-profile personnel include the following:

- Accion Ecologica: Ivonne Yanez, Esperanza Martinez
- BiofuelWatch: Rachel Smolker
- Carbon Trade Watch: Joanna Cabello
- Climate Justice Alliance: Bente Andersen, Stine Gry
- Corporate Europe Observatory: Olivier Hoedeman
- Democracy Center: Jim Shultz
- Earth in Brackets: Anjali Appadurai
- Ecologistas en Accion: Tom Kucharz
- Fern: Jutta Kill
- Focus on the Global South: Nicola Bullard, Dorothy Guerrero
- Friends of the Earth: Tord Björk, Michelle Chan, Siziwe Khanyile, Stephanie Long, Ricardo Navarro, Karen Orenstein, Lucia Ortiz, Bobby Peek, Asad Rehman, Joseph Zacune
- Gender CC: Nina Somera
- Global Alliance for Incinerator Alternatives: Ananda Tan, Neil Tangri, Mariel Vilella
- Global Exchange: Shannon Biggs
- Global Justice Ecology Project: Jeff Conant, Orin Langelle, Anne Petermann
- Grassroots Global Justice: Sha Grogan-Brown, Michael Guerrero, Jen Soriano, Cindy Wiesner
- Indigenous Environmental Movement: Ben Powless, Clayton Thomas-Muller
- Institute for Policy Studies: Daphne Wysham, Janet Redman
- Jubilee South: Beverly Keene, Lidy Nacpil
- Leave it in the Ground: Kjell Kuhne
- National Forum of Forest Peoples, Forest Workers: Soumitra Ghosh
- OilChange: Steve Kretzmann
- Our World is Not for Sale Trade, Climate Working Group: Deborah James, Karen Lang
- PanAfrican Climate Justice Alliance: Robert Chimambo, Michele Maynard, Mithika Mwenda, Noah Zimba
- Peoples Movement on Climate Change: Maria Theresa Nera-Lauron
- Platform: Kevin Smith
- REDD-Monitor: Chris Lang
- Red Ecologista Autónoma de la Cuenca de México: Miguel Valencia
- Rosa Luxemburg Foundation: Judith Dellheim, Tadzio Mueller
- South Asian Dialogue on Ecological Democracy: Soumya Dutta
- TransNational Institute: Praful Bidwai

- Via Campesina: Mary Lou Malig
- What Next: Niclas Hallstrom
- World Development Movement: Tim Jones, Kirsty Wright
- World Network: Lim Li Lin, Chee Yoke Ling, Meena Raman, Dale Wen
- World Rainforest Movement: Ana Filippini, Winnie Overbeek

It is, however, worth acknowledging that at least three well-regarded personalities whose climate advocacy has a very high profile – Kumi Naidoo of Greenpeace, Mary Robinson (ex-President of Ireland) and David Suzuki (geneticist and broadcaster) – are not Climate Justice proponents in terms of the definitions and movement priorities described previously, given that they (or their organisations) favour keeping the carbon trading option on the strategic table. For example, in relation to the Clean Development Mechanism, in spite of all the evidence to the contrary, Robinson argued in a 2011 London School of Economics lecture that carbon trading is 'finally starting to reap dividends for Africa and least developed countries' and that 'the experience gained through the design and implementation of success-ful regional cap-and-trade programs is hugely valuable if shared with developing country regional groups' (Robinson 2011). Other leading climate thinkers whose ambivalence about market mechanisms might also leave them outside the CJ camp include Tom Athanasiou, Mark Lynas, Peter Newell and Matthew Paterson (see Newell and Paterson 2010; Paterson, this volume). Another category of those concerned with much more legalistic notions of justice applied to climate (e.g., per capita pollution rights – hence not empowering base organisations or contemplating wider-scale socio-economic transformation) includes influ-ential lawyers such as Eric Posner and Cass Sunstein (2007), amongst others.

Another line of tension has developed over whether a 'right to development' should be invoked to permit higher levels of emissions in emerging market economies. Because cli-mate justice has always included an emphasis on South–North justice, and because interstate diplomatic negotiations over climate are the main site for this struggle, organisations such as the South Centre (led by Khor) and Third World Network (led by Meena Raman), as well as the Bolivian government, have stressed the ongoing importance of the UN COP terrain (Tandon 2009). In addition, Malaysian political economist Jomo Kwame Sundaram (2010) argued on behalf of the United Nations Department of Economic and Social Affairs that the semi-peripheral countries should have carbon-space rights to industrialise as part of climate justice. In contrast, Solon and Bello (2012) have argued strongly against the Brazil-Russia-India-China-South Africa (BRICS) countries' strategy of delaying binding emissions cuts: 'The elites of emerging economies are using the just demand of "historical responsibility" or "common but differentiated responsibility" in order to win time and have a weak bind-ing agreement by 2020 that they will be part of'. These are some of the areas where, from below, critical potentials exist to transcend older, nationalist framings, by ensuring that a full critique of the BRICS' copy-cat accumulation processes is offered by Climate Justice activ-ists across the Global South.

Critical potential

In order to overcome the barriers that exist to climate justice at the global scale and in the South–North confrontations discussed previously, and in order to build the climate justice movement from direct local experiences, the most sophisticated activists have redoubled ef-forts in key sites of struggle across the world, such as Nigerian and Ecuadorian oilfields,

Australia's main coal port, Britain's coal-fired power stations and main airport, Canada's tar sands, and U.S. coalfields, oil pipelines and corporate headquarters (see Price, Saunders and Olcese, and Watts and Peluso, this volume). To illustrate this in the most difficult setting – the United States – in 2010 the Detroit Social Forum began to consolidate progressive U.S. climate justice networking, featuring struggles led by people of colour. In a letter criticising the Washington-centric character of major environmental group lobbying, Movement Generation and its allies provided an impressive list of direct action events and resulting community organising victories in the United States, in various categories:

> stopping King Coal with community organising; derailing the build-up of coal power; preventing the proliferation of incinerators; defeating Big Oil in our own backyards; stopping false solutions like mega hydro; and building resilient communities through local action. (Movement Generation 2010)

Climate justice strategist Janet Redman (2012) noted how, just after Obama's re-election, North American activists were 'already building alternatives to our fossil-fueled economy while making their communities more resilient to climate disruption'. Examples of this grassroots activism, Redman (2012) observes, include

> WeACT in West Harlem, who are fighting for bus-rapid transit as a way to reduce greenhouse gas emissions, create public sector jobs and protect residents' health; the New York City Environmental Justice Alliance's Waterfront Justice Project – the Big Apple's first citywide community resiliency campaign – who are working to protect communities from toxic inundation during storm surges; the Right to the City and Grassroots Global Justice Alliance groups like CAAAV, Picture the Homeless, Make the Road and many more, who work to end displacement and economic inequality (which render families particularly vulnerable when climate disasters hit); Ironbound Community Corporation, a member of the Global Alliance for Incinerator Alternatives and the New Jersey Environmental Justice Alliance, who are crafting 'Zero Waste' solutions that create recycling and composting jobs while drastically reducing climate and toxic pollution from landfills and incinerators; and the Indigenous Environmental Network which has been working with Indigenous communities throughout Canada and the United States, fighting to protect their lands from fossil fuel development like tar sands mines and the Keystone XL, Kinder Morgan, and Enbridge Northern Gateway pipelines.

The highest-profile U.S. climate activism – albeit not Climate Justice in tone – was arranged by 350.org in August–September 2011, when 1,252 people were arrested at the White House during protests against the probable import of tar sands oil through the Keystone XL pipeline. This followed scores of localized victories against Big Coal, especially coal-fired power plants. According to the sub-movement's lead chronicler, Ted Nace (2011), '[S]ustained and passionate grassroots activism is challenging the idea that fossil fuels are the only option. Many governments have backtracked or shelved plans in response to political pressure or legal actions'. These reforms follow the strategy to 'Leave the Oil in the Soil, the Coal in the Hole, the Tar Sand in the Land, and the Fracking Shale Gas under the Grass'. Campaigns to prevent extraction from Yasuni Park in Ecuador, Norway's Lofoten region and various anti-fracking sites are indicative of the broad-based coalitions required (Bond 2012). The strategies of climate activists include the most progressive forms of juridical action to name and collect ecological debt (such as that Chevron owes Ecuador for Texaco's decades-old damage or that BP owes for its 2010 Gulf oil spill – both contested in the Ecuadoran courts). The activists can build transition towns, or generate plans to detox areas of carbon-intensive industry (as in sites such as Oakland, California and South Durban in South Africa). They can encourage extraction-site protests (such as in the Niger Delta and West Virginia) and work towards regional and then national bans on new emissions (even the first Obama administration made some minor progress on coal-fired power plants). They can foster a post-consumerist mentality (e.g., the *Story of Stuff* series, which has around 40 million internet downloads – http://www.storyofstuff.org; see also Brooks and Bryant, and Wapner, this volume), and they can also contemplate 'ecosocialist' argumentation and long-term environmental planning (e.g., http://ecosocialisthorizons.com/).

Some activists and theorists (for example, those associated with the journals *Capitalism Nature Socialism* and *Monthly Review*) anticipate that the linkage of red and green struggles under the climate justice banner will require society moving from a fossil fuel dependent capitalism to eco-socialism. This will entail, as Joel Kovel and Michael Lowy (2009) explain,

> a transformation of needs, and a profound shift toward the qualitative dimension and away from the quantitative . . . a withering away of the dependency upon fossil fuels integral to industrial capitalism. And this in turn can provide the material point of release of the lands subjugated by oil imperialism, while enabling the containment of global warming, along with other afflictions of the ecological crisis . . . The generalization of ecological production under socialist conditions can provide the ground for the overcoming of the present crises. A society of freely associated producers does not stop at its own democratization. It must, rather, insist on the freeing of all beings as its ground and goal.

Before such a vision can be properly articulated, several critical missing elements must be accounted for. Some of these issues include the question of how to achieve a stronger labour input, particularly given the potential for 'green jobs' to make up for existing shortfalls. British eco-socialists have taken the lead here, with demands for a million green jobs (Neale 2011). It is also necessary to draw an explicit connection between climate justice and anti-war movements, given that military activity is not only disproportionately concerned with supplies of oil and gas (Iraq and Afghanistan) but also uses vast amounts of CO_2 in the prosecution of war (Smolker 2010). There is also a requirement to foster a stronger presence of both environmentalists and socialists in many high emissions sites not yet suffused with grassroots climate justice movements, from China to the Arab oil world to petro-socialist Venezuela.

However, against eco-socialist orientations of the sort proposed by Kovel and Lowy, there are not only climate justice movement anarchists suspicious of central planning, but advocates of a bottom-up socialism who would preferably generate manifesto statements from actual practice – such as the efforts described briefly previously – and from generalised movement sensibility and demands, as opposed to top-down pronouncements. The forging of unity in movements that address climate and social justice from below is especially important during times of apparently intractable conflict and division, which at the time of writing appear to have disrupted and distracted the immediate future of climate justice politics.

Meanwhile, the feminist and socialist movements are engaged in dialogues with climate justice activists that are worth considering (see Cudworth, this volume). Teresa Brennan (2003) makes the link from the household scale to climate change, which is the biggest crisis women will face in the coming decades. Rearranging spatial and re/production arrangements is crucial to ending the unfair role of women in subsidising capitalism's destructive irrationality. In her book *Globalization and Its Terrors: Daily Life in the West,* Brennan wrote, '[t]he closer to home one's energy and raw material sources are, the more one's reproduction costs stay in line: paid and domestic labour will be less exploited, the environment less depleted' (2003: 8). The need now to limit the 'distance over which natural resources can be obtained' is obvious given how shipping, trucking and air transport contribute to carbon emissions (see Brooks and Bryant, and Litfin, this volume).

This is one of the insights an eco-feminist political economy gives climate justice strategists such as Nicola Bullard of Focus on the Global South. A typical debate with neoliberals is over whether the globalisation of industry has helped break up feudal-patriarchal relations, drawing women out of oppression into Mexican maquiladoras or Bangkok sweatshops. Such export-led growth is now an increasingly untenable 'development' strategy and, in any case, always generated extremely uneven development, drawing on the women's care economy for its hidden subsidies. Bullard (2009) likens the climate negotiations to those of the WTO: '[b]y and large, countries are defending their narrow economic interests and the rich countries in particular are trying to grab the last slice of the atmospheric pie'.

Bullard (2009) breaks down the climate policy narrative into three discourses: business as usual, catastrophism and climate justice. The first comes from business and most Northern governments, while the second, Bullard (2009) argues, is advanced by some smaller and vulnerable countries as well as many NGOs. Catastrophism also 'leads to dangerous last-gasp strategies such as geo-engineering, nuclear and carbon markets'. Third, feminists committed to climate justice are connecting the dots between these various oppressions, to warn how, in times of crisis, their opponents are emboldened. In a report, *Looking Both Ways,* the group Asian Communities for Reproductive Justice (2009) documents Hurricane Katrina's deeper political damage: '[f]ollowing a disaster, women of colour – particularly African American women, low-income women and immigrant women – are routinely targeted as burdens of the state and the cause of over population, environmental degradation, poverty, crime and economic instability' (see also Methmann and Oels, this volume). And more than for men, all eco-feminists with a climate justice orientation agree that ending women's economic instability is a vital component of the struggle for justice.

Conclusion

It has never been more important to draw together eco-feminist and eco-socialist insights to link issues, analyses, challenges and alliance-building efforts, for climate justice movements to fully thrive. Such a movement will have to emerge and rapidly build momentum if we are to survive, and *generational justice* will have to become more prominent, as the following challenges are addressed:

Red-green organisations are networking and expressing eco-socialist sentiments. The components of the eco-socialist movement are thousands of organisations in all parts of the world whose own assumptions about fighting environmental degradation are increasingly anti-capitalist. This is abundantly evident from the manifestos, analyses, press releases, demands, leaflets, slogans and other expressions of voice that they have generated in recent years. However, fragmentation and divisions prevent climate justice activists from having a coherent identity and impact.

The networks are typically single issue and do not sufficiently link across subsectors of environmental justice. The biggest intellectual problem these movements face is linking their concerns across other sectors. This is often because the networks come together around specific targets and because their funding sources or major in-house intellectual resources are extremely deep within the single issue they address, but unable to move beyond it (Harvey 1999).

Youth remain underrepresented in the movement. Although there are exceptions (e.g., Anjali Appadurai's high-profile role – at the Durban and Doha COPs – http://www.democracynow .org/2012/12/5/one_year_after_stirring_address_youth), the ability of young people to both organise and make major interventions in support of climate justice has been limited. Given the rise of universities as sites of fossil-fuel divestment campaigning, there are good prospects for a new cohort of intellectual, creative and strategic leadership to emerge.

The networks' analysis is sometimes delimited by the specific problem they are addressing. As single issue networks, the organisations generally view the attack by capitalism on nature as a problem that they may not be in a position to name, much less propose sweeping large-scale solutions to. That has generated a void, not only insofar as naming the problem (an environmentally voracious capitalism), but also naming a global-scale socialist solution – with, of course, profound respect for difference and the uneven development of both capitalism and the movements against it. A further problem is that most such manifestos by these movements have not been particularly conscious of gender. And finally, the other kinds of interlocking and overlapping oppressions and resistances – along lines of race, indigenous heritage, different ableness, sexual preference, generation and other divisions – are not sufficiently respected to generate a strong critique.

The networks' hunger to continue building links. The obvious next step for groups like CJN! is to make common cause with other movements addressing environmental issues where similar analysis, strategies, tactics, enemies and allies can be found. There is a huge gap, though, in information about each other, since with a few exceptions (for example, the World Social Forum, which had a vibrant 'Climate Space' in the 2013 Tunis meeting, or protests at major world summits or meetings of well-networked organisations such as Friends of the Earth International; see Solon 2013 and Death, this volume), these organisations have no opportunities to get together in a systematic way. And yet it is imperative that these links become ever stronger. It seems inexorable, too, that to properly address the challenge we face – nothing less than planetary and species survival – we confront the overarching power of patriarchal, racially divisive, uneven capitalist 'development'. Climate justice will require nothing less.

Further reading

In addition to books cited previously, especially by the key movement thinkers listed, there are other analysts who have studied climate justice activism – e.g., University of California-Santa Barbara sociologist John Foran at the International Institute for Climate Action and Theory (http://www.iicat.org/john-forans-iicat-research-portal/), University of Miami sociologist Ruth Reitan (http://www.as.miami.edu/international-studies/faculty/RuthReitan) and University of Pittsburgh sociologist Jackie Smith (http://mysite.verizon.net/vze182n3i/ id1.html).

Useful websites

International Institute for Climate Action and Theory: http://www.iicat.org/climate-justice-movements/
Earth in Brackets: http://www.earthinbrackets.org
Climate Space at the 2013 World Social Forum: http://climatespace2013.wordpress.com/
Durban Group for Climate Justice: http://www.durbanclimatejustice.org/
Climate Justice Now!: http://www.climate-justice-now.org/
Climate Justice Alliance: http://www.climate-justice-action.org/
Ecosocialist horizons: http://ecosocialisthorizons.com
Story of Cap and Trade: http://www.storyofstuff.org
Global Justice Ecology Project: http://globaljusticeecology.org/
World People's Conference on Climate Change and the Rights of Mother Earth: http://pwccc.wordpress
.com/

15 Limits

Gabriela Kütting

Introduction

This chapter is concerned with the concept of limits in global environmental politics and how it has been conceptualized over time. The idea of limits is fundamental, as the question of whether the finite nature of many of the world's resources needs to be overcome by cutting back on their usage, or can be overcome with technological progress, deeply divides many environmental researchers and thinkers. In this chapter, I will review and critically discuss the literature in this field and analyse how the conceptualization of limits has influenced environmental discourse.

The first major use of the concept of limits left the deepest imprint, namely the limits to growth debate in the early 1970s by Donatella Meadows and her co-authors, commissioned by the Club of Rome (Meadows, Meadows, Randers and Behrens III 1972). In the 1980s, with the rise of the environmental movement and the electoral success of green parties in some countries (see Price, Saunders and Olcese, this volume), the environmental discourse developed in two directions: one discourse embraced technological change and relegated to the side-lines the existence of physical limits, and the other continued to insist that there were physical limits to growth and that these needed to be heeded. This second perspective was explored from a variety of directions, such as the steady state economy (e.g., Daly 1991, 1996), the contradictions of the concept of sustainable development (e.g., Redclift 1987, 1992), critiques of capitalism (e.g., Merchant 1992) and several others discussed here. In the more management-oriented fields of resource politics and environmental security, the concept of scarcity (Homer-Dixon 1991, 1999) gained traction.

In this chapter, I will outline how the various debates developed over time, as well as the ideological differences over the role of limits in global environmental politics. The limits to growth debate will form a natural starting point, to be followed by a discussion of the division into techno-centric and eco-centric approaches to environmental politics and the role of limits in these discourses. In some ways or others, both the mainstream and more critical debates tended to apply concepts of natural limits or scarcity in a rather specialized way, namely limits on resource use. At the beginning of the new millennium, influenced by the increasing popularity of the study of civil society and a range of transnational actors, including individuals, in environmental politics, the debate has widened to encompass normative concerns with consumption and the sustainability of excessive consumption in industrialized countries (see Brooks and Bryant, this volume). Fundamentally, however, there is no constructive critical engagement finding common ground between those who see technological change as offering limitless opportunities and those who see the excessive use of finite resources (including air, water, atmosphere etc.) as the root cause of environmental problems and regard technological solutions as a 'band aid' treating superficial symptoms but not underlying causes.

Core ideas

The Club of Rome and limits to growth

The Club of Rome report was published at a time when the global environment and its precarious state first entered the spotlight. In 1972, the publication year of the report, the other big environmental event was the UN Conference on the Human Environment in Stockholm, which addressed the need for international cooperation on environmental problems for the first time (see Death and Whitehead, this volume). The Club of Rome report was the first highly methodical analysis to raise the issue that human and social organization relied on the consumption of finite natural resources and that these resources will come to an end at some stage. It is not as alarmist as it was portrayed by its critics, but rather aimed to start a debate on the finite nature of resources and how society should prepare for it.

The Club of Rome is an informal association of a group of scientists, academics, public officials and intellectuals as well as some representatives from the business world that formed in the 1960s around a common concern over global economic organization and its effects. They all felt that the rate of technological progress was based on the optimistic assumption that there was an unlimited range of possibilities for economic growth. However, the Club of Rome members argued in *The Limits to Growth* (Meadows et al. 1972) that the resources this expansion was built on had some clear natural limits and that society needed a view of the future and an awareness of the finite nature, or the limits, of the world's ecosystems and the resources society extracted from them. Their follow-up book, *Mankind at the turning point* (Mesarovic and Pestel 1974), put forward a revised version, but the original message that unlimited growth was unsustainable remained the same. While the Club of Rome's message was heatedly debated and often heavily criticized, it fueled a general debate and a political process examining environmental degradation and industrial activity.

A key theme in such neo-Malthusian debates (so-called because of their reference to an intellectual tradition dominated by Reverend Thomas Malthus, who in eighteenth-century England argued that human population growth would outrun food supply and lead to overshoot and collapse) is the metaphor of the 'tragedy of the commons'. Garrett Hardin (1968) was an American ecologist who argued that population growth would inevitably and tragically lead to the degradation of shared resources such as fish stocks, agricultural grazing land and so on. Referring to the practice of grazing land held in common – meaning free access of all – in medieval and early modern England, he claimed that each herdsman has a rational incentive to increase the size of their herd, but nobody has an incentive to protect or conserve the land. This is a classic collective action problem (see Wapner, this volume). Hardin argued that 'each man is locked into a system that compels him to increase his herd without limit – in a world that is limited. Ruin is the destruction to which all men rush, each pursuing his own best interest in a society that believes in the freedom of the commons. Freedom in a commons brings ruin to all' (1968: 1244).

Sustainable development

The dominant environmental discourse was thus framed around natural limits to economic growth. However, this concern with scarcity, and questioning growth, began to shift in the early 1980s towards more positive scenarios suggesting the possibility of sustainable economic growth. The *World Conservation Strategy* of the International Union for Conservation of Nature and Natural Resources (IUCN 1980) and the World Commission on Environment and Development's report *Our Common Future* (WCED 1987) shifted the discourse from 'limits to growth' to 'sustainable development' as the potential answer to the problems raised with the limits to growth debate (see Baker and Whitehead, this volume). Of these two reports, *Our Common Future* has become the seminal contribution of the 1980s to the subject of environmental degradation and economic development and introduced the concept of sustainable development into the mainstream debate. The chair of the Commission, Norwegian Prime Minister Gro Harlem Brundtland, was faced with competing interests and concerns. On the one hand, it was clear there was an ever more degraded natural environment and a clear threat to the quality of life of future generations; on the other hand, there were the interests of those (particularly in the developing world) who argued that continued economic growth was necessary to alleviate poverty and maintain standards of living. The Brundtland report reconciled these two camps by introducing a concept of growth that was sustainable and thus not harmful to the environment or future generations. This was achieved by a subtle position on the question of limits. As the report states,

> [t]he concept of sustainable development does imply limits – not absolute limits but limitations imposed by the present state of technology and social organization on environmental resources and by the ability of the biosphere to absorb the effects of human activities. But technology and social organization can be both managed and improved to make way for a new era of economic growth. (WCED 1987: 8)

The alternative to unlimited growth is thus defined not as zero growth but as sustainable growth. It is particularly noteworthy that the report denies the existence of 'absolute' limits as the quote suggests. This concept of sustainable development became hugely popular and has determined the direction of environmental and development discourses from the late 1980s onward (Baker 2006; Dryzek 2005; see also Baker and Whitehead, this volume).

However, the concept of sustainable development is quite often vaguely defined in terms of the needs of existing and future generations and has been interpreted by different political actors in often diametrically opposed ways (Death 2010; Dresner 2002). As a result, although sustainable development has become a household word, it does not have a concise or even consensual meaning. The definition used in the Brundtland report is that 'sustainable development is development that meets the needs of the present without compromising the ability of future generations to meet their own needs' (WCED 1987: 43). According to Redclift, there are at least two sets of contradictions that are evident once the concept is discussed in detail (1992: 399). First, there is a difference of emphasis in much of the debate. Some writers emphasize sustainability as a core issue because they see nature, or the environment, as being a natural constraint to economic growth and thus believe that the assumption of unlimited economic growth is fallacious and will exert a high price from society. These writers believe that the main challenge is to develop alternative technologies that do not rely on resource extraction to the same extent and will thus avoid the constraints of a limited resource base. Other writers find this strategy self-defeating as it does not address how human progress affects nature in itself and does not go to the root cause, namely the disconnect between nature and society.

To illustrate this with an example from the population debate, the Brundtland report (WCED 1987) states that present rates of population growth cannot continue and that population growth rates are the challenge solely of those nations with high rates of increase:

> Population growth and development are linked in complex ways. Economic development generates resources that can be used to improve education and health. These improvements, along with associated social changes, reduce both fertility and mortality

rates. On the other hand, high rates of population growth that eat into surpluses available for economic and social development can hinder improvements in education and health (chapter 4, point 7). When a population exceeds the carrying capacity of the available resources, it can become a liability in efforts to improve people's welfare (point 47).

However, the report does not take account of the fact that an additional person in an industrial country consumes far more and places far greater pressure on natural resources than an additional person in the developing world. Thus, the analysis put forward by the Brundtland Commission on the population issue rests on the assumption of two fundamental relationships, both of which must be balanced: there should be a balance between population size and available resources on the one hand, and between population growth and economic growth on the other.

Population is thus basically seen as an input problem at the national level. The question is whether there are enough natural resources to sustain a certain number of people within given national boundaries. There is also mention, in the report, of the fact that people should have equitable access to the overall resources pool, as such equitable access as well as further economic growth are both important means to lower fertility rates (WCED 1987: chapter 4).

While the Commission certainly pursues the laudable aim of providing equitable access to resources, this is combined with advocating further growth in order to eradicate poverty. For example, it proposed 'reviving growth' as the first 'critical objective' in the pursuit of sustainable development (WCED 1987: 49). Accordingly, the Report called for 'overall national income growth of around 5 per cent a year in the developing economies of Asia, 5.5 per cent in Latin America, and 6 per cent in Africa and West Asia' (WCED: 50). Yet, this is a problematic idea because the Commission's own figures in chapter one on poverty show that the rich are consuming the vast bulk of resources, which is the major reason for the environmental crisis to begin with. Thus, economic growth without redistribution cannot logically be sustainable; accordingly the Commission also called for a change in the character of economic growth to promote redistribution of resources. Yet the overall emphasis of the Brundtland Report tends to support the assumption that poverty is the cause of environmental degradation and that higher living standards will therefore reduce population growth and environmental degradation. Thus, the focus on human needs rejects the neo-Malthusian *Limits to Growth* argument that there are fundamental natural limits to human activity and progress.

Key thinkers

As such, there is a fundamental division of the environmental literature into those that believe in human progress/technology as the way forward out of the environmental crisis and the 'natural' limits to growth (encompassing positions from 'Promethean' rejections of environmental limits through to environment management proponents) and those that believe that the commodified relationship between society and nature has to change to ensure the survival of all on planet Earth (ranging from 'limits to growth' survivalists to political ecologists and green theorists). This dichotomy has persisted and still dominates the literature (see Dryzek 2005; and Whitehead, this volume).

The latter group implicitly accepts the existence of limits. Concepts here include Daly's notion of a 'steady state economy', which highlights the output of 'waste' in a fossil fuel economy as opposed to a steady state of material flows (1991), to Marxist critiques of industrial capitalism (Merchant 1992) and ecocentric critiques of human/nature dualism (Dobson

1990; Guha and Martinez Alier 1997). Traditionally, the literature focusing on the relationship between nature/environment and society/culture has identified the rise of modern capitalism and the associated rises of Enlightenment thinking, Newtonian science and the industrial revolution as the starting point of disturbed nature–society relations (see McShane, this volume). This view risks romanticizing the environmental impact of pre-industrial society (see Rudy and White, this volume). There have been several studies (Chew 2001; Ponting 1991) that have demonstrated that pre-industrial or pre-modern capitalist societies also engaged in practices resulting in widespread environmental degradation. However, it is often argued that these degrading practices had a local or regional rather than global impact and that modern capitalism and its social relations are the only forms of social organization that actually leads to *global* environmental degradation. The global nature of environmental degradation can largely be linked to the rise of the fossil fuel economy and the decreasing distance of time and space in the relations between different parts of the globe (Daly 1996). This point has been analysed in detail by global political economists such as ecological world systems writers (Chew 2001; Goldfrank, Goodman and Szasz 1999; Hornborg 1998).

Ecological world systems theory

The main argumentative thrust of this type of analysis suggests that the rise and fall of world civilizations can be traced to environmental degradation as a main contributory factor to the decline of empires and civilizations. Accordingly, they argue, the nature of capitalism can be understood through the social relations of production, labour and the environment. Ponting (1991), in his environmental history of the world, advances a similar argument. These are views of history that integrate an environmental or ecological perspective into predominantly social historical accounts. They are also views that include an account of environment-society relations as connections that are made between productive and consumptive relations and economic performance, as well as the negative impact of environmental degradation on economic performance. So from this point of view an ecological world systems approach can offer an interesting alternative to the historical materialist orthodoxy that argues that society–environment relations changed fundamentally with the rise of modern capitalism. Instead, it argues that environmental degradation is intrinsically linked to regimes of accumulation that existed in prior forms of economic organization.

The main argument of Chew's (2001) thesis, for example, is that different phases in world history and the rise and fall of trading relations can be analysed from a historical materialist perspective, as done by Wallerstein (1986) or Frank (1998), and can focus on the social relations of production. However, these approaches neglect the relationship between nature/natural resources and the material basis of production. In fact, the demise of most empires or large powers also coincides with a decline in the natural resource base through over-exploitation or other exhaustion, which he terms *dark ages* (see also Diamond 2005). Forensic research suggests that even the two historical periods of the dark ages are linked to the depletion of the natural resource base, and this has been documented in carbon testing from these areas (Chew 2001). So, for example, the dark ages in Germany and Sweden are accompanied by a decline in forestation, and the local economies started to recover once reforestation had taken place. This type of pattern is reproduced over time and over space, and a strong argument can be made that environmental degradation is an important factor in world system formation and decline, showing once again that social systems, whether global or local, are embedded in natural systems – and by extension the idea of natural limits.

Environmental security

Another influential thinker for the topic of limits is Thomas Homer-Dixon, whose research on security and global environmental politics introduces a slightly different perspective on the notion of scarcity. Environmental security became a popular field of study in the 1990s and is a significant element of the global environmental politics literature (see Dalby, this volume). The dominant approach here focuses on the impact of environmental problems and conflicts for the national security of states (Barnett 2001; Dalby 2009). Environmental problems are seen as the triggers of conflict, and the aim of the mainstream discipline of environmental security is to prevent or problematize such conflicts. A seminal writer in the field is Thomas Homer-Dixon who developed three hypotheses relating to environmental security and the relationship between environmental change, scarcity and conflict (1991, 1999). The first is that diminishing resources can lead to war and insurrection as distributional conflict, as found in traditional accounts of international conflict. However, the second hypothesis is that ecological collapse, the other side of the coin of diminishing resources, can cause losses of livelihoods and thus large scale migration, which can also lead to conflict. Thirdly, diminishing resources can lead to distributional conflict other than armed conflict between the inhabitants of the territory affected. Homer-Dixon uses a methodology that reduces environmental security to a single variable explanation, and his view has come under much scrutiny (see discussions in Barnett 2001 and Dalby 2009). In other words, he uses scarcity as the single explanatory variable for the existence of environmental security. Gleditsch (1999) and others in their research have not upheld this clear and direct relationship between environmental change and conflict, while Baechler (1999a) sees environmental security as a multi-factor issue, scarcity being one of the dominant ones. This position is close to Homer-Dixon but takes into account a broader range of factors.

Critical potential

The concept of limits is thus central to core environmental concerns about planetary health and civilizational survival, poverty and population, and environmental conflict. Many critical thinkers, in rejecting the notion of a fixed or essential nature, have also turned their back on the idea of limits (see Rudy and White, this volume). However, the fundamental environmental insight that we are part of a finite and bounded ecosystem has informed more recent critiques of the present day economy and its cultural component, the institution of consumption or the nature of global consumerism (see Brooks and Bryant, this volume).

The environmental dimensions of consumption are major considerations for several reasons. First of all, the social and structural origins of environmental degradation can be found in the excessive consumption of the planet's resources. Second, the dominant neoliberal or even liberal approach in global management institutions is based on the assumption that the current standard of living enjoyed by the richest 20 per cent of the world population can be extended to the whole globe. In terms of resource availability, this is clearly a myth and raises a multitude of questions regarding global equity and environmental feasibility (Wallis 2011). Third, consumption is not the last stage in the production chain as classic economic theory suggests; rather, the last stage is disposal of the product consumed. Waste is a serious environmental problem not just for local authorities but globally, and it affects the earth's capacity to act as a sink.

The early environmental movement in the 1970s, heavily influenced by the Club of Rome publications, questioned the contemporary ideology of consumerism and argued that excessive consumption would lead to the ecological collapse of the planet. Rather, there should be an ideological shift to considering what people actually *need* for a fulfilled life rather than *want,* i.e., a questioning of the possibility of unlimited economic growth and the belief in the further rise in the standard of living of those who had already achieved a high level (Daly 1996; Dresner 2002). This movement coincided with the first oil crisis in 1973 when the Arab oil exporting countries exposed an embargo and there were fuel shortages in the Western world. Since then, the idea that there are insufficient resources has often seemed to be discredited by the discovery of new oil fields and the introduction of more energy-efficient technologies, which have pushed back the projected date of 'peak oil'. The date when oil will run out (or become too expensive to extract) has been continually revised from a predicted '20 years from now' (in the 1970s) to somewhere in the middle of the twenty-first century (The Economist 2009).

Periodic energy crises have led to a lot of alternative energy forms being created, and some existing resources are being recycled. Technological advancements make it possible to find replacements for some materials when the need arises. However, all this does not change the fundamental truth that there is only a fixed amount of resources on this planet, and although we are not in danger of running out just yet, these resources are being used up at an unsustainable rate by only a small, but quickly growing, part of the world population. What is more, it is not only a question of using up resources but also of degrading sinks, i.e., using ecosystems to deposit the wastes of the industrial production process. As a result, while there are no pending energy or resource shortages as a result of 'running out', it is clearly the case that many ecological limits have been reached with soil, air or water degradation and local degraded environments as well as biodiversity loss (Millennium Ecosystem Assessment 2005).

The neoliberal economic order, like its precursors, treats the natural environment as if there was an unlimited supply of natural resources. The goods and services provided by the planet are not calculated, unlike capital goods and resources owned by a supplier, and therefore they are externalized by economists and taken for granted in economic valuations. Environmental economists such as David Pearce have overcome this shortcoming by integrating previously 'free' goods into the economic system through price mechanisms, but in essence, this still does not change the fundamental paradox of externalizing the resource or energy supply that underlies social survival (Pearce, Markandya and Barbier 1989; Pearce and Barbier 2001). In addition, the pricing of environmental goods means they can become luxury goods and therefore only available to those who can afford them, such as is the case with the privatization of water in many developing countries or the pricing mechanism where places with high air quality are luxury neighborhoods in many urban areas. This often makes environmental quality a preserve of the rich rather than a human right and raises questions of equity and access (see Bond, this volume). Every inhabitant of this planet has been exposed to some form of environmental degradation, and suffered a decline in conditions of living because of it, and is therefore aware of the limited capacity of the planet to cope with the rate of extraction of resources and depositing of waste. Therefore, the need for creating a careful balance between environmental and societal needs is abundantly clear. This leads us back to questions of consumption, agency and responsibility.

Whatever our perspective is on resources and their distribution, existing resource consumption can be likened to a 'global cake' that is eaten by the world population. The figure of the 80 per cent of resources being consumed by 20 per cent of the world's population should be re-stated (Worldwatch Institute 2011). If the current rate of consumption in the Western world is to be reproduced globally (which is, after all, the promise of the neoliberal free market economy), then five times as many resources or five additional planet Earths would be needed (Wallis 2011). Clearly, these are not available. That brings us back to the two solutions of the techno-centric versus the eco-centric view: either technological progress makes the resources stretch for such an expansion, or consumption rates have to be adjusted. Alternatively, the assumption that prosperity for all can be achieved has to be abandoned, and we need to acknowledge that there is a privileged pool of excessive consumers. In practice, these decisions are made by the ones for whom sacrifice would be a moral choice, not by those who sacrifice chronically and involuntarily (see Wapner, this volume). In other words, such choices would be made by the consumers of the 80 per cent of resources, not by the disempowered majority.

Thomas Princen's (2005) argument for sufficiency as one of the recent path-breaking texts on consumption issues does not suggest a notion of sacrifice or of a radical lifestyle change. Rather, it is based on questioning the logic that efficiency as defined by economies of scale, and that instant maximized profits without regard for the future, is the best organizing principle for economy and society. Princen approaches this as an eco-centric resource-use specialist and thus neatly slots into (and was indeed one of the founding thinkers of) a growing body of literature that addresses this point from a variety of disciplines. Consumer psychology writers have conducted studies that show that instant gratification and indiscriminate material consumption actually lead to less rather than more happiness (Kasser 2002; see Wapner, this volume). A burgeoning literature on the ethics of consumption has questioned neoliberal values underlying lifestyles (see Brooks and Bryant, this volume). Of course, there are also various civil society movements, such as the voluntary simplicity movement, the local currency movement, and others, doing similar things (see Price et al., this volume).

Thus, there are different levels at which the equity dimension of resource consumption/distribution is a problem at the international/global level. First, there is the agenda-setting power of the various states of the world when it comes to environmental degradation (see Death, this volume). Second, there is their position in the world economy. Third, there is the issue of purchasing power and consumption. Agenda-setting power is an indirect, structural type of power (on types of power relation see Lukes 1974; Barnett and Duvall 2005), but equity concerns are by no means limited to structural power. Equity problems can also be found in direct power relations between North and South or between any social groupings. Although coercion by violent means is a relatively rare phenomenon in the international system given the number of actors in it, the number of violent conflicts with an environmental or resource dimension is rising (Gleditsch 2001; see also Watts and Peluso, this volume). In addition, there are issues of financial and political coercion, which have become especially obvious through colonialism and modern forms of neo-colonialism. The framing of environmental limits is thus directly shaped by the exercise of power through global economic institutions. Thus, although the dominant framing of the sustainable development debate tends to focus on production, the existence of environmental limits forces us to consider questions of individual consumption. If the consumption side of the global political economy was included in economic analysis of environmental degradation, a different picture of responsibility and duty would arise, but also a different framework for the concept of limits would need to be devised.

When the political and economic elites met in Rio de Janeiro in June 2012 for the Rio+20 Summit to discuss new policies towards a more sustainable world, the hope placed in a green economy as a way forward towards more equity and a cleaner, healthier world featured prominently on the agenda (UN 2012; see also Death, this volume). Many economists, political scientists, the World Bank, the United Nations Environment Programme (UNEP) and the Organisation for Economic Co-operation and Development (OECD) have engaged with the notion of the green economy in recent years, and some have seemed to suggest that green growth may be a 'magic solution', offering new economic sectors with continued growth, new jobs and wealth increases while at the same time defusing the environmental crisis (OECD 2011).

However, critical voices have suggested a more cautious view, arguing that on a finite planet with an ever-increasing population and demands on existing resources, continued economic growth will not be able to guide the way to more equitable distributions of material well-being or environmental goods and bads, nor will it lead to a noticeable reduction in environmental degradation (Brand 2012; see also Whitehead, this volume). Most economists, political commentators and public policy makers see green growth as desirable and necessary. However, as Brand argues, 'what is usually described, is the potential of a green economy, whereas the obstacles and opposing interests are hardly addressed. There is a belief, akin to the beginning of the sustainable development discourse 20 years ago, that comprehensive win-win situations should be promoted. And there is firm trust in existing political and economic institutions and elites that are able and willing to guide this process' (2012: 20). The debates around the emerging concept of a green economy suggest that the concept reproduces the same difficulties associated with sustainable development in general, which is that between eco-centric and techno-centric world views. Moreover, the vital question of individual consumption is not generally addressed in such debates.

Conclusion

The concept of limits is one of the central issues both in environmental debates in general and in global environmental politics; indeed it lies at the heart of the philosophical debates underlying environmental studies. The environmental literature is ideologically divided over whether the finite nature of many of the earth's resources can be counterbalanced with technological advances and 'green' technologies that are less dependent on the resource base, or alternatively, if a fundamental change in the consumption habits of the planet's inhabitants is necessary to overcome the natural limits to economic growth. This ideological conflict can be traced through all debates, starting from the discourse on the limits to growth and the tragedy of the commons, to its supposed resolution with the concept of sustainable development, and through to more recent concerns with environmental security, individual consumption and the new green economy debate. Thus, 'limits' has inherently become an ideological concept, too, firmly entrenched in this ideological divide. The current debates on the green economy reproduce the same ideological divides, and differing interpretations of how society can address ecological limits is again at the heart of the conflict. Thus, the concept of limits is at the very core of environmental thought and policy. A critical environmental politics of limits will need to address the issue of inequitable consumption, and it will also need to rise above the seemingly intractable ideological disputes between eco-optimists and eco-pessimists.

Further reading

More detailed reading on limits includes Herman Daly (1991) *Steady State Economics,* Second edition, Washington DC: Island Press; Jared Diamond (2005) *Collapse: How Societies Choose to Fail or Survive,* London: Penguin; and Thomas Princen (2005) *The Logic of Sufficiency,* Cambridge, MA: MIT Press. For a historical treatment of the concept of limits, it would be useful to look at Gareth Hardin (1968), 'The tragedy of the commons', *Science* 162 (3859), 1234–1248; for a neo-Malthusian approach see Meadows et al. (1972), as well as the Brundtland Commission (WCED 1987). For current debates on the green economy, reports by the OECD (2011) as well as the UNEP (http://www.unep.org/greeneconomy/) are useful reading.

Useful websites

The United Nations Environment Programme: Green Economy: http://www.unep.org/greeneconomy/
OECD: Green Growth and Sustainable Development: http://www.oecd.org/greengrowth/oecd workongreengrowth.htm
Worldwatch Institute: http://www.worldwatch.org/
New Economics Institute: http://neweconomicsinstitute.org/
The Club of Rome: 40 Years 'Limits to Growth': http://www.clubofrome.org/?p=326

16 Localism

Karen Litfin

Introduction

'Eat local,' 'buy local,' 'it takes a village . . .' Paradoxically, just as trade, travel, and communication have been globalized, a broad and diverse movement of movements is calling for the relocalization of life. Globalization – or at least a certain disenchantment with it – has evidently spawned the resurgence of the local. Simultaneously, the social alienation engendered by other up-scaling trends like suburbanization and mega-urbanization fuels this resurgence of the local. Localism is therefore an inherently critical approach to environmental politics as well as other dimensions of political, economic, and cultural life.

This resurgence comes from three cross-cutting currents. First, globalization's critics promote relocalization on social, economic, and ecological grounds. A world where we know who grows our food, who produces our goods, and where our waste goes, they argue, will be a more just, convivial, and ecologically resilient world. Second, energy analysts make a more pragmatic argument: given that petroleum production has most likely reached its peak, we have now entered the era of energy decline (International Energy Agency 2010; see also Kütting, this volume). Relocalization, therefore, is not a choice; it is inevitable, and the sooner we embark upon the transition, the more graceful will be our descent. Third, top-down solutions to globalization's calamities have been too little, too late. Forty years of 'green diplomacy' have yielded little more than a host of toothless treaties and a planet on the verge of biospheric collapse (Barnosky et al. 2012; see also Death, this volume). No wonder, then, that so many people favor the near over the far. In contrast to the placeless and faceless global, the local holds out the promise of real relationships with real people and places. From all of these perspectives, localism is a healthy adaptive response to a rapacious and dysfunctional globalism.

Yet, as a purely reactive strategy, localism risks losing its progressive liberating potential. First, if the movement for a just sustainability reverts to the local, it effectively cedes the vast territory of the global to those forces that currently occupy that ground – most obviously multinational corporations and the political institutions serving their agenda. Second, the plain fact is that the lifestyles of the affluent have a global reach. Even if we pedal to the farmers market for our groceries, chances are that our bicycles were manufactured in China and our food grown with imported petroleum (see Brooks and Bryant, this volume). Third, there is something unseemly about the primary beneficiaries of globalization retreating to their local havens just as the planetary system reaches the precipice. Fourth, even in the improbable event that we could revert to the local, so long as transnational transportation exists, climate refugees and other uninvited guests will find their way into our communities (see Methmann and Oels, this volume). Finally, and most intriguingly, governance in the

Anthropocene will likely include a strong global component (see Baker, this volume). While the requisite political and economic institutions are nowhere in sight, this is the challenge before us. The global, therefore, is not so easily supplanted by valorizing the local.

For all its maladies, globalization is an unprecedented human one, I will argue, that may be far from complete if we choose wisely today. With greater integrative synergies, the resurgence of the local can serve as a progressive strategy rather than a mere recoil from the global. Indeed, in some important ways, it already is; my aim here is to amplify these efforts. In this chapter, I first describe the core ideas informing localism as a critical approach to environmental politics, distinguishing between its adaptive and regressive variants. I then trace the work of several key localist thinkers from the 1970s to the 2000s, showing how the case for localism has been strengthened by the twin phenomena of globalization and peak oil. Finally, I return to the question of progressive versus regressive variants. If localism is to actualize its critical potential, then it must move beyond – and not merely against – globalism as presently constituted. Organic globalism represents such a higher order synthesis, one that understands the world as a nested hierarchy of living systems, from the cell to the Earth system, and seeks to harmonize human systems with living systems at every level. We find evidence of such a higher order synthesis in the emergence of global activist networks with a strong localist agenda (see Bond and Price, Saunders, and Olcese, this volume). A plethora of Action Networks – Climate, Rainforest, Pesticide, Basel, etc. – and organizations ranging from the International Consortium of Local Environmental Initiatives (ICLEI) to La Via Campesina all point to an incipient organic globalism (see Bond, this volume). By simultaneously reinvigorating the local and democratizing the global, these groups are helping to realize localism's critical potential.

Core ideas

From an environmental vantage point, the rationale for localism is simple: all things being equal, a local economy will have lower energy requirements and therefore be ecologically friendlier (see Whitehead, this volume). Proponents of localism, however, are adamant that the psychological, social, cultural, political, and moral benefits are at least as significant. Localizers frequently deploy the term *human-scale,* implying that large-scale enterprises – multinational corporations, global supply chains, nuclear reactors, and the like – are fundamentally dehumanizing. This was E.F. Schumacher's point when he declared forty years ago that 'small is beautiful' (1973).

In the intervening years, the human and ecological consequences of 'bigness' have become more dire and far-reaching. The second half of the twentieth century saw a phenomenal rise in the speed, volume, and geographic scope of commerce, spurred on by new technologies as well as international trade, finance, and development institutions. A key function – arguably *the* key function – of most governments during this period was to facilitate the movement of goods and capital. Indeed, in the minds of many, the very notion of human progress was associated with bigger, faster, farther, and more. Globalization was fueled by nonrenewable fossil fuels, with petroleum at the helm. This extravaganza of energy consumption generated unprecedented growth in both human numbers and material wealth, but the attendant pollution, capital flight, and social displacement left in their wake devastated communities and ecosystems on every continent. No wonder, then, that the trickle of complaints in the 1980s became, by the turn of the century, a diverse movement for global justice and sustainability. As many as a million initiatives, from organic farms to labour unions to indigenous people's organizations, constitute this far-flung movement of movements (Hawken 2007; see also Bond and Price et al., this volume). Weaving through these movements is a strong thread of localism.

In their recent anthology on localization, Thomas Princen and Raymond DeYoung suggest that the primary concern is 'how to adapt institutions and behaviors to live within the limits of natural systems' (DeYoung and Princen 2012: xvii). They predict a shift from the *centrifugal* forces of globalization to the *centripetal* forces of localization. Whereas the former is associated with concentrated economic and political power, cheap and abundant resources, intensive commercialization, displaced wastes, and abstract modes of communication, the latter is associated with diffuse leadership, sustainable production and consumption, personal proficiency, and community self-reliance.

Ecological concerns are surely at or near the top of the localist agenda, particularly for those who foresee catastrophe and collapse (see Diamond 2005; Homer-Dixon 2006; Tainter 1988). Among localist concerns are climate change, the precipitous loss of biodiversity, and the depletion of freshwater. None, however, receives more attention than the zenith of global petroleum production sometime around 2007. With oil as the lifeblood of the global economy, this fact alone should make localizers of us all.

Key thinkers

For many of today's localizers, small is rendered inevitable by the reality of peak oil. A host of books such as *The Party's Over* (Heinberg 2005), *The Last Hours of Ancient Sunlight* (Hartmann 2000), and *Out of Gas* (Goodstein 2005) drive the point home. In laying out why 'small is inevitable', Rob Hopkins, a prominent localizer and founder of the Transition Towns movement, focuses on peak oil (Hopkins 2008: 68–78). As the master resource, energy propels every aspect of the economy: building, manufacturing, heating and cooling, and so on. And because the entire global economy – especially mining, transportation, and agriculture – is tied to petroleum, peak oil means *peak everything* (Heinberg 2007).

Aside from the inevitability of energy descent, there are other powerful arguments for localization. Again, the trickle of voices from decades past seems to be swelling into a flood. With growing concerns about climate and peak oil, for instance, Kirkpatrick Sale's bioregional writings from the 1980s enjoyed a revival in the new century (Thayer 2003). While Sale's bioregionalism, emphasizing both the psycho-social and ecological value of place-based identity, resonates well with contemporary localist movements, it lacks the thoroughgoing critique of global capitalism articulated during the same period by Murray Bookchin. In contrast to deep ecologists who tended to downplay social injustice, Bookchin's theory of social ecology roots environmental problems in social problems of domination and hierarchy. Likewise, Bookchin's notions of communalism and sustainable cities presage important elements of Transition Towns and other localist movements. Bookchin's recently reprinted seminal works, *Post-Scarcity Anarchism* (1971) and *The Ecology of Freedom* (1982), gained new relevance in the context of 'peak everything' and the anti-globalization movement.

Building upon the fact that place-based cultures have been the norm throughout human history, many localizers argue on anthropological grounds that people are more likely to flourish in place-based communities. Others promote local businesses and community ownership on the grounds of economic efficiency and social accountability (Shuman 2000). Still others see localization as a healthy response to the neocolonial model of development associated with globalization (Goldsmith and Mander 1997). And some, suggesting that democracy functions best in a regional context, claim that a powerful wave of decentralization is gaining momentum in the United States and other large countries (Alperovitz 2004). In their quest to green and humanize contemporary cities, urban planners are lending their voices to the growing choir (see Hamilton 2008 and Hess 2009). Localization is said to simultaneously foster ecological sustainability, social resilience, economic well-being, democratic participation, community values, and psychological health (see Whitehead, this volume). With all of these advantages, and given its inevitability in an energy descent world, one would be hard pressed to register serious objections to localism.

Alongside all of these good reasons, localization might arguably be the only viable game in town. The blunt reality is that the self-perceived mandate of national governments and international institutions was to expedite the flow of goods and capital, and this they have done. We might have hoped that the World Trade Organization (WTO) would make good on its mission of promoting sustainable development or that decades of negotiations would have stabilized our home planet's climate and forestalled the oncoming wave of mass extinctions, but things are as they are (see Okereke and Charlesworth, this volume). The recent Rio+20 Earth Summit is a case in point: lofty declarations and reams of hortatory documents but virtually no meaningful action. One veteran of so-called green diplomacy called the resulting international declaration 'the longest suicide note in history' (McDonald 2012). For many observers at Rio, the only shred of hope was the dynamism of nongovernmental side-events like the People's Sustainability Treaties (see Death, this volume).

It is said that nature abhors a vacuum, and this is no less true in the realm of politics and social action. The policy vacuum left by governments and intergovernmental organizations with respect to sustainability and social justice is giving rise to a host of local initiatives. National governments may have failed to reduce greenhouse gas emissions, for instance, but thousands of cities and businesses are taking up the effort. Ironically, subnational climate initiatives are proliferating in the United States, the world's most laggardly country on international climate governance (Hoffman 2011). In the face of a deep disenchantment with the top-down politics of globalization, the case for localization is compelling.

Yet some forms of localization are undesirable. Raymond DeYoung and Thomas Princen (2012) distinguish between positive localization, which they associate with cooperation and healthy communities, and negative localization, which they associate with survivalism and the fragmentation of communities. As Melanie DuPuis and David Goodman (2005) argue in their critique of the local food movement, 'unreflexive localism' can inadvertently foster inequality and hegemonic domination. In *The Crash Course* (2011), for instance, 'peak oil' analyst Chris Martenson prescribes stockpiling food and investing in gold. From a narrow individualistic standpoint, these strategies might be prudent, but they make little sense if we wish to build a just and sustainable world.

Fear is, no doubt, a valid response to the oncoming crises. If it prevails, though, more toxic forms of localization are likely to prevail. A telling anecdote illustrates the point. Soon after I returned from doing field research on the global ecovillage movement, I was speaking about my travels to an acquaintance and her twenty-something son. He began to ask some pointed questions about these communities' food and energy systems and their governance structures. As it turned out, he was a member of a local militia that was preparing for the coming collapse. Like the ecovillages I visited, his group was preparing for local self-reliance – growing and preserving food, building off-grid housing, etc. – but two key differences stood out. First, his group was stockpiling gasoline. Second, the men in his group gathered every Saturday for target practice. In his view, ecovillages were 'hippy communes' that would never survive because they lacked two essential things: strong hierarchy and guns. This conversation was an indelible reminder that localization comes in many flavors.

The exchange recalled my interview with Jonathan Dawson, president of the Global Ecovillage Network.[1] Jonathan observed that the most dynamic and long-lived ecovillages are the ones that put themselves at the service of the larger community and predicted that they will need to be of even greater service in the future. 'If we have a graceful transition to a new order', he said, 'ecovillages will be excellent training centers. They already are. If the transition is more catastrophic, ecovillages could be models – but only if they're not devoured by hungry hordes. They will need to be perceived by people as helpful to their own survival. So it's critical that they have strong local relationships'. Localization may be inevitable, but our near-term choices will determine whether cooperation and solidarity win out over violence and fragmentation.

DeYoung and Princen have little to say about negative localization, but some of their contributors make a strong case for rehabilitating associated terms that have a negative connotation. Wendell Berry (2001), for instance, champions the localization of food systems, finance, and economic life in general. To those who criticize his proposal as protectionist, he replies, '[T]hat is exactly what it is. It is a protectionism that is just and sound, because it protects local producers and is the best assurance of adequate supplies to local consumers' (2001: 37; quoted in DeYoung and Princen 2012: 333). Yet Berry is careful to distinguish this form of protectionism from isolationism. Rob Hopkins (2012) echoes Berry's rejection of isolationism. Self-reliance, he says, should not be equated with total self-sufficiency. Citing Shuman (2000: 48), Hopkins affirms that the goal of self-reliant communities 'is not to create a Robinson Crusoe economy in which no resources, people or goods enter or leave. A self-reliant community simply should seek to increase control over its own economy as far as is practicable' (Hopkins 2012: 66).

While some form of localization appears to be inevitable in an energy descent world, the mandate to 'go local' leaves many questions unanswered. When does local self-reliance become impracticable? What is the time frame for localizing? To what extent should we leverage resources from global markets today in order to build tomorrow's local economies and polities? If autarky is not the goal, then how do we decide when to buy local and when to buy from afar? Are there other values besides our own convenience and personal loyalties to people and place that should come into play as we go local?

Critical potential

The slogan 'Think globally, act locally' became popular in the 1990s just as globalization was shifting into high gear. The slogan suggests that if we truly care about global problems, we need to set our own house in order. The implication is that local actions, such as recycling, using mass transit, and buying local organic food, will get us out of the planetary mess we are in. Even more: a global perspective *compels* us to act locally. There are, no doubt, two powerful moments of truth to this claim. First, as a response to the destructive legacy of globalization, the slogan communicates a healthy wariness of large-scale action in challenging the core values of consumerist culture: speed and convenience. Second, if we profess a great concern for the human and ecological wreckage wrought by globalization yet persist in externalizing the negative consequences of our consumptive lifestyles, then we might rightly be accused of hypocrisy.

Both of these moments of truth, however, are matched and superseded by their converse. First, there is the incontrovertible fact that the most powerful global institution in the world today is the multinational corporation, with nation-states and international institutions like the WTO, the IMF, and the World Bank operating at its behest. Simply localizing leaves global action – and hence the primary levers of economic and political power – in the hands of these players. As Nicholas Low and Brendan Gleeson (1998) argue in their proposal for a nested hierarchy of cosmopolitan democratic governance, so long as global capitalism persists, there must be a countervailing power on a global scale. In their words,

> The slogan 'think globally, act locally' is no longer appropriate. Local action within an unchanged global order of production and governance rapidly reaches its limits. It is necessary today not only to think about the global consequences of local action, but to act to change the global context of local action: 'Think and act, globally and locally'. (Low and Gleeson 1998: 189)

Second, the localist impulse often discloses an underlying nostalgia for purity. While localism's emphasis on community values offers a healthy corrective to the values of speed, efficiency, and convenience associated with globalization, local producers are not necessarily any more deserving or trustworthy than peasants or factory workers overseas. Indeed, the anonymity and lack of accountability associated with globalization have been, for the most part, far more damaging in the Third World than the First. Affluence is highly concentrated, but its shadow ecologies are spread across the globe, which places the image of smart-phone addicts waxing eloquent about local food in an unsettling light. 'Going local' can serve as a kind of purification ritual, one that denies the human and material consequences of one's own lifestyle (Hawkins 2006).

Third, like it or not, billions of people are now highly dependent upon the global economy. A reflexive localist impulse, therefore, could have far-flung negative consequences. Consider a recent book whose title speaks for itself: *The Locavore's Dilemma: In Praise of the 10,000-Mile Diet* (Desrochers and Shimizu 2012). The authors view the local food movement as an elite-driven fad and a potentially dangerous distraction from serious global food issues. While they sidestep thorny issues regarding the environmental impact of industrial agriculture, they make a valid point: efficiencies of production have created a global food system that feeds more people than any other system in the past. This system, no doubt, is deeply flawed, but it should not be dismissed out of hand.

Fourth, given that the affluence of the global North was amassed through access to foreign natural and human resources, a fetishism of the local just as planetary systems are approaching a tipping point is, to say the least, an awkward strategy. If we retreat to our fortresses after wrecking the climate, we hardly have an ethical leg to stand on. To complicate matters, we are approaching 'peak everything' just as the global South is beginning to 'catch up'. The 80 per cent of humanity living in developing countries are unlikely to change their trajectories absent a compelling moral and practical exemplar – nor without assistance from the wealthy countries. Global justice, therefore, becomes a matter of 'geoecological realism' (Athanasiou and Baer 2002: 74). In this context, localization is a viable strategy only if it is pursued under the umbrella of global solidarity. Such a strategy requires not only *thinking* globally but also *acting* globally at an institutional level. A localist retreat in an era of climate refugees, geo-engineering, and species triage is a chimera.

We have entered a new era. Humanity is operating as a geophysical force, yet most of us are utterly unaware of our perilous entry into the Anthropocene (see Dalby, this volume). For the few who have registered this fact, there is a mighty temptation to see human survival itself as dependent upon relocalization. The threat of human extinction is like a dark cloud hanging over the discourse of localism, one that is rarely acknowledged but one that can also be fairly easily dispelled. A weedy species can inhabit and spread across a wide range of ecosystems, and humans are arguably the weediest species on the planet. While anything is possible, human extinction is probably not in the cards for the foreseeable future. In the event of global catastrophe, precluding a nuclear winter or an asteroid impact, we can expect human cultures to revert to their *modus operandi:* the local.

The local, then, is a given; the question at the dawn of the Anthropocene is whether we can devise a viable way of inhabiting the global. While we are very far from the requisite political and economic institutions, this is the challenge. It is at once a social, economic, political, ecological, and deeply personal challenge.

Conclusion

As we see the world, so shall we act. Today's global order is a concrete expression of an ontology of separation that constructs people as acquisitive individuals and nature as a vast storehouse of resources (see Hobden, and Rudy and White, this volume). Yet, as the story of separation reaches the end of its tether, the unfolding crisis carries within itself the seeds of a new story. Mechanistic globalism is not the end of the story. If *independence* was the byword of the old story, *interdependence* is the byword of the new. If the old metaphors were drawn from Newtonian physics, the new metaphors are rooted in ecology, where symbiosis is the rule. Whatever its political utility in the past, independence was always a biological fiction; current trends are driving that point home. The so-called individual turns out to be inextricably reliant on a vast web of social, ecological, and microbial networks. Organic globalism understands the world as a nested hierarchy of living systems, from the cell to the Earth system, and seeks to harmonize human systems with living systems at every level.

Harmonious integration is more straightforward in local economies. There may be greed and deception in a village, but it is more visible and the community has more power in the equation. If we are to persist as a global species, then, we must devise economies of care and connection that transcend the local, and we must do some serious number crunching. What should we acquire locally and what from afar? If I live in the western United States, for instance, I may need to consider that grass-fed beef from New Zealand might be more ecologically benign than corn-fed beef from California. And then we face an even more radical question: what do we forego (see Wapner, this volume)? Beef, perhaps. Besides rigorous ecological footprint analysis, economies of care and connection will also require relational modes of production and consumption that supplant the current norms of exploitive distancing (see Hinton, this volume). These relational networks are growing, with fair trade being the most obvious, but they account for only a tiny fraction of world markets (Stiglitz and Charlton 2007). For localists who see a role for international trade, governance and production decisions would be guided by the subsidiarity principle (DeYoung and Princen 2012: 333). Localizers and organic globalists could find common cause in mapping out how the subsidiarity principle would be implemented in practice. A key element of this mapping project would be determining the energetic requirements for a global civilization, a possibility that sociologist Stephen Quilley (2011) labels 'low-energy cosmopolitanism'.

First, however, they would have to grapple with the myopic approach of prevailing global institutions. The WTO, for instance, has been a lightning rod for localist sentiments, with many localizers arguing for its elimination. Yet, as the most powerful global political institution, a democratically restructured WTO would be the most likely candidate for an institutionally grounded organic globalism. Here, proponets of localism and organic globalism would find themselves on common ground, recognizing that the nation-state is neither large enough to inspire a planetary identity nor small enough to nurture the place-based identities that are essential to participatory governance. The nation-state would not necessarily disappear; rather, it would be incorporated into broader cross-cutting networks of supranational, regional, and local forms of governance (see Kuehls, this volume).

Indeed, we can already see evidence of these cross-cutting networks. Consider the International Consortium of Local Environmental Initiatives (ICLEI), a bottom-up network that emerged in the wake of failed international climate negotiations. The consortium serves as a forum for cities to not only respond to the international policy vacuum but to share their best practices on a host of other environmental concerns. Much of the environmental movement itself is organized on a network model, spanning geographic and political scales from the local to the global. Global action networks are in place for a range of issues, including rainforests, climate, pesticides, and hazardous waste. The global action network model is cropping up for other issues as well. La Via Campesina, for instance, is a global network of peasants' organizations calling for food sovereignty. Despite the strong localist overtones of its rallying cry, La Via Campesina has a cohesive global vision and a strong presence at international gatherings on food, climate, trade, and financial policy. Many of these local-to-global networks have a presence both at international civil society gatherings like the World Social Forum and at intergovernmental gatherings like Rio+20 (see Death, this volume). These bottom-up networks, aptly dubbed by Joshua Karliner (1997) as 'grassroots globalization', reflect the kind of higher order synergism that can help localism to realize its critical potential.

As valuable as these issue-based networks have been for fostering some semblance of global governance, they remain weak relative to the planetary reach of corporate capitalism. An intriguing initiative that seeks to lay the groundwork for the emergence of global democratic institutions was presented at Rio+20: The Widening Circles campaign (TWC) (2012). While acknowledging that partial and dispersed efforts, including efforts to build local resilience, are needed more than ever, TWC calls for a 'higher order synergy' responsive to the core condition of the twenty-first century: that 'humanity and Earth are now one community of fate'. TWC hopes to catalyse a polycentric global citizens movement comprising semi-autonomous territorial and issue circles linked through representative global circles. Rejecting the false dichotomy between top-down and bottom-up approaches to governance and trade, the campaign proposes a third way that, in essence, rearticulates the subsidiarity principle: 'as global as must be and as local as can be'. In other words, TWC seeks to change the global context of local action by thinking *and* acting globally *and* locally. Whether or not this particular campaign is successful, it can be read as an expression of an incipient organic globalism.

Ultimately, organic globalism is founded on an emerging form of identity: a sense of global citizenship that simultaneously transcends and includes our bounded self, our local and our national identities. While a resurgence of the local is a healthy response to the destructive legacy of mechanical globalism, the planetary phase of civilization calls for a larger sense of global identity and responsibility. In stretching our loyalties, we are simultaneously enlarged. As Robert Nozick says, 'The size of a soul, the magnitude of a person, is measured in part by the extent of what that person can appreciate and love' (1989: 258, quoted in Low and Gleeson 1998: 135). Globalization has given us the material infrastructure for planetary connectivity. The question now, as we cross the threshold into the Anthropocene, is whether we can develop the inner sense of connectivity to live as one species on our one Earth.

Further reading

Long before globalization entered the lexicon, social theorists were offering trenchant localist critiques of mass culture, urbanization, and capitalism. Robert Owen, a nineteenth-century British socialist, believed that worker collectives should form the basis of society. Owen emigrated to the United States, where he founded a socialist community, New Harmony, in Indiana. Across the diverse socialist and religious communitarian experiments in the United States (ranging from Owenites and Fourierites to Moravians and Shakers) is a unifying theme of localism (Kanter 1972). The rise of environmentalism in the 1970s rejuvenated localist thinking. Ivan Illich's *Tools for Conviviality* (1973, with a second edition in 2001) made the case for a low-tech, communitarian future. Presaging the discourses of environmental justice and climate equity, Illich's *Energy and Equity* (1974, second edition in 2000) offered a penetrating analysis of the relationship between energy consumption and social alienation. Drawing upon Gandhian ideas of local self-sufficiency and Buddhist ideas of deep interdependence, E.F. Schumacher's *Small is Beautiful* (1973) contributed to the appropriate technology and participatory development movements. In recent years, arguments for localization are increasingly rooted in a critique of globalization. Two prominent examples are Colin Hines (2000) *Localization: A Global Manifesto* and Walden Bello (2003) *Deglobalization: Ideas for a New Economy*. At the same time, in the face of unfolding realities of climate change and peak oil, a spate of practical books for localizers are available, including Sharon Astyk (2008) *Depletion and Abundance: Life on the New Home Front* and Alexis Rowell (2010) *Communities, Councils and a Low Carbon Future*. Integrating practical know-how and big picture theorizing are Stephen Morris (ed.) (2007), *The New Village Green: Living Light, Living Local, Living Large* and Karen Litfin (2013) *Ecovillages: Lessons for Sustainable Community*.

Useful websites

Community Solutions: http://www.communitysolution.org/
International Consortium for Local Environmental Initiative: http://www.iclei.org/
International Forum on Globalization: http://www.ifg.org/
New Economics Foundation: http://www.neweconomics.org/
PostCarbon Institute: http://www.postcarbon.org/
Resilience: Building a World of Resilient Communities: http://www.resilience.org/
Resurgence Magazine: http://www.resurgence.org/
Schumacher College: Transformative Learning for Sustainable Living: http://www.schumachercollege.org.uk/
Transition Network: http://transitionnetwork.org/

Note

1. 6 October 2007, Findhorn, U.K.

17 Movements

Stephan Price, Clare Saunders and Cristiana Olcese

Introduction

In December 2008, the UK Parliament became the first legislature in the world to turn climate mitigation targets into law. This step followed two-and-a-half years of increasingly intense campaigning for a law on climate change led by a coalition consisting largely of environment and development movement groups, but also including labour, peace, and church groups. After its success in the UK, the campaign for legislation in other European countries was taken on by Friends of the Earth Europe. In 2010 legislation was attempted in the United States (and failed), but was successfully passed in Mexico in 2012. But in 2009 the United Nations Framework Convention on Climate Change (UNFCCC) negotiations in Copenhagen failed to come up with the international framework that would make domestic action on climate change worthwhile globally (the challenges and opportunities posed by environmental summits are explored by Death, this volume); at the same time, messages hacked from email accounts at the Climate Research Unit at the University of East Anglia shook public confidence in climate concerns (see Okereke and Charlesworth, this volume). Combined with the more immediate problem of the economic crisis, these events contributed to a decline in protest and movement activity on climate change and environmental issues more widely. In 2009, just before the Copenhagen summit, London saw one of the largest public demonstrations of concern about climate change, The Wave, with 30,000 to 50,000 marchers. By 2012, in contrast, only 500 people marched through London to protest against the impact of shale gas on local communities and for climate mitigation targets.

Protests and phases of intense movement activity, like the campaign for climate legislation in the UK, come and go (Melucci 1989; Tarrow 1998). Unfortunately, perceived successes, such as achieving legislation, can contribute to demobilisation (Fillieule 2013). But the politics of climate change, and of environmental issues more widely, do not go away. Instead, UK climate change mitigation is now subject to institutionalised forms of decision-making that emphasise cost efficiency and threaten to produce undesirable consequences. For example, the latest 'dash to gas' may help to replace coal-fired power stations and reduce emissions in the short term, but it will also starve investment from the renewable energy infrastructure that is essential in the long term, as well as create risks for people living near 'fracking' sites.

Legislation on climate change has placed UK movement actors in a difficult position. They must now seek to promote the issue in a context in which, superficially, the problem is 'solved' by legislation. At the same time they must defend those values that are threatened by the outcomes of least-cost-highest-reward government decisions. But can the campaign for a climate law really be described as a 'movement' action, given that it was, in effect, asking government to take over? How much was it to do with a whole movement, given that more radical groups were not part of the campaign? Was there really anything else that could have been done?

Movement activists and scholars disagree about how much to engage with governments and the economy, and they also argue about what the movement is and who should be considered part of it, often on the basis of their arguments about politics and strategy. Central to these discussions is a tension between achieving meaningful social change and achieving anything at all. They are debates about how to define, and how to realise, a movement's critical potential.

In this chapter we define the critical potential of environmental movements as best achieved by creating spaces where dialogue between institutions, organisations, and activists with different identities can take place in a way that does not become reduced to economic instrumentalism. We focus particularly on movements engaging in climate action because of the centrality of climate change to many debates on contemporary environmental politics (Connelly, Smith, Benson, and Saunders 2012). Climate change is also an important issue because of its global scale and transboundary nature, and the long-term challenge it presents to society at every level, from the UN negotiations to the daily lives of ordinary people. As such it provides a useful context to explore the complex relations between states, environmental organisations, and activists. This definition of critical potential helps us to recognise that while the risks posed by dangerous climate change are best avoided, there are also dangers in trading climate mitigation goals off against broader human and social values. Instead of coming down on one side or the other in the debate between effectiveness and meaningful change, this definition bears the tension between them. It is drawn from the work of Andrew Jamison (2001), who has brought a critical perspective to the analysis of environmental movements. Jamison is concerned about strands of environmental thought and action oriented to seeking technical solutions to environmental problems. He argues that the real problem is a context in which the dominant culture aggressively promotes economic values over others, overriding other concerns (see Okereke and Charlesworth, Bond, and Paterson, this volume).

In the following section on 'Core Ideas', we discuss the different definitions of movements available within academic studies of environmental and social movements, identify which version is most appropriate for analysing critical potential as defined above, and outline how the analysis could be approached. In 'Key Thinkers' we look in more detail at how Jamison's (2001) ideas relate to some of the more important thinkers and activists in environmental politics around the world. The network approach to understanding environmental movements that we outline later requires that we assess critical potential in relation to specific movements, so in the final section we look at some examples of the extent to which the UK environmental movement has contributed to or created non-reductive spaces for dialogue in relation to climate change.

Core ideas

The range of vocabulary that scholars use in relation to 'movement' in environmental politics expresses the tensions within the politics of movements themselves. Although they are sometimes used interchangeably, the qualifiers 'environmental', 'ecology', and 'green' can indicate the extent to which scholars believe actors should be critical of the social and political order before they are considered part of a movement. By the same token, these terms can capture views on how far movements are thought of as inherently critical. The term *environmental movements* is the broadest concept and does not insist that those included under its umbrella are system-challenging. As such, it covers a broad range of environmental actors, from formally organised preservationist and conservationist organisations to de-centralised radical deep ecology and anti-capitalist networks (Connelly et al. 2012). In contrast, others have argued that a critical attitude to society is a defining characteristic of a social movement. The term *ecology movements* has been used by some academics to refer to the groups that emerged in Western democracies in the 1960s and 1970s (for example, Della Porta 2007; Giugni 2004; Kriesi, Koopmans, Duyvendak, and Giugni 1995). Such groups had roots in opposition to nuclear power. They grabbed the attention of scholars through their use of unconventional means to draw public and political attention to environmental issues. For example, Friends of the Earth (FoE), an organisation often considered representative of broader ecology movements, became famous overnight in the UK for dumping thousands of empty bottles on the doorstep of Schweppes in response to it phasing out its bottle re-use policy (Lamb 1996). At the time, 'ecology' movement groups were seen as radical, but the most successful organisations within the movement have also moderated their political critique and practices to develop and exploit institutional opportunities for change. In the late 1980s and early 1990s networks such as Earth First! emerged with a fresh radical critique, partly in reaction to the institutionalisation of the 'ecology' groups. Brian Doherty (2002) responds to this tension by re-affirming the importance of a critical attitude and arguing that groups must reject or challenge dominant forms of power if they are to be viewed as part of a 'green' movement.

Is it possible to find some common ground between different ideas of movement? Mario Diani has written one of the most useful articles on the 'concept of social movements' (Diani 1992). Diani noted that 'social and political phenomena as heterogeneous as revolutions, religious sects, political organisations, [and] single-issue campaigns are all, on occasion, defined as social movements' (1992: 2). Whilst this is not a problem as such, it means that one cannot be entirely sure that different scholars are talking about the same class of phenomena when deploying the term *social movement*. However, by looking at the four main branches of social movement theory, Diani was able to tease out elements of a consensus definition. Common to collective behaviour (Turner and Killian 1957), resource mobilisation (McCarthy and Zald 1977), political process (Tilly 1978), and new social movement (Melucci 1989) theories is emphasis on networks of informal interactions between individuals and organisations; solidarity, shared beliefs, or identity; political or cultural challenges to the social order; and action that 'primarily occurs outside of the institutional sphere and the routine procedures of social life' (Diani 1992: 11). Thus, for Diani, the consensual definition of a social movement becomes 'a network of informal interactions between a plurality of individuals, groups and/or organisations, engaged in a political or cultural conflict, on the basis of a shared collective identity' (1992: 13).

But although most environmental politics scholars can agree that a movement is best described as a network, they do not all agree that collective identity is a useful way to work out movement boundaries. Rootes (2000) suggests that the environmental movement includes people who do not share the values and beliefs necessary for a collective identity and so opts for the more inclusive criterion of 'shared concern'. Doherty (2002) believes that social movements are engaged in a specific type of conflict, challenging or rejecting the dominant social and/or political system; by extension, his idea implies a more exclusive collective identity. Part of the difficulty is that 'collective identity' is such a complex idea. As we argue later, this means that the more inclusive notion of 'shared concern' is more useful for our definition of movement potential.

Collective identity

The concept of collective identity is central to the social movement literature. Becoming a collective actor is considered a fundamental task of any social movement; how a movement achieves this, or fails to achieve it, is an important concern for scholars. Collective identity has been defined as an

> individual's cognitive, moral, and emotional connection with a broader community, category, practice, or institution. It is a perception of a shared status or relation, which may be imagined rather than experienced directly, and it is distinct from personal identities, although it may form part of a personal identity. (Polletta and Jasper 2001: 285)

However, there is disagreement about key aspects of collective identity. In particular, scholars differ over whether collective identity should be seen as a necessary condition for collective action (Hunt and Benford 2004; Polletta and Jasper 2001; Snow 2001), or the final result (Melucci 1995, 1996), and whether collective identity is an attribute of whole movements (Flesher Fominaya 2010), or only movement groups (Saunders 2008).

Is the construction of this 'we-ness' even relevant or necessary in contemporary social movements? Recent work by Melucci (2000), Touraine (2000), and Kevin McDonald (2002, 2006) argues that the question of identity in contemporary social movements is posed in quite a different way from the 'we-ness' model. Since neoliberal social models demand individual success, contemporary social conflicts emerge at the level of individual experience where new forms of domination are experienced. As a consequence, McDonald sees personal involvement, as opposed to acting out one's role as a member of a group, and a shift from representation to personal narration, as central to the actions and culture of contemporary social movements that are emerging out of the conflicts, including environmental ones, related to globalisation. However, for many organisations the concept of 'collective identity' is still a powerful mobiliser and a final aspiration, as well as a necessary condition for being taken seriously by other actors involved in the struggle, even though it can become detrimental for a movement as a whole (Saunders 2008) or be rejected by some movements (K. McDonald 2002, 2006) and/or organisations (Flesher Fominaya 2010). Some of the best research avoids a priori assumptions and engages with the analytical challenge of identifying the circumstances in which different relations between strategy and identity, personal and collective operate (Polletta and Jasper 2001). One of the most useful ways available to achieve this is to think of movements as networks.

Networks and institutions

The network-conception of movement put forward by Diani has been central to the debate about whether collective identity defines a movement (Diani 1992; Saunders 2007), or whether some looser notion, such as 'shared concern', is more appropriate (Rootes 2000; Saunders 2008). Empirical work has shown that 'external' boundaries of a movement are in fact highly fluid and contingent on 'internal' interactions (Saunders 2008), which in turn impact interactions with non-movement actors such as the state. These findings support the view that a loose network is more appropriate for understanding environmental movements. Saunders (2009) has shown, for example, how environmental organisations with an insider relationship with the polity will avoid overt links with more radical groups that could jeopardise their reputations. Her research takes a step towards breaking down the disciplinary boundary between social movement and political network scholars (c.f. Rootes 1999). This step is crucial because understanding movement potential requires consideration of the extent to which movements are able to create discourse spaces inclusive of the state, and with gatekeepers to reach a broader audience, such as the media (Huberts 1989).

Given the presence of links between the state and some actors within environmental movement networks, a useful definition of movement should include semi-institutionalised actors (see Baker, this volume). The fluidity and indeterminacy of movement boundaries mean that, if we accept that movements are networks, we must accept that they may be partially institutionalised. The environmental movement in the UK in 2007 provides a striking illustration of this. The National Trust has statutory powers to prevent land it wants to protect being sold or mortgaged: of all environmental organisations it is the most 'institutionalised'. In the run up to a planned direct action camp at Heathrow, the British Airports Authority (BAA) sought a court injunction against members of Airport Watch, an umbrella organisation for groups opposed to aviation expansion that includes Greenpeace, which carries out direct action and maintains links with radical groups as well as the National Trust. In effect, the BAA injunction would have prevented the three to four million members of the National Trust, including the judge hearing the case, from approaching Heathrow. As a relatively conservative organisation that rarely takes part in conventional forms of protest it would be easy and more convenient to exclude the National Trust from our treatment of the environmental movement. However, this case, and the National Trust's more recent protests against the UK coalition government's proposals to reform the planning system, show that 'institutionalised' organisations deserve much more careful consideration. Within the network perspective, boundaries to the environmental movement cannot easily be set according to system vs. challenger, institutional vs. non-institutional, mainstream vs. marginal, instrumental vs. expressive, or ideological simplifications. Consequently, when we think about movement potential, we need to consider, in a more joined up way, how different actors influence each other. Movement participants' interactions with the state, economy, and media affect movement participants' interactions with each other, and the process can also work the other way around. This means that if we draw on a network perspective to analyse critical potential, looking at conscious political ideologies and strategies alone and in theory is not enough. Movement potential must be assessed with empirical reference to specific movements in particular contexts.

In the final section of this chapter, we look at the particular example of the UK environmental movement actors engaged in climate campaigns and the extent to which they have created spaces for dialogue between widely differing actors and institutions that are resistant to instrumental/economic reductionism. First, we discuss how environmental thinkers have engaged with narrowly defined economic values, and how they relate to scholarly attempts to analyse environment movement potential.

Key thinkers

Economic growth has long been an underlying concern for environmentalists around the world. Any characterisation of the different overlying strands of thought and practice here risks oversimplification. One attempt that moves beyond straightforward developed–developing, First–Third, North–South type binaries is Doherty and Doyle's (2006) system of three categories. They describe the environmentalism dominant in the United States and Australia as 'post-materialist', in that it is primarily concerned with the protection of an 'other nature', or wilderness (although this, almost inevitably, overlooks the 50-year-old environmental justice movement; see Bond, this volume). They suggest the environmentalism dominant in Europe is post-industrialist, challenging the negative consequences of industry, whereas in the global South they argue that a post-colonial frame of reference is dominant (see Igoe, Watts and Peluso, and Rudy and White, this volume).

The first schism in U.S. environmental thought reflected the U.S. concern with wilderness. It came in 1913 over whether a dam should be built within a national park. The preservationist John Muir, co-founder of the Sierra Club, and Gifford Pinchot, who saw conservation as a way of managing natural resources for commercial use, differed over how pristine nature should remain. However, later U.S. environmentalists became less concerned about the siting of industry, challenging industry per se. In 1969 David Brower was spurred to leave the Sierra Club and founded FoE because of the Club Board's willingness to support nuclear power. Similarly, Rachel Carson, a biologist, published her concerns about the use of pesticides in agriculture in the book *Silent Spring* (1962), becoming widely cited as an inspiration for 'post-industrial' environmentalism. However, FoE remained the only group within the group of ten most influential environmental organisations in the United States not chiefly oriented to conservation (Rowell 1996); the 'post-industrial' concern was more successful in Europe.

From the 1970s, many environmentalists formalised their views and published their ideas about the relationships between the economy and the environment. These ideas fed into the positions of the 'ecology' movement that emerged in the late 1960s and early 1970s and that came to dominate European environmentalism. Fritz Schumacher, who argued for 'economics as if the world matters' (1973), the 'Club of Rome', the international think tank behind *The Limits to Growth* (Meadows, Meadows, Randers, and Behrens III 1972), and ecological economists such as Herman Daly, offered the intellectual references for environmentalists opposed to both population and economic growth. They recalled aspects of the work of liberal economists such as Adam Smith, John Stuart Mill, and John Maynard Keynes that had been forgotten by the mainstream, namely, the constraint future population increase would place on economic growth and the idea that economic growth was but a means to a steady-state economy in which humans could flourish (see Kütting and Whitehead, this volume).

Some 'ecology' groups, such as FoE and Greenpeace, targeted government, businesses, and consumers for environmental reforms of the economy, in particular around energy production and consumption. However, they often found they were fighting defensive actions against even more potentially destructive developments, such as nuclear power. Others sought more practical paths, developing alternative technologies, learning traditional crafts, and proposing economies based on small communities. They found inspiration in the writing and actions of Schumacher (1973), as well as William Morris, Ivan Illich (who wrote *Tools for Conviviality*, 1973), Mahatma Gandhi (Ruskin, Gandhi and Desai 1951), and Murray Bookchin (1982).

Emerging from within communist East Germany, Rudolf Bahro (1984) confirmed the concerns of many that Soviet-style socialism never represented a genuine alternative to capitalism. During the 1980s, Bahro led a move from the left towards green politics. However, the demise of Eastern European communism at the beginning of the 1990s resulted in the widely-held assumption that now capitalism was the only way of doing things, economically-speaking (Fukuyama 1992). This led many environmentalists to seek to reconcile economic growth and environmental concern. The ideas of the ecological modernisation school (Spaargaren and Mol 1992) created opportunities for powerful political coalitions to emerge between business and environmental movement entrepreneurs (Hajer 1995). As this strand of the movement grew in strength, activist groups such as Greenpeace and FoE found that their campaigning strategies had to become more heterogeneous. Peter Melchett at Greenpeace UK adopted a 'double-fisted approach' (Bennie 1998; Rawcliffe 1998), offering marketable solutions in collaboration with business and government, as well as criticism. Jonathon Porritt, who led FoE England, Wales, and Northern Ireland from 1984 to 1990 with an anti-growth position (Yearley 1991), turned away from his fundamentalist position. He headed the UK government's late Sustainable Development Commission and in 2005 published a book entitled *Capitalism as if the World Matters* (Porritt 2005).

Following the break-up of the Soviet Union, and the adjustment many Western environmental groups made to the new economic orthodoxy, tensions emerged between the post-materialist and post-industrial environmentalisms of the global North, and the post-colonial environmentalisms of the global South (Doherty 2006). Many groups in developing countries saw the northern groups as too close to their governments, and indeed, many saw themselves as Marxists who were involved in struggles for livelihoods, human and social rights, as well as environmental concerns (Doherty and Doyle 2006). For example, Chico Mendes, one of the leading figures of the Brazilian rubber tappers movement to conserve the Amazon rainforest during the 1970s and 1980s, was also a trade unionist and campaigned for the rights of indigenous peoples. The Chipko movement in northern India during the 1970s and 1980s drew on a legacy of Gandhian politics to resist industrial-scale deforestation that threatened their livelihoods. One of the leaders to emerge from this movement, Vandana Shiva, links concerns with feminism, agriculture, and globalisation in her work, for example, in her book *Soil Not Oil* (2009) (see Cudworth, this volume).

All of these writers and thinkers are concerned with the implications of limited material resources. But those for whom growth was only ever a means to an end also perceived that growth exploited human and social interaction, turning energy that could be used for creativity and relationships into productive labour and efficient consumption. Too often, efficient economic growth rests on a narrow, instrumental definition of the market that ignores its role as a social institution (Sandel 2012). In some places, the quality of life is merely degraded, in others, democratic and human rights are threatened or denied.

This insight is at the heart of the work of Jürgen Habermas (1987), which Andrew Jamison (2001) builds upon in his critical analysis of changes in the environmental movement in Europe and North America. For Habermas (1987), the types of rationality deeply embedded in our 'life and consciousness' during our earliest experiences of socialisation, when we learn our first language, are being replaced by methods of social co-ordination (such as money or formal power) that have developed in differentiated, specialised, and institutionalised spheres of social action. His work implies that people struggle with a tension between forms of action that connect to their life and consciousness but are redundant, and forms that are alienating yet (only) apparently effective. Even worse, this conflict is occurring in conditions in which opportunities to reflect on what is happening and develop responses within open free public discussion are in decline. Habermas (1987) and Jamison (2001) both argue for the creation and defence of space for public discourse (also see Hinton, this volume). In the context of the environmental movement, Jamison is concerned that discussion forums often lose their openness because, over time, some participants translate ideas into marketable products. Subsequently, their mode of interaction shifts to defending the interests invested in those products.

How does this type of process occur in practice, and how is it implicated in the limitations of an environmental movement's critical potential? In the remaining section of this chapter we explore these questions in relation to the UK environmental movement and the actions it has taken on climate change.

Critical potential

We begin this section with an external relationship, the interaction between the movement and the media. Ecology movements became popular through newspapers and exploited the opportunities of television to engage an audience and forge a constituency of support. Perhaps the news media could be a site for movement groups to build a space for dialogue between government, business, and civil society? Professionalised environmental actors have developed routinised interactions with the press that appear to ensure environmental movement groups at least some voice in press discourse on climate change. Yet the evidence is that this voice is clearly marginal. Analysis of UK press coverage of climate change suggests that there is a dominant 'light-green' consensus across the broadsheets that accepts technological and profitable 'solutions' for climate change (Saunders, Grasso, and Price 2012). On the one hand, the degree of consensus about climate change as an issue that requires action, coupled with a rising tide of coverage, could be seen as positive: more people can become aware of the issue and the options available (see Okereke and Charlesworth, this volume). On the other hand, this broad consensus could help to maintain and entrench a fallacy that the policies and proposals are sufficient to avoid dangerous climate change.

In this context, perhaps we would expect to find the most successfully diverse and non-reductive spaces are organised by more radical groups that are willing to challenge economic priorities. However, such events are unlikely to occur independently of wider discursive contexts, such as the news. The UK Climate Camp process demonstrates this. In yearly, week-long camps that took place between 2006 and 2010, the camps were set up with an open participatory principle and an explicit consensus decision-making model. However, the Camp was initially conceived as a direct action camp by its anti-authoritarian founders. When the Camp visited Heathrow in 2007, the media attention it received, largely as a result of the reaction of BAA to the protest (which we discussed earlier), led to a surge in popularity so that by 2008 participants from a wide spectrum of environmental political thought attended the Camp (Saunders and Price 2009; Saunders 2012), which on this occasion had been planned with the aim to include different voices and stimulate debate. The result was a discourse that crossed a number of ideological divides, reflecting the preponderant consensus for light green technical solutions in UK climate discourse (as represented in the news). However, this diversity ran counter to the initial vision of a number of activists, particularly as more liberal or mainstream views went unchallenged. A small group made a call for the Camp to associate itself with anarchist-inspired 'Peoples' Global Action Hallmarks' (PGA 2001), effectively excluding alternative, more liberal views from participation 'in' the process. The effort by a relatively small number of committed activists to set the ideological frame of the Camp cramped the space for open debate.

Perhaps a more formal mode of communication would help to reduce conflict and sustain dialogue, if a sufficiently open platform could be found? This is something that the Internet offers (see Hinton, this volume). Although barriers to inclusion remain, web-based campaigns can be open to all Internet users, but campaigners can influence the extent or nature of participation to help to achieve their goals. To date, the better resourced UK environmental groups have tended to use Internet participation in an instrumental fashion. For example, the crucial moment in the political struggle for a Climate Change Act in Britain arrived in the summer of 2007. The Climate Change Bill Committee had, before the parliamentary recess, voted against an 80 per cent reduction target. Over that summer the FoE 'Big Ask' campaigners created an online video march, which rapidly directed a digitally enhanced petition to MPs, creating the conditions for a face-saving deal to be struck when Parliament resumed in the autumn. There could not be a clearer example of the contribution Internet campaigners can make intervening in public debate and countering economic concerns that threatened to undermine the legislation. However, although this type of approach can deliver large numbers in support of movement positions, it demands little commitment, and there is little genuine dialogue. Aggregating such 'small asks' risks dissipating the moral feeling that something more must be done with policies that are ill-equipped to make a difference (such as the Climate Change Act). The case of the Climate Change Act shows that balancing economic priorities with wider concerns demands a sustained effort, rather than a temporary intervention.

Conclusion

If economic reductionism is the problem, then perhaps it makes sense to consider movement potential as the extent to which movements can foster social interaction on alternative values – social solidarity, for instance. But the idea of collective identity does not offer a clear starting point for considering movement potential. The concept is too unclear, collective identity itself could in fact hinder movements, and it may become less important as an element within political action as conditions change. Network analysis provides an open-ended way of approaching movements, and it leads us towards the consideration of particular movements, in context. When we do this, we discover continuous links and dynamics from within the most formal institutions to the most informal, system challenging groups (see Rudy and White, this volume). If these links did not exist, or could be avoided, movements could ignore economic priorities, but they cannot. So our understanding of how movements could realise their potential takes account of this, in spaces that neither exclude nor reduce to economic values.

In the UK, the passage of climate change legislation and the light-green consensus within national broadsheets are neither reasons for celebrating the success of the UK environmental movement nor for mourning its institutionalisation. Instead they are developments in the conditions that constrain or facilitate further movement action. The UK example shows ambiguous conditions in relation to the state and the press, and successes relative to previous achievements that are heavily qualified by failures in sustaining movement action. But failure is not the same as defeat. There is both the capacity and the need for action to create even more inclusive spaces of public discourse, which is absolutely vital for a project of critical environmental politics, as we see it.

Further reading

Andrew Jamison's (2001) account of the interface between environmental and economic values is both reflective and accessible. Those who wish to find out more about how Habermas viewed movements within his analysis of modern society should read his 1981 article 'New Social Movements', published in *Telos*. A present-day example of environmental movement participants reflecting on the more instrumental aspects of their strategies and seeking alternatives can be found in Stephen Hale's recent article in *Environmental Politics*, 'The new politics of climate change: Why we are failing and how we will succeed' (2010). *Environmental Politics* runs regular special issues on environmental movements and climate change politics. In particular, the 2006 issue 'Beyond Borders' places the issues discussed here, among others, in an international context, while the 2007 issue on the 'Politics of Unsustainability' places the challenge of economic imperatives in a stark light. Molly Scott Cato's (2009) *Green Economics: An Introduction to Theory, Policy and Practice* gives a broad-based introduction to alternative environmental perspectives on the economy; in contrast Tim Jackson's (2009) *Prosperity Without Growth* takes a more technical approach.

Useful websites

Campaign Strategy: http://www.campaignstrategy.org/
Climate Camp/Camp for Climate Action: http://climatecamp.org.uk/
Climate Outreach and Information Network: http://coinet.org.uk/
Heathrow Association for the Control of Aircraft Noise (HACAN Clearskies): http://www.hacan.org.uk/
The International Society for Ecological Economics: http://www.isecoeco.org/
Tools for Change: http://www.toolsforchange.net/

18 Posthumanism

Stephen Hobden

Introduction

The essence of posthumanism is to challenge the notion of human exceptionalism. In Donna Haraway's (2008: 11) words, human exceptionalism is 'the premise that humanity alone is not a spatial and temporal web of interspecies dependencies'. While relatively unknown in International Relations, it has become a major approach within sociology, has influenced thinkers within geography and has contributed enormously to the development of critical animal studies. It will be argued here that posthumanism is essential to a critical engagement with the politics of the environment. While posthumanism has made an impact on several disciplines, ideas about what is actually meant by the term are deeply contested and potentially contradictory. This chapter, while engaging with competing ideas about what is actually meant by the term, will advocate a particular perspective on posthumanism. This perspective makes an ontological claim – a challenge to humanocentrism by the decentring of the human, and an ethical one – our responsibilities extend not only to our kin, nationality, culture, ethnicity, and species, but also across species barriers (see McShane, this volume). The work of posthumanists challenges not only anthropocentrism but also the character of the species barrier itself. In the approach to thinking about posthumanism advocated here, the starting point is complexity theory, and particularly the overlapping and nested character of complex adaptive systems (see Baker, this volume). Complexity theory suggests that systems are 'open' rather than closed and emphasises their inter-dependence and cross-cutting character. It therefore highlights the human relationship with non-human nature and facilitates its analysis. The complexity approach is non-Newtonian and suggests that we reject humanocentric perspectives. The vast majority of work in the social sciences and International Relations provides a particularly vivid example, is human focused, accepting both religious and enlightenment notions that put the human (and usually male) subject at the centre of analysis. Posthumanism rejects such ideas and suggests that we see the human as 'of nature' rather than 'in nature'. This has profound implications for considerations of our relations with the rest of non-human nature, both animate and inanimate (see Rudy and White, this volume).

Core ideas

A central element of the posthuman move is the attempt to extinguish a perceived ontological dualism between human and non-human nature. Such dualist thinking has a very long pedigree. The religions of 'the book' all depicted the human as a special or chosen species, as indicated by the author of the book of Genesis, given special dominion over the rest of creation. While enlightenment thinkers challenged much of the grounds for the priority of religious beliefs, they did not seek to undermine the special position of the human. Descartes in the *Discourse on Method* drew a sharp distinction between animals and humans based on the possession of the latter of reason. Animals act not on the basis of intelligence or reason but only through 'nature which acts in them in accordance with the disposition of their organs' to operate like a 'clock' (Descartes 1999 [1637]). In a similar fashion, Kant depicted the human as distinct from the rest of nature in that beings with reason were ends in themselves, whereas beings without reason 'have only a relative, as means, and are therefore called things' (Kant 1998 [1785]: 37). Yet such humanocentric positions did not exist without question. Michel de Montaigne very famously queried his relationship with his cat, asking whether when he played with cat, was it not the other way round. For Spinoza, humans held no privileged position within nature (see Lloyd 1980, 1994). Such perspectives have been taken up by twentieth-century critical theorists. Horkheimer and Adorno in *Dialectic of Enlightenment* (2007) drew attention to the character of human non-human relations within nature, with the role of instrumental reason in extending its influence from control over nature to control over humans. More recently Dominic Pettman (2011: 7) has suggested we should 'focus on a collective attempt to retrofit our own self-understanding according to a less paranoid and fascistic logic of secured borders and pure typologies'.

Donna Haraway (2008: 11–12) discusses four 'wounds' that have challenged the perception of human centredness: the Copernican revolution that questioned the perception of the earth as the centre of the universe, Darwin's theory of evolution, Freud's work on the subconscious, and the development of the cyborg that questions human purity (see Rudy and White, this volume). Of these, perhaps the central contribution to challenging the edifice of humanocentrism has been the revolution in human conceptions of its place in nature brought about by Darwin's theory of evolution. Yet even this work has contributed to seeing the human as special as perhaps the most evolved, or 'fittest' species on the planet. Neil Shubin challenges such hubris by pointing out the traces in human anatomy that we have inherited from previous stages on the evolutionary journey. You should acknowledge, he suggests, *Your Inner Fish* (2009). The evolutionary process has not only left its traces in the makeup of the human organism, but also left humans with some rather problematic inheritances. Rather than being the most advanced organism on the planet, the evolutionary process has been the product of a 'convoluted history', leaving us subject to many ailments, from hiccups to haemorrhoids, that can be traced to our fish and other mammal ancestors. A designer creating a human body from scratch would probably come up with a rather different design, or, at a minimum, a more stream-lined one. As Shubin (2009: 185) observes, 'take the body plan of a fish, dress it up to be mammal, then twist and tweak that mammal until it walks on two legs, talks and has superfine control of its fingers – and you have a recipe for problems'. In a similar argument Gary Marcus points to the haphazard character of evolutionary development, with the process having a tendency to develop 'kluges'. A kluge is a 'clumsy or inelegant – yet surprisingly effective – solution to a problem' (Marcus 2008: 2). Many aspects of the human body, including the brain, are kluges, which likewise can be the source of a variety of problems.

The notion of the human has, however, been far from a pure one. It is also important to note that the quality of human is a contested one. Joanna Bourke (2011) points out that there has been a hierarchical perception of what it means to be human, with some humans regarded as less human than others. Bourke (2011: 67–70) points to the writing of an 'earnest English woman' who regarded the position of women as inferior even to that of animals and that to be considered at least as an animal would be something of an improvement.

Posthumanism itself has a number of perspectives. As Cary Wolfe (2010: xi) observes, the term 'generates different and even irreconcilable definitions'. For John Cairns (2005), a posthuman world is literally *after humanity* – we are confronting a world where the capacity exists for the species literally to become extinct either as the result of conflict or because of disastrous climate change. However, the *post* as meaning 'after humanity' is far from being the most widely used understanding of the term.

For the most part, other perspectives have used the term to indicate a questioning of the boundaries of what it means to be human. Agamben's work, to be discussed later, is at the forefront of questioning this divide. One way of categorizing these viewpoints would be to divide them between posthumanism as a historical development and posthumanism as a theoretical (and perhaps ethical) perspective. The first grouping might be considered to be in fact transhumanist (or perhaps even super-humanist) rather than specifically posthumanist. Writers within this group have examined the ways that technological developments have led to the questioning of the boundaries of what it means to be human. Chris Hables Gray's (2001) *Cyborg Citizen,* for example, examines the political implications for a human population that is increasingly a hybrid of human and machine. The focus of this literature is on the capacity for humans to extend the capabilities perhaps even by 'uploading' human consciousness into computers being able to extend human life indefinitely. For some this prospect opens up much in the way of possibilities; others (e.g., Fukuyama 2002) have expressed horror at this possibility as stripping away our essential human nature. Writing from a feminist perspective, Donna Haraway (1985, 1991) has argued that the appearance of the cyborg confronts us with the hybrid quality of life. Life is composed of various assemblages that are constantly shifting (see Rudy and White, this volume). Hence there are no fixed entities such as humans or animals. Yet, while her work questions the boundaries between human and non-human rather than celebrates the extension of human capabilities, she cautions against the use of posthumanism in this sense (Gane and Haraway 2006: 140).

While transhumanist approaches have raised questions about the meaning of the human, the posthumanism to be advocated here does not relate to a particular historical time period or level of technological development. Rather, based on recent work in complexity theory, it suggests that the attempt to isolate the human as distinct from the rest of nature has always been inherently mistaken. Human systems are embedded within other systems and crucially have co-evolved with them. This is not to say that we should abandon the study of human systems, or that issues of social exclusion are not fundamentally important. Rather it is to stress that human activity is pursued within, together with and with impacts on non-human nature. For example, it is frequently contended that human brain size co-evolved with more developed forms of tools. It wasn't that our ancestors with larger brains adopted tool use, it was more that tool usage led to increased brain size, which in turn led to the development of more complicated tools – an example of a positive feedback loop.

Like posthumanism, *complexity theory* is a deeply contested term, and complexity thinking within the social sciences has developed in a number of different ways (Cudworth and Hobden 2009). One way of distinguishing these differences is between a mathematically orientated approach, which suggests that given enough compute power the underlying patterns of complexity can be modelled, and a philosophical approach, which suggests that a complex world is essentially 'unknowable'. Edgar Morin (2007), who is discussed later, has distinguished these as 'restricted' and 'general' forms of complexity.

At the core of all approaches to thinking about complexity is the notion of the complex adaptive system. As the name suggests, these are systems that are complex and adaptive. They emerge from the interactions between their constituent units and have recognisable, though permeable, borders. Complex systems have 'emergent' features that appear from the interactions at a unit level but are not reducible to unit level properties (Mihata 1997: 31; see also Büscher, this volume). They are also complex because in such systems there is an expectation that interactions within and between systems will not necessarily follow linear patterns. A linear relationship is one where the pattern of interactions can be derived as a regular and predictable relationship. Non-linear relationships do not follow such regularities and are thus more difficult, and probably impossible to predict. Non-linear relationships can be significant because minor fluctuations can result in very large effects, whilst very large events can have rather minimal impacts. A frequently cited claim of the former is the question of whether a butterfly flapping its wings in Brazil could result in a tornado in Texas (Lorenz 1993 [1972]). Any pattern that does appear may also be short lived. While relations in and between complex adaptive systems may be unpredictable, this does not mean that they are chaotic. A further feature of such systems is that there is a tendency to self-organisation. In self-organising systems there is an expectation that there will be ever-higher levels of complexity. This is not a teleological feature as complex systems can suddenly flip or bifurcate, and there are plenty of examples of the collapse of complex social systems (Diamond 2005; Tainter 1988).

A further element of systems thinking in complexity analysis is the important role of feedback. In much traditional social analysis (for example, the work of Talcott Parsons) negative feedback brings systems back towards equilibrium, in a similar way that a central heating thermostat will switch on once a room falls below a certain temperature, and switches off once the room is warmed up again. Parsons argued that there are feedback systems in social systems that bring them back to equilibrium at times that they are disturbed. In International Relations theory, Realist accounts of the balance of power operate in a similar way (see, for example, Morgenthau 1960: 167). While acknowledging the operation of negative feedback, complexity theorists also argue that positive feedback can occur that takes systems further away from equilibrium. A frequently cited example is the concern that as a result of climate change brought about by the burning of fossil fuels, even higher levels of carbon dioxide will be released from oceans and previously frozen peat bogs, speeding up the effects of climate change even further (see Okereke and Charlesworth, this volume).

In distinction to much conventional systems theorising (for example, the work of Kenneth Waltz 1979), complex adaptive systems are perceived as having borders that are permeable, and as well as being subject to developments within the system, co-evolve in relation to other systems. This provides the adaptive part of the analysis. In this approach all other systems form an environment in which systems develop. Such a form of systems analysis allows the analysis of developments of and between systems, but also allows for the analysis of intersecting forms of power (Walby 2009).

A complexity view of the world therefore challenges many of the elements of the Newtonian model of science that have been imported rather unthinkingly into the social sciences. From a Newtonian perspective, the world is seen as exhibiting regular processes, systems are seen as closed, and the same rules apply regardless of time or space. It is, as Thomas Homer-Dixon (2009: 10) observes, somewhat bizarre that the main elements of the Newtonian worldview have been accepted into the social sciences at the very point in time when such accounts of reality are being challenged by physicists themselves (see Forsyth, this volume). In summary, such views challenge the mechanical and causal accounts of the social sciences, see historical development as core to understanding social phenomena, and dispute subject-object differentiation (Cudworth and Hobden 2012).

Furthermore, such approaches also open up the possibility of challenging humanocentric accounts of the social sciences. From a complexity perspective the environment of any one system is provided by all other systems (see McShane, this volume). Such systems are embedded within each other and coevolve. Hence humans exist within and are developing alongside a range of non-human systems.

Key thinkers

The posthumanism advocated here develops from the work of a number of writers, and here some of their central contributions are considered. While, as already noted, there is a considerable history of what we might call proto-posthumanist thought, posthumanism itself is a relatively recent development, and here contributions from three central authors will be summarised: Edgar Morin, Giorgio Agamben, and Donna Haraway.

Edgar Morin, the French sociologist, is, unfortunately, relatively unknown in the English speaking world. However, he is perhaps the most significant European thinker on the uses of complexity theory in the social sciences. His multi-volume work *La Méthode* is arguably the most sustained attempt to apply complexity thinking. Unfortunately, only one volume of *La Méthode* (Morin 1992) and very little of his other enormous output has been translated into English.

For Morin, complexity is a central feature of our existence. 'Complexity is in fact the fabric of events, actions, interactions, retroactions, determinations, and chance that constitute our phenomenal world' (Morin 2008: 5). We might describe this approach as cosmological, in that the phenomenal world exists between the cosmological and the quantum. Quantum physics introduced the notion of uncertainty to the study of the subatomic world, while at the cosmological level, physics introduced the notions of the collapse between space and time. However, these instances have been seen as borderline cases rather than as interwoven into the fabric of reality. 'Between the two, in the physical, biological and human domains, science reduced phenomenal complexity to simple order and elementary units' (Morin 2008: 20). Although science has made phenomenal leaps, these have been made on the basis of an oversimplification that has left us 'blind to the complexity of reality' (Morin 2008: 6).

In response, Morin's (2007) argument is that complexity requires a wholesale re-thinking of the ways in which we understand the world. Complexity approaches can be divided, he argues, between restricted approaches (by which he means essentially those that attempt to retain a Newtonian perspective) and generalised complexity. Morin is without doubt an advocate of a generalised complexity perspective, arguing that restricted accounts attempt to attach 'complexity as a kind of wagon behind the truth locomotive, that which produces laws' (Morin 2007: 10). Such approaches attempt to analyse complexity by taking the complexity out – while acknowledging complexity, they fail to recognise its implications: 'the breach is opened, then one tries to clog it' (Morin 2007: 10). Instead, complexity thinking requires a wholesale re-thinking of the knowledge enterprise.

In attempting to analyse the world, a central point is that nothing exists in isolation, and while some things exist in a tangle of causes and feedback loops, there are also events that are completely random. Ultimately, it is impossible to study events in isolation as everything is in some way interconnected. This, for Morin, is the 'primary complexity' (2008: 84).

Morin's work is not simply an attempt to engage with complexity; it also contains a deeply political element. We are citizens of 'homeland earth' and need to confront 'poly-crisical sets of interwoven and overlapping crises' (Morin 1999: 73). In dealing with these crises, 'we must learn to live with uncertainty' (Morin 2008: 97). Of course it is much more comfortable to operate in a world of certainty; however, 'if it is a false certainty, then this is very bad' (Morin 2008: 97). Instead what is needed is 'a complex form of thinking capable of understanding that politics has become multidimensional' (Morin 2008: 95). The profound re-thinking that engaging with complexity requires also then needs a re-envisioning of the way that politics operates. Ultimately, the work of Morin suggests that we need not develop the tools that allow us to simplify complexity because this only leads us to underestimate its effects, rather we need to work towards thinking about coping strategies. While perhaps not openly posthuman, Morin's work does point to posthuman conclusions by stressing the inter-connected and overlapping character of human and non-human systems. Human systems do not exist independently of non-human ones but are intimately interconnected.

While Morin's work provides the basis for an inclusion of complexity in posthuman thinking, a greater engagement is needed with an understanding of the creation of bound-aries between human and non-human animals, and a number of writers have contributed to this work. One example would be Giorgio Agamben's notion of the 'anthropological machine'. Agamben's work has been centrally concerned with the definition of what it means to be human and the operation of what he describes as sovereign power in terms of the creation of 'bare life' – a form of life outside of the normal practices of society and open to direct intervention by the sovereign power – the most immediate contemporary example being the detainees of Guantánamo Bay. Extending this analysis in *The Open,* Agamben asks 'in what way – within man – has man been separated from non-man, and the animal from the human' (2004: 16). This process he describes as the operation of the anthropological machine. A central contribution to the development of such a machine was the biologist Alfred Linnaeus, but even Linnaeus admitted that he found it difficult to dis-tinguish between the human and the non-human. As Agamben points out, Linnaeus found out how 'difficult it is to identify the specific difference between the anthropoid apes and man from the point of view of natural science' (2004: 23). It is the exclusion that makes the human, and those that do not recognise the exclusion (as with some of Linnaeus' crit-ics) do not make the human. '*Homo Sapiens,* then is neither a clearly defined species nor a substance; it is, rather a machine or device for producing the recognition of the human . . . *Homo is a* constitutively "anthropomorphous" animal . . . who must recognize himself in non-man in order to be human' (Agamben 2004: 26–7).

Working more specifically at the boundaries of the human, Donna Haraway has focussed on the boundary conditions that mark out the human. One of her most (in)famous works has used the idea of the cyborg as a way of questioning the boundaries of the human (Haraway 1991). The figure of the cyborg brings to our attention a number of boundary breakdowns: between human and animal; between organism and machine; and between physical and non-physical. With reference to the first, Haraway argues that 'the last beachheads of unique-ness have been polluted, if not turned into amusement parks – language, tool use, social behaviour, mental events. Nothing really convincingly settles the separation of human from animal' (1991: 151–2). While the 'cyborg manifesto' was primarily a means of advocating a feminist politics, Haraway has pursued the question of the human non-human animal bound-ary (which she sees as a feminist issue) in particular with her work on companion species (Haraway 2003; also see Cudworth, this volume).

The Companion Species Manifesto (2003) is a very wide ranging essay that focuses on a variety of issues in dog-human relations from Haraway's personal experiences through to dog training manuals. She examines the ways in which dogs and animals have co-evolved. People didn't just make a decision to tame wolves; 'dogs-to-be' also sought out ways to relate to humans, which was of benefit to both species. This working out is something that has continued: 'dogs are about the inescapable contradictory story of relationships – co-constitutive relationships in which none of the partners pre-exist the relating and the relating is never done once and for all' (Haraway 2003: 12). A key term that Haraway utilises is that of 'natureculture', which for her emphasises the impossibility of distinguishing between nature and culture. Nature, Haraway argues, is 'one of culture's most startling and non-innocent products' (1991: 109). Ultimately, 'we have never been human', and it is that construction of the human that is her source of interest, which an examination of cyborgs and companion animals allows her to explore. Separating culture from nature is an inherently political act, which is the central aim of a posthumanist approach to reveal and question.

Critical potential

The core of the posthumanist project is a critical one as it undermines one of the central delusions of modernity. For Bruno Latour a central aim of our claim to be modern has been the attempt to detach ourselves as a species from the rest of nature. That this has not been achieved means we have never been modern (Latour 2009: 75; 1993). Likewise for Haraway (2008), we have never been human. To conclude, this section will argue that posthuman approaches have a critical contribution to make in terms of analyses of the development of interacting forms of human and non-human exclusion and suggesting broad guidelines for practice. The central contribution of a posthuman approach is to emphasise the embedded character of human social systems. This leads to three overarching principles in terms of practice: precaution, humility, and the prioritisation of building resilience in human and non-human systems. Posthumanism also suggests the need to develop a posthuman politics that will require the re-thinking of the major concepts of political thought, such as sovereignty, the state, and justice (see Bond and Kuehls, this volume).

The posthumanism advocated in this chapter is built on a complexity form of thinking. Complexity thinking in itself has various implications for understanding environmental issues and developing a critical environmental politics. What has been highlighted in this chapter, however, is that the systems analysis that develops emphasises the overlapping and embedded character of systems, and thereby contributes to a posthuman form of thinking. Human systems do not exist independently of the rest of nature but are embedded and overlapping with multiple non-human systems, both animate and inanimate. Humans are 'of' nature rather than 'in' nature. Making this the basis for analysis opens the possibility of understanding the interactions between human and non-human systems as providing a basis for a critical environmental politics. Sylvia Walby (2009) has demonstrated that complexity thinking can be used to theorise multiple forms of exclusion. This can be extended across the species boundaries to theorise the exploitation of animal and non-animal systems. For example, an analysis of the global food production system links complex systems as diverse as the human digestive system, the (post-)colonial system of states, exploitative relations with other species, and the development of non-animate food products (see Cudworth and Hobden 2011: 97–109). Posthumanism, therefore, reflects a requirement to think of humans as being of nature, and, through an interlinking systems analysis, provides the means for thinking about this.

Yet this is not simply an attempt to provide a better form of analysis. Posthumanism is also underwritten with a particular critical political project, which could be described as a posthuman politics. This posthuman politics could be seen as having a number of elements. Firstly, it draws attention to the embedded character of our existence. Wolfe has suggested that what emerges from a posthuman approach 'is an increase in vigilance, responsibility and humility that might accompany living in a world' that is not understood 'humanocentrically' (2010: 47). A greater awareness of our co-existence and co-constitution with non-human nature should encourage greater humility in terms of our understanding of what it means to be human and our co-existence with non-human nature. Complexity thinking draws our attention to the implication that our actions have repercussions beyond their immediate location. Morin (2008: 96) has expressed this as action escaping 'the will of the actor'. In complex systems, very small actions can result in very large and unexpected outcomes in other systems.

Humility might draw our attention to a further element of a posthuman politics and that is to develop a precautionary principle. Confronted by the uncertainty that complexity implies, we need to think carefully about our actions. While a first reaction to thinking about complexity might be to draw the conclusion that all action is problematic given the unpredictability of outcomes, that is not the position taken here. Rather, the unpredictability of outcomes should suggest a need for a precautionary principle. Complexity itself might not provide an immediate solution to the problems we confront, but it does indicate why they are so difficult to resolve. An awareness that the outcomes of our actions may be very different from our intentions and that actions can spill across systems means that we need to learn to live and cope creatively with complexity. A whole field of studying the question of policy making under conditions of anarchy is appearing, and this work has considerable relevance for thinking about issues related to the environment (Mitchell 2009; see also Baker and Pellizzoni, this volume).

A further practical concern raised by thinking about complex systems would be to consider their resilience. Resilient systems have much more capability to withstand unexpected developments as opposed to systems where this feature has been undermined. Work in environmental sciences has focussed on the resilience of non-human systems as well as their interactions with human systems (Gallopín 2002). Hence, a priority in general social policy and with regard to thinking on environmental issues should be in terms of thinking about building the resilience of human and non-human systems and positively avoiding taking actions that might weaken their capacity to resist external shocks (see Grove, and Methmann and Oels, this volume).

The systems approaches associated with complexity thinking and the associated posthuman politics suggest ways of re-orientating our thinking about the embedded and embodied character of human existence. As we confront the major and inter-related crises of climate change and species extinction, posthumanism provides a framework for re-considering the human position within non-human nature (see Okereke and Charlesworth, this volume). Perhaps the writer who has engaged most directly with the politics of a posthuman position is Bruno Latour. Latour has advocated a 'parliament of things'. Such a parliament attempts to overcome the problems associated with simply human assemblies: 'By defending the rights of the human subject to speak and to be the sole speaker, one does not establish democracy; one makes it increasingly more impracticable every day' (Latour 2004a: 69). The kind of institution needed is one that can provide a voice to a collective of human and non-humans (see McShane, this volume). However, enabling those to speak who have no voice is not straightforward. Latour advocates 'trial by force' where those that cannot speak are repre-sented by scientists who must win the argument in order to carry a debate. The character of this posthuman politics is only beginning to be considered, and Latour's proposal for a parliament of things is perhaps the most thought through example of how this might operate (also see Rudy and White, this volume).

Conclusion

This chapter has introduced the notion of posthumanism and has considered the ways that it could make a contribution to a critical environmental politics. It is a central contention of all the writers considered here that a re-thinking of politics is needed, whatever form that might take, to reflect our growing awareness of our human situation as embedded and co-constituting. Such a re-thinking implies that the major concepts of politics, such as sov-ereignty, the state, justice, rights, and representation, take on a markedly different character from a posthuman perspective. This is why any consideration of a critical environmental politics needs, at its base, a posthuman politics.

Further reading

There is a large and expanding literature on posthumanism in its various forms. Under the editorship of Cary Wolfe, Minnesota University Press has launched an excellent series Post-humanities, and any of the books in this series are worthy of consideration. Cary Wolfe's *What is Posthumanism?* (2010) is a particularly good place to start for a general discussion of the topic. All of Donna Haraway's books are relevant to the issues discussed in this chap-ter, and *When Species Meet* (2008) provides a good summary of the development of her arguments to date. French speakers can engage with the enormous number of books written by Edgar Morin. For those of whose language skills render us incapable of engaging with academic literature in French, then, of the pitiful few of his works that have been translated into English, *On Complexity* (2008) provides a good introduction to the issues raised by his work in this area. In *Posthuman International Relations* (2011), Erika Cudworth and Stephen Hobden have suggested that complexity and posthuman thinking provides more effective ways of thinking about issues of the environment in international relations.

Useful websites

LSE Complexity Research Group: http://www.psych.lse.ac.uk/complexity/
Santa Fe Institute: http://www.santafe.edu/about/mission-and-vision/
Posthumanism at Academia.edu: http://www.academia.edu/Documents/in/Posthumanism

19 Resource violence

Michael Watts and Nancy Peluso

Introduction

Despite their anodyne moniker, many (most) natural resources are deeply enmeshed in complexes of wealth and violence. In view of its theoretical concern with political economy, political ecology has taken resources – especially systems of access and control – as key entry points for analysis (Neumann 2005; Robbins 2004). Recently, however, resources have emerged as central foci in development and policy questions concerning 'good governance', a trend most obviously seen in the large body of work operating under the sign of the 'resource curse' (see Collier 2007; Humphrey, Sachs and Stiglitz 2007). In this chapter, we draw upon political ecological analysis to suggest an alternative conceptual architecture, what we call the 'resource complex', as a more helpful way to understand the critical environmental politics of resources.

As a way to map out the ways in which resources have been construed, we begin with two brief case studies. Forests in Indonesia and oil and gas in Nigeria elucidate the ways in which resources are imbricated in, and shaped by, configurations of historically and geographically contingent institutional and political economic forces (the resource complex). They also demonstrate how and why, under some circumstances, resources often become sites and objects of violent and complex struggles. The two case study analyses are followed by a discussion of several prominent contributors and their stands on resource politics, before we set out the critical potential of a 'resource complex' approach.

Core ideas: Case studies of forests in Indonesia and oil in Nigeria

Indonesia's forests

Indonesia's forests are as famous for their violent histories as for their vast expanses of tropical biodiversity. Many of them have been sites of insurrections, insurgencies, separatist movements, and counter-insurgencies. These repeated episodes of political violence and what might be deemed civil war have not been related, for the most part, to the forests' extent and value, although Indonesian forests have also had their share of violence over access to and control of forest resources, land, and territory.

War in the forests of Indonesia was historically much more connected with territorial struggles. Prior to 1967, many forests were regarded as community, clan, or individual terrains, some planted or encouraged for their forest products, some reserve land for future generations of forest residents to cultivate. Since the Japanese Occupation (1942–45), after the subsequent Indonesian revolution (1945–49), the conflicts of 'Confrontation' between Indonesia and Malaysia (1963–66), and the internal wars of ideology, governance, and primitive accumulation (1965–68), the territories and boundaries of national forests and the Indonesian nation-state have been mutually constituted through violent engagements with 'insurgencies' and 'emergencies' staged from forested territories (Peluso and Vandergeest 2011). Many of these insurgencies represented completely different political visions for the nation and took place in historical moments and sites where the reach of 'the national' was still tentative. Rather than rendering them asunder and becoming the targets of insurgents for funding their alternative political projects, forested sites of war, insurgency, and counter-insurgency helped normalize the idea of 'political' forests and 'national forests'. They became symbolic, territorial components of the Indonesian nation-state, during and after the political violence (see Kuehls, this volume). In concert with the discourses of scientific forestry, state actors and institutions deployed these discourses to territorialize state control over forests, maintain national security, and create nationally controlled sites of revenue production. Political violence that was not only related to the value of the enclosed timbers enabled the national state to appropriate forested territories.

Counter-insurgency operations in the 'jungles' of West Kalimantan and elsewhere contributed to resource management ideologies that spatially separated forests from agriculture and called into being the 'jurisdictions' of very different government agencies, each benefitting distinct populations of users. Forests thus constitute a type of resource complex that has a historically contingent composition, involving a national state that took violent control of forests for timber extraction and its own territorial protection. The national or post-colonial version of the political forest superseded what had been, in practice and in law, historically decentralized forest governance; foresters reported to the governors of colonies and of early provinces (Soepardi 1974). Under centralized state institutions, most notably the Department of Forestry, the military and other elites in national government, domestic companies, and international corporations became the main beneficiaries of the forests: both as territorial 'lords' and as highly subsidized resource concessionaires (Barber, Afiff, and Purnomo 1995; Barr 1999). Unlike most other lands managed for agricultural crops, settlement, or water resources, the Indonesian forest resource complex depended on centralized control. It was the first time that the central state had had such extensive territorial power.

Forests had been rendered violently and suddenly 'national space' or 'state territories' by the legislative decree of the Basic Forestry Act in 1967. Though the Act was meant to improve economic growth and stimulate development through forest exploitation and management, it increased the marginalization of forest-based communities. The Act facilitated the issuance of large forestry concessions to corporations. Logging income increased by some 2,800 percent. So did the uses of the forest. Wright (2011: 126) reports that, 'in 1967, four million cubic meters of timber were extracted, the majority for domestic use, but ten years later this had increased to 28 million cubic meters, a majority of which was exported' (see also Sangaji 2000; Safitri and Bosko 2002). Moreover, with the passing of the New Forestry Law in 1999, forest-based communities became even more marginalized. *Adat,* or customary forest, is defined as 'State Forest situated in the territory of adat community', clearly delineating the national state as a holder of 'eminent domain' (Wright 2011: 127). Although in the wake of second president Suharto's fall, nearly every other aspect of Indonesian resource management was decentralized, the forest lands ('State Forest') remained the domain of the central state – and it was an extensive and lucrative domain.

To return to the question of history, the 'urgency' of counter-insurgency in the late 1960s and throughout the 1970s led to national and international institutions calling for 'forest-based development', including the Food and Agriculture Organization, United Nations Environment Program, the World Bank, and bilateral aid agencies. This 'hearts and minds' counter approach, in addition to the violence of nation-building, became the guiding governance logic of Cold War and post–Cold War politics. International agencies provided financial support to Indonesia's Department of Forestry from 1967, and entrepreneurs from all over the world were able to invest for the first time in Indonesia, an opportunity that was constrained by requirements for all foreign firms to have Indonesian partners. Forest-based development plus violent counter-insurgency measures also fit what the Indonesian state called the 'double function' of its national military: 'repression' plus 'development'. These policies increased the numbers of military personnel in and around the thousands of forest villages in Indonesia; it also helped militarize the parastatal forest 'service' (*Perum Perhutani*) on Java. In teak forests, forest guards and rangers were armed and became part and parcel of international conservation discourses that, in the late 1970s and 1980s, set up both resource production and conservation as necessitating national state 'wars' against 'encroaching' human populations (e.g., the IUCN's *World Conservation Strategy* [IUCN 1980]; see also Igoe, this volume). Globally, the crisis rhetoric of environmental security that emerged at this time articulated with international conservation and national security discourses and with the emergence and consolidation of nation-state forms all over the world (see Dalby, this volume). Forest conservation, global timber markets, the end of colonialism, and the rise of technological and strategic assistance also strengthened the territorial power and reach of national states such as Indonesia. Forested 'natures', by nature territorial, became critical domains of national state power.

Since 1967 and the shift in Indonesian national policy and government centralization, Indonesian forests have provided critical material and ideological bases for nation-state building. State territorialization plays a fundamental role. Indonesia's forests have generated a dominance of the tropical lumber and plywood trade, an acclaimed production of teak products (legal and illegal), and a forest products industry (paper, plywood, veneer, and other products) that in total generates 6–7 per cent of the nation's GDP, second only to the oil/gas sector. Forests have also constituted a majority of the national territory.

Tropical forest cover in Indonesia is the most extensive in Southeast Asia and third in the world, after Brazil and central Africa (Cameroon, CAR, Congo). In 1985, the forest cover of the five largest forested islands – Sumatra, Kalimantan, Sulawesi, 'Irian Jaya', and Maluku – totaled 115,885,000 hectares (World Bank 2011). Even this was less than the 88 per cent of Indonesian territory allegedly under mature forest cover in the 1950s. In addition, 21 per cent of the island of Java was designated for forest or forest plantations, totaling some 3 million hectares, and bringing the total under forest cover to 118,885,000 hectares, about 61 per cent of Indonesia's total land area (Government of Indonesia 1986). Today the total forest cover is 88,495,000 ha, or 48.8 per cent of the land area (Mongabay 2013). Most of these areas do not include privately or communally held forests, or 'agricultural' tree plantations such as oil palm, rubber, or coffee. While environmentalists fret that the forest cover of Indonesia has declined from 88 per cent to 49 per cent of the nation's territory, the ability to maintain so much national territory as political forest under centralized authority is rare on a global scale.

To understand the scale of state forestry, we need to understand national politics as deeply imbricated with resources. Since their emergence, nation-state authority has been partially defined by their territorial bounds and internally differentiated by political jurisdictions, including natural resource management areas. This territorial zoning has changed not only governance but also access, not least by transforming property rights on and around forested lands (see, e.g., Ribot and Peluso 2003). Under the regime of state-led development, the Indonesian military largely enforced forest security outside Java. Although neoliberalism has grown stronger in Indonesia since 1998, most 'new' security arrangements in forest areas still involve the police and the military in various capacities. Private militias have taken a much larger role in security, as they are often hired by plantation and forestry extraction companies, and these militias are often connected politically to either the military, the police or political parties.

While the forms of security are changing, the idea that forests could contribute to state security was initiated centuries ago, under colonial rule. As early as the eighteenth century, Dutch colonial military forces in Java used and valued teak as a strategic state resource, critical to 'colonial security' (Peluso 1992). Empire was then seaborne, and controlling a forest full of the most desirable shipbuilding material on the planet – teak – constituted a major political-economic resource (see, e.g., Boxer 1965). This critical strategic importance of teak, plus its concentration in semi-natural, mono-cultural stands in central-eastern Java, led to the Dutch colonial government drawing the first and strongest formal-legal territorial boundaries around teak stands in teak forest districts. Not insignificant was the fact that extraction technology in the nineteenth century largely consisted of corvée and wage laborers living in forest regions and teams of draft animals cobbled from smallholders to pull the cut logs to the water's edge for transport. Tens of thousands of landless and near landless people lived in these areas of Java and were deployed in extraction and, soon after, in planting and other production tasks. This was territorial forest protection at a grand scale: thousands of forest guards, many ex-military, were worth their wages, given the value of teak. In the 1970s, national claims to forests spread to more difficult access areas, including international borders. The task of security was given to the military. The vastness of the forests meant that forest and military guards were fewer and farther between but more violent, aggressive, armed, and representative of the state.

Since the Suharto regime began, forests have been contested sites of state-making and national power. Leading up to the establishment of the New Order, the massacres and pogroms of 1965–1967 were carried out in the name of national security (Cribb 1991). This violence preceded the national state's appropriation of millions of hectares of land and forests, a move that both benefited and empowered the national military and the Department of Forestry, and was one of the first big hits on the rights of smallholders by the New Order regime (Farid 2005).

The Suharto regime thus made resource history while it was remaking the Indonesian nation-state. Land grabbing and systematic dispossession of millions were inherent to the extensive commoditization of agrarian environments throughout Indonesia. The result was a bizarre amalgamation of state-led and private or semi-private capitalist enterprises on the one hand and rampant theft of 'state' resources on the other hand. Importantly, it was not only the ranks of the dispossessed 'stealing' from national forests, but also foresters, military, and police. The state's appointed territorial protectors were often equally involved in legal and illegal logging, legal and illegal forest product manufacturing, exports, and smuggling (Brown 1999; Obidzinski 2005; Obidzinski and Barr 2003).

Forests, the military, and the nation-state that they constitute and represent are profoundly imbricated in Kalimantan, though the manner of their imbrication has shifted since the fall of Suharto (1998). Since 1966 or so, the Indonesian military had a strong presence in West

Kalimantan. The army fought insurgents in these 'jungles' (1963–1974), all four military branches were awarded timber concessions when the first national forest law was passed (1967–1980s), military bases were located throughout the province, while retired soldiers and ex-combatants were given land to cultivate in recognition of their service (1980s–1990s) (Barber and Talbot 2003; Peluso and Vandergeest 2011). Indeed the national state divided the 1000-kilometer long, 20-kilometer wide international land border between Malaysia and Indonesia into concessions for these branches, which they 'managed' with contractors in 'joint' ventures (Barr 1998; Barber and Talbot 2003). All branches of the Indonesian military are required by law to finance more than 60 per cent of their operating budgets, hence the government's allocation of concessions to them. As managers, however, military units have not protected these resources for the state; rather, they have been shown repeatedly to be drivers of illegal logging and non-timber forest product networks (Barr 1998; Barber and Talbot 2003; Obidzinski 2005). Illegal logging and non-timber forest product collection in their own and others' concessions and parks, nature reserves, national forests, and the other sites they guard are not random acts. They are exemplars of the systematic thuggery, extortion, and other criminal acts condoned by whole military units. Organizationally, they constitute the state, yet they steal from the state. In a recent mapping activity, the World Resources Institute has shown that in this region, the 1000-kilometer border is still experiencing the most rapid clearing (Dan Hammer, World Resources Institute, pers. comm. 2012). This is not the curse of a natural resource, but the iniquity of the resource's claim by violent – and national – institutions.

Nigerian oil

Nigeria is an archetypical petro-state, the eleventh largest producer and the eighth largest exporter of crude oil in the world. The oil-producing Niger delta in the southeast of the country has provided 'sweet' (low sulphur) oil to the world market for more than half a century, during which time the Nigerian state has captured close to one trillion dollars. Since the return to civilian rule in 1999, Nigeria has been shaken by extraordinarily contentious and violent politics. After a decade of what resembles a form of violent democracy, Nigeria confronted not one but two home grown insurgencies: one emanating from the oilfields, the other from the Muslim heartland in the north (see Amnesty International 2012; Forest 2012; Isa 2010; Watts 2011a).

The vertiginous descent of the Niger delta oilfields into a strange and terrifying shadow-world of armed insurgency, organized crime, state violence, mercenaries and shady politicians, and massive oil theft casts a long shadow over Nigeria's purportedly rosy oil future. A powerful insurgent group called the Movement for the Emancipation of the Niger Delta (MEND) emerged from the creeks in 2006 (Courson 2009). Within two years of taking office in 2007, the new administration of President Yar'Adua saw oil revenues fall by 40 per cent due to audacious and well-organized attacks on the oil sector. Shell, the largest operator, accounting for almost half of all oil output, had already lost US$10.6 billion since late 2005. In the Port Harcourt and Warri regions – the two hubs of the oil industry – there were more than 5,000 pipeline breaks and ruptures in 2007 and 2008 perpetrated by insurgents and self-proclaimed militants. According to a 2008 report (NDTC 2008), the Nigerian government lost a staggering $23.7 billion in oil revenues in the first nine months of 2008 due to militant attacks and sabotage. By the summer of 2009, Shell's western operations were in effect closed down and more than 1 million barrels of oil were 'shut in' – the industry term for production capacity compromised by security problems. While a state-brokered amnesty was struck in late 2009 – almost 30,000 militants and their commanders signed up – and a demobilization, disarmament and reintegration (DDR) program initiated at the cost of $1.3 billion, the situation remains utterly precarious, marked by the dramatic car-bombing in the capital of Abuja in October 2010 attributed to delta militants.

Nigeria's oil complex was born in the mid-1950s when the first helicopters landed in Oloibiri in Bayelsa State near St Michael's Church to the astonishment of local residents. A camp was quickly built for oil workers; prefabricated houses, electricity, water, and a new road followed. In the subsequent decades, the Nigerian oil industry grew quickly in scale and complexity: 600 on and offshore fields, thousands of oil wells, 7,000 kilometers of pipelines, almost 300 flow stations, massive liquified natural gas plants, and related infrastructure. By the 1970s oil tankers lined the Cawthorne Channel near the oil city of Port Harcourt like participants in a local regatta, plying the same waterways that had housed slave-ships in the sixteenth century and palm oil hulks in the nineteenth. The petroleum frontier followed the slave and palm oil frontiers and the eighteenth and nineteenth centuries.

Oil converted Nigeria into a petro-state – but one constituted by vast shadow political and economic apparatuses in which the lines between public and private, state and market, government and organized crime are blurred and porous. A new study by the UN Office for Drugs and Crime, *Transnational Trafficking and the Rule of Law in West Africa*, estimates that 55 million barrels of oil are stolen each year from the Niger delta, a shadow economy in which high-ranking military and politicians are deeply involved. According to former World Bank President Paul Wolfo-witz (2005), around $300 billion of in oil revenues accumulated since 1960 have simply 'gone missing'. More than 80 per cent of oil revenues accrue to 1 per cent of the population. Poverty, meanwhile, increased: between 1970 and 2000, the number of income poor grew 19 million to a staggering 90 million. Over the last decade GDP per capita and life expectancy have both fallen, according to World Bank estimates. Petro-wealth has been squandered, stolen, and channeled to largely political, as opposed to productive, ends. In other words, rather than investing in infrastructure or health or education with oil wealth, surpluses have been allocated for the purpose of making alliances and buying off opponents. Oil resource wealth, in sum, has lubricated a catastrophic failure of secular national development (UNDP 2005).

How was the Nigerian oil resource complex assembled historically? The onshore oil frontier (the off-shore frontier began much later, and the first deepwater oil production only began in 2005) operated in a distinctive fashion. Oil bearing lands were in effect nationalized and leases and licenses awarded (typically with little or no transparency) to oil companies who were compelled to participate in joint ventures with a Nigerian state. A Memorandum of Understanding determined among other things the very substantial government take on every barrel of oil produced. Local communities across the delta lost access to their lands. They were typically compensated (in an *ad hoc* and disorganized fashion) for loss of land rights and for the cost of spillage. Communities deemed to be 'host communities' – there are more than 1,500 – in virtue of having oil within their customary territories or being directly affected by oil infrastructure, were to receive 'community benefits' from the oil companies that, in the absence of effective local state, came to be seen as local government (Nwajiaku 2012). The companies built alliances with local political forces, which in effect meant dealing directly with powerful chiefs and chieftaincy systems marked by the exercise of lineage-based gerontocratic powers. For the better part of three decades the companies could operate with impunity, cutting deals with chiefs and elders and the political classes, who, through direct cash payments, contracts, and community funds, acquired considerable wealth.

Two logics structured the operations of the oil resource complex. The first was the national state's capture of oil rents though a series of laws and statutory monopolies (the 1969 Petroleum Law being the foundation stone). As for forests in Indonesia at the same global historical moment, the conversion of oil into a *national* resource ignited a powerful duo of forces. First, it became the basis of differential claims making. That is, citizens could, in virtue of its national character, plausibly claim their share of this national cake as a citizenship right (a new individual status produced by the emergence of the nation-state). Second, oil became a means of state centralization. Government expropriation of oil flew in the face of robust traditions and institutions of customary rule and land rights. The continuity of so-called customary forms of rule and the authorization of community forms of rule in effect institutionalized a parallel system of governance associated with chieftaincy and the political institutions of the so-called city-states like Nembe and Brass that emerged from the palm oil boom of the nineteenth century. Oil nationalization also trampled on local property systems and land rights and complicated the already tense relations between first indigenes (first settlers in local parlance) and newcomers. In the Nigerian delta with its 60 ethno-linguistic groups, the national oil laws inevitably were construed as expropriation and dispossession. These claims and losses were inevitably expressed in ethnic terms ('our land', 'our oil') and marked the emergence of so-called oil minorities (a post-colonial invention) not only as a political category but as entities with strong territorial claims (Okonta 2005). The fact that oil companies, as co-signatories to joint ventures with state, were in turn compelled to pay rents – vague, indeterminate, and not transparent sums – to oil-bearing communities (which typically meant undisclosed cash payments to chiefs, councils of elders, and ruling royal or 'big houses'), also converted an already contested arena of land rights into a charnel house of violent struggles over 'who owned the oil' and on what sort of identity basis (lineage, clan, ethnicity, first settlers, and so on).

The second logic reflects the institutional mechanisms by which revenues were to be allocated with a complex multi-ethnic 36- state federal system (HRW 2007; Ikelegbe 2006). Oil revenues are the main source of public revenue, accounting for about 80 per cent to 85 per cent of the total receipts. The current vertical allocation of revenues for governance is 52.68 per cent, 26.72 per cent, and 20.60 per cent for federal, state, and local governments, respectively. These figures confirm the centralizing effect of capturing oil rents but hide the fact that the details, hammered out in a number of revenue commissions over half a century, are still subject to intense contestation and continuing controversy. The federal center captured a disproportionately large share of the revenues; the states and local governments depend heavily on the center's statutory allocations. Since the 1960s the principles of allocation radically reduced the principle of derivation, by which states producing the resource retained a share of the revenues. Fiscal centralization re-directed revenues away from the centers of oil production and towards powerful non-oil ethnic majority states, especially in the north of the country. Thus oil revenues, changes in allocations of revenues (based on new conceptions of property rights), and the ethnic politics that had long characterized the region were all constitutive of Nigeria's national politics. The federal center became a hunting ground for contracts and rents of various kinds. Derivation politics inevitably became a major axis of contention between the delta and the federal center, laying the basis for what became in the 1990s the delta's clamor for 'resource control'.

It was from these dynamics that a welter of violent struggles emerged. According to a UNDP report (2005), there are currently 120–150 'high risk and active violent conflicts' in the three core oil producing states. The field of violence operates at a number of levels. Some insurgent groups such as the MEND are engaged in armed struggle against the state and the oil companies (Obi and Rustaad 2011). Inter-community (both inter-ethnic and intra-ethnic) conflicts are often driven by land and jurisdictional disputes over oil-bearing lands (and correspondingly over access to cash payments and rents from the oil companies). Urban ethnic communities contend for access to oil wealth, seemingly preferring urban inter-ethnic warfare over an ethnic delineation of electoral wards and local government councils (undertaken by the states but with federal backing) (Ukiwo 2007). Oil wealth in urban areas comprises the rents paid by oil companies for land used for oil infrastructure (refineries, pipelines, and so on) and a part of the revenue allocation process that now ensures that local government coffers are awash with so-called 'excess oil profits'. Other communities are torn apart by intra-community youth violence: the famed city-state of Nembe is a case in point (Watts 2007), in which armed youth groups battle each other and their chiefs. They fight over the provision of protection services to the oil companies and access to various sorts of standby (a salary for doing nothing) and cash payments dolled out in the name of 'community development'. Many of these struggles have been financed by oil theft (bunkering) in which insurgent groups or militias inserted themselves (typically as underlings beneath high-ranking military and politicians). The militias resembled the mafias of mid-nineteenth-century Sicily, violent entrepreneurs who stood between a weak state and deep class struggles surrounding the *latifundia* (Bloc 1974); they have produced a ferocious battle over oil bunkering territories.

With prices for oil at $100 a barrel, the entire rickety structure can stagger on: the Nigerian government, the rebels, the international oil companies, the oil bunkerers, and the political godfathers can all get their cut in spite of, and because of, the ungovernability of the entire system. Violent accumulation within the Nigerian oil complex is, paradoxically, self-producing as an economy of violence (Watts 2011a).

Key thinkers: Are resources cursed?

How should we understand these two cases? Resources have typically provided an indispensable entry point for political ecological analysis, a field/approach developed by key thinkers such as Piers Blaikie, Judith Carney, Susanna Hecht, Richard Peet, Nancy Peluso, Michael Watts and others (see Robbins 2004; Neumann 2005). Central to political ecology was political economy, and integral to this perspective was access to and control over resources. Rather than examining the functional adequacies of static 'traditional cultures' or 'social structures' in adapting to various environments, as did some concurrently emerging approaches to human–environment relations, political ecology started with the relations of producers to the market, property and access relations, the commodification of land and labour, the forms of surplus extraction, and the prismatic forms of social differentiation within peasant communities, the breakdown of moral economies, emerging forms of class structure, and changing relations of production. In addition, they posed environmental questions *not* through the prism of society *and* nature or human action and biophysical effect, but mapped out a political ecology by drawing on Marxist ideas of the imbrications of labour process and first or second nature. In other words, they viewed nature and society as dialectically constituted (Smith 1984).

Political ecology had as its reference point what we would call *regimes of accumulation* that operated at and intersected across multiple scales. Its torch was turned on the uneven and dynamic commercializations of agrarian societies, the ways communities could be torn asunder and 'culture' retooled and redeployed (as a more dynamic 'cultural politics') under the conditions of development and post-colonial state power. Some of the earliest work in political ecology, such as Blaikie's (1985) analysis of soil erosion, Hecht's (1985; Hecht and Cockburn 1989) work on Brazilian ranching, and our own work on forests in Indonesia (Peluso 1992) and food in Nigeria (Watts 1983), engaged directly with resource dynamics in ways that were sensitive to the histories and geographies of the political economic settings in which the objects of analysis – Nepalese peasants, forest–pasture conversion on the Brazilian frontier, conflicts over forest and land control in Indonesia, and famine in the Sahel – were explored. For political ecologists, environment and resources became key sites where contradictory political economic and ecological tensions were constantly building and forcing change, often through media and mechanisms of cultural politics.

More recently, 'natural resources' and resource commodities have drawn the attention of development economists and political scientists, for two key reasons. One is the poor performance of resource-dependent states, especially but not exclusively in Africa (Collier and Ong 2005; Ross 2012), and the other is constituted by the geopolitical concerns surrounding 'resource scarcity' and global struggles over key strategic resources (Klare 2011; McKinsey and Company 2011). Poverty, security, and resources have been brought together in an important power line of 'policy research', operating under the sign of the 'resource curse'. Some of this work dates to the 1990s and the purported associations between a nation-state's heavy dependence on primary raw materials and a raft of what is customarily seen as state deficits and dysfunctions (see World Bank 2011). The 1990s studies offered a different interpretation of what was once called 'comparative advantage' in the 'modernization' literature (Rostow 1960). Governments captured rents from key resources – energy, minerals, agricultural commodities – in ways that produced bloated and centralized government, powerful patronage systems rather than democracy, corruption and a lack of transparency, and poor economic performance. Eventually, this so-called 'paradox of plenty' (Karl 1997) – i.e., resource wealth associated with developmental and governance failures – came to see particular resource-dependent nation-states as 'cursed': hence the 'resource curse' thesis (Basedau 2005; Brunnschweller and Bulte 2008; Ross 2012; Rosser 2006). In resource-dependent nation-states, this story goes, a combination of state pathologies and failures coupled to poor economic performance created conditions under which conflict was deemed almost inevitable. In some accounts the global or local scarcity of strategic resources made internal instability or inter-state conflict and destabilization more likely (see Klare 2011; Homer-Dixon 1999; Baechler 1998; see also Dalby and Kütting, this volume). The resource curse condemns the state to poor governance and simultaneously sentences the nation to civil wars over resources, contesting state power and both territorial and non-territorial means of resource control.

Paul Collier's influential book *The Bottom Billion* (2007) builds upon the analysis of oil-states and other resource-rich economies, arguing that most of the world's billion chronically poor live in 58 countries – almost three-quarters of which are African – distinguished by their lack of economic growth and the prevalence of civil conflict. Most are caught in a quartet of 'traps', two of which are integrally related: namely the civil war trap (the average cost of a typical civil war is about $64 billion) in which 73 per cent of the poor have been caught at one time or another, and a natural resource trap (resource wealth or dependency turned sour), which accounts for another 30 per cent (the other two traps are landlocked states with bad neighbors and bad governance in a small country). Collier claims to have identified a quantitative relation (based on a large-n statistical methodology) between resource wealth, poor economic performance, poor governance, and the likelihood of falling into civil conflicts. Resource wealth, once seen as a comparative advantage, turns out to be a 'curse'. For Collier (2007: 46) oil is a compelling case; 'Big Oil' engenders 'Big Patronage', or as he colorfully puts it: the 'law of the political jungle' is 'the survival of the fattest'. Oil wealth relaxes political constraints – most obviously by obviating the need to tax. The sort of democracy that resource rich states get is 'dysfunctional for economic development' – especially if they are low income and ethnically diverse. And to round out the story, the combustible mix of the law of the survival of the fattest under the dispensation of oil – and other resources, too – provides ideal grounds for resource predation and the illicit economy of rebellion (the economic basis of civil war). Rebellions, according to the greed over grievance theory promoted by Collier (2007), have much less to do with what rebel leaders have to say about their political projects (liberation, justice, equity) and much more to do with organized crime, shadow states, and mafia networks and the facility by which the 'fat' political classes in and outside of government can loot or predate these resources. Oil democracy, says Collier, is an oxymoron. In this rendering oil accounts for a delusional body politic, psychopathic criminals dressed up as freedom fighters, state institutions resembling those of Albanian socialism, rafts of Big-Men patrons armed with real estate in Nice and off-shore accounts in the Cayman islands, and ensures a descent into civil conflict that is likely to last seven years and make people 15 per cent poorer.

Of course there is a certain descriptive truth to Collier's analysis. Resource-dependent states are often corrupt. In most rebellions the line between liberation and 'crime' are fluid, in part because the terms of criminality are set by the state authorities in office. But nobody should be surprised at this finding. The great failing in the resource curse approach is its resource commodity determinism: oil or diamonds or timber is driving politics without a corresponding sensitivity to the cultural, historical, and political contexts into which timber, oil, and diamond revenues are inserted. Curiously, in his analysis of oil states, there are only two sets of actors: corrupt politicians and criminals dressed up as rebels. Oil companies have no agency and rarely appear; if they do they are only there to be predated or extorted. The wider array of actors, agents, and processes – in the case of oil this might include national oil companies, transnational oil service companies, banks, paramilitaries, criminal syndicates, local rulers, construction companies, and so on – are read out of the analysis. As a result, the curse of oil – and indeed other resources like diamonds and other minerals – overdetermines history and particular outcomes, producing a flat and lifeless account of both politics and violence (Cramer 2006).

In *Wars Of Plunder*, Le Billon (2012) offers an approach more in keeping with our own; he tries to link what he sees as three different approaches to resources – the resource curse, resource wars, and resource conflicts – by examining oil, timber, and diamonds. He treats the resource curse with caution since it does not apply to all sectors and resources but argues that some resources are more prone to violence because of the 'social relations of production' (2012: 5). Like the resource curse proponents, he emphasizes opportunities for armed insurgents associated with resources that can be looted or predated in some way to fund their activities – a physical access question. Le Billon's three approaches – which focus on vulnerability, risk, and opportunity – are capable of generating various forms of violence. Le Billon classifies resources according to whether they are point or diffuse and proximate or distant (to political power); this typology generates a four-fold typology of forms of conflict: coup d'etat, secession, mass rebellion, and warlordism. All of this adds a complexity we agree with, and he invokes political ecology because of its 'thick historical and geographical contextualization' (2012: 57). Yet, where complex cases fit into typologies is often hard to define, and critical historical analysis is more than simply contextualization. More critically, the specific ways in which neoliberalism and powerful actors and agents intersect and overlap, producing forms of spatial fragmentation and re-territorialization, are less evident in his analysis. That said, his critique of the large-n econometric analysis and the essential-ist of theorization of human motivations (greed or grievance) is surely right, and his claim that 'resources are social processes', that 'some resources make wars more likely', and that 'resource sectors' differ in their constitution clearly points away from the more simple-minded generalizations of the resource curse.

Critical potential and conceptual alternatives

The sorts of issues raised by Le Billon (2012) – and especially the relations between re-sources and conflict – can be seen as a starting point for our notion of 'resource complexes'. As recognized in an important World Bank report, *Conflict, Security, and Development* (World Bank 2011), the model of the Cold War insurgency – alternative civilizing projects or struggles for territory and ideology – seems no longer to hold. The Cold War's boundaries between war and peace, or between political and criminal violence, have become radically blurred. National states are still major players in political violence and development efforts, but in different ways and with more flexible financing. Meanwhile, poverty and violence are inextricably connected for Collier's (2007) bottom billion, according to the 2011 World Bank report. William Reno's (2011) notion of symmetrical irregular warfare – in which rebels hold no clear ideology and are fragmented, fluid, factionalized, dispersed, defensive, and parochial – seems consistent with much of what the Bank's report highlights. Poverty and political violence are both new and heterogeneous. The 'newness' of the field of violence is matched by a particular history and geography; there is a territoriality to it. The violence is spatially concentrated and historically recursive, especially in the neoliberalizing Global South. In other words, the territorialization, or spatialization, of organized violence falls disproportionately in some parts of the Global South, with devastating effect.

In many instances, the struggles over land, property, and territory in and around oil con-cessions in Nigeria and forests in Indonesia, and the vast footprints of forest or oil and gas industries have had the effect of fragmenting space and producing what Lefebvre (2005) called 'multiple and overlapping spaces'. Whether customary, chiefly, clan, or village territo-ries, these areas are contested by localities, bunkering territories, ethnic groups or migrants, and locals wishing to occupy land and gain or maintain control. These resentments have often been characterized by violent assertion of autochthony, citizenship, and other exclu-sionary attachments of individuals and groups to particular places and identities. In both countries, 'horizontal violence' has sometimes been directed at so-called strangers, migrants, or non-indigenes, and sometimes against state predators (Geschiere 2009). The multiplica-tion of oil spaces as well as political forests in Nigeria and Indonesia, respectively, often unruly and deeply conflicted, represent still ferocious struggles over nation-building and how it is to proceed; in whose name and interest.

One of the advantages of WDR 2011 is that it places resources on a much broader land-scape of institutions, actors, agents, and processes (legitimacy, authority, rule). In our view this is key to understanding the relations between resources and conflict: it requires shifting from the 'resource curse' to the 'resource complex'. Le Billon's (2001, 2012) earlier work on forests in Cambodia, his more recent work on oil producing regions, and Mitchell's (2012) book on oil and democracy calling analysts to 'closely follow the oil', echo Paul Robbins's (2004) call for political ecologists to seek answers by 'following the money and following the power'. These all state what we have in mind: namely the importance of exploring the links between production areas and their downstream sites of surplus accumulation and physical transformation. These are, of course, affected by the kinds of resources – in our examples, forests and oil – that are being extracted and produced: but they travel from production site to pipelines, pumping stations, and refineries; from forests, sawmills, and factories, plus shipping routes, road systems, and automobile and trucking cultures. The task is to discover how relations among resource access and management, violence, finance, expertise, and democracy are engineered and stabilized (see T. Mitchell 2009).

Seeing resources – especially those claimed by states as national (natural) capital – as constituting zones of political and economic calculation (i.e., state territories) requires encompassing multiple agents and institutions, place-based histories, cultures, and political formations associated with the resource, as well as the material and commodity qualities of the resource itself (oil is different from forests or food). In the case of oil, this complex includes the super-majors, the national oil companies (NOCs) and the service companies (Halliburton, Schlumberget), and the massive oil critical infrastructures, but also the appa-ratuses of the petro-states themselves, the enormous engineering companies and financial groups, the shadow economies (theft, money laundering, drugs, organized crime), the rafts of nongovernmental organizations (human rights organizations, monitoring agencies, corporate social responsibility groups, voluntary regulatory agencies), the research institutes and lob-bying groups, the landscape of oil consumption (from SUVs to pharmaceuticals), and not least the oil communities, the military and paramilitary groups, and the social movements that surround and shape the operations of the oil industry (Soares De Oliveira 2007). Forests are similarly complex assemblages, yet their territorial extents and locations next to popula-tion settlements, as well as next to many different kinds of agriculture, provoke different questions of security, access mechanisms, claims, and potential distributions. They also have different necessary infrastructures, different types of trade networks, and produce different sorts of vulnerabilities. On the institutional side, forests are equally plagued with conflicting claimants, historically fraught discourses of criminality and legality, social movements, and associations with war and political violence.

These connections, complex as they already seem, are only a start. The financial sector is key both in terms of project financing but also as oil, forests, and land have become financial-ized assets reflecting radical changes in resource markets (see Paterson, this volume). Again, the nature of and function of territory emerges in different ways with oil, forest, or food productions. With forests, financialization questions circulate around alternative land uses as well as competing claims, rights, and the power to see them through. New governance institutions include the commodity exchanges but also the newly emerging global gover-nance mechanisms such as the International Energy Forum and their critics such as Project Underground. And not least for every barrel of oil or board foot of timber produced, moved, refined, and consumed there are carbon emissions (and thereby carbon trading, carbon cred-its, offsets, and carbon markets), which is itself a complex market with its own politics and dynamics (see Paterson, this volume). And of course, there are questions of what new land uses and territorial concerns will ensue in the wake of massive extraction – and almost by definition – massive landscape transformation, if not total destruction.

Conclusion

A conceptual shift from a resource curse to a resource complex has two important concep-tual implications. First, political ecology's long-standing concern with the relations between resources and regimes of accumulation has been expanded to include what one might call (following Foucault) *regimes of truth* (Foucault 2007a, 2008; see also Anderson and Braun 2008; Johnson and Forsyth 2002) and (following Gramsci) *regimes of rule/hegemony* (Ekers, Hart, Kipfer, and Loftus 2012; Li 2007; Moore 2005). Changes in one of these regimes generally influence the others as well. For this reason alone, some kind of historical perspective must be central to the analysis. Again following Gramsci (1971), the historical trajectories of various processes, people, and places come together in particular ways, often violently, at certain key conjunctures. As students of society-environment relations, therefore, we need to attend to what exactly changed, when, and to what effect. Because so much is going on at once, we must also pay attention to contingencies as well as to how explanations are constructed and legitimated (the trajectories of regimes of truth and knowledge).

The resource complex, in other words, examines both how resources are made regulable objects, how they are governed as parts of particular systems of rule, and what are the political and power relations by which the complex is, or is not, stabilized and rendered self-reproducing. In addition, the resource complex is shaped by two relatively recent transformative processes: first, the concurrent centralization and neoliberalization of states and markets, unleashing brutal forces of accumulation by dispossession (Harvey 2005); second is the securitization of the resource complex by national states, even more so since September 11 (see Dalby, this volume). Many resources are draped in the languages of national security and other bunkering notions (food security, energy security, human security, and so on), which is to say they are strategic as well as wealth-producing assets (Floyd 2010). Both of these processes – neoliberalism and security – need to be seen historically: as moments in trajectories of capitalism and the nature of state power. They have come into being in part because of what Ash Amin (2010) calls 'the condition of calamity', or 'catastrophism', a dominant ideological motif of the current moment (see also Methmann and Oels, and Pellizzoni, this volume).

Discursively, in policy and academic circles, the resource complex is increasingly constituted by the language of security and by processes of securitization (Floyd 2010). Resource security in short resembles a state of emergency, not unlike the calamitous discourse calling for environmental and biodiversity protection; it involves a rallying of the technical and managerial 'troops' to wage war on un-sustainability. This goal is to be realized through state territorialization (see Kuehls, this volume), the creation of new sorts of property rights, and, as we have seen, the violence that accompanies these acts.

Further reading

Important conceptual and empirical work on resources and the ensemble of institutions and political economies of which they are part and perspectives can be found in Bohle and Funfgeld, (2007); and Soares De Oliveira (2007) *Oil and Politics in the Gulf of Guinea*, London: Hurst. On security and resources see Klare (2011) *The Race for What's Left*, New York: Metropolitan; Barnett (2001) *The Meaning of Environmental Security*, London: Zed Books Dalby (2009) *Security and Environmental Change*, Cambridge Polity; Floyd (2010) *Security and the Environment*, Cambridge: Cambridge University Press; and Matthew, Barnett, McDonald, and O'Brian (eds) (2010) *Global Environmental Change and Human Security*, Cambridge, MA MIT Press. For approaches using insights from Foucault see Dillon (2007b), Watts (2011b), Anderson (2012), and Li (2007). On resource conflicts see Peluso and Watts (2001) *Violent Environments*, Ithaca, NY: Cornell University Press, and Kosek (2006) *Understories*, Durham, NC: Duke University Press.

Useful websites

Global Witness: http://www.globalwitness.org/

Mongabay: http://www.mongabay.com/

Woodrow Wilson Center, Environmental Change and Security Program: http://www.wilsoncenter.org/
program/environmental-change-and-security-program

Forest Watch: http://www.globalforestwatch.org/english/index.htm

Human Rights Watch: http://www.hrw.org/

International Crisis Group: http://www.crisisgroup.org/

Friends of the Earth Indonesia is WALHI: http://www.foei.org/en/who-we-are/member-directory/
groups-by-region/asia-pacific/indonesia.html

ARUPA (English site): http://www.arupa.or.id/download/profileng.htm

Asia Forest Network via ARUPA: http://www.asiaforestnetwork.org/prog_nps_indonesia.html

Down to Earth: http://www.downtoearth-indonesia.org

20 Risk

Luigi Pellizzoni

Introduction

The expression *risk* is usually used to refer to possible harmful events, on which there exists some room for maneuver. A standard technical definition depicts risk as a concrete, quantifiable state of affairs: namely, the product of the probability and the 'magnitude' (import, severity) of the consequences of an adverse event. For there to be a risk there must be a hazard related to an object, situation or process, and the exposure of someone to such hazard. Some critics, however, contend that there is no risk as such in the 'real' world; or, whatever happens 'out there', we have only a socially and culturally mediated access to it. Others question the probabilistic character of the referent of the notion, or remark that the quantification of the consequences makes sense only within a subjectively variable threshold of catastrophe.

In pre-modern Europe, *risk* refers to the threats of sailing, such as storms or pirate attacks. As with metaphysical accounts of human vulnerability (magic, religion), human agency and responsibility is excluded. The modernization process leads to risk becoming used to designate events related to behavioural choices. This change is due to cultural and institutional factors, such as the emergence of the science of probability and statistics and the development of risk-focused regulations and organizations, such as insurance systems. In current everyday language, *risk* is a loose term covering a variety of situations. In specialized sectors, the notion has been increasingly challenged by, if not blurred with, connected yet competing concepts, such as uncertainty or indeterminacy.

In short, risk is an eminently convoluted issue. Its position is critical in the twofold sense that its potential for critique is strong but precarious. Discussing risk entails connecting conceptualizations and their historical milieus, specifications of the notion and the political questions such specifications address. Different approaches to risk emerge and compete under changing social and environmental conditions.

Core ideas and key thinkers

The connection between risk and the environment gains salience at the end of the Second World War. The Hiroshima and Nagasaki bombs suddenly make technology appear to rival (or put to work) the greatest forces of nature, showing a profound ambivalence, as both a creative and destructive power. The unrivalled account of this novel human condition remains Max Horkheimer and Theodor W. Adorno's *Dialectic of Enlightenment* (2007). Written during the war, the book detects in modern reason a tragic contradiction between human attempts to find protection from nature and the unknown through knowledge and technical control, and subjection to these very instruments of emancipation. Getting free from the hold of nature means falling prey to the same natural forces of domination.

This grand opening of the environmental question has no direct sequel. For years the environment fills the political agenda mostly in the form of specific policy issues. A variety of accidents strike the public opinion: from the nuclear releases of the Windscale (United Kingdom, 1957) and Three Mile Island (United States, 1978) power stations to the Torrey Canyon tanker wreckage in Cornwall (1967); from the dioxin release in Seveso (Italy, 1976) and the Love Canal (United States, 1979) residents' problems with toxic waste, to the chemical disaster of Bhopal (India, 1984). Other topics, however, gradually get momentum: Rachel Carson (1962) denounces the long-term effects of systematic abuse of pesticides. The physical limits to population growth and economic expansion are addressed by Paul Ehrlich (1968) and the MIT (Meadows, Meadows, Randers and Behrens III 1972). The Yom Kippur war (1973) inflicts an oil shock on Western countries. In the meantime, the environmental movement grows from niche to mass, with protests spreading at different scales on an assortment of topics (see Price, Saunders and Olcese, this volume).

It is through these events and voices that risk becomes a public matter. What was once taken for granted – a general support to technoscientific advancement and economic growth, and trust in expert assessments of relevant policy choices – is increasingly brought into question (see Forsyth, this volume). Policy-makers recognize that the matter is not just to 'get the numbers right', but that 'numbers' have to be publicized and explained. They soon realize, however, that this is often not enough to calm fears (Fischhoff 1995).

Risk perception and culture

Emerging in the 1970s, the 'psychometric paradigm' (Slovic 1992) represents an attempt to account for, and handle, this problem. If technologies, industrial facilities and infrastructures provide (alleged) major collective benefits against (purported) negligible risks, why is it that NIMBY/NIABY (not in my/anyone's backyard) protests proliferate? False beliefs, irrational fears and ignorance must be surely at play. Understanding the cognitive structure of risk evaluations becomes politically crucial. Research in risk perception (Slovic 2000) shows large, persistent biases in the way lay people process information, due to factors such as familiarity, novelty, dread or voluntary assumption, which lead to systematic over- or underestimation of actual risks. Communicating numbers is not enough. One needs to marketize environmental policies, for example, by offering suitable 'compensations' or showing that similar risks have been accepted in the past.

Yet the more that basic needs (jobs) are fulfilled, the spatial and social distribution of risks and benefits is regarded as unfair, and the main (political, scientific, corporate) institutions involved are perceived as mistrustful, the less the marketing strategies are likely to succeed. There is no compensation or justification for what is seen as an irreparable loss (of health, natural resources and amenities etc.). Above all, arguments appear to affect people with the same levels of information and similar interests in contrasting ways. Different rationalities seem at work, calling for more finely-tuned strategies. To this purpose, the 'cultural theory' of risk that develops roughly alongside the psychometric approach offers an alternative, politically appealing, framework. Grounded on the work of the anthropologist Mary Douglas, this approach addresses risk as a cultural construct, rather than a cognitive process. Following a Durkheimian rationale, Douglas argues that different forms of social organization entail different worldviews. The social order is protected and justified by the moral order: what people believe to be right or wrong. A given moral order leads to specific configurations of risks and threats and attributions of responsibility for its violation (Douglas 1992). In culturally heterogeneous societies different worldviews, thus different identifications of risks and responsibilities, coexist. Hence, the typical situation of environmental conflicts: techno-enthusiasts clash with techno-skeptics; supporters of experts' competence and reliability quarrel with critics; risk-takers are either admired or blamed; and nature is simultaneously described as fragile, resilient or menacing (Schwarz and Thompson 1990).

In short, the political framing of environmental risks is neither totally objective nor totally subjective. Appointing renowned experts to perform risk-benefit analyses may reassure some; others need to be 'listened to' and made 'partners'. Between the 1980s and the 1990s the emergent theme of public deliberation finds in the environment an elective terrain of application, while the major ecologist organizations are enrolled in the policy process, as collaborative rather than oppositional forces (see Hinton, this volume). The acknowledgment of the inevitably politicized character of risk leads also to devising a 'decisionist' strategy for the application of science to policy (European Commission [EC] 2000; NRC 1983). The direct link between scientific advice and policy-making, advocated since the end of World War II (Bush 1945), becomes a two-step process: a science-based risk assessment followed by a risk management phase, where decisions are taken by balancing scientific evidence with social and political considerations.

Uncertainty and the risk society

In synthesis, up until the end of the 1980s the dominant political question is how environmental risks – depicted as side effects of a generally benign growing intermingling with the biophysical world – can be managed through technical fixes, increasing 'eco-efficiency' and social mediation on the material and symbolic outcomes of such interaction. The climax of this approach is reached by the UN-sponsored 'Brundtland Report' (WCED 1987) and 1992 Rio de Janeiro Earth Summit, both sanctioning 'sustainability' as the general framework for collaborative environmental reforms (see Death and Whitehead, this volume). And yet the Chernobyl accident (1986), the discovery of the hole in the ozone layer (1987), the Bovine spongiform encephalopathy (BSE) crisis (1995), the persisting question of nuclear waste disposal, the appearance on the public scene of gene technologies, the increasing salience of climate change and biodiversity loss, indicate that a new season in environmental politics is opening up (see Büscher, Kütting, and Okereke and Charlesworth, this volume).

What these and other issues have in common is the uncertainty surrounding the causes and/or dynamics of phenomena and the results of policy action. For Silvio Funtowicz and Jerry Ravetz we have entered a phase of 'post-normal science', where typically 'facts are uncertain, values in dispute, stakes high and decisions urgent' (Funtowicz and Ravetz 1993: 744; see also Forsyth, this volume). Traditional experimental approaches prove difficult, or impracticable. Non-linear interactions make macro-effects impossible to derive from micro-dynamics (see Hobden, this volume). There can be a plurality of relevant views on problems, including those offered by 'lay' knowledge and insight into crucial local conditions. Sheer ignorance may surround the possible events and affecting factors, thus determining whether the right questions are put. Brian Wynne (1992) is most explicit in pointing to the reciprocal dependence of uncertainty and decision-stakes. The salience of uncertainty is related to our increasing expectations of control of nature. Moreover, expert knowledge implies assumptions about existing or desirable social arrangements and prescriptive models of individual and collective behaviour. Sheila Jasanoff talks of 'co-production' of the social and natural orders: '[t]he ways in which we know and represent the world (both nature and society) are inseparable from the ways we choose to live in it' (2004: 2). Hence, there is no clear-cut distinction between risk assessment and management, or between questions of knowledge and prediction and questions of rationale and implications of choices. The political case this scholarship often leads to is that decision-making must be 'democratized', in a twofold sense: by enlarging the review process of science and environment policy to include affected social groups, and by widening the scope of inquiry to a range of 'evidences' broader than those usually considered as 'scientific' (see Baker, this volume).

In short, the ecological crisis cannot be addressed on a case-by-case basis. It raises funda-mental questions. In a sense, we are back to Adorno and Horkheimer. At stake is the whole society–nature relationship; modern rationality in its scientific and political embodiments. Nowhere does this appear with greater clarity than in Ulrich Beck's account of the 'risk society' (1992). For the German sociologist, human-produced risks impinge profoundly on present society. They elude institutional control and rational calculation; often also sen-sorial perceptions. Their public salience has grown, also due to the individualization and de-traditionalization of society (cf. also Giddens 1990), which puts people in front of 'risky' everyday decisions that affect their health, wealth and happiness. This alters the charac-ter of conflict and solidarity, which increasingly concern the distribution of 'bads', rather than 'goods'. Risk today means uncertain hazard. This unsettles the calculative logic of sci-ence, enterprise, state bureaucracy and social security. Uncertainty about hazard description, causal chains, relevant evidence, entails major effects of 'organized irresponsibility' – the health and environmental costs of innovation are 'socialized' with no prior acknowledgment and agreement – which growing regulation, if anything, exacerbates. Politics, as understood in modern democracies, is under stress. Crucial decisions are taken, in full autonomy and shelter from public inquiry, by corporate managers, research groups and techno-bureau-cratic organisms. What we need, therefore, is to 'modernize modernity', promote a 'reflexive modernization' (Beck, Giddens and Lash 1994). Tradition and the authority principle must be replaced by a fully fledged application of modernity's core principle: critique and self-critique. This means a constant assessment of individual and collective practices; a full embracement of, rather than a retreat from, risk, acknowledging that there is no other choice than making choices (Giddens 1994); a de-monopolization of expertise and the development of a 'technological citizenship', that is alternative, citizen-based forms of expert knowledge (Beck 1996); and a growing inclusiveness of decision processes.

The totalizing assumptions of this approach are difficult to test in detail (yet cf. Tulloch and Lupton 2003). However, the 'risk society' argument finds correspondence in macro-scopic signs of change in environmental politics. Ecologism, for example, is taking novel forms. It often defies the advocacy and brokerage inclination of established organizations, focusing on single issues, building on loosely structured citizen groups and using unortho-dox means like consumer boycotts. The NIMBY stigma is increasingly deconstructed in the public arena in two ways: by showing that risks related to a particular resource, place or com-munity also affect general interests or widely shared values (Rootes 2007), and by producing scientifically grounded counter-arguments that challenge official statements and risk-benefit analyses (McCormick 2007; Moore, Kleinman, Hess and Frickel 2011; Pellizzoni 2011a). Partly in reply to this strengthened critical capacity, public dialogues and inclusive processes intensify to a remarkable extent, at a plurality of scales and on a variety of themes, from local waste repository siting to national biotechnology policy. Yet these processes typically consist of mere consultations with hardly any direct policy outcome; hence their success in containing sustained protests is often limited (see Price et al., this volume).

The rise of precaution as a key policy principle is another remarkable sign of change. The idea that policy action should focus not only on predictable risks but also on unquantifiable threats enters the global scene in the 1980s, enjoying growing public and regulatory success. Today references to precaution can be found in international declarations and agreements, European treaties and directives, national regulations and numberless citizen mobilizations. The most notable exception is in the United States, which has always remained resolutely adverse to the principle, at least in the environmental field. Actually, the idea of precaution suffers from an intrinsic opacity. Does it make sense to spend huge money on mere possibilities (Sunstein 2003)? Should a technology be regarded as potentially harmful until proven harmless? Isn't this too heavy a load for innovators? Is a negative proof ever producible? Doesn't a largely discretionary measure allow disguised forms of commercial protectionism? The European Commission's position (EC 2000) is emblematic of the contradictions that stem from attempting to ensure proportionate interventions in front of incalculable eventualities, or from recognizing the endemic presence of major uncertainties while simultaneously assuming that reliable scientific knowledge is only provisionally unavailable. Indeed, there is something ambiguous in an appeal to 'act' in anticipation of catastrophic events that cannot be consistently predicted. That the application of a 'heuristics of fear' may not always be so benign as philosophers (Jonas 1984) and a number of ecologists have imagined is testified by the U.S. invasion of Iraq, motivated precisely in terms of anticipatory response to an uncertain threat.

Risk as rationality of government

Whatever we think about risk – an objective state of the world, a psychological or cultural construct, a combination of material threats, human appraisal and social organization – its growing presence in society is undeniable. This makes it a crucial driver of meaning: about oneself, other people, biophysical entities, situations, events, actions. Risk constitutes a rationality of government and self-government – a 'govern-mentality' – of growing importance.

The notion of governmentality, as developed by Michel Foucault (2007a; see Lövbrand and Stripple, this volume), refers to the forms of reasoning around which the exercise of power is articulated. In a historical sense it indicates the growing role of expertise and administrative powers vis-à-vis traditional political authority and the rule of law; the growing relevance of the regulation and optimization of the biological life of people (see Grove, this volume); and the increasing focus of government on issues of individual and population security (Dalby, this volume). This includes also a growing attention to the biophysical milieu. Environment as a concept and a problem – ecological thinking; the perceived need of environmental governance; the idea of ecological crisis; the differently involved problems, knowledges, actors and forms of intervention – can actually be regarded as a key biopolitical driver, effect and arena (Darier 1999; Rutherford 2007).

Addressing risk as rationality of government is especially useful to account for the entanglement of environmental politics with the major project of political, economic and social change usually referred to as the advent of neoliberalism. The latter, as a set of ideas, programs and policies gaining ground since the 1980s, has enabled a renewed capital accumulation, leading to the privatization and marketization of previously unaffected aspects of biophysical reality. Yet the 'neoliberalization of nature' (Castree 2008; McCarthy and

Prudham 2004) entails a more profound change in the relationship with the biophysical world. Risk is a key element in this process.

Foucault and his scholarship stress that the neoliberal rationality of government engenders a major transformation of the social order. This in regard to the role of the market, capital and competition, the logic of which expands to encompass virtually any aspect and element of the social and natural world (Barry, Osborne and Rose 1996; Dean 1999; Lazzarato 2009; Nealon 2008). It is also in regard to risk. Decision-making under uncertainty is no more seen as an exceptional condition in the context of usually calculable risks, but as an everyday situation. Speculation prevails over prediction. Proper calculations of risk are the exception, while reasoned bets over unpredictable futures are the rule. Uncertainty is at the basis of entrepreneurial creativity, which requires intuition, foresight, flexibility, experiential judgment, rules of thumb and so on (O'Malley 2004). Turbulence and contingency, as produced by global trade, innovation-based competition and floating exchange rates, do not mean paralyzing uncontrollability but lack of limits, room for manoeuver, opening up of opportunities. The more unstable the world, the more manageable. The contrast with traditional environmental and social science understandings of uncertainty could not be starker. Indeterminacy, understood as *non-determinability,* has led in the past to either pessimistically acknowledging dramatic limits in our predictive abilities, as with chaotic systems (climate, for example), or to claiming capacities of control in spite of incomplete characterizations of physical states, as with quantum mechanics. Neoliberal rationality, instead, depicts indeterminacy as enabling *non-determination:* purposeful action is seen to expand its scope precisely thanks to the indefinite character of the state of affairs (Pellizzoni 2011b). The limits to knowledge and prediction are recast as chance for creative action, the worth of which is sanctioned ex-post by its very success. Major tenets of ecological thinking, like the idea of resilience as unpreventable, continuous adaptation to extreme, persistent turbulences (Holling 1973), is taken over by a rationality of government that replaces traditional planning and predictive forecasts with scenario techniques and regards as a core individual and collective requirement the ability to adapt to unknowable social and biophysical contingencies (Cooper 2010; Walker and Cooper 2011).

This cannot but affect the way in which the relationship with the biophysical world is understood and enacted. Discourses of limits to growth are replaced by narratives of growth of limits (see Kütting, this volume). It becomes possible to argue, for example, that biodiversity loss and population growth can be compensated by new genetically-engineered organisms (Gurian-Sherman 2009) or that climate change can be effectively addressed by means of 'geoengineering' technologies of solar radiation management and carbon dioxide removal (Royal Society 2009). There is more to the neoliberalization of nature than an increasing privatisation and marketisation of resources, therefore. There is a thorough reframing of the ontological condition of the biophysical world as indefinitely pliant to human agency, where risk as enabling indeterminacy plays a pivotal role.

The creation of 'carbon markets', that is markets in permits to emit greenhouse gases or in credits earned by not emitting them, provides an example (see Paterson, this volume). Carbon trading rests on the operators' acceptance – despite questionable theoretical assumptions and empirical estimates – of a conversion rate between CO_2 and other greenhouse gases: the 'global warming potential' (GWP). Reducing one's CO_2 emission or buying credits sold by someone else who, somewhere in the world, is reducing another greenhouse gas becomes in this way equivalent (MacKenzie 2009). The intractable complexity of the real impact of different quantities of diverse gases emitted in opposite parts of the world at different times is transformed into a matter of calculation. We have here not only a further expansion of the market logic, but also the appearance of an entity, GWP, provided with a peculiar ontological status. GWP is an abstraction, like money, since it works as an exchange rate. Yet it is also something allegedly happening in the atmosphere, a physical thing or phenomenon. Oscillating between reality and virtuality, matter and symbol, GWP is not just another 'fictitious commodity' (Polanyi 1944), as a tree becomes once disembedded from its socio-cultural meaning and biophysical function and placed in the market. GWP is more than an 'as if' – an abstraction of capital. It is an onto-logically indeterminate entity that did not exist beforehand and the reality of which is totally absorbed by, reduced to, its commodity status (Pellizzoni 2011b).

This rationality of government can be detected elsewhere. For example, by regarding a liv-ing entity as an artifact if its basic functional parameters can be controlled (thus reproduced), biotech patents establish a correspondence between information and matter so that rights in property over information can be subsumed into rights in property over the organisms incorporating such information, and vice versa (Carolan 2010). Moreover, by claiming that they are indistinguishable from nature for any practical purpose ('substantial equivalence' principle), patented artifacts are made simultaneously identical (hence no specific regula-tion required) and different (hence proprietary value assigned) to natural entities. Likewise, the properties of nanoparticles are typically analogous to their bulk variants only in some respects. Again, we are faced with things that are the same and different, with consequent controversies about the need and scope of specific regulations.

Critical potential

The contentious meaning of risk has historically offered a terrain on which opposing forces could deploy their interpretations of, and interests and commitments about, environmental issues. Risk, in other words, has represented a driver of power and domination but also of contestation and resistance. Its political significance rests on the variable assemblages of cognition and volition, descriptive assessment and value assignment it consists of; on the extent to, and the way in, which human finitude as existential openness to harm is addressed (see Methmann and Oels, this volume). More recent developments cannot but impinge on its critical capacity since they affect its constitutive mixture of rational knowledge and norma-tive orientation. It is impossible to anticipate what the eventual results of this will be. The literature on neoliberalism, however, offers plenty of evidence that the securitarian drift in which risk has been embroiled since the beginning is proceeding at a growing pace (Harvey 2005; Brown 2010; see also Dalby, this volume). In this context risk increasingly represents a potential driver of de-politicization.

In the public sphere, for example, risk discourses are frequently associated with the idea that environmental problems involve each and everybody, beyond differences and inequali-ties; a narrative already implied in the 'risk society' argument, which, however, is becoming increasingly pervasive. Climate change plays a major role in this respect. Its threats are typically depicted as incommensurable in the sense that they are impossible or pointless to specify in their distributional impacts, which may justify the assumption of quantifi-able risks, such as those of nuclear power. Hence, there is a plea for replacing 'ideological' disputes with stakeholder consensual reflection, within the unquestionable framework of capitalism (Swyngedouw 2010). In general, attempts at constructing 'inclusive' frameworks from above for a consensual handling of the multifarious sources and aspects of risk have become increasingly sophisticated (e.g., IRGC 2008).

At the regulatory level, the need for stronger international standards, stemming from the reduction of trade barriers, gives technical bodies increasing relevance. This is accompanied by a growing focus on issues of safety, quality and efficacy, to the detriment of socio-economic considerations of need, desirability and distribution (Kinchy, Kleinman and Autry 2008), which allegedly might divert investment and deter innovation.

At the level of local protests, scientific methods and languages are increasingly applied. This entails a growing relevance of risk/uncertainty-related counter-claims. Scientific arguments have critical leverage to the extent that they bring to the fore neglected issues and open spaces for questioning the political choices underlying appeals to 'sound science' (Frickel et al. 2010; Pellizzoni 2011a). Yet this comes at a cost. Grounding contestations on a scientific terrain means aligning with the treatment of environmental governance as a depoliticized, technical issue. Research shows that focusing on quality standards and scientific uncertainties may support but also limit the scope of citizen mobilizations (Drake 2010; Ottinger 2010). Such themes are simultaneously publicly resonant and attuned to neoliberal discourses of individual risk and responsibility in front of inexorable technological progress (see Luke, this volume).

In short, the political space of risk is increasingly becoming a minefield of manufactured, pliable realities, where oppositional forces may have more to lose than to gain. In a number of fields (gene/nanotechnologies, greenhouse gas emissions etc) organized interests appeal to scientific uncertainty or disagreement to question restrictive measures allegedly lacking a grounding in 'sound science' (Freudenburg, Gramling and Davidson 2008; Michaels 2006). Asking for precaution – that is for action in the absence of conclusive evidence of problems – means that environmentalism ends up playing the same game and talking the same language as the most conservative wings of capitalism.

In an illuminating conceptual exploration, Niklas Luhmann (1993) draws a distinction between risk and danger. The former is an event that the agent relates to its own behaviour; the latter is something on which the agent has (or believes to have) no influence. This clarifies in what sense modern society can be regarded as more 'risky' than, say, middle-age Europe – and indeed increasingly so. Risk expands together with our actual or presumed agency over the course of events. Yet Luhmann's account highlights another point. Regarding something as a risk or danger is a matter of social position, which dictates who has the legitimacy and capacity to act. What is a risk from the agent's viewpoint is a danger from the patient's. Risk is an eminently political question. Many environmental conflicts can be actually traced to this divide, which highlights the existence of institutionalized, systematic rather than contingent, discrepancies in the orientation towards risk (Pellizzoni and Ylönen 2008). On the one side there are those who have more to lose from what statisticians call false positives. Detecting problems that do not actually exist affects research, profits, national competitiveness and the health and environmental benefits of technology advancement. On the other side there are those who have more to lose from false negatives. Failing to detect problems that do actually exist affects technology end users, local communities and the environment at large. Experimental designs typically focus on exposure to single agents or conditions rather than mixtures. This is suitable for reducing false positives but may fail to grasp the multi-causal character of many biophysical processes. The presence of positional divergences about risks is however systematically obscured by the assumption that innovation and growth are beneficial to everyone, including those who bear the bulk of their drawbacks and 'side effects'; an assumption that leads to an interpretation of public fears and distrust as a demand of 'zero risk' (i.e., a misguided expectation of certainty from science).

These 'misunderstandings' have a well-documented history (Felt and Wynne 2007). Neoliberalism has certainly intensified them. Yet, as we have seen, it also raises new problems and challenges. Environmental politics seems increasingly embroiled not so much in the forms and limits of prediction, as in different – utopian and dystopian – visions of the future. Pleas for restraint are confronted with promissory anticipations of a brave new world, enabled by the unlimitedly pliable, 'improvable', character of nature (and humanity: Roco and Bainbridge 2002). Questions of risk, uncertainty and 'sound science', in this context, seem not so much questions about designing research and building policies appropriate to given goals; they rather involve moralized orientations towards a technological future (Berkhout 2006). The mutable, indeterminate character of nature mobilizes opposing parties in a battlefield increasingly populated by hype, expectations, anticipations and imaginaries (Pollock and Williams 2010). Ecologism is thus caught in the same speculative exercise as its scientific, corporate or political targets.

Conclusion

The destiny of risk as an instrument of critique, that is, as a means for opening up spaces of discussion, contestation and change, is therefore unclear. In philosophy and sociology several voices have recently arisen asking for critical attention to refocus on the agential materiality of nature: its active existence, its incessant becoming – from bacteria to geological processes, to humans' own bodily existence – as independent of, indifferent to, or overarching human appraisal and action (Barad 2007; Coole and Frost 2010; Clark 2011; Grosz 2011; Kirby 2011; see also Hobden, and Rudy and White, this volume). The growing reach of risk as related to the expanding scope of human agency might therefore be, to a significant extent, illusory.

Salutary as this discourse may sound against constructionist excesses (as well as straightforward realist assumptions of correspondence between things and cognitive representations), it does not come without problems. Whatever our conceptualization of nature, it cannot be other than our own: things exist *for us* only as we make physical and intellectual sense of them. Moreover, the case for an indeterminate, indifferent, performative materiality may find itself uncomfortably aligned with the neoliberal appropriative logic (which, as we have seen, builds precisely on the indeterminacy and fluidity of things) and, despite ostensibly opposite intentions, with its depoliticizing drift. This, at least, to the extent that politics remains the space of 'deliberation, decision making and human agency' (Hay 2007: 81) as opposed to fate, necessity, randomness, elusiveness, impassiveness.

The critical leverage of risk, in conclusion, rests on its connection with political agency, which means using the concept to reorient our attention to problems of choice and distribution against issues of safety and efficacy; to questions of 'whether or not' or 'for the benefit of whom', against questions of 'how'. At the same time it seems urgent to develop an account of nature and society, of humanity and non-humanity, which recognizes their plastic, never definitively determined character, yet contemporaneously claims the presence in them of a fundamental alterity and unattainableness that prevents their surreptitious reacquisition to human will. Cutting-edge philosophy and social science, from this viewpoint, may fall inadvertently prey to what Adorno (1973) calls 'identity thinking' – the overlap between concept and thing – forgetting that the thingness of the world (including our own constitution) can never be fully grasped or reconciled with us. This seems a relevant warning in front of a burgeoning conflation of ontology and epistemology, where the trademark neoliberal outlook of a fully manufacturable, hence appropriable, nature is mirrored in the case for the otherness and autonomy of materiality and, simultaneously, against representational filters – hence for the eventual disclosure of its actual constitution.

Further reading

Overviews of different aspects of, and approaches to, risk are provided by Deborah Lupton (1999) *Risk*, London: Routledge; Jens Zinn (ed.) (2008) *Social Theories of Risk and Uncertainty*, London: Blackwell; Carlo Jäger et al. (2001) *Risk, Uncertainty and Rational Action*, London: Earthscan; Matthias Gross (2010) *Ignorance and Surprise: Science, Society and Ecological Design*, Cambridge, MA: MIT Press. The classic references on the 'risk society' approach are Ulrich Beck (1992) *Risk Society: Toward a New Modernity*, London: Sage, and Anthony Giddens (1990) *The Consequences of Modernity*, Cambridge: Polity. More recent are: Ulrich Beck (2009) *World at Risk*, Cambridge: Polity, and Anthony Giddens (2009) *The Politics of Climate Change*, Cambridge: Polity. Equally classic is Luhmann's systems theory outlook: Niklas Luhmann (1993) *Risk: A Sociological Theory*, New Brunswick, NJ: Transaction Publishers. For the cultural theory of risk see Mary Douglas (1992) *Risk and Blame: Essays in Cultural Theory*, London: Routledge; Mary Douglas and Aaron Wildavsky (1982) *Risk and Culture*, Berkeley: University of California Press. For the risk perception approach see Paul Slovic (2000) *The Perception of Risk*, London: Earthscan. For the governmentality perspective see Mitchell Dean (1999) *Governmentality: Power and Rule in Modern Society*, London: Sage; Pat O'Malley (2004) *Risk, Uncertainty and Governance*, London: Glasshouse. For the neoliberal politics of nature see: Melinda Cooper (2008) *Life As Surplus: Biotechnology and Capitalism in the Neoliberal Era*, Washington: University of Washington Press; Luigi Pellizzoni and Marja Ylönen (eds) (2012) *Neoliberalism and Technoscience: Critical Assessments*, Farnham: Ashgate. For the new ontologies of matter see: Diana Coole and Samantha Frost (eds) (2010) *New Materialisms*, Durham, NC: Duke University Press.

Useful websites

International Risk Governance Council (IRGC): http://www.irgc.org/
United Nations Environment Programme (UNEP): http://www.unep.org/climatechange/
International Institute for Applied Systems Analysis (IIASA): http://www.iiasa.ac.at/web/home/
    research/researchPrograms/RiskPolicyandVulnerability/RPV-home.html
U.S. National Research Council (NRC): http://www.nationalacademies.org/nrc/index.html
European Food Safety Authority (EFSA): http://www.efsa.europa.eu/en/efsawhat/riskassessment.htm

21 Sacrifice

Paul Wapner

Introduction

Environmentalism has long preached the need to reduce humanity's ecological footprint, and this has often been translated into a call to sacrifice. We must reduce our material wants, restrict our forays into the natural world, and otherwise restrict ourselves from living out our materialist desires in the interest of environmental protection. This requires, at a minimum, foregoing immediate materialist pleasures for the higher goal of ecological well-being.

The push for environmental sacrifice comes from environmentalism's understanding that we live in a 'full world'. Human numbers, technological prowess, and affluence are enabling humanity to draw resources from and dump wastes into the furthest reaches of the earth at rates that are undermining the life-support systems of the planet (see Kütting, this volume). Today, three quarters of all ocean fisheries are overfished, the atmosphere is saturated with carbon dioxide due to the burning of fossil fuels by humans, the ozone layer is greatly compromised because of the release of ozone depleting substances, and biodiversity is nose-diving due to habitat destruction, introduction of invasive species, and other human actions. In the face of this, environmentalism calls for pulling back, restraining, limiting, or otherwise reducing our influence on the more-than-human world. This will only happen if humans give up our seemingly endless desire for material comforts and begin living smaller material lives more in tune with the ecological imperatives of the earth.

Despite its long history and strategic importance in environmentalist thought, the concept of sacrifice has recently come under attack. A new breed of environmentalism is emerging that sees sacrifice as an anachronistic term that lacks widespread appeal and strategic promise for creating genuine ecological protection. In the first instance, it is at odds with the consumerist culture that has been building for decades in the developing world and is increasingly globalizing (see Brooks and Bryant, this volume). Asking people to cut back on their materialist desires is a hard sell in prosperous consumer societies, and this is certainly the case in countries that are only recently coming to enjoy material prosperity. In the second instance, sacrifice, independent of its appeal and thus political relevance, seems increasingly inadequate to address the scale, pace, and magnitude of contemporary environmental challenges. Sacrifice involves acculturating people across the world into a sensibility of environmental restraint. Sadly, such a campaign will not happen within an adequate amount of time, nor will it dig deep enough into existing physical infrastructures, the world economy, and the international political system to alter our current tragic trajectory towards widespread environmental harm. To be sure, behavioral changes that involve cutting back our ecological footprint may be morally attractive and functionally important in terms of buying time to transition to a more sustainable future, but, in themselves, they will be unable to secure a sustainable world. To put it in contemporary parlance, sacrifice is 'so twentieth century.'

Instead of sacrificing materialist desires in the service of environmental well-being, the new breed of environmentalists counsels satisfying our desires in more intelligent ways. It calls on us, for example, to build more efficient buildings, design ecologically sound transportation systems, grow more food in ways that enhance soil fertility and crop productivity, and create more economical water distribution arrangements (see Baker, Luke, and Whitehead, this volume). Such efforts involve designing more ingenious and ecologically sound ways of maintaining current consumptive lifestyles. Put differently, they entail employing humanity's innovative, technological spirit in the service of environmental protection.

The new environmentalism holds much promise. We are in dire ecological straits and the push for greater technological, engineering, and design responses to environmental degradation should be embraced. The question arises, however, about the intensity of such an embrace. If the environmental movement fully endorses this new breed of environmental thought, it will shelve the concept of sacrifice. There will be no need to forego pleasures if we can satisfy them without curtailing our lifestyles. To some, this may not be a bad thing. Perhaps the whole concept of sacrifice *is* 'so twentieth century'. However, as I will argue in the following, such dismissal is misguided. The concept of sacrifice is valuable not simply because of its long historical intertwinement with environmentalism, but because, if viewed critically, sacrifice can be transformative. It can assist in creating a more sustainable future even in a hyper consumerist culture. And, it can do so by, ironically, providing a route toward greater individual and collective enrichment and happiness. Sacrifice may indeed be our salvation.

Core ideas and key thinkers

Within the environmental movement, there has been a long-standing debate between preservationists and conservationists (see Igoe, this volume). Preservationists call for protecting pristine landscapes, other species, and ecologically valuable and aesthetically pleasing sites. Seeking to safeguard wildlands (and rural ways of life) from the steady encroachment of an emerging industrial society, preservation found voice in poets such as Blake and Wordsworth, and thinkers such as Emerson and Thoreau, and was later promulgated by wilderness enthusiasts Muir, Roosevelt, and Leopold (see McShane, this volume). It still informs a significant branch of the environmental movement. Preservation wants to create and staff barriers between humans and the natural world to protect the latter from the former (Guha 2002).

Conservation is less interested in safeguarding certain regions from human intrusion and more committed to making sure that people use resources and emit waste in sustainable ways. It too emerged during the Industrial Revolution through the work of Humboldt (1996) and Brandis (2012) of Germany and Marsh (2012) in the United States, and later found expression in the thought of Pinchot (1998) and even later Carson (1962), Ehrlich (1968), and Commoner (1971). Conservationists call for maintaining the earth's ability to provide resources and absorb waste and advocate for efficient and wise use of the earth's bounty (Shabecoff 2003; Wapner 2010).

Despite differing orientations, preservation and conservation have historically shared a similar view of limits. Both have understood that the earth has biophysical thresholds and that the most important thing humans can do for environmental protection is to restrict their ecological imprint through restraining themselves individually and collectively from overrunning wilderness areas and/or overexploiting natural resources and sinks. Strategically, they have advocated for collective and individual sacrifice as the way to maintain and sustain ecosystem services and the more-than-human world.

Preservationists and conservationists have reluctantly promoted sacrifice. The call to sacrifice stems from a psycho-social understanding that humans have choices about their actions, and, given increasing environmental degradation, they must deliberately choose to deny themselves certain material pleasures in the service of environmental protection. Environmentalists encourage sacrifice individually through the many instructions of how to reduce one's ecological footprint (see Hinton, this volume). Books such as *True Green: 100 Everyday Ways you Can Contribute to a Healthier Planet* (McKay and Bonnin 2007) and *Green Made Easy: The Everyday Guide for Transitioning to a Green Lifestyle* (Prelitz 2009) seek to reveal the ecological ramifications of certain everyday activities and encourage people to shift their practices in more ecologically sound directions. Thus, environmentalists call on people to forego having additional children, buying excessive amounts of goods, and eating foods with large carbon or other ecological costs. Sacrifice, as such, is justified in the name of caring about the earth and its inhabitants. In words attributed to Gandhi: '[l]ive simply, so others may simply live'.[1]

Collective sacrifice involves communal sharing of the burden of environmental protection. It calls on countries, states, cities, and neighborhoods to shift budgets, alter planning, or otherwise direct their efforts towards environmental well-being rather than other social goals. This entails sacrifice insofar as it demands trade-offs. It requires collectivities to forego certain goods and practices in the service of environmental protection. Domestic and international policy-making is about deciding how to shift priorities and which social purposes must be forfeited in the interest of environmental well-being. Whether individual or collective, environmental sacrifice arises from the understanding that humanity cannot 'have it all'. On a finite planet, certain lifestyles, material desires, manufacturing techniques, food cultures, and so forth are incompatible with ecological realities. They must be 'sacrificed' in the name of environmental preservation and sustainability.

Post-sacrificial environmentalism

For preservationists and conservationists, environmental sacrifice is a necessary practice on a finite planet. Over the past few decades, a new breed of environmentalists has arisen that questions the very idea of limits. It does not ignore ecological thresholds but believes that these can be transcended through careful, innovative design, planning, and engineering. With roots in 'ecological modernization' and 'administrative rationalism', this new breed embraces humanity's footprint on earth and employs human ingenuity and technology to direct it towards sustainability (Dryzek 2005). For these thinkers and practitioners, sacrifice is not only unattractive as a strategy, but unnecessary. We can maintain high consumptive lifestyles by re-designing our buildings, products, transportation systems, and the like to enhance ecological well-being.

Architect Bill McDonough and chemist Michael Braungart represent this new breed (2002). They see environmental challenges not as structural or cultural defects but simply as design failures. To them, the Industrial Revolution is not the enemy of environmentalism so much as the demonstration of an ill-conceived design project. There is nothing wrong with industrialism or consumptive society per se. Rather, the flaws have to do with the kind of industrialism and consumption we engage in. McDonough and Braungart argue for and have created products and buildings that exemplify the safe and sustainable use of materials.

At the heart of McDonough and Braungart's (2002) vision is the idea that 'waste = food'. One of the reasons we face many current environmental challenges is that we have designed systems to take no account of materials after they have served their intended productive purpose. This is misguided insofar as it creates a throwaway society that literally wastes material goods. The results of such a society are mountains of trash, toxin-emitting incinerators, polluted waters, and a carbon-rich atmosphere, in addition to depleted stocks of natural resources. To counter this, McDonough and Braungart call for designing all products for infinite use. This means conceiving and fabricating products that can be broken down into their technical and biological components and reusing the components for other uses. For example, McDonough and Braungart have helped Shaw Carpet design a rug made of two parts, with two different future trajectories. The bottom layer is a synthetic that maintains its shape over time and can be sent back to the company for refurbishing. The top layer is a biological material that, when worn out, can be placed in a garden and used as fertilizer. The carpet is designed, then, as a technical and biological nutrient that feeds future uses. There is no waste. All material is valuable for indefinite use. McDonough and Braungart (2002) call this kind of design 'cradle to cradle,' in contrast to conventional 'cradle to grave' schemes. The key is that it involves no sacrifice. One need not forego carpeting on one's floors in an act of environmental stewardship. Rather, one can have floor coverings that actually enrich the earth.

Another set of thinkers who subscribe to the new environmentalism includes Ted Nordhaus and Michael Shellenberger. Authors of the somewhat famous essay 'The Death of Environmentalism' (2004), Nordhaus and Shellenberger reject the notion of ecological limits because humanity is capable of outsmarting the nonhuman world in the service of sustainability. They criticize the environmental movement for peddling in fear and doom and for berating people to change their habits *or else*. Nordhaus and Shellenberger see such fear-mongering not only counterproductive to building a movement but fundamentally mistaken about humanity's prospects.

According to Shellenberger and Nordhaus, one of the reasons environmentalism is so gloomy is that it sees an essential conflict between economic growth and ecological well-being. It believes that all forms of material productivity simply increase the amount of resources used and waste produced (Shellenberger and Nordhaus 2007). Like McDonough and Braungart (2002), they place their faith in industrial and post-industrial innovation that – with proper direction and design – can manufacture an infinitely sustainable future (creating alternative fuels, developing technologies to sequester carbon, generating green collar jobs, and so forth). Far from seeing a conflict, they claim that economic growth is actually a precursor to environmental protection. They advance this by pointing out that the environmental movement itself arose out of the post–World War II economic boom and, according to the Kuznets Curve (which advances a fairly well-accepted theory about the relationship between countries' GDP and their environmental conditions; see Whitehead, this volume), that societies need to grow economically before they can afford green technologies. Shellenberger and Nordhaus call on the environmental movement to embrace the coupling of economic growth and environmental protection. Sacrifice is therefore unnecessary since, with proper investment and guidance, society can have high production and consumption without ecological degradation.

Many other thinkers share the view that environmentalism can be compatible with contemporary economic and political practices and that we need not alter our lives dramatically to address environmental challenges. Differing only in degrees, thinkers as diverse as Thomas Friedman (2009), Paul Hawken and Amory and Hunter Lovins (2008), Jay Inslee and Bracken

Hendricks (2009), Dan Esty and Andrew Winston (2009), Diane MacEachern (2008), and scores of others believe that the route to environmental well-being is not through denying ourselves certain goods or familiar practices but, rather, through designing and investing in smarter ways to provision ourselves. MacEachern and Jones, for instance, argue that we can buy our way out of ecological challenges by simply buying smarter (MacEachern 2008; Jones 2008). Hawken, Lovins, and Lovins show how we can reengineer buildings, automobiles, and industrial processes to usher in a greener world (Hawken et al. 2008); Inslee and Hendricks write about how a green energy economy can produce jobs, boost profits, and enhance national security, all while combating climate change, a view shared by Friedman, Esty, and others (Esty and Winston 2009; Friedman 2009; Inslee and Hendricks 2009). These thinkers and this new breed of environmentalism in general embraces an upbeat view of technological possibility out of a faith in humanity's innovative spirit and a skepticism that people will actually sacrifice in the service of environmental protection. As Inslee and Hendricks put it, 'we can try to scold people into embracing sacrifice and change nothing . . . or offer choices that are cheaper and better' (2009: 11). Characterizing a part of their approach, they write, 'This is not about sacrifice; it is about economic growth, productivity, and investment' (18).

The new environmentalism may be right about the political and functional disadvantages of sacrifice. Social scientists have long understood that people and collectivities are unwilling to sacrifice for many common purposes. Collective action problems arise, for example, when people choose to 'free-ride' or otherwise not participate in common endeavors out of fear that their commitment to doing so will be unmatched by others. And, if this is the case, then they have sacrificed for little reason (Olson 1971). Furthermore, as Garrett Hardin explains, individual actors face tragic decisions when faced with addressing a common problem. In his famous essay 'The Tragedy of the Commons' (1968), Hardin points out that sacrificing one's potential benefit for the good of the whole is irrational since one reaps all the advantages of pursuing individual self-interest yet shares only a fraction of the costs of degradation of the commons (see also Kütting, this volume). In cases of collective action, sacrifice may be polite, compassionate, and even instrumentally beneficial; however, lacking guarantees that others will act similarly, it is illogical.

Sacrifice also becomes less attractive in the context of globalized commodity chains (see Paterson, Watts and Peluso, and Brooks and Bryant, this volume). Today, the production of goods is a global endeavor. Producers draw resources from across the globe, process and assemble products in multiple facilities, package and transport goods across national boundaries, and discard waste through numerous media and across various geographical regions. This makes it virtually impossible to trace, or even really know, the sources and routes of our manufactured world (Princen, Maniates, and Conca 2002). Without such knowledge and tracking, sacrifice becomes a nice gesture but functionally irrelevant. A globalized commodity system scrambles one's ability to have confidence that what one does in their corner of the world will actually have an ecological effect (Wapner and Willoughby 2005).

Such uncertainty currently fuels debate about the meaningful ways to shrink one's carbon footprint (see Hinton, this volume). Many recommend eating locally grown food to avoid carbon emissions involved with transportation. However, food's carbon footprint involves more than the petroleum burned needed for transportation. It also involves the amount of sunlight, soil fertility, pesticide use, water utilization, and human labour hours devoted to crop production, distribution, sales, and consumption. Such considerations led Michael Specter to suggest that people in England may be more ecologically responsible by buying lamb raised in New Zealand rather than Yorkshire, since New Zealand agricultural lands receive more sunlight and its famers use less pesticides and fertilizers (Specter 2008).

A final critique of environmental sacrifice comes from the view that the environmental movement itself is a child of economic success, and thus, foregoing material comforts in the service of environmental well-being is at odds with the historical trajectory and possibly the spirit of the movement. While the early days of environmentalism can be traced to the Industrial Revolution, the modern environmental movement rose to prominence after the post-World War II economic boom (see Price, Saunders, and Olcese, this volume). Social scientists like to refer to movements that arose during this period as 'post-material' because they are focused less on securing basic economic or security needs and more on quality of life issues (Inglehart 1977). To the degree that affluence accounts for the rise of the environmental movement, strategies that emphasize sacrifice, austerity, and decreasing materiality may sound off-key. It is challenging to preach asceticism to publics from groups that were raised on economic abundance. As Shellenberger and Nordhaus put it, 'the problem is that none of us, whether we are wealthy environmental leaders or average Americans, are willing to significantly sacrifice our standard of living' (Shellenberger and Nordhaus 2007: 125).

Critical potential

The new environmentalism is extremely attractive precisely because it eschews sacrificing. It claims that we can maintain our current lifestyles and enjoy ecological health without having to forgo any comforts or otherwise downsize our material desires. Who could argue with this? Who wants to sacrifice if we can have everything we want without hardship? This is where the critical potential of the concept of sacrifice comes into play.

Before explaining this, it must be said that, despite the hype of the new environmentalism, there is no guarantee that its proponents are accurate in their prognoses. Much of the new environmentalism is premised on rosy assumptions about investment payoffs, technological potential, and ecological resilience (see Luke and Pellizzoni, this volume). It is entirely possible that all the money in the world cannot produce absolutely clean sources of energy (e.g., the decades-long effort to produce nuclear fusion). Furthermore, ecological systems may not remain robust long enough for new technologies and practices to emerge. Many advocates of the new environmentalism admit as much insofar as they talk in terms of 'anticipatory design' – meaning that they are creating products, buildings, automobiles, and so forth that prefigure elements of envisioned, future, fully ecological goods but are not themselves those products. For example, even platinum Leadership in Energy and Environmental Design (LEED) buildings – the top tier of the LEED accreditation system – have a huge environmental footprint even though they are less impactful than non-LEED buildings (U.S. Green Building Council 2012; Newsham, Mancini, and Birt 2009). Despite the most innovatively designed structure, the best building still seems to be no building at all.

More generally, proponents of the new environmentalism may under-estimate the character of environmental thresholds. It is true that there are no absolute ecological limits (see Kütting, this volume). Indeed, humans can withstand much environmental assault and simply try to adjust. For example, air pollution has long fouled skies, but medical technologies that alleviate symptoms of asthma and related diseases render such thresholds less meaningful. Of course, human response to ecological limits disproportionately harms those of lower socio-economic status, but this does not negate the overall point that thresholds are somewhat malleable. This does not mean, however, that all thresholds are insignificant.

Many have warned that atmospheric carbon concentrations must not exceed 350 parts per million (ppm; carbon concentrations hovered around 270 ppm for most of human history). Above this amount, climate change ushers in a fundamentally new atmosphere in which all ecosystems on the planet are altered (McKibben 2010). Sadly, at the time of this writing, atmospheric carbon concentrations stand at 400 ppm and are still rising. What does this mean about the 350 threshold? A cynical interpretation is that we are simply willing to let those least able to adapt to a hotter, more storm-intensive world suffer the consequences, and we, the privileged, are going to hedge our bets (see Okereke and Charlesworth, this volume).

Another interpretation is that 350 ppm is an inaccurate threshold. Indeed, admitting that we have already exceeded 350 and are willing to live with current levels of climate disruption, many now point to 450 ppm as *the* threshold. Of course, before reaching 450 ppm, glaciers will melt, seas will rise, storms will be more frequent and powerful, the food supply will be more insecure, droughts will intensify, and vector-borne diseases will increase. However, these consequences will pale in comparison to the meaning of 450 ppm. At 450, we literally *bake.* Feedback loops become so coupled that we will experience runaway climate change with no chance to slow or reverse the trend.

This may, in fact, be true. But all such thinking ignores the human dimension of thresholds. What does 450 ppm (or even 350 ppm) mean to the victims of hurricane Katrina in 2005 or the Australian and Pakistani flood victims of 2010 or those killed by heat waves in Russia in 2010 (McKibben 2012: 9)? The new environmentalists may ignore biophysical constraints, but only because such limits have yet to reach thresholds that they themselves actually feel. The new environmentalists, in other words, may hold out promise for a greener world as innovative technologies are investigated and invented, economies shift to post-fossil sources of energy, and jobs are created in building sustainability. But, in the meantime, many people suffer without any assurance of genuinely transitioning to a sustainable world.

The new environmentalists rely on an optimism not shared by those who believe we must make sacrifices if we are to live sustainably. The critical potential of sacrifice is not about an exaggerated prognosis. Rather, it is about the quality of sacrifice itself. While functionally challenging, the world would, indeed, be materially better off if massive amounts of people forswore material comforts so that the less fortunate could enjoy higher levels of prosperity and the planet's ecosystems could catch a break. This is almost an absolute certainty. The promise of sacrifice, however, goes further. It offers the opportunity for enhancing the quality of human life.

Sacrifice signifies giving something up or, put differently, a loss. To the degree that it assumes a political face, it represents a politics of less. When it comes to environmental sacrifice, individuals and collectivities lose certain comforts or forego particular common goals in the interest of environmental protection. This is why critics of environmental sacrifice are so confident. They recognize that few people embrace the idea of reducing goods and practices that they currently enjoy. What critics fail to see, however, is that quantity and quality are different dimensions. It is not the case that an abundance of material quantity leads to enhanced quality of living. In fact, there is evidence that, over a certain economic threshold, one's happiness is completely unrelated to one's income.

One of the ironies of life in the affluent world is that, for all its material abundance, people report only modest levels of happiness. Surveys demonstrate that in the United States, for instance, people have grown increasingly less happy, even though, over the decades the economy and people's spending power have grown (McKibben 2007: 36). Surveys show that Americans were happiest in the 1950s and, despite significant economic growth (until very recently), their happiness level has decreased steadily since then (McKibben 2007: 36). A similar pattern exists in Japan. Between 1958 and 1986, Japan experienced a fivefold increase in per capita income but saw no change in people's satisfaction with their lives. Likewise, the United Kingdom saw a 66 percent increase in per capita gross domestic product between 1973 and 2001, yet people's satisfaction with their lives remained unchanged (McKibben 2007: 42). What is especially curious is that the relationship between financial abundance and happiness appears tenuous even among the super rich. *Forbes* magazine's richest Americans report happiness scores indistinguishable from those of the Pennsylvania Amish and only a fraction higher than those of the Swedes and Maasai tribesmen (McKibben 2007).

This has implications for thinking about sacrifice. It suggests that giving up material comfort may have little to no effect on the quality of one's life. In fact, it may – I stress 'may' – actually enhance one's experience. The Center for a New American Dream tries to capture this in its slogan, 'Less stuff, more fun'. This underlines the observation made by many that more material possessions can actually compromise our ability to pursue deeper levels of happiness (Segal 2003; Wann, Degraff, and Naylor 2005; Wann 2007). Caught in a consumerist culture, we need to spend greater amounts of time making money so that we can afford more things, larger homes to store all our stuff, and insurance plans and so forth to ensure that our things are protected. The irony is that many of us become trapped in a perpetual pursuit of greater economic might, while forfeiting many of the pleasures – time with friends and families, relaxation, and so on – that such efforts aim to provide.

In this sense, *giving up many material possessions may genuinely enhance our lives.* We can understand this when we appreciate that constraint is its own type of freedom. Many of us believe that freedom is being able to do anything we want. But this is a fairly immature notion. We all make choices in life, and, when we do so, we cut-off options as the cost of pursuing certain directions. To be sure, there may always be a feeling of regret in foreclosing alternative opportunities. But we also know that it is only by excluding certain preferences that we are able fully to experience the one's we have, in fact, chosen. For example, in choosing to be a professor, I have given up the possibility of being a full-time artist. I experience some regret over this. However, if I had not foreclosed the possibility of being a full-time artist, I would never have experienced the deep satisfactions of teaching and scholarship. Life is inextricably linked to sacrifice. It becomes meaningful when we realize that this does not always mean giving something up. Rather, more often than not, it entails gaining something else.

Environmental sacrifice assumes its critical potential insofar as it offers the possibility not only of contributing to environmental well-being (which is, itself, significant), but to the quality of our lives. Earlier I quoted the phrase attributed to Gandhi, 'Live simply, so others may simply live'. With the previous considerations in mind, we could invert this as: 'Live simply, so *you* can simply live'. Too many material possessions and the lifestyles needed to retain them rob many of us of the real juice of life. We are not simply living, but working endlessly to maintain an imagined level of material comfort. Maximally exhausted, stressed out, and otherwise frazzled by our contemporary, materially rich lives, environmental sacrifice suddenly appears not just green but transformative. Thus, while the new environmentalism may have a lot of promise, to the degree that it reinforces the lives many of us are used to, it may be in need of a healthy dose of sacrifice.

Environmental sacrifice offers a second critical role by serving as a practice of political resistance. Contemporary consumerist culture reproduces itself by the passive acquiescence of widespread publics. That is, consumerism is hegemonic to the degree that it instrumentalizes citizens to see their well-being wrapped up with material acquisition. Adopting a practice of sacrifice throws a cog in the wheel of contemporary consumerism and otherwise plants seeds of counterhegemonic activity. It circumscribes and develops a counterculture around nonmaterial values and even institutional structures, and therewith provides us with an oppositional narrative. In this sense, sacrifice is not simply an individual act or a collective expression about lifestyle, but a political action aimed at denying consumerism full cultural and social sway and at enabling the seeds of a different ethic to take root (Paterson 2000).

Conclusion

In this chapter, I tried to explain the importance of sacrifice in environmentalism and respond to criticisms of sacrifice arising from a new wing of the movement. In so doing, I may have suggested that there is a battle going on between old-time conservationist and preservationist environmentalism, on the one hand, and the new form of environmentalism that embraces technological prowess, economic growth, and the innovative dimension of the human spirit, on the other. I apologize if this is the impression I have given. The future of environmentalism will not tilt significantly in one direction or the other; one side will not bleach out the other. Environmentalism will continue to express both orientations. The transformative promise of the idea of sacrifice can be further appreciated within this tension.

The new environmentalism will continue to seek technological and economistic answers to our environmental woes. However, it will do so without an orienting compass. The concept of sacrifice can play an important role in providing guidance. It can remind us of *why* we are seeking environmental protection and *how* we might go about doing so in a way that aligns with our inner values. Sacrifice, if understood in a critical fashion, can positively intervene in environmental politics by blurring the distinction between altruistic behaviour focused on creating a more livable world for others and self-regarding action aimed at enhancing the quality of our own lives. Not two, one: environmental sacrifice involves making the world a better place for all beings, including ourselves.

Further reading

An important contribution to the literature on environmental sacrifice is Michael Maniates and John M. Meyer (eds) (2010) *The Environmental Politics of Sacrifice*, Boston: MIT Press. A classic work on sacrifice more generally is Marcel Mauss and Henri Hubert's (1981) *Sacrifice: Its Nature and Functions*, Chicago: University of Chicago Press. Classic treatments of ecological limits include Donella H. Meadows, Dennis L. Meadows, Jørgen Randers, and William W. Behrens III (1972) *The Limits to Growth*, New York: New American Library; Donella H. Meadows, Dennis L. Meadows, and Jørgen Randers (1992) *Beyond the Limits*, Post Mills, VT: Chelsea Green Publishing Company; Thomas Robert Malthus (1888) *An Essay on the Principle of Population: or, A View of Its Past and Present Effects on Human Happiness*, London: Reeves and Turner; Lester R. Brown (2009) *Plan B 4.0: Mobilizing to Save Civilization*, New York: W.W. Norton & Company; Richard Falk (1971) *This Endangered Planet: Prospects and Proposals for Human Survival*, New York: Vintage Books; and Paul Ehrlich (1968) *The Population Bomb*, New York: Ballantine. On the trade-offs between lifestyle and structural change, see Maniates (2001), Saunders (2008), and Seyfang (2005).

Useful websites

Center for a New American Dream: http://www.newdream.org/
Richard Louv: http://richardlouv.com/
No Impact Project: http://noimpactproject.org/
Slow Food USA: http://www.slowfoodusa.org/

Note

1. It is unsurprising that someone like Gandhi articulates self-sacrifice as a moral injunction. Almost every religious tradition has advanced sacrifice as a form of ethical practice (Peterson 2010).

22 Science

Tim Forsyth

Introduction

Science is a form of knowledge and inquiry that aims to be objective and authoritative. In environmental politics, science has often performed a crucial role in defining and supporting environmental objectives. But science has been analysed in different, and sometimes contradictory, ways.

This chapter discusses the different ways in which science has been used in critical environmental politics. In particular, it argues that environmental science has been treated as 'critical' in two crucial ways. The first places faith in the representativeness of scientific methods and uses science as a legitimization for environmentalism. The second sees science and scientific expertise as arenas of contested politics. This latter approach does not deny the need for concern about environment, but it looks critically at which political interests are represented within scientific practice and knowledge.

The chapter proceeds by identifying the key debates about science within critical environmental politics. The second section then discusses the key thinkers who have contributed to debates about the critical analysis of science. The chapter then describes key ways in which these debates can be used within critical environmental politics, especially concerning the analysis of knowledge, expertise, and social order.

Core ideas

The word *science* is usually meant to imply knowledge and understandings that have been made using appropriate and recognized scientific methods. In turn, science is also associated with information and propositions that are not biased by political opinion and, therefore, can be used as a source of reference in public debate. Scientists and scientific organizations are, therefore, often considered sources of neutral and policy-relevant expertise who can advise on, and sometimes adjudicate about, questions of political uncertainty. This viewpoint has supported much critical environmental politics in the past, especially from activists who wish to use science to demonstrate that urgent environmental protection is needed (see Büscher, Okereke and Charlesworth, and Price, Saunders, and Olcese, this volume).

But, in recent years, a growing number of social scientists have also pointed out that science itself is a source of political debate (see Hobden, and Rudy and White, this volume). These analysts do not suggest that science has no value, or that it cannot be used to explain complex events and problems. Rather, these analysts argue that science needs to be under-stood as a social process, and, therefore, the social influences on knowledge and expertise need to be understood as part of a critical environmental politics. This analysis of science can relate to the normative aspects of environmentalism as a social movement and to the operations of expert groups and scientists within the policy process (see Baker, this volume). In order to explain this tension, it is necessary to look at these different approaches in more detail.

Early approaches to critical environmental science

The first discussions of a critical environmental science – in Western debates – can be dated to the 1960s, when environmentalism began to rise as a critique of industrialization and modernity. Members of the Frankfurt School of critical theory (such as Herbert Marcuse and Jürgen Habermas; see the introduction to this volume) in particular argued that orthodox science and technology were the means by which modernity was alienating human nature and imposing the instrumental reason of cold economic logic and disempowering styles of bureaucratic government (Gandy 1997). In response, a new form of science was needed that was not so instrumental.

Writers such as Marcuse referred to *human* nature – or the essence of being alive under modern and industrial societies. But these same principles were also advanced to explore a new 'critical' environmental science that highlighted the human damage upon ecosystems and that sought an alternative, more caring relationship with environment. For example, the U.S. scientist Eugene Odum, the author of *Fundamentals of Ecology* (1953), also argued that a 'new' ecology could 'endanger the assumptions and practices accepted by modern societies' in order to restrain individualistic behaviour and make individuals more aware of the impacts of this behaviour (Sears 1964: 11–12). Similarly, another ecologist in the United States, Paul B. Sears (1964), argued that ecology was a 'subversive subject' because it challenged dominant human behaviours.

Accordingly, ecology – and environmental science more generally – has been associated with a political critique of rapid and uncaring economic growth (see Kütting, this volume). These ideas have been repeated since the 1960s in more specific environmental debates. Ecological feminists, for example, have used environmental scientific analysis to link the oppression of nature by modern societies to the similar oppression of women (Merchant 1980; see also Cudworth, this volume). Ecological Marxists have also connected this argument to the operations of global capitalism as a key driving force of environmental degradation (Gorz 1980; see also Paterson, this volume). And, more recently, environmental scholars have argued 'climate science offers an imminent critique of the industrial base of Western modernity' (Jacques 2012: 15). Indeed, Al Gore's film, *An Inconvenient Truth* (2006), about anthropogenic climate change presents science as a form of truth that society needs to listen to in order to reform itself.

There is, therefore, a long tradition of environmental science being used 'critically' of Western, modern societies. Much critical environmental politics has consequently relied upon the authority of science to strengthen its political engagement and to seek a different, better, world. Indeed, some analysts have argued that political actors and organizations that seek to criticize environmental concerns are '[a] betrayal of science and reason' (Ehrlich and Ehrlich 1996).

But, while this theme of critical environmental science is very vocal, especially in North American environmental politics, there are also concerns that this approach to critical environmental science can simplify the relationship of science and politics.

Later approaches to critical environmental science

These early approaches to 'critical' environmental science have been criticized by both ecologists and by social scientists. Many of these criticisms have been discussed more fully within the growing discipline of Science and Technology Studies (STS), which seeks to examine the political and social influences upon science, and vice versa. These approaches are therefore critical 'about' science, and the uses of science, in addition to using environmental science in order to be critical.

First, *science* itself is commonly defended on the grounds of the scientific method. But there are many scientific methods and approaches that have changed over time. Commonly, the scientific method is defined as a process of using neutral or random means of sampling in order to test theories and hypotheses, in order to find ways of identifying transferable explanations or scientific 'laws'. This approach is commonly called 'positivism'. But positivism itself has changed over time. The early positivists, such as the Austrian physicist Ernst Mach (1838–1916), saw 'positive science' as analysing datasets to find apparent trends. The so-called 'logical positivists' of the mid-twentieth century advanced this method by using verificationism – or the search for similar patterns in different datasets. Then, this approach was challenged by the writings of Karl Popper (1902–1994), who instead proposed falsificationism – or the testing of hypotheses in order to falsify them – as a way to establish truth claims. All of these different models of science indicate increasing levels of ambition about how scientific statements can represent complex situations and, consequently, make increasingly universal truth claims (Harré 1993).

Second, within ecology, there was a growing acknowledgement that 'ecology' was not necessarily a description of humanity's destructive impact on 'natural' ecosystems separate from human existence. The so-called 'new' ecologies have instead drawn upon the principles of chaos theory to demonstrate the chaotic and sometimes unpredictable ways in which change can occur in ecological systems such as forest and vegetation patchworks (Botkin 1990; Wu and Loucks 1995; see also Hobden, and Rudy and White, this volume). In turn, ecologists have argued that commonplace constructions of 'normality' or human impact can too easily be influenced by social values of what is an attractive or 'stable' landscape. For example, the poplar notion that 'wilderness' existed in North America before 1492 has been criticized (Adams 1997; Denevan 1989; see also Igoe, this volume). Other analysts have pointed out how forest ecosystems have changed over time as a result of non-anthropogenic climate change, and the difficulties of separating human and non-human causes of landscape change, such as through fire. Similarly, many analysts have now criticized the earlier beliefs that capitalism was the cause of environmental degradation alone. For example, the British scholar Piers Blaikie (1995: 12) noted that 'the case for the globalization of capital being causal in desertification looks rather amateur since the scientific evidence of permanent damage to the environment points in other directions.'

Thirdly, there has been greater attention to the interconnections of social norms and the generation of scientific knowledge. One theme here is the apparent tension between the normative purpose of early 'critical' ecology (which refers to a vision of how modern science ought to be) and the use of ecological science as a source of neutral and objective knowledge (which is meant to be knowledge that is free from social influence) (Yearley 1992). But more generally, STS and other political studies have highlighted that knowledge is deeply imbued with power – either in order to achieve a political objective, or as the result of pre-existing social orders and power imbalances. Accordingly, any ecology that seeks to be 'critical' and achieve social change needs to be assessed for which social influences exist in the knowledge created through ecological science, and who might win or lose accordingly.

These criticisms do not reject the need to be concerned about environmental degradation. Rather, they seek to assess how far 'science' might therefore appear to be neutral and representative of physical environmental change and all society and emphasize some viewpoints over others, or present images of 'fact' that might hide important additional changes.

For example, one early approach to analysing the social influences on scientific knowledge looked at environmental problems in the Himalayan Mountains. The classic text *Uncertainty on a Himalayan Scale* (Thompson, Warburton, and Hatley 1986) asked why most Western NGOs claimed there was a pressing environmental crisis in the Himalayan Mountains when estimates for deforestation in the region varied by a factor of 67 (even excluding apparent typing errors). This book argued that these differences did not result from the underlying complexity in rates of deforestation, but rather from the different worldviews of the people and organizations who collected and then presented these data. The point of this analysis was to argue that none of these representations were accurate – all contained elements of truth. Instead, there was a need to appreciate that all matters of environmental change are complex and uncertain, but that different actors will try to represent the problems as more certain than they are in order to justify these worldviews.

Another classic example concerns global climate change policy. In the early 1990s, there was a dispute between two think tanks that produced knowledge about climate change. On one hand, the World Resources Institute (WRI), a large and influential institute based in Washington DC, produced a report in 1990 that sought to identify national responsibilities for global warming based on current rates of carbon use and deforestation. This report identified Brazil, India, and China as among the six countries most responsible for combining deforestation and greenhouse gas emissions (Forsyth 2003: 166).

On the other hand, this report was criticized by an Indian organization, the Centre for Science and Environment (CSE) (Agarwal and Narain 1991), who argued that these stark statistics hid the facts that per capita carbon use was radically smaller in developing countries compared with the United States and other richer countries. They also pointed out that WRI's index did not differentiate between energy use for livelihoods versus luxury lifestyles, or how deforestation might be linked to food security rather than timber trade alone, or that richer countries have been emitting greenhouse gases for many years longer than poorer countries. Accordingly, CSE argued that WRI's statistical index gave the impression of scientific authority and universality but hid various normative questions about what kind of carbon use is appropriate for what kind of development.

These two early examples of critical environmental science demonstrated that many debates about environmental cause-and-effect were influenced by social and political factors. Moreover, the data used to define cause-and-effect can also hide or contribute to different power relations and inequalities that can have implications for who wins and loses under environmental policy, as well as for understanding the nature of environmental change itself. Much critical environmental science these days, therefore, considers how far statements claiming to be 'fact' or about something 'natural' might actually contain social and political influences.

In addition, STS does not only look at science in the traditional sense of what happens in laboratories or controlled experiments, but also at any form of knowledge that is treated as authoritative and legitimate. Indeed, as noted previously, some debates about environmental degradation have acknowledged that old visions of cause-and-effect need to be updated on the basis of newer scientific findings. Consequently, the continued belief in old explanations cannot be explained by science itself, as these have now been challenged or indeed falsified. Rather, there is a need to analyse all forms of knowledge that carry the authority of science, even if science itself does not necessarily support these claims.

Key thinkers

Some of the most influential thinkers for early approaches to critical environmental science were the social theorists of the Frankfurt School, such as Jürgen Habermas and Herbert Marcuse, who wrote about the need for a new science to challenge the instrumental rationality of modern, capitalist societies. These ideas have influenced later writing on environment and are still apparent today in some fields. For example, Carolyn Merchant (1980) and Val Plumwood (1993) used these ideas to write about ecofeminism by arguing that both women and nature were suppressed by the same instrumental rationality of capitalism.

The same principle has also been used to discuss climate change denial or opposition to all environmental regulation within the United States. Soulé and Lease (1995) have argued that ecological values represent an important criticism of the current political status quo, and therefore should not be challenged. Other writers have also linked the denial of climate change science by some politicians and think tanks as an organized unscientific campaign in order to prevent long-overdue regulation of Western, capitalist society (Jacques 2012).

But while these authors have tended to see environmental science as a truth that needs to be communicated more widely within political debates, authors within STS have looked at science as something that cannot escape social and political influence. STS scholars, therefore, analyse how scientific statements about the world reflect social structures and how these scientific statements in turn influence social order. There are various key thinkers within STS, – although identifying them is controversial because one has to ask how – and with what social support – did certain individuals gain status and authority?

Thomas Kuhn's *Structure of Scientific Revolutions* (1962) is often considered a starting point for the analysis of social influences on science. Kuhn argued that scientific progress occurred through changes in paradigms – or the guiding purposes and objectives of science – rather than through Popper's notions of falsification. Steven Shapin and Simon Schaffer's *Leviathan and the Air-Pump* (1985) is also considered a classic historical analysis of how scientific debates about vacuums during the 1660s were influenced by socially acceptable forms of experimentation and presentation of evidence, rather than simply through science identifying biophysical reality without social influence.

Various other authors have influenced ways of seeing the social and political influences on science. Roy Bhaskar's *A Realist Theory of Science* (1975) used the term *critical realism* to argue that all forms of knowledge can indicate some aspect of a complex reality – but that the knowledge produced by science should not be conflated with 'reality' itself. He proposed the concept of the 'epistemic fallacy', which exists when people assume that scientific knowledge is actually a true indication of underlying reality. He argued that knowledge could be divided into three types: the actual (or day-to-day experiences, such as changes in weather), the empirical (measured trends, such as long-term climatic records), and the real (or the underlying causal mechanisms, which might drive changes in climate, but which can never be known in their entirety). He also argued that most scientific explanations reflected a combination of social concern with slight glimpses of underlying reality, and, consequently, scientific inquiry should always seek to be critical of what it knows and why it knows it.

There are also key thinkers in social and political science. Much early STS was influenced by the Edinburgh-based 'strong programme' of sociology of scientific knowledge, typified by scholars such as David Bloor and Barry Barnes (Barnes, Bloor, and Henry 1996). This programme adopted the term *symmetry* to refer to the co-existence of scientific truth claims and social networks or solidarities to uphold it. As with Kuhn's (1962) work, this framework challenged the more orthodox idea that scientific propositions existed simply because they were based on evidence and had yet to be falsified.

Bruno Latour has influenced STS in many ways. His *Science in Action* (1987) analysed how scientific knowledge is 'made' in laboratories and how individual choice and values within scientists can influence the projection of wider systems of explanation. For example, he argued that the famous experiments of Louis Pasteur on anthrax led to the imposition of his laboratory-based assumptions all over France, with the tacit assumption that the laboratory results only succeeded in 'the field' when the same laboratory-type conditions are recreated. His later work theorized the social influences on the identification of things as 'natural' (Latour 1993), where he argued that commonplace distinctions between nature and society are not real and essential differences but reflect how societies have experienced and shaped non-human objects into 'purified' representations (see Rudy and White, this volume). Or, as Donna Haraway (1992: 296) has written, 'nature cannot pre-exist its construction'.

Latour's work also contributed to Actor Network Theory (ANT), which is a form of STS that seeks to explain the world based on the assumption that 'objects' and 'actors' always reflect social values and experiences. For example, Latour's colleague Michel Callon (1986) argued that the explanation of human impacts on scallop fishing in France usually adopted a familiar linear cause-and-effect formulation of how humans might or might not impact upon populations of scallops. An ANT approach, however, analyses how the objectives and assumptions of scientific enquiry attributes agency to non-human items. The resulting scientific explanations, therefore, can only be upheld if these underlying framings of research are maintained. Accordingly, scallops and other non-human artifacts can actually display agency (if not cognitive intentionality) if scientific explanations place them in a key causal role, and society accepts this explanation as unchallenged.

Sheila Jasanoff (1990, 2004) and Brian Wynne (Shackley and Wynne 1996; Wynne 1996, 2001) have analysed STS more specifically within policy contexts. Their emphasis has been less upon orthodox analyses of science within domains such as laboratories, but instead they have looked at the role of science-policy interactions such as risk assessments, expert bodies, and the social values underlying the creation of supposedly neutral databases or classifications such as the human genome project. Jasanoff (2004: 2) uses the term *coproduction* to refer to this 'proposition that the ways in which we know and represent the world (both nature and society) are inseparable from the ways in which we choose to live in it'. Accordingly, knowledge becomes stable and authoritative when it reflects, and in turn helps shape, social solidarities such as dominant discourses and hierarchies; social concepts such as class, gender, or caste; or more obvious structures such as expert bodies and organizations.

Critical potential

For many scholars, especially in the United States, critical environmental science still has the critical potential to challenge Western models of modern, capitalist living. Increasingly, however, STS and other forms of analysis are seeking to be critical about how science and scientific expertise are unexplored arenas of political influence. Three themes seem most apparent: the role of science as unquestioned or authoritative knowledge, the role of expertise as the source of scientific knowledge, and the implications of science and expertise for social order (and vice versa).

The key contribution of STS to environmental politics is that environmental science is not an apolitical or neutral representation of reality but is a reflection of social influences. These influences affect which knowledge is gathered; which interests or perspectives are reflected or excluded in this knowledge; and how this knowledge is used for political objectives. It should be noted that these statements do not imply that scientific knowledge is either futile, or never to be trusted – or that there are no environmental problems. Rather, the information gathered about environmental problems will always contain social influences and implications. The same conclusions are made for 'technologies' – which are considered separate and apolitical, but which are shaped by societies and can also express agency over humans, rather than only vice versa (Braun and Whatmore 2010; see also Luke, this volume).

For example, much current political debate concerns anthropogenic climate change. Some environmental analysts adopt the earlier approaches to critical environmental science by insisting that climate science is accurate and is resisted only because capitalist organizations wish to generate misleading information in order to avoid regulation (Jacques 2012). This stance is clearly critical because it seeks to challenge the existing social and political order in the world economy (see Okereke and Charlesworth, this volume).

Yet, an STS approach also seeks to be critical of what climate science means and of the analysts who seek to use it as a political tool. The purpose here is not to imply that anthropogenic climate change is not occurring, or that regulation is not needed, but to assess with more awareness what kinds of perspectives and insights are avoided in this argumentative strategy. For example, the earlier example of the Indian Centre for Science and Environment (Agarwal and Narain 1991) demonstrated that simply generating statistics about climate change policy can avoid many important questions about cause-and-effect, blame, and responsibility, which can have significant implications for which kinds of policies are considered appropriate and which countries should take action.

Much environmental research in STS has indicated the ways in which knowledge or apparent scientific 'laws' might contain hidden, unchallenged, or misleading assumptions (Forsyth 2003). Scholars have used the terms *environmental narratives* and *storylines* to describe common assumptions about environmental cause-and-effect that are not as accurate or inclusive as thought. These terms act as devices through which actors are positioned, and through which specific ideas of 'blame' and 'responsibility' and 'urgency' and 'responsible behavior' are attributed (Hajer 1995: 64–5).

For example, research in Africa has proposed that commonplace explanations of desertification place too much emphasis on the agency of smallholder farmers and pastoralists and allow states the opportunity to regulate land use and migration in rural zones on the basis of supposedly factual (yet questionable) science (Thomas and Middleton 1994). In West Africa, governments have often adopted a narrative of deforestation that blames small-holders; yet historical landscape research and questioning of farmers have proposed that smallholders have protected forest islands and that much change in forest cover can result from long-standing and complex fluctuations between savanna and closed forest (Fairhead and Leach 1996). In these cases, the generation and legitimization of scientific knowledge can reflect alliances (sometimes unwitting) between state bodies and international conserva-tionist NGOs, which lead to policies such as banning fire and other land-use practices, rather than assisting smallholders gain livelihoods.

A second theme is in environmental expertise. Expertise is the ability to speak with author-ity on matters of scientific or public concern (Jasanoff 1990; Turner 2001). Commonly, experts are assumed to be scientists or scientific organizations that have a clear reputation, training, and standing in a field of public concern. The political scientist Peter Haas (1992) used the term *epistemic community* to refer to scientific networks that can speak with author-ity and hence guide political debates about how to manage environmental problems.

But expertise is also highly politicized and contextual. Again, STS does not imply that there is no such thing as expertise, but that the status of expertise is often socially allocated and variable. The basis upon which people claim, or see, expertise needs to be opened to more public scrutiny in order to see how and why truth claims are considered authoritative or are assumed to be true when there is evidence to question them.

For example, the Intergovernmental Panel on Climate Change (IPCC) is an expert body with immense authority in influencing climate change policy. It is widely acknowledged as an epistemic community. In order to maintain this authority – especially against climate change deniers – it regularly makes statements such as 'the science has driven the politics ... if the science is to continue guiding the politics, it is essential to keep the politics out of the science' (Cutajar 2001). Yet, the IPCC found itself widely criticized in 2009 when emails from some of its members were leaked onto the internet, revealing some statements that some critics of climate change policy claimed were evidence to show that political objectives were indeed shaping scientific research.

Scholars in STS use the term *boundary work* to explain how scientific or expert bodies separate their work from political debate that cannot be considered to be as authoritative (Gieryn 1983). Boundary work might include strict rules of participation in scientific net-works or the exclusion of certain types of commentator or scientific information (such as research conducted by non-governmental organizations as opposed to peer-reviewed aca-demic papers). These steps constitute social acts of defining expertise, but also contribute to the appearance of scientific certainty when these organizations make announcements (Funtowicz and Ravetz 1993). STS scholars analyse boundary work in order to see how different voices and interests might be included or excluded and to assess the impacts on policy recommendations. For example, many analysts agree that the IPCC has generally adopted a model of risk based upon additional atmospheric greenhouse gas concentrations rather than how risks are experienced on the ground by societies with various levels of socio-economic vulnerability. Accordingly, much climate change policy to date has focused on global mitigation rather than building adaptive capacity. The IPCC is now changing to include a more diverse set of analysts, including specialists in economics and international development. Initially, however, it was largely composed of meteorologists (Beck 2011; Hulme 2009).

The third theme concerns the interrelationship of science and social order. The objective here is to assess what kinds of social orders generate different kinds of knowledge, and vice versa. Various analysts have proposed different ways of understanding this. One early approach to linking environmental knowledge to social structures was so-called Cultural Theory (which used a capital C and T to distinguish it from other theories). This work was based on the anthropologists Mary Douglas and Michael Thompson, and indeed the classic text, *Uncertainty on a Himalayan Scale* (Thompson et al. 1986), referred to previously, used this approach. Cultural Theory proposed that there were different worldviews based on how far individuals respond to the two criteria of 'grid' (the willingness to follow rules), and 'group' (the willingness to act with others). This rather simple classification led to four worldviews: 'Individualists', who see the world as resilient; 'egalitarians', who see the environment as threatened and fragile; 'hierarchists', who want to set rules for permissible environmental degradation; and 'fatalists', who are the group that live with rules without the chance to resist. In political terms, these groups classically are associated respectively with businesses, environmental NGOs, governments, and powerless groups such as hill farmers or factory workers. According to Cultural Theory, no one worldview is correct, but it is important to avoid any one group representing environmental problems in only their way. It is also worth noting that this analysis also forms a convenient explanation for the climate change deniers in the United States (individualists) and the so-called critical environmental scientists who adopt the earlier approach to environmental science in order to claim truth and reason on their side (egalitarians) (see Forsyth 2012).

Later approaches within STS, however, have avoided the suggestion that there are four worldviews and instead have sought to identify how social structures and scientific knowledge uphold each other on a more contextual and varied basis. Jasanoff (2004), for example, uses the concept of coproduction to refer to the mutual production of knowledge and social order. Accordingly, science is inherently linked to notions of democracy, and there is a constant need to question how far scientific certainty allows, on one hand, a useful insight into understanding complex environmental problems, or, on the other hand, a case where important voices and biophysical insights are excluded. Critical scientific analysis, therefore, seeks to identify which social structures and values allow knowledge to remain unchallenged and which new knowledge is deemed necessary. Epstein (1996), for example, argued that HIV research in the United States initially focused on seeking ways to destroy or prevent the transmission of HIV. Following activism from social campaigners, however, this research shifted to include ways of improving the lives of people with HIV. Batt (1994) also argued that activism by women's groups revealed the gender bias of research and surgery on breast cancer, resulting in a more diverse range of treatments (Harding 1986).

Conclusion

The role of science in critical environmental politics has therefore changed over time. Earlier approaches were based on the critical theory of writers such as Habermas, who argued that the problems of modern societies were based on the overwhelming domination of instrumental reason and economic exploitation. Environmental scientists and activists therefore adopted these ideas to claim that environmental science, and ecology in particular, played a crucial critical political role in undermining the hegemonic exploitative and economic order in modern capitalist societies. These ideas still have resonance today in some of the debates about the origins of climate change denial and the role of science in reforming modern society.

But the analysis of science within critical environmental politics is now changing towards the more convincing study of science as a political arena itself. This analysis – spearheaded by Science and Technology Studies (STS) – does not deny that there are worrying environmental problems, or a need for environmental regulation. But unlike the earlier style of critical science, it argues instead for analysing how science is made and used within environmental politics. It argues that all scientific methods are embedded in social processes that influence what is to be researched and for what purposes. Moreover, many statements that claim to be scientific often ignore scientific studies. In addition, the rules and ways of performing and reporting science can create additional social exclusions that can reduce the number of perspectives represented in scientific explanations, as well as miss important insights into underlying biophysical change.

Being critical about science in environmental politics therefore does not mean claiming that science is irrefutable and therefore should be followed. That would be an *uncritical* use of science. Rather, it means asking important questions about the mutual dependencies of science and politics. For example, how was a scientific statement made? Are important voices or perspectives excluded? How far is cause-and-effect foreclosed and, therefore, no longer discussed in environmental politics? What political capital and power is being invested in different speakers or organizations by repeating these scientific statements?

Asking these questions does not imply that science is not useful, or that it cannot assist in understanding complex and important problems. But it does mean that scientific statements should not be used in political debates without asking how politics infuse the science and how science empowers the politics. In addition, it also means asking what is meant by *science* more generally. Much environmental debate is based on allegedly scientific statements that many scientists question. Many assumptions or beliefs also occupy the same status as science but actually arise from factors unrelated to scientific inquiry. Sometimes *science* is identified more by who speaks, rather than which process is used.

These questions relate more generally to the importance of understanding knowledge within environmental politics debates. Understanding how less powerful voices in developed and developing societies can be rendered invisible, while others are more prominent, is a key part of environmental politics (see Bond and Hinton, this volume). Bringing critical environmental science more fully into environmental politics is therefore an important and highly influential part of democratic politics more generally.

Further reading

Good reviews of the relationships of environmental science and politics can be found in Forsyth (2003) *Critical Political Ecology: The Politics of Environmental Science*, London: Routledge; Jasanoff and Long-Martello (eds) (2005) *Earthly Politics: Local and Global in Environmental Governance*, Cambridge, MA: MIT Press; and Goldman, Nadasdy and Turner (2011) *Knowing Nature: Conversations at the Intersection of Political Ecology and Science Studies*, Chicago: University of Chicago Press. A book that focuses specifically on Africa is Leach and Mearns (eds) (1996) *The Lie of the Land: Challenging Received Wisdom on the African Environment*, Oxford: James Currey. Good introductions to Science and Technology Studies include Hackett, Amsterdamska, Lynch, and Wajcman (eds) (2007) *The Handbook of Science and Technology Studies*, Cambridge MA: MIT Press; Jasanoff (ed.)

(2006) *States of Knowledge: The Co-production of Science and Social Order*, Abingdon: Routledge; and Hess (1997) *Science Studies: An Advanced Introduction*, New York: New York University Press. A good introduction to the problems of expertise is Turner (2003) *Liberal Democracy 3.0: Civil-Society in an Age of Experts*, Thousand Oaks: Sage.

Useful websites

Centre for Science and Environment: http://www.cseindia.org/
IPCC: http://www.ipcc.ch/
Science and Democracy Network: http://www.hks.harvard.edu/sdn/
Society for Social Studies of Science: http://4sonline.org/
World Resources Institute: http://www.wri.org/

23 Security

Simon Dalby

Introduction

Security is at the heart of modern politics, a key concept and a series of practices that are frequently simply taken for granted. The term itself refers obviously to matters of safety and the protection of people and states from whatever might make them insecure. It is frequently understood in explicitly geographical tropes, where external threats are formulated in contrast to a domestic arena that is in need of protection from those foreign dangers; hence the language of 'national' security (Fierke 2007). But within states, *security* is also invoked in terms of such things as middle class fears of burglars and of crime and violence that specify threats 'out there' to domestic bliss 'in here'. Maintaining security is usually mostly about shoring up the existing social order; when it comes to international security, that usually requires non-violent resolution of international disputes unless states hugely violate international norms.

The assumption in most discussions of politics is that the maintenance of order and what is frequently now called *political stability* is the first pre-requisite for non-violent collective action, the sine qua non for political actions rather than for violence. Peaceful transitions of power are one of the goals of democratic states, a process of considerable importance, but one that also distances the provision of security from particular rulers; security is more than rule tied to one person or regime; it relates to the state more broadly conceived and is usually tied into an at least implicit assumption that the state is legitimate because of its provision of security, and this in turn is now also about the provision of economic prosperity for at least the middle classes in modern states.

The term *national security* is now widespread, incorporating the logic of 'reasons of state', which trump all dissent and usually evade democratic oversight, not least by invoking secrecy as a necessity for the protection of many things (see Kuehls, this volume). Security is the key overarching concept that links both matters of strategy and larger concerns with domestic politics within states into an encompassing concept that is very extensive, frequently highly elastic, and, as a result, both impossible to define in precise terms and immensely useful for political practitioners (Williams 2007). When it is stretched to matters of international security and global security, the terminology becomes even more elastic.

The United Nations has a Security Council at its heart, but nearly all its activities are discussed in terms of 'peace and security', even if this conjunction is rarely subject to the kind of critical analysis that such a telling phrase might reasonably be expected to generate. The linkage operates to perpetuate assumptions that the political economy of modernity, and the state system that effectively administers its activities, is the most important matter that needs to be secured, following which other matters can be dealt with as and when necessary. But it is precisely the consequences of that global economy and its transformations that now are endangering environments and their peoples in many places and, in turn, generating a series of discussions that directly link security to environment, and do so increasingly at the largest scale, that of the globe itself.

While environment has a long history as part of the United Nations system, the United Nations Environment Programme being effectively an offshoot of the 1972 United Nations conference on the human environment in Stockholm, the linkage of security to environmental matters has been slow to develop in either the United Nations process or in the policy formulation of most major states. However, in recent years a number of discussions in the Security Council have been triggered by members' concerns that climate change will have profound impacts in coming decades, a matter serious enough to be a priority and hence a matter for attention by the Security Council.

As the rest of this chapter will outline, how environment has become a matter of security, and with what political implications, is a long-standing and contentious debate among activists and academics. It has become all the more interesting in the last few years as climate change has forced state policy makers to confront environmental themes as a matter of security, although so far most states have, despite sometimes hyperbolic rhetoric, yet to securitise the environment, or, more specifically, matters of climate change, by making them a matter of state priority in terms of the allocation of resources or practical defence preparations (Oels 2012). Nonetheless climate concerns have been finding their way into official discussions of migration, their potential for aggravating conflicts and the need to prepare for dealing with disaster responses. As such environmental matters are now tied into many discussions of security.

Core ideas

Environmental themes have always been part of discussions of political economy, at least in so far as resources, food supplies and how these are distributed are key to any economic system (see Paterson, and Watts and Peluso, this volume). Thomas Malthus's pessimism about the human condition has remained a key part of the political discussion, and the assumption about scarcity is key to the modern understanding of economics and many other things (Xenos 1989; see also Kütting, this volume). In the 1990s, the discussion linking environmental change to potential conflicts repeatedly examined the assumption that scarcity would lead to conflict. In numerous ways the environmental problematique is a matter of the other side of the coin; rather than concerns with scarcity, it focuses on the detrimental effects of resource use and the problems of pollution and environmental destruction as a result of the expansion of economic activity. Both resources and environment are part of the discussion that has come to be simply called 'environmental security' over the last few decades, although how these are linked together isn't always clear. Especially so in the relentless stream of alarmist media headlines about resource wars, peak oil, climate refugees and general disruptions forecast by numerous reports on the human condition (see Methmann and Oels, this volume).

The alarm about contemporary trajectories is of course precisely why environment has been linked to security, notably by non-government organisations and advocates, rather than by states, at least until recently; these are big important trends and need much more attention from states than they have been getting. Hence the invocation of security rhetoric by those concerned to raise the profile of environmental matters in international affairs. These alarms about environmental issues crystallised in the late 1980s into what became the discussion of 'environmental security' (Barnett 2001). While these concerns were temporarily swept aside in the aftermath of 9/11 and the military response to these events by the United States, they returned later in the decade as numerous agencies began to think seriously about climate change specifically rather than more general environmental issues.

At least four major themes link environment and security, and they persist in the discussion, albeit with varying degrees of emphasis at different times. The first theme in the environmental security discussion suggests that warfare and preparations for warfare are a major cause of environmental destruction (Renner 1991). The obliteration of Hiroshima and Nagasaki at the end of the Second World War introduced the world to the phenomenon of radioactive fallout and environmental contamination (see Pellizzoni, this volume). Alarms about nuclear warfare in the 1980s were accentuated by discussions of the possibilities of nuclear winter. Studies suggested that this might result from soot and dust lofted into the high atmosphere by burning cities shading the planetary surface and cooling the planet (Sagan and Turco 1990). The results would disrupt agriculture and most terrestrial ecosystems. Preparations for warfare, not only nuclear facilities and testing ranges, but industrial facilities, waste dumps and fuel depots, left a toxic legacy in many places through the Cold War period (Hastings 2000). The term *environmental security* has been used widely in the U.S. military for practical engineering programmes of environmental remediation that might better be termed either environmental clean-up or simply pollution prevention (Floyd 2010).

The second theme in the environmental security discussion crystallised in the late 1980s when concerns over large scale environmental changes, not least the burning rainforests of the Amazon and the severe summer drought in the United States in 1988, compounded earlier concerns with the technological disasters of Bhopal and Chernobyl to suggest that the environmental matters were serious enough to be considered in terms of security (Mathews 1989). What wasn't clear then, and still isn't clear, is how such events might lead to overt violent conflict, the core theme of security, whether understood as national or international security. There was a frequently inchoate sense that this all mattered as a global concern even if the precise modalities that linked technological damage to human suffering were not well thought through. Soviet thinkers, alarmed by the fallout from Chernobyl and realising the extent of environmental degradation caused by their industrial model, began to raise matters of environment as security concerns (Dabelko 2008). This was part of their program of Perestroika, a comprehensive rethinking of many things, but one that was subsequently swept away by and mostly forgotten after the collapse of the Soviet Union in 1991.

Simultaneously, the discussion of sustainable development and attempts to make development less environmentally destructive was formulating suggestions to 'green' economic activity (see Whitehead, this volume). Part of the argument in the hugely influential 1987 World Commission on Environment and Development report on 'Our Common Future' was that sustainable development was necessary to prevent future conflict over resource scarcities that would occur, so the report's authors suggested, if sustainability wasn't factored in to development. This theme of future resource scarcity harkened back to 1970s debates about the 'Limits to Growth' and fears about fuel shortages in particular that had occurred in the aftermath of the 1973 Yom Kippur war and the OPEC petroleum export embargo on states that supplied weapons to Israel. Fears of resource shortages and conflict over diminishing supplies were simply taken for granted in much of this discussion, reprising matters in terms that are frequently called 'neo-Malthusian' (see Kütting, this volume).

Investigating the claims that environmental scarcities cause conflict became the third theme in the environmental security discourse; the question of the relationship between resources and conflict continues to be discussed in the literature. While research suggests some linkages, it is clear that social and political factors are more important than just environmental changes (see Watts and Peluso, this volume). Ironically, much evidence from the development literature suggests that violence is more closely related to resource abundance in places where there are few economic options other than the extraction of the resource (Le Billon 2012). In these circumstances, fighting to control the resource and the revenues that can be generated by its exploitation may make sense to local conflict entrepreneurs and disaffected ethnic populations. While violence is related to environmental scarcity, in many cases extreme scarcity leads to famine rather than to direct conflict, although it is important to remember that controlling food has long been part of warfare.

But, the critics asked, should the concern over environmental change be considered a matter of national security? Or at least Marc Levy (1995) pointedly asked if it mattered to the national security of the United States. Concerns with instabilities in marginal states were not a matter that should generate concern over major wars, and while interventions of a humanitarian nature might be important issues in their own right, they did not challenge the core competencies of major states and, hence, so the argument went, were not a matter of security concern. They might become so should large refugee flows from conflicts cause political instability, but this wasn't a matter of the same significance as preparing for a nuclear war or warfare with a major industrial power. Indeed while many militaries did pay some attention to environmental changes as a source of instability in the 1990s, few gave it any clear priority in terms of planning and policy formulation.

Most recently the preoccupation with climate has synthesised the three earlier themes into a fourth one loosely now called 'climate security'. While the Bush administration after 2001 was completely uninterested in matters of climate change, gradually security thinkers in the United States, Germany, and the United Kingdom began to work through the implications of climate change and came to the conclusion that it was a matter of long-term risks (CNA Corporation 2007; German Advisory Council on Global Change 2008; Mabey, Gulledge, Finel and Silverthorne 2011) and one that was likely to be a conflict multiplier in many places, although depending on whether the necessary anticipatory actions are set in place, not necessarily a cause of future wars (Dyer 2008). As a cause of insecurity in places that were vulnerable to climate change, and were inadequately equipped politically to deal with the disruptions, this obviously had implications for international security (see Okereke and Charlesworth, this volume).

Some of the analyses have suggested that metropolitan states are also vulnerable; the British in particular are concerned about rising sea levels, disruptions of water supplies due to possible changes in rainfall, and enhanced refugee migrations and political instabilities. Now climate security has taken over as the focal point for these discussions and is a matter taken seriously by at least some security planners (Webersik 2010). But if this new found concern with environment simply feeds into existing military planning for suppressing instabilities in the periphery of the global economy, then the more profound implications of linking security and environment will be foreclosed, and the opportunity to think in innovative ways about who is securing what kind of future will be lost.

Critical thinking requires challenging the assumption that environment can be added into conventional formulations of national security. Precisely the political and economic order that has rendered at least the peoples of modern states relatively secure is undermining the ecological basis on which that security has been built. Climate change makes this simple and alarming fact unavoidable now, but as the discussion in the rest of this chapter suggests, how to go about rethinking security in light of the growing awareness of the new ecological context for humanity requires much more than simply extending existing modes of analysis or policy practices.

Key thinkers

Environmental themes blossomed in the policy literature as the Cold War wound down in the late 1980s. Water wars, resource shortages, environmental disruptions and their inter-relationships made headlines and generated numerous calls to extend and rethink security. Michael Renner (1989) revived some earlier Worldwatch Institute concerns with pollution and environmental destruction as security issues (Brown 1977), and linked the discussion explicitly to the environmental devastation caused by military actions and preparations for war. Biologist Norman Myers published a series of papers and subsequently a popular book with the alarming title of *Ultimate Security* in 1993, arguing forcibly that environmental matters were the most important matter for consideration after the Cold War and that a sustainable planet was the sina qua non for everything else. Robert Kaplan's (1994) essay on 'The Coming Anarchy' in the *Atlantic Monthly* summarised the bleak fears of scarcity, violence and environmental change into a powerful image of imminent chaos, popularising the discussion without providing anything more than impressionistic fears about processes he failed to analyse.

The critics were quick to point out the weaknesses and dangers in linking environment and security. Daniel Deudney (1990) penned a paper that pointed out that the military, with primary responsibility for security provision, was an institution singularly ill-suited to dealing with environmental matters. Military training and technology was mostly about destroying things and killing people rather than environmental restoration and resource man-agement. He also argued that environmental matters needed a global view, not one devoted to protecting individual states. Indeed how these states used industrial means to build armed forces was in part the problem given the pollution and resources used by industrial militaries. Mathias Finger (1991) pointedly made the case that industrial states and their accumula-tion of power through resource extraction were precisely the security problem that needed addressing, as these modes of providing 'security' were what was causing environmental degradation in the first place. Jeremy Rifkin's popular discussion in his *Biosphere Politics* (1991) directly tackled the need to rethink security after the Cold War by abandoning the traditional geopolitical discourses and substituting an ecological sensibility instead.

What was noteworthy in the late 1980s was the lack of any clear empirical evidence that in fact environmental changes were related to conflict. While this assumption was repeated end-lessly in media and political commentary, it wasn't demonstrated in the scholarly literature. In North America, Thomas Homer-Dixon (1991, 1999) set out to research the link between environmental change and conflict. Given the amorphous nature of 'security', he narrowed the analysis to try to link environmental matters to acute conflict. In a series of empirical studies he suggested that while such links could be demonstrated, they required numerous 'intervening variables' related to a lack of governance capacities to sustain the argument. Simultaneously, a series of studies in Europe under Gunter Baechler's (1999b) overall direc-tion suggested that violence was related to environment, although principally in areas where elite discrimination and restricted access to resources aggravated social divisions. More so than Homer-Dixon's framework, these studies emphasised the huge transformations of rural economies as modernisation has spread world wide and focused on 'mal-development' as part of the problem.

Neither of these sets of studies suggested that security in the traditional sense of inter-state conflict was linked to these processes of environmental change. Colin Kahl's (2006) major attempt to synthesise the findings of empirical work and illustrate the conclusions with a comparative study of Kenya and the Philippines confirmed that political factors were key to violence that is somehow linked to environment and resources. He made it clear that the actions of elites are often much more important than what marginalised and impoverished peoples do. Recent research focusing on the potential for conflict related to climate change hasn't challenged the basic findings from the 1990s work; environmental change isn't a major direct cause of conflict despite some correlations between extreme conditions and political instability (O'Loughlin et al. 2012).

In the following decade the case that abundance was more important as a cause of conflict came to prominence. Indra De Soysa (2002) and other development researchers pointed to the importance of resource abundance and the control over the revenue streams as a more significant cause of conflict than environmental scarcity. Oil, diamonds, forest products, coltan and many other resources are now understood to be an integral part of the political economy of contemporary violence; frequently their sale provides funds for combatants to purchase weapons. This, too, is not a new phenomenon, as numerous imperial histories make clear; the rush for fast profits by extracting and harvesting resources to feed and fuel distant metropoles has frequently been a violent business (Le Billon 2012). Plantation agriculture too has displaced peoples through history, and the latest round of 'land grabbing' by rich states anxious to secure supplies of agricultural products in situations of global food crisis emphasises the importance of understanding the links between the expanding global economy and violence in peripheral regions.

Many of these themes have been thrown into sharp relief in recent years by the emergent discourse of climate security. Now the security establishments in Washington, as well as in Europe, are becoming concerned that rapid climate changes may have disruptive effects on many poorer states in the global south and, to a lesser extent, for metropolitan states as well, by accelerating or multiplying social stresses (CNA Corporation 2007; UNGA 2009). But while earlier concerns with environmental conflict discounted the possibilities of inter-state conflict, more recent security concerns in the war on terror portrayed climate disruptions as a conflict multiplier, and especially as a matter that might generate resentment at Western states that is expressed in terrorist activity. The unstable and peripheral parts of the global economy, the entities frequently classed as failed states are, so the argument goes, likely to be further disrupted by climate change-induced conflicts and migration, hence they are a security concern that needs to be taken seriously (Moran 2011).

How states adapt and what likely consequences will flow from various scenarios of future weather patterns matter; in these formulations, climate is a new driver of political instabilities. But the more important long-term issues are what is driving climate change in the first place and what might be done about it. This debate has become stymied in North America recently by the effective campaigns of the so-called climate deniers who have acted to prevent serious political initiatives at the federal level in the United States and in Canada, too (Boykoff 2011). However, a larger discussion of energy security, the possibility of 'green jobs' and a new post-carbon economy are tackling some of these issues. Ironically, given past practice, the American military is actively seeking to reduce its dependence on petroleum supplies, both in terms of using less by experimenting with solar powered electricity and diversifying fuel sources, all in the name of improving operational capabilities and reducing vulnerabilities to its supply lines. But this is mostly a matter of national security (Busby 2008), not a larger global concern with the transformation of the biosphere or a matter of security for all of humanity.

Critical potential

Reflecting on the 1990s debate, Jon Barnett (2000) posed the key question of who the environmental security discussion was for, and why impoverished Southern peoples were being constructed as a threat to Northerners in the first place. He then posed these questions as part of a larger discussion of *The Meaning of Environmental Security* (2001), linking the discussion to work on human rights, justice and the critical work on the environmental disruptions caused by development strategies (see Bond, this volume). His critique connected environmental security with perspectives drawing on the extensive discussion of human security that was started in the 1994 United Nations Development Report (UNDP 1994). Human security implicitly challenges much of the national security discourse, and does so by focusing on who specifically is insecure as a result of environmental transformation, rather than starting the analysis assuming states provide security (Matthew, Barnett, McDonald and O'Brian 2010).

Simon Dalby (2002) posed the questions of the geographies of the environmental security discourse by explicitly examining what order was being secured by the practices invoked in the name of environmental security. Drawing on critical work by Indian scholars of development and building on both Homer-Dixon (1999) and Baechler's (1999b) frameworks, he suggested that the processes of urbanisation were disrupting rural life and transforming peripheral places into suppliers of migrants and resources for the burgeoning cities in which humanity increasingly lives. More recently this framework has been extended (Dalby 2009) to link the discussion of climate security to matters of vulnerability, and, in particular, the vulnerabilities of urban dwellers, dependent on long commodity chains and functioning infrastructure, as well as political order to maintain their human security (see also Methmann and Oels, this volume).

This mode of thinking now needs to be put into the appropriate context if it is to be either intellectually coherent or make policy suggestions that are useful. Noteworthy in the last few years is the gradual acceptance by scientists that the sheer scale of human transformation of the earth's systems amounts to our now living in a new geological epoch, commonly called the Anthropocene (Steffen et al. 2011). This quite literally is the age of humanity. The significance of this is profound not just for the discussion of environmental security but also for much else besides. We are now quite literally making our collective future by how we reshape the biosphere for human ends (see Rudy and White, this volume). The environment is no longer a matter of a backdrop to human affairs; we are transforming it rapidly at a global scale, and any discussion of environmental security now has to consider such matters in terms of what might be called a 'political geo-ecology for the Anthropocene' (Brauch, Dalby and Oswald Spring 2011).

Critical voices linking all this to larger agendas for human security insist that we take humanity in all its multitudinous varieties seriously as that which is in need of security; simply invoking national populations as though they are homogenous wholes will not provide adequate understandings of the particular vulnerabilities of women, children and ethnic minorities, without which the specific human securities of large segments of today's peoples cannot be either discussed effectively or provided for (Oswald Spring 2008a). Linking this explicitly to environmental transformations and the social structures that link security to peace is also essential if the agenda for environmental security is to provide useful guidance as to how to handle change without resorting to violence in crisis situations (Brauch 2005).

The implications of all this suggest both that the early writers about environmental security and the importance of environmental matters were correct in raising the alarm about both its seriousness and the inappropriateness of thinking about any of this in terms of national security frameworks alone. Clearly humanity is transforming the globe but doing so both unequally in terms of who is making the decisions about what kind of transformations are being set in motion and also in terms of who will bear the costs of the new increasingly artificial circumstances in which we live (Scheffran, Broszka, Brauch, Link and Schilling 2012). This is brought into increasingly sharp relief by the simultaneous emergence of an awareness of climate change and the increasing inequalities within the global economy that ensure that some have the wherewithal to avoid the consequences of environmental change while others have little choice but to struggle for daily existence hoping that by chance they will not become a victim of either agricultural disruption or more directly of violent storms and resultant infrastructure failure. Insecurity is thus now unavoidably tied into matters of environmental injustice, too (Stoett 2012).

Conclusion

Recent security practices have focused on neo-liberal modes of governance and contemporary state and financial practices in addition to the war on terror (Duffield 2007). Contemporary security practices are now securing a form of political stability but an unsustainable one when viewed in light of current environmental transformations. Global financial governance has an uneasy relation to traditional forms of security with its notions of national security drawing boundaries and keeping threats at bay. But these modes of security link up with the theme of ensuring economic prosperity at home, and if the current policies tied to national specifications of threats and dangers originating in other places persist, then the prospect of a violent future looms as climate change accelerates, especially if elites use force to maintain their privileges (Welzer 2012).

Challenging the implicit geography of peripheral places threatening metropolitan prosperity is an essential intellectual task if security is to be rethought to include most humans rather than just the rich and powerful. The point about the Anthropocene is that it forces clear attention on what it is that is to be secured by policies of sustainable development and globalisation. It forces us to think of ourselves as part of earth, not apart from it. In doing so, one of the most basic dichotomies that structures modern thought, the distinction between humanity and environment, or between culture and nature, is rendered redundant as a premise for political thinking (see Hobden, McShane, and Rudy and White, this volume). What exactly it is that ought to be sustained is now an unavoidable political question at the heart of any discussion that links environment to security.

The Anthropocene also makes it very clear that production decisions, and land use decisions that go with this, are now the key to understanding what kind of environment humanity is making for itself. The global economy and what kind of energy systems power it, and what kinds of commodities it makes, are shaping the geology of the future of the planet, deciding such things as how many polar icecaps the planet will have in coming millennia. Given that the contemporary political economy is not reproducing a global environment that is similar to the conditions that gave rise to human civilisation in the first place, now the political issue for environmental security analysts and policy makers is nothing less than what kind of planet ought we be securing for what kind of humanity.

Considering security in light of global transformation requires rethinking other political concepts, too, and thinking about matters in terms of dynamic and increasingly artificial ecologies rather than taking environment as a stable backdrop. Much more than routine state environmental regulation is needed to deal with these large-scale transformations, and clearly, while states matter greatly in how this process is governed, corporate production decisions are also crucial to our future (see Baker, this volume). But these are not under effective democratic control in present circumstances; and insofar as they shape the future condition of human insecurity, clearly much further thought is needed about how they might be directed to make a secure habitat for the future of humanity.

Further reading

A large compendium of scholarly thinking on human security and climate change is presented in Scheffran et al. (2012) *Climate Change, Human Security and Violent Conflict: Challenges for Societal Stability.* In part this builds on the comprehensive overview report of the global climate change issue within a broad perspective on security by the German Advisory Council on Global Change (2008). A series of regional studies on how climate change might play out in various places is in Daniel Moran's (2011) edited volume *Climate Change and National Security.* A popular account of the climate security issue with particularly useful emphasis on the key matter of infrastructure planning is in Cleo Pascal's (2010) book *Global Warring: How Environmental, Economic and Political Crises Will Redraw the World Map.* The key study on how to apply risk analysis to climate and security is in Nick Mabey et al.'s (2011) report *Degrees of Risk: Defining a Risk Management Framework for Climate Security.* Gwynne Dyer's (2008) lucid popular introduction to military and climate science scenarios for the future is in his book *Climate Wars*, while Simon Dalby (2009) provides the framework for thinking about environmental security thinking for the Anthropocene epoch in his book on *Security and Environmental Change.*

Useful websites

Center for Climate and Security: http://climateandsecurity.org/
Institute for Environmental Security: http://www.envirosecurity.org/
Sustainable Security: http://sustainablesecurity.org/
Real Climate: http://www.realclimate.org/
Earth System Governance: http://www.earthsystemgovernance.org/
Wilson Center Environmental Change and Security Program: http://www.wilsoncenter.org/program/
  environmental-change-and-security-program

24 States

Thom Kuehls

Introduction

Since its origin in Europe in the sixteenth century, the state has reigned as the primary locus of political power in the modern world. It is, after all, the central legal and policy entity. Any collection on environmental politics cannot ignore the state's importance. The state makes decisions to allow or curb pollution, to protect or not protect various species, to pursue or not pursue 'green' technologies, and so on. Simply put, the state's impact on the environment, for better or worse, cannot go overlooked.

This chapter attempts to discuss the critical importance of the state with respect to environmental politics. In order to engage in this discussion, it is worth noting the historical and cultural specificity of this thing called the state. A disservice is done in political thought when the term *state* is used to refer to every political entity throughout time. I am, in this chapter, talking specifically about an entity that emerged in Europe some five centuries ago and has spread around the globe. Despite the ubiquity of the term *state* in political discourse, it is imperative that we recognize that not all political entities are states. And in order to do this, we need a better understanding of what constitutes the state.

Core ideas

A survey of introductory texts in the discipline of political science will present a reader with claims that attempts to define a state are 'always unsatisfactory' (Burgess 1994: 53). That said, the state is not an essentially contested concept. Definitions of the state are readily available, and while all are not identical, they tend to share at least four key features. Hedley Bull's description of states in *The Anarchical Society* (1977), a prominent text in international political theory, adequately sets out these components: 'each state possesses a government and asserts sovereignty in relation to a particular portion of the earth's surface and a particular segment of the human population' (8). In other words, the four key elements of a state are a government, sovereignty, a territory, and a people. While each of these elements may seem rather straightforward, they are not. Each contains a specificity worth exploring. In this section, I briefly describe each of these elements in an attempt to provide a basic sense of that entity known as a state.

Government

The term *government* can be understood in two ways. First, the term refers to a structured and hierarchical entity tasked with or possessing powers to make, enforce, and adjudicate disputes involving the law. This is the use of the term as presented in Bull's (1977) definition of the state. As with the state itself, the term *government* may appear to be rather generic. But as Bull (1977) points out, not all political communities possess governments: 'In parts of Africa, Australia and Oceana, before the European intrusion, there were independent political communities held together by ties of lineage or kinship, in which there was no such institution as government' (9). There may be an urge to dismiss Bull's claim here as Eurocentric bias – as simply a refusal to accept that the peoples living in these regions did possess governments in order to justify European colonization, or in Bull's case to at least not include them in the study of international politics since the international arena is made up of states and these political communities, lacking government, were/are not states. But I would recommend resisting this urge. Clearly Bull's (1977) description of these communities as not-states serves to exclude them from the discussion and in many ways serves to justify 'the European intrusion'. But Bull's use of the term *government* here is not inaccurate. It signals the specificity of the term. When we talk of states, we are talking about political communities that possess a particular entity known as government – a structured, organized, and hierarchical decision-making entity.

But government is more than a noun – a structured, organized, and hierarchical decision-making entity. Government is also a verb – a process whereby people and lands are governed. The second use of the term differs from the first in that it does not ask 'who possesses political power', or 'how is that power structured or organized', but focuses instead on 'how that power is used'. In his 'Discourse on Political Economy' written in 1775, Jean-Jacques Rousseau sought to differentiate political economy (what he called government) from domestic economy. While domestic economy sought to provide for the needs of a family, political economy, or government, according to Rousseau, had an essential duty to 'think of (the citizens') subsistence; and to provide for public needs' (Rousseau 1984: 164). In this regard, government is far more than just a decision-making entity organized in a particular fashion: it is a process, an approach, a science of caring for an entire citizenry, the people of a state (see also Baker, Grove, and Lövbrand and Stripple, this volume).

Sovereignty

As with government, *sovereignty* is intricately linked to the state. In his informative treatise on the concept, F. H. Hinsley noted, '[i]n a word, the origin and history of the concept of sovereignty are closely linked with the nature, the origin and history of the state' (Hinsley 1986: 2). Put simply, when we speak of sovereignty in the modern world, we are speaking of the state. Unlike government, which is an identifiable entity, or a process of ruling and directing the affairs of the state, sovereignty is simply a notion. Its existence depends on perception. Returning to Bull's description of the state (and not-states), '[t]he kingdoms and principalities of Western Christendom (Europe) in the Middle Ages were not states: they did not possess internal sovereignty because they were not supreme over authorities within their territory and population; and at the same time they did not possess external sovereignty since they were not independent of the Pope, or in some cases, the Holy Roman Emperor' (Bull 1977: 9). As presented by Bull in this passage, sovereignty has an internal and an external requirement. In order for a state to exist, it must 'possess' both internal and external sovereignty. But the possession of sovereignty is perceptual. In order for sovereignty to exist, it must be perceived both by those living inside and outside the boundaries of a state. Not only must the citizens within a particular territory recognize the sovereignty of the state within which they reside, but so must peoples living in other states recognize that the territory claimed by a particular state does in fact belong to that state – which brings us to the third element of the state.

Territory

As with government and sovereignty, *territory* is an essential element of a state. There can be, Bull maintains, 'a community in which a ruler asserts (a recognized) supremacy over a people but not over a distinct territory' (Bull 1977: 8). Such a community, he adds, 'can also not be said to be a state' (Bull 1977: 8). A church or a corporation might fit this description, and neither is a state. States require territory, a tract of land that is recognized as belonging to one group of people, or one government, in particular.

For most political thinkers, even environmental political thinkers, territory is a rather straightforward concept. It is simply the land over which sovereignty holds sway, or the land over which a government rules. But neither description captures the concept completely. Territory is a specific type of land. Territory is state land. Territory is land that is fixed, plotted, and mapped so that sovereignty can hold sway. There is a process of territorialization, if you will, that is necessary in order to transform land into a part of a state. In this respect, we can argue that territory is the result of governmental practices. Since an essential duty of government is to provide for public needs, government must make the land it administers useful to the state; it must transform the land into territory. Territory, then, is a particular type of land, structured, organized, and used in a particular way (see Watts and Peluso, this volume).

People

Of the four elements of the state, *people* may seem the most straightforward. States, as Bull (1977) put it, assert sovereignty over a particular segment of the human population – a citizenry. The relation between the state and its citizens is, in its most basic sense, a legal relationship. Those humans who meet the legal requirements of a state can be said to be citizens of that state (see Hinton, this volume). But the concept of people, as with territory, exceeds the simply legal. Just as states require territory and not simply lands, states require a people and not simply a segment of the human population. As the chapters on biopolitics (Grove, this volume) and governmentality (Lövbrand and Stripple, this volume) have made clear, people are not simply the inhabitants of a state: people are a product of the state. They are structured, organized, and used in a particular way. As I discuss later in the Critical Potential section, there is an intricate relationship between government as a process, territory, and people. Just as governmental processes must transform the land into something that can provide for the needs of the people, governmental processes must ensure that the people are disciplined in such a way that they can transform land into territory.

Key thinkers

In the Core Ideas section of this chapter I simply sought to describe in somewhat general terms the four main elements of the state. In this section I look briefly at analyses of these four elements of the state by some key thinkers. While none of these thinkers is explicitly an environmentalist, their work does provide pathways for environmental thought to follow. The thinkers I will focus on in this section are Jean-Jacques Rousseau, Michel Foucault, Gilles Deleuze, and Felix Guattari. Each offers an analysis of two or more of the four elements of the state.

Both Rousseau and Foucault frame their analyses of the state through the problem of government, understood as a process of governing the state rather than as a specific entity tasked with the governing of the state (see Baker, this volume). The problem of government, or governmentality as it was expressed by Foucault, has been examined in great detail in the chapter on governmentality (Lövbrand and Stripple, this volume). But a few remarks on Rousseau's and Foucault's thoughts on this issue are appropriate here. Rousseau, writing in the mid-eighteenth century, recognized the unusualness of using this sense of the term *government*. For most political thinkers of his era, government was (and still is today) thought solely in the first sense – how political power is organized – hence the long tradition in political thought of asking which form of government (democracy, aristocracy, monarchy, and so on) is best. But, Rousseau maintained, 'it is . . . necessary [for those involved in politics] to think of [the citizens'] subsistence; and to provide for public needs is an . . . essential duty of government' (1984: 164). Far from thinking of the problem of government as a problem of who should wield political power, Rousseau focused on how that power should be wielded. What ends should it attempt to accomplish? And far from seeing government as simply an entity tasked with ensuring that laws are followed, or that rights are protected, Rousseau maintained that the problem of government (the problem of providing for public needs) requires an examination of 'everything required by the locality, the climate, soil, moral customs, neighborhood, and all the particular relationships of the people . . . an infinity of details, of policy and *economy*' (Rousseau 1984: 150, emphasis in original). In thinking about government along these lines, Rousseau was examining a relatively new political discourse, one that had only begun to emerge as the state emerged in the sixteenth century.

As Michel Foucault articulated in a famous lecture from 1978, 'government as a general problem . . . explode[d] in the sixteenth century' as the state came into existence (Foucault 1991b: 87). Different from the problem of sovereignty, which is about imposing and enforcing the law over a people and a territory, Foucault argued that the problem of government is about 'managing individuals, goods, and wealth' (1991b: 92). This requires us to look at 'men in their relations, their links, their imbrications with . . . resources, means of subsistence, the territory with its specific qualities, climate, irrigation, fertility, etc.' (1991b: 93). In this respect, the problem of government takes us directly into the field of environmental politics. How a people relates to and engages the locality, the climate, the soil is, after all, an environmental question.

This analysis of government by Rousseau and Foucault opens the door to thoughts about how lands become the territory of a state and how groups of human beings become the people of a state. Both processes are governmental. Just as states require territories and not simply lands, and must code, map, and striate lands in order to make them into territories, states require a people, and not simply members of the human species. And the creation of both requires governmental actions.

In their late twentieth-century work *A Thousand Plateaus* (1987), Deleuze and Guattari approach the state by thinking, in part, of the non-state. Looking at the first sense of government, for instance, government as a structured, organized, hierarchical entity, Deleuze and Guattari draw out the specificity of this entity by pointing out that many political societies, while not possessing governments, still possess particular decision-making institutions that not only render them non-states, but actually prevent the formation of the state by preventing the formation of a government. Just as 'special institutions are . . . necessary to enable a chief to become a man of State', they write, 'diffuse collective mechanisms are just as necessary to prevent a chief from becoming one' (Deleuze and Guattari 1987: 357). Political communities can be organized in ways that prevent the formation of governments. Recognizing this fact is helpful in recognizing the specificity of this thing called government, and hence the specificity of the state.

Deleuze and Guattari (1987) also contrast the state and the non-state with regards to how each engages space and movement. The state, they maintain, '*parcels out a closed space to people,* assigning each person a share and regulating the communication between shares', while many non-states '*distribute people (or animals) in an open space,* one that is indefinite and noncommunicating' (1987: 386, emphasis in original). Put another way, Deleuze and Guattari maintain that 'movement (in state terms) is the characteristic of a 'moved body' going from one point to another in a striated space' rather than it being an essential element of a body existing in smooth space (1987). This understanding of the state's orientation to space and movement offers a slightly different way of thinking about territory and people than provided by the examination of the problem of government offered by Rousseau and Foucault – but an environmentally significant one nonetheless.

Finally, Deleuze and Guattari tie the concept of sovereignty into this analysis of space and movement. 'The State is sovereignty, but sovereignty only reigns over what it is capable of internalizing, of appropriating locally' (1987: 360). In other words, sovereignty has its limits. Politics (particularly environmental politics) quite regularly transgresses the limits of sovereignty. Because of this, Deleuze and Guattari suggest the need for a different understanding of political space. Using the metaphors of rhizomes and smooth space (in contrast to the metaphors of trees and striated spaces that represent the sovereign space of states), they suggest an alternative spatialization of politics. In doing so, they seek to problematize the all too easily configured inside-outside dichotomy of domestic and foreign political thought. 'The outside of States', they contend, 'cannot be reduced to "foreign policy", that is, to a set of relations among States . . . The outside appears simultaneously in two directions: huge worldwide machines . . . but also the local . . . segmentary societies [which stand] in opposition to the organs of State power' (1987: 360). Such a problematization of the space of politics can be of tremendous use to students of environmental politics as they analyse problems that cannot be confined to one state, or to simply the relations between states.

Critical potential

Unlike some of the other concepts analysed in this collection, which clearly carry a critical potential in and of themselves, I do not believe that the state, as such, possesses critical potential. This does not mean, however, that environmental political thinkers should not place the state at the center of their analysis. But in doing so, they need to take a critical stance towards the state. A great deal of discussion in the field of environmental politics concerning the state has focused on whether or not environmental political thought should be state-centered or anti-state in its orientation. To me, this is perhaps the wrong question to ask. Clearly, environmental politics exceeds the limits of the state and should be explored in not-state spaces, such as corporate activities, social movements, ecosystems, and so on (see Bond and Price, Saunders, and Olcese, this volume). But just as environmental politics exceeds the limits of the state, environmental politics clearly operates within the space of states, too. In this respect, I believe that Robin Eckersley (one of the leading critics of anti-state analysis) is on target in her work *The Green State: Rethinking Democracy and Sovereignty* (2004) when she begins by declaring that her project is to pose 'a fundamental challenge to traditional notions of the nation, of national sovereignty, and the organization of democracy in terms of an enclosed territorial space and polity' (3). Environmental political thought should not simply take the state as is. It needs to interrogate the state and question the environmental implications of its key elements: government, sovereignty, territory, and people. This, I believe, is where the critical potential of the state lies for environmental politics, in the critical engagement of its four key elements. To that end, in this section I offer some ways of thinking critically about the state by looking at examples of how environmental political thinkers have analysed and can analyse each of its four key elements. Some of the following glimpses draw specifically on the work of Rousseau, Foucault, Deleuze, and Guattari. Others are connected to the work of these four thinkers only tangentially.

Government

While the actions of governments are clearly of interest to environmental political thinkers, government as a particular organization of political power may not seem to be an environmental issue. Yet, for a host of environmentalists, often referred to as eco-anarchists, the elimination of government (and hence the state) is essential to the success of green politics. According to Murray Bookchin, the state exists 'only when coercion is *institutionalized* into a professional, systematic, and organized form of social control . . . with the backing of a monopoly of violence' (Bookchin 1990: 66, emphasis in original). In other words, the state exists only when a particular structure known as government is present. But government (and hence the state) is not essential to political existence, Bookchin adds. As Deleuze and Guattari (1987) maintained, political communities can exist without being states; they can exist without possessing governments. In fact, Bookchin maintains that the only hope for human survival is to end the reign of the state. Peace among humans and with the non-human world is only possible, Bookchin (1990) writes, if we eliminate the violence and coercion institutionalized in our political communities, that is, if we eliminate government (and again, the state).

While recognizing the environmental dangers present in coercive, hierarchical, and unreflexive governmental structures, Robin Eckersley (2004) cautions environmental political thinkers from simply seeking to reject government and hence the state. The state can be green, Eckersley argues. But to green the state, government must be re-organized, which requires 'new democratic procedures, new decision rules, new forms of political representation and participation' (2004: 3). Eckersley's promotion of an ecological democracy takes direct aim at the eco-anarchist argument. For Eckersley, government as a specifically organized entity is not inherently anti-green. But as it is currently organized, it tends not to work to further green goals. 'Institutional innovations' requiring 'more inclusive forms of representation and new, ecologically sensitive procedures and decisions rules' are necessary, she writes, 'if ecological justice is to be done' (Eckersley 2004: 137). The current organization of government in liberal democratic states is unsatisfying to many green political theorists, she argues. A turn to 'deliberative democracy . . . by which we *learn* of our dependence on others (and the environment) and the process by which we learn to recognize and respect differently situated others (including nonhuman others and future generations)' is imperative (2004: 115, emphasis in original).

Further opportunities for environmental political thought exist in looking at government as a process, as set out by Rousseau and Foucault. Again, since an entire chapter of this volume is devoted to governmentality, I do not feel it is necessary to examine the critical potential of government specifically. Instead, I attempt to do so somewhat indirectly in the following sections on territory and people, drawing on examples of how the process of government operates to create both territories and peoples.

Sovereignty

As noted in the previous discussion of the work of Deleuze and Guattari (1987), politics in general and environmental politics in particular exceeds the limits of sovereignty. The environmental problem of sovereignty seems to be best captured by the fact that many environmental issues exhibit no respect for claims of sovereignty as they slice across the pathetically porous borders of states. As Ken Conca has put it, '[e]nvironmental processes ignore borders and link places previously thought as separate, raising profound questions about the exclusive character of territorial rule' (2005: 184). In other words, environmental processes raise profound questions about sovereignty. If sovereignty means exclusive control over a particular territory and population, then many environmental processes have seemingly rendered sovereignty questionable, if not obsolete. If environmentally destructive policies by states in one part of the earth can impact the environments of other states, then what happens to claims of sovereignty? On the one hand, the sovereignty of a state is challenged when the actions taken in other states impact its environment. On the other hand, the sovereignty of a state is challenged when its sovereign right to engage in environmentally destructive action is challenged by other states due to the global effects of those actions. 'The transnational character of so many environmental problems', Conca adds, 'challenges the very distinction between what is domestic and what is international' (2005: 184). Because of this challenge, environmental political thinkers must look beyond the state to examine the potential role of international organizations and transnational non-governmental organizations. The critical potential of these non-state actors and organizations has been explored more fully in other chapters (see Bond, Cudworth, Hinton, Igoe and Price et al., this volume).

Territory

Territory is not simply the land over which sovereignty reigns. As Deleuze and Guattari put it, 'sovereignty only reigns over what it is capable of internalizing, of appropriating' (1987: 360). And the process of internalizing and appropriating lands, of transforming them into territories, takes us back to government. In her 1996 work *The Culture of Wilderness: Agriculture as Colonization in the American West,* Frieda Knobloch explores the governmental processes utilized in the settling of the American West. As the subtitle of her work suggests, the American West was settled (colonized) through the use of agriculture. Knobloch is quick to point out that agriculture is not simply about 'raising food crops'; agriculture is a governmental process intent not only on 'structuring social and political life' but on 'the transformation and improvement of nature' (Knobloch 1996: 2–3). In other words, agriculture, as a governmental process, is directly related to the transformation of lands into territories. It is no coincidence that the term *agriculture* was not invented until the start of the seventeenth century. Its emergence coincided with the emergence of the state. For states require not simply lands, but territories – lands that are organized in a specific way in order to meet the needs of the population. Mere lands (or what states often refer to as wilderness) are not sufficient for this task. Lands must be transformed into territories if the state is going to exist. The recognition of this fact by environmental political thinkers can open the door to yet another way to critically engage the state. It opens environmental analysis to what

James Scott calls the 'logic of the state', a logic that 'replaces the term 'nature' with the term 'natural resources', focusing on those aspects of nature that can be appropriated for human use' (Scott 1998: 13). This shift, Scott argues, is what is behind the transformation of forests into tree farms. It is what is behind the transformation of 'the wilderness' into the territory of a state (see Igoe, and Watts and Peluso, this volume).

In order for a state to exist, in order for claims of sovereignty to resonate, lands must not be simply lands. By recognizing that people have lived (and do live) on lands as lands and not as territories, environmental political thinkers can draw out the specificity of the term *territory*; they can draw out the profound environmental implications of the governmental processes of transforming lands into territories.

People

The transformation of lands into territories goes hand in hand with the process of developing a people. States require more than simply a segment of the human race to live within its geographic borders. States require humans capable of transforming lands into territories. The process of working the land in a way that territorializes it is part of what makes a people. 'States are in the business of *settling* territory', Knobloch informs us, 'in the sense of stilling it, stabilizing it, holding it under systems of sedentary occupation' (Knobloch 1996: 23). And in order for the state to settle territory, the state needs people disciplined for the task. Native Americans in the United States in the nineteenth century, if they were to become part of the American people, had to be 'agriculturalized'; they had to be 'actively and systematically compelled to change over to new methods' of living on the land, methods essential to the success of the State (Knobloch 1996: 57).

The process whereby humans become useful to the state, become a people, is a governmental process (see Grove, this volume). And the process is not simply about turning humans into agriculturalists. It is also about turning humans into consumers of the products of the state. As Knobloch notes, agriculture is all too often presented as something that was needed in order to meet the needs of the population. But, Knobloch adds, we all too often 'fail to ask the question of how such a need arose' (1996: 21). In basic terms, Knobloch asserts that a state cannot exist without the need for the products of the state. And the process of creating that need amongst the people is a governmental process. The consumption patterns and habits of human populations are not given. They are, in large part, the result of governmental processes. And they have profound environmental impacts (see Brooks and Bryant, this volume).

Conclusion

Because of the central role of the state, it is connected to virtually all of the other concepts addressed in this book. As noted previously, governmentality is a central element of my conception of the state (Lövbrand and Stripple, this volume). But clearly, concepts like citizenship (Hinton), justice (Bond), and security (Dalby) are intricately linked to the state, as are the 'ism' concepts discussed in this collection, such as eco-centrism (McShane), feminism (Cudworth), and localism (Litfin), and the movements that promote them (Price et al.) to the extent that they take the form of policies adopted or rejected by the state. And along these same lines, the concepts of biodiversity (Büscher), climate change (Okereke and Charlesworth), conservation (Igoe), consumption (Brooks and Bryant), sustainability (Whitehead), and so on are also linked to the state in terms of its policy decisions – decisions that are often shaped by dialogue between states, at the summit of international politics (Death). How each of these concepts develops, moreover, may determine the future of the state. Should citizenship, for instance, come to take on a broader, global, ecological meaning, what will become of the state? Or if a politics of ecosystems, movement, or becoming should develop, what would that do to the state's relationship to territory? Would it not, as Robin Eckersley remarks (quoting Gianfranco Poggi) 'strike at the state's relationship to a territory, to a geographically distinct part of the globe, which constitutes the unique physical base and referent of the state's institutional mission, its very body, the ground of its being' (Eckersley 2005: 178)? Would a truly environmental politics not mean, in other words, the end of the state?

Further reading

For a deeper look at the environmental implications of the process of government, see my *Beyond Sovereign Territory: The Space of Ecopolitics* (particularly chapter 3) (Kuehls 1996), as well as my 'The environment of sovereignty' in *A Political Space: Reading the Global Through Clayoquot Sound* (Kuehls 2003). Another text that parallels Knobloch's (1996) in many respects by focusing on the process of government in the colonization of the American West in the nineteenth century is Matthew Hannah's (2000) *Governmentality and the Mastery of Territory in Nineteenth-Century America.* R.B.J. Walker has examined the 'inside-outside' nexus of sovereignty and political thought in both *State Sovereignty, Global Civilization, and the Rearticulation of Political Space* (1988) and *Inside/Outside: International Relations as Political Theory* (1992). There has been a great deal of work that has explored the need for thinking of the entity of government beyond its current locus on the state, see for starters *The Global Predicament: Ecological Perspectives on World Order*, edited by David Orr and Marvin Soroos (1979), and compare it with *The Greening of Sovereignty in World Politics* edited by Karen Litfin (2003), or *The State and the Global Ecological Crisis*, edited by John Barry and Robin Eckersley (2005). A work that challenges much of the argument for extending the scope of government beyond the sovereign state is *Against Ecological Sovereignty* by Mick Smith (2011). Lastly, an examination of the World Commission on Environment and Development's *Our Common Future* (WCED 1987) with the issues explored in this chapter in mind might prove fruitful.

25 Summits

Carl Death

Introduction

Environmental summits are landmark moments in the evolution of global environmental governance. Over the past forty years, from Stockholm to Rio, Kyoto to Copenhagen, and Johannesburg back to Rio, they have highlighted the sheer scale of the environmental problems we confront and illuminated the relative successes and failures of political responses to these problems. They are a dominant mainstream technique of global environmental governance, but they also have a critical dimension. For better or worse they can act as 'change agents' (Schechter 2005: 8), shaping discourses, institutions, actors, and power relations. This chapter notes the prominence of summitry as a key technique of global environmental governance, highlights some of the most important thinkers and theoretical approaches to the study of summits, and discusses where critical perspectives on summitry might take us. Two avenues in particular are explored in this respect: the performative role of summits in 'sustaining the unsustainable' and the possibility of creating more open, non-hierarchical, egalitarian, and radically democratic summit spaces.

A brief history of environmental summits

The history of the last forty years of environmental politics can be (and frequently is) told through big international summits (Baker 2006: 54; Bernstein 2002; Brenton 1994: 13; Chasek 2001: 1; Dresner 2002; Kalhauge, Correll, and Sjöstedt 2005). In 1972 the UN Conference on the Human Environment (UNCHE) was held in Stockholm, Sweden, and was one of the first times environmental issues had been discussed internationally at the highest levels (Chasek 2001: 17). The outcomes of Stockholm included institutions such as the UN Environment Programme (UNEP), as well as a discursive framing of environmental debates that reflected a division between the desire of developed countries to raise environmental standards and protect 'nature' and developing countries' insistence that economic development and the alleviation of poverty were fundamental goals that could not be compromised for environmental reasons (see Whitehead, this volume).

Twenty years later the international community met again for a major summit. In 1992 the UN Conference on Environment and Development (UNCED) was held in Rio de Janeiro, Brazil, and was attended by 108 heads-of-state and heads-of-government, representatives of 172 governments, and a further 17,000 people who attended the parallel non-governmental organisation (NGO) forum (Dresner 2002: 41–5; Lanchberry 1996). Rio is remembered for establishing the global political significance of environmental issues and for being characterised by an optimism and sense of energy that was in part thanks to the size of the conference and the personalities driving it, and in part to the broader historical context in which it was located: the end of the Cold War, the emergence of a new world order, the apparent triumph of liberal democracy, and a much-trumpeted new era of global governance and multilateralism (Bernstein 2002). UNCED produced a lengthy blueprint for sustainable development known as *Agenda 21* and the Rio Declaration on Environment and Development (containing 27 principles that continue to inform international negotiations on environmental treaties) and was the stage for the launch of two legally binding conventions on biodiversity and climate change, a declaration on forests, and institutional mechanisms such as the Global Environmental Facility (GEF) and the Commission for Sustainable Development (CSD).

In the post-Rio era of multilateralism and global governance, summits and conferences proliferated (Fomerand 1996; Schechter 2005). Between 1992 and 2000 there were nine major UN summits and review conferences linked to the sustainable development agenda, including a review of progress since Rio in 1997, known as Earth Summit II, which was held in New York (Haas 2002: 83). The next really big international summit, however, was the UN World Summit on Sustainable Development (WSSD) held Johannesburg, South Africa, in 2002. Whilst it managed to attract plenty of high-level participants – more than 100 heads-of-state and representatives of more than 190 governments – and produced a voluminous 170-paragraph Plan of Implementation and a 37-point Johannesburg Declaration, the summit became embroiled in debates over implementation mechanisms and clashes between trade and environmental law, and it did not produce any new international agreements of substance (Baker 2006: 64–9; Death 2010; Dresner 2002: 59; Kalhauge et al. 2005; Middleton and O'Keefe 2003; Wapner 2003). It did, however, result in the announcement of 351 voluntary public–private partnerships for achieving sustainable development, and it further strengthened the precedent set in Rio in 1992 for the inclusion of non-state actors (known as UN Major Groups) in the official summit process (Bigg 2004; see also Baker and Hinton, this volume).

Despite the successes of Johannesburg – notably the South African hosts' delight at holding a smooth and trouble-free conference, especially considering they had been a pariah state when Rio had been held in 1992 (Death 2010: 110–15) – it was followed by a period of 'summit fatigue' and an ebbing of enthusiasm for major environmental summits (Death 2011: 12). Attention also began to shift away from sustainable development and towards climate change negotiations (see Okereke and Charlesworth, this volume). Notwithstanding the exception of COP17 in Copenhagen in 2009 where 120 heads-of-government met in the same building (Christoff 2010: 637), the Conferences of the Parties (COPs) to the UN Framework Convention on Climate Change (UNFCCC) and the Kyoto Protocol have usually occurred below the heads-of-government level. However, in 2012 the international community once more reconvened in Rio de Janeiro for the Rio+20 UN Conference on Sustainable Development (UNCSD), which sought to agree on new ways forward for the project of sustainable development. Negotiations over the text – entitled *The Future We Want* – focused on two themes: the green economy and the institutional architecture for sustainable development. Stalled negotiations in the preceding months meant that the Brazilian hosts eventually produced a new, watered-down text for the lead diplomats to approve, and little visible progress was made in key areas: making the UNEP 'fit-for-purpose', launching the Sustainable Development Goals (which some see as replacements for the Millennium Development Goals after 2015), or turning the 'green economy' rhetoric into concrete proposals, initiatives, and funds. Although 79 heads-of-state or heads-of-government attended, there was little global media enthusiasm or interest in the three-day event, and prominent international leaders such as Barack Obama (USA), Angela Merkel (Germany), and David Cameron (UK) did not attend. Mark Halle from the International Institute for Sustainable Development called for 'a moratorium on all global multilateral negotiations' and proposed focussing instead on addressing 'the thousands of unfulfilled promises and commitments we have made' (Halle 2012). Once again, interested observers found themselves asking what was the value or the utility of big multilateral summits (Reyes 2012).

Core ideas

The usual answer to this question about the value of high-level environmental summits highlights two key dimensions: universal multilateralism and participation at the highest political level. The UN-organised summits that have dominated the landscape of environmental politics have been multilateral and universal, in that all UN member states are invited to attend, speak, and negotiate (Chasek 2001; Eckersley 2012; Fomerand 1996; Schechter 2005). Moreover, many accredited non-state actors are also invited to attend and participate in some form, and summits have been a key forum in which NGO and social movement participation in world politics has been accelerated (Alger 2002; Baker 2006: 74; see also Price, Saunders, and Olcese, this volume). In this sense UN environmental summits are quite different from other international summits (such as the G8 or G20 meetings), which invite a limited group of key states and tend to exclude non-state actors (Putnam and Bayne 1987; Reynolds 2007). When addressing global environmental challenges, it is often argued that only inclusive multilateralism can muster sufficient international legitimacy to produce fair and equitable outcomes (Eckersley 2012).

The second core idea behind summits is that of 'diplomacy at the highest possible level' (Dunn 1996: 17). This is what technically distinguishes a summit from a conference or meeting, although in practice the terms can become blurred. A summit, quite literally, takes place at the peak or pinnacle of sovereign politics (see Kuehls, this volume). Participants frequently reflect that the urgency and 'political imperative' of a summit can break-through a diplomatic impasse (Lanchberry 1996: 226–33): one activist reflected that 'the only way to get anybody to do anything is through a high-level meeting like that, that's what they're motivated by' (in Death 2010: 91). The final stage of negotiations involves heads-of-government speaking to each other face-to-face and trying to resolve the crucial outstanding issues. In some cases, meetings that are technically conferences become summits when heads-of-state attend and take over the process. This happened at the 2009 COP17 Copenhagen Climate Conference, when the final Copenhagen Accord was announced after closed-door negotiations in the final hours between the Presidents of the United States, China, India, Brazil, and South Africa (Christoff 2010). Such last minute interventions constitute a familiar routine of summit drama (Death 2011: 9) and work to reinforce the perception that politics is ultimately about individual personalities and 'great men'. This is conveyed by the mountaineering metaphor: 'skilled and self-assured men' have 'climbed high and dangerously in the belief that at the summit they can change the world' (Reynolds 2007: 10).

The belief that it is only at the highest-level and with the inclusion of all legitimate political participants that urgent issues can be resolved in the final instance is one that has driven mainstream global environmental governance (Pianta 2001: 169). Indeed, the prevailing view is that, inadequate as these negotiations often are, they are the biggest and most important game in town (Chasek 2001: 8). And what would be the alternative? The prominence of Stockholm, Rio, and Johannesburg in histories of environmental politics is a reflection of this. Such perspectives on international politics are often referred to as liberal institutionalist perspectives: the view that international institutions (such as summits, as well as organisations like the UN or legal instruments like the UNFCCC) that work (or are supposed to work) according to liberal principles of multilateralism, democracy, fairness, free participation, openness, and transparency are the best ways to solve international problems (Bernstein 2002; Chasek 2001; Young 1994). Encapsulating this perspective, Keohane, Haas, and Levy argue that the Rio Earth Summit in 1992 'constituted the world's most comprehensive organised response to international environmental degradation' (1993: 3).

Many advocates of summitry go a step further, however, and suggest that even if summits are not always the most effective ways to solve problems, they have other inherent values. By including all states and also non-state participants together into a shared space of democratic deliberation and a mixing of culture and values, it is suggested that such meetings have a role to play in promoting cosmopolitan cultures of respect for difference, toleration, democracy, deliberation, and peace (Pianta 2001: 189; Schechter 2005: 9; Wapner 2003; see also Hinton, this volume). They could even be seen as a part of a civilising process, where states learn to conduct their affairs peaceably and to respect non-state participants such as indigenous peoples and civil society groups. For Jacques Fomerand, 'UN global conferences mirror the pluralism of the world as well as its increasing interdependence and globalisation. They reflect and perhaps amplify the ongoing changes of a revolutionary world seeking to be more equitable and democratic at one and the same time' (Fomerand 1996: 373). Such perspectives are often referred to as liberal cosmopolitan perspectives.

There is, of course, a tension between these two core ideas. On the one hand we have the principle of the widest possible participation, on the other the principle of participation at the highest political level. This tension is frequently reflected at summits themselves: as negotiations progress to the final and most sensitive stages, non-state actors and less powerful states find themselves increasingly excluded from discussions as the most powerful participants meet in ever-smaller groups to hammer out remaining differences (Chasek 2001: 198; Death 2010: 98–103). It is therefore widely accepted that – albeit in a rather narrow and conventional sense – summits are fundamentally political (Fomerand 1996: 371; Putnam and Bayne 1987: 18). They are about power, authority, interests, and compromises. According to a realist perspective on international relations, summits are seen as battlegrounds for hard-headed political contests (Brenton 1994; Chasek 2001: 14–15). As such one might predict that outcomes will usually reflect the interests and agendas of the most powerful negotiators, rather than any common interest or global good.

Key thinkers

These various different perspectives on the role and value of summits can be examined in more detail through the work of key authors and thinkers in this field. A key author from the liberal institutionalist perspective is Peter Haas, and this perspective has given rise to a wide range of research agendas designed to help explain or design better forms of summitry and environmental negotiation. In contrast, more critical Marxist perspectives have argued that institutions such as UN summits often tend to perpetuate inequitable power relations, favouring the rich and powerful over the poor and facilitating further environmental destruction. Finally, this section will explore a more poststructuralist critique of the theatrical and performative dimensions of power relations represented by summits, drawing upon the work of Costas Constantinou.

Peter Haas identifies a number of benefits or roles of conferences and summits that draw upon both liberal institutionalist and liberal cosmopolitan perspectives. These include agenda setting, popularising issues and raising consciousness, generating new information and identifying new challenges, providing early warning of new threats, galvanising administrative reform, adopting new norms and setting global standards, and promoting the involvement of new actors (Haas 2002: 83–6). In these ways, he argues, conferences can 'provide indirect effects that may be beneficial for inducing states to take more progressive steps towards governance and sustainable development', over and above their role in negotiating new legal regimes and formal institutions (2002: 73). Although they 'seldom have direct causal influences on members states' behaviour . . . their outcomes are part and parcel of this broader process of multilateral governance and may contribute towards stronger and more effective environmental governance by states' (2002: 74).

The approach of Haas and others to environmental summits and institutions has contributed to a very specific and clear research agenda. Illustrating this, Keohane, Haas, and Levy assert that 'the international community's ability to protect the quality of the planet for future generations depends upon international cooperation. Successful cooperation, in turn, requires effective international institutions to guide international behaviour along a path of sustainable development' (1993: 4). This means that research on what makes institutions effective 'could help the next generation of world leaders to design more effective international environmental institutions' (Keohane et al. 1993: 6; see also Baker, this volume).

Various authors have pursued this research agenda from a variety of perspectives: some emphasising the role of agency, others the importance of structure. Professional diplomats and foreign policy advisors have been concerned with mitigating the risk of heads-of-government taking unilateral discussions too quickly or being swayed by the force of personality of their opposite numbers when face-to-face (Benedick 1993; Berridge 2005: 175; Brenton 1994; Reynolds 2007: 16–17). Yet, such advisors are also aware that summits have the advantage of 'promoting friendly relations, clarifying intentions, information gathering, consular work (principally export promotion and interceding on behalf of detained nationals), and negotiation' (Berridge 2005: 180). Moreover, negotiators must also be aware of not only their opposites around the negotiating table, but also their domestic constituencies and lobbyists awaiting them when they return home (Putnam 1988; Putnam and Bayne 1987); and environmental summits also involve a large number of non-state actors who can influence proceedings (Alger 2002; Pianta 2001).

In terms of institutional structures, some work has concentrated on the phases and turning-points of the structure of negotiations and how these might relate to outcomes (Chasek 2001), whilst others have debated calls for a restructured UNEP or a new World Environmental Organisation (Ivanova 2012). There have been proposals for a Climate Change Council of 12 states to replace the more universal Conference of the Parties in the day-to-day work of negotiating climate change; an 'inclusive minilateralism', involving the most responsible, most capable, and most vulnerable (Eckersley 2012: 35). Motivating both these strands of research are the beliefs that better institutional designs, or clearer appreciations of the actors' strengths, weaknesses, and interests, will lead to more effective and desirable outcomes for people and the planet.

A similar concern with people and the planet is evident in the work of those influenced by more Marxist perspectives on environmental politics. However, key thinkers such as Matthew Paterson (2000) and Julian Saurin (1996) start from very different assumptions about the nature of international politics and come to very different conclusions about the role and function of environmental summits. Inspired by Marxist traditions of thought, which see the political economic relations established by capitalism as resulting in social and environmental alienation (see Bond, Cudworth, and Paterson, this volume), summits are interpreted either as irrelevant when they are unable to challenge prevailing structures of political and economic power, or as actively reinforcing the power of political and economic elites and exacerbating environmental and social inequalities. Thus, Saurin argues that 'a focus on inter-state relations is largely irrelevant to the explanation of global environmental degradation' (1996: 85), and Paterson argues that 'the politics of global environmental problems should be understood as phenomena internal to the logics of four main, interrelated, power structures of world politics: the state system; capitalism; knowledge; and patriarchy' (2000: 40). In a similar vein, Middleton and O'Keefe conclude that the outcomes of summits, such as discourses of sustainable development and documents such as *Agenda 21,* should be seen as 'polite meaningless words' that are often 'used to conceal a disagreeable reality' (2001: 31). More stridently, Chatterjee and Finger (1994) argued that the 1992 Rio Summit 'has boosted precisely the type of industrial development that is destructive for the environment, the planet, and its inhabitants . . . as a result of UNCED, the rich will get richer, the poor poorer, while more and more of the planet is destroyed in the process' (3). Middleton and O'Keefe concluded that the Johannesburg Summit of 2002 was a 'craven and flatulent' capitulation to the interests of transnational capital (2003: 107).

A common theme in some of these Marxist-inspired critiques is that summits are merely spectacles – distractions from the real problems or issues (Paterson 2000: 2). Middleton and O'Keefe suggest that at Johannesburg, 'as in all other summits, there is a degree of theatricality', and for the most part the NGOs in attendance are 'simply adding their bit-parts to the performance' (2003: 95). Similarly, Frank Furedi argued in the aftermath of the Copenhagen Climate Conference in 2009 that such meetings 'are essentially photo opportunities for politicians who want to be seen to be doing something', and given their 'routine of play-acting and posturing', they should be seen as merely 'a spectacle rather than as a venue for the conduct of global diplomacy' (Furedi 2009). Such critiques have certainly identified a crucial dimension of political summitry: their theatricality, symbolism, and stagecraft. However, closer attention to this theatricality and performance suggests that it is not simply a distraction from the main business of the negotiations, but is rather a key element of the politics of summitry (Death 2011).

For this it is useful to briefly examine the work of one more key thinker: Costas Constantinou. His work on diplomacy and summitry has emphasised its performative dimension: it is intersubjective and constitutive 'in the sense that the diplomatic process takes place between two constructed subjects whose very construction relies on the intercourse and mutual recognition of diplomacy' (Constantinou 1994: 23). This emphasis on performativity rejects the distinction between real politics and illusionary ritual – ritual, spectacle, and performance all have real political effects, and all real politics (and indeed all social interactions) involve a degree of performance, identity-construction, and 'play-acting' (Blühdorn 2007: 254; Butler 1990: 146). Summits have stages, scripts, casts, and audiences (Death 2011: 8). For Constantinou, 'the fictions and the dramas of diplomacy never end . . . they become the world of diplomacy, they are what there is' (1996: 103).

Summits are not, therefore, neutral spaces or technical institutions designed to facilitate cooperation between pre-existing parties. They are political in a much more fundamental sense as their existence constitutes – brings to life, makes real – the identity and subjectivity of the parties who participate in them. Without the opportunity to take part in international dialogue at the highest level, part of the fundamental *raison d'etre* of a state representative or diplomat would disappear (Watson 1984: 14–15). Given this, the metaphors that surround summits – the 'peaks' of global politics, referring to diplomats as the 'sherpas' who assist heads-of-government in reaching the pinnacle, lofty vantage points above mundane day-to-day level affairs – are particularly significant. This discourse 'fosters conventional ways of ordering the world, celebrates hierarchy and works to shape the global imaginary by recollecting popular stories or images of mountaineering, of high or noble objective, or control, of progress, of fortitude, and of human mastery' (Constantinou 1998: 24). Just as the sixteenth-century Swiss mountaineer and naturalist Conrad Gesner mused that 'the highest parts of the loftiest peaks seem to be above the laws that rule our world below, as if they belonged to another sphere' (in Macfarlane 2003: 201) – so, too, does our contemporary fascination with political summitry seem to assume (or at least hope) that higher political values and ideals will prevail here.

Critical potential

Such attention to the performativity of summitry leads us to ask what such summits do, and what they produce – rather than simply asking what they conceal. This section suggests two avenues of research into the effects of summits: their performative role in 'sustaining the unsustainable' and the possibility of creating more open, non-hierarchical, egalitarian, and radically democratic summit spaces.

Ingolfur Blühdorn and Ian Welsh (2007) argue that we have entered an era of 'post-ecologism' characterised by 'the politics of unsustainability', where the primary political challenge has become to devise ways to sustain forms of social life that we know are ecologically unsustainable. The central paradox here is marked by, 'on the one hand, a general acceptance that the achievement of sustainability requires radical change in the most basic principles of late-modern societies and, on the other hand, an equally general consensus about the non-negotiability of democratic consumer capitalism – irrespective of mounting evidence of its unsustainability' (Blühdorn and Welsh 2007: 198; see also Blühdorn 2011: 36). The prominence of environmental summits – at which all participants are united by their shared and loud commitment to sustainable development and 'saving the planet' – are an example of this (Death 2011). The failure of the Copenhagen Climate Conference in 2009 to substantially transform climate politics demonstrated the inertia of the established interstate political system and the difficulties faced by existing institutions in addressing ecological challenges (Blühdorn 2011: 35).

The role of theatre, drama, and symbolic politics is crucial in how this paradox is handled in contemporary society. For Blühdorn these are 'an integral part of the politics of simulation by means of which late-modern society manages to sustain – at least for the time being – what is known to be unsustainable' (2007: 253). Major international summits are a striking example of what he describes as 'show politics', which seek to demonstrate 'that the political class are still offering alternative visions, that electorates are still making a choice between these visions and that political institutions are still capable of then implementing their decisions' (Blühdorn 2007: 266). On the contrary, a whole range of recent problems – from the failure to achieve all of the Millennium Development Goals, to the complexity of the financial crisis and the apparent powerlessness of politicians and national governments in the face of endemic recessions, to runaway climate change – all point to the limitations of assuming that our elected leaders are in charge and can, in a few days of negotiations with other leaders at the summit of global politics, satisfactorily resolve these issues. The oft-cited failure of 'political will' is no longer a convincing explanation for why summits don't produce the solutions to global problems; rather the problem is the assumption that summits can function as the command-centre of political power. Contemporary power relations are far more dispersed and hybrid, and the powerlessness of politicians in the face of the finan-cial crisis – just as in dealing with climate change – should lead us to question the efficacy of the structures we have created (see Rudy and White, this volume). Archimedes famously claimed that with a place to stand and a lever long enough he could move the world; much of the history of environmental politics has assumed that summits provide a place to stand and politicians possess levers of sufficient length. Both of these assumptions now seem dubious at best.

Summits as spaces of radical democracy

As such, a more productive metaphor for thinking about the critical potential of summits might be that of a space, event, or forum, rather than a peak or pinnacle. Summits are not simply disembodied institutions for negotiations. They are broader events, encompassing a multitude of practices and interactions beyond the conference centre. Indeed, given their size and prominence, they are mega-events. In the academic literature the term *mega-event* refers to short-term, high-profile events associated with mass participation and global me-dia attention (Hiller 1998; Olds 1998; Roche 2000). Typical mega-events are world fairs (expos), the Olympics and other major sporting tournaments, and cultural events. UN envi-ronmental summits in Rio and Johannesburg, and the Copenhagen Climate Conference in 2009, have also had something of the flavour of a mega-event: mass participation of non-state actors in parallel civil society events, sideshows, talks, marches, protests, exhibitions, evening sessions, theatre, and music (O'Neill 2004; Pianta 2001; St John 2008). Some of the functions of these aspects can be captured in Haas's terms as popularising issues, raising consciousness, and promoting the involvement of new actors (Haas 2002: 83–6), but there is more going on here. Rather than simply being an adjunct to the negotiations, such aspects can be reconceived as the central purpose of environmental summits. Such spaces frequently become stages for the performance of an alternative sort of politics.

The parallel NGO forums at major UN summits provide one example of this sort of space and politics: involving a plurality of interests and a diversity of identities, non-representa-tional and non-decisional forms of politics, alternative practices, and radical ideas. Many other examples also exist elsewhere. In 2010 the Bolivian Government supported a Peoples' Climate Summit in Cochabamba in opposition to many of the outcomes from the COP17 Copenhagen Climate Conference (Reyes 2012). In late 2011 and 2012 the Occupy move-ments sought to create spaces for alternative forms of radical politics in city centres, parks, universities, schools, and fields (openDemocracy 2012; Reyes 2012).

Since 2001 the World Social Forum has also experimented with a variety of forms, styles, and locations, consciously invoking, parodying, and then rejecting the example of UN summits (Grzybowski 2006; Patomäki and Teivainen 2004). It has sought to create 'a pedagogical and political space that enables learning, networking and political organising' (Fisher and Ponniah 2003: 6). Held for the first three years in Porto Alegre, Brazil, it has subsequently been held in Mumbai, Nairobi, Belém, and Dakar. It has experimented with holding a 'polycentric' forum in Caracas, Bamako, and Karachi in 2006, and decentralised 'global' forums occurred simultaneously worldwide in 2008 and 2010. Whilst the World

Social Forum has also had its problems and debates – over the inclusion/exclusion of militant groups, the dominance of 'big men' and leftist politicians, and the perceived limits of
non-decisional forms of politics (Grzybowski 2006; Patomäki and Teivainen 2004) – it has
demonstrated its potential to create spaces where such questions can at least be discussed and
where alternative voices to UN diplomats and heads-of-state can be heard.

Such spaces can be incredibly valuable to social movements, activists, and protestors
'seeking visible, innovative forms of action', who have been able to hijack mega-events
to stage their own 'festivals of resistance' (Della Porta, et al. 2006: 120; see also O'Neill
2004; St John 2008; Price, Saunders, and Olcese this volume). The 'counter-summit' is able
to 'exploit the window of visibility offered by summits' (Della Porta et al. 2006: 147). But
to what ends, and what is at stake here? For some it is nothing less than the reinvention of
democracy. Fisher and Ponniah articulate this as the 'reinvention of society such that the
mode of economic production, the structures of political governance, the dissemination of
scientific innovation, the organization of the media, social relations and the relationships
between society and nature, are subjected to a radical, participatory and living democratic
process' (2003: 13). A key figure within the World Social Form describes it as 'a primary site
for building democratic planetary citizenship' (Grzybowski 2006: 9).

Tom Bigg from the International Institute for Environment and Development reflected on
similar themes in the aftermath of the 2002 Johannesburg WSSD: 'The activities of NGOs
at the Rio Summit in 1992 had focussed predominantly on the official negotiations. Whilst
this was still true of many in the WSSD process, the locus seems to have shifted significantly
towards a more decentralised understanding of where change comes from' (2004: 5). For
many observers these spaces of radical democracy, and the vibrant social movements that
inhabit them, are the best chance of moving past the apparent stalemate of inter-governmen-
tal summit negotiations. Ingolfur Blühdorn is a little more cautious, observing that in the
main, even these spaces of civil society activism have become pacified and incorporated, and
as such, they 'no longer represent any genuine challenge to the established politics of economic growth and material distribution' (2011: 37; see also Wapner 2003: 6). Yet, perhaps
it is only through the proliferation and multiplication of such spaces – whether at the peaks
of international politics or in everyday cities, towns, and villages – that the broader cultural
change required for a transition to sustainability can be achieved.

Conclusion

International summits and diplomacy have structured the politics of climate change (see
Okereke and Charlesworth, this volume), biodiversity (Büscher, this volume), conservation
(Igoe, this volume), and sustainability (Whitehead, this volume). They are a key technique
of environmental governance (Baker, this volume). Yet they frequently fall short of what is
expected, hoped for, and required. Pamela Chasek's (2001) book on environmental negotiations opens with a quote from a diplomat: 'Getting action in the United Nations', he said, 'is
like the mating of elephants. It takes place at a very high level, with an enormous amount
of huffing and puffing, raises a tremendous amount of dust and nothing happens for at least
23 months' (1).

Given this, why is summitry still such a prominent technique of global environmental governance? For Berridge, writing about political summits more generally, a summit
is 'valued chiefly for its enormous symbolic or propaganda potential' (2005: 179). This is
the reason why, despite their frequent alleged failures, summits continue to dominate the

landscape of environmental politics. Summits have a huge attraction for political elites – the mountaineering metaphor implies 'a dramatic act of will, opening up spectacular new vistas. A moment when a leader risks all before the gaze of the multitudes. A chance to make or break his reputation' (Reynolds 2007: 5). Critical perspectives on summitry must draw attention to their uses by political elites – as well as by other movements and NGOs – in ways that do not challenge but rather reinforce existing inequitable structures and power relations, be they gendered, class-based, racial, or ecological (see Bond, Cudworth, and McShane this volume). The task is also to think about how to create new, multiple spaces for different sorts of politics that can be more democratic and more ecologically sustainable.

Further reading

Interesting accounts of diplomatic life and perspectives can be found in Bo Kjellén (2008) *A New Diplomacy for Sustainable Development: The Challenge of Global Change*, Abingdon: Routledge; and relevant special issues of journals include *Environmental Politics* 2 (4) 1993 on the 1992 Rio conference, and *International Affairs* 88 (3) 2012 on Rio+20. The *Journal of Environment and Development* devoted two special issues to the themes of 'From Rio 1992 to Rio 2012 and Beyond' and 'Policy Instruments for Sustainable Development at Rio +20' in 2012, see issues 21(1) and 21(2). Up-to-date analysis of conference diplomacy can be found at the excellent *Earth Negotiations Bulletin* (see link under Useful Websites). Books by G.R. Berridge (2005) and David Dunn (1996) are the best introductions to diplomacy and summitry in general, whereas Pamela Chasek (2001) and Tony Brenton (1994) contain useful discussions of environmental diplomacy. More critical treatments of summitry in general can be found in the work of Costas Constantinou (1994, 1996, 1998), and environmental summits in Chatterjee and Finger (1994) and Middleton and O'Keefe (2003). An interesting and accessible discussion of civil society activism and protest at a recent climate conference is provided by David Hallowes, Trusha Reddy, and Oscar Reyes (2012).

Useful websites

Earth System Governance Project: http://www.earthsystemgovernance.org/
International Institute on Environment and Development: http://www.iied.org/
International Institute for Sustainable Development (including the Earth Negotiations Bulletin): http://www.iisd.org/
Johannesburg World Summit: http://www.un.org/jsummit/
Rio + 20: http://www.earthsummit2012.org/
Third World Network: http://www.twnside.org.sg/

26 Sustainability

Mark Whitehead

Introduction

Since the 1980s environmental politics, in its various forms, has been increasingly framed by the notion of sustainability. In 1987 the World Commission on Environment and Development (WCED) first established the modern codification of sustainability: commonly interpreted as a strategy for harmoniously combining the goals of socio-economic development and environmental conservation (WCED 1987). Since the WCED's intervention, sustainable development has become an organizing principle for global, supranational, national, regional and local environmental policies and development strategies. In many ways, however, it is wrong to conceive of sustainability as a late modern invention. Sustainability has been an enduring concern for societies throughout human history. At its heart, sustainability predominantly involves positioning human thought and planning in a reasonably long-term future orientation. This concern for the future operates at two levels. At one level, the politics of sustainability is about the struggle to avoid socio-ecological collapse. Diamond has recently defined collapse as '[a] drastic decrease in human population size and/or political/economic/social complexity over a considerable area, for an extended time' (2005: 3). In this eschatological context, sustainability is about avoiding the kinds of socio-ecological catastrophes that have afflicted ancient cultures such as the Mayan civilization or the people of Easter Island. At another level, however, sustainability is about a more focused concern with intergenerational equality and justice (see Barry 1997). On these terms, the politics of sustainability is a struggle to ensure that the needs and opportunities of future generations are not significantly undermined by the decisions and actions that we undertake now.

In order to appreciate the broader significance of theories of, and policies for, sustainability, it is important to distinguish it from environmental concerns more generally. The environmental movement, in its various shades and guises, has, of course, been concerned with the long-term welfare of the planet and its ecological sustainability for some time (see Igoe and McShane, this volume). What marks sustainability out from more green politics, however, is the consistent emphasis that it places on the connections that exist between human welfare and environmental justice (see Bond, Cudworth and Dalby, this volume). In this context, the principles of sustainability have established that not only is human socio-economic development environmentally tolerable, but that without such forms of development (and the relief from poverty and technological advances that development processes are associated with), long-term environmental sustainability may be threatened (Gray and Moseley 2005). On these terms, the threat of societal collapse at one level, or significant forms of intergenerational injustice at another, are seen to be the outcome of interconnected socio-environmental feedback loops, which connect deforestation and population growth, soil erosion and water management problems, poverty and overgrazing, invasive species and systems of colonial exploitation (Diamond 2005: 6).

We will talk at greater length about the ways in which the notions of sustainability connect questions of socio-economic development and environmental protection later in the chapter. At this point, however, it is necessary to establish the grounds upon which sustainability constitutes an object of critical political investigation. In this chapter, the politics of sustainability is explored at three levels. First, there are questions of the political struggles that determine the different variants of so-called *weaker* or *stronger* forms of sustainability that get adopted by agencies, states, and communities. Second, are questions concerning the political values (egalitarian/libertarian, eco-centric/techno-centric) that are engrained within different approaches to sustainability. A third set of political concerns relates to the forms of political system that are compatible with more or less sustainable societies. On these terms, some argue that the freedoms associated with liberal democracy, for example, are not compatible with long-term environmental sustainability and may be replaced in the longer term with various forms of eco-authoritarianism (see Ophuls 2011). Throughout this chapter we will return to the political dynamics of sustainability as we explore the concept in greater depth. Particular attention is drawn to the more radical interpretations of sustainability and how these approaches could guide future research in the field.

Core ideas

Sustainable yields

My preferred definition of sustainability is provided by the Merriam Webster's Collegiate Dictionary, which states that the concept has two basic forms:

> a. relating to, or being a method of harvesting or using a resource so that the resource is not depleted or permanently damaged; b. of or relating to a lifestyle involving the use of sustainable methods.

This definition of sustainability is useful because it indicates the scientific origins of the concept. The association of sustainability with the renewable harvest of natural resources takes us back to early forms of sustainable yield forestry, which first emerged in the United States of America in the early decades of the twentieth century. A sustainable yield is a measurement of the amount of resource that can be taken from an environmental system, up to which that system can naturally replenish what has been extracted (see Kütting, this volume). While sustainable yield management emerged first in the field of forest, it can also be applied to water extraction from aquifers, fish catches, or the exploitation of soil nutrients within agricultural systems (see Whitehead 2013). The science of sustainable yield forest management (and by definition the very notion of sustainable yields in themselves) can be traced back to the work of Gifford Pinchot. It was Teddy Roosevelt who appointed Pinchot the first director of the U.S. Forest Service (see Dresner 2002: 20). In advocating the conservation of forests through sustainable utilization, Pinchot established the practical foundations for modern sustainability. From Pinchot's perspective it was more likely that increased areas of woodland would be formally protected if such protections were associated with sustainable economic activity. Pinchot's pioneering work at the U.S. Forestry Service marked a broader schism within the early environmental movement that went beyond the issues of forest man-agement. This broader division opened up between old style preservationists (such as John Muir) and the new wave of conservationists (who were lead by Pinchot) (Dresner 2002; for more on the politics of conservation see Igoe and Wapner, this volume).

The pollution of poverty and just sustainabilities

By suggesting that the environment could be wisely used in ways that enabled nature to be protected, while also allowing for human resource needs to be met, the early conservationist movement suggested that there were ways of simultaneously achieving social and environ-mental justice. The connections between questions of social and environmental justice would become a prominent issue of international debate and conjecture some 70 years later, when the United Nations convened its first international conference on global environmental issues. The United Nations Conference on the Human Environment (UNCHE) was held in Stock-holm in 1972 (see Death, this volume). The aim of the conference was to establish an interna-tional framework that would enable enhanced forms of protection for the global biosphere and hydrosphere. It was in Stockholm that another key concept of sustainability would be estab-lished. In a speech that was delivered at the conference, Indira Gandhi, the Prime Minister of India, reflected on the fact that in Less Economically Developed Countries (hereafter LEDCs) 'poverty is the biggest polluter'. In introducing the idea of the 'pollution of poverty', Gandhi articulated a clear division that emerged at Stockholm between the global north and global south. While the global north were, in the main, keen to develop more effective agreements on environmental protection, the most pressing concerns of the global south were poverty allevia-tion and economic development. LEDCs were concerned that new international agreements on environmental protection could severely undermine their sovereign control over natural resources and thus inhibit their developmental potential.

The idea of the pollution of poverty can actually be interpreted in two different ways (see Whitehead 2013). First, as we have already established, it can be seen as a statement of existential anxiety, which emphasizes the fact that the most pressing concerns of many in the LEDCs are not environmental, but about escaping life-threatening poverty. At a second level, however, the concept suggests a counter-intuitive relationship between poverty and environ-mental degradation. Within this reading there is an assertion that it is not just wealth and over consumption that generate environmental degradation, but that poverty can also be a major driver of environmental harm. The connection between poverty and environmental degrada-tion is predicated upon the observed connection between short-term thinking and ecological exploitation. To put things another way, when confronted with a lack of financial resources and/ or a failing harvest, people are much more likely to think about immediate needs and exploit the environments upon which they depend without regard for the long-term ecological conse-quences of their actions. This line of argument provides the basis for *Time-Preference-Theory,* which suggests it is far easier for people to adopt sustainable environmental management strategies if they are allowed to escape the grip of poverty and disadvantage. While Time-Preference-Theory provides an important basis upon which the policies of sustainability have been promoted, it is important to note that some research questions the connections that are made between poverty and environmental degradation (see Gray and Moseley 2005). This research has shown that it is often those in positions of the greatest social disadvantage who plan most carefully for the future, while the wealthy, who are able to rely on their residual assets, are more inclined towards the pursuit of short-term need.

Rethinking development: from limits to growth to human development

Discussing the issue of poverty alleviation provides a convenient segue into the third and final key concept that undergirds sustainability thinking: development. Building upon the aforementioned ideas of sustainable yield management and the pollution of poverty, sustainability is wedded to the principle of socio-economic development for two main reasons. First, the science of sustainable yield management suggests that it should be possible for human societies to exploit natural resources as part of their own betterment, without undermining the ability of environmental systems to recover from their utilization. Second, the idea of development is the ethical imperative that derives from the high levels of persistent social poverty that are evident throughout the world and the associated recognition that these forms of poverty contribute to environmental destruction. While the pursuit of socio-economic development within policies for sustainability may seem now like a logical extension of evolving systems of environmental governance, at the time that it was first suggested it represented a radical break from green orthodoxy. In this context, it is important to realize that in its early iterations, particularly within the work of WCED, sustainability was a response to the impasse that had been generated by the Limits to Growth Report (Meadows, Meadows, Randers and Behrens III 1972). Based on computer-based scenario modeling carried out at the Massachusetts Institute of Technology (which predicted likely trajectories of population growth, industrial output, environmental pollution, and the availability of resources inter alia), the Limits to Growth Report suggested that there were absolute, ecological limits on the ability of human society to develop. An international impasse consequently emerged between those in pursuit of economic development and those concerned with ensuing environmental limits to economic growth (see Kütting, this volume).

Sustainability suggests that not only is development possible, but that it is an imperative if we are to have a secure socio-environmental future. To these ends, sustainability is, perhaps, best thought of as a fusion of environmentalism and international development. As an amalgam of green goals and international development strategy, it is, however, important to consider the assumed connections between environmental protection and development that sustainability implies. These connections are visually articulated in the form of the Environmental *Kutznets Curve* (see Figure 26.1). The Environmental Kuznets Curve charts

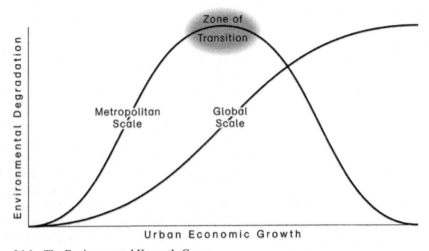

Figure 26.1   The Environmental Kuznet's Curve

an historical relationship that has been observed between different societies' levels of environmental degradation and their relative levels of socio-economic development. The curve suggests that, while early phases of development generally lead to heightened levels of environmental degradation, as development continues, environmental conditions improve. This graph has been derived from statistical observations that have been made of More-Economically Developed Countries. The gradual improvement in environmental conditions following continued socio-economic development is attributed to a series of interconnected factors (the dematerialization of the economy, the emergence of a green-conscious within new affluent classes, and the rise of improved systems of environmental monitoring and governance inter alia). Some have, however been critical of the Environmental Kuznets Curve as an indicative pathway for sustainability at a global level (see Marcotullio and McGranahan 2007; Whitehead 2012). Writers have been critical of the Curve because it fails to illustrate that the economies of the global north have become less environmentally degrading in part because they have been able to offshore their most polluting activities to low cost locations in the global south.

Recent debates around the concept of sustainable forms of development have not only questioned the connections that exist between socio-economic development and environmental conservation, but the very nature of development itself (Dresner 2002: 70–1; Sen 1987). At the centre of these discussions has been a concern that mainstream policies for sustainability tend to focus on a very narrow definition of development: one that concentrates on economic growth and the expansion of Gross Domestic Product (Bernstein 2000). Many argue, however, that the imperatives of economic growth will undermine the pursuit of sustainable levels of development while not, in and of itself, ensuring that the socio-economic needs of all are being met. It is in this context that the Indian Economist Amartya Sen proposed the idea of *human development* (see Dalby, and Methmann and Oels, this volume). Sen's work suggests that the pursuit of socio-economic development should not be judged in relation to absolute levels of economic growth – or related forms of average household income – but on the impacts that development was having on human welfare (Dresner 2002: 70). On these terms, *human development* is more about improving the capacities of individuals to live fulfilling lives and is measured in terms of education, health, self-determination and happiness. Sen's work was used to recalibrate UN measures of international development and sustainability in the *Human Development Index,* which was developed in the 1990s.

Key thinkers

Building on the key concepts that were introduced in the previous section, this section of the chapter explores emerging critiques of sustainability, drawing on the work of several key thinkers.

Unsteady states

Perhaps the most telling critique of sustainability targets the scientific principle upon which it is based: the sustainable yield. The idea of a sustainable yield has come under scrutiny from both biologists and ecologists. The biologist Daniel Botkin provides one of the most telling, popular critiques of sustainability thinking. In his influential 1990 book *Discordant Harmonies,* Botkin questions prevailing notions of steady-state ecology, which has had an enduring influence on environmental thought and policy. Botkin reflects that, '[C]hange now appears to be intrinsic and natural at many scales of time and space in the biosphere' (1990: 9). Of course, modern ecology's emerging sense of the complex and perpetually changing nature of environmental systems has significant implications for the practices of sustainable yield management. At one level, it suggests that the changes that the sustainable use of natural resources creates in an ecological system could be seen to be simply a healthy part of the ever-changing biosphere itself. At another level, however, non-steady-state ecology suggests that predicting, measuring, and thus observing levels of sustainable yield may be more difficult than was initially imagined. If ecosystems are perpetually going through processes of change and transformation, then it must be true that what counts as a sustainable yield in one year may change greatly in the following one (see Forsyth, and Rudy and White, this volume).

Beyond emerging critiques of sustainability within ecology, economists have also started to question the concept's reliance on a steady-state-assumption. One of the most vocal, and influential, voices of critique in this context has been the ecological economist Herman Daly. In a series of publications on steady-state-economics and environmental management, Daly suggests that the laws of physics undermine the ultimate goals of sustainable yield management (Daly 1996). Daly claims that the laws of physics (and in particular the nature of entropy) mean that economic growth and development cannot achieve the forms of stability suggested by sustainable yield management. Furthermore, Daly asserts that that continued dependence of modern economies on non-renewable resources, and the problems associated with the production of heightened levels of pollution, mean that the environment will place a limit on the ability of economic activity to grow and develop, even in the context of sustainable development practices (see Dresner 2002: 26). It is in this context that Daly proposes the idea of a *steady-state-economy* within which stable patterns of production and consumption (below sustainable thresholds) replace economic growth.

Sustainability and natural capital

A second set of critiques of sustainability has focused upon the economic assumptions of the paradigm. Arguably the most important intervention within this field of analysis has been made by the economic geography Eric Neumayer. According to Neumayer (2004), it is wrong to talk of sustainability as a singular policy strategy that has emerged from the World Commission on Environment and Development. While recognizing that various versions of sustainability actually exist that balance questions of social, economic and environmental needs in different ways (see Connelly 2007), Neumayer claims that there are actually two main categorical forms of sustainability: *weak sustainability* and *strong sustainability* (Neumayer 2004). *Weak sustainability* relates to those policies that are based upon a belief that human/technological capital can be used to replace depleted forms of natural capital. In Herman Daly's famous reflection of this form of sustainability, he suggests that it is akin to a policy of fishing, which suggests that declining fish catches caused by over fishing can be addressed by purchasing more fishing boats and improving fishing techniques (Daly 2005). Neumayer refers to this approach as a 'substitutability paradigm' and perceptively recognizes that, taken to its logical conclusion, it does not require sustainability practices to be adopted at all (as the sustainable yield is simply superseded by human technological ingenuity) (2004: 21).

Strong sustainability, on the other hand, is based upon the assertion that, in the long term at least, natural capital cannot be adequately substituted for human capital (Neumayer 2004 24).

Neumayer refers to this position as the 'non-substitutability paradigm'. Referring back to Herman Daly's (2005) fisheries example, a strong sustainability perspective would suggest that the ability to maintain a certain level of catch is not, in the long term, a product of the number of fishing boats that you have, but of the ability of the fish population to naturally replenish itself.

Acknowledging the key distinction between weak and strong forms of sustainability is important because it reveals that sustainability is as much about choosing a path of development, and the political struggles that surround that process, as it is a scientific discussion (see Kütting, this volume). The work of Steven Bernstein is particularly helpful when it comes to understanding the political framing of sustainability (Bernstein 2000, 2002). Steven Bernstein is a political scientist who has analysed the historical evolution of sustainability as an international norm complex. According to Bernstein, the form of sustainability that has emerged out of the WCED, and subsequently has been institutionalized within various UN programmes and agreements, is a weak version of sustainability. According to Bernstein, although strong forms of sustainability were discussed within the WCED, the Commission became increasingly subject to the influence of the Organization of Economic Cooperation and Development (OECD). The OECD were keen to promote growth-oriented forms of sustainability and worked hard to ensure that the principles of sustainability that were adopted by the UN were conducive to free-market principles and the promotion of an increasingly global economy. Bernstein has described the type of policy framework emerging from the WCED as a form of *liberal environmentalism* (Bernstein 2000). For Bernstein the notion of liberal environmentalism denotes an environmental policy regime that has been forged in the context of neoliberalism (see Paterson, and Lövbrand and Stripple, this volume). On these terms it is a form of environmental policy-making that assumes that economic growth, freedom and deregulation, at both global and local levels, provide the best opportunities to develop the types of commercial and technological innovations that will secure our collective futures. On these terms, and in accordance with Neumayer's definition of weak sustainability, liberal environmentalism assumes that natural capital can be effectively substituted by human ingenuity and technological development.

Anthropocentrism, scarcity and the post-political society

A third set of critical engagements with sustainability interrogate more directly its political implications and assumptions. One of the most telling political and philosophical critiques of modern forms of sustainability has emerged out of the work of the Norwegian philosopher Arne Naess. Naess (1994) claimed that despite appearing to represent an attempt to bring environmental considerations more directly in the political sphere, and the decision-making processes that inform it, sustainability represents a high degree of anthropocentrism, or human bias. On these terms, Naess argued that within policies for sustainability the environment is only able to enter political discussion in relation to its ability to support human economic development and the attainment of social justice. This represents a significant divergence from Arne Naess's principle of Deep Ecology: where nature is valued in isolation from its utility to humans and is allowed to enter the political sphere as an agent in its own right (see also Latour 1993, 2004a). While Naess's critique of sustainability could be applied to both its weak and strong iterations, it is clearly in its weaker manifestations that sustainability most marginalizes nature as a political consideration (see McShane, this volume).

If Arne Naess questions the nature of the political community that is defined within sustainability policy frameworks, William Ophuls's critique focuses more on the political assumptions that are associated with sustainability. William Ophuls is a political scientist and independent scholar who has written widely on the political implications of environmental change (Ophuls 1977, 1997, 2011). In his most recent volume, *Plato's Revenge* (2011), Ophuls considers the extent to which modern forms of liberal democracy are a unique feature of the period of relative ecological abundance through which we have been living over the last 200 years. Ophuls argues that liberal society, with its economic and political freedoms, is a product of a period characterized by a profusion of environmental resources (including coal, oil, gas and uranium). The relative abundance of these ultimately non-renewable resources has meant that, since the Industrial Revolution, the exploitation of these resources by one person, or corporation, has not impinged upon the freedoms of others to do the same. Crucially, however, Ophuls suggests that as access to precious resources declines, the use of resources by one party will infringe on the freedoms of another, thus exposing the precarious nature of our liberal traditions. It is in this context that Ophuls believes that scarcities will lead to a future that is increasingly characterized by forms of eco-authoritarianism, where more and more controls are placed on our economic freedoms (2011). This, of course, has critical implications for the political assumptions associated with sustainable development. Ophuls's analysis suggests that social innovations and technological revolutions that advocates of weaker forms of sustainability see emerging out of liberal societal forms, may be undermined by the gradual loss of those very liberal freedoms in a future of resource scarcity.

If Ophuls's work provides an insight into the likely impacts of weak patterns of sustainability on the political forms of future societies, the recent work of Erik Swyngedouw draws attention to its impacts on the political here and now. Swyngedouw is a Marxist geographer who has utilized the work of Chantal Mouffe and Slavoj Žižek (Mouffe 2005; Žižek 1999) on the post-political condition as a basis for analysing sustainability (Swyngedouw 2007b). Swyngedouw defines the post-political condition as '[a] political formation that actually forecloses the political, that prevents the politicization of particulars' (2007b: 23). On these terms, Swyngedouw argues that the hegemonic notions of sustainability are clear manifestations of an increasingly post-political society. As a master-concept, which is supported by science and underwritten by the UN and powerful international elites, sustainability now offers very little space for oppositional politics (see Price, Saunders and Olcese, this volume). The unquestionable status of sustainability as a paradigm for socio-environmental development would represent a democratic problem, even if the forms of sustainability that are currently being advocated were politically radical, and transformative, in their content and intent. But given that weak forms of sustainability, which are commensurable with an ethic of global capitalist expansionism, appear to be the accepted norm, Swyngedouw argues that sustainability makes it increasingly difficult for movements for social and environmental justice to occupy radical positions that enable them to question the impacts of neoliberalism (see also Bond, this volume).

Critical potential

In light of these varied critiques of sustainability, in this section I want to consider the more radical aspects of research that are framed around questions of sustainability. In using the term *radical sustainability*, I am referring to approaches to sustainability that do one of two things: (1) they explore the contradictions and limitations of the actually existing sustainabilities that surround us, and (2) they actively imagine and explore alternative visions of a sustainable society that challenge the social, economic and anthropocentric biases of our current political condition. To these ends, radical sustainabilities are unashamedly critical, abstract and change-oriented.

In recent work I have explored the potential for sustainability to redefine the nature of political subjectivity and citizenship (Bullen and Whitehead 2005; Whitehead 2007). At present, *citizenship,* broadly understood as the systems of rights and responsibilities in and through which human societies are ordered, has four key features: (1) it tends to define rights and responsibilities territorially on the basis of belonging to specific nation states, (2) it focuses on the rights and responsibilities of co-present citizens, (3) it defines humans as the political hubs around which rights are endowed and responsibilities expected, and (4) it defines citizenship as largely public acts, conducted in town-halls, welfare centres and voting booths (Bullen and Whitehead 2005; see also Hinton, this volume). My own work on emerging forms of education for global citizenship and sustainability in Wales has suggested that sustainability has the potential to radically redefine how citizenship is understood and enacted. In the context of sustainability's concerns with environmental justice, international development and the welfare of future generations, sustainability has the potential to re-orientate the traditional parameters of citizenship. In particular, it suggests a form of citizenship that stretches beyond narrow territorial and temporal systems of rights and responsibility and increasingly engages within the needs of the non-human world.

Arguably the most radical aspect of sustainability (weak or strong) is its insistence that we continually look at the links that exist between environmental justice, social welfare and economic development. These considerations have, of course, come into particularly sharp focus following the global financial crisis that took hold in 2008. While the global financial crisis has been seized on by some as an opportunity to reorient our social and environmental priorities in more sustainable directions (see New Economics Foundation 2008), formal political responses to the crises have thrown doubt on the commitment of political economic elites to questions of sustainability. In this context, the emphasis that has been placed within economic recovery plans on increasing economic output and restarting the consumer economy (through various mechanisms including tax breaks, state-sponsored construction projects and quantitative easing) has suggested that the real priority is not sustainability, but economic growth at whatever long-term costs. The axiomatic desire of economic elites to return a crisis ridden economy to the heady days of unfettered growth – growth that caused the crisis in the first place – has led some scholars of sustainability to look again at the connections between economic growth and prosperity (see Wapner, this volume). In his recent book, *Prosperity Without Growth: Economics for a Finite Planet* (2009), Tim Jackson (the Economics Commissioner of the erstwhile Sustainable Development Commission in the UK) questions whether economic growth can really be seen as a driver of increased prosperity. By trying to delink economic growth from the sustainability goals of socio-environmental justice, Jackson seeks to unpack the arbitrary link that has been forged between sustainability and the belief that its goals can only be met by a properly functioning global capitalist economy.

At one level Jackson (2009) argues that economic growth, and the emphasis that it ultimately puts on increasing economic output and consumption, does not contribute to all aspects of what we might call prosperity (including time spent with family, spiritual development and community-oriented work). At another level, Jackson suggests that economic development may actually be working against certain aspects of human prosperity (particular in relation to mental well-being and our ability to enjoy the natural world). Although Jackson's work clearly follows in the lineage of Sen, Daly, Bernstein and Swyngedouw, by questioning the very nature of prosperity, it brings an important reorientation to the sustainability debate.

Conclusion

In this chapter we have seen that sustainability represents a geopolitical compromise between the environmental and international development agendas. Critical analysis has, however, shown that while in principle sustainability reflects a desire to develop policy that simultaneously addresses pervading forms of social and environmental injustice, sustainability has, too often, been used as a basis for justifying the relative unreformed, expansionist ideology of the global market place and neoliberalism. It is only to be hoped that the political will and institutional capacity exists to transform our weak attachments to a sustainable future into a more radical programme of socio-economic and environmental change.

Further reading

For reviews of the origins and varied natures of sustainability see Mark Whitehead (2013) 'Sustainability' in Cloke et al. (eds) *Introducing Human Geographies*, London: Arnold, and (2007) *Spaces of Sustainability: Geographical Perspectives on the Sustainable Society*, Abingdon: Routledge. For a more detailed account of the relationship between sustainability and neoliberal politics see Bernstein (2002) *The Compromise of Liberal Environmentalism*, New York: Columbia University Press. Finally, for a fascinating discussion of the impacts of mainstream sustainability policies on environmental politics see Swyngedouw (2007b) 'Impossible "sustainability" and the postpolitical condition' in Krueger and Gibbs (eds) *The Sustainable Development Paradox: Urban Political Economy in the United States and Europe*, London: Guildford Press.

Useful websites

International Institute for Environment and Development: http://www.iied.org/
International Institute for Sustainable Development: http://www.iisd.org/
The United Nations Environment Programme: http://www.unep.org/
The Guardian newspaper's sustainable development site: http://www.guardian.co.uk/environment/
   sustainable-development

27 Technology

Timothy W. Luke

Introduction

This chapter outlines a cross-section of core ideas, key thinkers, and critical dimensions for understanding technology as an environmental concern. Whether one resorts, on the one hand, to classical notions of *technē,* which signifies a style and substance of human reasoning, learning, and acting tied to 'know-how', or retains, on the other hand, more modern ideas about *Zweckrationaltät,* which is anchored in purposive rationality dedicated to the demanding ends/means calculi of efficient action, it is clear that 'technology' must be a central concern for environmental politics (Barry 1998; Feenberg 1999). For many environmental movements, too much of nature is beyond the safe zones of care, community, and continuity needed to ensure the long-run sustainability of the Earth. Instead the natural life-world seems gripped unforgivably in the cool and cruel objectivity of instrumentally rational systems – or technology – focused on the project of sustaining its own machinic development rather than the planet itself. As the once wholly 'natural' sites, structures, and systems of everyday life are mentally and materially locked down more and more by the most 'artificial' workings of 'technology' in the operational imperatives of big cybernetic and mechanistic systems with their own highly complex path-dependent momenta (T. Hughes 2004), what is understood as 'nature' and 'society' both suffer.

The concept of technology in critical environmental politics, then, is as ambivalent as it is important. In some ways, many environmental movements have identified 'technology' as the nemesis of 'ecology'. Deep ecologists, ecofeminists, and wilderness defenders often argue the abolition or abridgement of modern technology as such would allow humanity to once again live in harmony with nature (Merchant 1980; Naess 1989; Zerzan 1994; see also Cudworth, Igoe, and McShane, this volume). On the other hand, cradle-to-cradle designers, ecosocialists, and social ecologists assert technology per se does not threaten nature, but how technology is used, what scale it adopts, or who controls its workings is the cause behind ecological environmental problems (Bookchin 1971; Gorz 1980; Lovins 1977; see also Rudy and White, and Wapner, this volume).

To gain 'know-how' about technology, as Foucault (2003) suggests, is also to acquire 'command, control, and communicate-how', because whatever powers and knowledges are implied by 'know-how' cannot easily, if ever, be divided from 'do-how'. Additionally, to speak of purposeful rational calculation is to assume there is a 'who' or 'what' whose purposes are well-served, along with a 'whom' whose ends are not being served or whose means will be abused. Many environmental thinkers recognize technical 'do-how' is in the hands of those who care little about people or nature; they seek only power and profit. Technology, therefore, is also essentially 'governmentality' (see Lövbrand and Stripple, this volume). Each and every technology, as Foucault (1991b) argues, channels a 'conduct of conduct' for its use and/or misuse, which becomes concretized in the tools, technics, and techniques of economies and societies (Ellul 1964; T. Hughes 2004; Luke 1989; Mumford 1932; Noble 1977; Virilio 1995). How, why, and what conduct is enabled, or disabled, for conduction where and when by technology, as it is socially constructed, are aspects of truly big political questions for ecologies and economies that few thinkers ever address (Hughes, Bijker, and Pinch 1987). Identifying technology's role in shaping the environment becomes a critical part of attempting to address these mental and material realities in the contemporary world economy (Beck 2000).

Core ideas

Technology is material stuff and mental systems of know-how that individuals and groups use to control both humanity and nature. Each technical act and artifact carries currents of ontic stability (setting the conditions of what is regarded as real), epistemic certainty (defining what can be known and how to know it), and axiological normality (fixing the common terms of intrinsic and extrinsic value) about human beings in nature. Indeed, through technology, environmentalists can investigate what occurs to environments behind, beneath, and between politics and economics in existing states and markets (Adas 1989; McKibben 2010). Hence, 'technocritique' must coevolve as part of 'ecocritique' (Luke 1997) because technology mediates the central workings of power over people and things for environments in the grip of bureaucracies, markets, and systems in today's world order (see Paterson, and Brooks and Bryant, this volume). Quite clearly, many environmental thinkers (Bookchin 1980; Gorz 1980; Merchant 1980; Sale 1991) have developed antipathies towards technologies as ecology-degrading forces to counteract the deeply embedded sense of powerlessness and inequality in economies and societies.

Whether they are appraised as surroundings or infrastructures, most people typically experience technology, like capital and corporations, as opaque dominating formations. Technics, in turn, operate under, across, over, and through collective groups of humans in ways yet to be fully understood (Virilio 1995). As he scrutinized how 'mechanization takes command' with capitalism, Giedion (1948) argued that modern technological systems and structures always have a very real, but quite determinant 'anonymous history'. Thinking through how such social forces function in technics, machinics, and logistics, it is clear they constitute most of humanity's natural and artificial space in equally anonymous economies, geographies, or sociologies (De Landa 1991). The recognition that 'know-how' also constitutes 'do-how' begins to crack open how environmentalists see the mediating systems of disorder and order in the Earth's ecologies. Technology, as techniques, technics, and tools, 'is not simply a means of reading or interpreting space: rather it is a means of living in that space, understanding, and producing it' (Lefebvre 1991: 47–8). That is, technology becomes an environmental force itself, as the constitutive space of social practices (Ong 1999) in its biopolitical articulations (Foucault 1980a; Barry 2001; Esposito 2008), in states and markets. Every human commodity contains and conceals technology, while each human technology reciprocally conceals and contains commodification (Luke 1999a; see also Paterson, this volume).

To deepen this biopolitical sense of 'technology' in environmental politics (see Grove, this volume), one must take Jameson's vision of 'the postmodern condition' as a decisive insight. Jameson (1992) observes today's basic natural and social reality is simple: it is all that is left 'when the modernization process is complete and nature is gone for good. It is allegedly a more fully human world than the modern era, but it also is one in which "culture" has become a veritable "second nature"' (ix). This condition of mixed hybrid coexistence of people, animals, plants, and technologies as second-nature environments (see Rudy and White, this volume) with the ecologies of first nature scrambles together the workings of human subjects and non-human objects in complex systems of systems (Luke 1994; see also Hobden, this volume).

Instead of being held forth as supreme in its own right, nature's infiltrations by technology, in which dense formations of capital and labour busily are building bigger markets for commodities, leaves new environments that are, in fact, a second nature, a processed world, or a machine of machines meant to make greater commodification (Lyotard 1984). In these spatial practices, those who own and control the material and mental means of enforcing order via technologies, as the 'do-how' embedded in 'know-how' always entails, concretize new degradations and inequalities on a global scale in many landscapes, places, and spaces – urban, rural, suburban, and exurban – that are neither metropolitan nor peripheral. As spatial practice, technification, then, morphs into an environmentalizing phenomenon. Both global and local, industrial and agricultural, urban and rural, built and unbuilt, the operations of technology force together humanity and nonhumanity in regimes of big, if brittle and bloated, embedded practices (Latour 1993; Law 1991; Virilio 2000).

A very suggestive characterization of such forces set-in-motion-and-in-place as 'technology' is often labeled obliquely as 'the grid', 'the apparatus', 'the system', 'the structure', or 'the network'. Its mechanism of ends–means action generates, distributes, and applies this or that clustered stream of energy, information, and matter in purposive applications. On the one hand, they can be celebrated as 'leading technologies' in delivering on the 'brand promise' of modernity; but, on the other hand, they also unfold as ecology despoiling degradations of nature (Luke 1989).

As technification unfolds with nation-building, technologies of building, power generation, or transport, for example, become parts of the spatial routines for imagined community (Anderson 1991). Basically, modernity itself is intertwined locally, regionally, and transnationally with technologies for environment-fabrication. The growth of technological systems – to the extent that they endanger human populations and natural ecologies in various territorial spaces in the unfolding of world capitalist markets – is what constitutes the artificial threats that concern many different types of environmentalists when the modernization process is complete and nature is gone for good.

Charles Perrow's *Normal Accidents: Living with High-Risk Technologies* (1984) spells out key insights into how innovative evolving technologies, such as electricity grids, jet aircraft, or space vehicles, imply intrinsically inescapable high-risk factors in their operation. Yet, he also concludes that this risk remains always already irreducible due to the inexorable dynamics in their very complexity. With technology, 'we create systems – organizations, and organizations of organizations – that increase risk for the operators, passengers, innocent bystanders, and for future generations' (Perrow 1984: 3).

Materialities in such risk-laden technics bear 'catastrophic potential' per se; but, still one finds 'every year there are more such systems' (Perrow 1984: 3). The catastrophic failures that he identifies as 'normal accidents' erupt because their material mechanisms and social systems carry innumerable conjunctures of repetitious risky contingency. Complexity is inescapable for these systems to operate.

'Normal accidents', therefore, happen. They expose and express the 'accidental normality' of modernity lying at the core of complex risky system-building (see Pellizzoni, this volume). New technological systems are constantly created, but each construct also is unavoidably an improvisational experiment (Beck 2009). Consequently, technological second nature's normality – for all of its apparent elegance, power, or order – is, ironically, both accidental and intentional. The normal accidents, such as the reactor mishaps at the Fukushima Daiichi (2011) and Chernobyl (1986) nuclear power plants, for example, register unintended costs in the unconscious acceptance of using nuclear fission for its intended benefits as an accidentally normalized way of generating electricity. Since technological catastrophes happen, societies only can, as Perrow (1984) argues, anticipate their occurrence, calculate costs, manage their risks, and contain environmental damage to the best of their systemic, albeit often equally improvisational abilities. Because catastrophic technics lie at the heart of modernity, critical environmental action should take into account this quasi-chaotic hybrid complexity. The destructive dynamics of technologies – as unsustainable air, earth, soil, and water polluting systems – are a perfect case in point of how ordinary and disastrous such accidental normality has become second nature, as Law (1991) and Latour (1993) maintain, in the coupled systems of nature/society.

While many environmental movements and critical environmentalist thinkers wish to maintain a strict division between nature and society, and thus environment and technology, it is plain that technology is essentially becoming an environment in itself (Luke 1997; Crutzen and Stoermer 2000). Moreover, the anthropogenic changes are already being felt in nature's confusions with technological by-products (Meadows, Meadows, Randers, and Behrens III 1972). Their effects will not dissipate; they instead continue to grow in scale and scope (Bourdieu 1998; Brown 1981; Falk 1999).

Bookchin's celebration of more ecological technologies rests upon finding less obtrusive, destructive, and abusive technics to perform essential tasks. Such 'ecotechnologies' also should be more empowering for individuals and communities by enhancing personal capabilities and individual self-reliance (Bookchin 1971). These technics should be human-scaled as well as made of 'flexible, versatile machinery whose productive applications would emphasize durability and quality, not built-in obsolescence, and insensate quantitative output of shoddy goods, and a rapid circulation of expendable commodities' (Bookchin 1980: 69). Here, Bookchin also puts his finger on the trouble with non-ecotechnologies whose corporate-scaled need for embedded waste, rapid replacement, and managerial control have led to the degradation of the environment (Smith 1984).

Seeing technology as environment, therefore, is an important development. For environmentalists and others, it is an outcome rooted in the ongoing operational imbrication of many human communities imagining, embedding, and engineering their lives together with technics (Hess 2009). When people aspire to occupy the same spaces, keep common times, run parallel lives, and experience comparable normalities in nature and society, complex technology cannot be avoided. Technology becomes more natural because it is like a force of nature, especially now in a world of rapid climate change (Barry 2012). Anderson (1991) suggests these syntopic and synchronic qualities in technics also evolve as part of the endless innovation of capitalist commodification with little regard to the planet's limits (also see Kütting, this volume). Continuous novelty, and normalization by material concretions of 'the endlessly new', however, 'arise historically only when substantial groups of people were in a position to think of themselves as living lives *parallel* to those of other substantial groups of people – if never meeting, yet certainly proceeding along the same trajectory. Between 1500 and 1800 an accumulation of technological innovations in the fields of shipbuilding, navigation, horology, and cartography, mediated through print capitalism, was making this type of imagining possible' (Anderson 1991: 188). Nature imagined as navigational mappings, ship transit times, or homogenized cartographical spaces exemplifies this environmental technification (Fuller 1969).

Key thinkers

When considering the role of technology in environmental politics, many key thinkers stand out as important figures, including Ulrich Beck, Michel Foucault, Thomas Hughes, John Law, Bruno Latour, Henri Lefebvre, and Paul Virilio. Living in societies of bureaucratically controlled consumption (Lefebvre 1984), which are organized on a transnational scale, discloses that consumption is a normative cluster of conduct that directly enables modes of bureaucratic control and control by corporate, government, and technoscientific bureaucracies (Giddens 1990). To critique 'everyday life in the modern world' is to recognize how much spatiality in 'the modern world' is an imagined community whose norms and designs that direct 'everyday life' in modes of global governance are ignored by far too many (Dean 2010). Industrial products, manufacturing processes, and transnational production are systems for conducting conduct by administering anxiety, power, and want. Second nature is neither natural nor wholly artificial, but it must be recognized as the true lifeworld (Ihde 1990), working as an assemblage (De Landa 1991) of engineered norms and embedded designs in all spaces. And, it is now more disturbing as its machinations drive our material and mental life in a much more occluded manner beyond the product potentials proffered in brand promises (Naess 1989; Baudrillard 1998).

The accidental normality of contemporary high-tech conditions now invests virtually everything in the human never-built, the built, and the yet-to-be-built environments in tangles of artificial logistics and engineered cultures. Nature, however, recedes as technology expands. As Hardt and Negri suggest, 'we continue to understand our psyches as driven by natural instincts and passions; but we have no nature in the sense that these forces and phenomena are no longer understood as outside, that is, they are not seen as original and independent of the civil order' (2000: 187). Technology entails normative imperatives in its ordinary material, operational, and spatial practice (Luke 2001). They are important in understanding how the reticulations of power and knowledge replicate and reinforce what Baudrillard (1996) has discovered to be 'the system of objects' evolving in local, national, or global markets. All of these terms, however, are mutable in their meanings, and they constantly are evolving every day in new objectified acts and artifacts of big technological systems at play as capitalism, nationalism, statism, and urbanism (Dean 2010).

Thinking about technology and the environment conceptually discloses a new historical a priori, or 'a series of complex operations that introduce the possibility of a constant order into the totality of representations. It constitutes a whole domain of empiricity as at the same time *describable* and *orderable*' (Foucault 1970: 158). As Foucault would indicate, concern for the environment as the 'framework of thought' for appraising technology should serve as the root structure of a historical a priori that 'delimits in the totality of experience a field of knowledge, defines the mode of being of the objects that appear in that field, provides man's everyday perception with theoretical powers, and defines the conditions in which he can sustain a discourse about things recognized to be true' (Foucault 1970: 158).

Reassessing liberal democratic capitalism's packaging of the technology found in nuclear energy technics, for example, returns one, at the same time, to the 'archaeological and genealogical study of practices envisaged simultaneously as a technological type of rationality and as strategic games of liberties' (Foucault 1984: 40). As they actualize each of the systems of systems that create some technically apt disposition between people and things embedded in uranium fuel, civilization becomes engineered for radioactive living and envisioned as greater energy consumption. All of these technological systems of machinic systems have been assembled in far too many contradictory ways. Over many decades, their accidental normality now ironically has come to constitute many structural limits imposed upon society, but which also enable some operational experiments at new possibilities for individuals to go, if only in part, beyond them (Foucault 1980b).

A regime of technology, like nuclear energy technics, materializes new modes of governmentality 'in which are articulated the effects of a certain type of power and the reference of a certain type of knowledge, the machinery by which the power relations give rise to a possible corpus of knowledge, and knowledge extends and reinforces the effects of this power' (Foucault 1980a: 29). Burning uranium fuel, typically, is seen as the gateway leading to greater dynamic freedom rather than the unfreedom of static submission to more primitive conditions of normality. When using less sophisticated technics, big crude technologies have not yet evolved into environmental forces. With nuclear power, however, one major mishap can bring this complexity all crashing down into primitive radioactive paralysis.

In this manner, technological practices serve as 'methods of power capable of optimizing forces, aptitudes, and life in general without at the same time making them more difficult to govern' (Foucault 1980a: 141). In fact, the most decisive environmental transformations are being made globally and locally, as Beck maintains, *'under the cloak of normality'* (1992: 186) in operational domains generated by technics and economics. Thus, 'in contemporary discussions' for policy change, 'the alternative society' is no longer expected to come from parliamentary debates on new laws, but rather from the application of microelectronics, genetic technology, and information media' (1992: 223). Technology is governance, and so, too, does it bring its own security and insecurity, power and vulnerability, risk and benefit (see Dalby, Pellizzoni, and Methmann and Oels, this volume).

Quite clearly, then, new formations to establish command, control, and communication through technics always constitute contradictory complexity. As Beck maintains, the challenges of artifice

> lie *across* the distinction between theory and practice, *across* the borders of specialties and disciplines, *across* the specialized competencies and institutional responsibilities, *across* the distinction between value and fact (and thus between ethics and science), and *across* the realms of politics, the public sphere, science and the economy, which are seemingly divided by institutions. (1992: 70)

Such mechanisms are complex, but the workings of technologies as governmentality unfold today at these intersections between the technics of domination and liberation (Mumford 1967, 1970).

The operations of technology reaffirm how completely environmental sites and systems are wholly embedded within 'a *sociotechnical* order' (Law 1991: 10). The networks of humans and machines, animals and plants, economies and ecologies, which have bound and shaped our environments, are mixed media of power and knowledge required for running high-tech civilization: 'what appears to be social is partly technical. What we usually call technical is partly social. In practice nothing is purely technical. Neither is anything purely social' (Law 1991: 10). Reappraising the larger technified elements of today's advanced built environments as a strong governmentality at work, nonetheless, reveals the degree to which the professional-technical agents of both government and business are, in many ways, trained consciously and unconsciously to operate technology's dark powers as 'object oriented ontologists'.

Critical potential

Environments, then, are world constructs. It is the terraformative characteristics of technologies, evolved into spatial systems with material quiddity, that make today's unstable and complex lifeworlds (Ihde 1990; Virilio 1997; Winner 1986). Who and/or what defines, directs, and develops that built environment and its products clearly must be a central concern of techno-cultural critique because states and societies both try to capture and contain these elusive social forces in dominating people and things (Jameson 1992). As the focus of power and locus of subjectivity in our world markets, the system of systems ironically is being built, and is already always accessible, in the essentially accidental anarchy of markets. One view of the accidents 'that gave birth to those things that continue to exist and have value for us' (Foucault 1977: 146) can be found in contemporary geopolitical celebrations of the environment-generating forces at work behind liberal capital democracy in today's world marketplace (Kennedy 1992). Following Adam Smith, careful ethical readings of technics also must trace out 'the productive powers of labour, and the order, according to which its produce is naturally distributed among the different ranks and conditions of men in the society' (Smith 1987: 105). Technologies are perhaps 'us/ing us', but this interrelation also affirms how capital is 'us/ing us'.

How does technology serve both as a generative system of order and disorder at almost any scale of contemporary global capitalism, and then how does its materiality serve as a basis for imagined, embedded, and engineered community – all at the same time? By tracking the spatial bases of technology as a system of globalizing change, one must soon realize how these material realities also then mystify commodification in technology (Virilio 2000). Technology is politics, but it is also property. Who defines, controls, owns, and creates technology, in turn, directs what is produced and consumed in economies and societies. Technology is 'so thoroughly biased in a particular direction that it regularly produces results as wonderful breakthroughs by social interests and crushing setbacks by others' (Winner 1999: 25–6). The extent to which this activity constitutes environments by drawing down resources, increasing risks, or sparking resistances is political as winners and losers come from these actions. This is true irrespective of whether many environmental problems are, in fact, technologically created as products and/or by-products of instrumentally rationally activities. Ecological activists famously have tended to defend nature by struggling to prevent or limit what 'drops out of the pipes' into nature from the economy and technology (see Baker, this volume). A critical environmental politics, however, should focus as much, or even more, on why there is a pipe, where it comes from, who controls what comes down it, what alternatives to the whole apparatus could be found at what cost, and finally who gains plus who loses from this technological complex being in operation (Luke 1999a).

Foucault's assessment of discursive formations suggests that 'truth values' are unstable. They also resonate more completely in the realm of operationality rather than as veracity *per se* (Foucault 1977: 150–1). That is, truth may well be taken as true due to its cultural utility rather than some abstract epistemic fidelity. Foucault hints that technology and discursivity cannot be captured as some 'primordial fact through the intermediary of perception or an image'; rather their influence is what 'arises between surfaces, where it assumes meaning, and in the reversal that causes every interior to pass to the outside and every exterior to the inside, in the temporal oscillation that always makes it precede and follow itself' (Foucault 1977: 169). Once flowing in this fashion, however, truth-like discursive formations also materialize crucial forms of technified spatiality in which services are found, circulation and exchange are practiced, transformations take hold, and scarcities are identified to be managed. It is true that burning coal adds to greenhouse gassing, but the 'living truths' of such power generation are what enable a fossil-fueled, high-tech existence. The epistemic regime of technology coincides with the regime of praxis. This is but one of the many commercial dialectics of big corporations' 'brand promises' and 'promised brands'. Human beings fashion their worlds out of words in disciplinary routines, discursive structures, and development texts, which they solidify in shared social materialities and mentalities.

As Law suggests, technology, once it constitutes the lifeworld, must work 'not only on inanimate physical materials, but on and through people, texts, devices, city councils, architectures, economics, and all the rest', such that if engineered designs are to work as well-imagined systems, then one always must have the material means to travel effectively 'between these different domains, weaving an emergent web which constituted and reconstituted bits and pieces that it brought together' (Law 1991: 9). For those fortunate enough to have access to the property that is technology, they effectively can embed their everyday life there.

The commercial artifacts circulating through webs of corporate commodification can be assayed as the media of '*a society of normalization*' (Foucault 1980a: 107) in which adding value to the artifacts of commerce and/or purchasing power over consumer goods becomes the sine qua non of being a good producer and consumer with normal technified tastes and attitudes. Living in this unsustainably developed system is 'enjoying the good life', while leaving the system's unsustainable regimen is regarded an antisocial act, retreating into premodern darkness and drudgery. Technological normality, of course, never unfolds as an ethical system in some univocal or monodirectional manner. Its essentially accidental quality is conflicted, multivocal, and polydirectional, as any strategic analysis of technological-driven corporate authorities intent upon exploiting global purchasing power in technified markets soon reveals (Bourdieu 1984).

While local, regional, and national variations recur in technology's concrete materiality, commodities still enforce the abstract social labour required by the unsustainable globalizing systems that contemporary markets, technics, and logistics continue to spin up (see Paterson, this volume). Fully enmeshed within technology's governmentality and its triadic assemblies of population, territory, and sovereignty for production, urban and rural environmental spaces usually become more repressive, antisensual, and decontextualized (Marcuse 1964). At these conjunctures, critical environmental thinking and resistant political action converge.

Conclusion

Technologies are intrinsic to the productions of the economy's and society's on-going commodification of the environment, which is actuated in the circuits of accumulation linking knowledge, money, and power. The systemic command, control, and communication functions of abstract technified space instead indicates how

> [t]he signification of this ensemble refers back to a sort of super-signification which escapes meaning's net: the functioning of capitalism, which contrives to be blatant and

covert at one and the same time. The dominant form of space, that of the centres of wealth and power, endeavors to mould the spaces it dominates (i.e. peripheral spaces) and it seeks, often by violent means, to reduce the obstacles and resistances it encounters there. (Lefebvre 1991: 49)

This technified spatial logic defines the world today: to aspire ideally to live beyond technology one first must, blatantly and covertly, act quite technologically.

As Lefebvre claims, the spatial practices of technologies in society secrete the space its residents and users occupy and utilize. These connections embrace

production and reproduction, and the particular locations and spatial sets characteristic of each social formation. Spatial practice ensures continuity and some degree of cohesion. In terms of social space, and of each member of a given society's relationship to that space, this cohesion implies a guaranteed level of *competence* and a specific level of *performance*. (1991: 33)

The technics, propounded and presupposed by the secretion of such space, will work only if people are accustomed to performing within them as lifeworlds (Ihde 1990). Amicable compliance – derived from individual competence and collective performance at particular locations with certain spatial settings – cannot be changed without remaking spatial and technical practices. Technologies create, and then conduct, strong normative expectations for human behaviour, while everyday commodification's spatial codes for exploitation of the environment as commercial exchange globally colonizes human and nonhuman being (Falk 1999). Every engineered system constitutes a normative order with its specific embedded materiality and mentality (Marcuse 1964). How to drive a car, operate electrical machines, or enjoy secure heated spaces brings new normative expectations to enjoy such services. And, this normativity always is recharging its services by circulating in today's accidental normality, whether it is leveraged daily as an element for governance either where it routinely sits or when it is flexibly deployed at other sites. The rules expressed through such normativity do not 'conform to the successive configurations of identical meaning; rather, they result from substitutions, displacements, disguised conquests, and systematic reversals' (Foucault 1977: 151). This fact is also true of all materials as well as any agents serving as their caretakers, managers, or vendors. Whether or not this technified normality is accidental, it plainly is materially normative in the production and consumption circuits of everyday urban life (see Brooks and Bryant, this volume).

With these social arrangements, the codes of power, wealth, and status rest upon owning, displaying, and using valorized technical objects, which are made, in turn, in many different collectivities of agents working as, or at times against, commodities in accord with those codes. As those codes provide a generalized system of decipherable signs for coherent communication amidst the instability of global commerce, a hard regime of inequitable social relations unfolds in the spatial manifolds of world trade (see Bond, this volume). New means of individual and group valorization are tied to technologies: what things people own, how those things are used, and where their enjoyment of thing-possession and thing-use develops all unfold their effects along with such things of order (Bourdieu 1998). While these codes of meaning may offer nothing but an ever-changing flux of sign value, they matter ethically and politically. Meanings are always 'complicitous and always opaque', but they also are 'the best means for the global social order to extend its immanent and permanent rule to all individuals' (Baudrillard 1996: 196).

Under the ordering influences circulating through the things of order, the everyday conditions for associating humans and nonhumans in technified collectives of theoretical self-understanding and practical joint-action are policed as the order of things known as 'the environment' (Foucault 1970; Latour 1993; see also Hobden, and Rudy and White, this volume). Through technologies, the control of commerce and powers of property are continuously rendered 'invisible, unthinkable, and unrepresentable' (Latour 1993: 34) to most people by their joint complicities with greater and greater commodification of 'the environment'. Indeed, occluding of who made what, where, when, and how in the diverse ecologies of the world environment spins up new illusions for tracking the visible, thinkable, and representable relationships in global trade. On a 'smarter planet', one finds most leave the sustainability and development of the environment in the hands of the 'latest technologies'.

Further reading

Interesting accounts of technology and the environment can be found in *Technology and Culture, Techné: Research in Philosophy and Technology, The Information Society: An International Journal*, and *E-The Environmental Magazine*. Another useful resource is *Philosophy of Technology* (Stanford Encyclopedia of Philosophy), available at http://plato.stanford. ed/entries/technology. Also see organizations such as *The Society for the Social Studies of Science* (4S), and PLOS One, an open access on-line resource on science, available at http://www.plosone.org. Also see Alfred Bergman (1984) *Technology and The Character of Contemporary Life: A Philosophical Inquiry*, Chicago: University of Chicago Press; Donna Haraway (1991) *Simians, Cyborgs and Women: The Reinvention of Nature*, New York: Routledge; Martin Heidegger (1977) *The Question Concerning Technology and Other Essays*, New York: Harper and Row; Lewis Mumford (1986) *The Lewis Mumford Reader*, ed. Donald Miller, New York: Pantheon; and Herbert Simon (1969) *The Sciences of the Artificial*, Cambridge, MA: MIT Press.

Useful websites

Appropedia – The Sustainability Wiki: http://www.appropedia.org
International Jacques Ellul Society: http://www.ellul.org/index.html
Green Technology: http://www.green-technology.org
Open Democracy (Science & Technology Section): http://www.opendemocracy.net/science_and_technology
Society for Philosophy and Technology: http://www.spt.org
The Union of Concerned Scientists: http://www.ucusa.org/mumford/mumford.html
United Nations Data Access System (UNdate): http://data.un.org

28 Vulnerability

Chris Methmann and Angela Oels

Introduction

For a long time, climate change was 'predominantly framed through weather events, charismatic megafauna and the movements of political actors and rhetoric, while few stories focused on climate justice and risk' (Boykoff 2008: 549). The concept of vulnerability attempts to correct this bias. It points to the fact that environmental change is not only a biological, geological or physical process. Whereas the planet as such is used to change, change can be a problem for some people. Even in the developed world, people are not equally affected by environmental change. Hurricane Katrina, which struck the city of New Orleans in August 2005, killed 1,800 people and made more than a million (at least temporarily) homeless. However, it was particularly the poor and members of the African American community that were hit hardest (Giroux 2006). When environmental change strikes, race and class obviously matter. Why are some people affected by environmental change while others not? Why do some people have the ability to cope with extreme weather events or gradual environmental change, whereas others lack it? What are the prerequisites for surviving an environmental disaster, and what do people need for coping with environmental stress? The concept of vulnerability aims to provide answers to these sorts of questions.

Scholars have started to engage with the notion of vulnerability since the 1970s. Today, the work of international institutions such as the United Nations Development Programme (UNDP), the World Bank, and the United Nations Framework Convention on Climate Change (UNFCCC) revolves around vulnerability. It is at the heart of large parts of the research on the impacts of environmental change. It features prominently in the reports of the Intergovernmental Panel on Climate Change (IPCC) (see Okereke and Charlesworth, this volume). And even high-ranking politicians use the concept to explain the (human) security concerns associated with environmental change, as, for example, in the climate-security debates in the UN Security Council (see Dalby, this volume). Today, vulnerability is an established but fragmented field of research (Adger 2006). In this chapter, we seek to trace the roots of the concept, outline the main currents of vulnerability research, and evaluate it in terms of its potential for human emancipation from inequality and domination that arises (not only) through environmental change. Throughout the text, we will use the example of climate-induced migration to illustrate our argument.

Core ideas

One of the few consensuses in the literature on vulnerability is that there are only a few consensuses. It is a highly disparate field with a lot of varying approaches (Janssen, Schoon, Ke and Börner 2006). However, there are several core features that almost all approaches to vulnerability share. First, all agree that 'vulnerability to environmental change does not exist in isolation from the wider political economy of resource use' (Adger 2006: 270; see also Watts and Peluso, this volume). The concept of vulnerability has its roots in the research on natural disasters. Put simply, it reflects the insight that natural disasters are in fact social disasters. Since the emergence of disaster research in the nineteenth century, for a long time the dominant consensus understood disasters such as earthquakes, floods or droughts as extreme physical events that require techno-scientific prediction and management (see Pellizzoni, this volume). This technocratic discourse privileges the position of scientists, bureaucrats or engineers (Hewitt 1983: 9–12) and tends to see affected populations or governments as guilty due to a lack of adequate knowledge and preparation (Varley 1994: 3). The concept of vulnerability, by contrast, argues that 'while hazards may be natural, disasters are generally not' (Bankoff 2001: 25). People are not at risk because they are simply exposed to hazard, but because of a certain 'marginality' (Bankoff 2001: 25), which depends on a variety of different factors such as race, class, gender, ethnicity and disability (Wisner and Luce 1993: 131–3). In other words, the adverse effects of natural hazards on people do not only lie within the hazard itself, but derive from the position of these individuals or groups within social, economic and political relations.

This results in the second consensus, namely, that vulnerability can be described as a function of three dimensions: exposure, sensitivity and adaptive capacity (Adger 2006: 270). This is also reflected in the famous definition of the IPCC, which is very influential within the literature on climate vulnerability (IPCCSR 2001). Exposure is, according to Adger (2006), the 'nature and degree to which a system experiences environmental or socio-political stress' (270). It contains the nature, degree, frequency and severity of environmental change that a certain population is facing. For example, a slow and gradual change in precipitation patterns will have a different effect on livelihoods than a sudden extreme weather event such as a storm flood. Sensitivity refers to the 'degree to which a system is modified or affected by perturbations' (Adger 2006: 270). A rural community living on small-scale subsistence farming may experience a lot more hardship from environmental changes than an urban industrial area. Adaptive capacity, finally, describes 'the ability of a system to evolve in order to accommodate environmental hazards or policy change and to expand the range of variability with which it can cope' (Adger 2006: 270). Having access to a broad variety of different types of crops that can be planted makes it easier to cope with environmental instability. These three concepts are important hallmarks within the field of vulnerability studies.

Key thinkers

In this section, we focus attention on some of the origins of the vulnerability literature and argue that since the 1970s, the field has evolved in three different branches that each put particular emphasis on exposure, sensitivity and adaptive capacity, respectively.

In a 1976 essay in *Nature,* Phil O'Keefe, Ken Westgate and Ben Wisner paradigmatically stated that 'disaster marks the interface between an extreme physical phenomenon and a vulnerable human population. It is of paramount importance to recognize both of these elements' (O'Keefe et al. 1976: 566). Some have seen this as the founding date of political ecology. Subsequent works developed this insight under a broadly Marxist framework (Blaikie and Brookfield 1987; Watts and Bohle 1993). These authors argued that the 'vulnerability' of people is often due to structural causes, such as integration into the world market, which undermine their capacity to adapt to extreme physical events. In other words, they were 'denying that these disasters were natural at all' (Wisner, O'Keefe and Westgate 1977: 48). These studies developed a critical perspective on disasters that aimed for the fundamental transformation of societies instead of a narrow focus on disaster prevention.

Yet vulnerability has also roots in liberal economic approaches that are less radical. In his seminal *Poverty and Famines,* Amartya Sen (1981) explains famines through a focus on entitlements. These are defined as 'the set of alternative commodity bundles that a person can command in a society using the totality of rights and opportunities that he or she faces' (Sen 1984: 497). His main argument is that famines are rarely caused by an actual lack of food, but by the inability of some parts of the population to get access to it – they lack sufficient entitlements. For example, the 1943 Bengal famine, which cost 3 million lives, was caused by a rise in prices, preventing the rural and urban poor from acquiring sufficient nutrition. This focus on contextual factors – declining wages, unemployment, rising food prices and poor food-distribution systems – inspired many of the subsequent writings on vulnerability. However, this perspective does not look at the structural causes or contextual determinants of vulnerability as the Marxist branch does, as Sen explicitly confines his analysis to non-political 'market failures'.

Another important contribution is the influential volume *Interpretations of Calamity* (Hewitt 1983). It criticized the focus on contextual factors, which resulted in technocratic (pre-)disaster management. Merging Marxist and Foucauldian thought, the book argued that vulnerability is merely the result of economic and social structures (e.g., race, class, gender) and that it is precisely the contextual knowledge of local populations that serves as an antidote against technocratic top-down management that sees populations as somehow deficient. Subsequent pioneers of vulnerability thinking have combined Sen's liberal approach with a Marxist political ecology perspective to broaden the focus beyond entitlements and operationalize the concept of vulnerability (Blaikie, Cannon, Davis and Wisner 1994; Watts and Bohle 1993). Such authors have argued that vulnerability is not only a feature of entitlements, but also defined by the relations between society and nature (ecosystem properties and usage, population growth etc.) as well as the results of long-term social developments such as the national regime of accumulation and the resulting class structure. Whether or not people suffer from famine thus depends both on, for example, their relationship with nature as well as their position within the social system. Here we already find the tripartite focus on exposure, sensitivity and adaptive capacity.

Based on these three dimensions of vulnerability, we can broadly discern three branches within the vulnerability literature: risk-hazard, social vulnerability and resilience (Eakin and Luers 2006). First, the risk-hazard approach is mostly interested in characterizing different physical sources of vulnerability, the expected consequences and the timing of these impacts (Eakin and Luers 2006: 369). In this sense, it understands vulnerability first and foremost as a biophysical phenomenon and does not pay much attention to its socio-economic context. A characteristic example for the risk-hazard approach is the U.S. Country Studies Programme during the early 1990s, which sought to assess the economic and social losses caused by climate change. Another prominent example, although not directly associated with the term vulnerability, would be the Stern Review (Stern 2007), which calculated the economic impacts of climate change. Vulnerability here simply measures the impact in terms of decreasing production or yield minus the capacity for adaptation in a given community. Therefore, some have labelled this approach an 'end point approach' (Kelly and

Adger 2000: 327) or 'outcome vulnerability' (O'Brien, Eriksen, Nygaard and Schjolden 2007: 75) as the 'assessment of vulnerability is the end point of a sequence of analyses beginning with projections of future emissions trends, moving on to the development of climate scenarios, thence to biophysical impact studies and the identification of adaptive options' (Kelly and Adger 2000: 327). It entails a rather linear perspective, moving from the natural to the social world, which are both understood as separate systems, based on a 'scientific framing' of environmental change (O'Brien et al. 2007: 76). It thus privileges the perspective of the natural sciences and, hence, focuses on the dimension of exposure (see Forsyth, this volume).

Second and by contrast, the social vulnerability approach sees vulnerability not as a natural, but a socio-economic phenomenon and is thus more interested in the dimension of sensitivity. It is closer to the aforementioned writings by Sen (1981; 1984). It does not stop at identifying particular vulnerabilities, but enquires into their causes beyond biophysical processes: Who is vulnerable? Why are some parts of the population vulnerable? And how are they vulnerable? In this sense, social vulnerability is a 'starting point' approach (Kelly and Adger 2000). It defines vulnerability as a preexisting state of populations – 'in terms of the ability or inability of individuals and social groupings to respond to, in the sense of cope with, recover from or adapt to, any external stress placed on their livelihoods and well-being' (Kelly and Adger 2000: 328). Environmental change is considered 'to occur in the context of political, institutional, economic and social structures and changes' (O'Brien et al. 2007: 76; see also Bond, this volume). This second approach thus can also be called 'contextual vulnerability' (O'Brien et al. 2007: 76). It tends to see nature and society as a coupled human-ecological system. And instead of a scientific framing, it is informed by a 'human security' discourse (O'Brien et al. 2007: 78; see Dalby, this volume). A good example of this is a study by Diana Liverman (1990). She shows that the differential impact of droughts in Mexico could not be explained only with precipitation patterns, but depended on land tenure and access to productive resources. The social vulnerability perspective also informs the very influential *Pressure and Release* model, which has been influential in emergency management (Blaikie et al. 1994). It has to be mentioned, though, that the (mostly Marxist) political ecology tradition of vulnerability research in this strand has been marginalized.

The third approach is rooted in the ecological concept of resilience and is relatively new to the field of vulnerability studies. It goes back to a paper by the ecologist C.S. Holling in 1973. He argued that the disciplines of ecology and resource management tend to view ecological systems as containing only one stable equilibrium, whereas in fact they have multiple and differing stable states (Holling 1973). This results in the notion that systems do not necessarily have to return to their initial equilibrium after experiencing a period of external stress, but can adopt a new, equally stable state. In this sense, resilience argues against a conservative perspective and for taking the creativity, flexibility and adaptability of ecological systems into account. Transferred to the sphere of the social sciences, it draws attention to the potential of social systems not to withstand change, but to actively shape it in order to survive. Society here is seen as a subsystem of ecological systems. Resilience expresses scepticism in central planning and management and seeks to increase the free flow of information in order to boost adaptive capacity (Folke et al. 2002; see also Baker, this volume). Case studies have argued for deploying community-based resource manage-ment systems that enhance dynamic learning and adaptation (Olsson, Folke and Berkes 2004). Thus, whereas other notions of vulnerability focus on factors that might endanger the preservation of the status quo in the face of environmental change, resilience looks for ways to utilize this change in order to promote creative adaptation measures (see Grove, this volume).

Critical potential

In this section, we critically evaluate the different notions of vulnerability. This critique is broadly inspired by the concepts of discipline, biopolitics, and governmentality that emerge from the writings of French philosopher Michel Foucault (see Grove, Kuehls, and Lövbrand and Stripple, this volume). In a nutshell, we ask how the three different schools of vulnerability thinking make human life governable in the face of environmental change. We follow a topological reading of governmentality (Collier 2009). Each of the three schools is analysed as a distinct configuration of governmental techniques and strategies, combining elements of sovereign power, discipline, biopolitics, and governmentality. The more recent configurations of governmentality have not replaced the earlier ones of sovereignty and discipline, but instead, they have governmentalized them, i.e., re-configured them for their purposes.[1] Excavating these configurations is crucial, as from a Foucauldian perspective being critical means resisting being governed in 'this' way and opening conceptual space for resistance and for thinking alternatives (Foucault 2007b). We will illustrate our critique drawing on the paradigmatic case of climate change induced migration.

First, the weakest notion of vulnerability is obviously found in its biophysical version of risk-hazard. Vulnerability is considered as decisively determined by the scope and scale of environmental change. The estimates of hazard probability and impact are often crude extrapolations of past trends, as seen in the debate on climate change induced migration. Myers and Kent, for example, have provided the most frequently cited estimate of 250 million climate change induced migrants by 2050 (Myers and Kent 1995). However, they do not consider how environmental drivers interact with and relate to economic, political and social drivers of migration but simply assume that 'environmental factors of unusual scope' (Myers and Kent 1995: 18–19) will be the determining variable (Jakobeit and Methmann 2012: 303). Furthermore, Myers and Kent use very crude measures to estimate the number of people who might migrate as a result of climate change. To assess the impact of sea-level rise on migration, for example, population trends in coastal areas are extrapolated in the future and then the total population of areas predicted to be under water by 2050 are projected as potential 'climate refugees'.

From a governmentality perspective, the political economy of power mobilized by the risk-hazard approach is predominantly, but by no means exclusively, one of discipline. The aim of this approach is to match calculations of environmental futures with responses in the form of social engineering. Affected populations are to be governed in such a way as to manage the most favourable distribution of human bodies in space so that least loss of human life will occur. There is no talk of choice or decision on the side of affected populations. Drawing on governmental techniques of identifying risk groups, those marked as vulnerable populations are conceptualized as passive bearers of their fate; they are deprived of their agency. Political options that could greatly modify the consequences of natural or man-made hazards are usually not at all or not adequately discussed. For this reason, the risk-hazard approach is often accused of environmental determinism (Hulme 2011). Alternative future scenarios are rendered unintelligible or at least marginalized.

This attempt to govern populations as 'vulnerable' and as in need of relocation has mobilized the resistance of target populations. UN ambassadors from low-lying small island states refuse to be conceptualized as 'climate refugees', as this tends to consider 'population mobility and loss of homelands' as 'unfortunate, but acceptable 'solutions' to the problems of the social impacts of climate change' (McNamara and Gibson 2009: 482). Moreover, it 'reduces the ability of Pacific ambassadors at the United Nations to pressure for change, lessening the onus on multilateral institutions to curb climate change at all' (ibid; see also Okereke and Charlesworth, this volume). This illustrates that the presumably technical and neutral exercise of mapping vulnerability to climate change with a focus on exposure to hazards implies far-ranging political visions about desirable futures. The underlying conflicts over desirable futures can be hidden by the technocratic innocence of this approach. The refusal of affected populations to be governed in this way brings the causes of climate change back into the picture.

Second, the notion of social vulnerability addresses these concerns more consciously and situates human life within its social, political and economic context. Vulnerability is an inherent feature of socio-economic systems and not something that only results from external stress. Read from a governmentality perspective, this contextual approach to vulnerability uses population statistics in order to identify 'risk groups'. Risk groups are those who have a higher than average risk of mortality or harm in the face of environmental change. The aim of a governmental intervention is then 'to bring the most unfavorable in line with the most favorable' (Foucault 2007a: 63). The idea of a governmental economy of power is to focus governmental interventions on risk groups in order to save the greatest number of lives with the available resources. This approach also involves careful monitoring and surveillance in order to identify climate change hotspots on the basis of a coupled analysis of social and biophysical systems. In these hotspots, freshwater resources may be degraded, food production could decline and storms and flood disasters might increase. From this perspective, climate change, for example, is not the single cause of possible harm and mortality. Instead, it is a 'threat multiplier' (UNGA 2009) that in conjunction with weak statehood and other pre-existing social conditions of vulnerability could produce 'environmentally induced migration' and 'conflict constellations' (WBGU 2007: 163). The main strategy of securing enabled by social vulnerability is the protection of risk groups. In the field of climate change, development assistance and adaptation projects are classic examples of measures that are financed by the international community of states for vulnerable communities. Changes in precipitation patterns are addressed with drought resistant crops; increasing numbers of 'king tides' with coastal defences. The aim of these measures is to allow affected populations to 'stay home' by assisting their adaptation. Moreover, if social vulnerability points to a nexus of socio-economic causes of vulnerabilities, it tends to ask more structural questions than the rather simple risk-hazard approach.

However, the social notion of vulnerability is not unproblematic, either. On the one hand, it still considers the state (or the international community of states) as the ultimate guarantor of security that needs to take care of risk groups (see Kuehls, this volume). The underlying discourse of human security produces '"humans" requiring securing' and mobilizes 'international institutions and actors to individuate, group and act upon Southern populations' (Duffield and Waddell 2006: 2–3). In the name of human security, military or civil interventions in southern states can be enacted. Even the most enthusiastic proponents of the concept admit that vulnerability is rarely invoked by those affected, but a concept deeply rooted in Western traditions of science (Furedi 2007: 487). It turns out that vulnerability is always something that resides within the 'other'. It is but the latest version of the old (post-)colonial story of 'tropicality' and 'development' (Bankoff 2001: 29). For example, 'climate refugees' from small island states in the Pacific are mostly presented 'as desperate and disempowered refugees', so that affected populations are conceptualized 'as something to either fear or control by those in the industrialised world' (Farbotko 2012: 135). In fact, 'islanders are reduced to being necessary recipients of the compassion and protection of the industrialised world, as fearful climate refugees' (Farbotko 2012: 135). Risk groups can be discriminated as unfit in the face of environmental change; they could be subjected to disciplinary or even coercive economies of power. The vulnerable are always on the brink of becoming dangerous. This climate-security discourse is thus underpinned by a neo-Malthusian discourse that tends to see the poor as drivers of conflict (Hartmann 2010; see also Kütting, this volume).

At best, the concept of social vulnerability, as well as the human security discourse on which it builds, provides a rather paternalistic framework for pro-active (Western) governmental intervention in order to reduce the vulnerability of those likely to be affected by environmental change. Yet this strength comes at the cost of rendering these affected populations as helpless victims, the upshot of which might even be a view of the vulnerable as becoming dangerous.

Third, the merits of the resilience notion of vulnerability lie precisely here: it puts the affected and their own interests and perspectives, their scope for action, right at the centre of the analysis. From a Foucaultian perspective, resilience is an advanced liberal governmental strategy that governs at a distance. Instead of direct governmental interventions, it uses technologies of agency (like participatory processes) and technologies of performance (like benchmarks) to mobilize affected populations to participate in their own securing. It renders affected populations responsible for their security and mobilizes them to transform themselves, to become flexible, adaptive subjects. In the name of security, individuals are put under close disciplinary surveillance to make sure that they use their liberties responsibly in ways preconceived by the state (see Grove, this volume).

The resilience paradigm opens conceptual space to rethink the affected populations as generally resourceful and capable. In the case of climate change induced migration, Carol Farbotko calls for highlighting 'the ways in which inhabitants of small islands represent themselves as they face the prospect of sea-level-rise related displacement' (2012: 140). She argues that contrary to Western perceptions of island people as rooted and stuck, most small island populations have a long tradition as great seafarers, but also as drifters on the ocean (Farbotko 2012). Both of these traditions could inform future resettlement strategies, promote a view of resourcefulness and tradition and offer an alternative to victimhood and disempowerment. In fact, many small island populations have taken their fate into their own hands. They prepare for self-organized, self-determined resettlement. This is clearly an act of resistance towards approaches seeking to victimize and/or 'rescue' small island populations. The Maldives have introduced a sovereign savings account with revenues from tourism to purchase land in Australia to resettle the 350,000 inhabitants in the near future. Papua New Guinea has begun the evacuation of the Carteret Islands in November 2003 as living conditions deteriorated there. Kiribati is planning to prepare its population for labour migration to New Zealand and Australia, for example, by training them as nurses.

Furthermore, the resilience paradigm has encouraged a reversal of traditional conceptualisations of climate change induced migration as an unfortunate condition that must be prevented by all means. The UK Government Office's Foresight Report on Migration and Global Environmental Change concludes that '"no migration" is not an option in the context of future environmental change' (Foresight 2011: 16). Instead, it is framed as an appropriate means of adaptation (Foresight 2011: 7). Circular and temporary migration can be important strategies of income diversification at times of drought or flood. The permanent migration of some who send remittances back home can enable those left behind to sustain their livelihood (Scheffran, Marmer and Sow 2011).

However, the resilience approach clearly underplays the structural causes of man-made and 'natural' disasters. The starting point for resilience is the failure of rational risk management in the face of uncertainty. Resilience operates in a world of endemic disaster. Disruptions to daily life are reconceptualized as inevitable and therefore as something to live with. What used to be extraordinary is now reconceptualized as 'normal', 'an extreme symptom of a general state of vulnerability' (Furedi 2007: 487). There is – again – little talk of political options that could prevent the occurrence of disasters in the first place; they are accepted as quasi-natural events. Resilience depoliticizes disasters and omits the structural causes of man-made hazards like climate change.

Moreover, some have remarked that the notion of vulnerability is closely connected to neoliberal thought (Walker and Cooper 2011; see also Rudy and White, this volume). Resilience thus runs the risk of becoming just another justification for conferring responsibility to the individual to govern herself in a responsible manner. As a case in point, the World Bank's World Development Report presents the neoliberal reforms in Vietnam from the 1980s onward as a forerunner for climate change resilience (World Bank 2010: 105). The fact that Vietnamese communities replaced former governmental activities when the state was dismantled becomes an advantage for these communities in dealing with climate change. In this sense, the notion of resilience is caught in a tension between actually empowering local populations to deal with environmental change themselves, on the one hand, and the tendency to obscure structural causes of vulnerability as well as individualizing those affected by climate change, on the other.

Take again the example of climate change induced migration, which has been reconceptualized as appropriate adaptation strategy. This is clearly not what most affected populations want. Interviews with UN ambassadors from small island states in 2004 revealed that 'the dominant view of these ambassadors was that climate change must be curbed to prevent them from having to flee their homelands. Exodus was simply not part of an acceptable future scenario' (McNamara and Gibson 2009: 479). The delegation of Tuvalu has frequently resisted such attempts of normalizing the loss of their homeland at UNFCCC climate negotiations, most notably at the Copenhagen summit 2009, where they demanded ambitious greenhouse gas emission reductions by industrialized countries (see Okereke and Charlesworth, and Death, this volume).

Conclusion

Vulnerability is a contested concept that has been employed by a variety of research traditions for different ends. In this chapter, we have distinguished between three distinct configurations of governmental techniques and strategies that are employed to govern 'vulnerable' populations and discussed their emancipatory potential. First, the risk-hazard perspective conceptualizes vulnerability as an outcome of exposure to natural or man-made hazards. We have accused this perspective of a tendency towards environmental determinism, as environmental changes are often depicted as inevitable while they could still be ameliorated at the political level. In our critique, we have argued that this perspective tends to overlook the pre-existing social, economic and political conditions that render people susceptible to harm by environmental change in the first place. Such a view of vulnerability as contextual condition is, however, introduced by the social vulnerability perspective. We have shown that this perspective conceptualizes vulnerable populations as problematic risk groups requiring governmental interventions for their protection. When the vulnerable become portrayed as 'dangerous', Northern governmental interventions on Southern populations might be enabled. However, some affected populations resist their victimisation, demand that the causes of climate change are addressed, and take their fate into their own hands. Third, we discussed the resilience approach to vulnerability, which addresses affected populations as capable of their own securing. Advanced liberal elements of resilience require vulnerable populations to become flexible, empowered, adaptive subjects in the face of inevitable disruptions to their daily lives. The resilience perspective tends to ignore the structural causes of man-made hazards and individual vulnerabilities. However, spontaneous coping strategies might still disrupt advanced liberal attempts to secure circulation in the liberal economic order. Finally, we suggest that one can discern a line of force within these transformations that increasingly seeks to govern vulnerability 'at a distance' (Rose and Miller 1992) – harnessing the capacities of the individual to cope with dramatic environmental change.

The concept of vulnerability is clearly implicated in North–South power relations, as it is first and foremost the vulnerability of the others, usually the poor in the global South, that is conceptualized as problematic and requiring governmental intervention. This construction of the vulnerable as potentially 'dangerous' has played an important role in the construction of climate change as a security issue (see Dalby, this volume). The construction of millions of climate refugees as a threat to Northern homeland security has facilitated the interest of the military sector in the geopolitical implications of climate change (Hartmann 2010). As we have revealed previously, there is little substance to back the claims made about future numbers of potential 'climate refugees', yet these constructions are highly influential in problematizing populations in the global South (and their governments) as 'dangerous' and as requiring interventions.

The recent proliferation of resilience in vulnerability debates is representative of a larger shift in risk management strategies in environmental politics (Oels 2011; Rothe 2011). Where traditional risk management based on probability calculations fail in the face of irresolvable uncertainty, a new strategy of risk management through contingency is emerging (Dillon 2008; see also Pellizzoni, this volume). In the face of indeterminacy, strategies of dealing with unknown unknowns like scenario planning are emerging, informing anticipation and preparedness. The study of critical environmental politics thus requires a reflexive and nuanced comprehension of the multiple dimensions of vulnerability, one that places marginalized and insecure populations at its heart.

Further reading

A very good introduction to the vulnerability literature is provided by W.N. Adger (2006) 'Vulnerability', *Global Environmental Change*, 16 (3): 268–81. Gregory Bankoff (2001) paints a somewhat more critical picture in 'Rendering the world unsafe: "Vulnerability" as western discourse', *Disasters*, 25 (1): 19–35. See also Bohle, Downing and Watts (1994). To get a first impression of vulnerability research 'in action' and its visualization, see O'Brien et al. (2004) 'Mapping vulnerability to multiple stressors: Climate change and globalization in India', *Global Environmental Change*, 14 (4): 303–13.

Useful websites

A collection of maps that illustrate vulnerability on a global scale can be found here: http://is.gd/
 HOPyPa
Environmental Vulnerability Index: http://www.vulnerabilityindex.net
Collectif Argos photo documentary on 'Climate Refugees': http://www.climaterefugees.eu/
Alliance of Small Island States (AOSIS): http://aosis.org/

Note

1. For reasons of space, we had to simplify our argument here, presenting three rather clear-cut categories. We provide a more detailed analysis of the three configurations of governmental techniques
   and strategies in Oels and Methmann (forthcoming).

Bibliography

Abélès, Marc (2010) *The Politics of Survival*, trans. Julie Kleinman, Durham: Duke University Press.

Ackerman, Frank, Stanton, Elizabeth A., Hope, Chris and Alberth, Stephane (2009) 'Did the Stern Review underestimate US and global climate damages?', *Energy Policy*, 37 (7): 2717–2721.

Adams, Carol J. (1990) *The Sexual Politics of Meat*, Cambridge: Polity.

Adams, Carol J. (ed.) (1993) *Ecofeminism and the Sacred*, New York: Continuum.

Adams, Carol J. (2003) *The Pornography of Meat*, London: Continuum.

Adams, Carol J. and Donovan, Josephine (eds) (1995) *Animals and Women: Feminist Theoretical Explorations*, London: Duke University Press.

Adams, Jonathan and McShane, Thomas (1996) *The Myth of Wild Africa: Conservation Without Illusions*, Berkeley: The University of California Press.

Adams, William (1997) 'Rationalization and conservation: Ecology and the management of nature in the United Kingdom', *Transactions of the Institute of British Geographers*, 22: 277–291.

Adams, William (2004) *Against Extinction: The Story of Conservation*, London: Earthscan.

Adas, Michael (1989) *Machines as the Measure of Men: Science, Technology, and Ideologies of Western Dominance*, Ithaca: Cornell University Press.

Adey, Peter (2008) 'Airports, mobility, and the calculative architecture of affective control', *Geoforum*, 39: 438–451.

Adey, Peter and Anderson, Ben (2012) 'Anticipating emergencies: Technologies of preparedness and the matter of security', *Security Dialogue*, 43 (2): 99–117.

Adger, W. Neil (2006) 'Vulnerability', *Global Environmental Change*, 16 (3): 268–281.

Adger, W. Neil, Arnell, Nigel and Tompkins, Emma (2005) 'Successful Adaptation to Climate Change Across Scales', *Global Environmental Change*, 15: 77–86.

Adger, W. Neil, Barnett, Jon, Chapin III, F. S. 'Terry' and Ellemor, Heidi (2011) 'This must be the place: Underrepresentation of identity and meaning in climate change decision making', *Global Environmental Politics*, 11 (2): 1–25.

Adorno, Theodor W. (1973) *Negative Dialectics*, New York: Seabury Press.

Agamben, Giorgio (1993) *The Coming Community*, Minneapolis: University of Minnesota Press.

Agamben, Giorgio (1998) *Homo Sacer: Sovereign Power and Bare Life*, Stanford: Stanford University Press.

Agamben, Giorgio (1999) *Remnants of Auschwitz: The Witness and the Archive*, Brooklyn: Zone Books.

Agamben, Giorgio (2004) *The Open: Man and Animal*, trans. Kevin Attell, Stanford CA: Stanford University Press.

Agamben, Giorgio (2005) *State of Exception*, Chicago: University of Chicago Press.

Agger, Ben (2004) *Speeding Up Fast Capitalism*, Boulder, CO: Paradigm Publishers.

Agarwal, Anil and Narain, Sunita (1991) *Global Warming in an Unequal World: A Case of Environmental Colonialism*, New Delhi: Centre for Science and Environment.

Agrawal, Arun (2005) *Environmentality: Technologies of Government and the Making of Subjects*, Durham, NC: Duke University Press.

Agrawala, Shardul (1998) 'Context and early origins of the Intergovernmental Panel on Climate Change', *Climatic Change* 39: 605–620.

Agyeman, Julian, Bullard, Robert D. and Evans, Bob (eds) (2003) *Just Sustainabilities: Development in an Unequal World,* London: Earthscan.

Ahmed, Sara (2004) 'Affective economies', *Social Texts,* 22 (2): 117–139.

Aitkenhead, Decca (2012) 'Žižek, Slavoj: Humanity is OK, but 99% of people are boring idiots', *The Guardian,* 10 June. Available at http://www.guardian.co.uk/culture/2012/jun/10/slavoj-zizek-humanity-ok-people-boring (accessed 27 March 2013).

Alaimo, Stacy (2000) *Undomesticated Ground: Recasting Nature as Feminist Space,* New York: Cornell University Press.

Alger, Chadwick (2002) 'The emerging roles of NGOs in the UN system: From Article 72 to a People's Millennium Assembly', *Global Governance,* 8 (1): 93–117.

Alperovitz, Gar (2004) *America Beyond Capitalism: Reclaiming Our Wealth, Our Liberty, and Our Democracy,* Hoboken, NJ: John Wiley & Sons.

Amazon Watch, International Rivers, Movimento Xingu Vivo (2012) 'Amazonian Indigenous Peoples Occupy Belo Monte Dam Site', *Press Release,* 23 June 2012. Available at http://amazonwatch.org/news/2012/0623-amazonian-indigenous-peoples-occupy-belo-monte-dam-site (accessed 27 March 2013).

Amin, Ash (2010) *Land of Strangers,* London: Polity.

Amnesty International (2012) *Nigeria: Trapped in a Cycle of Violence,* London: Amnesty International.

Amoore, Louise (2008) 'Foucault against the grain', *International Political Sociology,* 2 (3), 274–276.

Anderson, Ben (2010) 'Preemption, precaution, preparedness: Anticipatory action and future geographies', *Progress in Human Geography,* 34 (6): 777–798.

Anderson, Ben (2012) 'Affect and biopower: Towards a politics of life', *Transactions of the Institute of British Geographers,* 37: 28–43.

Anderson, Ben and Adey, Peter (2012) 'Governing events and life: "Emergency" in UK civil contingencies', *Political Geography,* 31 (1): 24–33.

Anderson, Benedict (1991) *Imagined Communities,* London: Verso.

Anderson, Kay and Braun, Bruce (eds) (2008) *Critical Essays in Human Geography,* London: Ashgate.

Anderson, Kevin and Bows, Alice (2008) 'Reframing the climate change challenge in light of post-2000 emission trends', *Philosophical Transactions of the Royal Society: A,* 366 (1882): 3863–3882.

Angermeier, Paul and Karr, James (1994) 'Biological Integrity versus Biological Diversity as policy directives protecting biotic resources', *Bioscience,* 44 (10): 690–697.

Angus, Ian (ed.) (2010) *The Global Fight for Climate Justice: Anticapitalist Responses to Global Warming and Environmental Destruction,* Toronto: Resistance Books.

Appadurai, Arjun (1986) 'Introduction: Commodities and the politics of value', in Arjun Appadurai (ed.) *The Social Lives of Things,* Cambridge: Cambridge University Press.

Appadurai, Arjun (1996) *Modernity at Large: Cultural Dimensions of Globalization,* Minneapolis: University of Minnesota Press.

Aradau, Claudia (2010) 'Security that matters: Critical infrastructure and objects of protection', *Security Dialogue,* 41 (5): 491–514.

Armour, Kyle C. and Roe, Gerard H. (2011) 'Climate commitment in an uncertain world', *Geophysical Research Letters,* 38 (1): L01707, DOI: 10.1029/2010GL045850.

Arsel, Murat (2012) 'Between "Marx and Markets"? The State, the "Left Turn" and Nature in Ecuador', *Tijdschrift voor Economische en Sociale Geografie,* 103 (2): 150–163.

Arsel, Murat and Büscher, Bram (2012) 'Nature™ Inc: Changes and continuities in neoliberal conservation and environmental markets', *Development and Change,* 43 (1): 53–78.

Ashley, Richard K. and Walker, R. B. J. (1990) 'Speaking the language of exile: Dissident thought in International Studies', *International Studies Quarterly,* 34 (3): 259–268.

Asian Communities for Reproductive Justice (2009) *Looking Both Ways: Women's Lives at the Crossroads of Reproductive Justice and Climate Justice,* Oakland. Available at http://www.reproductivejustice.org/ACRJ_Looking_Both_Ways.pdf (accessed 12 April 2013).

Astyk, Sharon (2008) *Depletion and Abundance: Life on the New Home Front,* Philadelphia: New Society.

Athanasiou, Thomas and Baer, Paul (2002) *Dead Heat: Global Justice and Global Warming,* New York: Seven Stories Press.

Attfield, Robin (2003) *Environmental Ethics: An Overview for the Twenty-First Century,* Cambridge: Polity.

Baber, Walter F. and Bartlett, Robert V. (2005) *Deliberative Environmental Politics: Democracy and Ecological Rationality,* Cambridge, MA: MIT Press.

Baechler, Günther (1998) 'Why environmental transformation causes violence: A synthesis', *Environmental Change and Security Project Report,* Issue 4 (Spring): 22–44.

Baechler, Günther (1999a) 'Environmental degradation in the South as a cause of armed conflict' in Alexander Carius and Kurt Lietzmann (eds) *Environmental Change and Security: A European Perspective,* Berlin: Springer Verlag, 107–129.

Baechler, Günther (1999b) *Violence through Environmental Discrimination: Causes, Rwanda Arena, and Conflict Model,* Dordrecht: Kluwer.

Bachram, Heidi (2004) 'Climate fraud and carbon colonialism: The new trade in greenhouse gases', *Capitalism, Nature, Socialism,* 15 (4): 5–20.

Bäckstrand, Karin and Lövbrand, Eva (2006) 'Planting trees to mitigate climate change: Contested discourses of ecological modernization, green governmentality and civic environmentalism', *Global Environmental Politics,* 6 (1): 50–75.

Bäckstrand, Karin, Khan, Jamil, Kronsell, Annika and Lövbrand, Eva (eds) (2010) *Environmental Politics and Deliberative Democracy: Examining the Promise of New Modes of Governance,* Cheltenham: Edward Elgar.

Bahro, Rudolf (1984) *From Red to Green: Interviews with the New Left Review,* London: Verso.

Bailey, Ronald (2005) *Liberation Biology: The Scientific and Moral Case for the Biotech Revolution,* Amherst, NY: Prometheus Books.

Baker, Susan (2006) *Sustainable Development,* Abingdon: Routledge.

Baker, Susan (2012) 'The governance of sustainable development', in Bitzer, Verena, Cörvers, Ron, Glasbergen, Pieter and Niestroy, Ingeborg (eds) *European Union, Governance and Sustainability,* Den Haag: Open University Press, 21–59.

Baker, Susan and Eckerberg, Katarina (eds) (2008) *In Pursuit of Sustainable Development: New Governance Practices at the Sub-national Level in Europe,* New York: Routledge.

Bakker, Karen (2005) 'Neoliberalizing nature? Market environmentalism in water supply in England and Wales', *Annals of the Association of American Geographers,* 95 (3): 542–565.

Baldwin, Andrew (2003) 'The nature of the boreal forest: Governmentality and forest-nature', *Space and Culture,* 6: 415–428.

Baldwin, Andrew (2013) 'Vital ecosystem security: Emergence, circulation, and the biopolitical environmental citizen', *Geoforum,* 45: 52–61.

Balsamo, Anne (1996) *Technologies of the Gendered Body: Reading Cyborg Women,* London: Duke University Press.

Bank of Natural Capital (2012a) 'Natural Capital'. Available at http://bankofnaturalcapital.com/category/natural-capital/ (accessed 16 May 2012).

Bank of Natural Capital (2012b) 'Ecosystems services'. Available at http://bankofnaturalcapital.com/ecosystem-services/ (accessed 15 May 2012).

Bankoff, Gregory (2001) 'Rendering the world unsafe: "Vulnerability" as western discourse', *Disasters,* 25 (1): 19–35.

Barad, Karen (1996) 'Meeting the Universe Halfway', in L. Nelson and J. Nelson (eds) *Feminism, Science, and the Philosophy of Science,* Dordrech: Kluwer Press.

Barad, Karen (2007) *Meeting the Universe Halfway: Quantum Physics and the Entanglement of Matter and Meaning,* Durham, NC: Duke University Press.

Barber, Charles, Afiff, Suraya and Purnomo, Agus (1995) *Tiger by the Tail? Reorienting Biodiversity Conservation and Development in Indonesia,* Washington DC: World Resources Institute.

Barber, Charles Victor and Talbot, Kirk (2003) 'The chainsaw and the gun: The role of military in deforesting Indonesia', *Journal of Sustainable Forestry,* 16 (3/4): 131–160.

Barker, Terry (2008) 'The economics of avoiding dangerous climate change: An editorial essay on The Stern Review', *Climatic Change,* 89 (3): 173–194.

Barkin, David (2002) *Wealth, Poverty and Sustainable Development,* Mexico City: Center for Ecology and Development.

Barnes, Barry, Bloor, David and Henry, John (1996) *Scientific Knowledge: A Sociological Analysis,* London: Athlone.

Barnett, Clive, Cloke, Paul, Clarke, Nick and Malpass, Alice (2005) 'Consuming ethics: Articulating the subjects and spaces of ethical consumption', *Antipode,* 37 (1): 23–45.

Barnett, Clive, Cloke, Paul, Clarke, Nick and Malpass, Alice (2010) *Globalizing Responsibility: The Political Rationalities of Ethical Consumption,* Chichester: John Wiley-Blackwell.

Barnett, Jon (2000) Destabilizing the environment-conflict thesis', *Review of International Studies,* 26: 271–288.

Barnett, Jon (2001) *The Meaning of Environmental Security: Ecological Politics and Policy in the New Security Era,* London: Zed Books.

Barnett, Michael and Duvall, Raymond (eds) (2005) *Power in Global Governance,* Cambridge: CUP.

Barnosky, Anthony D., Hadly, Elizabeth A., Bascompte, Jordi, Berlow, Eric L., Brown, James H., Fortelius, Mikael et al (2012) 'Approaching a state shift in Earth's biosphere,' *Nature* 486: 52–58.

Barr, Christopher M. (1998) 'Bob Hasan, the Rise of Apkindo, and the Shifting Dynamics of Control in Indonesia's Timber Sector', *Indonesia,* 65: 1–36.

Barr, Christopher M. (1999) 'Discipline and Accumulate: State Practice and Elite Consolidation in Indonesia's Timber Sector, 1967–1998', Master's Thesis, Cornell University.

Barr, Stewart (2011) 'Climate forums: Virtual discourses on climate change and the sustainable lifestyle', *Area,* 43 (1): 14–22.

Barry, Andrew (2001) *Political Machines: Governing a Technological Society,* London: Athlone Press.

Barry, Andrew, Osborne, Thomas and Rose, Nicholas (eds) (1996) *Foucault and Political Reason: Liberalism, Neo-liberalism, and Rationalities of Government,* Chicago: University of Chicago Press.

Barry, Brian (1997) 'Sustainability and Intergenerational Justice', *Theoria,* 45: 43–65.

Barry, John (1998) *Rethinking Green Politics, Nature, Virtue, and Progress,* London: Sage.

Barry, John (2006a) *Environment and Social Theory,* Second edition, Abingdon: Routledge.

Barry, John (2006b) 'Resistance is fertile: From environmental to sustainability citizenship', in Andrew Dobson and Derek Bell (eds) *Environmental Citizenship,* Cambridge MA: MIT Press.

Barry, John (2012) *The Politics of Actually Existing Unsustainability: Human Flourishing in a Climate-Changed, Carbon Constrained World,* Oxford: Oxford University Press.

Barry, John and Eckersley, Robyn (eds) (2005) *The State and the Global Ecological Crisis,* Cambridge MA: MIT Press.

Basedau, Matthias (2005) *Context Matters: Rethinking the Resource Curse in Sub-Saharan Africa,* Working Paper #1, Hamburg: German Overseas Institute.

Bassey, Nnimmo (2012) *To Cook a Continent,* Oxford: Pambazuka Press.

Batt, Sharon (1994) *Patient No More: The Politics of Breast Cancer,* Edinburgh: Scarlet.

Baudrillard, Jean (1981) *For a Critique of the Political Economy of the Sign,* St. Louis: Telos Press.

Baudrillard, Jean (1996) *The System of Objects,* London: Verso.

Baudrillard, Jean (1998) *The Consumer Society: Myths and Structures,* London: Sage.

Bauman, Zygmunt (1992) *Intimations of Postmodernity,* London: Routledge.

BBC News (2009) 'Maldives cabinet makes a splash', 17 October. Available at http://news.bbc.co.uk/1/hi/8311838.stm (accessed 27 March 2013).

Beck, Silke (2011) 'Moving beyond the linear model of expertise? IPCC and the test of adaptation', *Regional Environmental Change*, 2: 297–306.

Beck, Ulrich (1992) *Risk Society: Toward a New Modernity*, London: Sage.

Beck, Ulrich (1995) *Ecological Politics in an Age of Risk*, Cambridge: Polity Press.

Beck, Ulrich (1996) 'World risk society as cosmopolitan society? Ecological questions in a framework of manufactured uncertainties', *Theory, Culture & Society*, 13 (4): 1–32.

Beck, Ulrich (2000) *What is Globalization?*, Oxford: Blackwell.

Beck, Ulrich (2009) *World at Risk*, Cambridge: Polity.

Beck, Ulrich, Giddens, Anthony and Lash, Scott (1994) *Reflexive Modernization: Politics, Tradition and Aesthetics in the Modern Social Order*, Cambridge: Polity Press.

Bell, Derek R. (2003) 'Environmental Citizenship and the Political', paper presented at ESRC Seminar Series on Citizenship and the Environment, Newcastle, October.

Bell, Derek R. (2005) 'Liberal environmental citizenship', *Environmental Politics*, 14 (2): 179–194.

Bello, Walden (2003) *Deglobalization: Ideas for a New Economy*, London: Zed Books.

Benedick, Richard Elliott (1993) 'Perspectives of a negotiation practitioner', in Gunnar Sjostedt (ed.) *International Environmental Negotiation*, London: Sage, 219–243.

Benjamin, Walter (1999) *The Arcades Project*, trans. Howard Eiland and Kevin McLaughlin, Cambridge, MA: Harvard University Press.

Bennett, Jane (2007) *Vibrant Matter: A Political Ecology of Things*, Durham: Duke University Press.

Bennie, Lynn G. (1998) 'Brent Spar, Atlantic Oil and Greenpeace', in F.F. Ridley and Grant Jordan (eds) *Protest Politics: Cause Groups and Campaigns*, Oxford: Oxford University Press.

Benny, Norma (1983) 'All one flesh: The rights of animals', in Leonie Caldecott and Stephanie Leyland (eds) *Reclaim the Earth*, London: Women's Press.

Bentham, Jeremy (1948) *The Principles of Morals and Legislation*, New York: Hafner Press.

Benton, Ted (ed.) (1996) *The Greening of Marxism*, New York: Guilford Press.

Bergman, Alfred (1984) *Technology and The Character of Contemporary Life: A Philosophical Inquiry*, Chicago: University of Chicago Press.

Berkes, Fikret, Colding, Johan and Folke, Carl (eds) (2003) *Navigating Socio-ecological Systems: Building Resilience for Complexity and Change*, Cambridge: University Press.

Berkhout, Frans (2006) 'Normative expectations in systems innovation', *Technology Analysis and Strategic Management*, 18 (3/4): 299–311.

Bernstein, Steven (2000) 'Ideas, social structure and the compromise of liberal environmentalism' *European Journal of International Relations*, 6: 464–512.

Bernstein, Steven (2002) *The Compromise of Liberal Environmentalism*, New York: Columbia University Press.

Berridge, G. R. (2005) *Diplomacy: Theory and Practice*, Basingstoke: Palgrave.

Berry, Wendell (1977) *The Unsettling of America: Culture and Agriculture*, New York: Avon Books.

Berry, Wendell (2001) 'The idea of a local economy,' *Orion*, Winter. Available at http://www.orion-magazine.org/index.php/articles/article/299/ (accessed 3 March 2013).

Betsill, Michele and Hoffmann, Matthew J. (2011) 'The contours of "Cap and Trade": The evolution of emissions trading systems for greenhouse gases', *Review of Policy Research*, 28 (1): 83–106.

Bhabha, Homi (1994) *The Location of Culture*, London: Routledge.

Bhaskar, Roy (1975) *A Realist Theory of Science*, Leeds: Leeds Books.

Bidwai, Praful (2011) *The Politics of Climate Change and the Global Crisis: Mortgaging Our Future*, Hyderabad: Orient BlackSwan.

Biermann, Frank (2001) 'The emerging debate on the need for a World Environment Organization: A commentary', *Global Environmental Politics*, 1 (1): 45–55.

Biermann, Frank (2007) '"Earth system governance" as a crosscutting theme of global change research', *Global Environmental Change*, 17 (3–4): 326–337.

Biermann, Frank (2012) 'Greening the United Nations Charter: World politics in the Anthropocene', *Environment: Science and Policy for Sustainable Development*, 54 (3): 6–17.

Biermann, Frank and Bauer, Steffen (2005) (eds) *A World Environment Organization. Solution or Threat for Effective International Environmental Governance?* Aldershot, UK: Ashgate.

Biermann, Frank and Pattberg, Philippe (2008) 'Global environmental governance: Taking stock, moving forward', *Annual Review of Environment and Resources* 33: 277–294.

Biermann, Frank and Pattberg, Philipp (2012) *Global Environmental Governance Reconsidered* (Earth System Governance), Cambridge, MA: MIT Press.

Bigg, Tom (2004) 'The World Summit on Sustainable Development: Was it worthwhile?' in Tom Bigg (ed.) *Survival For a Small Planet: The Sustainable Development Agenda,* London: Earthscan, 1–22.

Black, Julia (2008) 'Constructing and contesting legitimacy and accountability in polycentric regulatory regimes', *Regulation & Governance,* 2: 137–164.

Blaikie, Piers (1985) *The Political Economy of Soil Erosion in Developing Countries,* London: Longman.

Blaikie, Piers (1995) 'Understanding environmental issues', in Stephen Morse and Michael Stocking (eds) *People and Environment,* London: UCL Press, 1–30.

Blaikie, Piers and Brookfield, Harold C. (1987) *Land Degradation and Society, Development Studies,* Berkeley: Taylor and Francis.

Blaikie, Piers, Cannon, Terry, Davis, Ian and Wisner, Ben (1994) *At Risk: Natural Hazards, People's Vulnerability and Disasters,* London: Routledge.

Blaikie, Piers and Jeanrenaud, Sally (1997) 'Biodiversity and human welfare', in K. B. Ghimire and M. P. Pimbert (eds) *Social Change and Conservation. Environmental Politics and Impacts of National Parks and Protected Areas,* London: Earthscan.

Bleischwitz, Raimund (2003) *Governance of Sustainable Development,* Wuppertal, Germany: Wuppertal Institute for Climate, Environment and Energy.

Bloc, Anton (1974) *The Mafia of a Sicilian Village: A Study of Violent Peasant Entrepreneurs,* Prospect Heights IL: Waveland Press.

Blühdorn, Ingolfur (2007) 'Sustaining the unsustainable: Symbolic politics and the politics of simulation', *Environmental Politics,* 16 (2): 251–275.

Blühdorn, Ingolfur (2011) 'The politics of unsustainability: COP15, post-ecologism, and the ecological paradox', *Organization & Environment,* 24 (1): 34–53.

Blühdorn, Ingolfur (2013) 'The governance of unsustainability: Ecology and democracy after the post-democratic turn', *Environmental Politics,* 22 (1): 16–36.

Blühdorn, Ingolfur and Ian Welsh (2007) 'Eco-Politics beyond the paradigm of sustainability: A conceptual framework and research agenda', *Environmental Politics,* 16 (2): 185–205.

Bodansky, Daniel (2010) 'The Copenhagen Climate Change Conference: A post-mortem,' *American Journal of International Law,* 104 (2): 130–139.

Bodansky, Daniel (2011) *W[h]ither the Kyoto Protocol? Durban and Beyond. Harvard Project on Climate Agreements.* Available at http://ssrn.com/abstract=1917603 (accessed 27 March 2013).

Borgerhoff Mulder, Monique and Coppolillo, Peter (2004) *Conservation: Linking Ecology, Economy, and Culture,* Princeton, NJ: Princeton University Press.

Bohle, Hans-Georg and Fünfgeld, Hartmut (2007) 'The political ecology of violence in eastern Sri Lanka', *Development and Change,* 38 (4): 665–687.

Bohle, Hans G., Downing, Thomas E. and Watts, Michael J. (1994) 'Climate change and social vulnerability: Toward a sociology and geography of food insecurity', *Global Environmental Change,* 4 (1): 37–48.

Böhm, Steffen and Dabhi, Siddhartha (eds) (2009) *Upsetting the Offset: The Political Economy of Carbon Markets,* London: Mayfly books.

Böhm, Steffan and Dabhi, Siddhartha (2011) 'Fault lines in climate policy: What role for carbon markets?' *Climate Policy,* 11 (6): 1389–1392.

Bond, Patrick (2002) *Unsustainable South Africa: Environment, Development and Social Protest,* London: Merlin Press.

Bond, Patrick (2012) *Politics of Climate Justice: Paralysis Above, Movement Below,* Pietermaritzburg: University of KwaZulu-Natal Press.

Bonner, Raymond (1994) *At the Hand of Man: Peril and Hope for Africa's Wildlife,* London: Simon & Schuster.

Bonneuil, Christophe (2002) 'The manufacture of species: Kew Gardens, The Empire, and the standardisation of taxonomic practices in late nineteenth century botany', in M.-N. Bourguet, C. Licoppe and O. Sibum (eds) *Instruments, Travel and Science: Itineraries of Precision from the 17th to the 20th century,* London: Routledge.

Bookchin, Murray (1971) *Post-Scarcity Anarchism,* Berkeley: Ramparts Books.

Bookchin, Murray (1980) *Toward an Ecological Society,* Montreal: Black Rose Books.

Bookchin, Murray (1982) *The Ecology of Freedom: The Emergence and Dissolution of Hierarchy,* Palo Alto, CA: Cheshire Books.

Bookchin, Murray (1990) *Remaking Society: Pathways to a Green Future,* Boston: South End Press.

Booker, Christopher (2009) *The Real Global Warming Disaster: Is The Obsession With 'Climate Change' Turning Out To Be The Most Costly Scientific Blunder In History?,* London: Continuum.

Botkin, Daniel (1990) *Discordant Harmonies: A New Ecology for the Twenty-First Century,* Oxford: Oxford University Press.

Bourdieu, Pierre (1984) *Distinction: A Social Critique of the Judgement of Taste,* Cambridge: Harvard University Press.

Bourdieu, Pierre (1998) *Acts of Resistance: Against the Tyranny of the Market,* New York: The New Press.

Bourke, Joanna (2011) *What It Means to Be Human: Historical Reflections from the 1800s to the Present,* London: Virago.

Bowker, Geoffrey C. and Star, Susan Leigh (1999) *Sorting Things Out: Classification and its Consequences,* Cambridge, MA: MIT Press.

Bowman, David (1998) 'Death of biodiversity – The urgent need for a global ecology', *Global Ecology and Biogeography Letters,* 7: 237–240.

Boxer, Charles Ralph (1965) *The Dutch Seaborne Empire, 160–1800,* New York: Alfred A. Knopf.

Boykoff, Maxwell T. (2008) 'The cultural politics of climate change discourse in UK tabloids', *Political Geography,* 27 (5): 549–569.

Boykoff, Maxwell T. (2011) *Who Speaks for the Climate? Making Sense of Media Reporting on Climate Change,* Cambridge: CUP.

Brand, Ulrich (2012) 'Green economy – The next oxymoron? No lessons learned from failures of implementing sustainable development', *GAIA,* 21 (1): 28–32.

Brandis, Dietrich (2012), *Indian Forestry,* New York: Ulan Press.

Brass, Paul R. (2000) 'Foucault steals political science', *Annual Review of Political Science,* 3 (1): 305–330.

Brassett, James (2009) 'British irony, global justice: A pragmatic reading of Chris Brown, Banksy and Ricky Gervais', *Review of International Studies,* 35 (1): 219–245.

Brauch, Hans-Guenter (2005) *Threats, Challenges, Vulnerabilities and Risks in Environmental and Human Security,* UNU-EHS Source No. 1/2005.

Brauch, Hans-Guenter, Dalby, Simon and Oswald Spring, Ursula (2011) 'Political Geoecology for the Anthropocene' in H. G. Brauch et al. (eds) *Coping with Global Environmental Change, Disasters and Security Threats, Challenges, Vulnerabilities and Risks,* Berlin: Springer-Verlag, 1453–1485.

Braun, Bruce (2000) 'Producing vertical territory: Geology and governmentality in late Victorian Canada', *Ecumene,* 7 (1): 7–46.

Braun, Bruce (2002) *The Intemperate Rainforest: Nature, Culture and Power on Canada's West Coast,* Minneapolis: University of Minnesota Press.

Braun, Bruce (2007) 'Biopolitics and the molecularization of life', *Cultural Geographies,* 14 (1): 6–28.

Braun, Bruce and Castree, Noel (eds) (1998) *Remaking Reality: Nature at the Millennium,* London: Routledge.

Braun, Bruce and Whatmore, Sarah J. (2010) *Political Matter: Technoscience, Democracy, and Public Life,* Minneapolis: University of Minnesota Press.

Brennan, Theresa (2003) *Globalization and Its Terrors: Daily Life in the West,* New York: Routledge.

Brenton, Tony (1994) *The Greening of Machiavelli: The Evolution of International Environmental Politics,* London: RIIA and Earthscan.

Bridge, Gavin (2007) 'Acts of enclosure: Claim staking and land conversion in Guyana's gold fields', in Nik Heynen, James McCarthy, Scott Prudham and Paul Robbins (eds) *Neoliberal Environments: False Promises and Unnatural Consequences,* Abingdon: Routledge, 74–88.

Brigg, Morgan and Bleiker, Roland (2010) 'Autoethnographic International Relations: Exploring the self as a source of knowledge', *Review of International Studies,* 36 (3), 779–798.

Brockington, Daniel (2002) *Fortress Conservation: The Preservation of the Mkomazi Game Reserve, Tanzania,* London: James Currey.

Brockington, Daniel (2009) *Celebrity and the Environment: Fame, Wealth, and Power in Conservation,* London: Zed Books.

Brockington, Daniel and Duffy, Rosaleen (2010) 'Capitalism and conservation: The production and reproduction of biodiversity conservation', *Antipode,* 42 (3): 469–484.

Brockington, Daniel and Duffy, Rosaleen (eds) (2011) *Capitalism and Conservation,* London: Blackwell Publishers.

Brockington, Daniel, Duffy, Rosaleen and Igoe, James (2008) *Nature Unbound: Conservation, Capitalism, and the Future of Protected Areas,* London: Earthscan.

Brockington, Daniel and Igoe, James (2006) 'Eviction for Conservation: a Global Overview', *Conservation and Society,* 4 (3): 424–470.

Brooks, Andrew (2013) 'Stretching global production networks: The international second-hand clothing trade', *Geoforum,* 44: 10–22.

Brosius, Peter (2004) 'Indigenous peoples at the World Parks Congress', *Conservation Biology,* 18 (5): 609–612.

Brown, Chris (1994) '"Turtles all the way down": Anti-foundationalism, Critical Theory and International Relations", *Millennium,* 23 (2): 213–236.

Brown, David (1999) *Addicted to Rent: Corporate and Spatial Distribution of Forest Resources in Indonesia: Implications for Forest Sustainability and Government Policy,* Jakarta: UK Tropical Forestry Mangement Programme.

Brown, Katrina (1998) 'The political ecology of biodiversity conservation and development in Nepal's Terai: Confused meanings, means and ends', *Ecological Economics,* 24: 73–87.

Brown, Lester (1977) *Redefining National Security,* Worldwatch Paper 14, Washington DC: Worldwatch Institute.

Brown, Lester (1981) *Building a Sustainable Society,* New York: Norton.

Brown, Lester (2009) *Plan B 4.0: Mobilizing to Save Civilization,* New York: W.W. Norton & Company.

Brown, Wendy (2010) *Walled States, Waning Sovereignty,* Cambridge, MA: MIT Press.

Brunnengräber, Achim (2006) 'The political economy of the Kyoto Protocol', in Leo Panitch and Colin Leys (eds) *Socialist Register 2007: coming to Terms with Nature,* London: Merlin Press, 213–230.

Brunnschweller, Christa and Bulte, Erwin (2008) 'Linking natural resources to slow growth', *Science,* 616–617.

Bryant, Raymond L. (1998) 'Power, knowledge and political ecology in the Third World', *Progress in Physical Geography,* 22 (1): 79–94.

Bryant, Raymond L. (2010) 'Consuming Burmese teak: Anatomy of a violent luxury resource', in M. Goodman, D. Goodman and M. Redclift (eds) *Consuming Space: Placing Consumption in Perspective,* Farnham: Ashgate, 239–256.

Bryant, Raymond L. and Goodman, Michael K. (2004) 'Consuming narratives: The political ecology of "alternative" consumption', *Transactions of the Institute of British Geographers,* 29: 344–66.

Bulkeley, Harriet and Schroeder, Heike (2012) 'Beyond state/non-state divides: Global cities and the governing of climate change', *European Journal of International Relations* 18 (4): 743–766.

Bulkeley, Harriet, Andonova, Liliana, Bäckstrand, Karin, Betsill, Michele, Compagnon, Daniel, Duffy, Rosaleen et al. (2012) 'Governing climate change transnationally: Assessing the evidence from a database of sixty initiatives', *Environment and Planning C: Government and Policy*, 30 (4): 591–612.

Bull, Hedley (1977) *The Anarchical Society: A Study of Order in Modern Politics*, New York: Columbia University Press.

Bullard, Nicola (2009) 'The state of climate politics', Speech delivered at a Rosa Luxemburg Foundation conference in Johannesburg, South Africa, 19 November.

Bullard, Robert D. (1990) *Dumping in Dixie: Race, Class and Environmental Quality*, Boulder, CO: Westview Press.

Bullard, Robert D. (2013) 'Environmental justice in the 21st century'. Available at http://www.ejrc.cau.edu/ejinthe21century.htm (accessed 12 April 2013).

Bullen, Anna and Whitehead, Mark (2005) 'Negotiating the networks of space, time and substance: A geographical perspective on the sustainable citizen', *Citizenship Studies*, 9: 499–516.

Bumpus, Adam G. and Liverman, Diana M. (2008) 'Accumulation by Decarbonization and the Governance of Carbon Offsets', *Economic Geography*, 84 (2): 127–155.

Burchell, Graham, Gordon, Colin and Miller, Peter (eds) (1991) *The Foucault Effect: Studies in Governmentality*, London: Harvester Wheatsheaf.

Burchell, Graham (1996) 'Liberal government and techniques of the self', in Andrew Barry, Thomas Osborne and Nicholas Rose (eds) *Foucault and Political Reason: Liberalism, Neo-Liberalism and Rationalities of Government*, Chicago: University of Chicago Press, 19–36.

Burgess, John W. (1994) *The Foundations of Political Science*, New Brunswick, NJ: Transaction Publishers.

Burgess, Jacquie, Harrison, C. M. and Filius, P. (1998) 'Environmental communication and the cultural politics of environmental citizenship', *Environment and Planning A*, 30 (8): 1445–1460.

Busby, Josh (2008) 'Who cares about the weather? Climate change and U.S. national security', *Security Studies*, 17: 468–504.

Büscher, Bram (2008) 'Conservation, Neoliberalism and Social Science: A critical reflection on the SCB 2007 Annual Meeting, South Africa', *Conservation Biology*, 22 (2): 229–231.

Büscher, Bram (2011) 'Derivative nature: Interrogating the value of conservation in "Boundless Southern Africa"', *Third World Quarterly*, 31 (2): 259–276.

Büscher, Bram (2012) 'Payments for ecosystem services as neoliberal conservation: (reinterpreting) Evidence from the Maloti-Drakensberg, South Africa', *Conservation & Society*, 10 (1): 29–41.

Büscher, Bram (2013) *Transforming the Frontier: Peace Parks and the Politics of Neoliberal Conservation in Southern Africa*, Durham, NC: Duke University Press.

Büscher, Bram (in press) 'Nature on the move: The emergence and circulation of liquid nature and fictitious conservation,' *New Proposals: Journal of Marxism and Interdisciplinary Enquiry*.

Büscher, Bram and Davidov, Veronica (eds) (2013) *The Ecotourism – Extraction Nexus: Political Economies and Rural Realities of (un)Comfortable Bedfellows*, Abingdon: Routledge.

Büscher, Bram and Igoe, James (2013, in press) 'Prosuming Conservation? Web 2.0, nature, and the intensification of value producing nature in late capitalism', *Journal of Consumer Culture*, 13 (3).

Büscher, Bram, Sullivan, Sian, Neves, Katja, Igoe, James and Brockington, Daniel (2012) 'Towards a synthesized critique of neoliberal biodiversity conservation', *Capitalism Nature Socialism*, 23 (2): 4–30.

Bush, Vannevar (1945) *Science – The Endless Frontier*, Washington DC: Government Printing Office.

Business and Biodiversity (2012) *Resource Center.* Available at http://www.businessandbiodiversity.org/index.html (accessed 16 May 2012).

Butler, Judith (1990) *Gender Trouble: Feminism and the Subversion of Identity*, London: Routledge.

Cahen, Harley (1988) 'Against the moral considerability of ecosystems', *Environmental Ethics*, 10: 195–216.

Caillon, Sophie and Degeorges, Patrick (2007) 'Biodiversity: Negotiating the border between nature and culture', *Biodiversity Conservation*, 16: 2919–2931.

Cairns, John (2005) 'Avoiding a posthuman world', *Science and Society,* 3 (1): 17–28.

Caldecott, Leonie and Leyland, Stephanie (eds) (1983) *Reclaim the Earth,* London: Women's Press.

Callicott, J. Baird (1980) 'Animal Liberation: A triangular affair', *Environmental Ethics,* 2: 311–328.

Callicott, J. Baird (1984) 'Non-Anthropocentric Value Theory and Environmental Ethics', *American Philosophical Quarterly,* 21: 299–309.

Callicott, J. Baird (ed.) (1987) *Companion to A Sand County Almanac: Interpretive and Critical Essays,* Madison: University of Wisconsin Press.

Callicott, J. Baird (1988) 'Animal Liberation and Environmental Ethics: Back together again', *Between the Species,* 4: 163–169.

Callicott, J. Baird (1999) 'Holistic Environmental Ethics and the problem of Ecofascism', in *Beyond the Land Ethic: More Essays in Environmental Philosophy,* Albany: SUNY Press.

Callon, Michel (1986) 'Some elements of a sociology of translation: Domestication of the scallops and the fishermen of Saint Brieuc Bay', in J. Law (ed.) *Power, Action and Belief: A new Sociology of Knowledge?* London: Routledge and Kegan Paul, 196–233.

Callon, Michel (2008) 'Civilizing markets: Carbon trading between in vitro and in vivo experiments', *Accounting, Organizations and Society,* 34 (3/4): 535–548.

Camacho, David (1998) *Environmental Injustices, Political Struggles: Race, Class, and the Environment,* Durham: Duke University Press.

Campbell, Timothy (2011) *Improper Life: Technology and Biopolitics from Heidegger to Agamben,* Minneapolis: University of Minnesota Press.

Carlassare, Elizabeth (1994) 'Essentialism in ecofeminist discourse', in Carolyn Merchant (ed.) *Ecology: Key Concepts in Cultural Theory,* Atlantic Highlands, NJ: Humanities Press.

Carolan, Michael (2010) 'The mutability of biotechnology patents: From unwieldy products of nature to independent "object/s"', *Theory, Culture & Society,* 27 (1): 110–129.

Carr, Edward Hallett (2001) [1939] *The Twenty Years' Crisis 1919–1939: An Introduction to the Study of International Relations,* Basingstoke: Palgrave Macmillan.

Carrier, James and Macleod, Daniel (2005) 'Bursting the bubble: The socio-cultural context of ecotourism,' *Journal of the Royal Anthropological Institute,* 11: 315–334.

Carrier, James and Luetchford, Peter G. (eds) (2012) *Ethical Consumption: Social Value and Economic Practice,* Berghahn: New York and Oxford.

Carroll, Patrick (2012) 'Water and technoscientific state formation in California,' *Social Studies of Science,* 42 (4): 489–516.

Carson, Rachel (1962) *Silent Spring,* Boston, MA: Houghton Mifflin.

Carter, Neil (2007) *The Politics of the Environment: Ideas, Activism, Policy,* Second edition, Cambridge: Cambridge University Press.

Carter, Neil (2013) 'Greening the mainstream: Party politics and the environment', *Environmental Politics,* 22 (1): 73–94.

Castells, Manuel (1997) *The Information Age: Economy, Society and Culture; Volume 2: The Power of Identity,* Oxford: Blackwell.

Castree, Noel (2003a) 'Commodifying what nature?' *Progress in Human Geography,* 27 (3): 273–297.

Castree, Noel (2003b) 'Bioprospecting: From theory to practice (and back again)', *Transactions of the Institute of British Geographers,* 28 (1): 35–55.

Castree, Noel (2006) 'A Congress of the World', *Science as Culture,* 15 (2): 159–170.

Castree, Noel (2008) 'Neoliberalising nature: The logics of deregulation and reregulation', *Environment and Planning A,* 40 (1): 131–152.

Castree, Noel and Braun, Bruce (1998) 'The construction of nature and the nature of construction: Analytical and political tools for building survivable futures', in Bruce Braun and Noel Castree (eds) *Remaking Reality: Nature at the Millennium,* London: Routledge.

Castree, Noel and Braun, Bruce (2001) *Social Nature,* London: Blackwell.

Cato Institute (2009) 'Global warming and climate change', Chapter 45, *Cato Handbook for Policymakers,* Seventh edition, Washington DC: Cato Institute.

Convention on Biological Diversity [CBD] (2010) *Global Biodiversity Outlook 3,* Montreal: CBD Secretariat.

Convention on Biological Diversity [CBD] (2012) *Article 1. Objectives.* Available at http://www.cbd.int/convention/articles/?a=cbd-01 (accessed 16 May 2012).

Chan, Michelle (2009) *Subprime Carbon? Re-thinking the World's Largest New Derivatives Market,* Washington DC: Friends of the Earth US.

Chandler, David (2012) 'Development as freedom? From colonialism to countering climate change', *Development Dialogue,* 58: 115–129.

Chapin, Mac (2004) 'A challenge to conservationists,' *Worldwatch,* Nov/Dec: 17–31.

Chappelles, Heather (2008) 'Systematically sustainable provision? The premises and promises of "joined-up" energy demand management', *International Journal of Environmental Technology and Management,* 9 (2/3): 259–275.

Charlesworth, Mark and Okereke, Chukwumerije (2009) 'A call to reason', *Nature Reports Climate Change,* 12 November, DOI:10.1038/climate.2009.118

Charlesworth, Mark and Okereke, Chukwumerije (2010) 'Policy responses to rapid climate change: An epistemological critique of dominant approaches', *Global Environmental Change,* 20 (1): 121–129.

Chasek, Pamela S. (2001) *Earth Negotiations: Analyzing Thirty Years of Environmental Diplomacy,* Tokyo: UNUP.

Chatterjee, Pratap and Finger, Matthias (1994) *The Earth Brokers: Power, Politics and World Development,* London: Routledge.

Chew, Sing C. (2001) *World Ecological Degradation: Accumulation, Urbanization and Deforestation 3000 BC–AD 2000,* Altamira: Walnut Creek CA.

Christensen, Henrik S. (2011) 'Political activities on the Internet: Slacktivism or political participation by other means?' *First Monday,* 16 (2). Available at http://firstmonday.org/htbin/cgiwrap/bin/ojs/index.php/fm/article/view/3336/2767 (accessed 16 July 2012).

Christoff, Peter (2010) 'Cold climate in Copenhagen: China and the United States at COP15', *Environmental Politics,* 19 (4): 637–656.

Clapp, Jennifer (2005) 'Global environmental governance for corporate responsibility and accountability', *Global Environmental Politics,* 5 (3): 23–34.

Clark, Brett and York, Richard (2005) 'Carbon metabolism: Global capitalism, climate change, and the biospheric rift', *Theory and Society,* 34 (4): 391–428.

Clark, Nigel (2011) *Inhuman Nature. Sociable Life on a Dynamic Planet,* London: Sage.

Clarke, Nick, Barnett, Clive, Cloke, Paul and Malpass, Alice (2007) 'Globalising the consumer: Doing politics in an ethical register', *Political Geography,* 26 (3): 231–249.

Clements, Frederic E. (1916) *Plant Succession: An Analysis of the Development of Vegetation,* Washington DC: Carnegie Institute.

CNA Corporation (2007) *National Security and the Threat of Climate Change,* Alexandria, VA: CNA Corporation.

Coe, Neil M., Dicken, Peter and Hess, Martin (2008) 'Global production networks: Realizing the potential', *Journal of Economic Geography,* 8 (3): 271–295.

Cohen, Maurice J. and Murphy, Joseph (2001) (eds) *Exploring Sustainable Consumption: Environmental Policy and the Social Sciences,* Pergmon: Oxford.

Coleman, Mathew and Grove, Kevin (2009) 'Biopolitics, biopower, and the "return" of sovereignty', *Environment and Planning D: Society and Space,* 27: 489–507.

Collard, Andrée with Contrucci, Joyce (1988) *Rape of the Wild: Man's Violence Against Animals and the Earth,* London: The Women's Press.

Collier, Paul (2007) *The Bottom Billion: Why the Pourest Countries are Failing and What Can Be Done About It,* London: Oxford University Press.

Collier, Stephen (2009) 'Topologies of power: Foucault's analysis of political government beyond 'governmentality'', *Theory, Culture & Society,* 26(6): 78–108.

Collier, Stephen and Lakoff, Andrew (2008) 'The vulnerability of vital systems: How "critical infrastructure" became a security problem', in Myriam Dunn and Kristian Kristensen (eds) *Securing the Homeland: Critical Infrastructure, Risk and (In)security,* Abingdon and New York: Routledge.

Collier, Stephen and Ong, Aihwa (2005) 'Global assemblages, anthropological problems', in Aihwa Ong and Stephen Collier (eds) *Global Assemblages: Technology, Politics and Ethics as Anthropological Problems,* Malden MA: Blackwell, 3–21.

Collins, Andrea, Cowell, Richard and Flynn, Andrew (2009) 'Evaluation and environmental governance: The institutionalisation of ecological footprinting', *Environment and Planning A,* 41 (7): 1707–1725.

Comaroff, Jean and Comaroff, John L. (2012) *Theory from the South; Or, How Euro-America is Evolving Toward Africa,* Boulder, CO: Paradigm.

Commoner, Barry (1971) *The Closing Circle: Nature, Man, and Technology,* New York: Knopf.

Conca, Ken (2005) 'Old states in new bottles? The hybridization of authority in global environmental governance', in John Barry and Robin Eckersley (eds) *The State and the Global Ecological Crisis,* Cambridge, MA: MIT Press.

Connaughton, Bernadette, Quinn, Brid and Rees, Nicholas (2008) 'Rhetoric or reality: Responding to the challenge of sustainable development and new governance patterns in Ireland', in S. Baker and K. Eckerberg (eds) *In Pursuit of Sustainable Development: New Governance Practices at the Sub-national Level in Europe,* Abingdon/New York: Routledge/ECPR studies in European Political Science, 145–168.

Connelly, James, Smith, Graham, Benson, David and Saunders, Clare (2012) *Politics of the Environment: From Theory to Practice,* Abingdon: Routledge.

Connelly, Steve (2007) 'Mapping sustainable development as a contested concept', *Local Environment,* 12: 259–278.

Constantinou, Costas M. (1994) 'Diplomatic representation … or Who framed the ambassadors?' *Millennium,* 23 (1): 1–23.

Constantinou, Costas M. (1996) *On the Way to Diplomacy,* Minneapolis: University of Minnesota Press.

Constantinou, Costas M. (1998) 'Before the summit: Representations of sovereignty on the Himalayas', *Millennium,* 27 (1): 23–53.

Constitution of Ecuador (2008) English text available from *Political Database of the Americas.* Available at http://pdba.georgetown.edu/Constitutions/Ecuador/english08.html (accessed 14 February 2013).

Cook, Ian (2004) 'Follow the thing: Papaya', *Antipode* 36 (4): 642–664.

Cook, Ian and Crang, Philip (1996) 'The world on a plate: Culinary culture, displacement and geographical knowledges', *Journal of Material Culture,* 1: 131–53.

Coole, Diana H. and Frost, Samantha (eds) (2010) *New Materialisms,* Durham NC: Duke University Press.

Cooper, Melinda (2006) 'Pre-empting emergence: The biological turn in the war on terror', *Theory, Culture & Society,* 23 (4): 113–135.

Cooper, Melinda (2008) *Life As Surplus: Biotechnology and Capitalism in the Neoliberal Era,* Seattle: University of Washington Press.

Cooper, Melinda (2010) 'Turbulent worlds: Financial markets and environmental crisis', *Theory, Culture & Society,* 27 (2–3): 167–190.

Cosgrove, Dennis (2008) *Geography and vision: Seeing, imagining and representing the world,* International Library of Human Geography, London: I. B. Tauris.

Courson, Elias (2009) *Movement for the Emancipation of the Niger Delta,* Uppsala: Nordic Africa Institute.

Cox, Robert W. (1981) 'Social forces, states and world orders: Beyond International Relations Theory', *Millennium: Journal of International Studies,* 10 (2): 126–155.

Cox, Robert W. (1997) 'Democracy in hard times: Economic globalisation and the limits to liberal democracy', in Anthony McGrew (ed.) *The Transformation of Democracy?* Cambridge: Polity Press, 49–72.

Cox, Robert W. (2001) 'The way ahead: Toward a new ontology of world order', in Richard Wyn Jones (ed.) *Critical Theory and World Politics,* Boulder, CO: Lynne Rienner.

Cramer, Christopher (2006) *Violence in Developing Countries,* Bloomington: Indiana University Press.

Crang, Philip, Jackson, Peter and Dwyer, Claire (2003) 'Transnationalism and the spaces of commodity culture', *Progress in Human Geography,* 27: 438–456.

Crenshaw, Kimberlé W. (1991) 'Mapping the margins: Intersectionality, identity politics, and violence against women of colour', *Stanford Law Review,* 43 (6): 1241–99.

Cribb, Robert (1991) *Gangsters and Revolutionaries: The Jakarta People's Militia and the Indonesian Revolution, 1945–1949,* Honolulu: University of Hawaii Press.

Cronon, William (1996) 'The trouble with wilderness or getting back to the wrong nature,' in William Cronon (ed.) *Uncommon Ground: Rethinking the Human Place in Nature,* New York: W.W. Norton.

Crosby, Alfred (1986) *Ecological Imperialism: The Biological Expansion of Europe, 900–1900,* Cambridge, Cambridge University Press.

Crutzen, Paul J. and Stoermer, Eugene F. (2000) 'The "Anthropocene"', *Global Change Newsletter,* 41: 17–18.

Cudworth, Erika (2005) *Developing Ecofeminist Theory: The Complexity of Difference,* Basingstoke: Palgrave.

Cudworth, Erika (2011) *Social Lives with Other Animals: Tales of Sex, Death and Love,* Basingstoke: Palgrave.

Cudworth, Erika and Hobden, Stephen (2009) 'More than a metaphor? Complexity in the social sciences', *International Journal of Interdisciplinary Social Sciences,* 4 (4): 59–70.

Cudworth, Erika and Hobden, Stephen (2011) *Posthuman International Relations: Complexity, Ecologism and Global Politics,* London: Zed.

Cudworth, Erika and Hobden, Stephen (2012) 'The foundations of complexity, the complexity of foundations', *Philosophy of the Social Sciences,* 42 (2): 163–187.

Cuomo, Christine (1998) *Feminism and Ecological Communities: An Ethic of Flourishing,* London: Routledge.

Cutajar, Michael Zammit (2001) 'Notes for closing session', in *Global Change Open Science Conference (IGBP – IHDP – WCRP),* Amsterdam: International Human Dimensions Program on Global Environmental Change.

Dabelko, Geoff (2008) 'An uncommon peace: Environment, development and the global security agenda', *Environment,* 50 (3): 32–45.

Dalby, Simon (2002) *Environmental Security,* Minneapolis: University of Minnesota Press.

Dalby, Simon (2009) *Security and Environmental Change,* Cambridge: Polity.

Dalby, Simon, Katz-Rosene, Ryan and Paterson, Matthew (2013) 'Ecological political economy', in Ronen Palan (ed.) *Global Political Economy: Contemporary Theories,* Second edition, Abingdon: Routledge, 219–231.

Daly, Herman (1973) *Toward a Steady-State Economy,* San Francisco: WH Freeman & Co.

Daly, Herman (1991) *Steady State Economics,* Second edition, Washington DC: Island Press.

Daly, Herman (1996) *Beyond Growth: The Economics of Sustainable Development,* Boston MA: Beacon Press.

Daly, Herman (2005) 'Economics in a full world', *Scientific American,* September: 100–107.

Daly, Herman and Townsend, Kenneth N. (1993) *Valuing the Earth: Economics, Ecology, Ethics,* Cambridge, MA: MIT Press.

Daly, Mary (1979) *Gyn/Ecology: The Metaethics of Radical Feminism,* London: The Women's Press.

Daly, Mary (1984) *Pure Lust,* London: Women's Press.

Daly, Mary with Caputi, Jane (1988) *Websters' First New Intergalactic Wickedary of the English Language,* London: Women's Press.

Darier, Eric (1999) 'Foucault and the environment: An introduction', in Eric Darier (ed.) *Discourses of the Environment,* Oxford: Blackwell, 1–33.

Darwin, Francis (ed.) (1911) [1887] *The Life and Letters of Charles Darwin, vol. 2,* London: John Murray Publishers.

Dauvergne, Peter (2008) *The Shadows of Consumption: Consequences for the Global Environment,* Cambridge, MA: MIT Press.

Davidov, Veronica (2012) 'From a Blind Spot to a Nexus: Building on Existing Trends in Knowledge Production to Study the Co-Presence of Eco-Tourism and Extraction', *Environment and Society: Advances in Research,* 3 (1): 78–102.

Davion, Victoria (1994) 'Is ecofeminism feminist?' in Karen Warren (ed.) *Ecological Feminism,* London: Routledge.

Dean, Hartley (2001) 'Green citizenship', *Social Policy & Administration,* 35 (5): 490–505.

Dean, Mitchell (1994) *Critical and Effective Histories: Foucault's Methods and Historical Sociology,* London: Routledge.

Dean, Mitchell (1999) *Governmentality. Power and Rule in Modern Society,* London: Sage.

Dean, Mitchell (2007) *Governing Societies,* Maidenhead: Open University Press.

Dean, Mitchell (2010) *Governmentality: Power and Rule in Modern Society,* Second edition, London: Sage.

Debord, Guy (1995) [1967] *The Society of the Spectacle,* New York: Zone Books.

Death, Carl (2010) *Governing Sustainable Development: Partnerships, Protests and Power at the World Summit,* Abingdon: Routledge.

Death, Carl (2011) 'Summit theatre: Exemplary governmentality and environmental diplomacy in Johannesburg and Copenhagen', *Environmental Politics,* 20 (1): 1–19.

De Landa, Manuel (1991) *War in the Age of Intelligent Machines,* New York: Zone Books.

Deleuze, Gilles and Foucault, Michel (2004) 'Intellectuals and power,' in David Lapoujade (ed.) *Desert Islands,* New York: Semiotext(e).

Deleuze, Gilles and Guattari, Félix (1987) *A Thousand Plateaus: Capitalism and Schizophrenia,* Minneapolis: University of Minnesota Press.

Della Porta, Donatella (2007) *The Global Justice Movement: Cross-national and Transnational Perspectives,* Boulder, CO: Paradigm.

Della Porta, Donatella, Andretta, Massimiliano, Mosca, Lorenzo and Reiter, Herbert (2006) *Globalization from Below: Transnational Activists and Protest Networks,* Minneapolis: University of Minnesota Press.

Demeritt, David (2002) '"What is the "social construction of nature"? A typology and sympathetic critique', *Progress in Human Geography,* 26 (6): 767–790.

Denevan, William (1989) 'The fragile lands of Latin America', in J. Browder (ed.) *The Fragile Lands of Latin America: Strategies for Sustainable Development,* Boulder: Westview Press, 3–25.

Denevan, William M. (1992) 'The Pristine Myth: The landscape of the Americas in 1492', *Annals of the Association of American Geographers,* 82 (3): 369–385.

Depledge, Joanne (2005) *The Organization of Global Negotiations: Constructing the Climate Change Regime,* London: Earthscan.

Descartes, René (1999) [1637] 'Discourse on the method for guiding one's reason and searching for truth in the sciences' in *Discourse on Method and Related Writings,* trans. Desmond M. Clarke, London: Penguin, 5–54.

De Soysa, Indra (2002) 'Ecoviolence: Shrinking Pie or Honey Pot?' *Global Environmental Politics,* 2(4): 1–34.

Desrochers, Pierre and Shimizu, Hiroko (2012) *The Locavore's Dilemma: In Praise of the 10,000-Mile Diet,* New York: PublicAffairs.

Deudney, Daniel (1990) 'The case against linking environmental degradation and national security', *Millennium,* 19: 461–476.

Devall, Bill (1990) *Simple in Means, Rich in Ends,* London: Greenprint.

Devall, Bill and Sessions, George (1985) *Deep Ecology: Living as if Nature Mattered,* Layton, UT: Gibbs M. Smith.

DeYoung, Raymond and Princen, Thomas (eds) (2012) *The Localization Reader: Adapting to the Coming Downshift,* Cambridge, MA: The MIT Press.

DeYoung, Raymond and Princen, Thomas (2012) 'Downshift/Upshift: Our Choice' in Raymond DeYoung and Thomas Princen (eds) *The Localization Reader: Adapting to the Coming Downshift,* Cambridge, MA: The MIT Press.

Diamond, Jared (2005) *Collapse: How Societies Choose to Fail or Survive,* London: Penguin.

Diani, Mario (1992) 'The concept of social movement', *The Sociological Review,* 40 (1): 1–25.

Dicken, Peter (2011) *Global Shift: Mapping the Changing Contours of the World Economy,* Sixth edition, London: Sage.

Dickens, Peter (1996) *Reconstructing Nature: Alienation, Emancipation and the Division of Labour,* London: Routledge.

Dillon, Michael (1995) 'Sovereignty and governmentality: From the problematics of the "new world order" to the ethical problematic of world order', *Alternatives,* 20: 323–368.

Dillon, Michael (1996) *Politics of Security: Towards a Political Philosophy of Continental Thought,* New York: Routledge.

Dillon, Michael (2007a) 'Governing terror: The state of emergency of biopolitical emergence', *International Political Sociology,* 1 (1): 7–28.

Dillon, Michael (2007b) 'Governing through contingency: The security of biopolitical governance', *Political Geography,* 26: 41–47.

Dillon, Michael (2008) 'Underwriting security', *Security Dialogue,* 39 (2–3): 309–332.

Dillon, Michael and Lobo-Guerrero, Luis (2008) 'Biopolitics of security in the 21st century: An introduction', *Review of International Studies,* 34: 265–292.

Dillon, Michael and Reid, Julian (2009) *The Liberal Way of War: Killing to Make Life Live,* Abingdon: Routledge.

Dobson, Andrew (1990) *Green Political Thought,* Second edition, London: Routledge.

Dobson, Andrew (1996) 'Democratising Green Theory: Preconditions and principles', in Brian Doherty and Marius de Geus (eds) *Democracy and Green Political Thought: Sustainability, Rights, and Citizenship,* London: Routledge.

Dobson, Andrew (1998) *Justice and the Environment: Conceptions of Environmental Sustainability and Dimensions of Social Justice,* Oxford: Oxford University Press.

Dobson, Andrew (ed.) (1999) *Fairness and Futurity: Essays on Environmental Sustainability and Social Justice,* Oxford: Oxford University Press.

Dobson, Andrew (2003) *Citizenship and the Environment,* Oxford: Oxford University Press.

Dobson, Andrew (2006) 'Ecological citizenship: A defence', *Environmental Politics,* 15 (3): 447–451.

Dobson, Andrew (2007) 'Environmental citizenship: Towards sustainable development', *Sustainable Development,* 15 (5): 276–285.

Dobson, Andrew (2009) 'Citizens, citizenship and governance for sustainability', in W. Neil Adger and Andrew Jordan (eds) *Governing Sustainability,* Cambridge: Cambridge University Press.

Dobson, Andrew and Bell, Derek (eds) (2006) *Environmental Citizenship,* Cambridge, MA: MIT Press.

Dobson, Andrew and Sáiz, Ángel V. (2005) 'Special Issue – Citizenship, Environment, Economy: Introduction', *Environmental Politics,* 14 (2): 157–162.

Doherty, Brian (2002) *Ideas and Actions in the Green Movement,* London: Routledge.

Doherty, Brian (2006) 'Friends of the Earth International: Negotiating a transnational identity', *Environmental Politics,* 15 (5): 860–880.

Doherty, Brian and de Geus, Marius (eds) (1996) *Democracy and Green Political Thought: Sustainability, Rights, and Citizenship,* London: Routledge.

Doherty, Brian and Doyle, Timothy (2006) 'Beyond borders: Transnational politics, social movements and modern environmentalisms', *Environmental Politics,* 15 (5): 697–712.

Dolan, Catherine S. (2011) 'Branding Morality: The Case of Fairtrade', in Meera Warrier (ed.) *The Politics of Fair Trade: A Survey,* Abingdon: Routledge, 37–52.

Domosh, Mona (2006) *American Commodities in an Age of Empire,* Abingdon: Routledge.

Doubiago, Sharon (1989) 'Mama coyote talks to the boys', in Judith Plant (ed.) *Healing the Wounds: The Promise of Ecofeminism,* London: Green Print.

Douglas, Mary (1992) *Risk and Blame: Essays in Cultural Theory,* London: Routledge.

Douglas, Mary and Wildavsky, Aaron (1982) *Risk and Culture,* Berkeley: University of California Press.

Dowie, Mark (2009) *Conservation Refugees: The 100-Year Conflict Between Global Conservation and Native Peoples,* Cambridge, MA: MIT Press.

Drake, Frances (2010) 'Protesting mobile phone masts: Risk, neoliberalism, and governmentality', *Science, Technology & Human Values,* 36 (4): 522–548.

Drengson, Alan and Inoue, Yuichi (eds) (1995) *The Deep Ecology Movement: An Introductory Anthology,* Berkeley: North Atlantic Books.

Dresner, Simon (2002) *The Principles of Sustainability,* London: Earthscan.

Dressler, Wolfram (2011) 'First to Third Nature: The rise of Capitalist Conservation in Palawan, The Philippines', *Journal of Peasant Studies,* 38 (3): 533–557.

Dryzek, John (1987) *Rational Ecology Environment and Political Economy,* Oxford: Blackwell.

Dryzek, John (1990) *Discursive Democracy: Politics, Policy, and Political Science,* Cambridge: CUP.

Dryzek, John (2005) *The Politics of the Earth: Environmental Discourses,* Oxford: Oxford University Press.

Dryzek, John, Norgaard, Richard and Schlosberg, David (2011) *The Oxford Handbook of Climate Change and Society,* Oxford: Oxford University Press.

Du Bois, W. E. B. (1903) *The Souls of Black Folk,* Chicago: A.C. McClurg & Co.

Duffield, Mark (2007) *Development, Security, and Unending War: Governing the World of Peoples,* Cambridge: Polity.

Duffield, Mark (2010) 'The liberal way of development and the development-security impasse: Exploring the global life-chance divide', *Security Dialogue,* 41(1): 53–76.

Duffield, Mark (2011) 'Total war as environmental terror: Linking liberalism, resilience, and the bunker', *The South Atlantic Quarterly,* 110 (3): 757–769.

Duffield, Mark and Waddell, Nicholas (2006) 'Securing humans in a dangerous world', *International Politics,* 43 (1): 1–23.

Duffy, Rosaleen (2010) *Nature Crime: How We're Getting Conservation Wrong,* New Haven, CT: Yale University Press.

Dunayer, Joan (1995) 'Sexist Words, Speciesist Roots', in Carol J. Adams and Josephine Donovan (eds) *Animals and Women,* London: Duke University Press.

Dunn, David H. (1996) 'What is summitry?' in David H. Dunn (ed.) *Diplomacy at the Highest Level: The Evolution of International Summitry,* Basingstoke: Macmillan.

DuPuis, E. Melanie and Goodman, David (2005) 'Should we go "home" to eat: Toward a reflexive politics of localism,' *Journal of Rural Studies,* 21 (3): 359–371.

Durant, John, Bauer, Martin W. and Gaskell, George (1998) *Biotechnology in the Public Sphere: A European Source Book,* London: Science Museum Publications.

Durkin, Martin (2007) *The Great Global Warming Swindle,* London: WAGTV. Available at http://www.wagtv.com/shows/detail/showid/38 (accessed 5 July 2013)

Dwyer, Claire and Jackson, Peter (2003) 'Commodifying difference: Selling EASTern fashion', *Environment and Planning D: Society and Space,* 21 (3): 269–291.

Dyer, Gwynne (2008) *Climate Wars,* Toronto: Random House.

Eakin, Hallie and Luers, Amy L. (2006) 'Assessing the vulnerability of social-environmental systems', *Annual Review of Environment and Resources,* 31 (1): 365–394.

Earth Charter Initiative (2000) The Earth Charter. Available at http://www.earthcharterinaction.org/content/pages/Read-the-Charter.html (accessed 27 March 2013).

Eckersley, Robyn (1992) *Environmentalism and Political Theory: Toward an Ecocentric Approach,* Albany: SUNY Press.

Eckersley, Robyn (2004) *The Green State: Rethinking Democracy and Sovereignty,* Cambridge MA: MIT Press.

Eckersley, Robyn (2005) 'Greening the Nation-State: From exclusive to Inclusive sovereignty', in John Barry and Robin Eckersley (eds) *The State and the Global Ecological Crisis,* Cambridge, MA: MIT Press.

Eckersley, Robyn (2012) 'Moving forward in the climate negotiations: Multilateralism or minilateralism?' *Global Environmental Politics,* 12 (2): 24–42.

Eder, Klaus (1993) *The New Politics of Class,* London: Sage.

Edkins, Jenny (1999) *Poststructuralism and International Relations: Bringing the Political Back In,* London: Lynne Rienner.

Ehrenfeld, David (1988) 'Why put a value on biodiversity?' in E. O. Wilson (ed.) *Biodiversity,* Washington DC: National Academy Press.

Ehrenfeld, David (2008) 'Neoliberalization of conservation', *Conservation Biology,* 22 (5): 1091–1092.

Ehrenfeld, David (2009) *Becoming Good Ancestors: How We Balance Nature, Community, and Technology,* Oxford: Oxford University Press.

Ehrlich, Paul (1968) *The Population Bomb,* New York: Ballantine.

Ehrlich, Paul and Ehrlich, Anne (1996) *Betrayal of Science and Reason: How Anti-environmental Rhetoric Threatens Our Future,* Washington DC: Island Books.

Ekers, Michael, Hart, Gillian, Kipfer, Stephan and Loftus, Alex (eds) (2012) *Gramsci: Space, Nature, Politics,* London: Wiley Blackwell.

Elden, Stuart (2001) *Mapping the Present: Heidegger, Foucault, and the Project of a Spatial History,* New York: Continuum.

Elden, Stuart (2007) 'Governmentality, calculation, territory', *Environment and Planning D: Society and Space,* 25: 562–580.

Ellerman, Denny, Convery, Frank and de Perthuis, Christian (2010) *Pricing Carbon: The European Emissions Trading Scheme,* Cambridge: Cambridge University Press.

Ellul, Jacques (1964) *The Technological Society,* New York: Knopf.

Elshtain, Jean, B. (1987) *Women and War,* Brighton: Harvester.

Engel, J. Ronald and Engel, Joan G. (eds) (1990) *Ethics of Environment and Development: Global Challenge, International Response,* London: Belhaven.

Epstein, Steven (1996) *Impure Science: AIDS Activism and the Politics of Knowledge,* Los Angeles: University of California Press.

Escobar, Arturo (1995) *Encountering Development: The Making and Unmaking of the Third World,* Princeton: PUP.

Escobar, Arturo (1999) 'After nature: Steps to an Anti-Essentialist Political Ecology', *Current Anthropology,* 40 (1): 1–30.

Esposito, Roberto (2008) *Bios: Biopolitics and Philosophy,* Minneapolis: University of Minnesota Press.

Esposito, Roberto (2009) *Communitas: The Origin and Destiny of Community,* Stanford: Stanford University Press.

Esposito, Roberto (2011) *Immunitas: The Protection and Negation of Life,* Cambridge: Polity Press.

Esty, Daniel C. (2006) 'Good Governance at the Supranational Scale: Globalizing Administrative Law', *The Yale Law Journal,* 115 (7), 1490–1562.

Esty, Daniel C. and Winston, Andrew (2009) *Green to Gold: How Smart Companies Use Environmental Strategy to Innovate, Create Value, and Build Competitive Advantage,* Hoboken: John Wiley & Sons.

European Commission (2000) *Communication from the Commission on the Precautionary Principle,* Brussels: European Commission, COM(2000) 1 Final.

Evans, David (2011) 'Consuming conventions: Sustainable consumption, ecological citizenship and the worlds of worth', *Journal of Rural Studies,* 27 (2): 109–115.

Fairhead, James and Leach, Melissa (1996) *Misreading the African Landscape: Society and Ecology in a Forest-Savanna Mosaic,* Cambridge: Cambridge University Press.

Fairhead, James, Leach, Melissa and Scoones, Ian (2012) 'Green grabbing: A new appropriation of nature,' *The Journal of Peasant Studies,* 39 (2): 235–261.

Falk, Richard (1971) *This Endangered Planet: Prospects and Proposals for Human Survival,* New York: Vintage Books.

Falk, Richard (1999) *Predatory Globalization: A Critique,* Cambridge: Polity Press.

Farbotko, Carol (2012) 'Skilful seafarers, oceanic drifters or climate refugees? Pacific people, news value and the climate refugee crisis', in Kerry Moore, Bernhard Gross, and Terry Threadgold (eds) *Migrations and the Media,* New York: Peter Lang.

Farbotko, Carol and McGregor, Helen V. (2010) 'Copenhagen, climate science and the emotional geographies of climate change', *Australian Geographer,* 41 (2): 159–166.

Farid, Hilmar (2005) 'Indonesia's Original Sin: Mass killings and capitalist expansion 1965–1966', *Inter-Asia Cultural Studies,* 6 (1): 3–16.

Farrell, Katharine, Kemp, Réne, Hinterberg, Friedrich, Rammel, Christian and Ziegler, Rafael (2005) 'From *for* to governance for sustainable development in Europe: What is at stake for future research?' *International Journal of Sustainable Development,* 8 (1–2): 127–151.

Featherstone, Mike (1991) *Consumer Culture and Postmodernism,* London: Sage.

Federici, Silvia (2012) *Revolution at Point Zero: Housework, Reproduction, and Feminist Struggles,* New York: PM Press.

Feenberg, Andrew (1999) *Questioning Technology,* New York: Routledge.

Felt, Ulrike and Wynne, Brian (eds) (2007) *Taking European Knowledge Society Seriously,* report for the European Commission, Luxembourg: Office for Official Publications of the European Communities. Available at http://ec.europa.eu/research/science-society/document_library/pdf_06/european-knowledge-society_en.pdf (accessed 12 June 2012).

Feschotte, Cédric (2010) 'Bornavirus enters the genome', *Nature,* 463 (7277): 39–40.

Fierke, Karin M. (2007) *Critical Approaches to International Security,* Cambridge: Polity.

Fillieule, Olivier (2013) 'Demobilization' in David A. Snow, Donatella Della Porta, Bert Klandermans and Doug McAdam (eds) *The Wiley-Blackwell Encyclopedia of Social and Political Movements,* Oxford: John Wiley and Sons Ltd.

Fine, Ben (1976) *Marx's Capital,* London: Macmillan Press.

Fine, Ben (2002) *The World of Consumption: The Material and Cultural Revisited,* Second edition, London: Routledge.

Finger, Matthias (1991) 'The military, the nation state, and the environment', *Ecologist,* 21 (5): 220–25.

Fischer, Frank (2003) *Reframing Public Policy: Discursive Politics and Deliberative Practices,* Oxford: Oxford University Press.

Fisher, William F. and Ponniah, Thomas (2003) 'Introduction: The World Social Forum and the reinvention of democracy', in William F. Fisher and Thomas Ponniah (eds) *Another World Is Possible: Popular Alternatives to Globalization at the World Social Forum,* London: Zed Books, 1–20.

Fischhoff, Baruch (1995) 'Risk perception and communication unplugged: Twenty years of process', *Risk Analysis,* 15 (2): 137–145.

Flesher Fominaya, Cristina (2010) 'Creating cohesion from diversity: The challenge of collective identity formation in the Global Justice Movement', *Sociological Inquiry,* 80 (3): 377–404.

Fletcher, Robert (2010) 'Neoliberal environmentality: Toward a post-structuralist political ecology of the conservationist debate,' *Conservation and Society,* 8(3): 171–181.

Floyd, Rita (2010) *Security and the Environment: Securitization Theory and US Environmental Security Policy,* Cambridge: Cambridge University Press.

FoEI-CFS (2008) *Who Benefits from GM Crops? The Rise in Pesticide Use,* London: Friends of the Earth International and the Center for Food Safety.

Folke, Carl (2006) 'Resilience: The emergence of a perspective for social-ecological systems analyses', *Global Environmental Change,* 16, 253–267.

Folke, Carl, Carpenter, Stephen, Walker, Brian, Scheffer, Marten, Chaplin, Terry and Rockström, Johan (2010) 'Resilience thinking: Integrating resilience, adaptability and transformability', *Ecology and Society,* 14 (4): 20.

Folke, Carl, Carpenter, Steve, Elmqvist, Thomas, Gunderson, Lance, Holling, C. S. and Walker, Brian (2002) 'Resilience and sustainable development: Building adaptive capacity in a world of transformations', *AMBIO: A Journal of the Human Environment*, 31 (5): 437–440.

Fomerand, Jacques (1996) 'UN conferences: Media events or genuine diplomacy?' *Global Governance*, 2(3): 361–375.

Ford, Lucy (2003) 'Challenging global environmental governance: Social movement agency and global civil society', *Global Environmental Politics* 3 (2): 120–134.

Foresight (2011) *Migration and Global Environmental Change*, London: The Government Office for Science.

Forest, James (2012) *Confronting Terrorism of Boko Haram in Nigeria*, JSOU Report 12–5 2012, Joint Operations University, Florida.

Forsyth, Tim (2003) *Critical Political Ecology: The Politics of Environmental Science*, London: Routledge.

Forsyth, Tim (2012) 'Politicizing environmental science does not mean denying climate science nor endorsing it without question', *Global Environmental Politics*, 12: 18–23.

Foster, John Bellamy (2002) 'Capitalism and ecology: The nature of the contradiction', *Monthly Review*, 54 (4): 6–16.

Foster, John Bellamy (2009) *The Ecological Revolution: Making Peace with the Planet*, New York: Monthly Review Press.

Foucault, Michel (1970) *The Order of Things: An Archaeology of the Human Sciences*, New York: Vintage.

Foucault, Michel (1977) 'Nietzsche, Geneaology, History', in Donald F. Bouchard (ed.) *Language, Counter-Memory, Practice: Selected Essays and Interviews*, Ithaca: Cornell University Press.

Foucault, Michel (1979) *History of Sexuality, Vol. I: An Introduction*, London: Penguin.

Foucault, Michel (1980a) *History of Sexuality, Vol. I: An Introduction*, New York: Vintage.

Foucault, Michel (1980b) *Power/Knowledge: Selected Interviews & Other Writings, 1972–1977*, New York: Pantheon.

Foucault, Michel (1982a) 'Afterword' in Hubert Dreyfus and Paul Rabinow (eds) *Michel Foucault: Beyond Structuralism and Hermeneutics*, Chicago: The University of Chicago Press, 208–226.

Foucault, Michel (1982b) 'The subject and power', in Hubert Dreyfus and Paul Rabinow (eds) *Michel Foucault: Beyond Structuralism and Hermeneutics*, Brighton: Harvester.

Foucault, Michel (1983) 'On the genealogy of ethics: An overview of work in progress', in Hubert Dreyfus and Paul Rabinow (eds) *Michel Foucault: Beyond Structuralism and Hermeneutics*, Chicago: University of Chicago Press.

Foucault, Michel (1984) 'What is Enlightenment,' in Paul Rabinow (ed.) *The Foucault Reader*, New York: Pantheon.

Foucault, Michel (1988) *Technologies of the Self*, Amherst: University of Massachusetts Press.

Foucault, Michel (1991a) *Discipline and Punish: The Birth of the Prison*, London: Penguin Books.

Foucault, Michel (1991b) 'Governmentality', in Graham Burchell, Colin Gordon and Peter Miller (eds) *The Foucault Effect: Studies in Governmentality*, London: Harvester Wheatsheaf, 87–104.

Foucault, Michel (1991c) 'Questions of Method', in Graham Burchell, Colin Gordon and Peter Miller (eds) *The Foucault Effect: Studies in Governmentality*, London: Harvester Wheatsheaf, 73–86.

Foucault, Michel (1997) 'On the ethics of the concern for self as a practice of freedom', in Paul Rabinow (ed.) *Ethics, Subjectivity and Truth: Essential Works of Foucault 1954–1984*, Vol. 1, New York: The New Press.

Foucault, Michel (2000) 'So it is important to think?' in James D. Faubion (ed.) *Power: Essential Works of Foucault 1954–1984*, Vol. 3, New York: The New Press.

Foucault, Michel (2003) *'Society Must Be Defended': Lectures at the Collège de France, 1975–1976*, New York: Picador.

Foucault, Michel (2007a) *Security, Territory, Population: Lectures at the Collège de France, 1977–1978*, New York: Picador.

Foucault, Michel (2007b) 'What is critique?' in Sylvère Lotringer (ed.) *The Politics of Truth*, Los Angeles: Semiotext(e).

Foucault, Michel (2008) *The Birth of Biopolitics: Lectures at the Collège de France, 1978–1979*, London: Palgrave Macmillan.

Foucault, Michel (2010) *The Government of Self and Others: Lectures at the Collège de France 1982–1983*, Basingstoke: Palgrave Macmillan.

Fox, Warwick (1995) *Toward a Transpersonal Ecology: Developing New Foundations for Environmentalism*, Albany: SUNY Press.

Frank, Andre Gunder (1998) *ReOrient, Global Economy in the Asian Age*, London: University of California Press.

Frank, David John, Hironaka, Ann and Schofer, Evan (2000) 'The nation-state and the natural environment over the twentieth century', *American Sociological Review*, 65: 96–116.

French, Duncan (2002) 'The role of the state and international organizations in reconciling sustainable development and globalization', *International Environmental Agreements: Politics, Law and Economics*, 2: 135–150.

Freudenburg, William, Gramling, Robert and Davidson, Debra (2008) 'Scientific certainty argumentation methods (SCAMs): science and the politics of doubt', *Sociological Inquiry*, 78 (1): 2–38.

Frickel, Scott, Gibbon, Sahra, Howard, Jeff, Kempner, Joanna, Ottinger, Gwen and Hess, David (2010) 'Undone science: Charting social movement and civil society challenges to research agenda settings', *Science, Technology & Human Values*, 35 (4): 444–473.

Fridell, Gavin (2006) 'Fair Trade and Neo-liberalism: Assessing emerging perspectives', *Latin American Perspectives* 33, 6: 8–28.

Friedberg, Susanne (2003) 'Cleaning up down South: Supermarkets, ethical trade and African horticulture', *Social and Cultural Geography*, 4: 27–43.

Friedman, Thomas L. (2009) *Hot, Flat, and Crowded*, New York: Picador / Farrar, Straus and Giroux.

Friel, Howard (2010) *Lomborg Deception: Setting the Record Straight About Global Warming*, New Haven and London: Yale University Press.

Fukuyama, Francis (1992) *The End of History and the Last Man*, New York: Free Press.

Fukuyama, Francis (2002) *Our Posthuman Future, Consequences of the Biotechnology Revolution*, London: Profile Books.

Fuller, R. Buckminster (1969) *Utopia or Oblivion: The Prospects for Humanity*, New York: Bantam Books.

Funtowicz, Silvio and Ravetz, Jerome (1993) 'Science for the post-normal age', *Futures*, 25 (7): 739–755.

Furedi, Frank (2007) 'The changing meaning of disaster', *Area*, 39 (4): 482–489.

Furedi, Frank (2009) 'This wasn't realpolitik. It was realitypolitik', 21 December. Available at http://www.spiked-online.com/index.php/site/author/Frank%20Furedi/ (accessed 12 January 2010).

Gaard, Greta (1993) 'Living interconnections with animals and nature', in Greta Gaard (ed.) *Ecofeminism: Women, Animals, Nature*, Philadelphia: Temple University Press.

Gallopín, Gilberto (2002) 'Planning? for resilience: Scenarios, surprises, and branch points', in Lance Gunderson and C. S. Holling (eds) *Panarchy: Understanding Transformations in Human and Natural Systems*, Washington DC: Island Press, 361–394.

Gandy, Matthew (1997) 'Ecology, modernity and the intellectual legacy of the Frankfurt School', in A. Light and J. Smith (eds) *Space, Place and Environmental Ethics: Philosophy and Geography I*, London: Rowman and Littlefield, 231–254.

Gandy, Matthew (2005) 'Cyborg urbanization: Complexity and monstrosity in the contemporary city,' *International Journal of Urban and Regional Research*, 29 (1): 26–49.

Gane, Nicholas and Haraway, Donna (2006) 'When we have never been human, what is to be done? An interview with Donna Haraway', *Theory, Culture and Society*, 23 (7/8): 135–158.

Gardiner, Stephen M. (2011) *A Perfect Moral Storm: The Ethical Tragedy of Climate Change*, Oxford: Oxford University Press.

Garvey, James (2008) *The Ethics of Climate Change: Right and Wrong in a Warming World*, London: Continuum.

Gaskell, George, Allum, Nick, Bauer, Martin W., Jackson, Jonathan, Howard, Susan and Lindsey, Nicolas (2003) *Ambivalent GM Nation? Public Attitudes to Biotechnology in the UK, 1991–2002*, London: London School of Economics and Political Science.

Gaskell, George, Stares, Sally, Allansdottir, Agnes, Allum, Nick, Castro, Paula, Esmer, Claude Fischler, et al. (2010) *Europeans and Biotechnology in 2010. Winds of change?* Luxembourg: Publications Office of the European Union.

Georgescu-Roegen, Nicholas (1971) *The Entropy Law and the Economic Process*, Cambridge MA: Harvard University Press.

Gereffi, Gary (1999) 'International trade and industrial upgrading in the apparel commodity chain', *Journal of International Economics*, 48 (1): 37–70.

German Advisory Council on Global Change (2008) *Climate Change as a Security Risk*, London: Earthscan.

Geschiere, Peter (2009) *The Perils of Belonging*, Chicago: University of Chicago Press.

Giddens, Anthony (1990) *The Consequences of Modernity*, Cambridge: Polity.

Giddens, Anthony (1994) *Beyond Left and Right. The Future of Radical Politics*, Cambridge: Polity.

Giddens, Anthony (2009) *The Politics of Climate Change*, Cambridge: Polity.

Giddens, Anthony (2011) *The Politics of Climate Change*, Second edition, Cambridge: Polity.

Giedion, Sigfried (1948) *Mechanization Takes Command: A Contribution to Anonymous History*, New York: Norton.

Gieryn, Thomas (1983) 'Boundary-Work and the demarcation of science from non-science: Strains and interests in professional ideologies of scientists', *American Sociological Review*, 486: 781–795.

Giffney, Noreen and Hird, Myra J. (eds) (2008) *Queering the Non/Human*, London, Ashgate.

Gilbertson, Tamra and Reyes, Oscar (2009) *Carbon Trading: How It Works and Why It Fails*, Critical Currents Volume 7, Uppsala: Dar Hammarskjöld foundation.

Gill, Steven R., Pop, Mihai, DeBoy, Robert T., Eckburg, Paul B., Turnbaugh, Peter J., Samuel, Buck S., et al. (2006) 'Metagenomic analysis of the human distal gut microbiome', *Science*, 312 (5778): 1355–1359.

Giroux, Henry A. (2006) 'Reading hurricane Katrina: Race, class, and the biopolitics of disposability', *College Literature*, 33 (3): 171–196.

Giugni, Marco G. (2004) *Social Protest and Policy Change: Ecology, Antinuclear, and Peace Movements in Comparative Perspective*, Lanham, MD: Rowman & Littlefield.

Gleditsch, N. (1999) 'Armed conflict and the environment: A critique of the literature'. *Journal of Peace Research*, 35 (3): 381–400.

Gleditsch, N. (2001) 'Armed conflict and the environment', in Paul Diehl and Nils Petter Gleditsch (eds) *Environmental Conflict*, Boulder: Westview Press, 251–272.

Goklany, Indur M. (2008) 'What to do about climate change', *Cato Policy Analysis No.609*. Available at http://www.cato.org/pubs/pas/pa-609.pdf (accessed 27 March 2013).

Goldfrank, Walter L., Goodman, David and Szasz, Andrew (eds) (1999) *Ecology and the World System*, London: Greenwood Press.

Goldman, Mara, Nadasdy, Paul and Turner, Matthew (2011) *Knowing Nature: Conversations at the Intersection of Political Ecology and Science Studies*, Chicago: University of Chicago Press.

Goldman, Michael (2005) *Imperial Nature: The World Bank and Struggles for Social Justice in the Age of Globalization*, New Haven, CT: Yale University Press.

Goldsmith, Edward and Mander, Jerry (eds) (1997) *The Case Against the Global Economy: And for a Turn toward the Local*, San Francisco: Sierra Club Books.

Golley, Frank B. (1996) *A History of the Ecosystem Concept in Ecology: More Than the Sum of the Parts*, New Haven, CT: Yale University Press.

Goodin, Robert (1992) *Green Political Theory*, Cambridge: Polity.

Goodman, Michael K. (2004) 'Reading fair trade: Political ecological imaginary and the moral economy of fair trade foods' *Political Geography*, 23 (7): 891–915.

Goodman, Michael K., Goodman, David and Redclift, Michael (2010) *Consuming Space: Placing Consumption in Perspective*, London: Ashgate.

Goodstein, David (2005) *Out of Gas: The End of the Age of Oil*, New York: Norton.

Gordon, Colin (1991) 'Governmental rationality: An introduction', in Graham Burchell, Colin Gordon and Peter Miller (eds) 1991) *The Foucault Effect: Studies in Governmentality*, Chicago: University of Chicago Press, 1–51.

Gordon, Colin (2001) 'Introduction', in James D. Faubion (ed.) *Power: The Essential Works of Foucault 1954–1984, Volume Three*, London: Allen Lane.

Gore, Al (2006) *An Inconvenient Truth: The Planetary Emergency of Global Warming and What We Can Do About It*, London: Bloomsbury.

Gorz, Andre (1980) *Ecology as Politics*, Montreal: Black Rose Books.

Goss, Jon (1999) 'Once-upon-a-time in the commodity world: An Unofficial guide to Mall of America', *Annals of the Association of American Geographers*, 89: 45–75.

Goss, Jon (2004) 'Geography of consumption I', *Progress in Human Geography*, 28: 369–380.

Gottleib, Roger S. (ed.) (1996) *This Sacred Earth: Religion, Nature and Environment*, London: Routledge.

Gough, Clair and Shackley, Simon (2001) 'The respectable politics of climate change: The epistemic communities and NGOs', *International Affairs*, 77: 329–345.

Gouldson, Andy (2009) 'Advances in environmental policy and governance', *Environmental Policy and Governance*, 19: 1–2.

Gouldson, Andy and Bebbington, Jan (2007) 'Corporations and the governance of environmental risk', *Environment and Planning C: Government and Policy*, 25: 4–20.

Government of Indonesia (1986) *Sejarah Kehutanan Indonesia (Indonesian Forestry History)*, Volumes 1–3, Jakarta: Ministry of Forestry.

Gramsci, Antonio (1971) *Prison Notebooks*, London: Lawrence and Wishart.

Gray, Leslie C. and Moseley, William C. (2005) 'A geographical perspective on poverty-environmental interactions', *The Geographical Journal*, 171: 9–23.

Gregson, Nicky (1995) 'And now it's all consumption?' *Progress in Human Geography*, 19: 135–141.

Griffin, Susan (1984) *Woman and Nature*, London: Women's Press.

Griffin, Susan (1988) *Pornography and Silence*, London: Women's Press.

Griffin, Susan (1994) *A Chorus of Stones: The Private Life of War*, London: Women's Press.

Griskevicius, Vladas, Tybur, Joshua M. and Van den Bergh, Bram (2010) 'Going Green to be Seen: Status, Reputation, and Conspicuous Conservation', *Journal of Personality and Social Psychology*, 98: 392–404.

Gross, Matthias (2010) *Ignorance and Surprise: Science, Society and Ecological Design*, Cambridge, MA: MIT Press.

Grosz, Elizabeth (2011) *Becoming Undone: Darwinian Reflections on Life, Politics, and Art*, Durham, NC: Duke University Press.

Grove, Kevin (2010) 'Insuring "our common future"? Dangerous climate change and the biopolitics of environmental security', *Geopolitics*, 15 (3): 536–563.

Grove, Kevin (2012a) 'Preempting the next disaster: Catastrophe insurance and the financialization of disaster management', *Security Dialogue*, 43 (2): 139–155.

Grove, Kevin (2012b) 'From emergency management to managing emergence: A genealogy of disaster management in Jamaica', *Annals of the Association of American Geographers*, DOI:10.1080/0004 5608.2012.740357

Grundmann, Reiner (2007) 'Climate change and knowledge politics', *Environmental Politics*, 16 (3): 414–432.

Grzybowski, Cândido (2006) 'The World Social Forum: Reinventing global politics', *Global Governance*, 12 (1): 7–13.

Guha, Ramachandra (2002) *Environmentalism: A Global History*, New York: Longman.

Guha, Ramachandra and Martinez-Alier, Juan (eds) (1997) *Varieties of Environmentalism; Essays North and South,* London: Earthscan.

Gunderson, Lance and Holling, Crawford Stanley (1995) *Barriers and Bridges to the Renewal of Ecosystems and Institutions,* New York: Columbia University Press.

Gunningham, Neil (2009) 'Environment law, regulation and governance: Shifting architectures', *Journal of Environmental Law,* 21 (2): 179–212.

Gurian-Sherman, Doug (2009) *Failure to Yield: Evaluating the Performance of Genetically Engineered Crops,* Cambridge, MA: Union of Concerned Scientists Publications.

Guyer, Jane and Richards, Paul (1996) 'The invention of biodiversity: Social perspectives on the management of biological variety in Africa', *Africa,* 66: 1–13.

Haas, Peter M. (1992) 'Introduction: Epistemic communities and international policy coordination', *International Organization,* 46 (1): 1–35.

Haas, Peter M. (2002) 'UN conferences and constructivist governance of the environment', *Global Governance,* 8 (1): 73–91.

Habermas, Jürgen (1981) 'New social movements', *Telos,* September 21: 33–37.

Habermas, Jürgen (1984) *The Theory of Communicative Action: Volume 1, Reason and the Rationalization of Society,* London: Heinemann Education.

Habermas, Jürgen (1987) *The Theory of Communicative Action. Volume 2: A Critique of Functionalist Reason,* trans. T. McCarthy, Polity Press: Cambridge.

Hables Gray, Chris (2001) *Cyborg Citizen: Politics in the Posthuman Age,* London: Routledge.

Hackett, Edward, Amsterdamska, Olga, Lynch, Michael and Wajcman, Judy (eds) (2007) *The Handbook of Science and Technology Studies,* Cambridge MA: MIT Press.

Haila, Yryö and Kouki, Jari (1994) 'The phenomenon of biodiversity in conservation biology', *Ann. Zool. Fennici,* 31: 5–18.

Hajer, Maarten A. (1995) *The Politics of Environmental Discourse: Ecological Modernization and the Policy Process,* Oxford: Oxford University Press.

Hale, Stephen (2010) 'The new politics of climate change: Why we are failing and how we will succeed', *Environmental Politics,* 19 (2): 255–275.

Hall, Stuart (1989) 'The meaning of new times', in Stuart Hall and Martin Jacques (eds) *New Times: The Changing Faces of Politics in the 1990s,* London: Lawrence and Wishart.

Halle, Mark (2012) 'Life after Rio: A commentary by Mark Halle, IISD', June 2012. Available at http://www.iisd.org/pdf/2012/com_life_after_rio.pdf (accessed 26 June 2012).

Hallowes, David, Reddy, Trusha and Reyes, Oscar (2012) *COP in, COP out, COP 17: A Review of Civil Society Participation in the UN Conference on Climate Change, Durban 2011,* Johannesburg: Earthlife Africa. Available at http://www.earthlife.org.za/?page_id=1808 (accessed 8 July 2013).

Hallstrom, Lars (2004) 'Eurocratising enlargement? EU elites and NGO participation in European environmental policy', *Environmental Politics,* 13 (1): 175–193.

Hallsworth, Ernest (1987) *Anatomy, Physiology and Psychology of Erosion,* Chichester: Wiley.

Hamilton, Marilyn (2008) *Integral City: Evolutionary Intelligences for the Human Hive,* Philadelphia: New Society Publishers.

Hannah, Matthew (2000) *Governmentality and the Mastery of Territory in Nineteenth-Century America,* Cambridge: Cambridge University Press.

Hannah, Matthew (2011) 'Biopower, life and left politics', *Antipode* 43 (4): 1034–1055.

Haraway, Donna J. (1976) *Crystals, Fabrics, and Fields: Metaphors of Organicism in Twentieth-Century Developmental Biology,* New Haven, CT: Yale University Press.

Haraway, Donna J. (1985) 'A manifesto for cyborgs: Science, technology, and socialist feminism in the 1980s', *Socialist Review,* 80: 65–108.

Haraway, Donna J. (1988) 'Situated knowledges: The science question in feminism and the privilege of partial perspective', *Feminist Studies,* 14: 575–599.

Haraway, Donna J. (1989) *Primate Visions: Gender, Race, and Nature in the World of Modern Science,* New York: Routledge.

Haraway, Donna J. (1991) *Simians, Cyborgs and Women: The Reinvention of Nature*, London/New York: Free Association Books/Routledge.

Haraway, Donna J. (1992) 'The promises of monsters: A regenerative politics for inappropriate/d others', in Lawrence Grossberg, Carey Nelson and Patricia A. Treichler (eds) *Cultural Studies*, New York: Routledge.

Haraway, Donna J. (1998) *Modest_Witness@Second_Millennium.FemaleMan©_Meets_Onco-Mouse™*, London: Routledge.

Haraway, Donna (2003) *The Companion Species Manifesto: Dogs, People and Significant Otherness*, Chicago IL: Prickly Paradigm Press.

Haraway, Donna (2008) *When Species Meet*, Minneapolis: University of Minnesota Press.

Haraway, Donna J. (2013) 'Sowing worlds: A seed bag for terraforming with Earth others', in Margret Grebowicz and Helen Merrick (eds) *Beyond the Cyborg: Adventures with Haraway*, New York: Columbia University Press.

Hardin, Garrett (1968), 'The tragedy of the commons', *Science*, 162 (3859), 1243–1248.

Harding, Sandra (1986) *The Science Question in Feminism*, Ithaca: Cornell University Press.

Hardt, Michael and Negri, Antonio (2000) *Empire*, Cambridge, MA: Harvard University Press.

Hardt, Michael and Negri, Antonio (2004) *Multitude: War and Democracy in the Age of Empire*, New York: Penguin.

Hardt, Michael and Negri, Antonio (2009) *Commonwealth*, Cambridge: Harvard University Press.

Hargreaves, Tom (2012) 'Questioning the virtues of pro-environmental behaviour research: Towards a phronetic approach', *Geoforum*, 43 (2): 315–324.

Harré, Rom (1993) *Laws of Nature*, London: Duckworth.

Hartmann, Betsy (2010) 'Rethinking climate refugees and climate conflict: Rhetoric, reality and the politics of policy discourse', *Journal of International Development*, 22 (2): 233–246.

Hartmann, Thom (2000) *The Last Hours of Ancient Sunlight: Waking Up to Personal and Global Transformation*, New York: Grove Press.

Hartwick, Elaine R. (1998) 'Geographies of consumption: A commodity-chain approach', *Environment and Planning D*, 16 (4): 423–437.

Harvey, David (1989) *The Condition of Postmodernity*, Oxford: Blackwell.

Harvey, David (1990) *The Condition of Postmodernity: An Enquiry into the Origins of Cultural Change*, Cambridge, MA: Blackwell.

Harvey, David (1996) *Justice, Nature and the Geography of Difference*, Oxford: Blackwell.

Harvey, David (1999) 'The environment of justice', in Frank Fischer and Maarten A. Hajer (eds) *Living With Nature: Environmental Politics as Cultural Discourse*, Oxford: OUP.

Harvey, David (2005) *A Brief History of Neoliberalism*, Oxford: Oxford University Press.

Harvey, David (2006) *Spaces of Global Capitalism: Towards a Theory of Uneven Geographical Development*, London: Verso.

Harvey, David (2010) *The Enigma of Capital and the Crises of Capitalism*, New York: Oxford University Press.

Harvey, L. D. Danny (2007), 'Allowable CO_2 concentrations under the United Nations Framework Convention on Climate Change as a function of the climate sensitivity probability distribution function', *Environmental Research Letters 2*, doi:10.1088/1748–9326/2/1/014001.

Hassler, Markus (2003) 'The global clothing production system: Commodity chains and business networks', *Global Networks*, 3 (4): 513–531.

Hastings, Tom H. (2000) *Ecology of War and Peace: Counting Costs of Conflict*, Lanham, MD: University Press of America.

Hawken, Paul (1993) *Ecology of Commerce: A Declaration of Sustainability*, New York: Harper Collins.

Hawken, Paul (2007) *Blessed Unrest: How the Largest Movement in the World Came Into Being and Why No One Saw It Coming*, New York: Viking.

Hawken, Paul, Lovins, Amory and Lovins, L. Hunter (2008) *Natural Capitalism: Creating the Next Industrial Revolution*, New York: Back Bay Books.

Hawkins, Gay (2006) *The Ethics of Waste,* Lanham, MD: Rowman & Littlefield.

Hay, Colin (2007) *Why We Hate Politics,* Cambridge: Polity Press.

Hayward, Tim (2006) 'Ecological citizenship: Justice, rights and the virtue of resourcefulness', *Environmental Politics,* 15 (3): 435–446.

Hecht, Susanna (1985) 'Environmental development and politics: Capital accumulation and the livestock center in Eastern Amazonia', *World Development,* 13(6): 663–684.

Hecht, Susanna and Cockburn, Alexander (1989) *The Fate of the Forest: Developers, Destroyers, and Defenders of the Amazon,* London: Verso.

Heidegger, Martin (1977) *The Question Concerning Technology and Other Essays,* New York: Harper and Row.

Heinberg, Richard (2005) *The Party's Over: Oil, War and the Fate of Industrial Societies,* Philadelphia: New Society.

Heinberg, Richard (2007) *Peak Everything: Waking Up to the Century of Declines,* Philadelphia: New Society.

Held, David (1987) *Models of Democracy,* Cambridge: Polity Press.

Helleiner, Eric and Thistlethwaite, Jason (2012) 'Subprime catalyst: Financial regulatory reform and the strengthening of US carbon market governance', *Regulation and Governance,* DOI: 10.1111/j.1748–5991.2012.01136.x.

Hendriks, Carolyn and Grin, John (2010) 'Contextualizing reflexive governance: The politics of Dutch transitions to sustainability', *Journal of Environmental Policy and Planning,* 9 (3–4): 333–350.

Hess, Carl (1979) *Community Technology,* New York: Harper and Row.

Hess, David (1997) *Science Studies: An Advanced Introduction,* New York: New York University Press.

Hess, David J. (2009) *Localist Movements in a Global Economy: Sustainability, Justice, and Urban Development,* Cambridge, MA: The MIT Press.

Hettinger, Ned and Throop, William (1999) 'Refocusing ecocentrism: De-emphasizing stability and defending wildness', *Environmental Ethics,* 21: 3–21.

Hewitt, Kenneth (1983) 'The idea of calamity in a technocratic age', in Kenneth Hewitt (ed.) *Interpretations of Calamity From the Viewpoint of Human Ecology,* Boston, MA: Allen and Unwin.

Heynen, Nik, McCarthy, James, Prudham, Scott and Robbins, Paul (eds) (2007) *Neoliberal Environments: False Promises and Unnatural Consequences,* Abingdon: Routledge.

Hiller, Harry (1998) 'Assessing the impact of mega-events: A linkage model', *Current Issues in Tourism,* 1 (1): 47–57.

Hinchliffe, Steve (2007) *Geographies of Nature,* London: Sage.

Hindess, Barry (1996) *Discourses of Power: From Hobbes to Foucault,* Oxford: Blackwell.

Hines, Colin (2000) *Localization: A Global Manifesto,* London: Routledge.

Hinsley, F.H. (1986) *Sovereignty,* Cambridge: Cambridge University Press.

Hinton, Emma D. (2011) 'Virtual Spaces of Sustainable Consumption: Governmentality and Third Sector Advocacy in the UK', unpublished thesis, King's College London.

Hird, Myra J. (2010) 'Indifferent globality: Gaia, symbiosis and "other worldliness"', *Theory Culture Society,* 27 (2–3): 54–72.

Hobson, Kersty (2002) 'Competing discourses of sustainable consumption: Does the "Rationalisation of lifestyles" make sense?' *Environmental Politics,* 11 (2): 95–120.

Hoffmann, Matthew J. (2011) *Climate Governance at the Crossroads: Experimenting With a Global Response after Kyoto,* New York: Oxford University Press.

Holling, Crawford S. (1973) 'Resilience and stability of ecological systems', *Annual Review of Ecology and Systematics,* 4: 1–23.

Holt, Flora (2005) 'The catch-22 of conservation, indigenous peoples, biologists and cultural change,' *Human Ecology,* 33(2): 199–215.

Holzinger, Katharina, Knill, Christoph and Schäfer, Ansgar (2006) 'Rhetoric or reality? "New Governance" in EU environmental policy', *European Law Journal,* 12 (3): 403–420.

Homer-Dixon, Thomas (1991) 'On the threshold: Environmental changes as causes of acute conflict', *International Security,* 16 (2): 76–116.

Homer-Dixon, Thomas (1999) *Environment, Scarcity and Violence,* Princeton: Princeton University Press.

Homer-Dixon, Thomas (2006) *The Upside of Down: Catastrophe, Creativity and the Renewal of Civilization,* Washington DC: Island Press.

Homer-Dixon, Thomas (2009) 'The newest science: Replacing physics, ecology will be the master science of the 21st century', *Alternatives Journal,* 35 (4): 8–38.

Hopkins, Rob (2008) *The Transition Handbook: From Oil Dependency to Local Resilience,* Totnes UK: Green Books.

Hopkins, Rob (2012) 'The arc of scenarios,' in Raymond DeYoung and Thomas Princen (eds) (2012) *The Localization Reader: Adapting to the Coming Downshift,* Cambridge, MA: The MIT Press, 59–68.

Hopkins, Terence K. and Wallerstein, Immanuel (1986) 'Commodity chains in the world economy prior to 1800', *Review,* 10 (1): 157–170.

Horkheimer, Max (1982) [1937] 'Traditional and critical theory', in Max Horkheimer, *Critical Theory: Selected Essays,* New York: Continuum.

Horkheimer, Max and Adorno, Theodor W. (2007) *Dialectic of Enlightenment: Philosophical Fragments,* Stanford, CA: Stanford University Press.

Hornborg, A. (1998) 'Ecosystems and world systems: Accumulation as an ecological process', *Journal of World-Systems Research,* 4 (2): 169–177.

HRW (2007) *Chop Fine,* New York: Human Rights Watch.

Huberts, Leo (1989) 'The influence of social movements on government policy', *International Social Movement Research,* 1: 395–426.

Hughes, James (2004) *Citizen Cyborg: Why Democratic Societies Must Respond to the Redesigned Human of the Future,* Boulder, CO: Westview Press.

Hughes, Thomas (2004) *Human-Built World: How to Think about Technology and Culture,* Chicago: University of Chicago Press.

Hughes, Thomas, Bijker, Wiebe E. and Pinch, Trevor J. (eds) (1987) *The Social Construction of Technological Systems: New Directions in the Sociology and History of Technology,* Cambridge, MA: MIT Press.

Hulme, Mike (2009) *Why We Disagree About Climate Change: Understanding Controversy, Inaction and Opportunity,* Cambridge: Cambridge University Press.

Hulme, Mike (2011) 'Reducing the future to climate: A story of climate determinism and reductionism', *Osiris,* 26 (1): 245–266.

Hulme, Mike, Doherty, Ruth, Ngara, Todd, New, Mark and Lister, David (2001) 'African climate change: 1900–2100', *Climate Research,* 17: 145–168.

Humboldt, Alexander von (1996) *Personal Narrative of a Journey to the Equinoctial Regions of the New Continent,* New York: Penguin Classics.

Humphrey, Macarten, Sachs, Jeffrey D., and Stiglitz, Joseph E. (eds) (2007) *Escaping the Resource Curse,* New York: Columbia University Press.

Hunn, Eugene, Johnson, Darryll R., Russell, Priscilla N. and Thornton, Thomas F. (2003) 'Huna Tlingit traditional environmental knowledge and the management of a wilderness park,' *Current Anthropology,* 44, supplement: S79–S103.

Hunt, Scott and Benford, Robert (2004) 'Collective identity, solidarity, and commitment', in David A. Snow, Sarah Soule and Hanspieter Kriesi (eds) *The Blackwell Companion to Social Movements,* Oxford: Blackwell.

Hutchings, Kimberly (2001) 'The nature of critique in critical international relations theory', in Richard Wyn Jones (ed.) *Critical Theory and World Politics,* Boulder, CO: Lynne Rienner.

Hutton, John, Adams, William and Murombedzi, James (2005) 'Back to the barriers? Changing narratives in biodiversity conservation', *Forum for Development Studies,* 2: 341–370.

Igoe, James (2004) *Conservation and Globalization: A Study of Indigenous Communities and National Parks from East Africa to South Dakota,* Belmont, CA: Wadsworth/Thompson.

Igoe, James (2005) 'Global indigenism and spaceship earth: Convergence, space, and re-entry friction,' *Globalizations* 2(3): 377–391.

Igoe, James (2010) 'The spectacle of nature in the global economy of appearances: Anthropological engagements with the spectacular mediations of transnational conservation', *Critique of Anthropology,* 30 (4): 375–397.

Igoe, James (2013) 'Consume, connect, conserve: Consumer spectacle and the technical mediation of neoliberal conservation's aesthetic of redemption and repair,' *Human Geography,* 6 (1): 16–28.

Igoe, James (in press) 'Nature on the move II: Contemplation becomes speculation,' *New Proposals: Journal of Marxism and Interdisciplinary Enquiry.*

Igoe, James and Brockington, Daniel (2007) 'Neoliberal conservation: A brief introduction,' *Conservation & Society,* 5 (4): 432–449.

Igoe, James, Neves, Katja and Brockington, Daniel (2010) 'A spectacular eco-tour around the historic bloc: Theorizing the current convergence of conservation and capitalism', *Antipode,* 42 (3): 486–512.

Ihde, Don (1990) *Technology and the Lifeworld: From Garden to Earth,* Bloomington: Indiana University Press.

Ikelegbe, Augustine (2006) 'The economics of conflict in oil rich Niger Delta region of Nigeria', *African and Asian Studies,* 5 (1): 23–55.

Iles, Alastair (2004) 'Mapping environmental justice in technology flows: Computer waste impacts in Asia', *Global Environmental Politics,* 4 (4): 76–107.

Illich, Ivan (1973) *Tools for Conviviality,* New York: Harper & Row.

Illich, Ivan (1974) *Energy and Equity,* New York: Harper & Row.

Inglehart, Ronald (1974) *Energy and Equity,* New York: Harper and Row.

Inglehart, Ronald (1977) *The Silent Revolution: Changing Values and Political Styles among Western Publics,* Princeton, NJ: Princeton University Press.

Ingold, Tim (2000) *The Perception of the Environment: Essays on Livelihood, Dwelling and Skill,* London: Routledge.

Inslee, Jay and Hendricks, Bracken (2009) *Apollo's Fire: Igniting America's Clean Energy Economy,* Washington DC: Island Press.

International Energy Agency (2010) *International Energy Outlook 2010.*Available at http://www.worldenergyoutlook.org/ (accessed 4 March 2013).

Inayatullah, Naeem and Blaney, David L. (2004) *International Relations and the Problem of Difference,* Abingdon: Routledge.

IPCCSR (Intergovernmental Panel on Climate Change Synthesis Report) (2001) *Climate Change 2001: Synthesis Report,* Cambridge: Cambridge University Press.

IPCCWG1 (Intergovernmental Panel on Climate Change Working Group 1) (2007) *Climate Change 2007: The Physical Science Basis,* Cambridge: Cambridge University Press.

IRGC (2008) *An Introduction to the IRGC Risk Governance Framework,* Geneva: International Risk Governance Council. Available at http://www.irgc.org/IMG/pdf/An_introduction_to_the_IRGC_Risk_Governance_Framework.pdf (accessed 11 December 2012).

Irwin, Alan (1995) *Citizen Science: A Study of People, Expertise and Sustainable Development,* London and New York: Routledge.

ITGLWF (International Textile, Garment and Leather Workers' Federation) (2012) *Fair Games? Human Rights of Workers in Olympic 2012 Supplier Factories,* Play Fair Campaign. Available at http://www.tuc.org.uk/tucfiles/291/sportswear.pdf (accessed 27 March 2013).

IUCN (International Union for the Conservation of Nature) (1980) *World Conservation Strategy,* Gland Switzerland: IUCN, UNEP and WWF.

Isa, Muhammed Kabir (2010) 'Militant Islamic groups in northern Nigeria', in Okumu, Wafula and Ikelegbe, Augustine (eds) *Militias, Rebels and Islamic Militants,* Pretoria: Institute of Security Studies.

Ivanova, Maria (2012) 'Institutional design and UNEP reform: Historical insights on form, function and financing', *International Affairs*, 88 (3): 565–584.

Jackson, Peter (1999) 'Commodity cultures: The traffic in things', *Transactions of the Institute of British Geographers*, 24: 95–108.

Jackson, Tim (2009) *Prosperity Without Growth: Economics for a Finite Planet*, London: Earthscan.

Jacques, Peter J. (2012) 'A general theory of climate denial', *Global Environmental Politics*, 12: 9–17.

Jägel, Thomas, Keeling, Kathy, Reppel, Alexander and Gruber, Thorsten (2012) 'Individual values and motivational complexities in ethical clothing consumption: A means-end approach', *Journal of Marketing Management*, 28 (3–4): 373–396.

Jäger, Carlo, Renn, Ortwin, Rosa, Eugene and Webler, Thomas (2001) *Risk, Uncertainty and Rational Action*, London: Earthscan.

Jakobeit, Cord and Methmann, Chris (2012) '"Climate refugees" as a dawning catastrophe? A critique of the dominant quest for numbers', in Jürgen Scheffran, Michael Brzoska, Hans Günter Brauch, Peter Michael Link and Janpeter Schilling (eds) *Climate Change, Human Security and Violent Conflict: Challenges for Societal Stability*, Berlin, Heidelberg: Springer.

Jameson, Fredric (1992) *Postmodernism, or the Cultural Logic of Late Capitalism*, Durham: Duke University Press.

Jamieson, Dale (1992) 'Ethics, public policy, and global warming', *Science, Technology and Human Values*, 17 (2): 139–153.

Jamison, Andrew (2001) *The Making of Green Knowledge: Environmental Politics and Cultural Transformation*, Cambridge: Cambridge University Press.

Janssen, Marco A., Schoon, Michael L., Ke, Weimao and Börner, Katy (2006) 'Scholarly networks on resilience, vulnerability and adaptation within the human dimensions of global environmental change', *Global Environmental Change*, 16 (3): 240–252.

Jasanoff, Sheila (1990) *The Fifth Branch: Science Advisers as Policymakers*, Cambridge, MA: Harvard University Press.

Jasanoff, Sheila (2004) 'The idiom of co-production', in Sheila Jasanoff (ed.) *States of Knowledge: The Co-production of Science and Social Order*, Abingdon: Routledge, 1–12.

Jasanoff, Sheila (ed.) (2006) *States of Knowledge: The Co-production of Science and Social Order*, New Edition, Abingdon: Routledge.

Jasanoff, Sheila and Long-Martello, Marybeth Long (eds) (2005) *Earthly Politics: Local and Global in Environmental Governance*, Cambridge MA: MIT Press.

Johns, David (2009) *New Conservation Politics: Power, Organization Building, and Effectiveness*, Oxford: Oxford University Press.

Johnson, Craig and Forsyth, Tim (2002) 'In the eyes of the state: Negotiating a "Rights-Based Approach" to forest conservation in Thailand', *World Development*, 30 (9): 1591–1605.

Johnson, Lawrence E. (1991) *A Morally Deep World*, Cambridge: Cambridge University Press.

Johnston, Josée (2008) 'The citizen-consumer hybrid: Ideological tensions and the case of Whole Foods Market', *Theory and Society*, 37 (3): 229–270.

Jonas, Hans (1984) *The Imperative of Responsibility: In Search of An Ethics for the Technological Age*, Chicago, IL: University of Chicago Press.

Jones, Ellis (2008) *The Better World Shopping Guide: Every Dollar Makes a Difference*, Boston: New Society.

Jordan, Andrew (2008) 'The governance of sustainable development: Taking stock and looking forwards', *Environment and Planning C: Government and Policy*, 26 (1): 17–23.

Jordan Andrew, Wurzel, Rüdiger and Zito, Anthony (2003) (eds) *New Instruments of Environmental Governance? National Experiences and Prospects*, London: Frank Cass.

Joseph, Jonathan (2009) 'Governmentality of what? Populations, states and international organisations', *Global Society*, 23 (4): 413–419.

Kaara, Wahu (2010) 'Reclaiming peoples' power in Copenhagen 2009: A victory for ecosocialist ecofeminism,' *Capitalism Nature Socialism*, 21 (2): 107–111.

Kahl, Colin (2006) *States, Scarcity and Civil Strife in the Developing World,* Princeton: Princeton University Press.

Kalhauge, Angela Churie, Correll, Elisabeth and Sjöstedt, Gunnar (2005) 'The multilateral process for sustainable development: Past, present and future', in Angela Churie Kalhauge, Gunnar Sjöstedt and Elisabeth Correll (eds) *Global Challenges: Furthering the Multilateral Process for Sustainable Development,* Sheffield: Greenleaf, 16–30.

Kant, Immanuel (1949) [1784] 'What is Enlightenment?' in Immanuel Kant, *The Philosophy of Kant: Immanuel Kant's Moral and Political Writings,* New York: Modern Library.

Kant, Immanuel (1998) [1785] *The Groundwork for the Metaphysics of Morals,* trans. Mary J. Gregor, Cambridge: Cambridge University Press.

Kanter, Rosemary (1972) *Commitment and Community: Communes and Utopias in Sociological Perspective,* Cambridge, MA: Harvard University Press.

Kaplan, Martha (2007) 'Fijian water in Fiji and New York: Local politics and a global commodity', *Cultural Anthropology,* 22: 685–706.

Kaplan, Robert (1994) 'The coming anarchy', *Atlantic Monthly,* 273 (2): 44–76.

Kaplan, Robert (1996) *The Ends of the Earth: A Journey at the Dawn of the 21st Century,* New York: Random House.

Kaplinsky, Raphael (2000) 'Globalisation and unequalisation: What can be learned from value chain analysis?' *Journal of Development Studies,* 37 (2): 117–146.

Kappeler, Susanne (1995) 'Speciesism, racism, nationalism… . or the power of scientific subjectivity', in Carol J. Adams and Josephine Donovan (eds) *Animals and Women,* London: Duke University Press.

Karl, Terry L. (1997) *The Paradox of Plenty: Oil Booms and Petrol States,* Berkeley: University of California Press.

Karliner, Joshua (1997) *The Corporate Planet: Ecology and Politics in the Age of Globalization,* San Francisco: Sierra Club Books.

Karliner, Joshua (2000) 'Climate justice summit provides alternative vision,' CorpWatch. Available at http://www.corpwatch.org/article.php?id=977 (accessed 12 April 2013).

Kasser, T. (2002) *The High Price of Materialism,* Cambridge, MA: MIT Press.

Katz, Eric (1997) *Nature as Subject: Human Obligation and Natural Community,* Lanham, MD: Rowman & Littlefield.

Kelly, P. Michael and Adger, W. Neil (2000) 'Theory and practice in assessing vulnerability to climate change and facilitating adaptation', *Climatic Change,* 47 (4): 325–352.

Kemp, René, Parto, Saeed and Gibson, Robert (2005) 'Governance for sustainable development: Moving from theory to practice', *International Journal of Sustainable Development,* 8 (1–2): 13–30.

Kemp, René and Martens, Pim (2007) 'Sustainable development: How to manage something that is subjective and never can be achieved?' *Sustainability; Science, Practice, & Policy,* 3 (2): 5–14.

Kennedy, Paul (1992) *Preparing for the Twenty-First Century,* New York: Random House.

Keohane, Robert O., Haas, Peter M. and Levy, Marc A. (1993) 'The effectiveness of international environmental institutions', in Peter M. Haas, Robert O. Keohane and Marc A. Levy (eds) *Institutions for the Earth: Sources of Effective International Environmental Protection,* Cambridge, MA: MIT Press, 3–24.

Keohane, Robert O. and Victor, David G. (2011) 'The regime complex for climate change', *Perspectives on Politics,* 9 (1): 7–23.

Kheel, Marti (2008) *Nature Ethics: An Ecofeminist Perspective,* Lanham MD: Rowland and Littlefield.

Kinchy, Abby J., Kleinman, Daniel L. and Autry, Robyn (2008) 'Against free markets, against science? Regulating the socio-economic effects of biotechnology', *Rural Sociology,* 73 (2): 147–179.

King, David (2004) 'Climate change science: Adapt, mitigate, or ignore?' *Science,* 303: 176–7.

King, Ynestra (1983) 'The eco-feminist imperative', in Leonie Caldecott and Stephanie Leyland (eds) *Reclaim the Earth,* London: Women's Press.

Kingsbury, Noel (2009) *Hybrid: The History and Science of Plant Breeding,* Chicago: University of Chicago Press.

Kirby, Vicky (2011) *Quantum Anthropologies,* Durham, NC: Duke University Press.

Kjellén, Bo (2008) *A New Diplomacy for Sustainable Development: The Challenge of Global Change,* Abingdon: Routledge.

Klare, Michael (2011) *The Race for What's Left,* New York: Metropolitan.

Klein, Naomi (2000) *No Logo,* London: Flamingo.

Klein, Naomi (2008) *Shock Doctrine,* New York: Henry Holt.

Kohler-Koch, Beate and Rittberger, Berthold (2006) 'The governance turn in EU studies', *Journal of Common Market Studiess,* 44 (S1): 27–49.

Kooiman, Jan (2000) 'Societal governance: Levels, modes, and orders of social-political interaction', in Jon Pierre (ed.) *Debating Governance,* Oxford: Oxford University Press, 138–166.

Kosek, Jake (2006) *Understories,* Durham, NC: Duke University Press.

Kovel, Joel (2007) *The Enemy of Nature: The End of Capitalism or the End of the World?,* London: Zed Books.

Kovel, Joel and Lowy, Michael (2001) *An Ecosocialist Manifesto,* pamphlet, Paris. Available at http://www.cnsjournal.org/manifesto.html (accessed 8 July 2013).

Kriesi, Hanspieter, Koopmans, Ruud, Duyvendak, Jan Willem and Giugni, Marco G. (1995) *New Social Movements in Western Europe: A Comparative Analysis,* Minneapolis: University of Minnesota Press.

Knobloch, Frieda (1996) *The Culture of Wilderness: Agriculture as Colonization in the American West,* Chapel Hill: University of North Carolina Press.

Knutti, Reto (2008) 'Should we believe model predictions of future climate change?' *Philosophical Transactions of the Royal Society A,* 366 (1885): 4647–4664.

Kuehls, Thom (1996) *Beyond Sovereign Territory: The Space of Ecopolitics,* Minneapolis: University of Minnesota Press.

Kuehls, Thom (1998) 'Between sovereignty and environment: An exploration of the discourse of government', in Karen Litfin (ed.) *The Greening of Sovereignty in World Politics,* Cambridge, MA: MIT Press.

Kuehls, Thom (2003) 'The environment of sovereignty', in Warren Magnusson and Karena Shaw (eds) *A Political Space: Reading the Global Through Clayoquot Sound,* Minneapolis: University of Minnesota Press.

Kuhn, Thomas (1962) *The Structure of Scientific Revolutions,* Chicago: University of Chicago Press.

Kurki, Milja (2011) 'The limitations of the critical edge: Reflections on critical and philosophical IR scholarship today', *Millennium,* 40 (1): 129–146.

Lafferty, William (ed.) (2004) *Governance for Sustainable Development: The Challenge of Adapting Form to Function,* Cheltenham: Edward Elgar.

Lamb, Robert (1996) *Promising the Earth,* London: Routledge.

Lander, Edgardo (2010) 'Reflections on the Cochabamba climate summit,' Caracas, 27 April. Available at http://www.tni.org/article/reflections-cochabamba-climate-summit (accessed 12 April 2013).

Landström, Catharina, Whatmore, Sarah, Lane, Stuart, Odoni, Nicholas, Ward, Neil and Bradley, Susan (2011) 'Coproducing flood risk knowledge: Redistributing expertise in critical "participatory modelling"', *Environment and Planning A,* 43 (7): 1617–1633.

Lane, Stuart, Odoni, Nicholas, Landström, Catharina, Whatmore, Sarah, Ward, Neil and Bradley, Susan (2011) 'Doing flood risk science differently: An experiment in radical scientific method', *Transactions of the Institute of British Geographers,* 36 (1): 15–36.

Landen, Laura (2003) 'Biotic community – Real or unreal: A philosophical dilemma', *Worldviews,* 7: 58–79.

Lapid, Yosef (1989) 'The third debate: On the prospects of international theory in a post-positivist era', *International Studies Quarterly,* 33 (3): 235–254.

Latour, Bruno (1987) *Science in Action: How to Follow Scientists and Engineers through Society,* Cambridge, MA: Harvard University Press.

Latour, Bruno (1992) 'Where are the missing masses? The sociology of a few mundane artifacts', in Wiebe E. Bijker and John Law (eds) *Shaping Technology/Building Society,* Cambridge MA: MIT Press.

Latour, Bruno (1993) *We Have Never Been Modern,* London: Harvester-Wheatsheaf.

Latour, Bruno (1996) 'On Actor-Network Theory: A few clarifications plus more than a few complications', *Soziale Welt,* 47: 369–381.

Latour, Bruno (1999) *Pandora's Hope: Essays on the Reality of Science Studies,* Cambridge, MA: Harvard University Press.

Latour, Bruno (2004a) *The Politics of Nature: How to Bring the Sciences into Democracy,* Cambridge, MA: Harvard University Press.

Latour, Bruno (2004b) 'Why has critique run out of steam? From matters of fact to matters of concern', *Critical Enquiry,* 30: 225–248.

Latour, Bruno (2007) *Reassembling the Social: An Introduction to Actor-Network Theory,* Oxford: Oxford University Press.

Latour, Bruno (2009) 'A plea for earthly sciences', in Judith Burnett, Syd Jeffers, and Graham Thomas (eds) *New Social Connections: Sociology's Subjects and Objects,* Basingstoke: Palgrave, 72–84.

Latour, Bruno (2010) 'An attempt at a "compositionist manifesto"', *New Literary History,* 41 (3): 471–490.

Lanchberry, John (1996) 'The Rio Earth Summit', in David H. Dunn (ed.) *Diplomacy at the Highest Level: The Evolution of International Summitry,* Basingstoke: Macmillan.

Law, John (ed.) (1991) *A Sociology of Monsters: Essays on Power, Technology, and Domination,* London: Routledge.

Lawson, Nigel (2009) *An Appeal to Reason: A Cool Look at Global Warming,* London: Duckworth.

Lazzarato, Maurizio (2009) 'Neoliberalism in action: Inequality, insecurity and the reconstitution of the social', *Theory, Culture & Society,* 26 (6): 109–133.

Leach, Melissa and Mearns, Robin (eds) (1996) *The Lie of the Land: Challenging Received Wisdom on the African Environment,* Oxford: James Currey.

Le Billon, Philippe (2001) 'The political ecology of war: Natural resources and armed conflicts', *Political Geography,* 20(5): 561–584.

Le Billon, Philippe (2006) 'Fatal transactions: Conflict diamonds and the (anti) terrorist consumer', *Antipode,* 38: 778–801.

Le Billon, Philippe (2012) *Wars of Plunder: Conflicts, Profits and the Politics of Resources,* London: Hurst.

Lee, Michael S.W., Moron, Judith and Conroy, Denise (2008) 'Anti-consumption and brand avoidance', *Journal of Business Research,* 62: 169–180.

Lee-Sanchez, Carol (1993) 'Animal, vegetable and mineral', in Carol J. Adams (ed.) *Ecofeminism and the Sacred,* New York: Continuum.

Lefebvre, Henri (1984) *Everyday Life in the Modern World,* New Brunswick, NJ: Transaction.

Lefebvre, Henri (1991) *The Production of Space,* Oxford: Blackwell.

Lefebvre, Henri (2005) *The Production of Space,* London: Verso.

Lemke, Thomas (2011) *Biopolitics: An Advanced Introduction,* New York: New York University Press.

Lenschow, Andrea (1999) 'Transformation in European Environmental Governance', in Beate Kohler-Koch and Rainer Eising (eds) *The Transformation of Governance in the European Union,* London: Routledge, 39–60.

Lentzos, Filippa and Rose, Nikolas (2009) 'Governing insecurity: Contingency planning, protection, resilience', *Economy and Society,* 38 (2): 230–254.

Leonard, Annie (2009) *The Story of Cap and Trade.* Available at http://www.storyofstuff.org (accessed 12 April 2013).

Leonard, Annie (2010) *The Story of Stuff,* New York: Free Press.

Leopold, Aldo (1970) *A Sand County Almanac with Essays on Conservation from Round River,* New York: Ballentine Books.

Lepawsky, Josh and Mather, Charles (2011) 'From beginnings and endings to boundaries and edges: Rethinking circulation and exchange through electronic waste', *Area* 43 (3): 242–249.

Lévêque, Christian and Mounolou, Jean-Claude (2003) *Biodiversity,* Sussex: Wiley.

Levin, Kelly, Cashore, Benjamin, Bernstein, Steven and Auld, Graeme (2012) 'Overcoming the tragedy of super wicked problems: constraining our future selves to ameliorate global climate change' *Policy Sciences,* 45 (2) 123–152.

Levy, Marc A. (1995) 'Is the environment a national security issue?' *International Security,* 20 (2): 35–62.

Levy, David L. and Egan, Daniel (2003) 'A Neo-Gramscian approach to corporate political strategy: Conflict and accommodation in the climate change negotiations', *Journal of Management Studies,* 40 (4): 803–830.

Leyland, Stephanie (1983) 'Feminism and ecology: Theoretical considerations', in Leonie Caldecott and Stephanie Leyland (eds) *Reclaim the Earth,* London: Women's Press.

Lezaun, Javier (2011) 'Bees, beekeepers, and bureaucrats: Parasitism and the politics of transgenic life', *Environment and Planning D: Society and Space,* 29: 738–756.

Li, Tania Murray (2007) *The Will to Improve: Governmentality, Development and the Practice of Politics,* Raleigh, NC: Duke University Press.

Linklater, Andrew (1990) *Beyond Realism and Marxism: Critical Theory and International Relations,* Basingstoke: Macmillan.

Linklater, Andrew (2001) 'The changing contours of critical international relations theory', in Richard Wyn Jones (ed.) *Critical Theory and World Politics,* Boulder, CO: Lynne Rienner.

Linklater, Andrew (2007) *Critical Theory and World Politics: Citizenship, Sovereignty and Humanity,* Abingdon: Routledge.

Lipow, Gar (2012) *Cooling It! No Hair Shirt Solutions to Global Warming,* Boulder, CO: Praeger Press.

Litfin, Karen (ed.) (2003) *The Greening of Sovereignty in World Politics,* Cambridge, MA: MIT Press.

Litfin, Karen (2013) *Ecovillages: Lessons for Sustainable Community,* Cambridge: Polity.

Liverman, Diana M. (1990) 'Drought impacts in Mexico: Climate, agriculture, technology, and land tenure in sonora and puebla', *Annals of the Association of American Geographers,* 80 (1): 49–72.

Lloyd, Genevieve (1980) 'Spinoza's environmental ethics', *Inquiry,* 23 (3): 293–311.

Lloyd, Genevieve (1994) *Part of Nature: Self-Knowledge in Spinoza's Ethics,* Ithaca NY: Cornell University Press.

Lobo-Guerrero, Luis (2010) *Insuring Security: Biopolitics, Security, and Risk,* Abingdon: Routledge.

Lodziak, Conrad (2000) 'On explaining consumption', *Capital and Class,* 72: 111–133.

Lohmann, Larry (2005) 'Marketing and making carbon dumps: Commodification, calculation and counterfactuals in climate change mitigation', *Science as Culture,* 14 (3): 203–235.

Lohmann, Larry (2006) 'Carbon trading: A critical conversation on climate change, privatization and power', *Development Dialogue,* 48: 1–356.

Lohmann, Larry (2008) 'Carbon trading, climate justice and the production of ignorance: Ten examples', *Development,* 51 (3): 359–365.

Lohmann, Larry (2009) 'Climate as investment', *Development and Change,* 40 (6): 1063–1083.

Lohmann, Larry (2010) 'Uncertainty markets and carbon markets: Variations on Polanyian themes', *New Political Economy,* 15 (2): 225–254.

Lomborg, Bjørn (2001) *The Skeptical Environmentalist: Measuring the Real State of the World,* Cambridge: Cambridge University Press.

Loorbach, Derk (2010) 'Transition management for sustainable development: A prescriptive, complexity-based governance framework, *Governance: An International Journal of Policy, Administration, and Institutions,* 23 (1): 161–183.

Lorenz, Edward (1993) [1972] 'Predictability: Does the flap of a butterfly's wings in Brazil set off a tornado in Texas', Presented to the 139th meeting of the American Association for the Advancement of Science, reprinted in Edward Lorenz, *The Essence of Chaos*, Seattle: University of Washington Press, 181–184.

Lorimer, John (2009) 'Posthumanism/posthumanistic geographies', in Rob Kitchin and Nigel Thrift (eds) *International Encyclopaedia of Human Geography, Vol. 8*, Oxford: Elsevier.

Louden, Robert B. (1984) 'On some vices of virtue ethics', *Philosophical Quarterly*, 21 (3): 227–236.

Lövbrand, Eva and Stripple, Johannes (2006) 'The climate as political space: Territorialization of the global carbon cycle', *Review of International Studies*, 32: 217–235.

Lövbrand, Eva and Stripple, Johannes (2011) 'Making climate change governable: Accounting for carbon as sinks, credits and personal budgets', *Critical Policy Studies*, 5 (2): 187–200.

Lövbrand, Eva and Stripple, Johannes (2012) 'Disrupting the public-private distinction: Excavating the government of carbon markets', *Environment and Planning C*, 30: 658–674.

Lövbrand, Eva, Stripple, Johannes and Wiman, Bo (2009) 'Earth system governmentality: Reflections on science in the Anthropocene', *Global Environmental Change*, 19 (1): 7–13.

Lovell, Heather, Bulkeley, Harriet and Liverman, Diana (2009) 'Carbon offsetting: Sustaining consumption?' *Environment and Planning A*, 41 (10): 2357–2379.

Lovins, Amory (1977) *Soft Energy Paths*, New York: Ballinger.

Low, Nicholas and Gleeson, Brendan (1998) *Justice, Society and Nature: An Exploration of Political Ecology*, London: Routledge.

Lowy, Michael (2001) *The Politics of Combined and Uneven Development: The Theory of Permanent Revolution*, London: Verso Books.

Luhmann, Niklas (1993) *Risk: A Sociological Theory*, New Brunswick, NJ: Transaction Publishers.

Luke, Timothy W. (1989) *Screens of Power: Ideology, Domination, and Resistance in Informational Society*, Urban: University of Illinois Press.

Luke, Timothy W. (1994) 'Placing Powers, Siting Spaces: The Politics of Global and Local in the New World Order', *Environment and Planning A: Society and Space*, 12: 613–628.

Luke, Timothy W. (1995a) 'New World Order or Neo-World Orders: Power, politics and ideology in informationalizing glocalities' in Mike Featherstone, Scott Lash, and Roland Robertson (eds) *Global Modernities*, London: Sage Publications, 91–107.

Luke, Timothy W. (1995b) 'On environmentality: Geo-power and eco-knowledge in the discourses of contemporary Environmentalism', *Cultural Critique*, 31: 57–81.

Luke, Timothy W. (1996) 'Liberal society and cyborg subjectivity: The politics of environments, bodies, and nature', *Alternatives*, 21: 1–30.

Luke, Timothy W. (1997) *Ecocritique: Contesting the Politics of Nature, Economy and Culture*, Minneapolis: University of Minnesota Press.

Luke, Timothy W. (1998) '"Moving at the speed of life"? A cultural kinematics of telematic times and corporate values,' *Cultural Values*, 2 (2 and 3): 320–339.

Luke, Timothy W. (1999a) *Capitalism, Democracy, and Ecology: Departing from Marx*, Urbana: University of Illinois Press.

Luke, Timothy (1999b) 'Environmentality as green governmentality', in Eric Darier (ed.) *Discourses of the Environment*, Oxford: Blackwell Publishers, 121–151.

Luke, Timothy W. (2001) 'Real interdependence: Discursivity and concursivity in global politics', in Francois Debrix (ed.) *Language, Agency and Politics in a Constructed World*, New York: M.E. Sharpe.

Luke, Timothy W. (2009) 'Situating knowledges: The politics of globality, locality, and green statism', in Gabriela Kütting and Ronnie Lipschutz (eds) *Environmental Governance*, New York: Routledge.

Lukes, Steven (1974) *Power: A Radical View*, Basingstoke: Macmillan.

Lulka, David (2009) 'The residual humanism of hybridity: Retaining a sense of the earth', *Transactions of the Institute of British Geographers*, 34: 378–393.

Lundborg, Tom and Vaughan-Williams, Nick (2011) 'Resilience, critical infrastructure, and molecular security: The excess of "life" in biopolitics', *International Political Sociology*, 5: 367–383.

Lupton, Deborah (1999) *Risk*, London: Routledge.

Lury, Celia (2004) *Brands: The Logos of the Global Cultural Economy*, Abingdon: Routledge.

Lyotard, Jean-Francois (1984) *The Postmodern Condition*, Minneapolis: University of Minnesota Press.

Mabey, Nick, Gulledge, Jay, Finel, Bernard and Silverthorne, Katherine (2011) *Degrees of Risk: Defining a Risk Management Framework for Climate Security*, London: E3G.

McAfee, Kathleen (1999) 'Selling nature to save it? Biodiversity and green developmentalism', *Society and Space*, 17 (2): 203–219.

McCall, Leslie (2005) 'The complexity of intersectionality', *Signs*, 30 (3): 171–180.

McCarthy, James and Prudham, Scott (2004) 'Neoliberal nature and the nature of neoliberalism', *Geoforum*, 35 (3): 275–283.

McCarthy, John D. and Zald, Mayer N. (1977) 'Resource mobilization and social movements: A partial theory', *American Journal of Sociology*, 82: 1212–1241.

McCormick, Sabrina (2007) 'Democratizing science movements: A new framework for mobilization and contestation', *Social Studies of Science*, 37 (4): 609–623.

McDonald, David A. (ed.) (2002) *Environmental Justice in South Africa*, Athens: Ohio University Press.

MacDonald, Kenneth (2010a) 'Business, biodiversity, and the new "fields" of conservation: The World Conservation Congress and the renegotiation of organizational order,' *Conservation and Society*, 8 (4): 256–275.

MacDonald, Kenneth (2010b) 'The devil is in the (bio)diversity: Private sector "engagement" and the restructuring of biodiversity conservation', *Antipode*, 42 (3): 513–550.

MacDonald, Kenneth and Corson, Catherine (2012) '"TEEB Begins Now": A virtual moment in the production of natural capital', *Development and Change*, 43 (1): 159–184.

McDonald, Kevin (2002) 'From solidarity to fluidity: Social movements beyond "collective identity", the case of globalization conflicts', *Social Movement Studies*, 1 (2): 109–128.

McDonald, Kevin (2006) *Global Movements: Action and Culture*, Oxford: Blackwell.

McDonald, Mark (2012) 'U.N. Report from Rio on Environment "a Suicide Note"', *The New York Times*, 24 June. Available at http://rendezvous.blogs.nytimes.com/2012/06/24/u-n-report-from-rio-on-environment-a-suicide-note/ (accessed 5 March 2013).

McDonough, William and Braungart, Michael (2002) *Cradle to Cradle*, New York: North Point Press.

MacEachern, Diane (2008) *Big Green Purse*, New York: Avery Publishing.

Macfarlane, Robert (2003) *Mountains of the Mind: A History of a Fascination*, London: Granta Books.

McIntosh, Robert P. (1985) *The Background of Ecology: Concept and Theory*, Cambridge: Cambridge University Press.

MacIntyre, Alasdair (1990) *Three Rival Versions of Moral Enquiry*, London: Duckworth.

McKay, Kim and Bonnin, Jenny (2007) *True Green: 100 Everyday Ways you Can Contribute to a Healthier Planet*, Washington DC: National Geographic.

MacKenzie, Donald (2009) 'Making things the same: Gases, emission rights and the politics of carbon markets', *Accounting, Organizations and Society*, 34 (3–4): 440–455.

McKibben, Bill (1989) *The End of Nature*, New York: Anchor.

McKibben, Bill (2007) *Deep Economy: The Wealth of Communities and the Durable Future*, New York: Times Books.

McKibben, Bill (2010) *Eaarth*, New York: Times Books.

McKibben, Bill (2012) 'Introduction', in Bill McKibben (ed.) *The Global Warming Reader*, New York: Penguin Books, 9–18.

McKinsey and Company (2011) *Resource Revolution*, McKinsey Global Institute.

McNamara, Karen E. and Gibson, Chris (2009) '"We do not want to leave our land": Pacific ambassadors at the United Nations resist the category of climate refugees', *Geoforum*, 40 (3): 475–483.

McShane, Katie (2004) 'Ecosystem health', *Environmental Ethics*, 26: 227–245.

McWhorter, Ladell (2011) 'Decapitating power', *Foucault Studies*, 12: 77–96.

Malthus, Thomas Robert (1888) *An Essay on the Principle of Population: or, A View of Its Past and Present Effects on Human Happiness,* London: Reeves and Turner.

Magnusson, Warren (2003) 'The puzzle of the political', in Warren Magnusson and Karena Shaw (eds) *A Political Space: Reading the Global Through Clayoquot Sound,* Minneapolis: University of Minnesota Press.

Maniates, Michael F. (2001) 'Individualization: Plant a tree, buy a bike, save the world?' *Global Environmental Politics* 1: 31–52.

Maniates, Michael (2002) 'Individualisation: Plant a tree, buy a bike, save the world?' in Thomas Princen, Michael Maniates and Ken Conca (eds) *Confronting Consumption,* Cambridge MA: MIT Press.

Maniates, Michael and Meyer, John M. (eds) (2010) *The Environmental Politics of Sacrifice,* Boston: MIT Press.

Mann, Charles C. (2005) *1491: New Revelations of the Americas Before Columbus,* New York: Random House.

Mann, Charles C. (2011) *1493: Uncovering the New World Columbus Created,* New York: Knopf.

Mansvelt, Juliana (2005) *Geographies of Consumption,* London: Sage.

Marcotullio, Peter J. and McGranahan, Graham (eds) (2007) *Scaling Urban Environmental Challenges: From Local to Global and Back,* London: Earthscan.

Marcus, George E. (1995) 'Ethnography in/of the world system: The emergence of multi-sited ethnography', *Annual Review of Anthropology,* 24 (1): 95–117.

Marcus, Gary (2008) *Kluge: The Haphazard Construction of the Human Mind,* London: Faber.

Marcuse, Herbert (1964) *One-Dimensional Man: Studies in the Ideology of Advanced Industrial Society,* Boston: Beacon.

Marres, Noortje (2008) 'The making of climate publics: Eco-homes as material devices of publicity', *Distinktion,* 9 (1): 27–45.

Marsh, George Perkins (2012) *The Earth As Modified By Human Action,* New York: Forgotten Books.

Martenson, Chris (2011) *The Crash Course: The Unsustainable Future of our Economy, Energy, and Environment,* New York: John Wiley & Sons.

Martinez-Alier, Joan (2005) *The Environmentalism of the Poor,* New Delhi: Oxford University Press.

Marx, Karl (1843) 'Letter from Marx to Arnold Ruge in Dresden'. Available at http://www.marxists.org/archive/marx/works/1843/letters/43_09-alt.htm (accessed 1 February 2013).

Marx, Karl (1857) *Outline of the Critique of Political Economy (Grundrisse).* Available at http://www.marxists.org/archive/marx/works/1857/grundrisse/ch01.htm (accessed 27 March 2013).

Marx, Karl (1976) *Capital: A Critique of Political Economy,* Harmondsworth: Penguin.

Marx, Karl and Engels, Friedrich (1848) *The Communist Manifesto.* Available at http://www.marxists.org/archive/marx/works/1848/communist-manifesto/ (accessed 1 February 2013).

Marx, Karl and Engels, Friedrich (1978) 'The Communist Manifesto', in Robert C. Tucker (ed.) *The Marx-Engels Reader,* New York: Norton.

Massumi, Brian (2005) 'Fear (the spectrum said)', *Positions,* 13 (1): 31–48.

Massumi, Brian (2007) 'Potential politics and the primacy of preemption', *Theory & Event,* 10 (2). Available at http://muse.jhu.edu/journals/theory_and_event/v010/10.2massumi.html (accessed 2 January 2013).

Massumi, Brian (2009) 'National enterprise emergency: Steps toward an ecology of powers', *Theory, Culture & Society,* 26 (6): 153–185.

Mathews, Jessica T. (1989) 'Redefining security,' *Foreign Affairs,* 68 (2): 162–177.

Matthew, Richard A., Barnett, Jon, McDonald, Bryan and O'Brian, Karen L. (eds) (2010) *Global Environmental Change and Human Security,* Cambridge, MA: MIT Press.

Mauss, Marcel and Hubert, Henri (1981) *Sacrifice: Its Nature and Function,* Chicago: University of Chicago Press.

Meadows, Donella H., Meadows, Dennis L., Randers, Jørgen and Behrens III, William W. (1972) *The Limits to Growth,* New York: New American Library.

Meadows, Donella H., Meadows, Dennis L. and Randers, Jørgen (1992) *Beyond the Limits,* Post Mills, VT: Chelsea Green Publishing Company.

Meadowcroft, James (2007a) 'Who is in charge here? Governance for sustainable development in a complex world', *Environmental Policy and Planning,* 9 (3–4): 193–212.

Meadowcroft, James (2007b) 'National sustainable development strategies: Features, challenges and reflexivity, *European Environment,* 17: 152–163.

Meine, Curt, Soulé, Michael and Noss, Reed (2006) '"A mission-driven discipline": The growth of conservation biology', *Conservation Biology,* 20 (3): 631–651.

Mellor, Mary (1992) *Breaking the Boundaries: Towards a Feminist Green Socialism,* London: Virago Press.

Mellor, Mary (1997) *Feminism and Ecology,* Cambridge: Polity.

Melucci, Alberto (1989) *Nomads of the Present,* London: Hutchinson Radius.

Melucci, Alberto (1995) 'The Process of Collective Identity', in Hank Johnston and Bert Klandermans (eds) *Social Movements and Culture,* Minneapolis: University of Minnesota Press.

Melucci, Alberto (1996) *Challenging Codes,* Cambridge: Cambridge University Press.

Melucci, Alberto (2000) *Culture in Gioco: Differenze per Convivere,* Milan: Saggiatore.

Merchant, Carolyn (1980) *The Death of Nature: Women, Ecology and the Scientific Revolution,* New York: Harper and Row.

Merchant, Carolyn (1985) *Ecological Revolutions,* New York: Harper and Row.

Merchant, Carolyn (1992) *Radical ecology: The Search for a Liveable World,* London: Routledge.

Mesarovic, Mihaljo and Pestel, Eduard (1974) *Mankind at the Turning Point,* New York: EP Dutton.

Methmann, Chris and Rothe, Delf (2012) 'Politics for the day after tomorrow: The logic of apocalypse in global climate policy', *Security Dialogue,* 43(4): 323–344.

Meuleman, Louis and in't Veld, Roeland (2009) *Sustainable Development and the Governance of Long-Term Decisions,* Den Haag: RMNO.

Meyer, Warren (2012) 'Understanding the global warming debate', *Forbes.* Available at http://www.forbes.com/sites/warrenmeyer/2012/02/09/understanding-the-global-warming-debate/ (accessed 27 March 2013).

Michael, Michael (2000) *Reconnecting Culture, Technology, and Nature: From Society to Heterogeneity,* London: Routledge.

Michaels, David (2006) 'Manufactured uncertainty: Protecting public health in the age of contested science and product defense', *Annals of the New York Academy of Sciences,* 1076: 149–162.

Michaels, Patrick J. (2012) *The Current Wisdom: Throwing Science Overboard to get a Sea-Level Disaster,* Cato Institute, 11 July. Available at http://www.cato.org/publications/commentary/current-wisdom-throwing-science-overboard-get-sealevel-disaster (accessed 27 March 2013).

Middleton, Neil and O'Keefe, Phil (2001) *Redefining Sustainable Development,* London: Pluto Press.

Middleton, Neil and O'Keefe, Phil (2003) *Rio Plus Ten: Politics, Poverty and the Environment,* London: Pluto Press.

Mies, Maria (1997) *Patriarchy and Accumulation on a World Scale: Women in the International Division of Labour,* London: Zed Books.

Mihata, Kevin (1997) 'The persistence of "emergence"', in Raymond A. Eve, Sara Horsfall and Mary Lee (eds) *Chaos, Complexity and Sociology: Myths, Models, and Theories,* London: Sage.

Mill, John Stuart (1962) *Utilitarianism and Other Writings,* New York: Meridian.

Millennium Ecosystem Assessment (2005) *Ecosystems and Human Well-Being: Synthesis,* Washington DC: Island Press.

Miller, Clark A. and Edwards, Paul N. (eds) (2001) *Changing the Atmosphere: Expert Knowledge and Environmental Governance,* Cambridge, MA: MIT Press.

Miller, Daniel (1998) 'Coca-Cola: A black sweet drink from Trinidad', in Daniel Miller (ed.) *Material Cultures: Why Some Things Matter,* Chicago: University of Chicago Press, 169–187.

Miller, Daniel (2008) *The Comfort of Things,* London: Polity Press.

Miller, Daniel, Jackson, Peter, Thrift, Nigel, Holbrook, Beverley and Rowlands, Michael (1998) *Shopping, Place and Identity,* London: Routledge.

Miller, Peter and Rose, Nikolas (2008) *Governing the Present: Administering Economic, Social and Personal Life,* Cambridge: Polity Press.

Mills, Sara (2003) *Michel Foucault,* Routledge Critical Thinkers, London: Routledge.

Mintz, Sidney (1986) *Sweetness and Power: The Place of Sugar in Modern History,* London: Penguin.

Mitchell, Don (2005). 'The S.U.V. model of citizenship: Floating bubbles, buffer zones, and the rise of the "purely atomic" individual', *Political Geography,* 24 (1): 77–100.

Mitchell, Sandra (2009) *Unsimple Truths: Science, Complexity and Policy,* Chicago, IL: University of Chicago Press.

Mitchell, Timothy (2002) *Rule of Experts: Egypt, Technopolitics, Modernity,* Berkeley: University of California Press.

Mitchell, Timothy (2009) 'Carbon Democracy', *Economy and Society,* 38 (3): 399–432.

Mitchell, Timothy (2012) *Carbon Democracy: Political Power in the Age of Oil,* London: Verso.

Monbiot, George (2006) *Heat,* London: Penguin.

Mongabay (2013) 'Indonesian Forests'. Available at http://www.mongabay.com/ (accessed 27 March 2013).

Moore, Donald (2005) *Suffering for Territory: Race, Place and Power in Zimbabwe,* Durham and London: Duke University Press.

Moore, Hilary and Russell, Joshua Kahn (2011) *Organizing Cools the Planet,* San Francisco: PM Press.

Moore, Kelly, Kleinman, Daniel L., Hess, David and Frickel, Scott (2011) 'Science and neoliberal globalization: A political sociological approach', *Theory and Society,* 40 (5): 505–532.

Moore, Niamh (2004) 'Ecofeminism as third wave feminism: Essentialism, activism and the academy', in Stacy Gills, Gillian Howie, and Rebecca Munford (eds) *Third Wave Feminism: A Critical Exploration,* Basingstoke: Palgrave.

Moran, Daniel (ed.) (2011) *Climate Change and National Security: A Country-Level Analysis,* Washington: Georgetown University Press.

Moran, Katy, King, Steven and Carlson, Thomas (2001) 'Biodiversity prospecting: Lessons and prospects', *Annual Review of Anthropology,* 30: 505–526.

Morgenthau, Hans (1960) *Politics Among Nations: The Struggle for Power and Peace,* Third edition, New York: Knopf.

Morin, Edgar (1992) *Method: Towards a Study of Humankind, Vol.1, The Nature of Nature,* trans. Roland Bélanger, New York: Peter Lang.

Morin, Edgar (1999) *Homeland Earth: A Manifesto for the New Millennium,* trans. Sean Kelly and Roger LaPointe, Cresskill NJ: Hampton Press.

Morin, Edgar (2007) 'Restricted complexity, general complexity', in Carlos Gershenson, Diederik Aerts and Bruce Edmonds (eds) *Worldviews, Science and Us: Philosophy and Complexity,* Singapore: World Scientific Publishing, 5–29.

Morin, Edgar (2008) *On Complexity,* Cresskill NJ: Hampton Press.

Morito, Bruce (2003) 'Intrinsic value: A modern albatross for the ecological approach', *Environmental Values,* 12: 317–336.

Morris, Stephen (ed.) (2007) *The New Village Green: Living Light, Living Local, Living Large,* Philadelphia: New Society.

Morris, Meaghan and Patton, Paul (eds) (1979) *Michel Foucault: Power, Truth, Strategy,* Sydney: Feral Publications.

Mouffe, Chantal (2005) *On the Political,* Abingdon: Routledge.

Movement Generation (2010) 'Open letter to 1 Sky,' Oakland, 24 October. Available at http://grist.org/article/2010-10-23-open-letter-to-1-sky-from-the-grassroots/ (accessed 8 July 2013).

Muir, John (1997) *Nature Writings,* New York: Library of America.

Muir, John (2003) [1911] *My First Summer in the Sierra,* New York: The Modern Library.

Muller, Benito (2001) 'Varieties of distributive justice in climate change', *Climatic Change,* 48 (2–3): 273–288.

Muller, Benito (2002) *Equity in Climate Change: The Great Divide,* Oxford: Oxford Institute for Energy Studies.

Mumford, Lewis (1932) *Technics and Civilization,* New York: Harcourt Brace Jovanovich.

Mumford, Lewis (1967) *The Myth of the Machine, Vol. 1 Technics and Human Development,* New York: Harcourt Brace Jovanovich.

Mumford, Lewis (1970) *The Myth of the Machine: Vol. 2 The Pentagon of Power,* New York: Harcourt Brace Jovanovich.

Mumford, Lewis (1986) *The Lewis Mumford Reader,* New York: Pantheon.

Murdoch, Jonathan and Ward, Neil (1997) 'Governmentality and territoriality: The statistical manufacture of Britain's "national farm"', *Political Geography,* 16 (4): 307–324.

Myanna, Lahsen (2005) 'Seductive simulations? Uncertainty distribution around climate', *Social Studies of Science,* 35 (6): 895–922.

Myers, Norman (1993) *Ultimate Security: The Environmental Basis of Political Stability,* New York: Norton.

Myers, Norman and Kent, Jennifer (1995) *Environmental Exodus: An Emergent Crisis in the Global Arena,* Washington DC: Climate Institute.

Nace, Ted (2009) *Climate Hope: On the Front Lines of the Fight Against Coal,* San Francisco: CoalSwarm.

Nace, Ted (2011) 'Down with coal', *Grist,* 27 May. Available at http://grist.org/coal/2011-05-27-down-with-coal-the-grassroots-anti-coal-movement-goes-global/ (accessed 13 April 2013).

Naess, Arne (1973) 'The shallow and the deep, long-range ecology movement: A summary', *Inquiry,* 16: 95–100.

Naess, Arne (1989) *Community, Ecology, and Lifestyle,* Cambridge: Cambridge University Press.

Naess, Arne (1994) 'The shallow and deep long-range ecological movement' in L.P. Pojman and P. Pojman (eds) *Environmental Ethics: Reading in Theory and Application,* Independence, KY: Wadsworth Publishing.

Naess, Arne (2009) 'Identification as a source of deep ecological attitudes', in Eldon Soifer (ed.) *Ethical Issues: Perspectives for Canadians,* Third edition, Peterborough, Ontario: Broadview Press.

Narain, Sunita (1990) *Global Warming in an Unequal World,* New Delhi: Centre for Science and Environment.

Nature Inc (2011) *Nature Inc.: Questioning the Market Panacea in Environmental Policy and Conservation,* conference at the Institute of Social Science, Hague, Netherlands, 30 June–3 July 2011. Available at http://www.iss.nl/research/conferences_and_seminars/previous_iss_conferences_and_seminars/naturetm_inc_questioning_the_market_panacea_in_environmental_policy_and_conservation/ (accessed 27 March 2013).

NDTC (Niger Delta Technical Committee) (2008) *Report of the Technical Committee of the Niger Delta,* Abuja: Federal Government of Nigeria.

Neale, Jonathan (2008) *Stop Global Warming,* London: Bookmarks Publications.

Neale, Jonathan (ed.) (2011) *One Million Climate Jobs: Solutions to the Economic and Environmental Crises,* A report by the Campaign against Climate Change trade union group in conjunction with the Communication Workers Union (CWU), Public and Commercial Services Union (PCS), Transport Salaried Staffs Association (TSSA) and the University and College Union (UCU), London.

Nealon, Jeffrey (2008) *Foucault Beyond Foucault. Power and Its Intensification Since 1984,* Stanford, CA: Stanford University Press.

Nederveen Pieterse, Jan (2004) *Globalization and Culture: Global Mélange,* Oxford: Rowman & Littlefield.

Neocleous, Mark (2008) *Critique of Security,* Edinburgh: Edinburgh University Press.

Neumann, Roderick (1998) *Imposing Wilderness: Struggles over Livelihoods and Nature Preservation in Africa,* Berkeley: University of California Press.

Neumann, Roderick (2005) *Making Political Ecology,* London: Hodder.

Neumayer, Eric (2004) *Weak Versus Strong Sustainability: Exploring The Limits Of Two Opposing Paradigms,* Cheltenham: Edward Elgar.

Neumayer, Eric (2007) 'A missed opportunity: The Stern Review on climate change fails to tackle the issue of non-substitutable loss of natural capital', *Global Environmental Change,* 17 (3–4): 297–301.

New Economics Foundation (2008) *Green New Deal,* London: New Economics Foundation.

Newell, Peter (2001) 'Managing multinationals: The governance of investment for the environment', *Journal of International Development,* 13 (7): 907–919.

Newell, Peter and Paterson, Matthew (1998) 'A climate for business: Global warming, the state and capital', *Review of International Political Economy,* 5 (4): 679–703.

Newell, Peter and Paterson, Matthew (2010) *Climate Capitalism: Global Warming and the Transformation of the Global Economy,* Cambridge: Cambridge University Press.

Newsham, Guy R., Mancini, Sandra and Birt, Benjamin J. (2009) 'Do LEED-certified buildings save energy? Yes, but . . . ', *Energy and Building,* 41: 897–905.

Nibert, David (2002) *Animal Rights/Human Rights: Entanglements of Oppression and Liberation,* Lanham, MD: Rowman and Littlefield.

Noble, David (1977) *America by Design: Science, Technology, and the Rise of Corporate Capitalism,* New York: Knopf.

Nordhaus, William (2007) 'Review of the Stern Review on the Economics of Climate Change', *Journal of Economic Literature,* 45 (3): 686–702.

Nordhaus, Ted and Shellenberger, Michael (2007) *Break Through: From the Death of Environmentalism to the Politics of Possibility,* New York: Houghton Press.

Norgaard, Richard B. (1994) *Development Betrayed: The End of Progress and a Coevolutionary Revisioning of the Future,* London: Routledge.

Norton, Bryan G. (1984) 'Environmental ethics and weak Anthropocentrism', *Environmental Ethics,* 6: 131–148.

Norton, Bryan G. (2005) *Sustainability: A Philosophy of Adaptive Ecosystem Management,* Chicago: University of Chicago Press.

Nozick, Robert (1989) *The Examined Life,* New York: Simon and Schuster.

NRC (National Research Council) (1983) *Risk Assessment in the Federal Government: Managing the Process,* Washington DC: National Academy Press.

Nwajiaku, Kathryn (2012) 'The political economy of oil and rebellion in Nigeria's Niger delta', *Review of African Political Economy,* 132: 295–314.

Oberthür, Sebastian and Gehring, Thomas (eds) (2006) *Institutional Interaction in Global Environmental Governance: Synergy and Conflict among International and EU Policies,* Cambridge: MIT Press.

Obi, Cyril and Rustad, Siri Aas (eds) (2011) *Oil and Insurgency in the Niger Delta: Managing the Complex Politics of Petro-violence,* London: Zed Press.

Obidzinski, Krystof (2005) 'Illegal logging in Indonesia: Myth and reality', in Budy P. Resosudarmo (ed.) *The Politics and Economics of Indonesia's Natural Resources,* Singapore: The Institute of Southeast Asian Studies with Australian National University, 193–205.

Obidzinski, Krystof and Barr, Christopher (2003) *The Effects of Decentralisation on Forests and Forest Industries in Berau District, East Kalimantan,* Bogor, Indonesia: CIFOR.

O'Brien, Karen, Eriksen, Siri, Nygaard, Lynn P. and Schjolden, Ane (2007) 'Why different interpretations of vulnerability matter in climate change discourses', *Climate Policy,* 7 (1): 73–88.

O'Brien, Karen, Leichenko, Robin, Kelkar, Ulka, Venema, Henry, Aandahl, Guro, Tompkins, Heather et al. (2004) 'Mapping vulnerability to multiple stressors: Climate change and globalization in India', *Global Environmental Change,* 14 (4): 303–313.

O'Connor, James (1991) 'On the two contradictions of capitalism', *Capitalism, Nature, Socialism,* 2 (3): 107–109.

O'Connor, James (1996) 'The second contradiction of capitalism', in Ted Benton (ed.) *The Greening of Marxism,* New York: Guildford Press, 197–221.

O'Connor, Martin (1994) *Is Capitalism Sustainable? Political Economy and the Politics of Ecology,* New York: Guilford Press.

Odum, Eugene (1953) *Fundamentals of Ecology,* Chicago: W.B. Saunders.

Odum, Eugene (1964) 'The new ecology', *Bioscience,* 14: 14–16.

OECD (2011), *Towards Green Growth*. Available at http://www.oecd.org/greengrowth/48224539.pdf (accessed 27 March 2013).

Oels, Angela (2005) 'Rendering climate change governable: From biopower to advanced liberal government?' *Journal of Environmental Policy and Planning*, 7 (3): 185–207.

Oels, Angela (2011) 'Rendering climate change governable by risk: From probability to contingency', *Geoforum*, DOI:10.1016/j.geoforum.2011.09.007

Oels, Angela (2012) 'Comparing three theoretical perspectives on climate change as a security issue: From the "securitisation" of climate change to the "climatisation" of the security field', in Jürgen Scheffran, Michael Brzoska, Hans-Günter Brauch, Michael Link, and Jan-Peter Schilling (eds) *Climate Change, Human Security and Violent Conflict: Challenges for Societal Stability*, Berlin: Springer, 185–205.

Oels, Angela and Methmann, Chris (forthcoming) 'The vulnerable becoming dangerous: Rethinking the history of environmental security from conflict to resilience', in Christopher Daase, Gabi Schlag and Julian Junk (eds) *Dialogues on Security*, New York: Routledge.

O'Keefe, Phil, Westgate, Ken and Wisner, Ben (1976) 'Taking the naturalness out of natural disasters', *Nature*, 260: 566–567.

Okereke, Chukwumerije (2008) *Global Justice and Neoliberal Environmental Governance: Sustainable Development, Ethics and International Co-operation*, Abingdon: Routledge.

Okereke, Chukwumerije (2010a) 'Climate justice and the international regime', *WIREs Interdisciplinary Review*, 1: 462–474.

Okereke, Chukwumerije (2010b) 'Ethics and global environmental governance' in *The Environment Encyclopaedia and Directory 2010*, Fifth edition, Abingdon: Routledge, 22–32.

Okereke, Chukwumerije (2011) 'Moral foundations for global environmental and climate justice', *Royal Institute of Philosophy Supplements*, 69 (69): 117–135.

Okereke, Chukwumerije, Bulkeley, Harriet and Schroeder, Heike (2009) 'Conceptualizing climate change governance beyond the international regime', *Global Environmental Politics*, 9 (1): 58–78.

Okereke, Chukwumerije and Dooley, Kate (2010) 'Principles of justice in proposals and policy approaches to avoided deforestation: Towards a post-Copenhagen climate agreement', *Global Environmental Change*, 20: 82–95.

Okereke, Chukwumerije and Schroeder, Heike (2009) 'How can the objectives of justice, development and climate change mitigation be reconciled in the treatment of developing countries in a post-Kyoto settlement?' *Climate and Development*, 1: 10–15.

Okereke, Chukwumerije, Wittneben, Bettina and Bowen, Frances (2012) 'Climate change: Challenging business, transforming politics', *Business & Society*, 51 (1): 7–30.

Okonta, Ike (2005) *When Citizens Revolt: Nigerian Elites, Big Oil and the Ogoni Struggle for Self-Determination*, Trenton NJ: World Africa Press.

Olds, Kris (1998) 'Urban mega-events, evictions and housing rights: The Canadian case', *Current Issues in Tourism*, 1 (1): 2–46.

O'Loughlin, John, Witmer, Frank D. W., Linke, Andrew M., Laing, Arlene, Gettelman, Andrew and Dudhia, Jimmy (2012) 'Climate variability and conflict risk in East Africa, 1990–2009', *Proceedings of the National Academy of Sciences*, 109 (45): 18344–18349.

Olson, Mancur (1971) *The Logic of Collective Action: Public Goods and the Theory of Groups*, Cambridge, MA: Harvard University Press.

Olsson, Per, Folke, Carl and Berkes, Fikret (2004) 'Adaptive comanagement for building resilience in social-ecological systems', *Environmental Management*, 34 (1): 75–90.

O'Malley, Pat (2004) *Risk, Uncertainty and Governance*, London: Glasshouse.

O'Malley, Pat (2010) 'Resilient subjects: uncertainty, warfare, and liberalism', *Economy and Society*, 39(4): 488–509.

O'Neill, Kate (2004) 'Transnational protest: States, circuses, and conflicts at the frontline of global politics', *International Studies Review*, 6 (2): 233–251.

Ong, Aihwa (1999) *Flexible Citizenship: The Cultural Logics of Transnationality,* Durham, NC: Duke University Press.

openDemocracy (2012) 'Occupy!' Available at http://www.opendemocracy.net/ourkingdom/collections/occupy (accessed 17 January 2012).

Ophuls, William (1977) *Ecology and the Politics of Scarcity: Prologue to a Political Theory of the Steady State,* San Francisco: W.H. Freeman.

Ophuls, William (1992) *Ecology and the Politics of Scarcity Revisited,* New York: W.H. Freeman.

Ophuls, William (1997) *Requiem for Modern Politics: The Tragedy of the Enlightenment and the Challenge of the New Millennium,* Boulder, CO: Westview Press.

Ophuls, William (2011) *Plato's Revenge: Politics in the Age of Ecology,* London: MIT Press.

Oppenheimer, Michael (2005), 'Defining dangerous Anthropogenic interference: The role of science, the limits of science', *Risk Analysis,* 25 (6): 1399–1407.

Oreskes, Naomi and Conway, Eric, M. (2010) *Merchants of Doubt: How a Handful of Scientists Obscured the Truth on Issues from Tobacco to Global Warming,* New York; Bloomsbury Press.

O'Riordan, Tim (ed.) (2001) *Globalism Localism, and Identity: Transition to Sustainability,* London: Earthscan.

Orr, David and Soroos, Marvin (eds) (1979) *The Global Predicament: Ecological Perspectives on World Order,* Chapel Hill: University of North Carolina Press.

Ostrom, Elinor (2009) 'A general framework for analyzing sustainability of social-ecological systems', *Science,* 325: 419–422.

Oswald Spring, Úrsula (2007) 'Human, gender and environmental security: A HUGE challenge', in Úrsula Oswald Spring (ed.) *International Security, Peace, Development, Environment: Encyclopaedia on Life Support Systems/UNESCO,* Oxford: Oxford University Press.

Oswald Spring, Úrsula (2008a) *Gender and Disasters: Human, Gender and Environmental Security: A HUGE Challenge,* Bonn: UNU-EHS, Intersection.

Oswald Spring, Úrsula (2008b) 'A HUGE gender security approach: Towards human, gender and environmental security', in Hans Günter Brauch, John Grin, Czeslaw Mesjasz, C., Heinz Krummenacher, Navitna Chadha, Béchir Choru et al. (eds) *Facing Global Environmental Change: Environmental, Human, Energy, Food, Health and Water Security Concept,* Hexagon Series on Human and Environmental Security and Peace, Berlin: Springer-Verlag.

Ottinger, Gwen (2010) 'Buckets of resistance: Standards and the effectiveness of citizen science', *Science, Technology, & Human Values,* 35 (2): 244–270.

Owens, Susan (2000) '"Engaging the public": Information and deliberation in environmental policy', *Environment and Planning A,* 32 (7): 1141–1148.

Paavola, Jouni, Gouldson, Andy and Kluvánková-Oravská, Tatiana (2009) 'Interplay of actors, scales, frameworks and regimes in the governance of biodiversity', *Environmental Policy and Governance,* 19 (3): 148–158.

Pachauri, Rajendra K. (2006) 'Avoiding dangerous climate change', in Hans-Joachim Schellnhuber (ed.) *Avoiding Dangerous Climate Change,* Cambridge: Cambridge University Press, 3–5.

Palmer, Martin and Finlay, Victoria (2003) *Faith in Conservation: New Approaches to Religions and the Environment,* Washington DC: The World Bank.

Parenti, Christian (2012) *Tropic of Chaos: Climate Change and the New Geography of Violence,* New York: Nation Books.

Pascal, Cleo (2010) *Global Warring: How Environmental, Economic and Political Crises Will Redraw the World Map,* Toronto: Key Porter.

Pasquino, Pasquale (1978) 'Theatrum politicum: the genealogy of capital–police and the state of prosperity', *Ideology and Consciousness,* 4: 41–53.

Paterson, Matthew (1996) *Global Warming and Global Politics,* London: Routledge.

Paterson, Matthew (2000) *Understanding Global Environmental Politics: Domination, Accumulation, Resistance,* New York/London: Macmillan Palgrave.

Paterson, Matthew (2007) *Automobile Politics: Ecology and Cultural Political Economy,* Cambridge: Cambridge University Press.

Paterson, Matthew and Stripple, Johannes (2010) 'My space: Governing individuals' carbon emissions', *Environment and Planning D: Society and Space,* 28: 341–362.

Patomäki, Heikki and Teivainen, Teivo (2004) 'The World Social Forum: An open space or movement of movements?' *Theory, Culture and Society,* 21 (6): 145–154.

Pearce, David and Barbier, Edward (2001) *Blueprint for a Sustainable Economy,* London: Earthscan.

Pearce, David, Markandya, Anil and Barbier, Edward (1989) *Blueprint for a Green Economy,* London: Earthscan.

Peet, Richard and Watts, Michael (eds) (1996a) *Liberation Ecologies: Environment, Development and Social Movements,* London: Routledge.

Peet, Richard and Watts, Michael (1996b) 'Liberation ecology: Development, sustainability, and environment in an age of market triumphalism,' in Richard Peet and Michael Watts (eds) *Liberation Ecologies: Environment, Development and Social Movements,* London: Routledge.

Peet, Richard, Robbins, Paul and Watts, Michael (2011) 'Global nature', in Richard Peet, Paul Robbins and Michael J. Watts (eds) *Global Political Ecology,* Abingdon: Routledge.

Pellizzoni, Luigi (2011a) 'The politics of facts: Local environmental conflicts and expertise', *Environmental Politics,* 20 (6): 765–785.

Pellizzoni, Luigi (2011b) 'Governing through disorder: Neoliberal environmental governance and social theory', *Global Environmental Change,* 21 (3): 795–803.

Pellizzoni, Luigi and Ylönen, Marja (2008) 'Responsibility in uncertain times: An institutional perspective on precaution', *Global Environmental Politics,* 8 (3): 51–73.

Pellizzoni, Luigi and Ylönen, Marja (eds) (2012) *Neoliberalism and Technoscience: Critical Assessments,* Farnham: Ashgate.

Peluso, Nancy L. (1992) *Rich Forests, Poor People: Resource Control and Resistance in Java,* Berkeley: University of California Press.

Peluso, Nancy L. (2012) 'What's nature got to do with it? A situated historical perspective on socionatural commodities', *Development and Change,* 43: 79–104.

Peluso, Nancy L. and Vandergeest, Peter (2011) 'The political ecology of war and forests: Counterinsurgency and the making of national natures', Annals of the Association of American Geographers, 101 (3): 587–608.

Peluso, Nancy L. and Watts, Michael (eds) (2001) *Violent Environments,* Ithaca, NY: Cornell University Press.

Perrow, Charles (1984) *Normal Accidents: Living with High Risk Technologies,* New York: Basic Books.

Petermann, Anne (2009) 'What is climate justice?' Vermont, Global Justice Ecology Project. Available at http://globaljusticeecology.org/climate_justice.php (accessed 12 April 2013).

Peterson, Anna (2010) 'Ordinary and extraordinary sacrifices: Religion, everyday life, and environmental practice', in Michael Maniates and John M. Meyer (eds) *The Environmental Politics of Sacrifice,* Boston: MIT Press, 91–116.

Petrina, Stephen (2000) 'The political ecology of design and technology Education: An inquiry into methods', *International Journal of Technology and Design Education,* 10: 207–237.

Pettman, Dominic (2011) *Human Error: Species Being and Media Machines,* Minneapolis: University of Minnesota Press.

Pflughoeft, Kathryn J. and Versalovic, James (2012) 'Human Microbiome in Health and Disease', *Annual Review of Pathology: Mechanisms of Disease,* 7: 99–122.

PGA (2001) *Hallmarks of Peoples' Global Action.* Available at http://www.nadir.org/nadir/initiativ/agp/free/pga/hallm.htm (accessed 4 Feb 2013).

Philo, Chris (2012) 'A "new Foucault" with lively implications – or "the crawfish advances sideways"', *Transactions of the Institute of British Geographers,* DOI: 10.1111/j.1475–5661.2011.00484.x.

Phoenix, Ann and Pattynama, Pamela (2006) 'Editorial: Intersectionality', *European Journal of Women's Studies,* 13 (3): 187–192.

Pianta, Mario (2001) 'Parallel summits of global civil society', in Helmet Anheier, Marlies Glasius and Mary Kaldor (eds) *Global Civil Society 2001*, Oxford: OUP, 169–194.

Pielke, Roger A. Jr (2000) 'Policy history of the US Global Change Research Programme: Part I. Administrative Development', *Global Environmental Change*, 10: 9–25.

Pielke, Roger A. Jr (2007) 'Mistreatment of the economic impacts of extreme events in the Stern Review Report on the Economics of Climate Change', *Global Environmental Change*, 17 (3–4): 302–310.

Pierre, Jon (2000) 'Introduction: Understanding governance', in Jon Pierre (ed.) *Debating Governance*, Oxford: Oxford University Press: 1–12.

Pierre, Jon, and Peters, Guy (2000) *Governance, Politics and the State*, London: Macmillan.

Pinchot, Gifford (1998) *Breaking New Ground*, Washington DC: Island Press.

Plant, Judith (1989) *Healing the Wounds: The promise of Ecofeminism*, Philadelphia: New Society Publishers.

Plant, Judith (1997) 'The challenge of ecofeminist community,' in Karen Warren (ed.) *Ecofeminism: Women, Nature, Culture*, Philadelphia: New Society.

Plumwood, Val (1991) *Nature, Self and Gender*, London: Routledge.

Plumwood, Val (1993) *Feminism and the Mastery of Nature*, London: Routledge.

Plumwood, Val (1994) 'The ecopolitics debate and the politics of nature,' in Karen Warren (ed.) *Ecological Feminism*, London: Routledge.

Plumwood, Val (1997) 'Androcentrism and anthropocentrism: Parallels and politics,' in Karen Warren (ed.) *Ecofeminism: Women, Nature, Culture*, Philadelphia: New Society.

Plumwood, Val (2004) 'Ecofeminism,' in Robert White (ed.) *Controversies in Environmental Sociology*, Cambridge: Cambridge University Press.

Polanyi, Karl (1944) *The Great Transformation: The Political and Economic Origins of Our Time*, Boston: Beacon Press.

Polletta, Francesca and Jasper, James (2001) 'Collective identity and social movements', *Annual Review of Sociology*, 27: 283–305.

Pollock, Neil and Williams, Robin (2010) 'The business of expectations: How promissory organizations shape technology and innovation', *Social Studies of Science*, 40 (4): 525–548.

Ponting, Clive (1991) *A Green History of the World*, London: Penguin.

Pool, Robert (1997) *Beyond Engineering: How Society Shapes Technology*, Oxford: Oxford University Press.

Popke, Jeff (2006) 'Geography and ethics: Everyday mediations through care and consumption', *Progress in Human Geography*, 30 (4): 504–512.

Porritt, Jonathon (2005) *Capitalism as if the World Matters*, London: Earthscan.

Posner, Eric and Sunstein, Cass (2007) 'Climate Change Justice', John M. Olin Law & Economics Working Paper No. 354, University of Chicago Law School, Chicago.

Postrel, Virgina (1998) *The Future and Its Enemies: The Growing Conflict Over Creativity, Enterprise, and Progress*, New York: Free Press.

Prelitz, Chris (2009) *Green Made Easy: The Everyday Guide for Transitioning to a Green Lifestyle*, Carlsbad: Hay House.

Price, Jennifer (1995) 'Looking for nature in the mall: A field guide to the Nature Company', in William Cronon (ed.) *Uncommon Ground*, New York: WW Norton, 186–202.

Princen, Thomas (2005) *The Logic of Sufficiency*, Cambridge MA: MIT Press.

Princen, Thomas, Maniates, Michael and Conca, Ken (eds) (2002) *Confronting Consumption*, Cambridge, MA: MIT Press.

Putnam, Robert D. (1988) 'Diplomacy and domestic politics: The logic of two-level games', *International Organization*, 42 (3): 427–460.

Putnam, Robert D. and Bayne, Nicholas (1987) *Hanging Together: Cooperation and Conflict in the Seven-Power Summits*, London: Sage.

Quilley, Stephen (2011) 'Entropy, the anthroposphere and the ecology of civilization: An essay on the problem of "liberalism in one village" in the long view', *Sociological Review*, 59: 65–90.

Rajamani, Lavanya (2011) 'The Cancun Climate Agreements: Reading the text, subtext, and tea leaves', *International and Comparative Law Quarterly*, 60 (2): 499–519.

Rawcliffe, Peter (1998) *Environmental Pressure Groups in Transition*, Manchester: Manchester University Press.

Rayner, Steve (2010) 'How to eat an elephant: A bottom-up approach to climate policy', *Climate Policy*, 10 (6): 615–621.

Redclift, Michael (1987) *Sustainable Development: Exploring the Contradictions*, London: Routledge.

Redclift, Michael (1992) 'The meaning of sustainable development', *Geoforum*, 23 (3): 395–403.

Redclift, Michael (2000) *Wasted: Counting the Cost of Global Consumption*, London: Earthscan.

Redford, Kent (1990) 'The ecologically noble savage,' *Orion*, 9: 24–29.

Redford, Kent (2011) 'Misreading the conservation landscape', *Oryx*, 45: 324–330.

Redman, Janet (2012) 'Now will Obama break his climate silence?' *Huffington Post*, 8 November. Available at http://www.huffingtonpost.com/janet-redman/obama-climate-change_b_2091210.html (accessed 12 April 2013).

Rees, William E. (1992) 'Ecological footprints and appropriated carrying capacity: What urban economics leaves out', *Environment and Urbanisation*, 4 (2): 121–130.

Regan, Tom (1983) *The Case for Animal Rights*, Berkeley: University of California Press.

Reich, Robert (1991) *The Work of Nations: Preparing Ourselves for 21st Century Capitalism*, New York: Knopf.

Reid, Julian (2007) *The Biopolitics of the War on Terror: Life Struggles, Liberal Modernity and the Defence of Logistical Societies*, Manchester: Manchester University Press.

Reid, Julian (2010) 'The biopoliticization of humanitarianism: from saving bare life to securing the biohuman in post-interventionary societies', *Journal of Intervention and Statebuilding*, 4 (4): 391–411.

Reid, Julian (2012) 'The disastrous and politically debased subject of resilience', *Development Dialogue*, 58: 67–79.

Renner, Michael (1989) *National Security: The Economic and Environmental Dimensions*, Worldwatch Paper 89, Washington DC: Worldwatch Institute.

Renner, Michael (1991) 'Assessing the Military's War on the Environment', in Lester Brown, *State of the World 1991*, New York: Norton, 132–152.

Reno, William (2011) *Warfare in Independent Africa*, Cambridge: Cambridge University Press.

Reyes, Oscar (2012) 'After Durban: All talked out?' *Red Pepper*, January 2012. Available at http://www.redpepper.org.uk/after-durban-all-talked-out/?utm_source=Pepperista&utm_campaign=74a8693f2b-96035f6d2dc1a0ab8d89ff1b8516f23b&utm_medium=email (accessed 6 February 2012).

Reynolds, David (2007) *Summits: Six Meetings that Shaped the Twentieth Century*, London: Allen Lane.

Ribot, Jesse C. and Peluso, Nancy L. (2003) 'A theory of access', *Rural Sociology*, 68 (2): 153–181.

Rice, Jennifer (2010) 'Climate, carbon, and territory: Greenhouse gas mitigation in Seattle, Washington', *Annals of the Association of American Geographers*, 100 (4): 929–937.

Rifkin, Jeremy (1991) *Biospheric Politics: A New Consciousness for a New Century*, New York: Crown.

Rivoli, Petra (2009) *The Travels of a T-shirt in the Global Economy*, Second edition, Hoboken, NJ: Wiley & Sons.

Roberts, J. Timmons and Parks, Bradley C. (2007) *Climate of Injustice: Global Inequity, North-South Politics and Climate Policy*, Cambridge: MIT Press.

Robertson, Morgan (2004) 'The neoliberalization of ecosystem services: Wetland mitigation banking and problems in environmental governance', *Geoforum*, 35 (3): 361–373.

Robertson, Morgan (2006) 'The nature that capital can see: Science, state, and market in the commodification of ecosystem services', *Society and Space*, 24 (3): 367–387.

Robbins, Paul (2004) *Political Ecology: A Critical Introduction*, Malden, MA: Blackwell Publishing.

Robbins, Paul, and Luginbuhl, April (2007) 'The last enclosure: resisting privatization of wildlife in the western United States,' in Nik Heynen, James McCarthy, Scott Prudham and Paul Robbins (eds) *Neoliberal Environments: False Promises and Unnatural Consequences,* Abingdon: Routledge, 25–37.

Robinson, John (2012) 'Common and conflicting interests in the engagements between conservation NGOs and corporations,' *Conservation Biology,* 26 (6): 967–977.

Robinson, Mary (2011) 'Protecting the most vulnerable', Speech at the London School of Economics Centre for the Study of Human Rights, London, 10 March. Available at http://www.mrfcj.org/news_centre/2011/mary_robinson_lecture_lse.html (accessed 12 April 2013).

Roche, Maurice (2000) *Mega-Events and Modernity: Olympics and Expos in the Growth of Global Culture,* London: Routledge.

Rockström, Johan, Steffen, Will, Noone, Kevin, Persson, Åsa, Chapin, F. Stuart, Lambin, Eric F., et al. (2009) 'A safe operating space for humanity', *Nature,* 461 (7263): 472–475.

Roco, Mihail C. and Bainbridge, William S. (eds) (2002) *Converging Technologies for Improving Human Performance,* Arlington, VA: National Science Foundation.

Rolston, Holmes, III (1988) *Environmental Ethics: Duties to and Values in the Natural World,* Philadelphia: Temple University Press.

Rootes, Christopher (1999) '"Political opportunity structures": Promise, problems and prospects', *La Lettre de la Maison Française d'Oxford,* 10: 75–97.

Rootes, Christopher (2000) 'Environmental movements and green parties in western and eastern Europe', in M. R. Redclift and G. Woodgate (eds) *The International Handbook of Environmental Sociology, Part 4,* Cheltenham: Edward Elgar.

Rootes, Christopher (2007) 'Acting locally: The character, contexts and significance of local environmental mobilisations', *Environmental Politics,* 16 (5): 722–741.

Rose, Nikolas (1999) *Powers of Freedom: Reframing Political Thought,* Cambridge: CUP.

Rose, Nikolas and Miller, Peter (1992) 'Political power beyond the state: Problematics of government', *The British Journal of Sociology,* 43 (2), 173–205.

Rose, Nikolas, O'Malley, Pat and Velverde, Marina (2006) 'Governmentality', *Annual Review of Law and Social Science,* 2 (1): 83–104.

Ross, Annie, Sherman, Richard, Snodgrass, Jeffrey G. and Delcore, Henry D. (2011) *Indigenous Peoples and Collaborative Stewardship of Nature: knowledge binds and institutional conflicts,* Walnut Creek, CA: Left Coast Press.

Ross, Michael L. (2012) *The Oil Curse: How Petroleum Wealth Changes the Development of Nations,* Princeton: Princeton University Press.

Rosser, Andrew (2006) 'Escaping the resource curse', *New Political Economy,* 11 (4): 557–569.

Rostow, Walt W. (1960) *The Stages of Economic Growth: A Non-Communist Manifesto,* Cambridge: Cambridge Universtiy Press.

Rothe, Delf (2011) 'Managing climate risks or risking a managerial climate', *International Relations,* 25 (3): 330–345.

Rousseau, Jean-Jacques (1984) *Of the Social Contract and Discourse on Political Economy,* trans. C. Sherover, New York: Harper and Row.

Routley, Richard and Routley, Val (1979) 'Against the inevitability of human chauvinism', in K. E. Goodpaster and K. M. Sayre (eds) *Ethics and Problems of the 21st Century,* Notre Dame, IN: University of Notre Dame Press.

Rowell, Alexis (2010) *Communities, Councils and a Low Carbon Future,* Totnes UK: Green Books.

Rowell, Andrew (1996) *Green Backlash: Global Subversion of the Environment Movement,* London: Routledge.

Royal Society (2009) *Geoengineering the Climate. Science, Governance and Uncertainty,* RS Policy Document 10/09, London: The Royal Society.

Royal Society (2012) *People and the Planet,* The Royal Society Science Policy Centre report 01/12, London: The Royal Society.

Ruddick, Sarah (1990) *Maternal Thinking,* London: Women's Press.

Ruskin, John, Gandhi, Mohandas K. and Desai, Valji Govindji (1951) *Unto this Last: A Paraphrase by MK Gandhi,* Ahmedabad: Navajivan Publishing House.

Rutherford, Paul (1999) 'The entry of life into history', in Eric Darier (ed.) *Discourses of the Environment,* Malden MA: Blackwell Publishers, 37–62.

Rutherford, Stephanie (2007) 'Green governmentality: Insights and opportunities in the study of nature's rule', *Progress in Human Geography,* 31 (3): 291–307.

Rutland, Ted and Aylett, Alex (2008) 'The work of policy: Actor networks, governmentality, and local action on climate change in Portland, Oregon', *Environment and Planning D: Society and Space,* (26): 627–646.

Sachs, Wolfgang (1992) 'Environment', in Wolfgang Sachs (ed.) *The Development Dictionary: A Guide to Knowledge as Power,* London: Zed.

Safitri, Myrna and Bosko, Rafael (2002) *Indigenous Peoples/Ethnic Minorities and Poverty Reduction-Indonesia 17,* Manila: Environment and Social Safeguard Division Regional and Sustainable Development Department, Asian Development Bank.

Sagan, Carl and Turco, Richard (1990) *A Path Where No Man Thought: Nuclear Winter and the End of the Arms Race,* New York: Random House.

Said, Edward (1978) *Orientalism,* London: Penguin.

Sáiz, Ángel V. (2005) 'Globalisation, cosmopolitanism and ecological citizenship', *Environmental Politics,* 14 (2): 163–178.

Salamone, Constantia (1982) 'The prevalence of natural law within women: women and animal rights', in Pam McAllister (ed.) *Reweaving the Web of Life: Feminism and Non-violence,* San Francisco: New Society.

Sale, Kirkpatrick (1985) *Dwellers in the Land: The Bioregional Vision,* New York: Random House.

Sale, Kirkpatrick (1991) *Dwellers in the Land: The Bioregional Vision,* Philadelphia: New Society Press.

Salleh, Ariel K. (1984) 'Deeper than deep ecology: The eco-feminist connection', *Environmental Ethics,* 6 (4): 339–345.

Salleh, Ariel K. (1997) *Ecofeminism as Politics: Nature, Marx and the postmodern,* London: Zed.

Salleh, Ariel K. (2009) 'Ecological debt: Embodied debt', in Ariel K. Salleh (ed.) *Eco-Sufficiency and Global Justice: Women Write Political Ecology,* London: Pluto Press/Spinnifex Press.

Sandel, Michael (2012) *What Money Can't Buy: The Moral Limits of Markets,* London: Allen Lane.

Sanderson, Steven and Redford, Kent (1997) 'Biodiversity politics and the contest for ownership of the world's Biota', in R. Kramer, C. P. van Schaik, and J. Johnson (eds) *Last Stand: Protected Areas and the Defense of Tropical Biodiversity,* New York: Oxford University Press.

Sandilands, Catriona (1999) 'Sex at the limits', in Eric Darier (ed.) *Discourses of the Environment,* Malden MA: Blackwell Publishers, 79–94.

Sandler, Ronald and Cafaro, Philip (eds) (2005) *Environmental Virtue Ethics,* Lanham, MD: Rowman and Littlefield.

Sangaji, Anto (2000) *Orang Katu di Behoa Kakau: Korban Politik Konservasi, makalah, tidak.* Cited in Safitri, Myrna and Bosko, Rafael (2002) *Indigenous Peoples/Ethnic Minorities and Poverty Reduction-Indoneisa 17,* Manila: Environment and Social Safeguard Division Regional and Sustainable Development Department, Asian Development Bank.

Sarkar, Sahotra (2005) *Biodiversity and Environmental Philosophy: An Introduction,* Cambridge: Cambridge University Press.

Saunders, Clare (2007) 'Using social network analysis to explore social movements: A relational approach', *Social Movement Studies,* 6 (3): 227–243.

Saunders, Clare (2008) 'Double-edged swords? Collective identity and solidarity in the environment movement', *The British Journal of Sociology,* 59 (2): 227–253.

Saunders, Clare (2009) 'It's not just structural: Social movements are not homogenous responses to structural features, but networks shaped by organisational strategies and status', *Sociological Research Online,* 14 (1).

Saunders, Clare (2012) 'Reformism and radicalism in the Climate Camp in Britain: Benign coexistence, tensions and prospects for bridging', *Environmental Politics*, 21 (5): 829–846.

Saunders, Clare and Price, Stephan (2009) 'One person's eu-topia, another's hell: Climate Camp as a heterotopia', *Environmental Politics*, 18 (1): 117–122.

Saunders, Clare, Grasso, Maria and Price, Stephan (2012) 'From Issue Attention Cycle to Carbon Consensus: British Reporting of Climate Change 1997–2009', Comparing Climate Policy Networks Working Paper, University of Southampton.

Saurin, Julian (1994) 'Global environmental degradation, modernity and environmental knowledge', in Caroline Thomas (ed.) *Rio: Unravelling the Consequences*, London: Frank Cass.

Saurin, Julian (1996) 'International relations, social ecology and the globalisation of environmental change', in John Vogler and Mark F. Imber (eds) *The Environment and International Relations*, London: Routledge, 77–98.

Schechter, Michael G. (2005) *United Nations Global Conferences*, Abingdon: Routledge.

Scheffran, Jürgen, Marmer, Elina and Sow, Papa (2011) *Migration as a Resource for Resilience and Innovation in Climate Adaptation: Social Networks and Co-development in Northwest Africa*, Working Paper CLISEC-16, Hamburg: University of Hamburg.

Scheffran, Jürgen, Broszka, Michael, Brauch, Hans-Günter, Link, Peter Michael, and Schilling, Janpeter (eds) (2012) *Climate Change, Human Security and Violent Conflict: Challenges for Societal Stability*, Berlin: Springer Verlag.

Schlosberg, David (1999) *Environmental Justice and the New Pluralism*, Oxford: OUP.

Schlosberg, David (2013) 'Theorising environmental justice: The expanding sphere of a discourse', *Environmental Politics*, 22 (1): 37–55.

Schnaiberg, Allan, Pellow, David N. and Weinberg, Adam (2002) 'The Treadmill of Production and the Environmental State', *Research in Social Problems and Public Policy*, (10): 15–32.

Schneider, Stephen (2008) '"Dangerous" climate change: Key vulnerabilities' in Ernesto Zedillo (ed.) *Global Warming: Looking Beyond Kyoto*, Washington DC: Brookings Institution Press and Yale Center for the Study of Globalization.

Schor, Juliet (2008) 'Tackling turbo consumption', *Cultural Studies*, 22: 588–598.

Schumacher, Ernst F. (1973) *Small is Beautiful: A Study of Economics As If People Mattered*, New York: Harper and Row.

Schumpeter, Joseph A. (1975) [1942] *Capitalism, Socialism and Democracy*, New York: Harper.

Schurman, Rachel (2004) 'Fighting Frankenfoods: Industry structures and the efficacy of the anti-biotech movement in Western Europe', *Social Problems*, 51 (2): 243–269.

Schurman, Rachel and Munro, William (2003) 'Making biotech history: Social resistance to agricultural biotechnology and the future of the agricultural biotechnology industry,' in Rachel Schurman and Daniel Kelso (eds) *Engineering Trouble: Biotechnology and Its Discontents*, Berkeley: University of California Press.

Schwarz, Michiel and Thompson, Michael (1990) *Divided We Stand: Redefining Politics, Technology and Social Choice*, Hemel Hempstead: Harvester Wheatsheaf.

Scott, James (1998) *Seeing Like a State: How Certain Schemes to Improve the Human Condition Have Failed*, New Haven, CT: Yale University Press.

Scott Cato, Molly (2009) *Green Economics: An Introduction to Theory, Policy and Practice*, London: Earthscan.

Scruggs, Lyle and Benegal, Salil (2012) 'Declining public concern about climate change: Can we blame the great recession?' *Global Environmental Change*, 22 (2): 505–515.

Seagle, Caroline (2012) 'Inverting the impacts: Mining, conservation and sustainability claims near the Rio Tinto/QMM ilmenite mine in Southeast Madagascar', *Journal of Peasant Studies*, 39 (2): 447–477.

Sears, Paul B. (1964) 'Ecology – a subversive subject', *Bioscience*, 14: 11–13.

Segal, Jerome (2003) *Graceful Simplicity: The Philosophy and Politics of the Alternative American Dream*, Berkeley: University of California Press.

Segal, Lynne (1987) *Is the Future Female? Troubled Thoughts on Contemporary Feminism*, London: Virago.

Sen, Amartya (1987) *On Ethics and Economics:* Oxford, Basil Blackwell.

Sen, Amartya (1981) *Poverty and Famines: An Essay on Entitlement and Deprivation*, Oxford: Clarendon Press.

Sen, Amartya (1984) *Resources, Values, and Development*, Cambridge, MA: Harvard University Press.

Senellart, Michel (2007) 'Course context', in Michel Foucault, *Security, Territory, Population: Lectures at the Collège de France, 1977–1978*, Basingstoke: Palgrave Macmillan, 369–401.

Seyfang, Gill (2005) 'Shopping for sustainability: Can sustainable consumption promote ecological citizenship?' *Environmental Politics*, 14 (2): 290–306.

Shabecoff, Philip (2003) *A Fierce Green Fire: The American Environmental Movement*, Washington DC: Island Press.

Shackley, Simon and Wynne, Brian (1996) 'Representing uncertainty in global climate change science and policy: Boundary-ordering devices and authority', *Science, Technology and Human Values*, 21: 275–302.

Shahriari, Sara (2012) 'Bolivia enacts new law for Mother Earth', *Indian Country Today Media Network*. Available at http://indiancountrytodaymedianetwork.com/gallery/photo/bolivia-enacts-new-law-for-mother-earth-141899 (accessed 14 February 2013).

Shantu Riley, Shamara (1993) 'Ecology is a sistah's issue too', in Carol J. Adams (ed.) *Ecofeminism and the Sacred*, New York: Continuum.

Shapin, Steven and Schaffer, Simon (1985) *Leviathan and the Air-Pump: Hobbes, Boyle, and the Experimental Life*, Princeton: Princeton University Press.

Shaw, Chris (2009) 'The dangerous limits of dangerous limits: Climate change and the precautionary principle', *The Sociological Review*, 57: 103–123.

Shell, Ellen R. (2009) *Cheap: The High Cost of Discount Culture*, Harmondsworth: Penguin.

Shellenberger, Michael and Nordhaus, Ted (2004) *The Death of Environmentalism*. Available at http://www.thebreakthrough.org/images/Death_of_Environmentalism.pdf (accessed 5 February 2013).

Shellenberger, Michael and Nordhaus, Ted (2007) *Break Through: From the Death of Environmentalism to the Politics of Possibility*, New York: Houghton Mifflin.

Shiva, Vandana (1988) *Staying Alive: Women, Ecology and Development*, London: Zed.

Shiva, Vandana (1993) *Monocultures of the Mind*, London: Zed.

Shiva, Vandana (1998) *Biopiracy: The Plunder of Nature and Knowledge*, Dartington: Green Books.

Shiva, Vandana (2009) *Soil Not Oil: Climate Change, Peak Oil and Food Insecurity*, London: Zed.

Shrader-Frechette, Kristin S. (2002) *Environmental Justice: Creating Equality, Reclaiming Democracy*, Oxford: Oxford University Press.

Shove, Elizabeth (2010) 'Beyond the ABC: Climate change policy and theories of social change', *Environment and Planning A*, 42 (6): 1273–1285.

Shubin, Neil (2009) *Your Inner Fish: The Amazing Discovery of Our 375 Million Year Old Ancestor*, London: Penguin.

Shue, Henry (1992) 'The unavoidability of justice', in Andrew Hurrell and Benedict Kingsbury (eds) *International Politics of the Environment: Actors Interests and Institutions*, Oxford: Clarendon Press.

Shuman, Michael (2000) *Going Local: Creating Self-reliant Communities in a Global Age*, New York: Routledge.

Shuman, Michael (2012) 'Locally owned business' in Raymond DeYoung and Thomas Princen (eds) *The Localization Reader: Adapting to the Coming Downshift*, Cambridge, MA: MIT Press, 85–108.

Simon, Herbert (1969) *The Sciences of the Artificial*, Cambridge, MA: MIT Press.

Singer, Peter (1990) *Animal Liberation*, New York: Avon Books.

Skocpol, Theda (2013) 'You can't change the climate from inside Washington', *Foreign Policy*, 24 January. Available at http://www.foreignpolicy.com/articles/2013/01/24/you_can_t_change_the_climate_from_inside_washington_barack_obama (accessed 12 April 2013).

Slocum, Rachel (2004) 'Consumer citizens and the Cities for Climate Protection campaign', *Environment and Planning A*, 36 (5): 763–782.

Sloterdijk, Peter (2009) *Terror from the Air*, Los Angeles: Semiotext(e).

Slovic, Paul (1992) 'Perception of risk: Reflections on the psychometric paradigm', in Sheldon Krimsky and Dominic Golding (eds) *Social Theories of Risk*, Westport, CT: Praeger, 117–152.

Slovic, Paul (2000) *The Perception of Risk*, London: Earthscan.

Smith, Adam (1987) *The Wealth of Nations*, London: Penguin.

Smith, David M. (2000) *Moral Geographies: Ethics in a World of Difference*, Edinburgh: Edinburgh University Press.

Smith, Kevin (2007) *The Carbon Neutral Myth: Offset Indulgences for your Climate Sins*, Amsterdam: Carbon Trade Watch.

Smith, Mark J. and Pangsapa, Piya (2008) *Environment & Citizenship: Integrating Justice, Responsibility and Civic Engagement*, London and New York: Zed Books.

Smith, Mick (2011) *Against Ecological Sovereignty: Ethics, Biopolitics and Saving the Natural World*, Minneapolis: University of Minnesota Press.

Smith, Neil (1984) *Uneven Development: Nature, Capital and the Production of Space*, Oxford: Oxford University Press.

Smith, Neil (2006) 'Nature as accumulation strategy', in Leo Panitch and Colin Leys (eds) *The Socialist Register 2007: Coming To Terms with Nature*, London: Merlin Press, 16–37.

Smith, Susan J. (2000) 'Citizenship', in Ron J. Johnston, Derek Gregory, Geraldine Pratt and Michael Watts (eds) *The Dictionary of Human Geography*, Fourth edition, Oxford: Blackwell.

Smolker, Rachel (2010) 'Militarism and climate change', *Climate Justice Now!-lists.riseup.net* [Internet], Seattle, 22 November. Available at https://lists.riseup.net/www/info/cjn (accessed 12 April 2013).

Snow, David A. (2001) 'Collective identity and expressive forms', *University of California, Irvine, eScholarship Repository*. Available at http://repositories.cdlib.org/csd/01–07 (accessed 18 Sep 2004).

Soares De Oliveira, Ricardo (2007) *Oil and Politics in the Gulf of Guinea*, London: Hurst.

Soepardi (1974) *Hutan dan Kehutanan Dalam Tiga Jaman*, Jakarta: Perum Perhutani.

Solon, Pablo (2013) 'How to overcome the climate crisis', *Focus on the Global South, Bangkok*. Available at http://climatespace2013.wordpress.com/2013/03/14/a-contribution-to-the-climate-space-2013-how-to-overcome-the-climate-crisis/ (accessed 12 April 2013).

Solon, Pablo and Walden Bello (2012) 'Why are climate negotiations locked in stalemate?,' *Bangkok Post*, 4 September. Available at http://www.bangkokpost.com/opinion/opinion/310683/why-are-climate-negotiations-locked-in-a-stalemate (accessed 12 April 2013).

Soper, Kate (1995) *What is Nature?* Oxford: Blackwell.

Soper, Kate (2000) 'Other pleasures: The attractions of post-consumerism'. *Socialist Register*, 36: 116–132.

Sørensen, Eva (2006) 'Metagovernance: The changing role of politicians in processes of democratic governance', *American Review of Public Administration*, 36 (1): 98–114.

Soulé, Michael and Lease, Gary (1995) *Reinventing Nature? Responses to Postmodern Deconstruction*, Washington DC: Island Press.

Spaargaren, Gert, and Mol, Arthur P. (1992) 'Sociology, environment, and modernity: Ecological modernization as a theory of social change', *Society & Natural Resources*, 5 (4): 323–344.

Spaargaren, Gert and Oosterveer, Peter (2010) 'Citizen-consumers as agents of change in globalizing modernity: The case of sustainable consumption', *Sustainability*, 2 (7): 1887–1908.

Specter, Michael (2008) 'Big Foot: In measuring carbon emissions, it is easy to confuse morality and science', *The New Yorker*, February 25. Available at http://www.newyorker.com/reporting/2008/02/25/080225fa_fact_specter (accessed 27 March 2013).

Spelman, Elizabeth V. (1990) *Inessential Woman: Problems of Exclusion in Feminist Thought*, London: The Women's Press.

Spence, Mark (1999) *Dispossessing the Wilderness: Indian Removal and the Making of National Parks*, Oxford: Oxford University Press.

Spitzner, Meike (2009) 'How global warming is gendered', in Arielle K. Salleh (ed.) *Eco-Sufficiency and Global Justice: Women Write Political Ecology*, London: Pluto Press/Spinnifex Press.

Stabile, Carol A. (1994) '"A garden enclosed is my sister": ecofeminism and eco-Valences', *Cultural Studies*, 8 (1): 56–73.

Stahel, Andri (1999) 'Time contradictions of capitalism', *Capitalism Nature Socialism*, 10 (1): 101–132.

Staeheli, Lynn A. and Mitchell, Don (2006) 'USA's destiny? Regulating space and creating community in American shopping malls', *Urban Studies*, 43: 977–992.

Starhawk (1990) *Truth or Dare*, San Francisco: Harper Collins.

Statman, Daniel (ed.) (1997) *Virtue Ethics: A Critical Reader*, Edinburgh: Edinburgh University Press.

Steffen, Will, Persson, Asa, Deutsch, Lisa, Zalasiewicz, Jan, Williams, Mark, Richardson, Katherine, et al. (2011) 'The Anthropocene: From global change to planetary stewardship', *Ambio*, 40: 739–761.

Steffensen, Jørgen Peder, Andersen, Katrine K., Bigler, Matthias, Clausen, Henrik B., Dahl-Jensen, Dorthe, Fischer, Hubertus et al. (2008) 'High-resolution Greenland Ice Core data show abrupt climate change happens in few years', *Science*, 321: 680–684.

Stern, Nicholas (2007) *The Economics of Climate Change*, Cambridge: Cambridge University Press.

Stevenson, Nick (2006) 'Technological citizenship: Perspectives in the recent work of Manuel Castells and Paul Virilio', *Sociological Research Online*, 10 (3). Available at http://www.socresonline.org.uk/11/3/stevenson.html (accessed 27 March 2013).

Stiegler, Bernard (2011) 'Suffocated desire or how the cultural industry destroys the individual: Contribution to a theory of mass consumption', *Parrhesia*, 13: 52–61.

Stiglitz, Joseph (1988) *Economics of the Public Sector*, New York: Norton and Company.

Stiglitz, Joseph and Charlton, Andrew (2007) *Fair Trade for All: How Trade Can Promote Development*, New York: Oxford University Press.

St John, Graham (2008) 'Protestival: Global days of action and carnalivalized politics in the present', *Social Movement Studies*, 7 (2): 167–190.

St. Martin, Kevin (2008) 'The difference that class makes: Neoliberalization and non-capitalism in the fishing industry of New England', in Becky Mansfield (ed.) *Privatization*, Oxford: Blackwell, 133–155.

Stoett, Peter (2012) 'What are we really looking for? From ecoviolence to environmental injustice', in Matthew Schnurr and Larry Swatuk (eds) *Natural Resources and Social Conflict: Towards Critical Environmental Security*, London: Palgrave Macmillan, 15–32.

Stokke, Olav (1997) 'Regimes as governance systems', in Oran Young (ed.) *Global Governance: Drawing Insights from the Environmental Experience*, Cambridge, MA: MIT Press, 27–63.

Stripple, Johannes and Lövbrand, Eva (2010) 'Carbon market governance beyond the public–private divide', in Frank Biermann, Philipp Pattberg and Fariborz Zelli (eds) *Global Climate Governance Post 2012: Architectures, Agency and Adaptation*, Cambridge: Cambridge University Press, 165–183.

Sturgeon, Nöel (2009) *Environmentalism and Popular Culture: Gender, Race, Sexuality and the Politics of the Natural*, Tempe: University of Arizona Press.

Sullivan, Sian (2009) 'Green capitalism and the cultural poverty of constructing nature as service provider', *Radical Anthropology*, 3: 18–27.

Sullivan, Sian (2011) 'On bioculturalism, shamanism and unlearning the creed of growth', *Geography and You*, March–April 2011: 15–19.

Sullivan, Sian (2013) 'Banking nature? The spectacular financialisation of environmental conservation', *Antipode*, 45 (1): 198–217.

Sullivan, Sian (in press) 'Nature on the move III: Recountenancing an animate nature', *New Proposals: Journal of Marxism and Interdisciplinary Enquiry*.

Sullivan, Sian (2013) 'After the green rush: Biodiversity offsets, uranium power, and the calculus of casualties in greening growth', *Human Geography*, 6 (1): 80–101.

Sundaram, Jomo Kwame (2010) 'Climate Change and Industrial Development', presentation to the University of KwaZulu-Natal, South Africa, 17 May.

Sundaraman, Narasimhan (1995) 'Impact of climate change', *Nature*, 377 (6549): 472.

Sunstein, Cass (2003) 'Beyond the precautionary principle', *University of Pennsylvania Law Review*, 151: 1003–1058.

Sutter, Paul S. (2002) *Driven Wild: How the Fight Against Automobiles Launched the Modern Wilderness Movement*, Seattle: University of Washington Press.

Swanson, Timothy (1999) 'Why is there a biodiversity convention? The international interest in centralized development planning', *International Affairs*, 75 (2): 307–331.

Swyngedouw, Erik (2005) 'Governance innovation and the citizen: The Janus face of governance-beyond-the-state', *Urban Studies*, 42 (11): 1991–2006.

Swyngedouw, Erik (2007a) 'Dispossessing H$_2$O: The contested terrain of water privatization', in Nik Heynen, James McCarthy, Scott Prudham and Paul Robbins (eds) *Neoliberal Environments: False Promises and Unnatural Consequences*, Abingdon: Routledge, 51–62.

Swyngedouw, Erik (2007b) 'Impossible "sustainability" and the postpolitical condition', in Rob Krueger and David Gibbs (eds) *The Sustainable Development Paradox: Urban Political Economy in the United States and Europe*, London: Guildford Press.

Swyngedouw, Erik (2009) 'The Antinomies of the postpolitical city: In search of a democratic politics of environmental production', *International Journal of Urban and Regional Research*, 33 (3): 601–620.

Swyngedouw, Erik (2010) 'Apocalypse forever? Post-political populism and the spectre of climate change', *Theory Culture & Society*, 27 (2–3): 213–232.

Tabb, William (2000) *The Amoral Elephant: Globalization and the Struggle for Social Justice in the Twenty-First Century*, New York: Monthly Review Press.

Tainter, Joseph (1988) *The Collapse of Complex Societies*, Cambridge: Cambridge University Press.

Takacs, David (1996) *The Idea of Biodiversity: Philosophies of Paradise*, Baltimore: The Johns Hopkins University Press.

Tandon, Yash (2009) 'Dangers and opportunities: Political, economic and climatic crises of Western civilization', *Pambazuka News*, 426. Available at http://pambazuka.org/en/category/features/55334 (accessed 12 April 2013).

Tarrow, Sidney (1998) *Power in Movement: Social Movement and Contentious Politics*, Cambridge: Cambridge University Press.

TEEB (2012) 'The economics of ecosystems and biodiversity'. Available at http://www.teebweb.org/about/ (accessed 16 May 2012).

Terborgh, John (2004) 'Reflections of a scientist on the World Parks Congress', *Conservation Biology*, 18: 619–620.

Thatcher, Margaret (1989) Provisional Verbatim Record of the 48th Meeting, Held at Headquarters, New York, On Wednesday, 8 November 1989: General Assembly, 44th Session A/44/PV.48. Availableat www.margaretthatcher.org/document/107817 (accessed 27 March 2013).

Thayer, Robert (2003) *LifePlace: Bioregional Thought and Practice*, Berkeley: University of California Press.

The Economist (2009) *The Peak Oil Debate*, 10 December. Available at http://www.economist.com/node/15065719 (accessed 13 February 2013).

The Widening Circle Campaign (2012). Available at http://www.wideningcircle.org/ (accessed 6 July 2013).

Thomas, David and Middleton, Nick (1994) *Desertification: Exploding the Myth*, Chichester: Wiley.

Thompson, Craig J. and Arsel, Zeynep (2004) 'The Starbucks brandscape and consumers' (anticorporate) experiences of glocalization', *Journal of Consumer Research*, 31 (3): 631–642.

Thompson, Michael, Warburton, Michael and Hatley, Tom (1986) *Uncertainty on a Himalayan Scale: An Institutional Theory of Environmental Perception and a Strategic Framework for the Sustainable Development of the Himalaya*, London: Milton Ash Editions.

Tierney, Kathleen, Bevc, Christine and Kuligowski, Erica (2006) 'Metaphors matter: Disaster myths, media frames, and their consequences in hurricane Katrina', *The Annals of the American Academy of Political and Social Science,* 604 (1): 57–81.

Tilly, Charles (1978) *From Mobilization to Revolution,* Reading, MA: Addison-Wesley.

Tingley, Martin P., Craigmile, Peter F., Haran, Murali, Li, Bo, Mannshardt-Shamseldin, Elizabeth and Rajaratnam, Bala (2012) 'Piecing together the past: Statistical insights into paleoclimatic reconstructions', *Quaternary Science Reviews,* 35: 1–22.

Tokar, Brian (2010) *Toward Climate Justice,* Vermont: Communalism Press.

Tol, Richard S. J. and Yohe, Gary W. (2009) 'The Stern Review: A deconstruction', *Energy Policy,* 37 (3): 1032–1040.

Touraine, Alain (2000) *La Recherche de Soi, Dialogue sur le Sujet,* Paris: Fayard.

Trentmann, Frank (ed.) (2006) *The Making of the Consumer,* Oxford: Berg.

Tulloch, John and Lupton, Deborah (2003) *Risk and Everyday Life,* London: Sage.

Turner, Ralph H. and Killian, Lewis M. (1957) *Collective Behavior,* Oxford: Prentice-Hall.

Turner, Stephen (2001) 'What is the problem with experts?' *Social Studies of Science,* 31: 123–149.

Turner, Stephen (2003) *Liberal Democracy 3.0: Civil-Society in an Age of Experts,* Thousand Oaks, CA: Sage.

Ukiwo, Ukoha (2007) 'From "pirates" to "militants": A historical perspective on anti-state and anti-oil company mobilisation among the Ijaw of Warri, western Niger Delta', *African Affairs,* 106 (425): 587–610.

UN (1992a) *Agenda 21.* Available at http://www.unep.org/Documents.Multilingual/Default.asp?documentid=52 (accessed 27 March 2013).

UN (1992b) *Annex I: Rio Declaration on Environment and Development, Report of the United Nations Conference on Environment and Development,* Rio de Janeiro, Brazil 3–4 June.

UN (2012) *The Future We Want.* Rio+20: United Nations Conference on Sustainable Development. Rio de Janeiro, Brazil 20–22 June 2012. Available at http://www.uncsd2012.org/content/documents/727The%20Future%20We%20Want%2019%20June%201230pm.pdf (accessed 27 March 2013).

UNDP (1994) *Human Development Report,* New York: Oxford University Press.

UNDP (2005) *Niger Delta Human Development Report,* Abuja: United Nations Development Program.

UNGA (2009) *Climate Change and Its Possible Security Implications,* Report of the Secretary-General, A/64/350, New York: UN.

UNODC (2009) *Transnational Trafficking and the Rule of Law in West Africa.* UN Office for Drugs and Crime: Vienna. Available at http://www.unhcr.org/refworld/docid/4a54bc3e0.html (accessed 27 March 2013).

U.S. Green Building Council (2012) *LEED.* Available at https://new.usgbc.org/leed (accessed 16 November 2012).

Uranium-network (2012), *Press Release Regarding World Heritage Committee Decision on Selous Game Reserve Boundary in Tanzania.* Available at http://www.uranium-network.org/index.php/mkuju-river-important (accessed 17 February 2013).

van de Hove, Sybille (2000) 'Participatory approaches to environmental policy-making: The European Commission Climate Policy Process as a case study', *Ecological Economics,* 33 (3): 457–472.

van Vilet, Bas, Chappells, Heather and Shove, Elizabeth (2005) *Infrastructures of Consumption,* London: Earthscan.

van Zeijl-Rozema, Annemarie, Cörvers, Ron, Kemp, René and Martens, Pim (2008) 'Governance for sustainable development: A framework', *Sustainable Development,* 16 (6): 410–421.

Varley, Ann (1994) 'The exceptional and the everyday: Vulnerability in the international decade for disaster reduction', in Ann Varley (ed.) *Disaster, Development and Environment,* Chichester: Wiley.

Varner, Gary (1991) 'No holism without pluralism', *Environmental Ethics,* 13: 175–179.

Varner, Gary (1998) *In Nature's Interests? Interests, Animal Rights, and Environmental Ethics,* Oxford: Oxford University Press.

Verweij, Marco, Douglas, Mary, Ellis, Richard, Engel, Christoph, Hendriks, Frank, Lohmann, Susanne et al (2006) 'Clumsy solutions for a complex world: The case of climate change', *Public Administration,* 84 (4): 817–843.

Victor, David (2001) *The Collapse of the Kyoto Protocol and the Struggle to Slow Global Warming,* Princeton: Princeton University Press.

Victor, Peter A. (2008) *Managing Without Growth: Slower by Design, Not Disaster,* Cheltenham: Edward Elgar Publishing.

Virilio, Paul (1995) *The Art of the Motor,* Minneapolis: University of Minnesota Press.

Virilio, Paul (1997) *Open Sky,* London: Verso.

Virilio, Paul (2000) *A Landscape of Events,* Cambridge, MA: MIT Press.

Voß, Jan-Peter, Bauknecht, Dierk, Kemp, René (2006) (eds) *Reflexive Governance for Sustainable Development,* Cheltenham: Edward Elgar.

Voß, Jan-Peter and Kemp, René (2006) 'Introduction', in Jan-Peter Voß, Dierk Bauknecht and René Kemp (eds) *Reflexive Governance for Sustainable Development,* Cheltenham: Edward Elgar.

Wackernagel, Mathis and Rees, William (1996) *Our Ecological Footprint: Reducing Human Impact on the Earth,* Gabriola Island BC: New Society Publishers.

Walby, Sylvia (1990) *Theorizing Patriarchy,* Oxford: Basil Blackwell.

Walby, Sylvia (2009) *Globalization and Inequalities: Complexity and Contested Modernities,* London: Sage.

Walker, Brian, Holling, Crawford Stanley, Carpenter, Stephen and Kinzig, Ann (2004) 'Resilience, adaptability and transformability in social-ecological systems', *Ecology and Society,* 9 (2): 5.

Walker, Gordon and Shove, Elizabeth (2007) 'Ambivalence, sustainability and the governance of socio-technical transitions', *Journal of Environmental Policy and Planning,* 9 (3–4): 213–225.

Walker, Jeremy and Cooper, Melinda (2011) 'Genealogies of resilience: From systems ecology to the political economy of crisis adaptation', *Security Dialogue,* 14 (2): 143–160.

Walker, R. B. J. (1988) *State Sovereignty, Global Civilization, and the Rearticulation of Political Space,* Princeton: Center of International Studies, Princeton University.

Walker, R. B. J. (1992) *Inside/Outside: International Relations as Political Theory,* New York: Cambridge University Press.

Walker, R. B. J. (2003) 'They seek it here, they seek it there: Locating the political in Clayoquot Sound' in Warren Magnusson and Karena Shaw (eds) *A Political Space: Reading the Global Through Clayoquot Sound,* Minneapolis: University of Minnesota Press.

Wall, Derek (2010) *The Rise of the Green Left: Inside the Worldwide Ecosocialist Movement,* London: Pluto Press.

Wallerstein, Immanuel (1986) *Africa and the Modern World,* Trenton, NJ: Africa World Press.

Wallis, Stuart (2011) *The Great Transition,* London: New Economics Foundation.

Walsh, Andrew (2012) *Made in Madagascar: Sapphires, Ecotourism, and the Global Bazaar,* Toronto: University of Toronto Press.

Walters, William (2012) *Governmentality: Critical Encounters,* New York: Routledge.

Waltz, Kenneth (1979) *Theory of International Politics,* New York: Random House.

Wann, David (2007) *Simple Prosperity: Finding Real Wealth in a Sustainable Lifestyle,* New York: St. Martin's Griffin.

Wann, David, Degraff, John and Naylor, Thomas (2005) *Affluenza: The All-Consuming Epidemic,* Second edition, New York: Berrett-Koehler Publishers.

Wapner, Paul (2003) 'World Summit on Sustainable Development: Toward a post-Jo'burg environmentalism', *Global Environmental Politics,* 3 (1): 1–10.

Wapner, Paul (2010) *Living through the End of Nature: The Future of American Environmentalism,* Cambridge MA: MIT Press.

Wapner, Paul and Willoughby, John (2005) 'The irony of environmentalism: The ecological futility but political necessity of lifestyle change', *Ethics and International Affairs,* 19 (2): 77–89.

Warren, Karen J. (1987) 'Feminism and ecology: Making connections,' *Environmental Ethics,* 9: 3–20.

Warren, Karen J. (1994) *Ecological Feminism,* Abingdon: Routledge.

Warren, Karen J. (1997) 'Taking empirical data seriously: An ecofeminist philosophical perspective' in Karen J. Warren (ed.) *Ecofeminism: Women, Nature, Culture,* Philadelphia: New Society.

Warrier, Meera (ed.) (2011) *The Politics of Fair Trade: A Survey,* Abingdon: Routledge.

Watson, Adam (1984) *Diplomacy: The Dialogue Between States,* London: Routledge.

Watts, Michael (1983) *Silent Violence: Food, Famine and Peasantry in Northern Nigeria,* Berkeley: University of California Press.

Watts, Michael (2007) 'Petro-insurgency or criminal syndicate?', *Review of African Political Economy,* 144: 637–660.

Watts, Michael (2011a) 'Blood oil', in Andrea Behrends, Stephen Reyna and Gunther Schlee (ed.) *Crude Domination: An Anthropology of Oil,* Oxford: Berghahn, 49–80.

Watts, Michael (2011b) 'Ecologies of rule', in C. Calhoun and G. Derlugian (eds) *The Deepening Crisis,* New York: New York University Press, 67–92.

Watts, Michael and Bohle, Hans G. (1993) 'The space of vulnerability: The causal structure of hunger and famine', *Progress in Human Geography,* 17 (1): 43–67.

WBGU (2007) *World in Transition: Climate Change As a Security Risk,* Berlin, Heidelberg: Springer.

WCED (World Commission on Environment and Development) (1987) *Our Common Future,* Oxford: Oxford University Press.

Webersik, Christian (2010) *Climate Change and Security: A Gathering Storm of Global Challenges,* Santa Barbara, CA: Praeger.

Welchman, Jennifer (1999) 'The virtues of stewardship', *Environmental Ethics,* 21 (4): 411–423.

Welzer, Harald (2012) *Climate Wars: What People will be Killed for in the Twenty First Century,* Cambridge: Polity.

West, Paige (2006) *Conservation is Our Government Now: The Politics of Ecology in Papua New Guinea,* Durham, NC: Duke University Press.

West, Paige and Carrier, James (2004) 'Ecotourism & authenticity: Getting away from it all?' *Current Anthropology,* 45 (4): 483–498.

West, Paige, Igoe, James and Brockington, Daniel (2006) 'Parks and people: The social impacts of protected areas', *Annual Review of Anthropology,* 35: 251–277.

Weston, Anthony (1996) 'Beyond intrinsic value: Pragmatism in Environmental Ethics', in Andrew Light and Eric Katz (eds) *Environmental Pragmatism,* London: Routledge.

Whatmore, Sarah (2002) *Hybrid Geographies,* London: Sage Publications.

White, Damian F., Rudy, Alan P. and Gareau, Brian (forthcoming) *The Environment, Nature and Social Theory: Hybrid Approaches,* London: Macmillan.

White, Damian F. and Wilbert, Chris (2009) *Technonatures: Technologies, Spaces and Places in the 21st Century,* Waterloo: Wilfrid Laurier Press.

Whitehead, Mark (2007) *Spaces of Sustainability: Geographical Perspectives on the Sustainable Society,* Abingdon: Routledge.

Whitehead, Mark (2009) *State, Science and the Skies: Governmentalities of the British Atmosphere,* Chichester: Wiley-Blackwell.

Whitehead, Mark (2011) 'The sustainable city: an obituary? Critical reflections on the future of sustainable urbanism' in John Flint and Mike Raco (eds) *Sustaining Success: The New Politics of Sustainable Urban Planning,* Bristol: Policy Press.

Whitehead, Mark (2012) 'Urban sustainability and economic development', in T. Hutton and R. Paddison (eds) *Handbook of Urban Economic Development,* London: Sage.

Whitehead, Mark (2013) 'Sustainability' in Paul Cloke, Phil Crang and Mark Goodwin (eds) *Introducing Human Geographies,* London: Arnold.

Whitehead, Mark, Jones, Rhys and Jones, Martin (2007) *The Nature of the State: Excavating the Political Ecologies of the Modern State,* New York: Oxford University Press.

Wilk, Richard R. (2010) 'Consumption embedded in culture and language: Implications for finding sustainability', *Sustainability: Science, Practice and Policy,* 6 (2): 1–11.

Wilkinson, Richard and Pickett, Kate (2009) *The Spirit Level: Why Equality is Better for Everyone,* Harmondsworth: Penguin.

Williams, Chris (2011) *Ecology and Socialism: Solutions to Capitalist Ecological Crisis,* Chicago: Haymarket Books.

Williams, Michael (2007) *Culture and Security: Symbolic Power and the Politics of International Security,* Abingdon: Routledge.

Wilson, Edward (ed) (1988) *Biodiversity,* Washington DC: National Academy Press.

Winner, Langdon (1999) 'Do artifacts have politics', in Donald A. Mackenzie and Judy Wajcman (eds) *The Social Shaping of Technology,* Second edition, London: Open University Press.

Winner, Langdon (1986) *The Whale and the Reactor: A Search for Limits in an Age of High Technology,* Chicago: University of Chicago Press.

Wisner, Ben and Luce, Henry R. (1993) 'Disaster vulnerability: Scale, power and daily life', *GeoJournal,* 30 (2): 127–140.

Wisner, Ben, O'Keefe, Phil and Westgate, Ken (1977) 'Global systems and local disasters: The untapped powers of peoples' science', *Disasters,* 1 (1): 47–57.

Wissenburg, Marcel and Levy, Yoram (eds) (2004) *Liberal Democracy and Environmentalism: The End of Environmentalism?* Abingdon: Routledge.

Wolfe, Cary (2010) *What is Posthumanism?* Minneapolis: University of Minnesota Press.

Wolfowitz, Paul (2005) An address to the National Press Club, Washington DC, 7 December. Available at http://web.worldbank.org/WBSITE/EXTERNAL/EXTABOUTUS/ORGANIZATION/EXTPRESIDENT2007/EXTPASTPRESIDENTS/EXTOFFICEPRESIDENT/0,contentMDK:20747792~menuPK:64343271~pagePK:51174171~piPK:64258873~theSitePK:1014541,00.html (accessed 20 March 2013).

World Bank (2010) *Development and Climate Change,* World Development Report, Washington DC: World Bank.

World Bank (2011) *Conflict, Security and Development,* Washington DC: The World Bank.

World Bank (2012) 'New initiatives give hope to a carbon market facing challenges', Press Release, *World Bank.* Available at http://web.worldbank.org/WBSITE/EXTERNAL/NEWS/0,contentMDK:23206021~menuPK:34463~pagePK:34370~piPK:34424~theSitePK:4607,00.html (accessed 6 June 2012).

Worldwatch Institute (2011) *State of the World,* Washington DC: The Worldwatch Institute.

Worster, Donald (1977) *Nature's Economy: The Roots of Ecology,* Garden City, NJ: Anchor Books.

Wright, Glen (2011) 'Indigenous people and customary landownership under Domestic REDD PLUS frameworks: A case study of Indonesia', *Law, Environment and Development,* 7(2): 117–131.

Wu, Jiangu and Loucks, Orie (1995) 'From balance of nature to hierarchical patch dynamics: A paradigm shift in ecology', *The Quarterly Review of Biology,* 70: 439–466.

Wyn Jones, Richard (1999) *Security, Strategy and Critical Theory,* Boulder, CO: Lynne Rienner.

Wynne, Brian (1992) 'Uncertainty and environmental learning', *Global Environmental Change,* 6 (2): 111–127.

Wynne, Brian (1996) 'May the sheep safely graze? A reflexive view of the expert-lay knowledge divide', in Scott Lash, Bron Szersynski and Brian Wynne (eds) *Risk, Environment and Modernity: Towards a New Ecology,* London: Sage, 44–83.

Wynne, Brian (2001) 'Creating public alienation: Expert cultures or risk and ethics on GMOs', *Science as Culture,* 10: 445–481.

Xenos, Nicholas (1989) *Scarcity and Modernity,* London: Routledge.

Yearley, Steven (1991) *The Green Case: A Sociology of Environmental Issues, Arguments, and Politics,* London: HarperCollinsAcademic.

Yearley, Steven (1992) 'Green ambivalence about science: Legal-rational authority and the scientific legitimization of a social movement', *The British Journal of Sociology,* 43: 511–532.

Young, Oran R. (1994) *International Governance: Protecting the Environment in a Stateless Society,* Cornell: Cornell University Press.

Young, Robert M. (1979) 'Science is a labour process' *Science for People,* 43/44: 31–37.

Young, Robert M. (1985) 'Is nature a labour process?' in Les Levidow and Robert M. Young (eds) *Science, Technology and the Labour Process: Marxist Studies, Vol. 2,* London: Free Association Books.

Yuval-Davis, Nira (1997) *Gender and Nation,* London: Sage.

Yuval-Davis, Nira (2010) *The Intersectional Politics of Belonging,* London: Sage.

Zerzan, John (1994) *Future Primitive,* New York: Autonomedia.

Zinn, Jens (ed.) (2008) *Social Theories of Risk and Uncertainty,* London: Blackwell.

Žižek, Slavoj (1999) *The Ticklish Subject: The Absent Centre of Political Ontology,* London: Verso.

Žižek, Slavoj (2009) *First as Tragedy, Then as Farce,* London: Verso.

Index